CLYMER®

SUZUKI

GSX-R600 • 1997-2000

The world's finest publisher of mechanical how-to manuals

INTERTEC PUBLISHING
P.O. Box 12901, Overland Park, Kansas 66282-2901

Copyright ©2001 Intertec Publishing

FIRST EDITION
First Printing May, 2001

Printed in U.S.A.

CLYMER and colophon are registered trademarks of Intertec Publishing.

ISBN: 0-89287-775-8

Library of Congress: 2001090061

Technical photography by Ron Wright. Technical photographic assistance by Katie Wright.

Technical illustrations by Stephen Amos and Robert Caldwell.

COVER: Photographed by Mark Clifford, Mark Clifford Photography, Los Angeles, California.

PRODUCTION: Susan Hartington.

CONTENTS

QUICK REFERENCE DATA

VEHICLE HISTORY DATA

MODEL:_____YEAR:_____

VIN NUMBER:_____

ENGINE SERIAL NUMBER:_____

CARBURETOR SERIAL NUMBER OR I.D. MARK:_____

Record the numbers here for your reference.

TIRE SPECIFICATIONS

Item	Front	Rear
Tire type	Tubeless	Tubeless
Size	120/70 ZR17 (58W)	180/55 ZR17 (73W)
Minimum tread depth	1.6 mm (0.06 in.)	2.0 mm (0.08 in.)
Inflation pressure (cold)*		
Solo	250 kPa (36 psi)	250 kPa (36 psi)
Rider and passenger	250 kPa (36 psi)	250 kPa (36 psi)

*Tire inflation pressure is for original equipment tires. Aftermarket tires may require different inflation pressure. The use of tires other than those specified by Suzuki may cause instability.

RECOMMENDED LUBRICANTS AND FLUIDS

Fuel	Unleaded
Octane	87 [(R + M)/2 method] or research octane of 91 or higher
U.S.A., California, and Canada models	87 [(R + M)/2 method] or research octane of 91 or higher
Non- U.S.A., California, and Canada models	85-95
1997-1998	85-95
1999-on	91 or higher
Fuel tank capacity, including reserve	18.0 L (4.8 U.S. gal., 4.0 Imp. gal.)
Engine oil	
Grade	API SF or SG
Viscosity	SAE 10W40
Capacity	
Oil change only	2.6 L (2.7 U.S. qt., 2.3 Imp. qt.)
Oil and filter change	2.8 L (3.0 U.S. qt., 2.5 Imp. qt.)
When engine completely dry	3.5 L (3.7 U.S. qt., 3.1 Imp. qt.])
Brake fluid	DOT 4
Fork oil	
Viscosity	Suzuki No. 10 fork oil or equivalent
Capacity per leg	533 ml (18.0 U.S. oz., 18.8 Imp. oz.)

(continued)

RECOMMENDED LUBRICANTS AND FLUIDS (continued)

Engine coolant	
Type	Antifreeze/coolant that is compatible with an aluminum radiator.
Ratio	50:50 with distilled water
Capacity	2550 ml (2.7 U.S. qt., 2.2 Imp. qt.)

MAINTENANCE AND TUNE-UP TIGHTENING TORQUES

Item	N•m	in.-lb.	ft.-lb.
Engine sprocket bolt	120	–	89
Oil hose banjo bolt			
Upper side	20	–	15
Lower side	25	–	18
Oil drain plug	28	–	21
Oil pan bolt	14	–	10
Main oil gallery plug	40	–	29
Exhaust pipe bolt	23	–	17
Muffler mounting bolt	23	–	17
Valve timing inspection cap	23	–	17
Spark plug	12	106	–
Rear axle nut	100	–	74
Front axle	100	–	74
Front axle pinch bolt	23	–	17
Rear brake master cylinder locknut	18	–	13
Cylinder head cover bolt	14	–	10

COOLING SYSTEM SPECIFICATIONS

Item	Specification
Coolant type	Antifreeze/coolant compatable with aluminum radiator. Mixed with distilled water at 50:50 ratio.
Coolant capacity	2.5 L (2.7 U.S. qt., 2.2 Imp qt.)
Thermostat valve opening temperature	74.5-78.5° C (166.1-173.3° F)
Thermostat valve lift	Over 7.0 mm at 90° C (over 0.28 in. at 194° F)
Radiator cap valve opening pressure	110 kPa (15.6 psi)

DRIVE CHAIN SPECIFICATIONS

Drive chain	
Type	Takasago RK525SMOZ$_2$ (108 links, continuous)
20-pin length	319.4 mm (12.6 in.)
Chain slack	20-30 mm (0.8-1.2 in.)

REPLACEMENT BULBS

Item	Voltage/wattage
Headlight (high/low beam)	
U.S.A., California, Canada, Australia, U.K.	12 V 55/50 W x 2
Austria, Belgium, Brazil, France, Finland,	
Germany, Italy, Netherlands, Norway, Spain,	
Sweden, Switzerland	12 V 55/55 W
(continued)	

REPLACEMENT BULBS (continued)

Item	Voltage/wattage
Position light	
Austria, Belgium, Brazil, France, Finland,	
Germany, Italy, Netherlands, Norway, Spain,	
Sweden, Switzerland, U.K.	12 V 5 W
Tail/brake light	12 V 5/21 W x 2
Turn signal	12 V 21 W
Tachometer light	12 V 1.7 W
Speedometer light	12 V 1.7 W
Neutral indicator light	12 V 1.7 W
High beam indicator light	12 V 1.7 W
Turn signal indicator light	12 V 1.7 W
Fuel indicator light	12 V 1.7 W

CHAPTER ONE

GENERAL INFORMATION

This detailed and comprehensive manual covers the Suzuki GSX-R600 model from 1997-on.

The text provides complete information on maintenance, tune-up, repair and overhaul. Hundreds of photos and drawings guide the reader through every job.

A shop manual is a reference tool and as in all Clymer manuals, the chapters are thumb tabbed for easy reference. Important items are indexed at the end of the book. All procedures, tables and figures are designed for the reader who may be working on the motorcycle for the first time. Frequently used specifications and capacities from individual chapters are summarized in the *Quick Reference Data* at the front of the book.

Tables 1-7 are at the end of this chapter.

Table 1 lists serial numbers.

Table 2 lists vehicle dimensions.

Table 3 lists decimal and metric equivalents.

Table 4 lists conversion tables.

Table 5 lists general torque specifications.

Table 6 lists technical abbreviations.

Table 7 lists metric tap and drill sizes.

MANUAL ORGANIZATION

All dimensions and capacities are expressed in metric and U.S. standard units of measurement.

This chapter provides general information on shop safety, tool use, service fundamentals and shop supplies. The tables at the end of the chapter include general vehicle information.

Chapter Two provides methods for quick and accurate diagnosis of problems. Troubleshooting procedures present typical symptoms and logical methods to pinpoint and repair the problem.

Chapter Three explains all routine maintenance necessary to keep the vehicle running well. Chapter Three also includes recommended tune-up procedures, eliminating the need to constantly consult the chapters on the various assemblies.

Subsequent chapters describe specific systems such as engine, transmission, clutch, drive system, fuel and exhaust systems, suspension and brakes. Each disassembly, repair and assembly procedure is discussed in step-by-step form.

Some of the procedures in this manual specify special tools. In most cases, the tool is illustrated in use. Well-equipped mechanics may be able to substitute similar tools or fabricate a suitable replacement. However, in some cases, the required specialized equipment or expertise may make it impractical for the home mechanic to attempt the procedure. When necessary, such operations are identified in the text with the recommendation to have a dealership or specialist perform the task. It may be less expensive to have a professional perform these jobs, especially when considering the cost of the equipment.

WARNINGS, CAUTIONS AND NOTES

The terms, WARNING, CAUTION and NOTE have specific meanings in this manual.

A WARNING emphasizes areas where injury or even death could result from negligence. Mechanical damage may also occur. WARNINGS *are to be taken seriously*.

A CAUTION emphasizes areas where equipment damage could result. Disregarding a CAUTION could cause permanent mechanical damage, though injury is unlikely.

A NOTE provides additional information to make a step or procedure easier or clearer. Disregarding a NOTE could cause inconvenience, but would not cause equipment damage or personal injury.

SAFETY

Professional mechanics can work for years and never sustain a serious injury or mishap. Follow these guidelines and practice common sense to safely service the vehicle.

1. Do not operate the vehicle in an enclosed area. The exhaust gasses contain carbon monoxide, an odorless, colorless, and tasteless poisonous gas. Carbon monoxide levels build quickly in small enclosed areas and can cause unconsciousness and death in a short time. Make sure the work area is properly ventilated or operate the vehicle outside.

2. *Never* use gasoline or any extremely flammable liquid to clean parts. Refer to *Cleaning Parts* and *Handling Gasoline Safely* in this chapter.

3. *Never* smoke or use a torch in the vicinity of flammable liquids, such as gasoline or cleaning solvent.

4. If welding or brazing on the vehicle, remove the fuel tank, carburetor and shock to a safe distance at least 50 ft. (15 m) away.

5. Use the correct type and size of tools to avoid damaging fasteners.

6. Keep tools clean and in good condition. Replace or repair worn or damaged equipment.

7. When loosening a tight fastener, be guided by what would happen if the tool slips.

8. When replacing fasteners, make sure the new fasteners are of the same size and strength as the original ones.

9. Keep the work area clean and organized.

10. Wear eye protection *anytime* the safety of your eyes is in question. This includes procedures involving drilling, grinding, hammering, compressed air and chemicals.

11. Wear the correct clothing for the job. Tie up or cover long hair so it can not get caught in moving equipment.

12. Do not carry sharp tools in clothing pockets.

13. Always have an approved fire extinguisher available. Make sure it is rated for gasoline (Class B) and electrical (Class C) fires.

14. Do not use compressed air to clean clothes, the vehicle or the work area. Debris may be blown into your eyes or skin. *Never* direct compressed air at yourself or someone else. Do not allow children to use or play with any compressed air equipment.

15. When using compressed air to dry rotating parts, hold the part so it cannot rotate. Do not allow the force of the air to spin the part. The air jet is capable of rotating parts at extreme speed. The part may be damaged or disintegrate, causing serious injury.

16. Do not inhale the dust created by brake pad and clutch wear. These particles may contain asbestos. In addition, some types of insulating materials and gaskets may contain asbestos. Inhaling asbestos particles is hazardous to health.

17. Never work on the vehicle while someone is working under it.

18. When placing the vehicle on a stand, make sure it is secure before walking away.

Handling Gasoline Safely

Gasoline is a volatile flammable liquid and is one of the most dangerous items in the shop.

Because gasoline is used so often, many people forget that it is hazardous. Only use gasoline as fuel for gasoline internal combustion engines. Keep in mind, when working on a vehicle, gasoline is always present in the fuel tank, fuel line and carburetor. To avoid a disastrous accident when working around the fuel system, carefully observe the following precautions:

1. *Never* use gasoline to clean parts. See *Cleaning Parts* in this chapter.

2. When working on the fuel system, work outside or in a well-ventilated area.

3. Do not add fuel to the fuel tank or service the fuel system while the vehicle is near open flames, sparks or where someone is smoking. Gasoline vapor is heavier than air. It collects in low areas and is more easily ignited than liquid gasoline.

4. Allow the engine to cool completely before working on any fuel system component.

5. When draining the carburetor, catch the fuel in a plastic container and then pour it into an approved gasoline storage devise.

6. Do not store gasoline in glass containers. If the glass breaks, a serious explosion or fire may occur.

7. Immediately wipe up spilled gasoline with rags. Store the rags in a metal container with a lid until they can be properly disposed of, or place them outside in a safe place for the fuel to evaporate.

8. Do not pour water onto a gasoline fire. Water spreads the fire and makes it more difficult to put out. Use a class B, BC or ABC fire extinguisher to extinguish the fire.

9. Always turn off the engine before refueling. Do not spill fuel onto the engine or exhaust system. Do not overfill the fuel tank. Leave an air space at the top of the tank to allow room for the fuel to expand due to temperature fluctuations.

Cleaning Parts

Cleaning parts is one of the more tedious and difficult service jobs performed in the home garage. There are many types of chemical cleaners and solvents available for shop use. Most are poisonous and extremely flammable. To prevent chemical exposure, vapor buildup, fire and serious injury, observe each product warning label and note the following:

1. Read and observe the entire product label before using any chemical. Always know what type of chemical is being used and whether it is poisonous and/or flammable.

2. Do not use more than one type of cleaning solvent at a time. If mixing chemicals is called for, measure the proper amounts according to the manufacturer.

3. Work in a well-ventilated area.

4. Wear chemical-resistant gloves.

5. Wear safety glasses.

6. Wear a vapor respirator if the instructions call for it.

7. Wash hands and arms thoroughly after cleaning parts.

8. Keep chemical products away from children and pets.

9. Thoroughly clean all oil, grease and cleaner residue from any part that must be heated.

10. Use a nylon brush when cleaning parts. Metal brushes may cause a spark.

11. When using a parts washer, only use the solvent recommended by the manufacturer. Make sure the parts washer is equipped with a metal lid that will lower in case of fire.

Warning Labels

Most manufacturers attach information and warning labels to the vehicle. These labels contain instructions that are important to personal safety when operating, servicing, transporting and storing the vehicle. Refer to the owner's manual for the description and location of labels. Order replacement labels from the manufacturer if they are missing or damaged.

SERIAL NUMBERS

Serial numbers are stamped onto the frame and engine. Record these numbers in the *Quick Reference Data* section at the front of the book. Have these numbers available when ordering parts.

The frame number (**Figure 1**) or vehicle identification number (VIN) is stamped on the right side of the steering tube.

The engine number (**Figure 2**) is stamped on a pad on the rear of the upper crankcase half.

Table 1 list model years and numbers.

FASTENERS

Proper fastener selection and installation is important to ensure that the vehicle operates as designed, and can be serviced efficiently. The choice of original equipment fasteners is not arrived at by chance. Make sure that replacement fasteners meet all the same requirements as the originals.

Threaded Fasteners

Threaded fasteners secure most of the components on the vehicle. Most are tightened by turning them clockwise (right-hand threads). If the normal rotation of the component would loosen the fastener, it may have left-hand threads. If a left-hand threaded fastener is used, it is noted in the text.

Two dimensions are required to match the size of the fastener: the number of threads in a given distance and the outside diameter of the threads.

Two systems are currently used to specify threaded fastener dimensions: the U.S. Standard system and the metric system (**Figure 3**). Pay particular attention when working with unidentified fasteners; mismatching thread types can damage threads.

> *NOTE*
> *To ensure that the fastener threads are not mismatched or cross-threaded, start all fasteners by hand. If a fastener is hard to start or turn, determine the cause before tightening with a wrench.*

The length (L, **Figure 4**), diameter (D) and distance between thread crests (pitch) (T) classifies metric screws and bolts. A typical bolt may be iden-

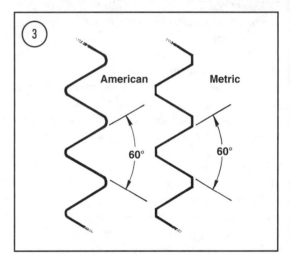

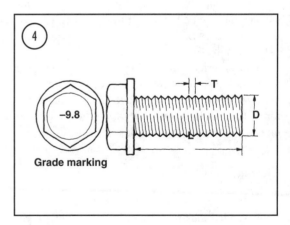

tified by the numbers, 8—1.25 × 130. This indicates the bolt has diameter of 8 mm, the distance between thread crests is 1.25 mm and the length is 130 mm. Always measure bolt length as shown in **Figure 4** to avoid purchasing replacements of the wrong length.

The numbers located on the top of the fastener (**Figure 4**) indicate the strength of metric screws

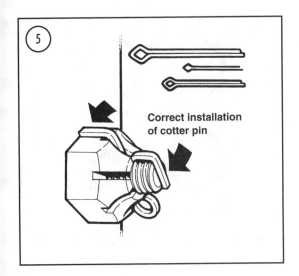

Correct installation of cotter pin

and bolts. The higher the number, the stronger the fastener. Unnumbered fasteners are the weakest.

Many screws, bolts and studs are combined with nuts to secure particular components. To indicate the size of a nut, manufacturers specify the internal diameter and the thread pitch.

The measurement across two flats on a nut or bolt indicates the wrench size.

> *WARNING*
> *Do not install fasteners with a strength classification lower than what was originally installed by the manufacturer. Doing so may cause equipment failure and/or damage.*

Torque Specifications

The materials used in the manufacture of the vehicle may be subjected to uneven stresses if the fasteners of the various subassemblies are not installed and tightened correctly. Fasteners that are improperly installed or work loose can cause extensive damage. It is essential to use an accurate torque wrench, described in this chapter, with the torque specifications in this manual.

Specifications for torque are provided in Newton-meters (N•m), foot-pounds (ft.-lb.) and inch-pounds (in.-lb.). Refer to **Table 5** for torque conversions and **Table 6** for general torque specifications. To use **Table 6**, first determine the size of the fastener as described in *Fasteners* in this chapter. Torque specifications for specific components

are at the end of the appropriate chapters. Torque wrenches are covered in the *Basic Tools* section.

Self-Locking Fasteners

Several types of bolts, screws and nuts incorporate a system that creates interference between the two fasteners. Interference is achieved in various ways. The most common is the nylon insert nut and a dry adhesive coating on the threads of a bolt.

Self-locking fasteners offer greater holding strength than standard fasteners, which improves their resistance to vibration. Most self-locking fasteners cannot be reused. The materials used to form the lock become distorted after the initial installation and removal. It is a good practice to discard and replace self-locking fasteners after their removal. Do not replace self-locking fasteners with standard fasteners.

Washers

There are two basic types of washers: flat washers and lockwashers. Flat washers are simple discs with a hole to fit a screw or bolt. Lockwashers are used to prevent a fastener from working loose. Washers can be used as spacers and seals, or to help distribute fastener load and to prevent the fastener from damaging the component.

As with fasteners, when replacing washers make sure the replacement washers are of the same design and quality.

Cotter Pins

A cotter pin is a split metal pin inserted into a hole or slot to prevent a fastener from loosening. In certain applications, such as the rear axle on an ATV or motorcycle, the fastener must be secured in this way. For these applications, a cotter pin and castellated (slotted) nut are used.

To use a cotter pin, first make sure the diameter is correct for the hole in the fastener. After correctly tightening the fastener and aligning the holes, insert the cotter pin through the hole and bend the ends over the fastener (**Figure 5**). Unless instructed to do so, never loosen a torqued fastener to align the holes. If the holes do not align, tighten the fastener just enough to achieve alignment.

Cotter pins are available in various diameters and lengths. Measure length from the bottom of the head to the tip of the shortest pin.

Snap Rings and E-clips

Snap rings (**Figure 6**) are circular-shaped metal retaining clips. They are required to secure parts and gears in place on parts such as shafts, pins or rods. External type snap rings are used to retain items on shafts. Internal type snap rings secure parts within housing bores. In some applications, in addition to securing the component(s), snap rings of varying thickness also determine endplay. These are usually called selective snap rings.

Two basic types of snap rings are used: machined and stamped snap rings. Machined snap rings (**Figure 7**) can be installed in either direction, since both faces have sharp edges. Stamped snap rings (**Figure 8**) are manufactured with a sharp edge and a round edge. When installing a stamped snap ring in a thrust application, install the sharp edge facing away from the part producing the thrust.

E-clips and circlips are used when it is not practical to use a snap ring. Remove these clips with a flat blade screwdriver by prying between the shaft and clip. To install an E-clip, center it over the shaft groove and push or tap it into place.

Observe the following when installing circlips:

1. Remove and install snap rings with snap ring pliers. See *Snap Ring Pliers* in this chapter.
2. In some applications, it may be necessary to replace snap rings after removing them.
3. Compress or expand snap rings only enough to install them. If overly expanded, they lose their retaining ability.
4. After installing a snap ring, make sure it seats completely.
5. Wear eye protection when removing and installing snap rings.

SHOP SUPPLIES

Lubricants and Fluids

Periodic lubrication helps ensure a long service life for any type of equipment. Using the correct type of lubricant is as important as performing the lubrication service, although in an emergency the wrong type is better than none. The following sec-

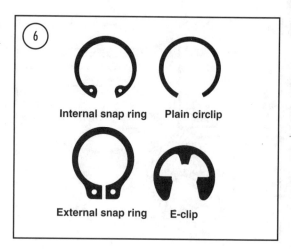

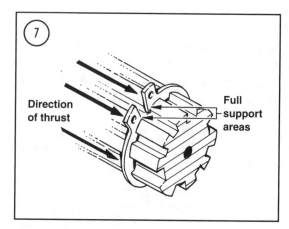

tion describes the types of lubricants most often required. Make sure to follow the manufacturer's recommendations for lubricant types.

Engine oils

Engine oil is classified by two standards: the American Petroleum Institute (API) service classification and the Society of Automotive Engineers (SAE) viscosity rating. This information is on the oil container label. Two letters indicate the API service classification. The number or sequence of numbers and letter (10W-40 for example) is the oil's viscosity rating. The API service classification and the SAE viscosity index are not indications of oil quality.

The service classification indicates that the oil meets specific lubrication standards. The first letter in the classification (*S*) indicates that the oil is for gasoline engines. The second letter indicates the

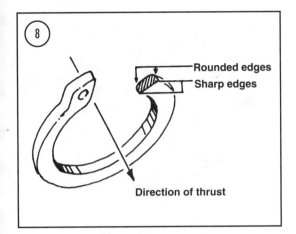

Rounded edges
Sharp edges

Direction of thrust

standard the oil satisfies. The classification started with the letter (*A*) and is currently at the letter (*J*).

Always use an oil with a classification recommended by the manufacturer. Using an oil with a classification different than that recommended can cause engine damage.

Viscosity is an indication of the oil's thickness. Thin oils have a lower number while thick oils have a higher number. Engine oils fall into the 5- to 50-weight range for single-grade oils.

Most manufacturers recommend multigrade oil. These oils perform efficiently across a wide range of operating conditions. Multigrade oils are identified by a (*W*) after the first number, which indicates the low-temperature viscosity.

Engine oils are most commonly mineral (petroleum) based; however synthetic and semi-synthetic types are used more frequently. When selecting engine oil, follow the manufacturer's recommendation for type, classification and viscosity.

Greases

Grease is lubricating oil with thickening agents added to it. The National Lubricating Grease Institute (NLGI) grades grease. Grades range from No. 000 to No. 6, with No. 6 being the thickest. Typical multipurpose grease is NLGI No. 2. For specific applications, manufacturers may recommend water-resistant type grease or one with an additive such as molybdenum disulfide (MoS_2).

Brake fluid

Brake fluid is the hydraulic fluid used to transmit hydraulic pressure (force) to the wheel brakes. Brake fluid is classified by the Department of Transportation (DOT). Current designations for brake fluid are DOT 3, DOT 4 and DOT 5. This classification appears on the fluid container.

Each type of brake fluid has its own definite characteristics. Do not intermix different types of brake fluid. DOT 5 fluid is silicone-based. DOT 5 is not compatible with other fluids or systems for which it was not designed. Mixing DOT 5 fluid with other fluids may cause brake system failure. When adding brake fluid, *only* use the fluid recommended by the vehicle manufacturer.

Brake fluid will damage any plastic, painted or plated surface it contacts. Use extreme care when working with brake fluid and remove any spills immediately with soap and water.

Hydraulic brake systems require clean and moisture free brake fluid. Never reuse brake fluid. Keep containers and reservoirs properly sealed.

> *WARNING*
> *Never put a mineral-based (petroleum) oil into the brake system. Mineral oil will cause rubber parts in the system to swell and break apart, resulting in complete brake failure.*

Chain lubricant

There are many types of chain lubricants available. Which type of chain lubricant to use depends on the type of chain.

On O-ring (sealed) chains, the lubricant keeps the O-rings pliable and prevents corrosion. The actual chain lubricant is enclosed in the chain by the O-rings. Recommended types include aerosol sprays specifically designed for O-ring chains, and conventional engine or gear oils. When using a spray lubricant, make sure it is suitable for O-ring chains.

Do not use a high-pressure washer, solvents or gasoline to clean an O-ring chain; clean only with kerosene.

Foam air filter oil

Filter oil is specifically designed for use in foam air filters. The oil is blended with additives making it easy to pour and apply evenly to the filter. These additives evaporate quickly, making the filter oil very tacky. This allows the oil to remain suspended within the foam pores, trapping dirt and preventing it from being drawn into the engine.

Do not use engine oil as a substitute for foam filter oil. Engine oils will not remain in the filter. Instead, they will be drawn into the engine, leaving the filter ineffective.

Cleaners, Degreasers and Solvents

Many chemicals are available to remove oil, grease and other residue from the vehicle.

Before using cleaning solvents, consider how they will be used and disposed of, particularly if they are not water-soluble. Local ordinances may require special procedures for the disposal of many types of cleaning chemicals. Refer to *Safety and Cleaning Parts* in this chapter for more information on their use.

Use brake parts cleaner to clean brake system components when contact with petroleum-based products will damage seals. Brake parts cleaner leaves no residue. Use electrical contact cleaner to clean electrical connections and components without leaving any residue. Carburetor cleaner is a powerful solvent used to remove fuel deposits and varnish from fuel system components. Use this cleaner carefully, as it may damage finishes.

Generally, degreasers are strong cleaners used to remove heavy accumulations of grease from engine and frame components.

Most solvents are designed to be used in a parts washing cabinet for individual component cleaning. For safety, use only nonflammable or high flash point solvents.

Gasket Sealant

Sealants are used in combination with a gasket or seal and are occasionally used alone. Follow the manufacturer's recommendation when using sealants. Use extreme care when choosing a sealant different from the type originally recommended. Choose sealants based on their resistance to heat, various fluids and their sealing capabilities.

One of the most common sealants is RTV, or room temperature vulcanizing sealant. This sealant cures at room temperature over a specific time pe-

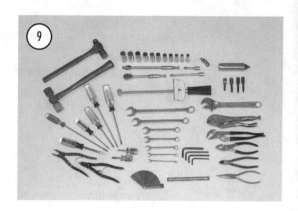

riod. This allows the repositioning of components without damaging gaskets.

Moisture in the air causes the RTV sealant to cure. Always install the tube cap as soon as possible after applying RTV sealant. RTV sealant has a limited shelf life and will not cure properly if the shelf life has expired. Keep partial tubes sealed and discard them if they have passed the expiration date.

Applying RTV sealant

Clean all old gasket residue from the mating surfaces. Remove all gasket material from blind threaded holes; it can cause inaccurate bolt torque. Spray the mating surfaces with aerosol parts cleaner and then wipe with a lint-free cloth. The area must be clean for the sealant to adhere.

Apply RTV sealant in a continuous bead 2-3 mm (0.08-0.12 in.) thick. Circle all the fastener holes unless otherwise specified. Do not allow any sealant to enter these holes. Assemble and tighten the fasteners to the specified torque within the time frame recommended by the RTV sealant manufacturer.

Gasket Remover

Aerosol gasket remover can help remove stubborn gaskets. This product can speed up the removal process and prevent damage to the mating surface that may be caused by using a scraping tool. Most of these types of products are very caustic. Follow the gasket remover manufacturer's instructions for use.

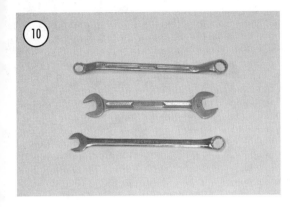

ish and are comfortable to use. Quality tools are a good investment.

When purchasing tools to perform the procedures covered in this manual, consider the tools potential frequency of use. If a tool kit is just now being started, consider purchasing a basic tool set (**Figure 9**) from a large tool supplier. These sets are available in many tool combinations and offer substantial savings when compared to individually purchased tools. As work experience grows and tasks become more complicated, specialized tools can be added.

Threadlocking Compound

A threadlocking compound is a fluid applied to the threads of fasteners. After tightening the fastener, the fluid dries and becomes a solid filler between the threads. This makes it difficult for the fastener to work loose from vibration, or heat expansion and contraction. Some threadlocking compounds also provide a seal against fluid leakage.

Before applying threadlocking compound remove any old compound from both thread areas and clean them with aerosol parts cleaner. Use the compound sparingly. Excess fluid can run into adjoining parts.

Threadlocking compounds are available in different strengths. Follow the particular manufacturer's recommendations regarding compound selection. Two manufacturers of threadlocking compound are ThreeBond and Loctite. They both offer a wide range of compounds for various strength, temperature and repair applications.

BASIC TOOLS

Most of the procedures in this manual can be carried out with simple hand tools and test equipment familiar to the home mechanic. Always use the correct tools for the job at hand. Keep tools organized and clean. Store them in a tool chest with related tools organized together.

Quality tools are essential. The best are constructed of high-strength alloy steel. These tools are light, easy to use and resistant to wear. Their working surface is devoid of sharp edges and the tool is carefully polished. They have an easy-to-clean fin-

Screwdrivers

Screwdrivers of various lengths and types are mandatory for the simplest tool kit. The two basic types are the slotted tip (flat blade) and the Phillips tip. These are available in sets that often include an assortment of tip sizes and shaft lengths.

As with all tools, use a screwdriver designed for the job. Make sure the size of the tip conforms to the size and shape of the fastener. Use them only for driving screws. Never use a screwdriver for prying or chiseling metal. Repair or replace worn or damaged screwdrivers. A worn tip may damage the fastener, making it difficult to remove.

Wrenches

Box-end, open-end and combinations wrenches (**Figure 10**) are available in a variety of types and sizes.

The number stamped on the wrench refers to the distance between the work areas. This size must match the size of the fastener head.

The box-end wrench is an excellent tool because it grips the fastener on all sides. This reduces the chance of the tool slipping. The box-end wrench is designed with either a 6 or 12-point opening. For stubborn or damaged fasteners, the 6-point provides superior holding ability by contacting the fastener across a wider area at all six edges. For general use, the 12-point works well. It allows the wrench to be removed and reinstalled without moving the handle over such a wide arc.

An open-end wrench is fast and works best in areas with limited overhead access. It contacts the fastener at only two points, and is less subject to slipping under heavy force, or if the tool or fastener is worn. A box-end wrench is preferred in most instances, especially when breaking loose and applying the final tightness to a fastener.

The combination wrench has a box-end on one end, and an open-end on the other. This combination makes it a very convenient tool.

Adjustable Wrenches

An adjustable wrench or Crescent wrench (**Figure 11**) can fit nearly any nut or bolt head that has clear access around its entire perimeter. Adjustable wrenches are best used as a backup wrench to keep a large nut or bolt from turning while the other end is being loosened or tightened with a box-end or socket wrench.

Adjustable wrenches contact the fastener at only two points, which makes them more subject to slipping off the fastener. The fact that one jaw is adjustable and may loosen only aggravates this shortcoming. Make certain the solid jaw is the one transmitting the force.

Socket Wrenches, Ratchets and Handles

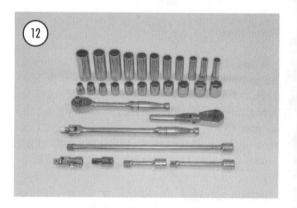

Sockets that attach to a ratchet handle (**Figure 12**) are available with 6-point (A, **Figure 13**) or 12-point (B) openings and different drive sizes. The drive size indicates the size of the square hole that accepts the ratchet handle. The number stamped on the socket is the size of the work area and must match the fastener head.

As with wrenches, a 6-point socket provides superior-holding ability, while a 12-point socket needs to be moved only half as far to reposition it on the fastener.

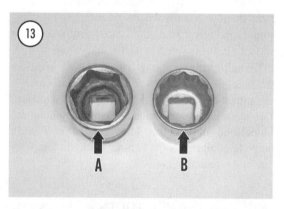

Sockets are designated for either hand or impact use. Impact sockets are made of thicker material for more durability. Compare the size and wall thickness of a 19-mm hand socket (A, **Figure 14**) and the 19-mm impact socket (B). Use impact sockets when using an impact driver or air tools. Use hand sockets with hand-driven attachments.

> *WARNING*
> *Do not use hand sockets with air or impact tools, as they may shatter and cause injury. Always wear eye protection when using impact or air tools.*

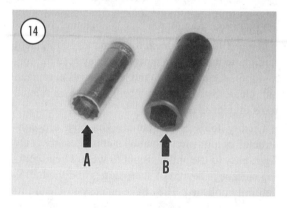

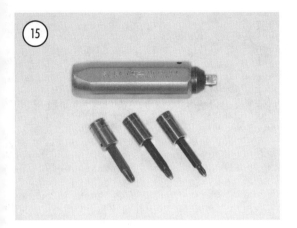

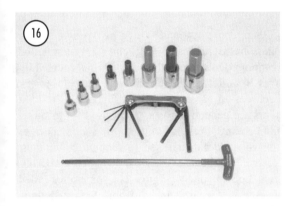

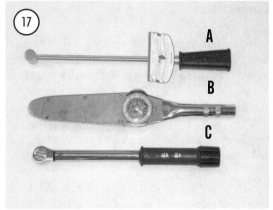

Various handles are available for sockets. The speed handle is used for fast operation. Flexible ratchet heads in varying lengths allow the socket to be turned with varying force, and at odd angles. Extension bars allow the socket setup to reach difficult areas. The ratchet is the most versatile handle. It allows the user to install or remove the nut without removing the socket.

Sockets combined with any number of drivers make them undoubtedly the fastest, safest and most convenient tool for fastener removal and installation.

Impact Driver

An impact driver provides extra force for removing fasteners by converting the impact of a hammer into a turning motion. This makes it possible to remove stubborn fasteners without damaging them. Impact drivers and interchangeable bits (**Figure 15**) are available from most tool suppliers. When using a socket with an impact driver make sure the socket is designed for impact use. Refer to *Socket Wrenches, Ratchets and Handles* in this section.

WARNING
Do not use hand sockets with air or impact tools as they may shatter and cause injury. Always wear eye protection when using impact or air tools.

Allen Wrenches

Allen or setscrew wrenches (**Figure 16**) are used on fasteners with hexagonal recesses in the fastener head. These wrenches are available in L-shaped bar, socket and T-handle types. Allen bolts are sometimes called socket bolts.

Torque Wrenches

A torque wrench is used with a socket, torque adapter or similar extension to tighten a fastener to a measured torque. Torque wrenches come in several drive sizes (1/4, 3/8, 1/2 and 3/4) and and have various methods of reading the torque value. The drive size indicates the size of the square drive that accepts the socket, adapter or extension. Common methods of reading the torque value are the deflecting beam (A, **Figure 17**), the dial indicator (B) and the audible click (C).

When choosing a torque wrench, consider the torque range, drive size and accuracy. The torque specifications in this manual provide an indication of the range required.

A torque wrench is a precision tool that must be properly cared for to remain accurate. Store torque wrenches in cases or separate padded drawers within a toolbox. Follow the manufacturer's instructions for their care and calibration.

Torque Adapters

Torque adapters or extensions extend or reduce the reach of a torque wrench. The torque adapter shown in **Figure 18** is used to tighten a fastener that cannot be reached due to the size of the torque wrench head, drive, and socket. If a torque adapter changes the effective lever length (**Figure 19**), the torque reading on the wrench will not equal the actual torque applied to the fastener. It is necessary to recalibrate the torque setting on the wrench to compensate for the change of lever length. When a torque adapter is used at a right angle to the drive head, calibration is not required, since the effective length has not changed.

To recalculate a torque reading when using a torque adapter, use the following formula, and refer to **Figure 19**.

$$TW = \frac{TA \times L}{L + A}$$

TW is the torque setting or dial reading on the wrench. TA is the torque specification and the actual amount of torque that will be applied to the fastener. A is the amount that the adapter increases (or in some cases reduces) the lever length as measured along the centerline of the torque wrench (**Figure 19**). L is the lever length of the wrench as measured from the center of the drive to the center of the grip. The effective length of the torque wrench is the sum of L and A.

Example:

TA = 20 ft.-lb.

A = 3 in.

L = 14 in.

$$TW = \frac{20 \times 14}{14 + 3} = \frac{280}{17} = 16.5 \text{ ft. lb.}$$

In this example, the torque wrench would be set to the recalculated torque value (TW = 16.5 ft.-lb.). When using a beam-type wrench, tighten the fastener until the pointer aligns with 16.5 ft.-lb. In this example, although the torque wrench is preset to 16.5 ft.-lb., the actual torque is 20 ft.-lb.

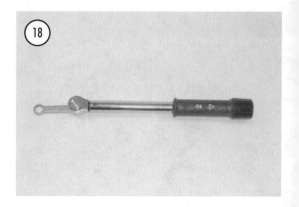

Pliers

Pliers come in a wide range of types and sizes. Pliers are useful for holding, cutting, bending, and crimping. Do not use them to turn fasteners. **Figures 20 and 21** show several types of useful pliers. Each design has a specialized function. Slip-joint pliers are general-purpose pliers used for gripping and bending. Diagonal cutting pliers are needed to cut wire and can be used to remove cotter pins. Needlenose pliers are used to hold or bend small objects. Locking pliers (**Figure 21**), sometimes called Vise-grips, are used to hold objects very tightly. They have many uses ranging from holding two parts together, to gripping the end of a broken stud. Use caution when using locking pliers, as the sharp jaws will damage the objects they hold.

Snap Ring Pliers

Snap ring pliers (**Figure 22**) are specialized pliers with tips that fit into the ends of circlips to remove and install them.

Circlip pliers are available with a fixed action (either internal or external) or convertible (one tool works on both internal and external circlips). They may have fixed tips or interchangeable ones of various sizes and angles. For general use, select a convertible type plier with interchangeable tips.

> *WARNING*
> *Circlips can slip and fly off when removing and installing them. Also, the circlip plier tips may break. Always wear eye protection when using circlip pliers.*

⑲ # HOW TO MEASURE TORQUE WRENCH EFFECTIVE LENGTH

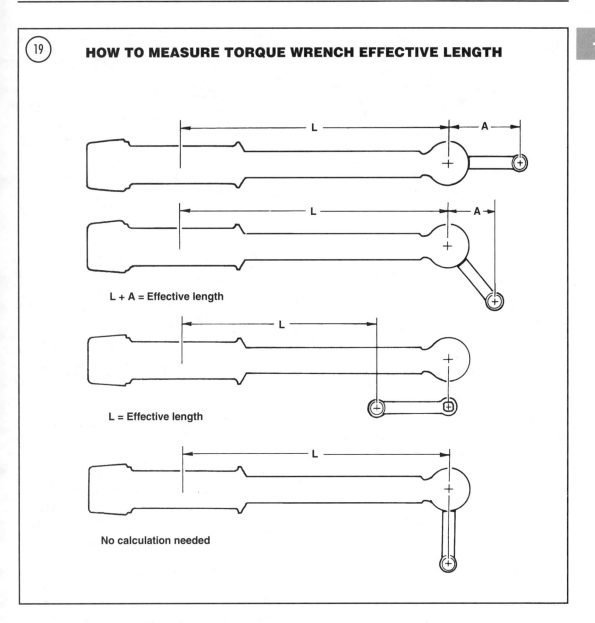

L + A = Effective length

L = Effective length

No calculation needed

⑳

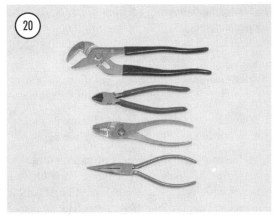

㉑

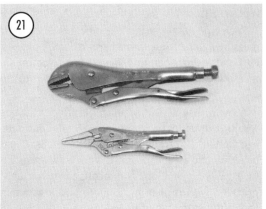

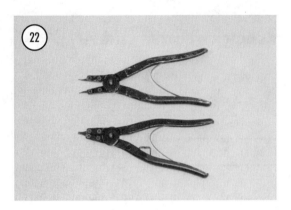

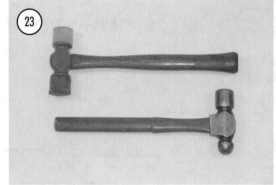

Hammers

Various types of hammers (**Figure 23**) are available to fit a number of applications. A ball-peen hammer is used to strike another tool, such as a punch or chisel. Soft-faced hammers are required when a metal object must be struck without damaging it. *Never* use a metal-faced hammer on engine and suspension components, as damage will occur in most cases.

Always wear eye protection when using hammers. Make sure the hammer face is in good condition and the handle is not cracked. Select the correct hammer for the job and make sure to strike the object squarely. Do not use the handle or the side of the hammer to strike an object.

PRECISION MEASURING TOOLS

The ability to accurately measure components is essential to successfully rebuild an engine. Equipment is manufactured to close tolerances, and obtaining consistently accurate measurements is essential to determining which components require replacement or further service.

Each type of measuring instrument is designed to measure a dimension with a certain degree of accuracy and within a certain range. When selecting the measuring tool, make sure it is applicable to the task.

As with all tools, measuring tools provide the best results if cared for properly. Improper use can damage the tool and result in inaccurate results. If any measurement is questionable, verify the measurement using another tool. A standard gauge is usually provided with measuring tools to check accuracy and calibrate the tool if necessary.

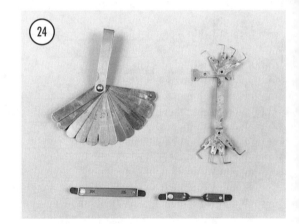

Precision measurements can vary according to the experience of the person performing the procedure. Accurate results are only possible if the mechanic possesses a feel for using the tool. Heavy-handed use of measuring tools may produce inaccurate results. Hold the tool gently by the fingertips so the point at which the tool contacts the object is easily felt. This feel for the equipment will produce more accurate measurements and reduce the risk of damaging the tool or component. Refer to the following sections for specific measuring tools.

Feeler Gauge

The feeler or thickness gauge (**Figure 24**) is used for measuring the distance between two surfaces.

A feeler gauge set consists of an assortment of steel strips of graduated thickness. Each blade is marked with its thickness. Blades can be of various lengths and angles for different procedures.

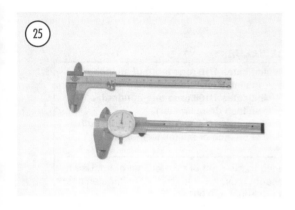

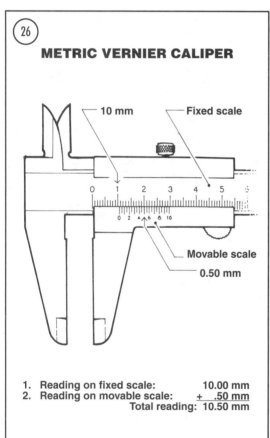

METRIC VERNIER CALIPER

10 mm

Fixed scale

Movable scale

0.50 mm

1.	Reading on fixed scale:	10.00 mm
2.	Reading on movable scale:	+ .50 mm
	Total reading:	10.50 mm

A common use for a feeler gauge is to measure valve clearance. Wire (round) type gauges are used to measure spark plug gap.

Calipers

Calipers (**Figure 25**) are excellent tools for obtaining inside, outside and depth measurements. Although not as precise as a micrometer, they allow reasonable precision, typically to within 0.05 mm (0.001 in.). Most calipers have a range up to 150 mm (6 in.).

Calipers are available in dial, vernier or digital versions. Dial calipers have a dial readout that provides convenient reading. Vernier calipers have marked scales that must be compared to determine the measurement. The digital caliper uses an LCD to show the measurement.

Properly maintain the measuring surfaces of the caliper. There must not be any dirt or burrs between the tool and the object being measured. Never force the caliper closed around an object; close the caliper around the highest point so it can be removed with a slight drag. Some calipers require calibration. Always refer to the manufacturer's instructions when using a new or unfamiliar caliper.

To read a vernier caliper refer to **Figure 26**. The fixed scale is marked in 1 mm increments. Ten individual lines on the fixed scale equal 1 cm. The moveable scale is marked in 0.05 mm (hundredth) increments. To obtain a reading, establish the first number by the location of the 0 line on the movable scale in relation to the first line to the left on the fixed scale. In this example, the number is 10 mm. To determine the next number, note which of the lines on the movable scale aligns with a mark on the fixed scale. A number of lines will seem close, but only one will align exactly. In this case, 0.50 mm is the reading to add to the first number. The result of adding 10 mm and 0.50 mm is a measurement of 10.50 mm.

Micrometers

A micrometer is an instrument designed for linear measurement using the decimal divisions of the inch or meter (**Figure 27**). While there are many types and styles of micrometers, most of the procedures in this manual require an outside micrometer. The outside micrometer is used to measure the outside diameter of cylindrical forms and the thickness of materials.

A micrometer's size indicates the minimum and maximum size of a part that it can measure. The usual sizes (**Figure 28**) are 0-1 in. (0-25 mm), 1-2 in. (25-50 mm), 2-3 in. (50-75 mm) and 3-4 in. (75-100 mm).

Micrometers that cover a wider range of measurement are available. These use a large frame with interchangeable anvils of various lengths. This type

(27)

DECIMAL PLACE VALUES*

0.1	Indicates 1/10 (one tenth of an inch or millimeter)
0.010	Indicates 1/100 (one one-hundreth of an inch or millimeter)
0.001	Indicates 1/1,000 (one one-thousandth of an inch or millimeter)

*This chart represents the values of figures placed to the right of the decimal point. Use it when reading decimals from one-tenth to one one-thousandth of an inch or millimeter. It is not a conversion chart (for example: 0.001 in. is not equal to 0.001 mm).

of micrometer offers a cost savings; however, its overall size may make it less convenient to use.

Reading a Micrometer

When reading a micrometer, numbers are taken from different scales and added together. The following sections describe how to read the measurements of various types of outside micrometers.

For accurate results, properly maintain the measuring surfaces of the micrometer. There cannot be any dirt or burrs between the tool and the measured object. Never force the micrometer closed around an object. Close the micrometer around the highest point so it can be removed with a slight drag. **Figure 29** shows the markings and parts of a standard inch micrometer. Be familiar with these terms before using a micrometer in the following sections.

Standard inch micrometer

The standard inch micrometer is accurate to one-thousandth of an inch or 0.001. The sleeve is marked in 0.025 in. increments. Every fourth sleeve mark is numbered 1, 2, 3, 4, 5, 6, 7, 8, 9. These numbers indicate 0.100, 0.200, 0.300, and so on.

The tapered end of the thimble has twenty-five lines marked around it. Each mark equals 0.001 in. One complete turn of the thimble will align its zero mark with the first mark on the sleeve or 0.025 in.

When reading a standard inch micrometer, perform the following steps while referring to **Figure 30**.
1. Read the sleeve and find the largest number visible. Each sleeve number equals 0.100 in.

(28)

2. Count the number of lines between the numbered sleeve mark and the edge of the thimble. Each sleeve mark equals 0.025 in.
3. Read the thimble mark that aligns with the sleeve line. Each thimble mark equals 0.001 in.

NOTE
If a thimble mark does not align exactly with the sleeve line, estimate the amount between the lines. For accurate readings in ten-thousandths of an inch (0.0001 in.), use a vernier inch micrometer.

4. Add the readings from Steps 1-3.

Vernier inch micrometer

A vernier inch micrometer is accurate to one ten-thousandth of an inch or 0.0001 in. It has the same markings as a standard inch micrometer with an additional vernier scale on the sleeve (**Figure 31**).

1

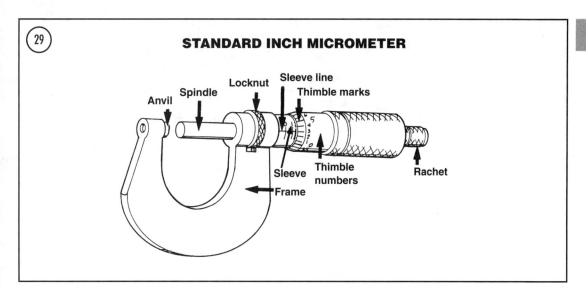

STANDARD INCH MICROMETER

Anvil — Spindle — Locknut — Sleeve line — Thimble marks — Sleeve — Thimble numbers — Rachet — Frame

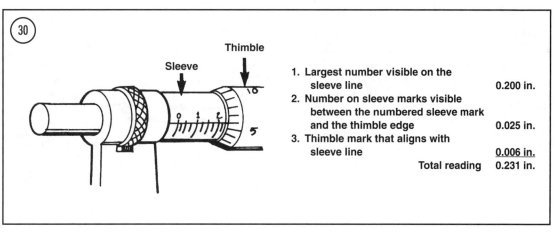

Sleeve — Thimble

1. Largest number visible on the sleeve line — 0.200 in.
2. Number on sleeve marks visible between the numbered sleeve mark and the thimble edge — 0.025 in.
3. Thimble mark that aligns with sleeve line — 0.006 in.
   Total reading — 0.231 in.

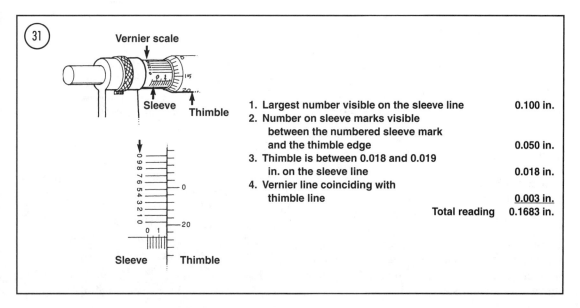

Vernier scale — Sleeve — Thimble — Sleeve — Thimble

1. Largest number visible on the sleeve line — 0.100 in.
2. Number on sleeve marks visible between the numbered sleeve mark and the thimble edge — 0.050 in.
3. Thimble is between 0.018 and 0.019 in. on the sleeve line — 0.018 in.
4. Vernier line coinciding with thimble line — 0.003 in.
   Total reading — 0.1683 in.

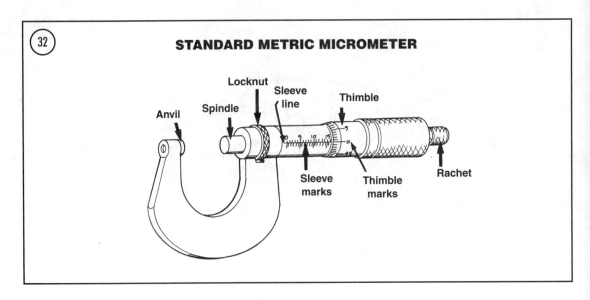

STANDARD METRIC MICROMETER

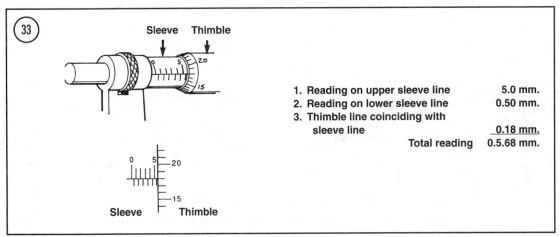

1. Reading on upper sleeve line   5.0 mm.
2. Reading on lower sleeve line   0.50 mm.
3. Thimble line coinciding with
        sleeve line   <u>0.18 mm.</u>
             Total reading   0.5.68 mm.

The vernier scale consists of 11 lines marked 1-9 with a 0 on each end. These lines run parallel to the thimble lines and represent 0.0001 in. increments.

When reading a vernier inch micrometer, perform the following steps while referring to **Figure 31**.

1. Read the micrometer in the same way as a standard micrometer. This is the initial reading.

2. If a thimble mark aligns exactly with the sleeve line, reading the vernier scale is not necessary. If they do not align, read the vernier scale in Step 3.

3. Determine which vernier scale mark aligns with one thimble mark. The vernier scale number is the amount in ten-thousandths of an inch to add to the initial reading from Step 1.

Metric micrometer

The standard metric micrometer (**Figure 32**) is accurate to one one-hundredth of a millimeter (0.01-mm). The sleeve line is graduated in millimeter and half millimeter increments. The marks on the upper half of the sleeve line equal 1.00 mm. Every fifth mark above the sleeve line is identified with a number. The number sequence depends on the size of the micrometer. A 0-25 mm micrometer, for example, will have sleeve marks numbered 0 through 25 in 5 mm increments. This numbering sequence continues with larger micrometers. On all metric micrometers, each mark on the lower half of the sleeve equals 0.50 mm.

The tapered end of the thimble has fifty lines marked around it. Each mark equals 0.01 mm.

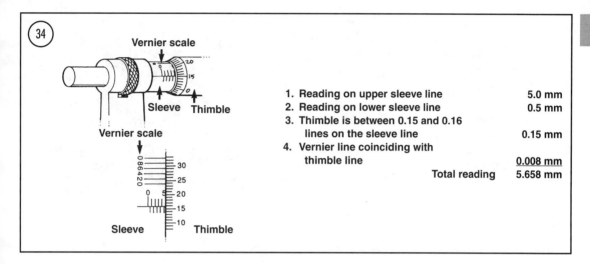

1. Reading on upper sleeve line	5.0 mm
2. Reading on lower sleeve line	0.5 mm
3. Thimble is between 0.15 and 0.16 lines on the sleeve line	0.15 mm
4. Vernier line coinciding with thimble line	<u>0.008 mm</u>
Total reading	5.658 mm

One complete turn of the thimble aligns its 0 mark with the first line on the lower half of the sleeve line or 0.50 mm.

When reading a metric micrometer, add the number of millimeters and half-millimeters on the sleeve line to the number of one one-hundredth millimeters on the thimble. Perform the following steps while referring to **Figure 33**.

1. Read the upper half of the sleeve line and count the number of lines visible. Each upper line equals 1 mm.

2. See if the half-millimeter line is visible on the lower sleeve line. If so, add 0.50 to the reading in Step 1.

3. Read the thimble mark that aligns with the sleeve line. Each thimble mark equals 0.01 mm.

NOTE
If a thimble mark does not align exactly with the sleeve line, estimate the amount between the lines. For accurate readings in two-thousandths of a millimeter (0.002 mm), use a metric vernier micrometer.

4. Add the readings from Steps 1-3.

Metric vernier micrometer

A metric vernier micrometer (**Figure 34**) is accurate to two-thousandths of a millimeter (0.002-mm). It has the same markings as a standard metric micrometer with the addition of a vernier scale on the sleeve. The vernier scale consists of five lines marked 0, 2, 4, 6, and 8. These lines run parallel to the thimble lines and represent 0.002-mm increments.

When reading a metric vernier micrometer, perform the following steps and refer to **Figure 34**.

1. Read the micrometer in the same way as a standard metric micrometer. This is the initial reading.

2. If a thimble mark aligns exactly with the sleeve line, reading the vernier scale is not necessary. If they do not align, read the vernier scale in Step 3.

3. Determine which vernier scale mark aligns exactly with one thimble mark. The vernier scale number is the amount in two-thousandths of a millimeter to add to the initial reading from Step 1.

Micrometer Adjustment

Before using a micrometer, check its adjustment as follows.

1. Clean the anvil and spindle faces.

2A. To check a 0-1 in. or 0-25 mm micrometer:
  a. Turn the thimble until the spindle contacts the anvil. If the micrometer has a ratchet stop, use it to ensure that the proper amount of pressure is applied.
  b. If the adjustment is correct, the 0 mark on the thimble will align exactly with the 0 mark on the sleeve line. If the marks do not align, the micrometer is out of adjustment.
  c. Follow the manufacturer's instructions to adjust the micrometer.

2B. To check a micrometer larger than 1 in. or 25 mm use the standard gauge supplied by the manufacturer. A standard gauge is a steel block, disc or rod that is machined to an exact size.

a. Place the standard gauge between the spindle and anvil, and measure its outside diameter or length. If the micrometer has a ratchet stop, use it to ensure that the proper amount of pressure is applied.

b. If the adjustment is correct, the 0 mark on the thimble will align exactly with the 0 mark on the sleeve line. If the marks do not align, the micrometer requires adjustment.

c. Follow the manufacturer's instructions to adjust the micrometer.

Micrometer Care

Micrometers are precision instruments. They must be used and maintained with great care.

Note the following:

1. Store micrometers in protective cases or separate padded drawers in a toolbox.

2. When in storage, make sure the spindle and anvil faces do not contact each other or another object. If they do, temperature changes and corrosion may damage the contact faces.

3. Do not clean a micrometer with compressed air. Dirt forced into the tool will cause wear.

4. Lubricate micrometers with WD-40 to prevent corrosion.

Telescoping and Small Bore Gauges

Use telescoping gauges (**Figure 35**) and small hole gauges (**Figure 36**) to measure bores. Neither gauge has a scale for direct readings. An outside micrometer must be used to determine the reading.

To use a telescoping gauge, select the correct size gauge for the bore. Compress the movable post and carefully insert the gauge into the bore. Carefully move the gauge in the bore to make sure it is centered. Tighten the knurled end of the gauge to hold the movable post in position. Remove the gauge and measure the length of the posts. Telescoping gauges are typically used to measure cylinder bores.

To use a small-bore gauge, select the correct size gauge for the bore. Carefully insert the gauge into the bore. Tighten the knurled end of the gauge to carefully expand the gauge fingers to the limit within the bore. Do not overtighten the gauge, as there is no built-in release. Excessive tightening can damage the bore surface and damage the tool. Remove the gauge and measure the outside dimension

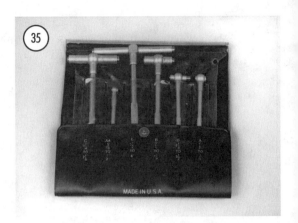

(**Figure 37**). Small hole gauges are typically used to measure valve guides.

Dial Indicator

A dial indicator (A, **Figure 38**) is a gauge with a dial face and needle used to measure variations in dimensions and movements. Measuring brake rotor runout is a typical use for a dial indicator.

Dial indicators are available in various ranges and graduations and with three basic types of mounting bases: magnetic, clamp, or screw-in stud. When

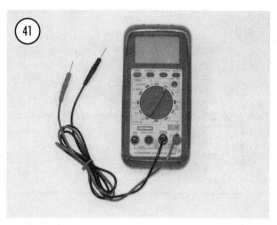

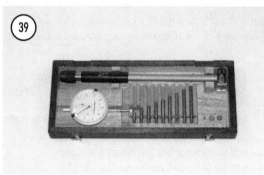

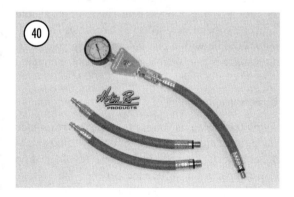

purchasing a dial indicator, select the magnetic stand type (B, **Figure 38**) with a continuous dial.

Cylinder Bore Gauge

A cylinder bore gauge is similar to a dial indicator. The gauge set shown in **Figure 39** consists of a dial indicator, handle, and different length adapters

(anvils) to fit the gauge to various bore sizes. The bore gauge is used to measure bore size, taper and out-of-round. When using a bore gauge, follow the manufacturer's instructions.

Compression Gauge

A compression gauge (**Figure 40**) measures combustion chamber (cylinder) pressure, usually in psi or kg/cm^2. The gauge adapter is either inserted or screwed into the spark plug hole to obtain the reading. Disable the engine so it will not start and hold the throttle in the wide-open position when performing a compression test. An engine that does not have adequate compression cannot be properly tuned. See Chapter Three.

Multimeter

A multimeter (**Figure 41**) is an essential tool for electrical system diagnosis. The voltage function indicates the voltage applied or available to various electrical components. The ohmmeter function tests circuits for continuity, or lack of continuity, and measures the resistance of a circuit.

Some manufacturers'specifications for electrical components are based on results using a specific test meter. Results may vary if using a meter not recommend by the manufacturer. Such requirements are noted when applicable.

Ohmmeter (analog) calibration

Each time an analog ohmmeter is used or if the scale is changed, the ohmmeter must be calibrated.

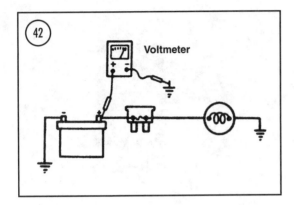

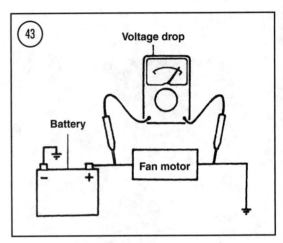

Digital ohmmeters do not require calibration.
1. Make sure the meter battery is in good condition.
2. Make sure the meter probes are in good condition.
3. Touch the two probes together and observe the needle location on the ohms scale. The needle must align with the 0 mark to obtain accurate measurements.
4. If necessary, rotate the meter ohms adjust knob until the needle and 0 mark align.

ELECTRICAL SYSTEM FUNDAMENTALS

A thorough study of the many types of electrical systems used in today's vehicles is beyond the scope of this manual. However, a basic understanding of electrical basics is necessary to perform simple diagnostic tests.

Voltage

Voltage is the electrical potential or pressure in an electrical circuit and is expressed in volts. The more pressure (voltage) in a circuit, the more work that can be performed.

Direct current (DC) voltage means the electricity flows in one direction. All circuits powered by a battery are DC circuits.

Alternating current (AC) means that the electricity flows in one direction momentarily then switches to the opposite direction. Alternator output is an example of AC voltage. This voltage must be changed or rectified to direct current to operate in a battery powered system.

Measuring voltage

Unless otherwise specified, perform all voltage tests with the electrical connectors attached.

When measuring voltage, select the meter range that is one scale higher than the expected voltage of the circuit to prevent damage to the meter. To determine the actual voltage in a circuit, use a voltmeter. To simply check if voltage is present, use a test light.

> *NOTE*
> *When using a test light, either lead can be attached to ground.*

1. Attach the negative meter test lead to a good ground (bare metal). Make sure the ground is not insulated with a rubber gasket or grommet.
2. Attach the positive meter test lead to the point being checked for voltage (**Figure 42**).
3. Turn on the ignition switch. The test light should light or the meter should display a reading. The reading should be within one volt of battery voltage. If the voltage is less, there is a problem in the circuit.

Voltage drop test

Resistance causes voltage to drop. This resistance can be measured in an active circuit by using a voltmeter to perform a voltage drop test. A voltage drop test compares the difference between the voltage available at the start of a circuit to the voltage at the end of the circuit while the circuit is operational. If the circuit has no resistance, there will be no voltage drop. The greater the resistance, the greater the voltage drop will be. A voltage drop of one volt or more indicates excessive resistance in the circuit.
1. Connect the positive meter test lead to the electrical source (where electricity is coming from).
2. Connect the negative meter test lead to the electrical load (where electricity is going). See **Figure 43**.

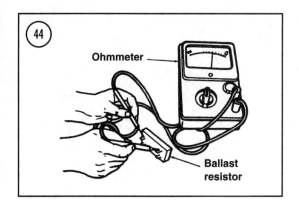

Ohmmeter

Ballast resistor

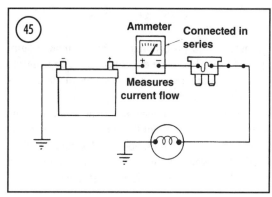

Ammeter Connected in series

Measures current flow

1

3. If necessary, activate the component(s) in the circuit.
4. A voltage reading of 1 volt or more indicates excessive resistance in the circuit. A reading equal to battery voltage indicates an open circuit.

Resistance

Resistance is the opposition to the flow of electricity within a circuit or component and is measured in ohms. Resistance causes a reduction in available current and voltage.

Resistance is measured in an inactive circuit with an ohmmeter. The ohmmeter sends a small amount of current into the circuit and measures how difficult it is to push the current through the circuit.

An ohmmeter, although useful, is not always a good indicator of a circuit's actual ability under operating conditions. This is due to the low voltage (6-9 volts) that the meter uses to test the circuit. The voltage in an ignition coil secondary winding can be several thousand volts. Such high voltage can cause the coil to malfunction, even though it tests acceptable during a resistance test.

Resistance generally increases with temperature. Perform all testing with the component or circuit at room temperature. Resistance tests performed at high temperatures may indicate high resistance readings and result in the unnecessary replacement of a component.

Measuring resistance and continuity testing

CAUTION
Only use an ohmmeter on a circuit that has no voltage present. The meter will be damaged if it is connected to a live circuit. An analog meter must be

*calibrated each time it is used or the scale is changed. See **Multimeter** in this chapter.*

A continuity test can determine if the circuit is complete. Perform this type of test using an ohmmeter or a self-powered test lamp.
1. Disconnect the negative battery cable.
2. Attach one test lead (ohmmeter or test light) to one end of the component or circuit.
3. Attach the other test lead to the opposite end of the component or circuit (**Figure 44**).
4. A self-powered test light will come on if the circuit has continuity or is complete. An ohmmeter will indicate either low or no resistance if the circuit has continuity. An open circuit is indicated if the meter displays infinite resistance.

Amperage

Amperage is the unit of measure for the amount of current within a circuit. Current is the actual flow of electricity. The higher the current, the more work that can be performed up to a given point. If the current flow exceeds the circuit or component capacity, the system will be damaged.

Measuring amps

An ammeter measures the current flow or amps of a circuit (**Figure 45**). Amperage measurement requires that the circuit be disconnected and the ammeter be connected in series to the circuit. Always use an ammeter that can read higher than the anticipated current flow to prevent damage to the meter. Connect the red test lead to the electrical source and the black test lead to the electrical load.

SPECIAL TOOLS

Some of the procedures in this manual require special tools. These are described in the appropriate chapter and are available from either the manufacturer or a tool supplier.

In many cases, an acceptable substitute may be found in an existing tool kit. Another alternative is to make the tool. Many schools with a machine shop curriculum welcome outside work that can be used as practical shop applications for students.

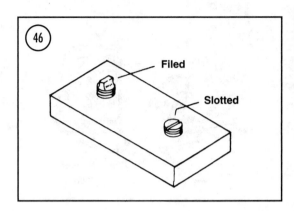

BASIC SERVICE METHODS

Most of the procedures in this manual are straightforward and can be performed by anyone reasonably competent with tools. However, consider personal capabilities carefully before attempting any operation involving major disassembly of the engine.

1. Front, in this manual, refers to the front of the vehicle. The front of any component is the end closest to the front of the vehicle. The left and right sides refer to the position of the parts as viewed by the rider sitting on the seat facing forward.

2. Whenever servicing an engine or suspension component, secure the vehicle in a safe manner.

3. Tag all similar parts for location and mark all mating parts for position. Record the number and thickness of any shims as they are removed. Identify parts by placing them in sealed and labled plastic bags.

4. Tag disconnected wires and connectors with masking tape and a marking pen. Do not rely on memory alone.

5. Protect finished surfaces from physical damage or corrosion. Keep gasoline and other chemicals off painted surfaces.

6. Use penetrating oil on frozen or tight bolts. Avoid using heat where possible. Heat can warp, melt or affect the temper of parts. Heat also damages the finish of paint and plastics.

7. When a part is a press fit or requires a special tool for removal, the information or type of tool is identified in the text. Otherwise, if a part is difficult to remove or install, determine the cause before proceeding.

8. To prevent objects or debris from falling into the engine, cover all openings.

9. Read each procedure thoroughly and compare the illustrations to the actual components before starting the procedure. Perform the procedure in sequence.

10. Recommendations are occasionally made to refer service to a dealership or specialist. In these cases, the work can be performed more economically by the specialist than by the home mechanic.

11. The term *replace* means to discard a defective part and install a new part. *Overhaul* means to remove, disassemble, inspect, measure, repair and/or replace parts as required to recondition an assembly.

12. Some operations require the use of a hydraulic press. If a press is not available, have these operations performed by a shop equipped with the necessary equipment. Do not use makeshift equipment that may damage the vehicle.

13. Repairs are much faster and easier if the vehicle is clean before starting work. Degrease the vehicle with a commercial degreaser; follow the directions on the container for the best results. Clean all parts with cleaning solvent as they are removed.

> *CAUTION*
> *Do not apply a chemical degreaser to an O-ring drive chain. These chemicals will damage the O-rings. Use kerosene to clean O-ring type chains.*

> *CAUTION*
> *Do not direct high-pressure water at steering bearings, carburetor hoses, wheel bearings, suspension and electrical components, or O-ring drive chains. The water will force the grease out of the bearings and possibly damage the seals.*

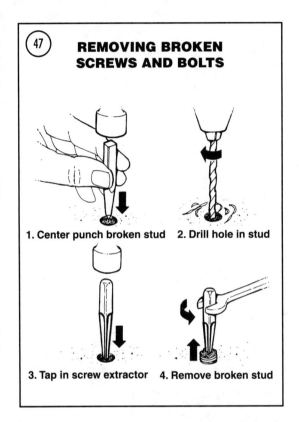

47 REMOVING BROKEN SCREWS AND BOLTS

1. Center punch broken stud   2. Drill hole in stud

3. Tap in screw extractor   4. Remove broken stud

14. If special tools are required, have them available before starting the procedure. When special tools are required, they will be described at the beginning of the procedure.

15. Make diagrams of similar-appearing parts. For instance, crankcase bolts are often not the same lengths. Do not rely on memory alone. It is possible that carefully laid out parts will become disturbed, making it difficult to reassemble the components correctly without a diagram.

16. Make sure all shims and washers are reinstalled in the same location and position.

17. Whenever a rotating part contacts a stationary part, look for a shim or washer.

18. Use new gaskets if there is any doubt about the condition of old ones.

19. If self-locking fasteners are used, replace them with new ones. Do not install standard fasteners in place of self-locking ones.

20. Use grease to hold small parts in place if they tend to fall out during assembly. Do not apply grease to electrical or brake components.

Removing Frozen Fasteners

If a fastener cannot be removed, several methods may be used to loosen it. First, apply penetrating oil such as Liquid Wrench or WD-40. Apply it liberally and let it penetrate for 10-15 minutes. Rap the fastener several times with a small hammer. Do not hit it hard enough to cause damage. Reapply the penetrating oil if necessary.

For frozen screws, apply penetrating oil as described, then insert a screwdriver in the slot and rap the top of the screwdriver with a hammer. This loosens the rust so the screw can be removed in the normal way. If the screw head is too damaged to use this method, grip the head with locking pliers and twist the screw out.

Avoid applying heat unless specifically instructed, as it may melt, warp or remove the temper from parts.

Removing Broken Fasteners

If the head breaks off a screw or bolt, several methods are available for removing the remaining portion. If a large portion of the remainder projects out, try gripping it with locking pliers. If the projecting portion is too small, file it to fit a wrench or cut a slot in it to fit a screwdriver (**Figure 46**).

If the head breaks off flush, use a screw extractor. To do this, centerpunch the exact center of the remaining portion of the screw or bolt. Drill a small hole in the screw and tap the extractor into the hole. Back the screw out with a wrench on the extractor (**Figure 47**).

Repairing Damaged Threads

Occasionally, threads are stripped through carelessness or impact damage. Often the threads can be repaired by running a tap (for internal threads on nuts) or die (for external threads on bolts) through the threads (**Figure 48**). To clean or repair spark plug threads, use a spark plug tap.

If an internal thread is damaged, it may be necessary to install a Helicoil or some other type of thread insert. Follow the manufacturer's instructions when installing their insert.

If it is necessary to drill and tap a hole, refer to **Table 8** for metric tap and drill sizes.

Stud Removal/Installation

A stud removal tool is available from most tool suppliers. This tool makes the removal and installation of studs easier. If one is not available, thread two nuts onto the stud and tighten them against each other. Remove the stud by turning the lower nut (**Figure 49**).

1. Measure the height of the stud above the surface.
2. Thread the stud removal tool onto the stud and tighten it, or thread two nuts onto the stud.
3. Remove the stud by turning the stud remover or the lower nut.
4. Remove any threadlocking compound from the threaded hole. Clean the threads with an aerosol parts cleaner.
5. Install the stud removal tool onto the new stud or thread two nuts onto the stud.
6. Apply threadlocking compound to the threads of the stud.
7. Install the stud and tighten with the stud removal tool or the top nut.
8. Install the stud to the height noted in Step 1 or its torque specification.
9. Remove the stud removal tool or the two nuts.

Removing Hoses

When removing stubborn hoses, do not exert excessive force on the hose or fitting. Remove the hose clamp and carefully insert a small screwdriver or pick tool between the fitting and hose. Apply a spray lubricant under the hose and carefully twist the hose off the fitting. Clean the fitting of any corrosion or rubber hose material with a wire brush. Clean the inside of the hose thoroughly. Do not use any lubricant when installing the hose (new or old). The lubricant may allow the hose to come off the fitting, even with the clamp secure.

Bearings

Bearings are used in the engine and transmission assembly to reduce power loss, heat and noise resulting from friction. Because bearings are precision parts, they must be maintained by proper lubrication and maintenance. If a bearing is damaged, replace it immediately. When installing a new bearing, take care to prevent damaging it. Bearing replacement procedures are included in the individ-

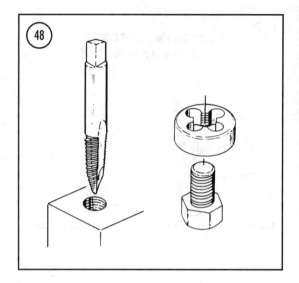

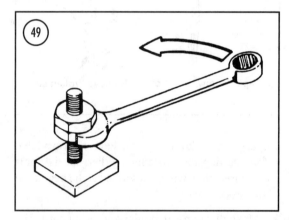

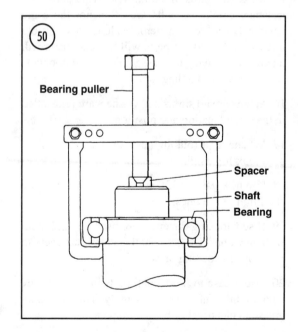

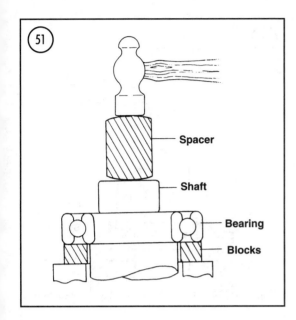

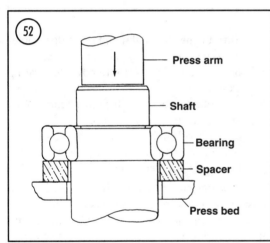

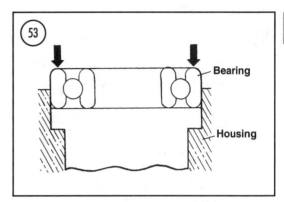

ual chapters where applicable; however, use the following sections as a guideline.

NOTE
Unless otherwise specified, install bearings with the manufacturer's mark or number facing outward.

Removal

While bearings are normally removed only when damaged, there may be times when it is necessary to remove a bearing that is in good condition. However, improper bearing removal will damage the bearing and maybe the shaft or case half. Note the following when removing bearings.

1. When using a puller to remove a bearing from a shaft, take care that shaft is not damaged. Always place a piece of metal between the end of the shaft and the puller screw. In addition, place the puller arms next to the inner bearing race. See **Figure 50**.

2. When using a hammer to remove a bearing from a shaft, do not strike the hammer directly against the shaft. Instead, use a brass or aluminum rod between the hammer and shaft (**Figure 51**) and make sure to support both bearing races with wooden blocks as shown.

3. The ideal method of bearing removal is with a hydraulic press. Note the following when using a press:

   a. Always support the inner and outer bearing races with a suitable size wooden or aluminum ring (**Figure 52**). If only the outer race is supported, pressure applied against the balls and/or the inner race will damage them.

   b. Always make sure the press arm (**Figure 52**) aligns with the center of the shaft. If the arm is not centered, it may damage the bearing and/or shaft.

   c. The moment the shaft is free of the bearing, it will drop to the floor. Secure or hold the shaft to prevent it from falling.

Installation

1. When installing a bearing in a housing, apply pressure to the *outer* bearing race (**Figure 53**). When installing a bearing on a shaft, apply pressure to the *inner* bearing race (**Figure 54**).

2. When installing a bearing as described in Step 1, some type of driver is required. Never strike the bearing directly with a hammer or the bearing will be damaged. When installing a bearing, use a piece

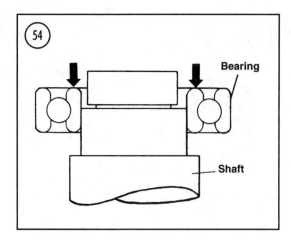

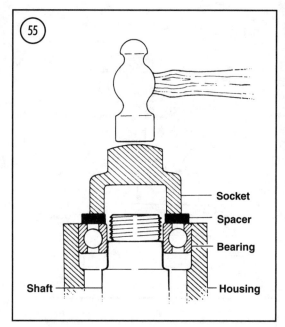

of pipe or a driver with a diameter that matches the bearing race. **Figure 55** shows the correct way to use a driver and hammer to install a bearing.

3. Step 1 describes how to install a bearing in a case half and over a shaft. However, when installing a bearing over a shaft and into a housing at the same time, a tight fit will be required for both outer and inner bearing races. In this situation, install a spacer underneath the driver tool so that pressure is applied evenly across both races. See **Figure 55**. If the outer race is not supported as shown, the balls will push against the outer bearing race and damage it.

Interference Fit

1. Follow this procedure when installing a bearing over a shaft. When a tight fit is required, the bearing inside diameter will be smaller than the shaft. In this case, driving the bearing on the shaft using normal methods may cause bearing damage. Instead, heat the bearing before installation. Note the following:

 a. Secure the shaft so it is ready for bearing installation.

 b. Clean all residues from the bearing surface of the shaft. Remove burrs with a file or sandpaper.

 c. Fill a suitable pot or beaker with clean mineral oil. Place a thermometer rated above 120° C (248° F) in the oil. Support the thermometer so that it does not rest on the bottom or side of the pot.

 d. Remove the bearing from its wrapper and secure it with a piece of heavy wire bent to hold it in the pot. Hang the bearing in the pot so it does not touch the bottom or sides of the pot.

 e. Turn the heat on and monitor the thermometer. When the oil temperature rises to approximately 120° C (248° F), remove the bearing from the pot and quickly install it. If necessary, place a socket on the inner bearing race and tap the bearing into place. As the bearing chills, it will tighten on the shaft so installation must be done quickly. Make sure the bearing is installed completely.

2. Follow this step when installing a bearing in a housing. Bearings are generally installed in a housing with a slight interference fit. Driving the bearing into the housing using normal methods may damage the housing or cause bearing damage. Instead, heat the housing before the bearing is installed. Note the following:

CAUTION
Before heating the housing in this procedure, wash the housing thoroughly with detergent and water. Rinse and rewash the cases as required to remove all traces of oil and other chemical deposits.

 a. Heat the housing to approximately 212° F (100° C) in an oven or on a hot plate. An easy way to check that it is at the proper temperature is to place tiny drops of water on the housing; if they sizzle and evaporate immedi-

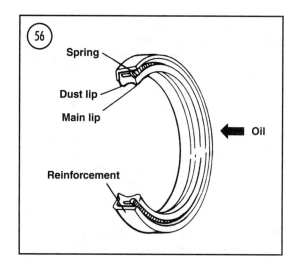

ately, the temperature is correct. Heat only one housing at a time.

CAUTION
Do not heat the housing with a propane or acetylene torch. Never bring a flame into contact with the bearing or housing. The direct heat will destroy the case hardening of the bearing and will likely warp the housing.

b. Remove the housing from the oven or hot plate, and hold onto the housing with a kitchen potholder, heavy gloves or heavy shop cloth. It is hot!

NOTE
Remove and install the bearings with a suitable size socket and extension.

c. Hold the housing with the bearing side down and tap the bearing out. Repeat for all bearings in the housing.

d. Before heating the bearing housing, place the new bearing in a freezer if possible. Chilling a bearing slightly reduces its outside diameter while the heated bearing housing assembly is slightly larger due to heat expansion. This will make bearing installation easier.

NOTE
Always install bearings with the manufacturer's mark or number facing outward.

e. While the housing is still hot, install the new bearing(s) into the housing. Install the bearings by hand, if possible. If necessary, lightly tap the bearing(s) into the housing with a socket placed on the outer bearing race (**Figure 53**). Do not install new bearings by driving on the inner-bearing race. Install the bearing(s) until it seats completely.

Seal Replacement

Seals (**Figure 56**) are used to contain oil, water, grease or combustion gasses in a housing or shaft. Improper removal of a seal can damage the housing or shaft. Improper installation of the seal can damage the seal. Note the following:

1. Prying is generally the easiest and most effective method of removing a seal from a housing. However, always place a rag underneath the pry tool (**Figure 57**) to prevent damage to the housing.

2. Pack waterproof grease in the seal lips before the seal is installed.

3. In most cases, install seals with the manufacturer's numbers or marks facing out.

4. Install seals with a socket placed on the outside of the seal as shown in **Figure 58**. Drive the seal squarely into the housing. Never install a seal by hitting against the top of the seal with a hammer.

STORAGE

Several months of non-use can cause a general deterioration of the vehicle. This is especially true in areas of extreme temperature variations. This deterioration can be minimized with careful preparation for storage. A properly stored vehicle will be much easier to return to service.

Storage Area Selection

When selecting a storage area, consider the following:
1. The storage area must be dry. A heated area is best, but not necessary. It should be insulated to minimize extreme temperature variations.
2. If the building has large window areas, mask them to keep sunlight off the vehicle.
3. Avoid buildings in industrial areas where corrosive emissions may be present. Avoid areas close to saltwater.
4. Consider the area's risk of fire, theft or vandalism. Check with an insurer regarding vehicle coverage while in storage.

Preparing the Vehicle for Storage

The amount of preparation a vehicle should undergo before storage depends on the expected length of non-use, storage area conditions and personal preference. Consider the following list the minimum requirement:
1. Wash the vehicle thoroughly. Make sure all dirt, mud and road debris are removed.
2. Start the engine and allow it to reach operating temperature. Drain the engine oil regardless of the

riding time since the last service. Fill the engine with the recommended type of oil.
3. Drain all fuel from the fuel tank, run the engine until all the fuel is consumed from the lines and carburetor(s).
4. Remove the spark plug(s) and pour a teaspoon of engine oil into the cylinder(s). Place a rag over the opening(s) and slowly turn the engine over to distribute the oil. Reinstall the spark plug(s).
5. Cover the exhaust and intake openings.
6. Reduce the normal tire pressure by 20%.
7. Apply a protective substance to the plastic and rubber components, including the tires. Make sure to follow the manufacturer's instructions for each type of product being used.
8. Place the vehicle on a stand or wooden blocks, so the wheels are off the ground. If this is not possible, place a piece of plywood between the tires and the ground. Inflate the tires to the recommended pressure if the vehicle can not be elevated.
9. Cover the vehicle with old bed sheets or something similar. Do not cover it with any plastic material that will trap moisture.

Returning the Vehicle to Service

The amount of service required when returning a vehicle to service after storage depends on the length of non-use and storage conditions. In addition to performing the reverse of the above procedure, make sure the brakes, clutch, throttle and engine stop switch work properly before operating the vehicle. Refer to Chapter Three and evaluate the service intervals to determine which areas require service.

Table 1 FRAME SERIAL NUMBERS

Model	Year	Frame number
GSX-R600V	1997	JS1GN78A V2100001-on
GSX-R600W	1998	JS1GN78A W2100001-on
GSX-R600X	1999	JS1GN78A X2100001-on
GSX-R600Y	2000	JS1GN78A Y2100001-on

Table 2 VEHICLE DIMENSIONS AND WEIGHT

Overall length	
Australia, Austria, Germany and	
Switzerland models	2100 mm (82.7 in.)
All other models	2065 mm (81.3 in.)
Overall width	720 mm (28.3 in.)
Overall height	
1997 models	1135 mm (44.7 in.)
1998-on	1165 mm (45.9 in.)
Seat height	830 mm (32.7 in.)
Wheelbase	
1997	1390 mm (54.7 in.)
1998-on	1385 mm (54.5 in)
Ground clearance	130 mm (5.1 in.)
Dry mass	
Austria, California and	
Switzerland models	175 kg (386 lb.)
All other models	174 kg (386 lb.)

Table 3 DECIMAL AND METRIC EQUIVALENTS

Fractions	Decimal in.	Metric mm	Fractions	Decimal in.	Metric mm
1/64	0.015625	0.39688	33/64	0.515625	13.09687
1/32	0.03125	0.79375	17/32	0.53125	13.49375
3/64	0.046875	1.19062	35/64	0.546875	13.89062
1/16	0.0625	1.58750	9/16	0.5625	14.28750
5/64	0.078125	1.98437	37/64	0.578125	14.68437
3/32	0.09375	2.38125	19/32	0.59375	15.08125
7/64	0.109375	2.77812	39/64	0.609375	15.47812
1/8	0.125	3.1750	5/8	0.625	15.87500
9/64	0.140625	3.57187	41/64	0.640625	16.27187
5/32	0.15625	3.96875	21/32	0.65625	16.66875
11/64	0.171875	4.36562	43/64	0.671875	17.06562
3/16	0.1875	4.76250	11/16	0.6875	17.46250
13/64	0.203125	5.15937	45/64	0.703125	17.85937
7/32	0.21875	5.55625	23/32	0.71875	18.25625
15/64	0.234375	5.95312	47/64	0.734375	18.65312
1/4	0.250	6.35000	3/4	0.750	19.05000
17/64	0.265625	6.74687	49/64	0.765625	19.44687
9/32	0.28125	7.14375	25/32	0.78125	19.84375
19/64	0.296875	7.54062	51/64	0.796875	20.24062
5/16	0.3125	7.93750	13/16	0.8125	20.63750
21/64	0.328125	8.33437	53/64	0.828125	21.03437
11/32	0.34375	8.73125	27/32	0.84375	21.43125
23/64	0.359375	9.12812	55/64	0.859375	22.82812
3/8	0.375	9.52500	7/8	0.875	22.22500
25/64	0.390625	9.92187	57/64	0.890625	22.62187
13/32	0.40625	10.31875	29/32	0.90625	23.01875
27/64	0.421875	10.71562	59/64	0.921875	23.41562
7/16	0.4375	11.11250	15/16	0.9375	23.81250
29/64	0.453125	11.50937	61/64	0.953125	24.20937
15/32	0.46875	11.90625	31/32	0.96875	24.60625
31/64	0.484375	12.30312	63/64	0.984375	25.00312
1/2	0.500	12.70000	1	1.00	25.40000

Table 4 CONVERSION TABLES

Multiply	By	To get equivalent of
Length		
Inches	25.4	Millimeter
Inches	2.54	Centimeter
Miles	1.609	Kilometer
Feet	0.3048	Meter
Millimeter	0.03937	Inches
Centimeter	0.3937	Inches
Kilometer	0.6214	Mile
Meter	3.281	Mile
Fluid volume		
U.S. quarts	0.9463	Liters
U.S. gallons	3.785	Liters
U.S. ounces	29.573529	Milliliters
Imperial gallons	4.54609	Liters
Imperial quarts	1.1365	Liters
Liters	0.2641721	U.S. gallons
Liters	1.0566882	U.S. quarts
Liters	33.814023	U.S. ounces
Liters	0.22	Imperial gallons
Liters	0.8799	Imperial quarts
Milliliters	0.033814	U.S. ounces
Milliliters	1.0	Cubic centimeters
Milliliters	0.001	Liters
Torque		
Foot-pounds	1.3558	Newton-meters
Foot-pounds	0.138255	Meters-kilograms
Inch-pounds	0.11299	Newton-meters
Newton-meters	0.7375622	Foot-pounds
Newton-meters	8.8507	Inch-pounds
Meters-kilograms	7.2330139	Foot-pounds
Volume		
Cubic inches	16.387064	Cubic centimeters
Cubic centimeters	0.0610237	Cubic inches
Temperature		
Fahrenheit	$(F - 32) \times 0.556$	Centigrade
Centigrade	$(C \times 1.8) + 32$	Fahrenheit
Weight		
Ounces	28.3495	Grams
Pounds	0.4535924	Kilograms
Grams	0.035274	Ounces
Kilograms	2.2046224	Pounds
Pressure		
Pounds per square inch	0.070307	Kilograms per square centimeter
Kilograms per square centimeter	14.223343	Pounds per square inch
Kilopascals	0.1450	Pounds per square inch
Pounds per square inch	6.895	Kilopascals
Speed		
Miles per hour	1.609344	Kilometers per hour
Kilometers per hour	0.6213712	Miles per hour

Table 5 GENERAL TORQUE SPECIFICATIONS*

Thread diameter	N.m	in.-lb.	ft.-lb.
5 mm bolt and nut	5	44	–
6 mm bolt and nut	10	88	–
8 mm bolt and nut	22	–	16
10 mm bolt and nut	34	–	25
12 mm bolt and nut	54	–	40
5 mm screw	4	35	–
6 mm screw	9	80	–
6 mm flange bolt with 8 mm head (small flange surface)	9	80	–
6 mm flange bolt with 8 mm head (large flange surface)	12	106	–
6 mm flange bolt with 10 mm head and nut	12	106	–
8 mm flange bolt and nut	26	–	20
10 mm flange bolt and nut	39	–	29

*This table lists general torque specifications for metric fasteners. Use this table when a specific torque specification is not listed for a fastener at the end of the appropriate chapter. The torque specifications listed in this table are for threads that are clean and dry.

Table 6 TECHNICAL ABBREVIATIONS

ABDC	After bottom dead center
ATDC	After top dead center
BBDC	Before bottom dead center
BDC	Bottom dead center
BTDC	Before top dead center
C	Celsius (Centigrade)
cc	Cubic centimeters
cid	Cubic inch displacement
CDI	Capacitor discharge ignition
cu. in.	Cubic inches
F	Fahrenheit
ft.	Feet
ft.-lb.	Foot-pounds
gal.	Gallons
H/A	High altitude
hp	Horsepower
in.	Inches
in.-lb.	Inch-pounds
I.D.	Inside diameter
kg	Kilograms
kgm	Kilogram meters
km	Kilometer
kPa	Kilopascals
L	Liter
m	Meter
MAG	Magneto
ml	Milliliter
mm	Millimeter
N•m	Newton-meters
O.D.	Outside diameter
oz.	Ounces
psi	Pounds per square inch
PTO	Power take off
pt.	Pint
qt.	Quart
rpm	Revolutions per minute

Table 7 METRIC TAP AND DRILL SIZES

Metric size	Drill equivalent	Decimal fraction	Nearest(mm)
3 × 0.50	No. 39	0.0995	3/32
3 × 0.60	3/32	0.0937	3/32
4 × 0.70	No. 30	0.1285	1/8
4 × 0.75	1/8	0.125	1/8
5 × 0.80	No. 19	0.166	11/64
5 × 0.90	No. 20	0.161	5/32
6 × 1.00	No. 9	0.196	13/64
7 × 1.00	16/64	0.234	15/64
8 × 1.00	J	0.277	9/32
8 × 1.25	17/64	0.265	17/64
9 × 1.00	5/16	0.3125	5/16
9 × 1.25	5/16	0.3125	5/16
10 × 1.25	11/32	0.3437	11/32
10 × 1.50	R	0.339	11/32
11 × 1.50	3/8	0.375	3/8
12 × 1.50	13/32	0.406	13/32
12 × 1.75	13/32	0.406	13/32

CHAPTER TWO

TROUBLESHOOTING

The troubleshooting procedures described in this chapter provide typical symptoms and logical methods for isolating the cause(s). There may be several ways to solve a problem, but only a systematic approach will be successful in avoiding wasted time and possibly unnecessary parts replacement.

Gather as much information as possible to aid in diagnosis. Never assume anything and do not overlook the obvious. Is there fuel in the tank? Has a spark plug wire fallen off? Learning to recognize symptoms will make troubleshooting easier. In most cases, expensive and complicated test equipment is not needed to determine whether repairs can be performed at home. On the other hand, be realistic and do not start procedures that are beyond your experience and equipment on hand. Many service departments will not take work that involves the reassembly of damaged or abused equipment. If they do, expect the cost to be high. If the motorcycle does require the attention of a professional, describe symptoms and conditions accurately and fully. The more information a technician has available, the easier it will be to diagnose the problem.

Proper lubrication, maintenance and periodic tune-ups reduce the chance that problems will occur. However, even with the best of care the motorcycle may require troubleshooting.

OPERATING REQUIREMENTS

An engine needs three basic elements (**Figure 1**) to run properly: correct air/fuel mixture, compression and a spark at the correct time. If any one element is missing, the engine will not run. Four-stroke engine operating principles are described in Chapter Four.

If the machine has been sitting for any length of time and refuses to start, check and clean the spark plugs and then inspect the fuel delivery system. This includes the fuel tank, fuel valve, fuel pump and fuel lines to the carburetor. Gasoline deposits may have gummed up the carburetor jets and air passages. Gasoline tends to lose its potency after standing for long periods. Condensation may contaminate the fuel with water. Drain the old fuel (fuel tank, fuel lines and carburetor) and start with fresh fuel.

STARTING THE ENGINE

The ignition and starting circuits use a switch interlock system. The position of the sidestand, clutch lever and gear selector affect starting. The engine cannot turn over if the transmission is in gear and the sidestand is down. If the transmission is in gear and the sidestand is up, the clutch must be fully disengaged. To start the engine, refer to the starting conditions that best meet the conditions.

> *CAUTION*
> *The oil pressure warning light should go out a few seconds after the engine starts. If not, stop the engine **immediately**. Check the oil level as described in Chapter Three. If the oil level is correct, determine whether insufficient oil pressure (Chapter Three) or an electrical problem (Chapter Nine) is the cause.*

Starting a Cold Engine

1. Shift the transmission into NEUTRAL.
2. Set the engine stop switch (A, **Figure 2**) to RUN.
3. Turn the ignition switch ON.
4. Make sure the neutral indicator and oil pressure warning lights are illuminated.
5. Pull the choke lever (A, **Figure 3**) all the way back to the ON position.
6. Pull the clutch lever (B, **Figure 3**) all the way to the handlebar grip to disengage the clutch.
7. With the throttle completely closed, push the START button (B, **Figure 2**).
8. When the engine starts, work the throttle slightly to keep it running.
9. Idle the engine for approximately 30-60 seconds or until the throttle responds cleanly, and then push the choke lever all the way forward to the OFF position.

Starting a Warm or Hot Engine

1. Shift the transmission into NEUTRAL.
2. Set the engine stop switch (A, **Figure 2**) to RUN.
3. Turn the ignition switch ON.
4. Make sure the neutral indicator and oil pressure warning lights are illuminated.
5. Make sure the choke lever (A, **Figure 3**) is all the way forward to the OFF position.

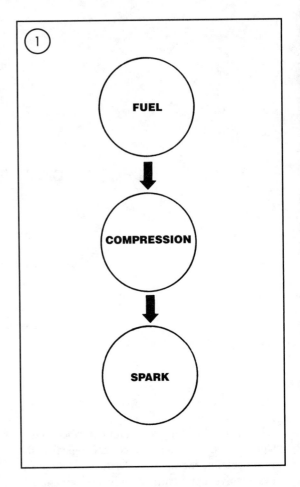

6. Pull the clutch lever (B, **Figure 3**) all the way to the handlebar grip to disengage the clutch.

7. Open the throttle slightly and operate the START button (B, **Figure 2**).

Starting a Flooded Engine

If the engine does not start and there is a strong gasoline smell, the engine may be flooded. If so, open the throttle all the way and operate the starter. Do not open the choke. Holding the throttle open allows more air to reach the engine.

> *NOTE*
> *If the engine refuses to start, check the carburetor overflow hose attached to the bottom of the float bowl. If fuel runs out the end of the hose, the float is stuck open, allowing the carburetor to overfill. If this problem exists, remove the carburetor and correct the*

problem as described in Chapter Eight.

STARTING DIFFICULTIES

If the engine turns over but does not start, check for obvious problems first. Go down the following list step by step. Perform each step while remembering the three engine operating requirements described earlier in this chapter.

If the engine still does not start, refer to the appropriate troubleshooting procedure that follows in this chapter.

1. Make sure the choke lever is in the correct position.

> *WARNING*
> *Do not use an open flame to check for fuel in the tank. A serious explosion is certain to result.*

2. Make sure there is fuel in the tank. Open the fuel filler cap and rock the bike. Listen for the fuel sloshing around. Fill the tank if necessary. If the fuel condition is in doubt, drain the fuel from the tank, and fill it with fresh fuel.

3. If the engine is flooded, open the throttle all the way and operate the START button. If the engine is severely flooded (fouled or wet spark plugs), remove the spark plugs and dry the base and electrode thoroughly with a soft cloth or with an aerosol electrical contact cleaner. Reinstall the plugs and attempt to start the engine.

> *NOTE*
> *If fuel is reaching the carburetor, the fuel system could still be the problem. The jets (pilot and main) could be plugged from fuel deposits. This is especially true if the motorcycle has not been used recently. However, before removing the carburetors, make sure the ignition provides adequate spark.*

4. Make sure the ENGINE STOP switch (A, **Figure 2**) is not stuck or working improperly. Also make sure the switch wire is not broken or shorted. If necessary, test the engine stop switch as described under *Switches* in Chapter Nine.

5. Make sure the clutch is disengaged and the clutch switch (**Figure 4**) operates properly.

6. Make sure the ignition coil/plug cap is securely on each spark plug. Make sure the spark plug wires are in good condition. Remove the air box, as described in Chapter Eight, and push all four caps and boots (**Figure 5**) and slightly rotate them to clean the electrical connection between the plug and the connector.

> *NOTE*
> *If the engine still does not start, continue with the following.*

7. Perform a spark test as described under *Engine Fails to Start (Spark Test)* in this chapter. If there is a strong spark, perform Step 8. If there is no spark or if the spark is very weak, test the ignition system as described under *Ignition System* in this chapter.

8. Check cylinder compression as follows:

NOTE
Refer to Chapter Three for spark plug removal information.

CAUTION
To prevent damage to the ignition system, ground the spark plugs when performing the following steps. Do not ground the spark plug to the cylinder head cover, clutch cover, starter clutch cover, idler gear cover or the alternator cover. An electrical spark will damage these magnesium covers.

   a. Remove and ground the ignition coil/plug cap against the crankcase.
   b. Put your finger tightly over the spark plug hole.
   c. Operate the START button. When the piston comes up on the compression stroke, pressure in the cylinder should force your finger from the spark plug hole. If your finger pops off, the cylinder probably has sufficient compression to start the engine. Repeat for the other cylinders.

NOTE
*A compression problem may still exist, even though the cylinder passed the previous test. Check engine compression with a compression gauge as described under **Tune-up** in Chapter Three.*

   d. Install the spark plugs and ignition coil/plug caps. Reconnect the vacuum line to the fuel shutoff valve.

Engine Fails to Start
(Spark Test)

Perform a spark test to determine if the ignition is producing adequate spark. This test can be performed with a spark plug or a spark tester. A spark tester (**Figure 6**) is used as a substitute for the spark plug and allows the spark to be more easily ob-

served between the adjustable air gap. The tool shown is available from Motion Pro (part No. 08-0122).

CAUTION
Before removing the spark plugs in Step 1, clean all dirt and debris away from the plug base. Dirt that falls into the cylinder causes rapid engine wear.

1. Refer to Chapter Three and disconnect all four ignition coil/plug caps (**Figure 5**) and remove all four spark plugs.

CAUTION
Do not ground the spark plug to the cylinder head cover, clutch cover, starter clutch cover, idler gear cover or the alternator cover. An electrical spark will damage these magnesium covers.

2. Insert the spark plug, or spark tester, into its cap and touch the spark plug base against the crankcase to ground it. Position the spark plug so the electrode can be observed.

NOTE
If not using a spark tester, always use a new spark plug for this test.

WARNING
Mount the spark plug, or tester, away from the spark plug hole in the cylinder so the spark cannot ignite the gasoline vapors in the cylinder. If the engine is flooded, do not perform this test. Fuel that is ejected through the spark plug hole can be ignited by the firing of the spark plug.

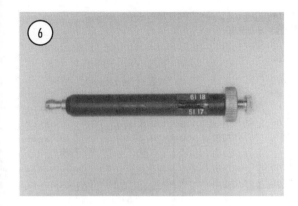

3. Turn the ignition switch ON.

> *WARNING*
> *Do **not** hold the spark plug, wire or connector or a serious electrical shock may result.*

4. Turn the engine over. A fat blue spark should be evident across the spark plug electrode or spark tester terminals. If there is strong sunlight on the plug, shade the plug to improve visability. Repeat for all other cylinders.

5. If the spark is good, check for one or more of the following possible malfunctions:

   a. Obstructed fuel line or fuel filter or a malfunctioning fuel pump.

   b. Low compression or engine damage.

   c. Flooded engine.

6. If the spark is weak or if there is no spark, refer to *Engine is Difficult to Start* in this chapter.

> *NOTE*
> *If the engine backfires while starting, the ignition timing may be incorrect. A signal generator rotor, loose signal generator or a defective ignition component will change the ignition timing. Refer to **Ignition System** in this chapter for more information.*

ENGINE IS DIFFICULT TO START

The following section groups the three main engine operating systems with probable causes.

Electrical System

The electrical system is a common source of engine starting problems. Trouble usually occurs at the wiring harness and connectors.

1. *Spark plugs*:
   a. Fouled spark plug(s).
   b. Incorrect spark plug gap.
   c. Incorrect spark plug heat range; see Chapter Three.
   d. Worn or damaged spark plug electrodes.
   e. Damaged spark plug(s).
   f. Damaged ignition coil/plug cap(s) or wire(s).

> *NOTE*
> *Refer to **Reading Spark Plugs** in Chapter Three for additional information.*

2. *Ignition coil*:
   a. Loose or damaged primary wire leads.
   b. Cracked ignition coil body.
   c. Loose or corroded ground wire.
3. *Switches and wiring*:
   a. Dirty or loose-fitting terminals.
   b. Damaged wires or connectors.
   c. Damaged start switch.
   d. Damaged engine stop switch.
   e. Damaged ignition switch.
4. *Electrical components*:
   a. Damaged signal generator and/or rotor.
   b. Damaged CDI unit.

Fuel System

A contaminated fuel system causes engine starting and performance related problems. It only takes a small amount of dirt in the fuel valve, fuel line or carburetor to cause problems.

1. *Air filter*:
   a. Clogged air filter.
   b. Clogged air filter housing.
   c. Leaking or damaged air filter housing-to-carburetor boots.
2. *Fuel shutoff valve*:
   a. Clogged fuel hose.
   b. Clogged fuel valve filter.
   c. Clogged or leaking vacuum hose.
3. *Fuel tank*:
   a. No fuel.
   b. Clogged fuel filter.

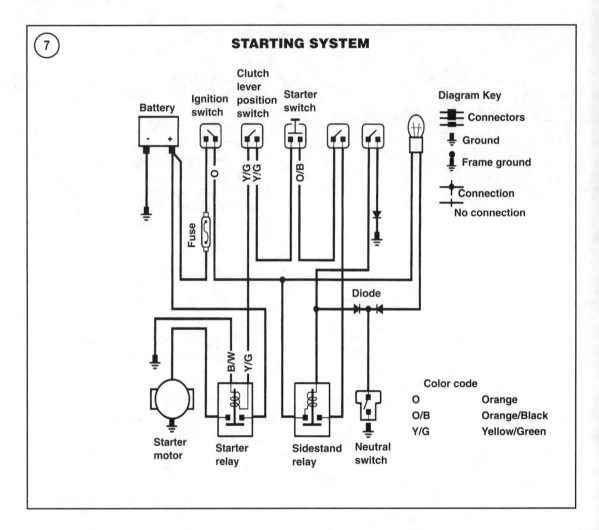

STARTING SYSTEM

c. Contaminated fuel.

d. Clogged fuel tank breather.

4. *Carburetor*:

   a. Clogged or damaged choke system.

   b. Clogged main jet(s).

   c. Clogged slow jet(s).

   d. Loose slow jet(s) or main jet(s).

   e. Clogged slow jet air passages.

   f. Incorrect float level(s).

   g. Leaking or otherwise damaged float(s).

   h. Worn or damaged needle valve(s).

5. *Fuel pump*:

   a. Fuel pump filter clogged.

   b. Fuel pump electrical connector corroded or disconnected.

   c. Defective fuel pump relay.

Engine Compression

Check engine compression with a compression gauge as described in Chapter Three.

1. *Cylinder and cylinder head*:

   a. Loose spark plug(s).

   b. Missing spark plug gasket(s).

   c. Leaking cylinder head gasket.

   d. Leaking cylinder block base gasket.

   e. Excessively worn or seized piston(s), piston rings and/or cylinder walls.

   f. Loose cylinder block and/or cylinder head fasteners.

   g. Cylinder head incorrectly installed and/or tightened.

   h. Warped cylinder head.

   i. Blown head gasket.

   j. Blown cylinder block base gasket.

   k. Loose cylinder fasteners.

    l. No valve clearance.

    m. Incorrect valve timing.

2. *Piston and piston rings*:

    a. Worn piston rings.

    b. Damaged piston rings.

    c. Piston seizure or piston damage.

3. *Crankcase and crankshaft*:

    a. Seized connecting rod(s).

    b. Damaged crankcases.

    c. Damaged oil seals.

POOR IDLE SPEED PERFORMANCE

If the engine starts but off-idle performance is poor (hesitation, cutting out, etc.), check the following:

1. Clogged or damaged air filter.

2. *Carburetor*:

    a. Clogged slow jet(s).

    b. Loose slow jet(s).

    c. Damaged choke system.

    d. Incorrect throttle cable adjustment.

    e. Incorrect carburetor adjustment.

    f. Flooded carburetor (visually check carburetor overflow hose for fuel).

    g. Vacuum piston not sliding smoothly in carburetor bore.

    h. Clogged fuel hose.

3. *Fuel*:

    a. Water and/or alcohol in fuel.

    b. Old fuel.

    c. Defective fuel pump or fuel pump relay.

4. *Engine*:

    a. Low engine compression.

    b. Incorrect valve clearance.

    c. Poor valve seating.

    d. Defective valve guides.

    e. Worn tappet/cam surface.

5. *Electrical system*:

    a. Damaged spark plug(s).

    b. Damaged ignition coil/plug cap(s).

    c. Damaged signal generator rotor and/or signal generator.

    d. Damaged CDI unit.

POOR MEDIUM AND HIGH SPEED PERFORMANCE

Refer to *Engine is Difficult to Start* in this chapter, then check the following:

1. *Carburetor(s)*:

    a. Incorrect fuel level.

    b. Incorrect jet needle clip position (if adjustable).

    c. Clogged or loose main jet(s).

2. Clogged air filter.

3. Defective fuel pump or fuel pump relay.

4. *Engine:*

    a. Weakened valve springs.

    b. Worn camshafts.

    c. Incorrect valve timing.

    d. Incorrect valve adjustment.

5. *Electrical:*

    a. Spark gap too narrow.

    b. Insufficient ignition advance.

    c. Defective ignition coil/plug cap(s).

    d. Defective signal generator or CDI unit.

6. *Other considerations*:

    a. Overheating.

    b. Clutch slippage.

    c. Brake drag.

    d. Engine oil viscosity too high or oil level too high.

STARTING SYSTEM

The starting system consists of the starter motor, battery, starter relay and switch. This section describes procedures for troubleshooting the system. A fully charged battery, ohmmeter and jumper cables are required to perform these tests. Refer to the schematic in **Figure 7** throughout the tests.

If the starter does not operate, perform the following tests. After each test, reconnect any connector that was disconnected before proceeding.

CAUTION
Do not operate the starter motor for more than five seconds. Allow the starter motor to cool for 15 seconds between starting attempts.

1. Make sure the battery is fully charged and the cables are not damaged. Make sure the battery-to-cable connections are clean and secure. Test the battery as described in Chapter Three.

2. Make sure all electrical connections are clean and secure.

3. Inspect the wiring harness and socket connections for damage.

4. Check the main fuse mounted next to the starter relay on the left side.

    a. Remove the left rear frame cover.

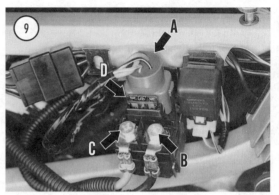

b. Remove the starter relay cover (**Figure 8**).

c. Pull up and remove the fuse (D, **Figure 9**). Visually inspect it. If the fuse is blown (**Figure 10**), refer to *Fuse* in Chapter Nine. If the main fuse is good, reinstall it, or install a new one, then go on to the next step.

5. Disconnect the following switches one by one (in the sequence provided) and test them as described in Chapter Nine. If the switch operates correctly, reinstall the switch and test the next one. If the switch does not operate correctly, replace it.

    a. Main switch.

    b. Start switch.

    c. Engine stop switch.

    d. Sidestand switch.

    e. Clutch switch.

6. Inspect the sidestand relay as described in Chapter Nine. Replace the relay if it is defective.

7. Remove the cover from the starter relay. Disconnect the starter relay primary connector (A, **Figure 9**).

8. Disconnect the black starter motor lead (B, **Figure 9**) and the red battery lead (C, **Figure 9**) from the starter relay.

9. Connect an ohmmeter and a 12 volt battery to the starter relay terminals as shown in **Figure 11**. When the battery is connected, there should be continuity (low to zero ohms) across the two terminals. When the battery is disconnected, there should be no continuity (infinity).

10. Connect an ohmmeter to the starter relay terminals as shown in **Figure 12** and measure the resistance across these terminals. The resistance should be 3-5 ohms.

    a. If the starter circuit relay tested correctly, perform Step 11.

    b. If the starter circuit relay did not test correctly, replace the relay and retest.

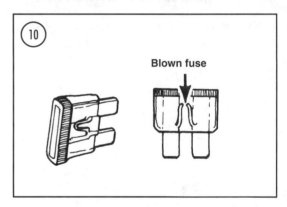

Blown fuse

11. If the starting system problem has not been found, recheck the wiring system for dirty or loose-fitting terminals or damaged wires. Clean and repair the wiring/terminals as required. If all the connectors and wires are in good condition, the starter motor is probably faulty. Remove and overhaul the starter motor as described under *Starter* in Chapter Nine.

12. Make sure all connectors disassembled during this procedure are free of corrosion and are reconnected properly.

CHARGING SYSTEM

A malfunction in the charging system generally causes the battery to remain undercharged. **Figure 13** shows a schematic of the charging system and its components.

Test each of the following items and refer to the appropriate chapter if applicable.

1. Make sure the battery is fully charged and the cables are not damaged. Make sure the battery-to-cable connections are clean and secure. Test the battery as described in Chapter Three. If the bat-

12-volt battery

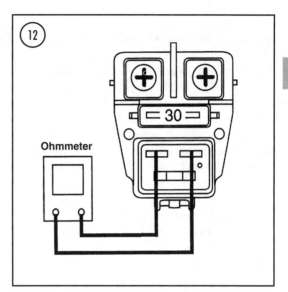

2

tery cable polarity is reversed, check for a damaged regulator/rectifier.

2. Make sure all wiring and connections between the battery and alternator are clean, secure and undamaged.

3. Perform the *Charging System Output Test* as described in Chapter Nine.

4. Test the regulator/rectifier as described under *Regulator/Rectifier* in Chapter Nine.

IGNITION SYSTEM

All models are equipped with a transistorized ignition system. This solid state system uses no con-

tact breaker points or other moving parts. Because of the solid state design, problems with the transistorized system are rare. If a problem occurs, it generally causes a weak spark or no spark at all. An ignition system with a weak spark or no spark is relatively easy to troubleshoot. It is difficult, however, to troubleshoot an ignition system that only malfunctions when the engine is hot or under load. Use the troubleshooting procedure in **Figure 14** to isolate an ignition system malfunction. Refer to Chapter Nine for specific electrical system tests, and the wiring diagrams at the end of the book for the specific model and year.

WARNING
High voltage is present during ignition system operation. Do not touch ignition components, wires or test leads while cranking or running the engine.

FUEL SYSTEM

Many riders automatically assume that the carburetors are at fault when the engine does not run properly. While fuel system problems are not uncommon, carburetor adjustment is seldom the answer. In many cases, adjusting the carburetors only compounds the problem by making the engine run worse.

Start fuel system troubleshooting at the fuel tank and work through the system, reserving the carburetor assembly as the final point. Most fuel system problems result from an empty fuel tank, a plugged fuel filter or fuel valve, fuel pump failure or contaminated fuel. Fuel system troubleshooting is also covered under *Engine Is Difficult To Start, Poor Idle Speed Performance* and *Poor Medium and High Speed Performance* in this chapter.

The carburetor choke system can also present problems. Check choke operation by moving the choke lever back and forth by hand. The choke should move freely without binding or sticking in one position. If necessary, remove the choke as described under *Carburetor Disassembly* in Chapter Eight and inspect its plunger and spring for severe wear or damage.

ENGINE OVERHEATING

Engine overheating can quickly cause engine seizure and damage. The following section groups five main systems with probable causes that can lead to engine overheating.

1. *Ignition system*:
   a. Incorrect spark plug gap.
   b. Incorrect spark plug heat range; see Chapter Three.
   c. Defective CDI unit/incorrect ignition timing.
2. *Engine compression*:
   a. Cylinder head gasket leakage.
   b. Heavy carbon buildup in combustion chamber.
3. *Engine cooling*:
   a. Improper spark plug heat range.
   b. Incorrect coolant level.
   c. Cooling system malfunction.
   d. Clogged radiator.
   e. Thermostat stuck closed.
   f. Worn or damaged radiator cap.
   g. Fan switch, relay or thermoswitch malfunction.
   h. Damaged cooling fan blades.
   i. Clogged or blocked coolant passages in radiator, hoses or engine.
   j. Oil level low.
   k. Oil not circulating properly.
   l. Valves leaking.
   m. Dragging brakes.
   n. Clutch slippage.
   o. Heavy carbon deposits.
4. *Fuel system*:

a. Clogged air filter element.
b. Carburetor fuel level too low.
c. Incorrect carburetor adjustment or jetting.
d. Loose carburetor hose clamps.
e. Leaking or damaged carburetor-to-air filter housing air boot(s).
f. Incorrect air/fuel mixture.
5. *Engine load*:
   a. Dragging brake(s).
   b. Damaged drivetrain components.
   c. Slipping clutch.
   d. Engine oil level too high.
   e. Improper grade engine oil.

ENGINE

Engine troubles generally indicate something wrong in a suspect system, such as ignition, fuel or starting.

Preignition

Preignition is the premature burning of fuel and is caused by hot spots in the combustion chambers. Glowing deposits in the combustion chambers, inadequate cooling or an overheated spark plug(s) can all cause preignition. This is first noticed as a power loss but eventually results in damage to the internal parts of the engine because of higher combustion chamber temperatures.

Detonation

Commonly called spark knock or fuel knock, detonation is the violent explosion of fuel in the combustion chamber before the proper time of ignition. Severe damage can result. Use of low octane gasoline is a common cause of detonation.

Even when using a high octane gasoline, detonation can still occur. Other causes are over-advanced ignition timing, lean air/fuel mixture at or near full throttle, inadequate engine cooling, or the excessive accumulation of carbon deposits in the combustion chamber (cylinder head and piston crowns).

Power Loss

Several factors can cause a lack of power and speed. Look for a clogged air filter or fouled or

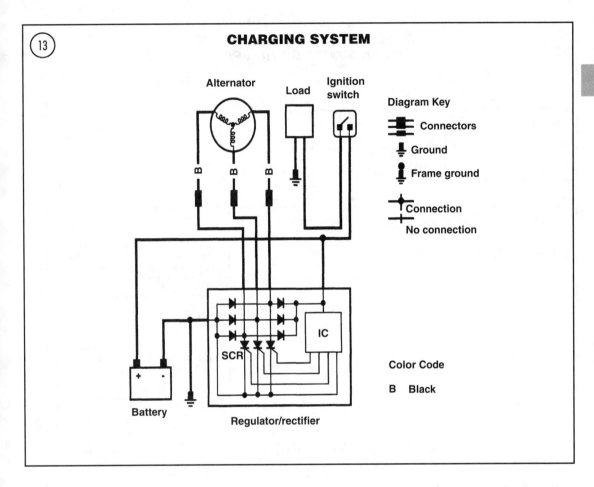

CHARGING SYSTEM

⑬

Alternator

Load

Ignition switch

Diagram Key

Connectors

Ground

Frame ground

Connection

No connection

B

IC

SCR

Color Code

B Black

Battery

Regulator/rectifier

damaged spark plugs. A piston or cylinder that is galled, incorrect piston clearance or worn or sticky piston rings may be responsible. Look for loose bolts, defective gaskets or leaking machined mating surfaces on the cylinder head, cylinder block or crankcase.

Piston Seizure

This is caused by incorrect bore clearance, piston rings with an improper end gap, compression leak, incorrect air/fuel mixture, spark plugs of the wrong heat range or incorrect ignition timing. Overheating may result in piston seizure.

Piston Slap

Piston slap is an audible slapping or rattling noise resulting from excessive piston-to-cylinder clearance. When allowed to continue, piston slap eventually causes the piston skirt to shatter.

To prevent piston slap, clean the air filter on a regular schedule. When piston slap is heard, disassemble the engine top end, measure the cylinder bore and piston diameter, and check for excessive clearance. Replace parts that exceed wear limits or show damage.

ENGINE NOISES

1. *Knocking or pinging during acceleration*—Can be caused by using a lower octane fuel than recommended or a poor grade of fuel. Incorrect carburetor jetting and a too hot spark plug can also cause pinging. Refer to *Spark Plug Heat Range* in Chapter Three. Check also for excessive carbon buildup in the combustion chamber or a defective ignition system component.

2. *Slapping or rattling noises at low speed or during acceleration*—Can be caused by excessive piston-to-cylinder wall clearance. Check also for bent

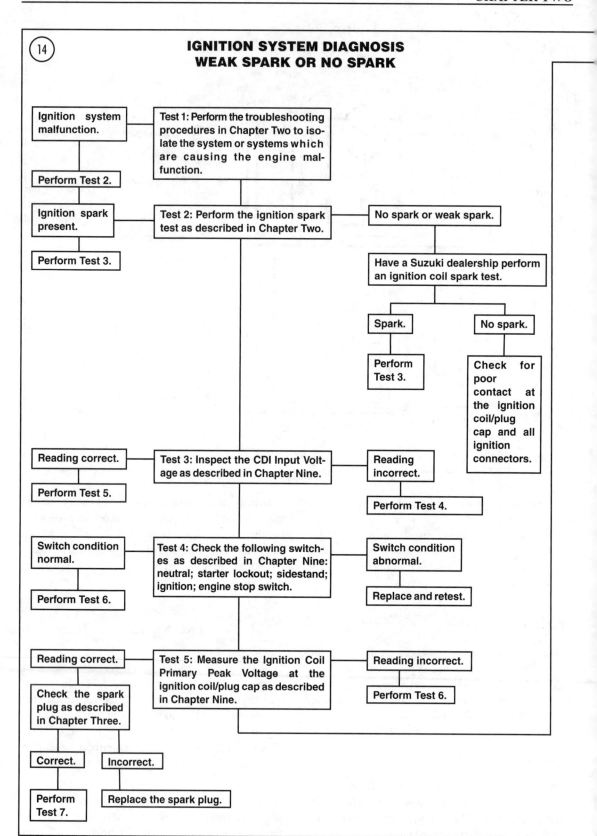

⑭ **IGNITION SYSTEM DIAGNOSIS**
WEAK SPARK OR NO SPARK

| Ignition system malfunction. | Test 1: Perform the troubleshooting procedures in Chapter Two to isolate the system or systems which are causing the engine malfunction. |

Perform Test 2.

| Ignition spark present. | Test 2: Perform the ignition spark test as described in Chapter Two. | No spark or weak spark. |

Perform Test 3.

Have a Suzuki dealership perform an ignition coil spark test.

| Spark. | No spark. |

| Perform Test 3. | Check for poor contact at the ignition coil/plug cap and all ignition connectors. |

| Reading correct. | Test 3: Inspect the CDI Input Voltage as described in Chapter Nine. | Reading incorrect. |

Perform Test 5.

Perform Test 4.

| Switch condition normal. | Test 4: Check the following switches as described in Chapter Nine: neutral; starter lockout; sidestand; ignition; engine stop switch. | Switch condition abnormal. |

Perform Test 6.

Replace and retest.

| Reading correct. | Test 5: Measure the Ignition Coil Primary Peak Voltage at the ignition coil/plug cap as described in Chapter Nine. | Reading incorrect. |

Check the spark plug as described in Chapter Three.

Perform Test 6.

| Correct. | Incorrect. |

| Perform Test 7. | Replace the spark plug. |

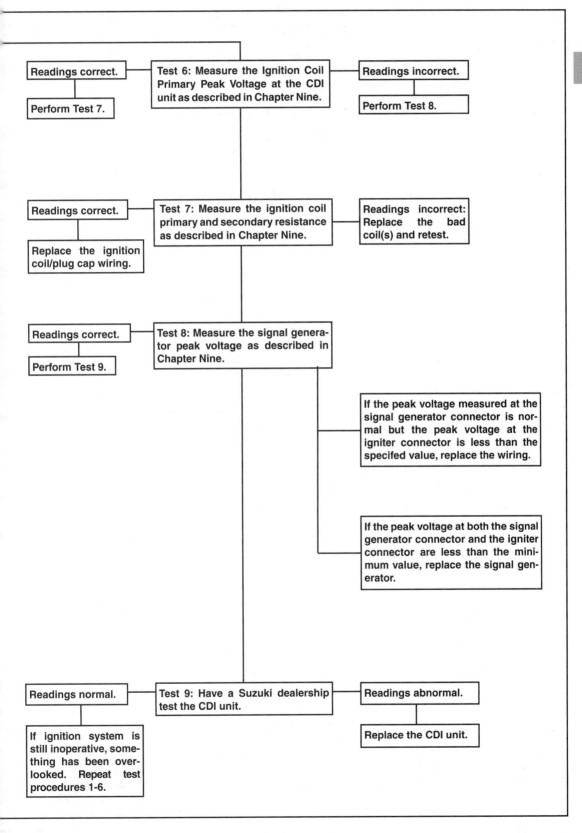

Readings correct.

Perform Test 7.

Test 6: Measure the Ignition Coil Primary Peak Voltage at the CDI unit as described in Chapter Nine.

Readings incorrect.

Perform Test 8.

2

Readings correct.

Replace the ignition coil/plug cap wiring.

Test 7: Measure the ignition coil primary and secondary resistance as described in Chapter Nine.

Readings incorrect: Replace the bad coil(s) and retest.

Readings correct.

Perform Test 9.

Test 8: Measure the signal generator peak voltage as described in Chapter Nine.

If the peak voltage measured at the signal generator connector is normal but the peak voltage at the igniter connector is less than the specifed value, replace the wiring.

If the peak voltage at both the signal generator connector and the igniter connector are less than the minimum value, replace the signal generator.

Readings normal.

If ignition system is still inoperative, something has been overlooked. Repeat test procedures 1-6.

Test 9: Have a Suzuki dealership test the CDI unit.

Readings abnormal.

Replace the CDI unit.

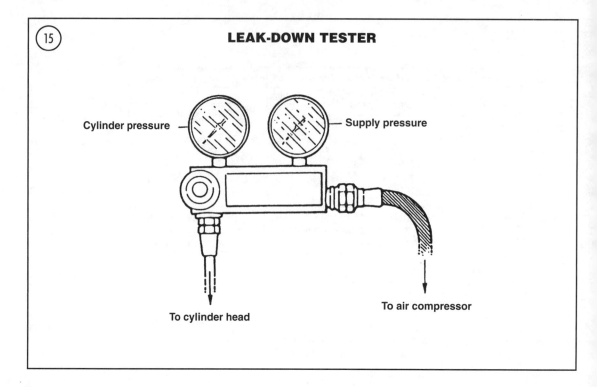

LEAK-DOWN TESTER

Cylinder pressure — Supply pressure

To cylinder head

To air compressor

connecting rods or worn piston pins and/or piston pin holes in the pistons.

3. *Knocking or rapping while decelerating*—Usually caused by excessive rod bearing clearance.

4. *Persistent knocking and vibration or other noise*—Usually caused by worn main bearings. If the main bearings are good, consider the following:

    a. Loose engine mounts.
    b. Cracked frame.
    c. Leaking cylinder head gasket.
    d. Exhaust pipe leakage at cylinder head.
    e. Stuck piston ring(s).
    f. Broken piston ring(s).
    g. Partial engine seizure.
    h. Excessive connecting rod bearing clearance.
    i. Excessive crankshaft runout.
    j. Worn or damaged primary drive gear.

5. *Rapid on-off squeal*—Compression leak around cylinder head gasket or spark plug.

CYLINDER LEAKDOWN TEST

A cylinder leakdown test can locate engine problems from leaking valves, blown head gaskets or broken, worn or stuck piston rings. This test is performed by applying compressed air to the cylinder and then measuring the percent of leakage. Use a cylinder leakdown tester (**Figure 15**) and an air compressor to perform this test.

Follow the manufacturer's directions along with the following information when performing a cylinder leak down test.

1. Start and run the engine until it reaches normal operating temperature. Then turn off the engine.

2. Remove the air filter assembly. Open and secure the throttle so it remains in the wide open position.

3. Set the piston for the cylinder being tested to TDC on its compression stroke. See *Valve Clearance Check and Adjustment* in Chapter Three.

4. Remove the ignition coil/plug cap and the spark plug as described in Chapter Three.

5. Install the leakdown tester into the cylinder spark plug hole. Connect an air compressor to the tester fitting.

NOTE
The engine may turn over when air pressure is applied to the cylinder. To prevent this from happening, shift the transmission into fifth gear and set the parking brake.

6. Apply compressed air to the leakdown tester. Read the rate of leakage on the gauge. Record the leakage rate for that cylinder.

7. After recording the leakage rate of the cylinder, listen for air escaping from the engine.

   a. Air leaking through the exhaust pipe points to a leaking exhaust valve.

   b. Air leaking through the carburetor points to a leaking intake valve.

   c. Air leaking through the crankcase breather tube indicates worn piston rings.

   d. Air leaking into the cooling system causes the coolant to bubble in the radiator. If this occurs, check for a damaged cylinder head gasket and/or a warped or cracked cylinder head or cylinder block surface.

8. Repeat Steps 3-7 for the remaining cylinders.

   a. For a new or rebuilt engine, a leakage rate of 0 to 5 percent per cylinder is desirable. A leakage rate of 6 to 14 percent is acceptable and means the engine is in good condition.

   b. If testing a used engine, the critical parameter is not each cylinder's actual leakage rate, but the difference in the leakage rates between the various cylinders. On a used engine, a difference of 10 percent or less between cylinders is acceptable.

   c. If the leakage rate of any two cylinders differs by more than 10 percent, the engine is in poor condition and further testing is required.

CLUTCH

The two basic clutch troubles are:

1. Clutch slipping.
2. Clutch dragging.

All clutch troubles require partial engine disassembly to identify and repair the problem. Refer to Chapter Six for procedures.

Clutch Slipping

1. *Clutch wear or damage*:
   a. Loose, weak or damaged clutch spring.
   b. Worn friction plates.
   c. Warped steel plates.
   d. Excessively worn clutch hub and/or clutch housing.
   e. Incorrectly assembled clutch.
   f. Incorrectly adjusted clutch.

2. *Engine oil*:
   a. Low oil level.
   b. Oil additives.
   c. Low viscosity oil.

Clutch Dragging

1. *Clutch wear or damage*:
   a. Warped steel plates.
   b. Swollen friction plates.
   c. Warped pressure plate.
   d. Incorrect clutch spring tension.
   e. Incorrectly assembled clutch.
   f. Incorrectly adjusted clutch.
   g. Loose clutch nut.
   h. Damaged clutch boss.

2. *Engine oil*:
   a. Oil level too high.
   b. High viscosity oil.

TRANSMISSION

The basic transmission troubles are:

1. Difficult shifting.
2. Gears pop out of mesh.

Transmission symptoms can be hard to distinguish from clutch symptoms. Be sure that the clutch is not causing the trouble before working on the transmission.

Difficult Shifting

If the shift shaft does not move smoothly from one gear to the next, check the following.

1. *Shift shaft*:
   a. Incorrectly installed shift lever.
   b. Stripped shift lever-to-shift shaft splines.
   c. Bent shift shaft.
   d. Damaged shift shaft return spring.
   e. Damaged shift shaft where it engages the shift drum.
   f. Loose shift return spring pin.
   g. Shift drum positioning lever binding on pivot bolt.

2. *Stopper lever*:
   a. Seized or damaged stopper lever roller.
   b. Broken stopper lever spring.
   c. Loose stopper lever mounting bolt.

3. *Shift drum and shift forks*:
   a. Bent shift fork(s).

b. Damaged shift fork guide pin(s).

c. Seized shift fork (on shaft).

d. Broken shift fork or shift fork shaft.

e. Damaged shift drum groove(s).

f. Damaged shift drum bearing.

g. Worn shift pawls.

Gears Pop Out of Mesh

If the transmission shifts into gear but then slips or pops out, check the following:

1. *Shift shaft*:
   a. Incorrect shift lever position/adjustment.
   b. Stopper lever fails to move or set properly.
2. *Shift drum*:
   a. Excessively worn or damaged shift drum groove(s).
   b. Worn shift pawls.
3. Bent shift fork(s).
4. *Transmission*:
   a. Worn or damaged gear dogs.
   b. Excessive gear thrust play.
   c. Worn or damaged shaft circlips and/or thrust washers.

Transmission Overshifts

If the transmission overshifts when shifting up or down, check for a weak or broken shift mechanism arm spring or a weak or broken shift drum positioning lever.

DRIVETRAIN NOISE

This section deals with noises restricted to the drivetrain assembly, clutch and transmission. While some drivetrain noises have little meaning, abnormal noises may indicate a developing problem. The difficulty is recognizing the difference between a normal and abnormal noise. A new noise, no matter how minor, should be investigated.

1. *Drive chain noise*—Normal drive chain noise can be considered a low-pitched, continuous whining sound. The noise will vary, depending on the speed of the bike, as well as proper lubrication, wear (both chain and sprockets) and alignment. When checking abnormal drive chain noise, consider the following:

   a. *Inadequate lubrication*—A dry chain will gives off a loud whining sound. Clean and lu-

bricate the drive chain at regular intervals; see Chapter Three.

   b. *Incorrect drive chain adjustment*—Check and adjust the drive chain as described in Chapter Three.

   c. *Worn drive chain*—Check drive chain wear at regular intervals and replace it when its overall length reaches the wear limit specified in Chapter Three.

   d. *Worn or damaged sprockets*—Worn or damaged engine and rear sprockets accelerate drive chain wear. Inspect both sprockets carefully as described in Chapter Three.

   e. *Worn swing arm /drive chain guide or slider*—A damaged chain guard or worn through buffer will allow the chain to contact the frame or swing arm. If this occurs, the chain will wear rapidly and damage the frame and/or swing arm. Inspect the guard and buffer at regular intervals and replace them if worn or damaged.

2. *Clutch noise*—Investigate any noise that develops in the clutch. First, drain the engine oil, checking for bits of metal or clutch plate material. If the oil is contaminated, remove the clutch cover and clutch (Chapter Six) and check for the following:

   a. Worn or damaged clutch housing gear teeth.
   b. Excessive clutch housing axial play.
   c. Excessive clutch housing-to-friction plate clearance.
   d. Excessive clutch housing gear-to-primary drive gear backlash.
   e. Worn splines on the mainshaft or hub.
   f. Distorted clutch or friction plates.
   g. Worn clutch release bearing.
   h. Weakened clutch dampers.

3. *Transmission noise*—The transmission exhibits more normal noises than the clutch, but like the clutch, investigate any new noise. Drain the engine oil into a clean container. Check for the presence of metallic particles. Inspect the drain container for signs of water separation from the oil. Transmission associated noises can be caused by:

   a. Insufficient engine oil level.
   b. Contaminated engine oil.
   c. Engine oil viscosity too thin. A low viscosity oil will raise the transmission operating temperature.
   d. Worn transmission gear(s).
   e. Chipped or broken transmission gear(s).

f. Excessive transmission gear side play.

g. Worn or damaged crankshaft-to-transmission bearing(s).

HANDLING

Investigate handling problems immediately. Minor symptoms can develop into problems that may have an adverse effect on motorcycle control and result in a crash. Check the following items:

1. If the handlebars are hard to turn, check for the following:

a. Low tire pressure.

b. Incorrect front brake hydraulic hose routing.

c. Incorrect throttle cable routing.

d. Incorrect handlebar switch cable routing.

e. Steering stem adjustment is too tight.

f. Bent steering stem.

g. Improperly lubricated steering stem bearings.

h. Damaged or worn steering stem bearings.

2. If there is excessive handlebar shake or vibration, check for the following:

a. Loose or damaged handlebar holder bolts.

b. Incorrect handlebar holder and bolt installation.

c. Bent or cracked handlebar.

d. Loose steering stem nut.

e. Worn wheel bearing(s).

f. Damaged tire.

g. Excessively worn front tire.

h. Damaged rim.

i. Loose, missing or broken engine mount bolts and mounts.

j. Cracked frame, especially at the steering head.

k. Incorrect tire inflation pressure for prevailing riding conditions.

l. Imbalance between the left and right fork legs.

m. Distorted front fork.

n. Bent front axle.

3. If the rear suspension is too soft, check for the following:

a. Incorrect shock absorber adjustment.

b. Damaged shock absorber damper rod.

c. Leaking shock absorber damper housing.

d. Sagged shock spring.

e. Loose or damaged shock mount bolts and nuts.

4. If the rear suspension is too hard, check for the following:

a. Incorrect shock absorber adjustment.

b. Rear tire inflation pressure too high.

c. Shock linkage binding or damaged.

d. Bent shock absorber shaft.

FRAME NOISE

Noises traced to the frame or suspension are usually caused by loose, worn or damaged parts. Various noises that are related to the frame are listed below:

1. *Disc brake noise*—A screeching sound during braking is the most common disc brake noise. Some other disc brake associated noises can be caused by:

a. Glazed brake pad surface.

b. Severely worn brake pads.

c. Warped brake disc(s).

d. Loose brake disc mounting bolts.

e. Loose or missing caliper mounting bolts.

f. Damaged caliper(s).

g. Cracked wheel flange or bosses, where the brake disc mounts to the wheel.

2. *Front fork noise*:

a. Contaminated fork oil.

b. Fork oil level too low.

c. Broken fork spring.

d. Worn front fork bushings.

e. Loose bolts on the suspension.

3. *Rear shock absorber noise*:

a. Loose shock absorber mounting bolts and nuts.

b. Cracked or broken shock spring(s).

c. Damaged shock absorber.

d. Loose shock absorber linkage mounting bolts and nuts.

e. Damaged shock absorber linkage.

f. Worn swing arm or shock linkage bearings.

4. *Some other frame associated noises can be caused by:*

a. Cracked or broken frame.

b. Broken swing arm or shock linkage.

c. Loose engine mounting bolts.

d. Damaged steering bearings.

e. Loose mounting bracket(s).

⑯ **DISC BRAKE TROUBLESHOOTING**

Disc brake fluid leakage

Check:
- Loose or damaged line fittings
- Worn caliper piston seals
- Scored caliper piston or bore
- Loose banjo bolts
- Damaged brake line washers
- Leaking master cylinder diaphragm
- Leaking master cylinder secondary seal
- Cracked master cylinder housing
- Brake fluid level too high
- Loose or damaged master cylinder cover

Brake overheating

Check:
- Warped brake disc
- Incorrect brake fluid
- Caliper piston and/or brake pads binding
- Riding brakes during riding

Brake chatter

Check:
- Warped brake disc
- Incorrect caliper alignment
- Loose caliper mounting bolts
- Loose front axle nut and/or clamps
- Worn wheel bearings
- Damaged hub
- Restricted brake hydraulic line
- Contaminated brake pads

Brake locking

Check:
- Incorrect brake fluid
- Plugged passages in master cylinder
- Caliper piston and/or brake pads binding
- Warped brake disc

Insufficient brakes

Check:
- Air in brake lines
- Worn brake pads
- Low brake fluid level
- Incorrect brake fluid
- Worn brake disc
- Worn caliper piston seals
- Glazed brake pads
- Leaking primary cup seal in master cylinder
- Contaminated brake pads and/or disc

Brake squeal

Check:
- Contaminated brake pads and/or disc
- Dust or dirt collected behind brake pads

BRAKES

The front and rear brake units are critical to riding performance and safety. Inspect the brakes frequently and repair any problem immediately. When replacing or refilling the disc brake fluid, use only DOT 4 brake fluid from a closed and sealed container. Refer to Chapter Fourteen for additional information on brake fluid selection and disc brake service. Use the troubleshooting procedures in **Figure 16** to isolate the majority of disc brake troubles.

When checking brake pad wear, check that the brake pads in each caliper contact the disc squarely. If one of the brake pads is wearing unevenly, suspect a warped or bent brake disc or damaged caliper.

2

CHAPTER THREE

LUBRICATION, MAINTENANCE AND TUNE-UP

This chapter covers lubrication, maintenance and tune-up procedures. **Figure 1** and **Figure 2** show the locations of various components relating to service. A schedule, specifications, lubricants and capacities are listed in **Tables 1-5** at the end of this chapter.

To maximize the service life of the motorcycle and gain the utmost in safety and performance, it is necessary to perform periodic inspections and maintenance. Minor problems found during routine service can be corrected before they develop into major ones.

PRE-RIDE CHECK LIST

Perform the following checks before the first ride of the day. Each check is described in this chapter. If a component requires service, refer to the appropriate section.

1. Check the engine oil level in the oil inspection window (**Figure 3**) located on the clutch cover. The oil level must be between the upper and lower lines.

WARNING
When performing any service work to the engine or cooling system, never remove the radiator cap, coolant drain screws or disconnect any coolant hose when the engine and radiator are hot. Scalding fluid and steam will blow out under pressure and cause serious injury.

2. Check the coolant level when the engine is cold. Check the cooling system for leaks and make sure the coolant is between the FULL and LOW marks on the coolant reservoir (**Figure 4**). If the fluid level is below the LOW mark, add coolant to the reservoir until the fluid level is at the FULL mark. Always add coolant to the reservoir, not the radiator.

3

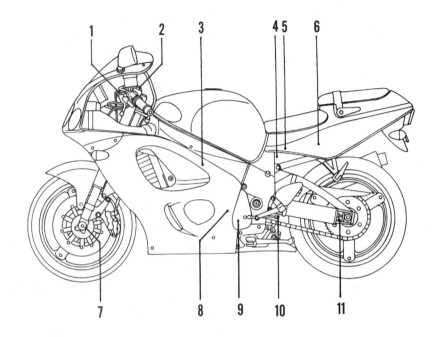

COMPONENT LOCATION

1. Clutch cable adjustment
2. Fork spring preload and rebound damping adjustment
3. Idle adjust knob
4. Shock absorber compression damping adjustment
5. Battery
6. Main 30 amp fuse
7. Fork compression damping adjustment
8. Coolant reservoir
9. Clutch mechanism adjustment
10. Shock absorber rebound damping adjustment
11. Drive chain adjustment

3. Turn the handlebar from side to side and check for steering play. Check that the control cables are properly routed and do not interfere with the handlebar or the handlebar controls.

4. Check the throttle operation. Open the throttle all the way and release it. The throttle should close quickly with no binding or roughness. Repeat this step with the handlebar facing straight ahead and at both full lock positions.

5. Check that the clutch and the brake levers operate properly with no binding. Replace damaged levers. Check the lever housings for damage.

WARNING
When checking the brake and clutch levers, check the ball on the end of the lever. If it is broken off, replace the lever immediately.

② **COMPONENT LOCATION**

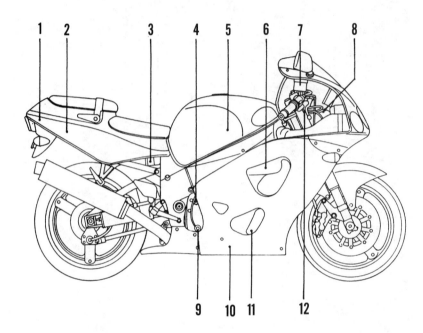

1. Tool kit
2. Fuel tank prop stay
3. Rear brake master cylinder reservoir
4. Engine oil fill cap
5. Air filter air box and element
6. Spark plugs

7. Front brake master cylinder reservoir
8. Auxiliary fuse panel
9. Engine oil level inspection window
10. Engine oil drain plug
11. Engine oil filter
12. Throttle cable adjustment

6. Inspect the front and rear suspension. Make sure they have a good solid feel with no looseness.

7. Check both wheels and tires for damage.

8. Inspect the drive chain for wear, correct tension and proper lubrication.

9. Check the drive chain guide for wear or damage; replace if necessary.

10. Lubricate the drive chain.

11. Make sure the air filter element is clean and the air box and carburetor boots are secured tightly.

12. Check tire pressure (**Table 2**).

13. Check the exhaust system for looseness or damage.

14. Check the tightness of all fasteners, especially engine, steering and suspension mounting hardware.

15. Check the rear driven sprocket bolts and nuts for tightness.

16. Make sure the fuel tank is full of fresh gasoline.

17. Inspect the fuel lines and fittings for wetness.

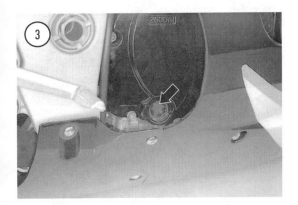

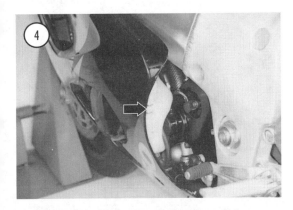

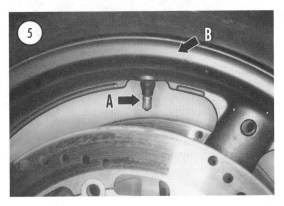

18. Check the brake fluid level in both front and rear brake master cylinder reservoirs. Add fluid if necessary.

MAINTENANCE SCHEDULE

Table 1 is a recommended schedule. Strict adherence to these recommendations ensures long service from the bike. However, if the bike is run in an area of high humidity, perform the lubrication and service procedures more frequently to prevent possible rust damage.

For convenience when maintaining the vehicle, most of the services shown in **Table 1** are described in this chapter. However, some procedures which require more than minor disassembly or adjustment are covered in the appropriate chapter.

TIRES AND WHEELS

Tire Pressure

Check and adjust tire pressure (**Table 2**) to maintain good traction and handling and to prevent rim damage.

> *NOTE*
> *After checking and adjusting the tire pressure, make sure to install the valve stem cap (A, **Figure 5**). The cap prevents debris from collecting in the valve stem. This could allow air leakage or result in incorrect tire pressure readings.*

Tire Inspection

Inspect the tires for excessive wear, cuts, abrasions, etc. If an object has punctured the tire, mark its location with a light crayon before removing it. This will help locate the hole for repairs. Refer to the tire changing procedure in Chapter Eleven.

Measure the tread depth at the center of the tire (**Figure 6**) using a tread depth gauge or small ruler. Replace the original equipment tires when the tread has worn to the dimensions specified in **Table 2**.

Rim Inspection and Runout

Frequently inspect wheel rims (B, **Figure 5**) for cracks, warpage or dents. A damaged rim may leak or knock the wheel out of balance. If the rim portion of an alloy wheel is damaged, replace the wheel. It *cannot be serviced or repaired.*

Wheel rim runout is the amount of wobble a wheel shows as it rotates. Check runout with the wheels on the bike by supporting the bike with the wheel off the ground. Slowly turn the wheel while holding a pointer solidly against a fork leg or the swing arm with the other end against the wheel rim. If you suspect that rim runout is excessive, measure the runout by following the procedure described in Chapter Eleven. If the runout is excessive, replace the wheel.

BATTERY

Most electrical system troubles can be traced to battery neglect. Clean and inspect the battery at periodic intervals. All models are equipped with a maintenance free battery. This is a sealed battery so the electrolyte level cannot be checked.

When removing the battery, disconnect the negative (–) cable first, and then disconnect the positive (+) cable. This minimizes the chance of a tool shorting to ground when disconnecting the battery positive cable.

Battery Removal/Installation

1. Remove the seats as described in Chapter Fifteen.
2. Disconnect the negative battery cable (A, **Figure 7**).
3. Remove the red protective cap (B, **Figure 7**) from the positive terminal, and disconnect the positive battery cable.

> *NOTE*
> *The battery is held in place by the rear fuel-tank-mounting bracket (C, **Figure 7**).*

4. Remove the fuel tank as described in Chapter Eight.
5. Remove the battery.
6. Inspect the cushion pads (**Figure 8**) in the battery compartment for wear or deterioration. Replace any if necessary.
7. Position the battery with the negative battery terminal (A, **Figure 7**) on the right side of the frame.
8. Reinstall the battery into the battery compartment in the frame.

> *CAUTION*
> *Make sure the battery cables are properly connected. The red battery cable must be connected to the positive battery terminal and the black, or black/white, battery cable must be connected to the negative battery terminal. Reversing the polarity will damage the rectifier.*

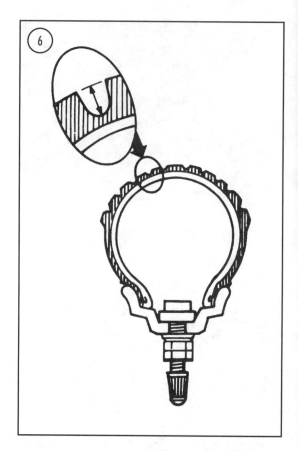

9. Install and tighten the positive battery cable (B, **Figure 7**).
10. Install and tighten the negative battery cable (A, **Figure 7**).
11. Coat the battery connections with dielectric grease or petroleum jelly to retard corrosion.
12. Install the red protective cap (A, **Figure 7**) over the positive terminal.
13. Install the fuel tank as described in Chapter Eight.

Inspection and Testing

The battery electrolyte level cannot be serviced. *Never* attempt to remove the sealing bar from the top of the battery. This bar was removed for the initial filling of electrolyte before delivery of the bike, or the installation of a new battery, and is not to be removed thereafter. The battery does not require periodic electrolyte inspection or water refilling.

Even though the battery is a sealed type, protect eyes, skin and clothing in case the battery is cracked and leaking electrolyte. Battery electrolyte is very

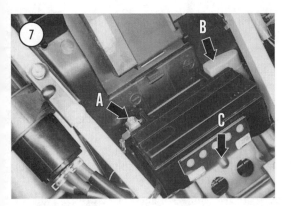

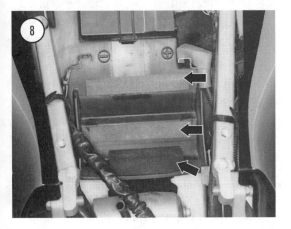

3

4. Check the entire battery case (**Figure 9**) for cracks or other damage. If the battery case is warped, discolored or has a raised top, the battery has been suffering from overcharging or overheating.

5. Check the battery terminal bolts, spacers and nuts (A, **Figure 9**) for corrosion or damage. Clean parts thoroughly with a solution of baking soda and water. Replace severely corroded or damaged parts.

6. Clean the top of the battery with a stiff bristle brush using the baking soda and water solution.

7. Check the battery cable clamps for corrosion and damage. If corrosion is minor, clean the battery cable clamps with a stiff wire brush. Replace excessively worn or damaged cables.

8. Connect a voltmeter between the battery negative and positive terminals. Note the following:

    a. If the battery voltage is 12.6 volts (at 20° C [68° F]), or greater, the battery is fully charged.

    b. If the battery voltage is 12.0 to 12.5 volts (at 20° C [68° F]), or less, the battery is undercharged. Recharge it as described in this chapter.

    c. Once the battery is fully charged, test the charging system as described in Chapter Two.

corrosive and can cause severe chemical burns and permanent injury. If electrolyte spills onto clothing or skin, immediately neutralize the electrolyte with a solution of baking soda and water, and then flush the area with an abundance of clean water.

> *WARNING*
> *Always wear safety glasses while working with a battery. If you get electrolyte in your eyes, call a physician immediately. Force your eyes open and flood them with cool, clean water for approximately 15 minutes and seek medical attention.*

1. Remove the battery as described in this chapter. Do not clean the battery while it is mounted in the frame.

2. Place the battery on a stack of newspapers or shop cloths to protect the surface of the workbench.

3. Inspect the battery compartment cushion pads (**Figure 8**) for contamination or damage. Clean with a solution of baking soda and water.

Charging

Refer to *Battery Initialization* in this chapter if the battery is new.

If recharging is required on a maintenance-free battery, a digital voltmeter and a charger with an adjustable amperage output are required. If this equipment is not available, it is recommended that battery charging be entrusted to a shop with the proper equipment. Excessive voltage and amperage from an unregulated charger can damage the battery and shorten service life.

The battery should only self-discharge approximately one percent each day. If a battery not in use, with no loads connected, loses its charge within a week after charging, the battery is defective.

If the motorcycle is not used for long periods of time, an automatic battery charger with variable voltage and amperage outputs is recommended for optimum battery service life.

CAUTION
Always disconnect the battery cables from the battery and remove the battery from the bike before connecting charging equipment. If the cables are left connected, the charger may damage the diodes within the voltage regulator/rectifier.

WARNING
During charging, highly explosive hydrogen gas is released from the battery. Charge the battery only in a well-ventilated area that has no open flames (including pilot lights on some gas home appliances). Do not allow any smoking in the area. Never check the charge of the battery by arcing across the terminals. The resulting spark can ignite the hydrogen gas.

1. Remove the battery from the bike as described in this chapter.
2. Set the battery on a stack of newspapers or shop cloths to protect the surface of the workbench.
3. Connect the positive charger lead to the positive battery terminal and the negative charger lead to the negative battery terminal.
4. Set the charger to 12 volts. If the output of the charger is variable, it is best to select the low setting.

CAUTION
Never set the battery charger to more than 4 amps. The battery will be damaged if it is charged at a rate exceeding 4 amps.

5. The charging time depends on the discharged condition of the battery. Use the suggested charging amperage and length of charge time on the battery label (C, **Figure 9**). Normally, a battery should be

charged at a slow charge rate of 1/10th its given capacity.
6. Turn the charger ON.
7. After the battery has been charged for the pre-determined time, turn the charger off and disconnect the leads.
8. Wait 30 minutes, and then measure the battery voltage. Refer to the following:
    a. If the battery voltage is 12.6 volts (at 20° C [68° F]), or greater, the battery is fully charged.
    b. If the battery voltage is 12.0 to 12.5 volts (at 20° C [68° F]), or less, the battery is undercharged and requires additional charging time.
9. If the battery remains stable for one hour, the battery is charged.
10. Install the battery into the bike as described in this chapter.

Battery Initialization

When replacing the old battery, make sure the new battery is charged completely before installing it in the bike. Failure to do so reduces the life of the battery. Using a new battery without an initial charge will result in a battery never holding more than an 80 percent charge. Charging a new battery after it has been used will not bring its charge to 100 percent. When purchasing a new battery, verify its charge status. If necessary, have the supplier perform the initial or booster charge to bring the battery up to 100 percent charge.

NOTE
Recycle the old battery. Most motorcycle dealerships accept old batteries in trade. Never place a battery in the household trash. It is illegal to place any acid or lead (heavy metal) contents in landfills. There is also the danger of the battery being crushed in the trash truck and spraying acid on the truck or landfill operator.

PERIODIC LUBRICATION

Perform the services listed in this section at the maintenance intervals listed in **Table 1**. If the vehicle is exposed to harder than normal use with constant exposure to water and high humidity, perform

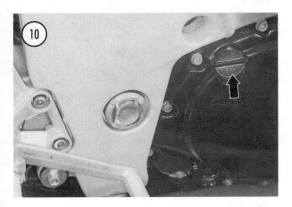

the services more frequently. Refer to *Shop Supplies* in Chapter One for information on lubricants and cleaners.

Engine Oil Level Check

Engine oil level is checked with the oil level gauge located on the clutch cover.

1. If the bike has not been run, start the engine and let it warm up approximately 2-3 minutes.
2. Park the bike on the sidestand on level ground.
3. Shut off the engine and let the oil settle for 2-3 minutes.

CAUTION
Do not take this oil level reading with the bike on the sidestand as the oil will flow away from the gauge giving a false reading.

4. Have an assistant sit on the bike to hold it vertically on level ground.
5. Check the engine oil level in the oil inspection window (**Figure 3**) on the clutch cover. The oil level must be between the upper and lower lines.
6. If the oil level is low, unscrew the oil filler cap (**Figure 10**) from the clutch cover. Insert a small funnel into the hole. Add the recommended grade and viscosity oil (**Table 3**) to correct the level.
7. Inspect the O-ring seal on the oil filler cap. Replace the O-ring if it is starting to deteriorate or harden.
8. Install the oil filler cap, and tighten it securely.

NOTE
*Refer to **Engine Oil and Filter Change** in this chapter for additional information on oil selection.*

9. If the oil level is too high, remove the oil filler cap and draw out the excess oil with a syringe or suitable pump.
10. Recheck the oil level and adjust if necessary.
11. Install the oil filler cap, and tighten it securely.

Engine Oil and Filter Change

Regular oil and filter changes contribute more to engine longevity than any other maintenance service. The recommended oil and filter change interval is listed in **Table 1**. This assumes that the bike is operated in moderate climates. If it is operated under dusty conditions, the oil gets dirty more quickly and should be changed more frequently than recommended.

Use only a high-quality detergent motor oil with an API classification of SF or SG. Use SAE 10W-40 weight oil in all models. Use a lighter viscosity oil in cool climates and the heavier viscosity oil in warm climates. Use the same brand of oil at each oil change.

To change the engine oil and filter use the following:

  a. Drain pan.
  b. Funnel.
  c. Can opener or pour spout.
  d. Wrench and sockets.
  e. 3-4 quarts of oil (**Table 3**).
  f. New oil filter.
  g. Socket-type oil filter wrench.

NOTE
Use a socket-type oil filter wrench to remove the oil filter because of the small working area between the oil filter, the exhaust system and the engine.

NOTE
*Never dispose of motor oil in the trash, on the ground, or down the storm drain. Many service stations accept used motor oil and waste haulers provide curbside used motor oil collection. Do not combine other fluids with motor oil to be recycled. To locate a recycler, contact the American Petroleum Institute (API) at **www.recycleoil.org**.*

1. Remove the right lower fairing side panel as described in Chapter Fifteen.
2. Start the engine and let it warm up approximately 2-3 minutes. Shut the engine off.

NOTE
Warming the engine heats up the oil so it flows freely and carries out contamination and sludge.

3. Place the bike on the sidestand on level ground.
4. Place a drain pan under the engine.
5. Remove the oil drain plug (**Figure 11**) and gasket from the bottom of the oil pan.
6. Loosen the oil filler cap (**Figure 10**). This speeds up the flow of oil.
7. Allow the oil to completely drain.
8. Inspect the condition of the drained oil for contamination. After it has cooled down, check for any metal particles or clutch friction disc particles. Remove the oil pan from the bottom of the engine. Clean the pan and the pick up screen as described in this chapter.

WARNING
The exhaust system must be completely cool before removing the oil filter. The working area between the oil cooler and exhaust system is very small.

9. To replace the oil filter, perform the following:
   a. Move the drain pan under the oil filter (**Figure 12**).
   b. Install a socket-type oil filter wrench onto the oil filter, and turn the filter *counterclockwise* until oil begins to run out. Wait until the oil stops then loosen the filter until it is easy to turn.
   c. Due to limited space, remove the oil filter wrench from the end of the filter then com-

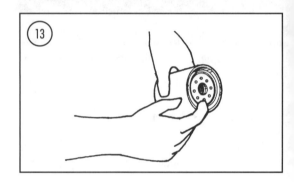

pletely unscrew and remove the filter. Hold it with the open end facing up.
   d. Hold the filter over the drain pan and pour out any remaining oil. Place the old filter in a heavy-duty, freezer-grade reclosable plastic bag and close the bag. Discard the old filter properly.
   e. Thoroughly clean the filter-to-crankcase surface. This surface must be clean to prevent leakage.
   f. Apply a light coat of clean engine oil to the rubber seal on the new filter (**Figure 13**).
   g. Install the new oil filter onto the threaded fitting on the oil cooler.
   h. Tighten the filter by hand until the rubber gasket contacts the crankcase surface, and then tighten it an additional two full turns.

10. Inspect the drain plug gasket for damage. Replace the gasket if necessary.

11. Install the drain plug (**Figure 11**) and its gasket. Tighten the oil drain plug to the torque specification in **Table 5**.

12. Insert a funnel into the oil filler hole, and add the quantity of oil specified in **Table 3**.

13. Remove the funnel and screw in the oil filler cap securely.

14. Usually some oil will leak onto the exhaust pipes during this procedure. Wipe off as much as possible with a shop rag, and then spray some aerosol parts cleaner onto the pipes.

NOTE
If servicing a rebuilt engine, check the engine oil pressure as described in this chapter.

15. Start the engine, and let it idle.

16. Check the oil filter and drain plug for leaks. Tighten either if necessary.

17. Turn off the engine, and check the engine oil level as described in this chapter. Adjust the oil level if necessary.

18. Install the right lower fairing side panel as described in Chapter Fifteen.

WARNING
Prolonged contact with oil may cause skin cancer. Wash your hands thoroughly with soap and water as soon as possible after handling or coming in contact with motor oil.

Engine Oil Pan and Oil Sump Filter

The engine oil pan and oil sump strainer can be removed and installed with the engine in the frame. This procedure is shown with the engine removed for clarity.

1. Drain the engine oil as described in this chapter.

2. Remove the lower fairing side panel from each side as described in Chapter Fifteen.

3. Remove the oil pan bolts from the bottom of the crankcase. Watch for the gasket washers installed with the three bolts (B, **Figure 14**) in the rear right corner of the oil pan.

4. Remove the oil pan (A, **Figure 14**) and gasket from the bottom of the crankcase. Account for the two locating dowels.

5. Remove the bolts (**Figure 15**) securing the oil inlet guide, and remove the guide.

6. Remove the oil sump filter (**Figure 16**) from the crankcase.

7. If still in place, remove the oil sump gasket from the sump mount. Make sure to replace this gasket with a new one.

8. Check the oil sump filter screen for debris buildup or damage. Thoroughly clean the oil inlet guide and screen with solvent. Dry them with compressed air.

NOTE
If the screen was contaminated with metal or clutch friction disc material, clean as much of this contamination from the oil pan area of the lower crankcase as possible. Also, thoroughly clean the oil line of any debris.

9. Inspect the screen for broken areas or damage. Replace the oil sump filter if necessary.

10. Install a new gasket and the sump filter (**Figure 16**) onto the sump mount.

11. Install the oil inlet guide, and tighten the bolts securely (**Figure 15**).

12. Thoroughly clean old gasket material from the gasket surfaces of the crankcase and oil pan. Clean the crankcase gasket surface with an aerosol parts cleaner.

13. If removed, install the locating dowels (A, **Figure 17**) into the crankcase.

14. Apply a *small amount* of gasket sealer to the crankcase gasket surface, and set the new gasket (B, **Figure 17**) onto this surface.

15. Install the oil pan and bolts. Make sure to install the gasket washers under the three bolts (B, **Figure 14**) at the rear right corner of the oil pan. Tighten the oil pan bolts to the torque specification listed in **Table 5**.

Engine Oil Pressure Test

Perform this procedure after reassembling the engine or when troubleshooting the lubrication system.

To check the oil pressure a Suzuki oil pressure gauge (part No. 09915-74510), gauge attachment (09915-74540) and high pressure meter (09915-77300) are required.

1. Remove the right, lower fairing side panel as described in Chapter Fifteen.

2. Check that the engine oil level is correct as described in this chapter. Add oil if necessary.

3. Start the engine and allow it to reach normal operating temperature. Turn off the engine.

4. Place a drain pan under the main oil gallery plug to catch the oil that drains out during the test.

5. Unscrew and remove the main oil gallery plug (**Figure 18**) from the crankcase.

6. Install the adapter, and then the gauge into the main oil gallery. Make sure the fitting is tight to avoid an oil loss.

> *CAUTION*
> *Keep the gauge hose away from the exhaust pipe during this test. If the hose contacts the exhaust pipes, it may melt and spray hot oil onto the hot exhaust pipe, resulting in a fire.*

7. Start the engine and let it idle. Increase engine speed to 3,000 rpm. The oil pressure should be within the range specified in **Table 4** when the oil temperature is 60° C (140° F).

8. If the oil pressure is lower than specified, check the following:

  a. Clogged oil filter.

  b. Oil leak from oil passageway.

  c. Damaged oil seal(s).

  d. Defective oil pump.

  e. Combination of the above.

9. If the oil pressure is higher than specified check the following:

  a. Oil viscosity too heavy (drain oil and install lighter weight oil).

  b. Clogged oil passageway.

  c. Combination of the above.

10. Shut off the engine and remove the test equipment.

11. Apply a light coat of gasket sealer to the main oil gallery plug, then install the plug (**Figure 18**) onto the crankcase. Tighten it to the torque specification listed in **Table 5**.

12. Check oil level and adjust if necessary.

13. Install the right lower fairing section as described in Chapter Fifteen.

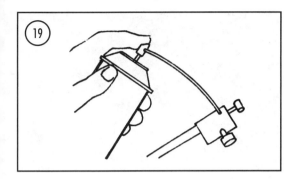

General Lubrication

At the service intervals listed in **Table 1**, lubricate the brake lever, the clutch lever and the drive chain with engine oil. Lubricate the brake pedal pivot, gearshift lever pivot, footpeg pivots, and the sidestand pivot and springs with waterproof grease.

Control Cable Lubrication

Clean and lubricate the throttle cables and clutch cable at the intervals indicated in **Table 1**. In addition, check the cables for kinks and signs of wear and damage or fraying that could cause the cables to fail or stick.

The most positive method of control cable lubrication involves the use of a cable lubricator (**Figure 19**). A can of cable lube or an aerosol general lubricant is required. Do *not* use chain lube as a cable lubricant.

1. Remove the fuel tank and air box as described in Chapter Eight.
2. Disconnect both throttle cables from the right handlebar switch. Refer to *Throttle Cable Replacement* in Chapter Eight.
3. Disconnect the clutch cable from the left handlebar switch. Refer to *Clutch Cable Replacement* in Chapter Six.
4. Attach a cable lubricator to the end of the cable following the manufacturer's instructions.

NOTE
Place a shop cloth at the end of the cables to catch the oil as it runs out.

5. Insert the lubricant can nozzle into the lubricator. Press and hold the button on the can until the lubricant begins to flow out of the other end of the cable. If the cable lube will not flow through the cable at one end, remove the lubricator from the cable end.

Disconnect the cable from the carburetor assembly or the clutch, and try at the opposite end of the cable.
6. Disconnect the lubricator.
7. Apply a light coat of grease to the cable ends before reconnecting them. Reconnect the cable(s), and adjust them as described in this chapter.
8. After lubricating the throttle cables, operate the throttle at the handlebar. It should open and close smoothly.
9. After lubricating the clutch cable, operate the clutch lever at the handlebar. It should open and close smoothly.

Drive Chain Cleaning and Lubrication

Clean and lubricate the drive chain at the interval indicated in **Table 1** or whenever it becomes dry. If the drive chain tends to rust between cleanings, clean and lubricate the chain at more frequent intervals. A properly maintained drive chain provides maximum service life and reliability.

1. Place the bike on level ground on the sidestand.
2. Shift the transmission into NEUTRAL.
3. Place a suitable size jack or wooden blocks under the engine to securely support the bike with the rear wheel off the ground.

CAUTION
Do not use gasoline or solvent to clean the chain. Only use kerosene. Other fluids can attack the O-rings in the chain.

4. Carefully and thoroughly clean the drive chain with kerosene and a soft brush. Dry with clean cloth and then with compressed air.

CAUTION
Use SAE 20W-50 weight motor oil to lubricate the chain. Do not use a lighter weight oil. It will not stay on the chain as long.

5. Apply SAE 20W-50 motor oil to the bottom chain run. Concentrate on getting the oil down between the side plates on both sides of the chain. Do not overlubricate the chain. This causes dirt to collect on the chain and sprockets.
6. Rotate the rear wheel and continue lubricating until the entire chain is lubricated.

7. Turn the wheel slowly, and wipe excess oil from the chain with a clean shop cloth. Also wipe any oil off the rear hub, wheel and tire.

Swing Arm Bearing Assembly Lubrication

Frequent lubrication of the swing arm bearings is vital to keep the rear suspension in peak condition. Lubricate the swing arm bearing assemblies whenever they are disassembled. Use a waterproof grease.

The swing arm must be removed and partially disassembled to lubricate the needle bearings and collars. To clean, examine and lubricate the swing arm bearings and bushings, remove the swing arm as described in Chapter Thirteen. Clean, inspect and lubricate the bearings while they are installed in the swing arm. Do *not* remove the bearings. They will be damaged during removal.

Shock Linkage Lubrication

The shock linkage rocker arm must be removed and partially disassembled to lubricate the needle bearings and collars as described in Chapter Thirteen.

To clean, examine and lubricate the rocker arm bearings and bushings, remove the shock linkage as described in Chapter Thirteen. Clean, inspect and lubricate the bearings while they are installed in the shock linkage component. Do *not* remove the bearings during lubrication. The bearings will be damaged during removal.

Wheel Bearings

Routinely inspect the front and rear wheel bearings and seals for wear or damage. Pack the lip of each seal with waterproof bearing grease. Clean and repack non-sealed bearings once a year; decrease the time between services if the bike is frequently operated in wet conditions. The service procedures are covered in Chapter Eleven.

PERIODIC MAINTENANCE

Periodic maintenance intervals are listed in **Table 1**.

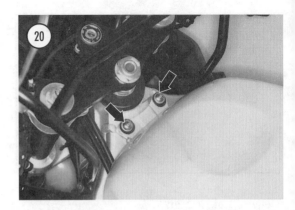

Air Filter Cleaning

Remove and clean the air filter at the interval indicated in **Table 1**. Replace the element at the interval indicated in **Table 1** or whenever it is damaged or starting to deteriorate.

The air filter removes dust and abrasive particles before the air enters the carburetors and the engine. Without the air filter, very fine particles will enter the engine and cause rapid wear of the piston rings, cylinder bores and bearings. They also might clog

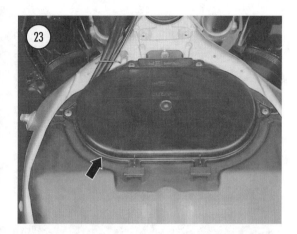

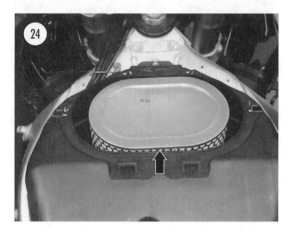

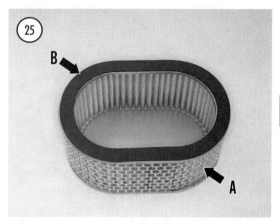

3

6. Place a clean shop cloth into the opening in the air box to prevent the entry of debris.

NOTE
If the air filter is extremely dirty or if there are any holes in the element, wipe out the interior of the air box with a shop rag dampened in cleaning solvent. Remove any debris that may have passed through a broken element.

7. Gently tap the air filter to loosen the trapped dirt and dust.

CAUTION
In the next step, do not apply compressed air toward the inside surface of the filter. Air directed at the inside surface forces the dirt and dust into the pores of the element thus restricting air flow.

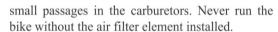

small passages in the carburetors. Never run the bike without the air filter element installed.

1. Place the bike on the sidestand on level ground.

2. Raise and support the fuel tank by performing the following:

   a. Remove the seats as described in Chapter Fifteen.

   b. Remove the bolts (**Figure 20**) securing the fuel tank at the front.

   c. Remove the fuel tank stay (**Figure 21**) from the tray under the rear seat.

   d. Lift the front of the fuel tank, insert the crank end of the stay into the steering stem and the other end onto the fuel tank mount (**Figure 22**).

3. Thoroughly clean any debris from the area surrounding the air box cover.

4. Remove the screws securing the air box cover (**Figure 23**) and remove the cover.

5. Remove the air filter (**Figure 24**) from the air box.

8. Apply low-pressure compressed air to the outside surface (A, **Figure 25**) of the air filter element, and remove all loosened dirt and dust.

9. Thoroughly and carefully inspect the filter element. If it is torn or broken in any area, replace the air filter. Do not run the bike with a damaged air filter element. It may allow dirt to enter the engine. If the element is good, use it until the indicated time for replacement listed in **Table 1**.

10. Make sure the foam gasket (B, **Figure 25**) is in place and is not broken, creased or damaged.

11. Install the air filter (**Figure 24**) so the foam side faces down into the air box. Make sure the filter is properly seated so there is no air leak.

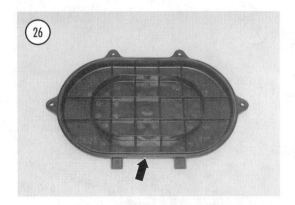

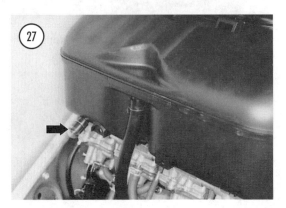

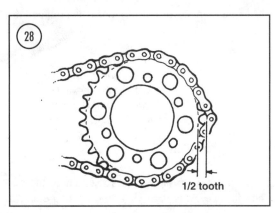

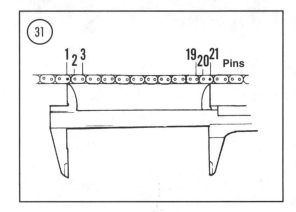

12. Make sure the O-ring (**Figure 26**) is in place in the air box cover.

13. Install the air filter cover and screws. Tighten the screws securely.

14. Lower the fuel tank by performing the following:

   a. Lift up on the fuel tank and remove the tank stay (**Figure 22**).

   b. Lower the fuel tank and install the bolts. Tighten the bolts securely.

   c. Install the tank stay (**Figure 21**) onto the locating clips on the tray under the rear seat.

   d. Install the seats as described in Chapter Fifteen.

Air Box Drain

1. Place the bike on the sidestand on level ground.

2. Raise and support the fuel tank as described above in *Air Filter Cleaning*.

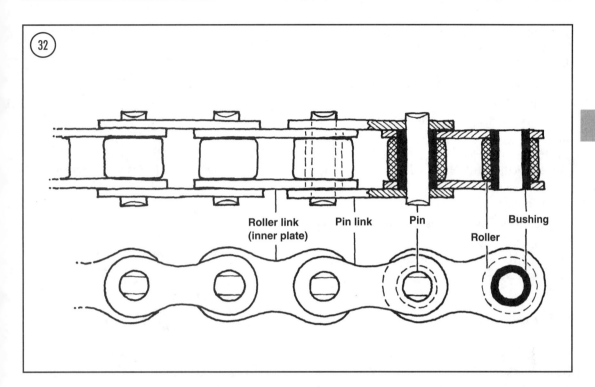

Roller link (inner plate) Pin link Pin Bushing Roller

3. Place a rag under the drain (**Figure 27**) on the left side of the air box. Remove the cap, and drain out water and other debris collected in the air box.

4. Reinstall the drain cap. Make sure it is clamped in place.

5. Lower the fuel tank as described above in *Air Filter Cleaning*.

6. Install the seat as described in Chapter Fifteen.

Drive Chain and Sprocket Wear Inspection

Check the drive chain frequently and replace it when it is excessively worn or damaged.

A quick check gives an indication of when to actually measure chain wear. At the rear sprocket, pull one of the links away from the sprocket. If the link pulls away more than 1/2 the height of a sprocket tooth as shown in **Figure 28**, the chain is probably worn beyond the service limit. Measure the drive chain wear as described below.

To measure drive chain wear, perform the following:

1. Place the bike on the sidestand on level ground.

2. On U.S.A., California and Canada models, remove the cotter pin (A, **Figure 29**) from the rear axle nut. Discard the cotter pin. Install a new one during assembly.

3. Loosen the rear axle nut (B, **Figure 29**).

4. On each side, loosen the chain adjuster locknut (A, **Figure 30**) and tighten the chain adjusters (B, **Figure 30**) to move the wheel rearward until the chain (C, **Figure 29**) is tight with no slack.

5. Place a vernier caliper along the chain run and measure the distance between 21 pins (20 links) in the chain as shown in **Figure 31**. If the 21-pin. length exceeds the specification in **Table 4**, install a new drive chain as described in Chapter Thirteen.

6. Inspect the inner plate chain faces (**Figure 32**). They should be lightly polished on both sides. If they show considerable uneven wear on one side, the engine and rear sprockets are not aligned properly. Excessive wear requires replacement of not only the drive chain but also the engine and rear sprockets.

NOTE
The engine sprocket cover must be partially removed to visually inspect the drive sprocket.

7. To inspect the engine sprocket, refer to *Sprockets* in Chapter Eleven and partially remove the engine sprocket cover.

8. If the drive chain is excessively worn, inspect both the engine and rear sprockets for the following defects:

    a. Undercutting or sharp teeth (**Figure 33**).

    b. Broken teeth.

9. If wear is evident, replace the drive chain, the engine sprocket and the rear sprocket as a complete set. If only the drive chain is replaced, the worn sprockets will quickly wear out the new chain. Refer to the engine and rear sprocket removal/installation procedures in Chapter Eleven.

10. Adjust the drive chain as described in this chapter.

11. Install the engine sprocket cover as described in Chapter Eleven.

Drive Chain Free Play Adjustment

The drive chain must have adequate play so the chain is not strung tight when the swing arm is horizontal. On the other hand, too much slack may cause the chain to jump off the sprockets with potentially dangerous results.

Check and adjust the drive chain at the interval listed in **Table 1**. A properly lubricated and adjusted drive chain provides maximum service life and reliability.

When adjusting the chain, check the free play at several places along its length by rotating the rear wheel. The chain rarely wears uniformly and as a result will be tighter at some places than at others. Measure the chain free play when the chain's tightest point is halfway between the sprockets.

1. Roll the bike back and forth and check the chain for tightness at several points on the chain. Identify the tightest point, and mark this spot with a piece of chalk.

2. Turn the wheel until this mark is on the lower chain run, midway between the engine and drive sprockets.

3. Place the bike on the sidestand on level ground.

4. Grasp the chain at the center of the chain run, and move the chain up and down. Measure the distance the chain moves vertically (**Figure 34**). Compare the measurement to the drive chain free play specified in **Table 4**. If necessary, adjust the free play by performing the following.

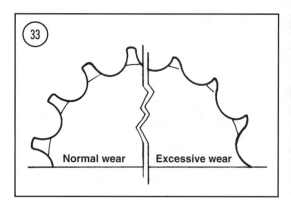

Normal wear   Excessive wear

NOTE
When adjusting the drive chain free play, make sure to maintain rear wheel alignment. A misaligned rear wheel can cause poor handling. All models are equipped with alignment marks on the swing arm and the chain adjusters.

5. On U.S.A., California and Canada models, remove the cotter pin (A, **Figure 29**) from the rear axle nut. Discard the cotter pin. Install a new one during assembly.

6. Loosen the rear axle nut (B, **Figure 29**).

7. On each side, loosen the chain adjuster locknut (A, **Figure 30**).

8. Tighten or loosen the adjuster bolt (B, **Figure 30**) on each side an equal amount until the chain free play is within the range specified in **Table 4**. Make sure the edge of each adjuster (D, **Figure 29**) aligns with the same mark on each side of the swing arm.

9. When drive chain free play is correct, check the wheel alignment by sighting along the top of the drive chain from the rear sprocket. The chain should form a straight line as it leaves the rear sprocket and travels to the front sprocket (A, **Figure 35**). If the chain veers to one side or the other (B and C, **Figure 35**), perform the following:

    a. Check that the adjusters are set to the same positions on the swing arm (D, **Figure 29**).

    b. If not, readjust the drive chain so the adjusters are at the same position on both sides and the free play is within specification.

10. Tighten the rear axle nut to the torque specification listed in **Table 5** and then tighten the adjuster locknuts securely.

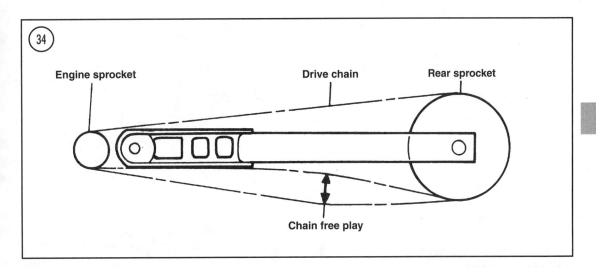

(34)

Engine sprocket — Drive chain — Rear sprocket

Chain free play

3

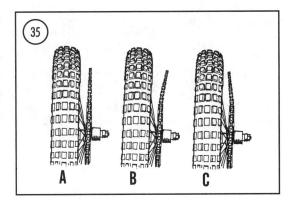

(35)

A B C

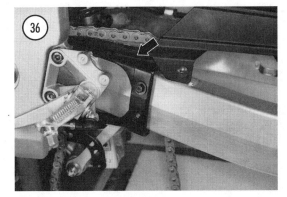

(36)

11. On U.S.A., California and Canada models, install a new cotter pin and bend the ends over completely.

12. If the drive chain cannot be adjusted to the correct measurement, the drive chain is excessively worn and must be replaced as described in Chapter Thirteen. Replace both the engine and rear sprockets when replacing the drive chain. Never install a new drive chain over worn sprockets.

Drive Chain Slider

Inspect the drive chain slider (**Figure 36**) on the left side of the swing arm for wear. Replace the slider if it is excessively worn.

Routine inspection and replacement of the drive chain slider prevents the drive chain from damaging the swing arm. A chain that is too loose causes rapid wear to the slider. To replace the drive chain slider, remove the swing arm as described in Chapter Thirteen and remove the slider. Whenever the swing

arm is removed for slider replacement, inspect and lubricate the swing arm bearings.

Engine and Rear Sprockets

NOTE
Replace the engine (front) and rear sprockets whenever the drive chain is replaced. Always replace both sprockets and the drive chain as a set. Never install a new chain over worn sprockets.

To replace the engine and rear sprockets, refer to the *Sprockets* section of Chapter Eleven.

CAUTION
When installing a new rear sprocket, check the torque on the rear sprocket nuts after 10 minutes of riding and after each 10 minute riding period until the nuts have seated to the new

sprocket and remain tight. Failure to keep the sprocket nuts correctly tightened damages the rear hub.

Throttle Operation

Check the throttle operation at the interval indicated in **Table 1**.

Operate the throttle grip. Check for smooth throttle operation from fully closed to fully open and then back to the fully closed position. The throttle should automatically return to the fully closed position without any hesitation.

Check the throttle cables for damage, wear or deterioration. Make sure the throttle cables are not kinked at any place.

If the throttle does not return to the fully closed position smoothly and if the exterior of the cable sheaths appears to be in good condition, lubricate the throttle cables as described in this chapter. Also apply a light coat of grease to the throttle cable spool at the hand grip.

If cable lubrication does not solve the problem, replace the throttle cables as described in Chapter Eight.

Throttle Cable Free Play

Check the throttle cable free play at the interval indicated in **Table 1**. The throttle cable free play specification appears in **Table 4**.

In time, the throttle cable free play becomes excessive from cable stretch. This delays throttle response and affects low speed operation. On the other hand, insufficient throttle cable free play can lead to an excessively high idle.

Minor adjustments can be made at the throttle grip end of the throttle cables. If proper adjustment cannot be achieved at this location, the cables must be adjusted at the throttle wheel on the carburetor assembly.

1. Shift the transmission into NEUTRAL.
2. Start the engine and allow it to idle.
3. With the engine at idle speed, slowly twist the throttle to raise engine speed. Note the amount of rotational movement (**Figure 37**) required to raise the idle. This is the throttle cable free play.
4. If throttle cable free play is outside the range specified in **Table 4**, adjust it by performing the following procedure.

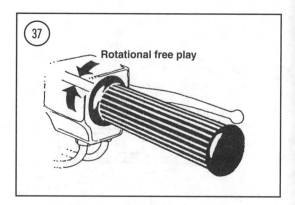

5. Shut off the engine.

6A. On 1997 models, perform the following:

  a. Loosen the locknut on the push cable (A, **Figure 38**) and turn the adjuster (B, **Figure 38**) in either direction until the correct amount of free play is achieved.

  b. Hold onto the push cable adjuster and tighten the locknut.

  c. Loosen the locknut on the pull cable (C, **Figure 38**) and turn the adjuster (D, **Figure 38**) in either direction until the correct amount of free play is achieved.

  d. Hold onto the pull cable adjuster and tighten the locknut.

6B. On 1998-on models, perform the following:

  a. Loosen the locknut on the push cable (A, **Figure 38**) and turn the adjuster (B, **Figure 38**) all the way in.

  b. Loosen the locknut on the pull cable (C, **Figure 38**) and turn the adjuster (D, **Figure 38**) in either direction until the correct amount of free play is achieved. Hold the pull cable adjuster, and tighten the locknut securely.

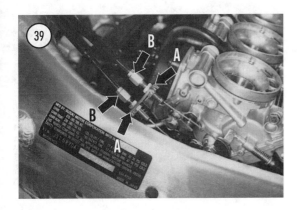

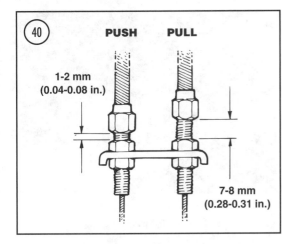

c. Hold the throttle grip in the fully closed position.

d. Slowly turn the adjuster on the push cable (B, **Figure 38**) until there is resistance, then stop. Hold onto the push cable adjuster (B) and tighten the locknut (A).

7. Restart the engine and repeat Steps 2-5 to make sure the adjustment is correct.

8. If throttle cable free play cannot be properly adjusted with the adjusters at the throttle grip end of the cables, continue with the following steps.

9. Raise and support the fuel tank as described in Chapter Eight.

10. At the throttle cables on the carburetor assembly, perform the following:

a. Loosen both throttle cable adjuster locknuts (A, **Figure 39**) on each side of the cable bracket.

b. Rotate the adjuster (B, **Figure 39**) on each cable in either direction until the correct clearance shown in **Figure 40** is attained.

c. Hold onto the adjusters and securely tighten the locknuts.

11. Recheck the throttle cable free play. If necessary, readjust free play with the adjusters at the throttle grip (Step 6).

12. If the throttle cable free play cannot be adjusted to specification, the cable(s) is stretched beyond the wear limit and must be replaced. Refer to Chapter Eight for this service procedure.

13. Check the throttle cables from grip to carburetor. Make sure they are not kinked or chafed. Replace as necessary.

14. Lower the fuel tank as described in Chapter Eight.

> *WARNING*
> *With the engine idling, move the handlebar from side to side. If the idle speed increases during this movement, the throttle cables may need adjusting or may be incorrectly routed through the frame. Correct this problem immediately. Do **not** ride the bike in this unsafe condition.*

15. Test ride the bike, slowly at first, and make sure the throttle cables are operating correctly. Readjust if necessary.

Disc Brakes

Check the brake fluid in each disc brake master cylinder at the interval listed in **Table 1**. Also check the brake pads for wear at the same time. Bleeding the system, servicing the brake system components and replacing the brake pads are covered in Chapter Fourteen.

Disc Brake Fluid Level
Check and Fill

Keep the brake fluid in the reservoirs at the upper line. **Figure 41** shows the front brake reservoir; **Figure 42** shows the rear brake reservoir. If necessary, correct the level by adding fresh brake fluid.

> *CAUTION*
> *Brake fluid will damage most surfaces it contacts. Immediately wash off any spilled brake fluid with soapy water. Thoroughly rinse the area with clean water.*

1. Place the bike on level ground on the sidestand.

2. Clean any dirt from the area around the cover before removing the cover.

3. On the front master cylinder, perform the following:

    a. Position the handlebar so the front master cylinder is horizontal.

    b. Remove the mounting screw and lift the reservoir cap retaining clip (A, **Figure 43**) from the top cover.

    c. Unscrew and remove the top cover (B, **Figure 43**), diaphragm plate and diaphragm from the master cylinder reservoir.

4. On the rear master cylinder, perform the following:

    a. Remove the rear frame cover as described in Chapter Fifteen.

    b. Clean all dirt and debris from the top of the master cylinder reservoir.

    c. Remove the screws securing the top cover (**Figure 44**). Remove the top cover and diaphragm.

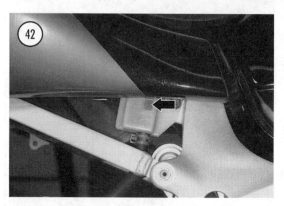

> *NOTE*
> *To control the flow of fluid, punch a small hole into the seal of a new container of brake fluid next to the edge of the pour spout. This helps eliminate fluid spillage while adding fluid to the very small reservoirs.*

> *WARNING*
> *Use DOT 4 brake fluid from a sealed container. Other types may vaporize and cause brake failure. Always use the same brand of brake fluid. Do not intermix different brands. They may not be compatible. Do not use silicone based (DOT 5) brake fluid. It can cause brake component damage leading to brake system failure.*

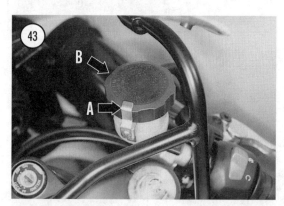

5. Refill the master cylinder reservoir, if necessary, to maintain the correct fluid level as indicated on the side of the reservoir.

6. On the front master cylinder, perform the following:

    a. Install the diaphragm, diaphragm plate and cover. Tighten the cover securely.

    b. Move the reservoir cap retaining clip back into position and tighten the mounting screw securely.

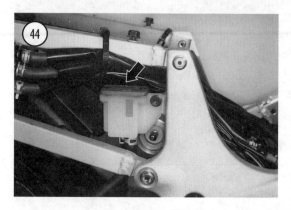

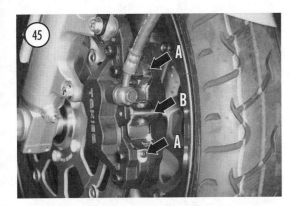

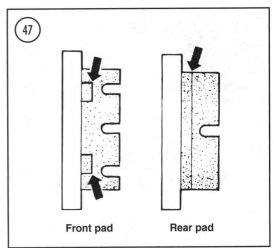

Front pad   Rear pad

45). Look into the top portion of the caliper assembly and inspect the brake pads for excessive or uneven wear. Install the pad spring and tighten the screws securely.

On the rear caliper, look down into the caliper from behind the rear wheel. Inspect the brake pads (**Figure 46**) for excessive wear.

If any pad is worn to the wear limit (**Figure 47**), replace the pads. Follow the pad replacement procedure in Chapter Fourteen.

> *NOTE*
> *Always replace both pads in each caliper at the same time to maintain even pressure on the brake disc. On the front brakes, replace the brake pads on both calipers at the same time to maintain even braking.*

Disc Brake Fluid Change

Brake fluid is hygroscopic (absorbs moisture). Moisture in the brake fluid will vaporize at the high temperatures created during hard braking efforts, which will reduce hydraulic pressure. If this occurs brake performance will be impaired. Moisture that remains in the system will eventually corrode and damage the internal brake components.

To maintain peak braking efficiency, change the brake fluid at the interval listed in **Table 1**. To change brake fluid, follow the *Bleeding The System* procedure in Chapter Fourteen. Continue adding new brake fluid to the master cylinder and bleed the

7. On the rear master cylinder, perform the following:
    a. Install the diaphragm and cover. Tighten the cover screws securely.
    b. Install the rear frame cover as described in Chapter Fifteen.

Disc Brake Hoses

Check the brake hoses between each master cylinder and each brake caliper assembly.

If there is any leakage, tighten the connections and bleed the brakes as described in Chapter Fourteen. If tightening the connection does not stop the leak or if the brake hose(s) is obviously damaged, cracked or chafed, replace the brake hose(s) and bleed the system as described in Chapter Fourteen.

Disc Brake Pad Wear

Inspect the brake pads for wear at the interval indicated in **Table 1**.

On the front brake caliper, remove the screws (A, **Figure 45**) and remove the pad spring (B, **Figure**

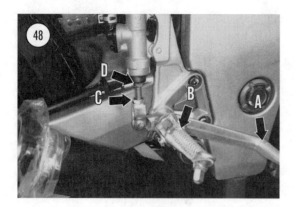

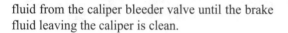

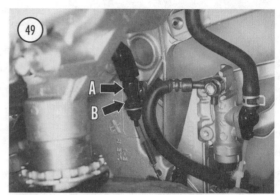

fluid from the caliper bleeder valve until the brake
fluid leaving the caliper is clean.

> *WARNING*
> *Use DOT 4 brake fluid from a sealed
> container. Other types may vaporize
> and cause brake failure. Always use
> the same brand of brake fluid. Do not
> intermix different brands. They may
> not be compatible. Do not use silicone
> based (DOT 5) brake fluid. It can
> cause brake component damage lead-
> ing to brake system failure.*

Rear Disc Brake Pedal Height Adjustment

Adjust the brake pedal height at the interval listed
in **Table 1**. The pedal height will change as the
brake pads wear. The top of the brake pedal (A, **Figure 48**) should be positioned below the top surface
of the footpeg (B, **Figure 48**). The distance between
the top of the brake pedal and the top of the footpeg
should equal the specification listed in **Table 4**. If
the dimension is incorrect, adjust the brake pedal
height by performing the following.

1. Place the bike on level ground on the sidestand.

2. Make sure the brake pedal is in the at-rest position.

3. At the rear brake master cylinder, loosen the
locknut (C, **Figure 48**) and turn the pushrod (D,
Figure 48) in either direction until the brake pedal
height equals the dimension specified in **Table 4**.

4. Tighten the rear brake master cylinder locknut to
the torque specification listed in **Table 5**.

Rear Brake Light Switch Adjustment

1. Turn the ignition switch to the ON position.

2. Depress the brake pedal and watch the brake
light. The brake light should come on just before
feeling pressure at the brake pedal. If necessary, adjust the rear brake light switch by performing the
following.

> *NOTE*
> ***Figure 49*** *is shown with the swing
> arm removed for clarity.*

3. To adjust the brake light switch, hold the switch
body (A, **Figure 49**) and turn the adjusting locknut
(B, **Figure 49**). To make the light come on earlier,
turn the adjusting locknut and move the switch body
up. Move the switch body *down* to delay the light
coming on.

4. Check that the brake light comes on when the
pedal is depressed and goes off when the pedal is released. Readjust if necessary.

5. Turn the ignition switch to the OFF position.

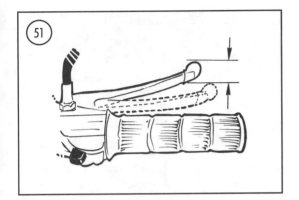

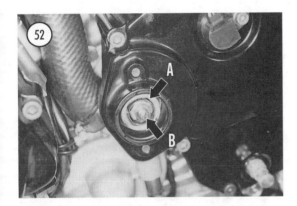

Clutch Lever Free Play Adjustment

Adjust the clutch cable at the interval listed in **Table 1**. For the clutch to fully engage and disengage, there must be free play at the tip of the clutch lever. The clutch lever free play specification is listed in **Table 4**.

For minor adjustments, turn the adjuster (**Figure 50**) at the clutch lever until the amount of free play at the end of the clutch lever (**Figure 51**) is within the range specified in **Table 4**.

If the clutch lever free play cannot be adjusted to within specification at the clutch lever, perform the following.

1. Remove the left lower fairing side panel as described in Chapter Fifteen.
2. At the clutch lever, turn the adjuster (**Figure 50**) all the way into the clutch lever assembly.
3. Remove the coolant reservoir tank as described in Chapter Ten.
4. Remove the clutch release cover from the engine sprocket cover.
5. At the clutch release mechanism, loosen the locknut (A, **Figure 52**) and turn the adjust screw out (B, **Figure 52**) two or three complete turns.

6. Turn the adjust screw in slowly until resistance is felt, and then stop. From this position, turn the adjust screw out 1/4 turn. Hold onto the adjust screw and tighten the locknut securely.
7. At the engine sprocket cover, loosen the clutch cable locknut (A, **Figure 53**) and turn the adjuster (B, **Figure 53**) in either direction until the clutch lever free play (**Figure 51**) is within the range specified in **Table 4**. Hold onto the adjuster (B, **Figure 53**) and tighten the locknut (A, **Figure 53**) securely.
8. If necessary for fine adjustment, at the clutch lever, turn the cable adjuster (**Figure 50**) in either direction to obtain the specified amount of free play at the clutch lever (**Figure 51**).
9. Install the clutch release lever cover onto the engine sprocket cover. Tighten the mounting screws securely.
10. Install the coolant reservoir tank as described in Chapter Ten.
11. Install the left lower fairing section as described in Chapter Fifteen.

Crankcase Breather

1. Remove the fuel tank as described in Chapter Eight.
2. Inspect the breather hose (**Figure 54**) from the cylinder head cover to the air box. If it is cracked or deteriorated, replace it. Make sure the hose clamps are in place and are tight.
3. Install the fuel tank.

Evaporative Emission Control System (California Models Only)

The evaporative emissions control system captures fuel vapors and stores them so they will not be released into the atmosphere. The fuel vapors are routed through the roll-over valve and stored in the charcoal canister (A, **Figure 55**), located on the right side of the rear sub-frame. When the engine is started, these stored vapors are drawn from the canister, through the purge control valves and into the carburetors. Make sure all evaporative emission control hoses (B, **Figure 55**) are correctly routed and properly attached. Refer to the Emission Control label located under the seat. Inspect the hoses and replace any if necessary as described in Chapter Eight.

PAIR Emission Control System (1997-on Calif. Models, 1999-on U.S.A., Canada, Austria and Switzerland models)

The PAIR system introduces fresh air into the exhaust ports to reduce the exhaust emission level.

Refer to *PAIR (Air Supply) System* in Chapter Eight for complete inspection and service procedures.

Cooling System Inspection

Once a year, or whenever the cooling system requires repeated refilling, check the following items. If the test equipment is not available, the tests can be done by a Suzuki dealership, automobile dealership, radiator shop or competent service station.

> *WARNING*
> *When performing any service work to the engine or cooling system, never remove the radiator cap, coolant drain screws or disconnect any hose while the engine and radiator are hot. Scalding fluid and steam may blow out under pressure and cause serious injury.*

1. Remove the lower fairing side panel on each side as described in Chapter Fifteen.
2. With the engine *cold*, remove the radiator cap (**Figure 56**).
3. Check the rubber sealing washers on the radiator cap (**Figure 57**). Replace the cap if the washers show signs of deterioration, cracking or other damage. If the radiator cap is acceptable, perform Step 3.

> *NOTE*
> *Apply water to the rubber washer in the radiator cap before installing the cap onto the pressure gauge.*

4. Pressure test the radiator cap (**Figure 58**). The radiator cap release pressure is listed in **Table 4**. The cap must be able to hold this pressure for at least 10 seconds. Replace the cap if it does not hold

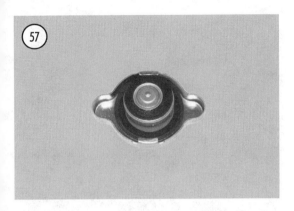

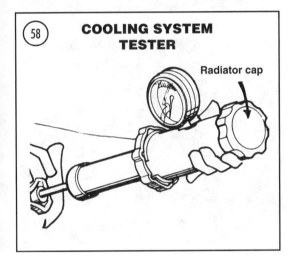

COOLING SYSTEM TESTER

Radiator cap

pressure or if the relief pressure is too high or too low.

5. Pressure test the radiator and cooling system. The specific radiator and cooling system pressure is listed in **Table 4**. If the cooling system will not hold this pressure, determine the source of leakage and make the appropriate repairs.

6. With the engine cold, remove the radiator cap and test the specific gravity of the coolant. Use an antifreeze tester following the manufacturer's instructions. This ensures adequate temperature and corrosion protection. Never let the mixture become less than 50 percent antifreeze or corrosion protection will be impaired. Never use a mixture of 60 percent or greater or the cooling efficiency will be reduced.

7. Check all cooling system hoses and the radiator for damage or deterioration as described in Chapter Ten.

8. Install the radiator cap. Turn the radiator cap clockwise to the first stop. Then push down and turn it clockwise until it stops.

9. Install the lower fairing panel on each side as described in Chapter Fifteen.

Coolant

Use only a high-quality ethylene-glycol based coolant formulated for aluminum radiators and engines. Mix the coolant with distilled water at a 50:50 ratio. Coolant capacity is listed in **Table 3**. When mixing antifreeze and water, make sure to use only a soft or distilled water. *Never* use tap water as this damages engine parts. Distilled (or purified) water can be purchased at supermarkets stores in gallon containers.

Coolant Change

Completely drain and refill the cooling system at the interval listed in **Table 1**.

It is sometimes necessary to drain the coolant from the system to perform a service procedure on some part of the engine. If the coolant is in good condition (and not due for replacement), it can be reused if it remains clean. Drain the coolant into a *clean* drain pan and then pour the coolant into a *clean* sealable container (milk or bleach bottle) and screw on the cap. This coolant can then be reused.

WARNING
Antifreeze is an environmental toxic waste. Do not dispose of it by flushing down a drain or pouring it onto the ground. Place old antifreeze into a suitable container and dispose of it properly. Do not store coolant where it is accessible to children or pets.

WARNING
Do not remove the radiator cap when the engine is hot. The coolant is very hot and under pressure. Severe scalding could result if the coolant comes in contact with your skin.

CAUTION
Be careful not to spill coolant on painted, plated or plastic surfaces. It may damage the finish and/or surface. Wash any applicable area with

soapy water and rinse thoroughly with clean water.

Perform the following procedure when the engine is *cold*.

1. Place the bike on level ground on the sidestand.
2. Remove the lower fairing panel on each side as described in Chapter Fifteen.
3. With the engine *cold*, remove the radiator cap (**Figure 56**).
4. On the left side, place a drain pan under the water pump housing.
5. Loosen the clamp screw and disconnect the coolant hose (A, **Figure 59**) from the water pump fitting, and drain the coolant into the pan.
6. Tip the bike from side to side to drain residual coolant from the cooling system.

> *NOTE*
> *If the coolant is dirty, place another drain pan under the water pump and disconnected coolant hose, and flush the system with clean water. Drain out all water from the system.*

7. Install the coolant hose onto the water pump fitting and tighten the clamp screw securely.
8. Remove the bolt securing the coolant reservoir in place.
9. Remove the reservoir cap (B, **Figure 59**) and drain the old coolant into a suitable container.
10. If necessary, clean the inside of the reservoir with a liquid detergent. Thoroughly rinse it with clean water.
11. Reinstall the reservoir, and tighten the hardware securely. If disconnected, attach both hoses to the reservoir tank.

> *CAUTION*
> *Do not use a coolant-to-water ratio higher than 50:50. A higher concentration of coolant (60 percent or greater) actually **decreases** the performance of the cooling system.*

12. Place a funnel into the radiator filler neck and refill the radiator and engine.
13. Use a 50:50 mixture of coolant and distilled water. Slowly add the coolant through the radiator filler neck. Add it slowly so it expels as much air as possible from the engine and radiator. Top off the coolant to the bottom of the filler neck. Do not install the radiator cap at this time.

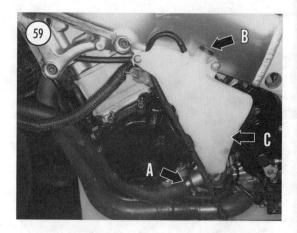

14. Remove the fill cap (B, **Figure 59**) from the reservoir. Refill the reservoir tank to the FULL mark (C, **Figure 59**) and install the cap.
15. Tip the bike from side to side several times. This helps bleed off some of the air trapped in the cooling system. If necessary, add additional coolant to the system until the coolant level is to the bottom of the filler neck.

> *CAUTION*
> *If the radiator cap is not installed correctly, coolant loss and engine damage will occur.*

16. Install the radiator cap. Turn the radiator cap clockwise to the first stop. Then push down and turn it clockwise until it stops.
17. Start the engine and run it at idle until it reaches operating temperature. Make sure there are no air bubbles in the coolant and that the coolant level has stabilized at the correct level. Add coolant if necessary.

18. Test ride the bike and readjust the coolant level in the reservoir tank if necessary.

19. Install the lower fairing panel on each side as described in Chapter Fifteen.

Exhaust System

1. Inspect the exhaust system for cracks or dents which could alter performance.

2. Check all exhaust system fasteners and mounting points for loose or damaged parts.

3. Make sure all mounting bolts and nuts are tight. If loose, refer to Chapter Eight for torque specifications.

Fuel Line Inspection

Inspect the fuel lines from the fuel tank to the carburetor assembly and other remaining hoses. If any hoses are cracked or deteriorated, replace them. Make sure the small hose clamps are in place and holding securely.

> *WARNING*
> *A damaged or deteriorated fuel line presents a dangerous fire hazard to the rider and the bike if fuel should spill onto a hot engine or exhaust pipe.*

Steering Head Adjustment Check

The steering head on all models consists of upper and lower caged ball bearings. A loose bearing adjustment will hamper steering. In severe conditions,

a loose bearing adjustment can cause loss of control.

1. Place the bike on the sidestand on level round.

2. Remove the lower fairing as described in Chapter Fifteen.

3. Place wooden blocks under the engine.

4. Have an assistant sit on the seat to raise the front wheel off the ground.

5. Hold onto the front fork tubes and gently rock the fork assembly back and forth. If there is looseness, adjust the steering head bearings as described in Chapter Twelve.

Handlebars

Inspect the individual handlebar assemblies weekly for any signs of damage. Replace a bent or damaged handlebar. Check the tightness of the clamping bolts.

> *CAUTION*
> *If any of the previously mentioned bolts and nuts are loose, refer to Chapter Twelve for correct procedures and torque specifications.*

Handlebar Grips

Inspect the handlebar grips for tearing, looseness or excessive wear. Install new grips when required. Use a grip adhesive (ThreeBond Griplock TB1501C, or equivalent) to prevent them from slipping.

Front Suspension Inspection

1. Apply the front brake and pump the front fork up and down vigorously. Check for smooth operation and oil leaks.

2. Make sure the upper (**Figure 60**) and lower (**Figure 61**) fork bridge clamp bolts are tight.

3. On the right side, make sure the front axle clamp bolts (A, **Figure 62**) are tight.

4. Check the tightness of the front axle nut (B, **Figure 62**).

5. On the left-hand side, make sure the front axle clamp bolts (**Figure 63**) are tight.

> *CAUTION*
> *If any of the previously mentioned bolts and nuts are loose, refer to*

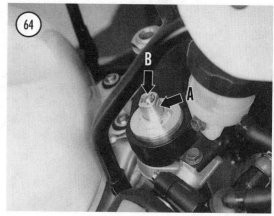

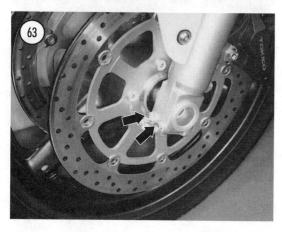

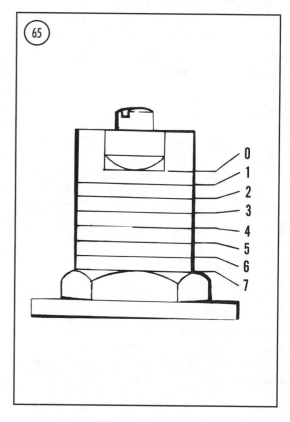

Chapter Twelve for correct proce-
dures and torque specifications.

Front Suspension Adjustment

The front fork spring preload and rebound damping can be adjusted on all models. On 1998-on, the
compression rebound can also be adjusted. The following procedures describe adjustment.

> *WARNING*
> *Each fork leg must be set to the **same***
> ***setting***. *If the fork legs are set differ-*
> *ently, it will adversely affect the han-*
> *dling. Make sure all three settings are*
> *identical on both fork leg assemblies.*

Fork spring preload adjustment

Adjust the spring preload by turning the spring
adjuster (A, **Figure 64**) on the top of each fork tube.
The adjuster is marked with eight (0-7) equally

spaced grooves as shown in **Figure 65**. Position 0
provides the maximum spring preload; position 7
provides the minimum.

The standard setting is when groove No. 4 aligns
with the top of the hexagon surface on the fork cap.
Turn the spring adjuster clockwise to increase
preload. Turn the adjuster counterclockwise to decrease preload. Use the grooves to ensure that the
spring preload is set to the same level on each fork
leg.

66

| U.S.A, California and Canadian models | Non U.S.A, California and Canadian models |

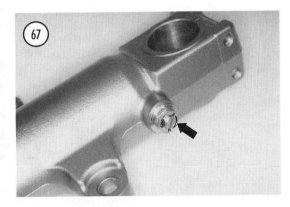

67

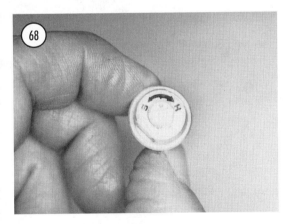

68

Rebound damping adjustment

Rebound damping affects the speed at which the front suspension returns to the fully extended position after compression.

Each front fork is equipped with a rebound damping adjuster (B, **Figure 64**) in the middle of the spring preload adjuster. The top of the adjuster is marked with a directional arrow and an **S** (soft) and **H** (hard) designations.

CAUTION
Do not turn the rebound damping adjuster past the point where it stops at its full clockwise or counterclockwise positions. Doing so damages the adjuster screw.

1. To set the rebound damping to the standard setting, perform the following:
   a. Turn the rebound damping adjuster clockwise until it stops. This is the hardest setting.
   b. Turn the adjuster counterclockwise the number of turns indicated in **Table 4**. The rebound damping is now adjusted to the standard setting.
2. To further adjust the rebound damping, perform the following:
   a. To reduce rebound damping, turn the adjuster counterclockwise toward the **S** (**Figure 66**).
   b. To increase rebound damping, turn the adjuster clockwise toward the **H** (**Figure 66**).
3. Make sure to adjust the rebound damping to the same setting on both fork legs.

Compression damping adjustment (1998-on)

Compression damping affects the speed at which the front suspension compresses. The compression damper (**Figure 67**) is mounted in the bottom of each slider. The adjuster is marked with a directional arrow and an **S** (solt) and **H** (hard) designations (**Figure 68**).

CAUTION
Do not turn the compression damping adjuster past the point where it stops at its full clockwise or counterclockwise positions. Doing so damages the adjuster screw.

1. To set the compression damping to the standard setting, perform the following:
   a. Turn the compression damping adjuster clockwise until it stops. This is the hardest setting.
   b. Turn the adjuster counterclockwise the number of turns indicated in **Table 1**. The compression damping is now adjusted to the standard setting.
2. To further adjust the compression damping, perform the following:

a. To reduce compression damping, turn the adjuster counterclockwise toward the **S** (**Figure 68**).

b. To increase rebound damping, turn the adjuster clockwise toward the **H** (**Figure 68**).

3. Make sure the compression damping is adjusted to the same setting on both fork legs.

Rear Suspension Check

1. Place the bike on level ground on the sidestand.
2. Remove the lower fairing as described in Chapter Fifteen.
3. Place wooden blocks under the engine.
4. Have an assistant sit forward on the seat to raise the rear wheel off the ground.
5. Push hard on the rear wheel (sideways) to check for side play in the rear swing arm bearings.
6. On the left side, make sure the swing arm pivot bolt nut is tight (**Figure 69**).
7. Remove the seat as described in Chapter Fifteen.
8. Make sure the shock absorber upper (A, **Figure 70**) and lower (A, **Figure 71**) hardware is tight.
9. Make sure the shock absorber lever assembly hardware is tight (B, **Figure 71**).
10A. On U.S.A., California and Canada models, make sure the rear axle nut cotter pin (A, **Figure 72**) is in place and that the nut (B, **Figure 72**) is tight.
10B. On models other than U.S.A., California and Canada, make sure the rear axle nut is tight.

> *CAUTION*
> *If any of the previously mentioned bolts and nuts are loose, refer to Chapter Thirteen for correct procedures and torque specifications.*

Rear Shock Absorber Adjustment

The spring preload and shock absorber rebound damping can be adjusted to suit the load and rider preference.

Spring preload adjustment

Set the spring preload by adjusting the spring length. A longer spring length provides a softer ride; a shorter spring length provides a stiffer ride. The preload must remain between the minimum and maximum specification (**Table 4**) at all times. Do

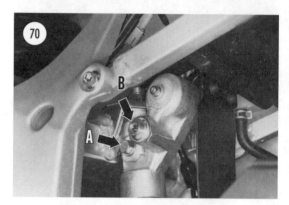

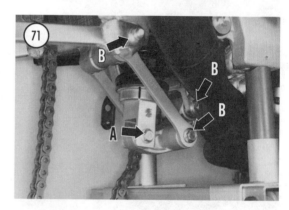

not operate the bike with the preload set below the minimum specification.

Two Steering Stem Nut Wrenches (Suzuki part No. 57001-1100) or equivalents are required for this procedure.

1. Remove the shock absorber as described in this chapter.

2. Using the special wrenches, completely loosen the upper locknut then the lower adjust nut (**Figure 73**) until there is no pressure being applied to the spring.

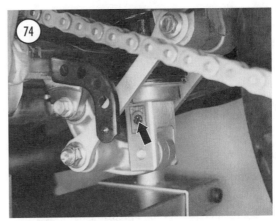

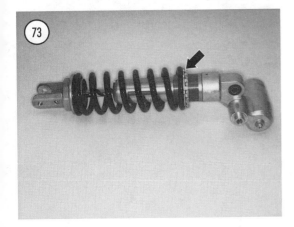

3

a. Turn the rebound adjuster (**Figure 74**) clockwise until it stops. This is the hardest setting.

b. Back the adjuster out (counterclockwise) the number of turns indicated in **Table 4** or until the punch mark on the adjuster aligns with the reference mark on the shock housing.

2. To fine tune the rebound damping, perform the following:

NOTE
When fine tuning the suspension, do so gradually. Turn the rebound damping adjuster in 1/8-turn increments and then test ride the motorcycle.

a. To reduce the rebound damping, turn the adjuster counterclockwise toward the **S** (soft) mark on the shock housing.

b. To increase the rebound damping, turn the adjuster clockwise toward the **H** (hard) mark on the shock housing.

3. Tighten the lower adjust nut to achieve the desired amount of spring preload.

4. Once the correct amount of spring preload is achieved, hold the lower adjust nut and tighten the upper locknut securely.

5. Install the shock absorber as described in this chapter.

Rebound damper force adjustment

Rebound damping affects the rate at which the shock absorber returns to its extended position after compression. Rebound damping does not affect the action of the shock on compression.

NOTE
When turning the adjuster, make sure it clicks into one of the detent positions. Otherwise the adjuster automatically sets to the stiffest position.

1. To adjust the rebound damping to the standard setting, perform the following:

Compression damping force adjustment

Compression damping affects the rate at which the shock compresses when the rear wheel hits a bump. This adjustment does not affect the action of the shock absorber on rebound.

1. To adjust the compression damping to the standard setting, perform the following:

a. Turn the compression damping adjuster (B, **Figure 70**) clockwise until it stops. This is the hardest setting.

b. Back the adjuster out (counterclockwise) the number of turns indicated in **Table 4**. Or until the punch mark on the adjuster aligns with the reference mark on the shock housing.

2. To fine tune the compression damping, perform the following:

> *NOTE*
> *When fine tuning the suspension, do so gradually. Turn the compression damping adjuster in 1/8-turn increments and then test ride the motorcycle.*

a. To reduce the compression damping, turn the adjuster counterclockwise toward the **S** (soft) marked on the shock housing.

b. To increase the compression damping, turn the adjuster clockwise toward the **H** (hard) mark on the shock housing.

Frame Inspection

Inspect the frame for cracks or other damage. Check all areas where welded sections attached to the main frame spar. Check the tightness of the rear sub-frame mounting bolts (**Figure 75**), and tighten securely if necessary.

Nuts, Bolts and Other Fasteners

Constant vibration can loosen many of the fasteners on the bike. Check the tightness of all fasteners, especially those on:

1. Engine mounting hardware.
2. Engine crankcase covers.
3. Handlebar and front fork.
4. Gearshift lever.
5. Brake pedal and lever.
6. Exhaust system.

ENGINE TUNE-UP

The following section describes tune-up procedures. Perform these tasks in the following order:

1. Clean or replace the air filter element.
2. Check and adjust the valve clearances (engine must be cold).
3. Perform a compression test.
4. Check or replace the spark plugs.
5. Check and adjust the carburetor idle speed and synchronization.

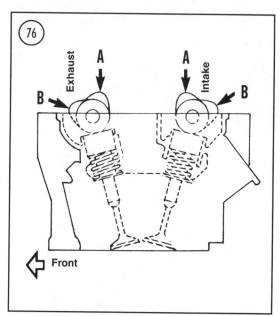

Valve Clearance Measurement

The valve clearance for all models is listed in **Table 4**. The exhaust valves are located at the front of the engine and the intake valves are located at the rear of the engine.

The cylinders are numbered from left to right, 1-4. The left and right sides refer to the position of the parts as viewed by the rider siting on the seat facing forward.

The figures in this procedure show the engine removed from the frame for clarity. It is not necessary to remove the engine to adjust the valves.

Use a flat metric feeler gauge to check the valve clearance. The engine *must* be cold (below 35° C/95° F) to obtain accurate results.

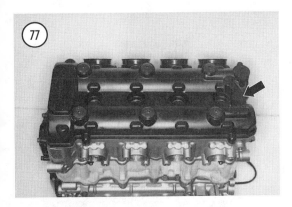

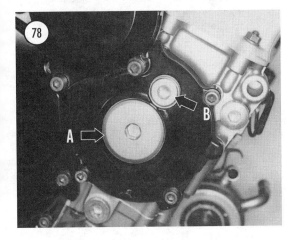

NOTE
*The camshaft lobes must point away from the tappet as shown in either position A or B, **Figure 76**. Clearance dimensions taken with the camshaft in any other position gives a false reading, leading to incorrect valve clearance adjustment and possible engine damage.*

1. Remove the seat and the lower fairing side panel on both sides as described in Chapter Fifteen.

2. Remove the air box and carburetor assembly as described in Chapter Eight.

3. Remove all four spark plugs as described in this chapter. This makes it easier to turn the engine by hand.

4. Following a crisscross pattern, evenly loosen the cylinder head cover bolts (**Figure 77**).

5. Remove the bolts, and then remove the cover and gasket.

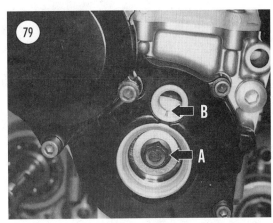

6. Remove the starter clutch cover cap (A, **Figure 78**) and the valve timing inspection cap (B, **Figure 78**).

NOTE
In Step 7, both the TOP line on the starter clutch and the camshaft notches on the left side must be correctly aligned and positioned. Several complete engine revolutions may be necessary to achieve this alignment.

NOTE
Use a mirror to observe the camshaft notches on the left side.

7. Correctly position the camshafts as follows:
   a. Use a 14 mm wrench on the starter clutch mounting bolt (A, **Figure 79**). Rotate the engine *clockwise*, as viewed from the right side of the engine, until the TOP line on the starter clutch aligns with the mark on the timing inspection hole (B, **Figure 79**).
   b. At the same time, bring the camshaft notches, on the left side of each camshaft, to the position shown in **Figure 80**. If the camshaft notches are not positioned as shown, rotate the engine 360° (one full revolution) until the camshaft notches are positioned correctly.
   c. If it was necessary to rotate the engine an additional revolution, recheck that the TOP line on the starter clutch is once again aligned with the mark on the timing inspection hole (B, **Figure 79**). Realign this mark if necessary.

8. With the engine in this position, check the valve clearance on the following valves (1, **Figure 81**):
   a. No. 2 cylinder: Intake valves.

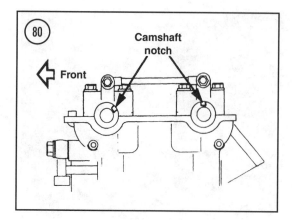

Camshaft notch
Front

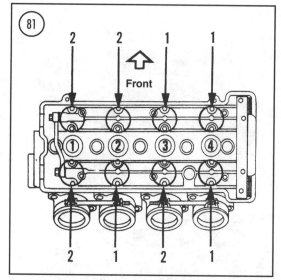

2   2   1   1
Front
① ② ③ ④
2   1   2   1

b. No. 3 cylinder: Exhaust valves.

c. No. 4 cylinder: Intake and exhaust valves.

NOTE
When checking the clearance, start out with a feeler gauge of the specified clearance thickness. If this thickness is too large or small, change the gauge thickness until there is a drag on the feeler gauge when it is inserted and withdrawn.

9. Check the clearance by inserting the feeler gauge between the tappet and the camshaft lobe (**Figure 82**). When the clearance is correct, there will be a slight resistance on the feeler gauge when it is inserted and withdrawn. Record the clearance dimension. Identify the clearance by cylinder number and by intake or exhaust valve. The clearance dimension is needed if adjustment is necessary.

10. Continue on to Step 11 even if some of the valves in this group require adjustment. Measure the clearance of all valves before beginning the valve adjustment procedure.

11. For measuring the remaining valves, perform the following:

a. Use the 14 mm wrench on the starter clutch mounting bolt (A, **Figure 79**) and rotate the engine 360° (one full revolution) *clockwise*, when viewed from the right side of the bike. Rotate the engine until the TOP line on the starter clutch once as aligns with the mark on the timing inspection hole (B, **Figure 79**).

b. At the same time, bring the notches on the left side of the camshafts to the position shown in **Figure 83**.

12. With the engine in this position, check the valve clearance on the following valves (2, **Figure 81**):

a. No. 1 cylinder: Intake and exhaust valves.

b. No. 2 cylinder: Exhaust valves.

c. No. 3 cylinder: Intake valves.

13. Check the clearance by inserting a flat metric feeler gauge between the tappet and the camshaft lobe (**Figure 82**). When the clearance is correct, there will be a slight resistance on the feeler gauge when it is inserted and withdrawn. Record the clearance dimension. Identify the clearance by cylinder number and by intake or exhaust valve. The clearance dimension is needed if adjustment is necessary.

14. If the valves require adjustment, follow the adjustment procedure described below.

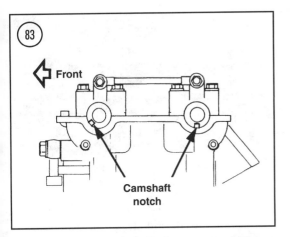

83

Front

Camshaft
notch

84

85

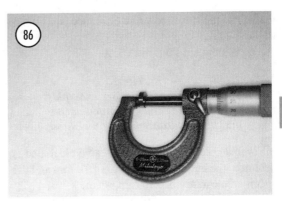

86

3

NOTE
*Measure the thickness of the shims
that are removed from the engine to
confirm their dimensions. If the shim
is worn to less than its indicated size,
the valve clearance calculations will
be inaccurate. Also measure replacement shims to make sure they are correctly marked.*

1. Remove the camshaft(s) as described in Chapter
Four.
2. To avoid confusion adjust one valve at a time.
3. Remove the tappet(s) (**Figure 84**) for the valve
requiring adjustment.
4. Use needlenose pliers or tweezers to remove the
shim(s) (**Figure 85**) from the top of the valve spring
retainer.
5. Check the number on the bottom of the shim. If
the number is no longer legible, measure the shim
with a micrometer (**Figure 86**).

NOTE
*Table 4 lists the valve clearance spec-
ification as a range. When performing
the calculation in Step 6, use the
mid-point of the specified range. For
example the specified intake valve
clearance is 0.10-0.20 mm. The
mid-point is 0.15 mm.*

6. Using the measured valve clearance, the specified valve clearance listed in **Table 4** and the old
shim thickness, calculate the new shim thickness by
using the following equation:
   $a = (b-c) + d$
   Where:
   a equals the new shim thickness.
   b equals the measured valve clearance.

Valve Clearance Adjustment

   To adjust the valve clearance, replace the shim located under the tappet with a shim of a different
thickness. The camshaft(s) must be removed to gain
access to the shims. The shims are available from
Suzuki dealerships in thickness increments of 0.05
mm that range from 1.20 to 2.20 mm in thickness.

c equals the specified valve clearance (mid-point of the specified range).

d equals the old shim thickness.

> *NOTE*
> *The following numbers are **examples only**. Use the values recorded during the valve clearance check procedure.*

For example: if the measured valve clearance is 0.23 mm, the old shim thickness is 1.70 mm and the specified clearance is 0.15 mm, then:

a = (0.23 − 0.15) + 1.70

a = 1.78

Since the shims are sold in increments of 0.05 mm, round the calculated shim thickness up to the nearest 5 hundredths of a millimeter. In the example, round the 1.78 up to 1.80, therefore the new shim should be 1.80 mm thick.

> *NOTE*
> *If the shim thickness exceeds 2.20 mm, the valve seat is heavily carboned and should be refaced.*

7. Apply clean engine oil to both sides of the new shim and to the receptacle on top of the valve spring retainer. Position the shim so the side with the printed number faces down, and install the shim(s) (**Figure 85**) into the recess in the valve spring retainer.

8. Install the tappet(s) (**Figure 84**) into the cylinder head receptacle.

9. Repeat this procedure for all valve assemblies that are out of specification.

10. Install the camshaft(s) as described in Chapter Four.

11. Use a 14 mm wrench on the starter clutch mounting bolt (A, **Figure 79**) and rotate the engine several complete revolutions *clockwise*, as viewed from the right side of the bike. This seats the new shims and squeezes any excess oil from between the shim, the spring retainer and the tappet.

12. Recheck all valve clearances as described in the preceding procedure. If there is any clearance outside the specified range, repeat this procedure until all clearances are correct.

13. Install the cylinder head cover as follows:

   a. Inspect the rubber gasket (A, **Figure 87**) around the perimeter of the cylinder head cover. Also inspect the rubber gasket at each spark plug hole (B, **Figure 87**). If they are

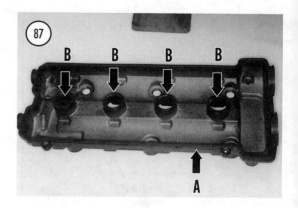

starting to deteriorate or harden, replace them. Replace the gaskets as a set even if only one requires replacement. If replacement is necessary, refer to *Cylinder Head Cover Installation* in Chapter Four.

   b. Thoroughly clean the gasket mating surface on the cylinder head.

   c. Apply a light coat of sealant (Suzuki Bond No. 1207B, or equivalent) to the four camshaft end caps where they fit into the receptacles in the cylinder head.

   d. Install the cylinder head cover.

   e. Install a *new* gasket under the cylinder head cover mounting bolts, then install the bolts.

   f. Tighten the bolts in a crisscross pattern to the torque specification listed in **Table 5**.

14. Inspect the O-ring seals on the caps, and replace them if necessary. Install the starter clutch cover cap (A, **Figure 78**) and the valve timing inspection cap (B, **Figure 78**).

15. Install all four spark plugs as described in this chapter.

16. Install the carburetor assembly and air box as described in Chapter Eight.

17. Install the lower fairing side panels and seat as described in Chapter Fifteen.

Cam Chain Adjustment

An automatic cam chain tensioner assembly is attached to the backside of the cylinder head. No adjustment is possible nor required.

Cylinder Compression

A cylinder cranking compression check is one of the quickest ways to check the internal condition of the engine, including the piston rings, pistons, and head gasket. Check the compression at each tune-up, record the readings and compare them with the readings at the next tune-up. This helps spot any developing problems.

1. Before starting the compression test, make sure the following items are correct:

    a. The cylinder head bolts are tightened to the specified torque. Refer to Chapter Four.

    b. The valves are properly adjusted as described in this chapter.

    c. The battery is fully charged to ensure proper engine cranking speed.

2. Warm the engine to normal operating temperature. Turn the engine off.

3. Remove the fuel tank and air box as described in Chapter Eight.

4. Remove all four spark plugs as described in this chapter.

> *NOTE*
> *A screw-in type compression gauge with a flexible adapter is required for this procedure. Before using this gauge, check the condition of the rubber gasket on the end of the adapter. This gasket must seal the spark plug hole and cylinder to ensure accurate compression readings. Replace the seal if it is cracked or starting to deteriorate.*

5. Thread the tip of a compression gauge into the No. 4 cylinder following the manufacturer's instructions.

> *CAUTION*
> *Do not crank the engine over more than absolutely necessary. When the spark plug leads are disconnected, the electronic ignition will produce the highest voltage possible and the coils may overheat and be damaged.*

6. *Open the throttle completely* and turn the engine over until there is no further rise in pressure. Maximum pressure is usually reached within 4-7 seconds. Record the pressure reading for that cylinder. The recommended cylinder compression and the maximum allowable difference between cylinders is listed in **Table 4**.

7. Remove the compression gauge from that cylinder.

8. Repeat Steps 5-7 for the remaining cylinders and record the readings.

9. Install the spark plugs, plug caps, air box and the fuel tank.

10. Compression between cylinders should not vary by more than the specification. If it does, the low-reading cylinder has a valve or ring problem. To determine which, pour about a teaspoon of engine oil into the spark plug hole of the low-reading cylinder and repeat Step 6.

    a. If the compression increases significantly, the piston rings are probably worn.

    b. If the compression does not increase, the valves are leaking.

11. Install the spark plugs, plug caps, air box and the fuel tank.

SPARK PLUGS

Spark Plug Removal

A spark plug can be used to help determine the operating condition of its cylinder when properly read. As each spark plug is removed, label it with its cylinder number.

The cylinders are numbered from left to right, 1-4. The left and right sides refer to the position of the parts as viewed by the rider siting on the seat facing forward.

1. Remove the seat as described in Chapter Fifteen.

2. Remove the fuel tank and air box as described in Chapter Eight.

> *CAUTION*
> *Whenever the spark plug is removed, dirt around it can fall into the plug hole. This can cause serious engine damage*

3. Blow away all loose dirt, and wipe off the top surface of the cylinder head cover. Remove all loose debris that could fall into the cylinder head spark plug tunnels.

> *CAUTION*
> *Handle the ignition coil/plug cap assemblies carefully. Remove the electrical coupler before removing the ignition coil/plug cap. Do not use any type of tool to pry the ignition coil/plug cap from the spark plug, remove them by hand. Any damage to*

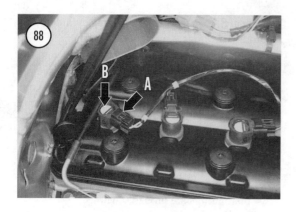

*the assembly could result in an open
or short circuit.*

4. Carefully disconnect the electrical coupler (A,
Figure 88) from each ignition coil/plug cap.

5. The ignition coil/plug caps form a tight seal on
the cylinder head cover as well as the spark plugs.
Grasp the ignition coil/plug cap (B, **Figure 88**), and
twist it from side-to-side to break the seal loose.
Carefully pull the ignition coil/plug cap up and off
the spark plug. If it is stuck to the plug, twist it
slightly to break it loose.

6. As each ignition coil/plug cap is removed, label
it with its cylinder number.

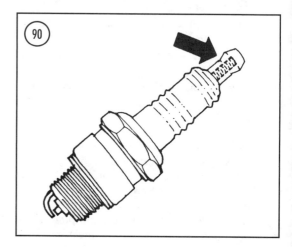

> *NOTE*
> *Use a special spark plug socket
> equipped with a rubber insert that
> grabs the side of the spark plug. This
> type of socket is included in the stan-
> dard tool kit and is necessary for both
> removal and installation since the
> spark plugs are located down deep in
> their cylinder head receptacles. You
> cannot use your fingers to remove or
> install the spark plugs.*

> *NOTE*
> *Do not clean the spark plugs with a
> sand-blasting type device. Any clean-
> ing material left on the plug will fall
> into the cylinder during operation and
> cause damage.*

10. Inspect the ignition coil/plug caps (**Figure 89**)
for damage. If visually damaged, inspect the assembly as described in Chapter Nine.

11. Inspect each electrical coupler (A, **Figure 88**)
and wiring for corrosion and/or damage. If damaged, the wiring and electrical couplers are part of
the main wiring harness and cannot be replaced separately.

7. Install the spark plug socket onto the spark plug.
Make sure it is correctly seated on the plug. Install
an open end wrench or socket handle and remove
the spark plug. Label the spark plug with the cylinder number.

8. Repeat the above procedure for the remaining
three spark plugs.

9. Inspect the plugs carefully. Look for a broken
center porcelain insulator, excessively eroded electrodes and excessive carbon or oil fouling.

Spark Plug Gap and Installation

Carefully gap the spark plug to ensure a reliable,
consistent spark. Use a special spark plug gaping
tool and a wire feeler gauge.

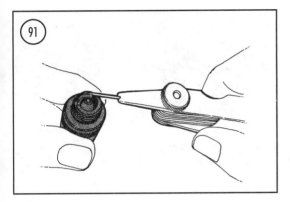

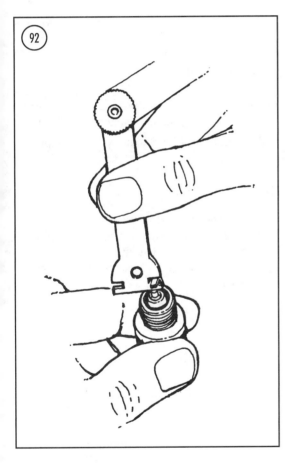

3. Apply a *light* coat of antiseize compound onto the threads of the spark plug before installing it. Do not use engine oil on the plug threads.

> *CAUTION*
> *The cylinder head is aluminum. The spark plug hole threads can be easily damaged by cross-threading of the spark plug.*

4. The spark plugs are recessed into the cylinder head and cannot be started by hand. Attach a length of vinyl or rubber hose to the top end of the spark plug. Screw the spark plug in by hand until it seats. Very little effort is required. If force is necessary, the plug is cross threaded. Unscrew it and try again. Once the plug is screwed in several revolutions, remove the hose.

5. Use the same tool set-up used during removal and hand-tighten the plug until seated. Tighten the plug to the torque specification listed in **Table 5**.

> *NOTE*
> *Do not overtighten the spark plug. This only squashes the gasket and destroys its sealing ability.*

> *CAUTION*
> *Handle the ignition coil/plug cap assemblies carefully. Install them onto the spark plugs by hand.*

> *NOTE*
> *Make sure to push the ignition coil/plug cap all the way down to make full contact with the spark plug post. If the cap does not completely contact the plug, the engine may develop an ignition misfire.*

6. Refer to the marks made during removal and install each ignition coil/plug cap onto the correct spark plug. Press the ignition coil/plug cap (B, **Figure 88**) onto the spark plug, rotate the assembly slightly in both directions and make sure it is attached to the spark plug and to the sealing surface of the cylinder head cover.

7. Position the electrical connector receptacle on the ignition coil/plug cap so the No. 1 and No. 2 cylinders are facing toward each other and the No. 3 and No. 4 cylinders are facing toward each other (**Figure 93**).

1. Unscrew the small adapter from the end of the plug (**Figure 90**). This adapter is *not* used.

2. Insert a wire feeler gauge between the center and side electrode of the plug (**Figure 91**). The specified gap is listed in **Table 4**. If the gap is correct, there will be a slight drag as the wire is pulled through. If there is no drag or if the gauge will not pass through, bend the side electrode with a gaping tool (**Figure 92**) and set the gap to specification.

8. Carefully connect the electrical coupler (A, **Figure 88**) onto each ignition coil/plug cap. Position the electrical coupler so it does not contact the raised portion of the cylinder head cover as shown in **Figure 93**.

9. Make sure the electrical connectors are free of corrosion and are on tight.

10. Install the air box and fuel tank as described in Chapter Eight.

11. Install the seat as described in Chapter Fifteen.

Spark Plug Reading

Reading the spark plugs can provide a significant amount of information regarding engine performance. Reading plugs that have been in use will give an indication of spark plug operation, air/fuel mixture composition and engine condition (oil consumption, pistons, etc.). Before checking the spark plugs, operate the motorcycle under a medium load for approximately 6 miles (10 km). Avoid prolonged idling before shutting off the engine. Remove the spark plugs as described in this chapter. Examine each plug and compare it to those in **Figure 94**.

If the plugs are being read to determine if carburetor jetting is correct, start with new plugs and operate the bike at the load that corresponds to the jetting information desired. For example, if the main jet is in question, operate the bike at full throttle and shut the engine off and coast to a stop.

Spark Plug Heat Range

Spark plugs are available in various heat ranges, hotter or colder than the plugs originally installed by the manufacturer.

Select a plug with a heat range designed for the loads and conditions under which the bike will be operated. A plug with an incorrect heat range can foul, overheat and cause piston damage.

In general, use a hot plug for low speeds and low temperatures. Use a cold plug for high speeds, high engine loads and high temperatures. The plug should operate hot enough to burn off unwanted deposits, but not so hot that it is damaged or causes preignition. To determine if plug heat range is correct, remove each spark plug and examine the insulator.

Do not change the spark plug heat range to compensate for adverse engine or carburetion conditions. Compare the insulator to those in **Figure 94** when reading plugs.

When replacing plugs, make sure the reach (**Figure 95**) is correct. A longer than standard plug could interfere with the piston, causing engine damage.

Refer to **Table 4** for recommended spark plugs.

Normal condition

A light tan- or gray-colored deposit on the firing tip and no abnormal gap wear or erosion indicates good engine, ignition and air/fuel mixture conditions. The plug in use is of the proper heat range. It may be serviced and returned to use.

Carbon fouled

Soft, dry, sooty deposits covering the entire firing end of the plug are evidence of incomplete combustion. Even though the firing end of the plug is dry, the plug's insulation decreases when in this condition. The carbon forms an electrical path that bypasses the electrodes resulting in a misfire condition. Carbon fouling can be caused by one or more of the following conditions:

1. Rich air/fuel mixture.

2. Spark plug heat range too cold.

3. Clogged air filter.

4. Improperly operating ignition component.

5. Ignition component failure.

6. Low engine compression.

7. Prolonged idling.

94

SPARK PLUG CONDITIONS

NORMAL USE

OIL FOULED

CARBON FOULED

OVERHEATED

GAP BRIDGED

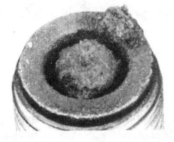

SUSTAINED PREIGNITION

WORN OUT

3

Oil fouled

An oil fouled plug has a black insulator tip, a damp oily film over the firing end and a carbon layer over the entire nose. The electrodes are not worn. Common causes for this condition are:
1. Incorrect air/fuel mixture.
2. Low idle speed or prolonged idling.
3. Ignition component failure.
4. Spark plug heat range too cold.
5. Incomplete engine break-in.
6. Worn valve guides.
7. Worn or broken piston rings.

Oil fouled spark plugs may be cleaned in an emergency, but it is better to replace them. It is important to correct the cause of fouling before the engine is returned to service.

Gap bridging

Plugs with this condition have deposits building up between the electrodes. The deposits reduce the gap and eventually close it entirely. If this condition is encountered, check for excessive carbon buildup or oil entering the combustion chamber. Make sure to locate and correct the cause of this condition.

Overheating

Badly worn electrodes and premature gap wear are signs of overheating, along with a gray or white blistered porcelain insulator surface. This condition is commonly caused by a spark plug heat range that is too hot. If the standard heat range spark plug is being used and the plug is overheated, consider the following causes:
1. Lean fuel/air mixture.
2. Improperly operating ignition component.
3. Engine lubrication system malfunction.
4. Cooling system malfunction.
5. Engine air leak.
6. Improper spark plug installation (overtightening).
7. No spark plug gasket.

Worn out

Corrosive gases formed by combustion and high voltage sparks have eroded the electrodes. A spark plug in this condition requires more voltage to fire under hard acceleration. Install a new spark plug.

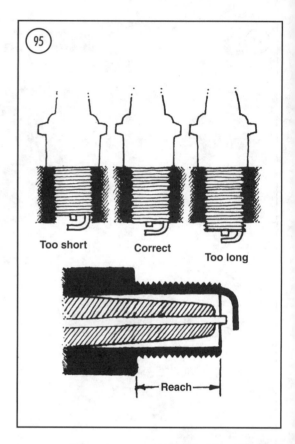

Too short   Correct   Too long

Reach

Preignition

If the electrodes are melted, preignition is almost certainly the cause. Check for carburetor mounting or intake manifold leaks and advanced ignition timing. The plugs heat range may also be too hot. Find the cause of the preignition before returning the engine into service. For additional information on preignition, refer to *Preignition* in Chapter Two.

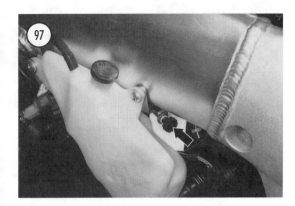

Ignition Timing

The engine is equipped with a fully transistorized ignition system. This solid state system uses no breaker points or other moving parts. The ignition timing is not adjustable. There are no procedures available from the manufacturer to check the ignition timing. Because of the solid state design, problems with the transistorized system are rare. If there seems to be an ignition related problem; inspect the ignition components as described in Chapter Nine.

Incorrect ignition timing can cause a drastic loss of engine performance and efficiency. It may also cause overheating.

Idle Speed Adjustment

Before making this adjustment, the air filter element must be clean and the engine must have adequate compression. See *Compression Test* in this chapter. Otherwise this procedure cannot be done properly.

1. Make sure the throttle cable free play is adjusted correctly. Check and adjust if necessary as described in this chapter.

2. Start the engine and let it warm up approximately 2-3 minutes. Shut off the engine and make sure the carburetor choke lever (**Figure 96**) is all the way forward in the OFF position.

3. Connect a tachometer following the manufacturer's instructions.

4. The idle speed knob (**Figure 97**) is on the left side of the motorcycle. Turn the idle speed knob in or out to adjust the idle speed to the specification in **Table 4**.

5. Open and close the throttle a couple of times. Check for variations in idle speed, and readjust if necessary.

> *WARNING*
> *With the engine running at idle speed, move the handlebar from side to side. If idle speed increases during this movement, the throttle cable needs adjusting or may be incorrectly routed through the frame. Correct this problem immediately. Do not ride the bike in this unsafe condition.*

6. Turn off the engine.
7. Disconnect the tachometer.

Carburetor Idle Mixture

The idle mixture (pilot screw) is pre-set by the manufacturer and *is not to be reset*. Do not adjust the pilot screws unless the carburetors have been overhauled. Refer to Chapter Eight.

Carburetor Synchronization

To ensure maximum engine performance, the carburetors must be synchronized. This procedure ensures that each carburetor is opening the same amount throughout the throttle range.

Synchronization tools are available in a number of different styles; some measure engine vacuum with a traditional vacuum gauge or by the movement of mercury within a glass tube, while some perform this function electronically. In addition to the synchronization tool, an auxiliary fuel tank and tachometer are required for this procedure. If this equipment is not available, have a Suzuki dealership or motorcycle specialist perform the operation. Do not attempt to synchronize the carburetors without the proper equipment. Doing so will result in misadjustment and poor engine performance.

> *NOTE*
> *Prior to synchronizing the carburetors, clean the air filter element and adjust the valve clearance.*

1. Start the engine and let it reach normal operating temperature.
2. Adjust the idle speed as described in this chapter, and then shut off the engine.

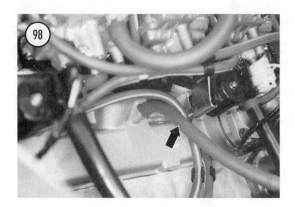

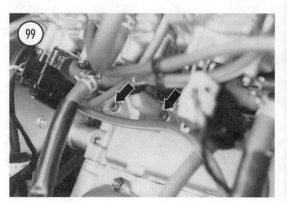

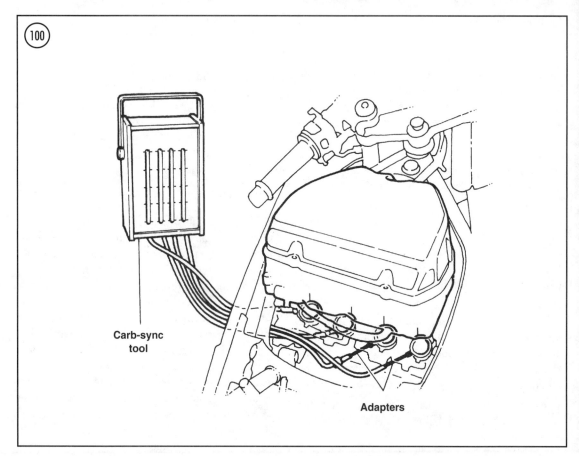

Carb-sync
tool

Adapters

3. Install a portable tachometer following the manufacturer's instructions.

4. Remove the fuel tank as described in Chapter Eight.

> *WARNING*
> *When using an auxiliary fuel tank, make sure the tank is secure and all fuel lines are tight to prevent leaks.*

5. Disconnect the No. 3 cylinder vacuum hose (**Figure 98**) from the fitting.

6. Remove the No. 1, 2 and 4 cylinder vacuum screws (**Figure 99**). Use an impact driver and a No. 3 Philips bit to loosen the screws. Do not lose the sealing washer behind each vacuum screw.

7. Install the synchronization tool to the vacuum fittings following the manufacturer's instructions (**Figure 100**).

8. Start the engine. Turn the idle adjust knob (**Figure 97**) until the engine idles at 1750 rpm.

9. If the carburetors are correctly balanced, the gauge set will have equal readings for each cylinder.

NOTE
The No. 3 carburetor is the base carburetor. It has no synchronization screw. The other carburetors must be synchronized to the No. 3 carburetor.

10. Turn the adjusting screws (**Figure 101**) with a Philips screwdriver, and adjust the No. 1, 2 and 4 carburetors so they each have the same gauge reading as the No. 3 carburetor. Snap the throttle a few times and recheck the synchronization readings. Readjust synchronization if required.

11. Reset the idle speed to the specification in **Table 4**.

12. Shut off the engine.

13. Disconnect the auxiliary fuel tank and the vacuum gauge set from the carburetors.

14. Install the vacuum hose (**Figure 98**) onto the No. 3 carburetor vacuum fitting.

15. Reinstall the vacuum screws (**Figure 99**) for the No. 1, 2 and 4 cylinders and tighten them securely. Make sure a sealing washer is installed with each screw to avoid a vacuum leak.

16. Install the fuel tank as described in Chapter Eight.

17. Restart the engine and reset the engine idle speed to the value specified in **Table 4**, if necessary.

18. Shut off the engine.

Table 1 MAINTENANCE SCHEDULE

Weekly/gas stop
  Check tire pressure cold; adjust to suit load and speed
  Check condition of tires
  Check brakes for a solid feel
  Check throttle grip for smooth operation and return
  Check for smooth but not loose steering
  Check axles, suspension, controls, linkage nuts, bolts and fasteners; tighten if necessary
  Check engine oil level; add oil if necessary
  Check lights and horn operation, especially brake light
  Check for any abnormal engine noise and leaks
  Check coolant level
  Check kill switch operation
Every 600 miles (1000 km) or 1 month
  Change engine oil and replace oil filter
  Check idle speed; adjust if necessary
  Check throttle cable free play; adjust if necessary
  Clean and lubricate drive chain
  Check brake pads for wear and rear pedal height
  Check brake discs thickness; replace if necessary
  Check brake discs for rust and corrosion; clean if necessary
  Check steering play; adjust if necessary
  Check and tighten all nuts, bolts and fasteners on exhaust system
  Check tightness of all chassis bolts and nuts; tighten if necessary
  On California models, synchronize the carburetors
Every 4000 miles (6000 km) or 6 months
  Check air filter element for contamination; clean or replace if necessary
  Check spark plugs; replace if necessary

(continued)

Table 1 MAINTENANCE SCHEDULE (continued)

Every 4000 miles (6000 km) or 6 months (continued)
  Check all fuel system hoses for leakage; repair or replace if necessary
  Change engine oil
  Check idle speed; adjust if necessary
  Check throttle cable free play; adjust if necessary
  Check clutch lever free play adjustment; adjust if necessary
  Check radiator and all coolant hoses for leakage
  Check battery charge and condition
  Clean and lubricate drive chain
  Check drive chain and sprockets for wear or damage
  Check drive chain free play; adjust if necessary
  Check brake pads for wear
  Check brake discs thickness; replace if necessary
  Check brake discs for rust and corrosion; clean if necessary
  Check brake system for leakage; repair if necessary
  Check brake fluid level in both reservoirs; add fluid if necessary
  Check tire and wheel rim condition
  Lubricate all pivot points
  Check tightness of all chassis bolts and nuts; tighten if necessary
Every 7500 miles (12,000 km) or 12 months
  All of the checks listed in 4000 miles (6000 km) or 6 months and the following:
  Replace the spark plugs
  Synchronize carburetors
  Check front fork operation and for leakage
  Check EVAP hoses (California models)
  Check PAIR (air supply) hoses, 1998-on California models)
  Lubricate control cables
Every 11,000 miles (18,000 km) or 18 months
  All of the checks listed in 7500 miles (12,000 km) or 12 months and the following:
  Replace air filter element
  Replace oil filter
Every 15,000 miles (24,000 km) or 24 months
  All of the checks listed in 7500 miles (12,000 km) or 12 months and the following:
  Check valve clearance; adjust if necessary
Every 2 years
  Replace coolant
  Replace brake fluid
Every 4 years
  Replace all brake hoses
  Replace EVAP hoses (California models)

Table 2 TIRE SPECIFICATIONS

Item	Front	Rear
Tire type	Tubeless	Tubeless
Size	120/70 ZR17 (58W)	180/55 ZR17 (73W)
Minimum tread depth	1.6 mm (0.06 in.)	2.0 mm (0.08 in.)
Inflation pressure (cold)*		
Solo	250 kPa (36 psi)	250 kPa (36 psi)
Rider and passenger	250 kPa (36 psi)	250 kPa (36 psi)

*Tire inflation pressure is for original equipment tires. Aftermarket tires may require different inflation pressure. The use of tires other than those specified by Suzuki may cause instability.

Table 3 RECOMMENDED LUBRICANTS AND FLUIDS

Fuel	Unleaded
Octane	87 [(R + M)/2 method] or research octane of 91 or higher
U.S.A., California, and Canada models	87 [(R + M)/2 method] or research octane of 91 or higher
Non- U.S.A., California, and Canada models	85-95
1997-1998	85-95
1999-on	91 or higher
Fuel tank capacity, including reserve	18.0 L (4.8 U.S. gal., 4.0 Imp. gal.)
Engine oil	
Grade	API SF or SG
Viscosity	SAE 10W40
Capacity	
Oil change only	2.6 L (2.7 US qt., 2.3 Imp. qt.)
Oil and filter change	2.8 L (3.0 US qt., 2.5 Imp. qt.)
When engine completely dry	3.5 L (3.7 US qt., 3.1 Imp. qt.])
Brake fluid	DOT 4
Fork oil	
Viscosity	Suzuki No. 10 fork oil or equivalent
Capacity per leg	533 ml (18.0 U.S. oz., 18.8 Imp. oz.)
Engine coolant	
Type	Antifreeze/coolant that is compatible with an aluminum radiator.
Ratio	50:50 with distilled water
Capacity	2550 ml (2.7 U.S. qt., 2.2 Imp. Qt.)

3

Table 4 MAINTENANCE AND TUNE-UP SPECIFICATIONS

Battery	
Type	FTX9-BS Maintenance free (sealed)
Capacity	12 volt 8 amp hour
Spark plug	
Standard	NGK CR9E, ND U27ESR-N
Hotter	NGK CR8E, ND U24ESR-N
Colder	NGK CR10E, ND U31ESR-N
Spark plug gap	0.7-0.8 mm (0.028-0.031 in.)
Idle speed	
U.S.A., California, Canada, Austria, and 1999-on Australia models	1200-1400 rpm
Switzerland models	1250-1400 rpm
All other models	1100-1300 rpm
Ignition timing	5 B.T.D.C at 1500 rpm
Valve clearance (cold)	
Intake	0.10-0.20 mm (0.004-0.008 in.)
Exhaust	0.20-0.30 mm (0.008-0.012 in.)
Compression pressure (at sea level)	
Standard	1100-1500 kPa (156-213 psi)
Service limit	900 kPa (128 psi)
Maximum difference between cylinders	200 kPa (28 psi)
Engine oil pressure (hot)	200-500 kPa (28-71 psi) at 3000 rpm
Brake pedal height	55 mm (2.2 in.)
Throttle cable free play	
1997 models	0.5-1.0 mm (0.02-0.04 in.)
1998-on models	2.0-4.0 mm (0.08-0.16 in.)
Clutch lever free play	10-15 mm (0.4-0.6 in.)

(continued)

Table 4 MAINTENANCE AND TUNE-UP SPECIFICATIONS (continued)

Rim runout (front and rear)	
Axial	2.0 mm (0.08 in.)
Radial	2.0 mm (0.08 in.)
Radiator cap release pressure	110 kPa (15.6 psi)
Radiator and cooling system test pressure	120 kPa (17 psi)
Drive chain 21-pin length	319.4 mm (12.6 in.)
Drive chain free play	20-30 mm (0.8-1.2 in.)
Fork spring preload adjuster	4th groove from top
Fork spring damping adjuster	
1997 U.S.A., California, and Canada models	
Rebound damping	1 1/8 turns out
1997 non-U.S.A., California	
and Canada models	
Rebound damping	1 turn out
1998-on models	
Rebound damping	1 1/8 turns out
Compression damping	1 turn out
Shock Absorber	
Spring preload	
1997 models	
Standard preload (spring length)	193.9 mm (7.6 in.)
Maximum preload (spring length)	188.9 mm (7.4 in.)
Minimum preload (spring length)	198.9 mm (7.9 in.)
1998-on	
Standard spring length	195.4 mm (7.7 in.)
Maximum spring preload	190.4 mm (7.5 in.)
Minimum spring preload	204.4 mm (8.0 in.)
Damping	
1997 U.S.A., California,	
and Canada models	
Rebound damping	1 1/8 turns out
Compression damping	7/8 turns out
1997 non U.S.A., California	
and Canada models	
Rebound damping	1 1/8 turns out
Compression damping	3/4 turns out
1998 models	
Rebound damping	1 turn out
Compression damping	1 3/8 turns out

Table 5 MAINTENANCE AND TUNE-UP TORQUE SPECIFICATIONS

Item	N•m	in.-lb.	ft.-lb.
Cylinder head cover bolt	14	–	10
Engine sprocket bolt	120	–	89
Exhaust pipe bolt	23	–	17
Front axle	100	–	74
Front axle pinch bolt	23	–	17
Main oil gallery plug	40	–	29
Muffler mounting bolt	23	–	17
Oil drain plug	28	–	21
Oil hose banjo bolt			
Upper side	20	–	15
Lower side	25	–	18
(continued)			

Table 5 MAINTENANCE AND TUNE-UP TORQUE SPECIFICATIONS (continued)

Item	N•m	in.-lb.	ft.-lb.
Oil pan bolt	14	–	10
Rear axle nut	100	–	74
Rear brake master cylinder locknut	18	–	13
Spark plug	12	106	–
Valve timing inspection cap	23	–	17

3

CHAPTER FOUR

ENGINE TOP END

ENGINE PRINCIPLES

Figure 1 explains basic four-stroke engine operation. This is helpful when troubleshooting or repairing the engine.

EXHAUST SYSTEM

Check the exhaust system for deep dents and fractures. Repair or replace damaged parts immediately. Check the muffler frame mounting flanges for fractures and loose bolts. Check the cylinder head mounting flanges for tightness. Loose exhaust pipe connections will cause excessive exhaust noise and rob the engine of power.

Muffler

Removal/installation

Refer to **Figure 2** for this procedure.
1. Securely support the bike on level ground.
2. Remove the nuts and washers (A, **Figure 3**) securing the muffler to the exhaust pipe assembly.

3. Remove the muffler mounting bolt, washers and nut (B, **Figure 3**) securing the muffler clamp to the rear footpeg bracket.
4. Pull the muffler out from the exhaust pipe and remove the muffler (C, **Figure 3**). Remove the gasket from the exhaust pipe.
5. Check the rubber grommet at the rear mounting bracket. Replace the rubber grommet if it is starting to harden or deteriorate.
6. Installation is the reverse of removal.
   a. Install a *new* gasket over the end of the exhaust pipe.
   b. Tighten the hardware to the specifications in **Table 3**.
   c. After installation is complete, start the engine and make sure there are no exhaust leaks.

Removal/Installation

Refer to **Figure 2** for this procedure.
1. Remove the lower fairing side panel from each side as described in Chapter Fifteen.

FOUR-STROKE ENGINE PRINCIPLES

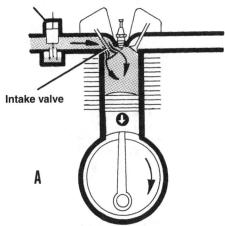

Carburetor

Intake valve

A

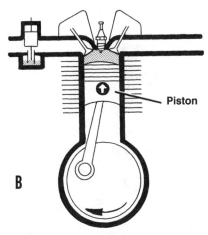

Piston

B

As the piston travels downward, the exhaust valve is closed and the intake valve opens, allowing the new air/fuel mixture from the carburetor to be drawn into the cylinder. When the piston reaches the bottom of its travel (BDC) the intake valve closes and remains closed for the next 1 1/2 revolutions of the crankshaft.

While the crankshaft continues to rotate, the piston moves upward, compressing the air/fuel mixture.

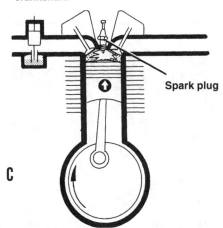

Spark plug

C

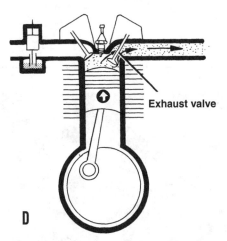

Exhaust valve

D

As the piston almost reaches the top of its travel, the spark plug fires, igniting the compressed air/fuel mixture. The piston continues to top dead center (TDC) and is pushed downward by the expanding gases.

When the piston almost reaches BDC, the exhaust valve opens and remains open until the piston is near TDC. The upward travel of the piston forces the exhaust gases out of the cylinder. After the piston has reached TDC, the exhaust valve closes and the cycle repeats.

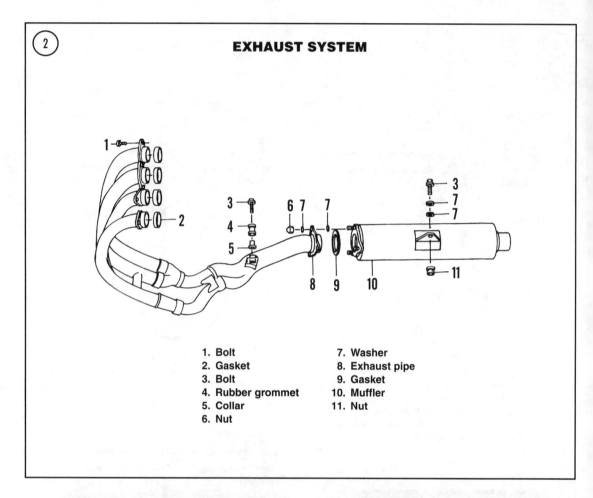

EXHAUST SYSTEM

1. Bolt
2. Gasket
3. Bolt
4. Rubber grommet
5. Collar
6. Nut
7. Washer
8. Exhaust pipe
9. Gasket
10. Muffler
11. Nut

2. Remove the radiator as described in Chapter Ten.

3. Remove the muffler as previously described in this chapter.

NOTE
*Only one exhaust header bolt is visible at each exhaust port in **Figure 4**.*

Make sure to remove two bolts from each cylinder outlet.

4. Remove the two header bolts (**Figure 4**) from each exhaust port.

5. Pull the exhaust pipe assembly forward and out of the cylinder head, and then remove the exhaust

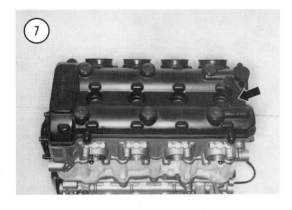

pipe assembly from the bike. Remove the sealing gaskets from the exhaust ports in each cylinder.

6. Inspect the mounting bracket on the muffler for cracks or damage.

7. Check the exhaust pipe-to-cylinder head flange for corrosion, burned areas or damage.

8. Inspect all of the welds for leakage or corrosion.

9. If any of the black painted areas are worn off, clean old paint from these areas. Repaint them with a *heat resistant* paint.

10. Install a *new* exhaust pipe sealing gasket into each exhaust port (**Figure 5**). Apply a small amount of cold grease to the gaskets to hold them in place.

11. Install the exhaust pipe assembly onto the cylinder head and frame.

12. Install the exhaust header bolts (**Figure 4**). Finger-tighten them at this time.

13. Install the muffler as previously described in this chapter. Finger-tighten the hardware at this time.

14. Tighten the exhaust system hardware to the specifications in **Table 3** and in the following sequence:

    a. Exhaust header bolts.

    b. Exhaust pipe-to-muffler nuts.

    c. Exhaust pipe mounting bolt.

    d. Muffler mounting bolt.

15. After installation is complete, start the engine and make sure there are no exhaust leaks.

CYLINDER HEAD COVER

The cylinder head cover can be removed with the engine mounted in the frame. However, for clarity, some of this procedure shows the engine removed.

Removal

1. Place the bike on level ground on a stand or wooden blocks.

2. Remove the seats and lower fairing side panels on each side as described in Chapter Fifteen.

3. Disconnect the negative battery cable as described in Chapter Three.

4. Remove the fuel tank as described in Chapter Eight.

5. Remove the air box as described in Chapter Eight.

6. Remove the carburetor assembly as described in Chapter Eight. Make sure to install lint-free cloths into the intake manifolds (**Figure 6**) to prevent the entry of debris.

7. Disconnect the spark plug wires and caps and move the wires out of the way. Refer to Chapter Three.

8. Using a crisscross pattern, loosen then remove the bolts securing the cylinder head cover (**Figure 7**).

9. Pull the cover straight up and off the cylinder head and remove the cover. Watch for the two dowels.

10. The gasket (A, **Figure 8**) will usually stay attached to the cylinder head cover. Remove the gasket even if its appears to be in good condition, as the gasket must be sealed to the cylinder head cover during installation.

11. Do not lose the rubber sealing gaskets (B, **Figure 8**) on each spark plug tower in the cylinder head.

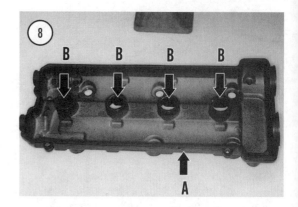

Inspection and Gasket Replacement

1. Make sure the gasket sealing surface in the cover groove is clean and free of any oil. This surface must be clean and smooth to provide a tight seal.

2. Inspect the cylinder head cover gasket around its perimeter for wear or damage. Replace the gasket if it is not in excellent condition.

3. Remove all old gasket sealer residue from the gasket sealing surface around the perimeter of the cylinder head. Make sure to clean off all old sealer from the crescent-shaped machined surfaces at each end of the cylinder head.

4. Check the cylinder head cover (**Figure 9**) for warp, cracks or damage. Replace if necessary.

5. Inspect the cover bolts for thread damage and rubber/metal sealing rings for damage or hardness. Replace as necessary.

6. Install the new gasket onto the cylinder head cover. Make sure it is completely seated around the perimeter.

7. Apply a light coat of Suzuki Bond No. 1207B, or equivalent, to the crescent shaped portions of the gasket. This ensures a tight seal between the cylinder head cover and the cylinder head.

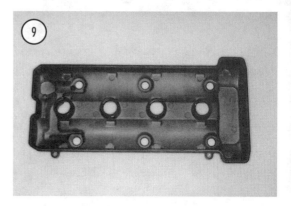

Installation

1. Make sure the gasket (A, **Figure 8**) is installed correctly in the cylinder head cover.

2. If removed, install the rubber sealing gaskets (B, **Figure 8**) on each spark plug tower in the cylinder head cover.

3. If removed, install the two locating dowels (**Figure 10**) into the cylinder head.

4. Install the cylinder head cover onto the cylinder head (**Figure 7**). Make sure the four crescent por-

tions of the cover gasket properly engage the crescent shaped areas of the cylinder head.

5. Install the cover bolts making sure the gaskets are installed under each bolt. Tighten the bolts in a crisscross pattern to the torque specification listed in **Table 3**.

6. Connect the spark plug wires and caps to the correct cylinders as described in Chapter Three.

7. Remove the lint-free cloths from the intake manifolds.

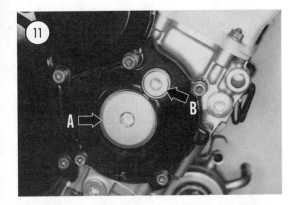

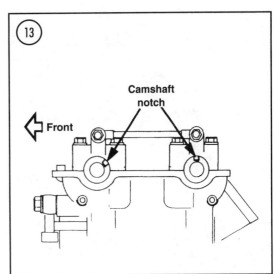

Camshaft
notch

Front

8. Install the carburetor assembly as described in Chapter Eight.

9. Install the air box as described in Chapter Eight.

10. Install the fuel tank as described in Chapter Eight.

11. Connect the negative battery cable as described in Chapter Three.

12. Install the lower fairing side panels on each side and install the seats as described in Chapter Fifteen.

CAMSHAFT

NOTE
The camshafts can be removed with the engine in the frame. However, installing the camshaft and setting the cam timing is very difficult if the engine is in the frame because the wide frame side rail restricts visibility. Consequently, it is recommended that this procedure be performed with the engine removed from the frame, which is how it is described below.

Removal

1. Remove the engine as described in Chapter Five.

2. Remove the cylinder head cover as described in this chapter.

3. Remove the spark plugs as described in Chapter Three. This makes it easier to turn the engine by hand.

4. Remove the cam chain tensioner as described below.

5. Remove the starter clutch cover cap (A, **Figure 11**) and the valve timing inspection cap (B, **Figure 11**).

6. Correctly position the camshafts as follows:

   a. Use a 14 mm wrench on the starter clutch mounting bolt (A, **Figure 12**). Rotate the engine *clockwise*, as viewed from the right side of the bike, until the TOP line on the starter clutch aligns with the mark on the timing inspection hole (B, **Figure 12**).

   b. Make sure the camshaft notches, on the left side, are positioned as shown in **Figure 13**. If the camshaft notches are not positioned as shown, rotate the engine one full revolution (360°) until the camshaft notches are positioned correctly.

   c. If it was necessary to rotate the engine an additional revolution, recheck that the TOP line on the starter clutch is once again aligned with the mark on the timing inspection hole (B, **Figure 12**). Realign if necessary.

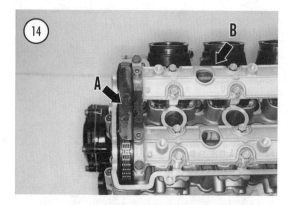

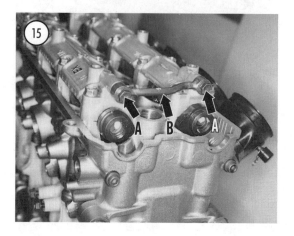

7. Remove the bolts securing the top cam chain guide (A, **Figure 14**) and remove the guide.

8. Remove the banjo bolts and sealing washers (A, **Figure 15**) securing the oil pipe (B, **Figure 15**) and remove the pipe.

9. Using a crisscross pattern, loosen then remove the bolts securing the camshaft holders (B, **Figure 14**). Pull the holders straight up and off the camshafts.

> *NOTE*
> *There is no need to secure the camshaft drive chain to the exterior of the engine. The cam chain stopper bolt (**Figure 16**) prevents the chain from dropping into the crankcase.*

10. Disengage the cam chain from the camshaft sprockets and remove the intake and the exhaust camshafts (**Figure 17**) from the cylinder head one at a time. Do not drop the ball bearing retaining C-rings (A, **Figure 18**) into the crankcase. Remove both C-rings at this time.

> *CAUTION*
> *If the crankshaft must be rotated while the camshafts are removed, pull up on the cam chain so it properly engages the crankshaft timing sprocket. Hold the chain taut on the timing sprocket while rotating the crankshaft. If this is not done, the cam chain could become kinked, which could cause damage to the chain, timing sprocket and surrounding crankcase area.*

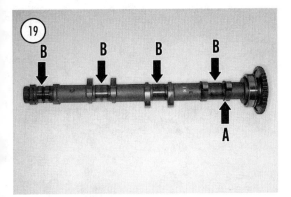

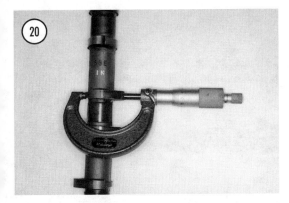

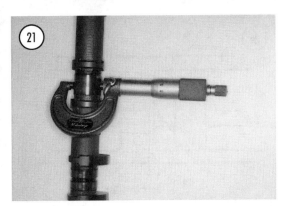

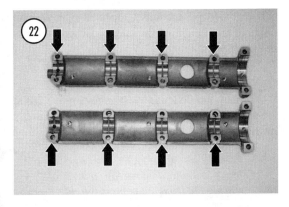

Inspection

When measuring the camshafts in this section, compare the actual measurements to the new and wear limit specifications listed in **Table 2**. Replace parts that are out of specification or show damage as described in this section.

1. Check each camshaft lobe (A, **Figure 19**) for wear. The lobes should not be scored and the edges should be square.

2. Measure the height of each lobe (**Figure 20**) with a micrometer. Replace the camshaft if any lobe is out of specification.

3. Check each camshaft bearing journal (B, **Figure 19**) for wear and scoring.

4. Measure the diameter of each camshaft bearing journal (**Figure 21**) with a micrometer. Record each measurement. It is necessary to have them when measuring camshaft bearing clearance. Replace the camshaft if any journal diameter is out of specification.

5. If the bearing journals are excessively worn or damaged, check the bearing journals in the cylinder head (B, **Figure 18**) and in the camshaft holders (**Figure 22**). They should not be scored or excessively worn. If any of the bearing surfaces are worn or scored, replace the cylinder head assembly and camshaft holders as a set.

6. Inspect the ball bearing (A, **Figure 23**) on each camshaft. The bearing must rotate freely with no binding or excessive play. If necessary, replace the camshaft(s); the ball bearing cannot be replaced.

7. Place the camshaft on a set of V-blocks and check the runout with a dial indicator. Replace the camshaft if its runout is out of specification.

8. Inspect the camshaft sprocket (B, **Figure 23**) for broken or chipped teeth. Also check the teeth for cracking or rounding. If the camshaft sprocket(s) is damaged or excessively worn, replace the camshaft. Also, inspect the camshaft timing sprocket mounted on the crankshaft as described in Chapter Five.

> *NOTE*
> *If the camshaft sprockets are worn, check the cam chain, chain guides and chain tensioner for damage.*

9. Inspect the sliding surface of the top cam chain guide (**Figure 24**) for wear or damage. Also check both ends of the guide. Replace the top guide as necessary.

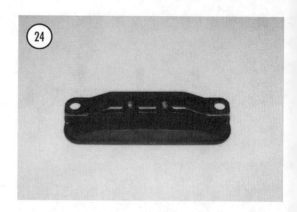

Camshaft Bearing Clearance Measurement

This procedure requires the use of Plastigage. The camshafts must be installed into the cylinder head. Before installing the camshafts, wipe all oil residue from each camshaft bearing journal and from the bearing surface of the cylinder head and camshaft holders.

1. Do not install the drive chain onto the camshafts for this procedure.

2. Install the camshafts into the cylinder head in the correct location. Refer to the **IN** and **EX** marks (**Figure 25**) on each camshaft. Install the exhaust camshaft in the front of the engine and the intake camshaft in the rear.

3. Place a strip of Plastigage onto each bearing journal (**Figure 26**). The Plastigage must be parallel to the camshaft.

4. Install each camshaft holder in its correct location. Refer to the **IN** and **EX** marks (**Figure 27**) on each holder. Install the exhaust camshaft holder in the front of the engine and the intake camshaft holder in the rear.

5. Install the bolts and evenly tighten them in the sequence indicated by the raised numbers adjacent to each bolt hole. Torque the bolts *in sequence* to the specification listed in **Table 3**.

> *CAUTION*
> *Do not rotate the camshafts with the Plastigage in place.*

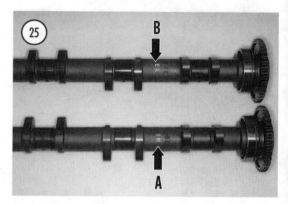

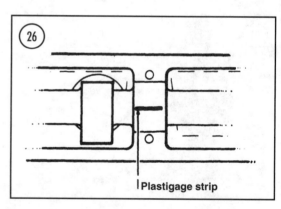

Plastigage strip

6. Refer to Step 5 and loosen the bolts in the *reverse order* of the tightening sequence. Loosen the bolts in 2-3 stages.

7. Pull straight up and carefully remove both camshaft holders.

8. Measure the flattened Plastigage (**Figure 28**) at the widest point, according to the manufacturer's instructions.

> *CAUTION*
> *Make sure to remove all traces of Plastigage from the camshaft holders*

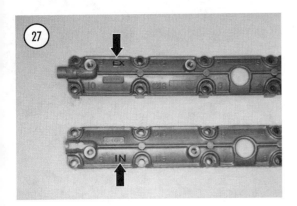

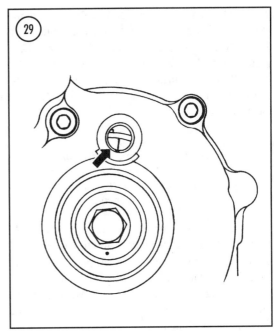

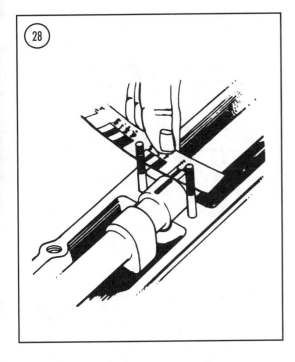

and from the camshaft bearing journal. If any of the material is left in the engine, it can plug an oil control orifice and cause severe engine damage.

9. Remove *all* Plastigage from the camshafts and camshaft holders.

10. If the camshaft bearing oil clearance is greater than specified in **Table 2**, refer to the camshaft bearing outer diameter dimension recorded in *Inspection* Step 4. If the bearing surface is worn to the service limit; replace the camshaft. If the camshaft is within specification; replace the cylinder head assembly.

Camshaft Installation

NOTE
*The camshafts are identified by a letter code stamped on the end of each shaft. When replacing a camshaft, install the correct one for the particular model. The camshaft codes for all models are listed in **Table 4**.*

1. Pull up on the cam chain and make sure it is properly meshed with the crankshaft timing sprocket.

NOTE
*If the crankshaft has not been disturbed since the camshafts were removed, the engine may still be at the correct position for camshaft installation. If the TOP line on the starter clutch is still aligned with the mark on the timing inspection hole (**Figure 29**) then the engine is in the correct position for camshaft installation. If alignment is incorrect, perform Step 2.*

2. Use a 14 mm wrench on the starter clutch mounting bolt (A, **Figure 12**). Rotate the engine *clockwise*, as viewed from the right side of the bike, until

the TOP line on the starter clutch is aligned with the mark on the timing inspection hole (B, **Figure 12**).

3. Apply a light coat of molybdenum disulfide grease to each camshaft journal (B, **Figure 19**). Coat all bearing surfaces in the cylinder head (B, **Figure 18**) and camshaft holders (**Figure 22**) with clean engine oil.

CAUTION
The bearing retaining C-rings control the end float of the camshafts. If not installed, the camshafts can float sideways and cause damage.

4. Install both ball bearing retaining C-rings (A, **Figure 18**) into the cylinder head grooves.

5. Set the exhaust camshaft (B, **Figure 25**) into the cam chain and install the camshaft onto the cylinder head bearing surface (**Figure 30**). Make sure the groove in the ball bearing properly engages the C-ring in the cylinder head.

6. Lift up on the chain and rotate the exhaust camshaft until the No. 1 arrow mark is level with the top surface of the cylinder head (**Figure 31**). The No. 2 arrow mark is now pointing straight up. Properly mesh the cam chain with the sprocket and install a short cable tie to secure the cam chain to the cam sprocket (A, **Figure 32**).

7. Fit the intake camshaft (A, **Figure 25**) through the cam chain and install the camshaft onto the cylinder head bearing surface (**Figure 33**). Make sure the groove in the bearing properly engages the C-ring in the cylinder head.

8. Note that the No. 2 arrow on the exhaust cam sprocket points to a pin on the cam chain. This is the first pin (**Figure 31**). Starting at this pin, count back to the 15th pin. Properly mesh the cam chain with the intake cam sprocket so the 15th pin is opposite the No. 3 arrow on the intake cam sprocket (**Figure 34**). Install a short cable tie to secure the cam chain to the sprocket (B, **Figure 32**).

CAUTION
Engine damage is likely if the cam chain-to-camshaft installation and alignment is incorrect. Recheck the work several times to make sure alignment is correct.

NOTE
The cam chain is now riding on the crankshaft timing sprocket, the ex-

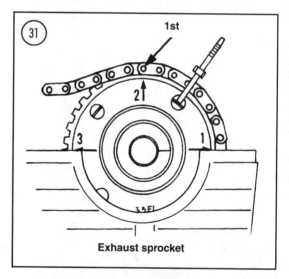

Exhaust sprocket

haust cam sprocket and the intake cam sprocket. Do not disturb this alignment until the camshaft holders and cam chain tensioner are properly installed.

9. Install the camshaft holders (B, **Figure 14**) onto the correct camshaft. Refer to the **IN** and **EX** marks

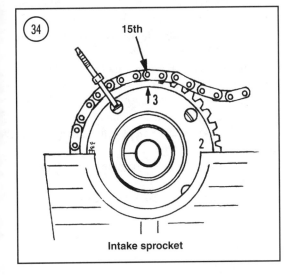

15th

↑3

2

Intake sprocket

(**Figure 27**) and install the exhaust camshaft holder in the front of the engine. Install the intake camshaft holder into the rear.

> **CAUTION**
> *Do not substitute any other type of bolt for the original camshaft holder bolts. These special bolts are marked with a 9 on the head and are of a superior strength grade. Substitute bolts may not have the required strength.*

10. Install the camshaft holder bolts finger-tight at this time.

> **CAUTION**
> *Failure to tighten the bolts in the specified sequence will result in damage to the bearing surfaces in the cylinder head and camshaft holders.*

11. Refer to the raised number next to the bolt holes on the camshaft holders. Evenly tighten the bolts sequentially in ascending order. Tighten the bolts in 2-3 stages to slowly pull the camshaft holder down onto its camshaft. Torque the bolts, in sequence, to the specification listed in **Table 3**.

12. Remove the cable ties (A and B, **Figure 32**).

13. As a final check, insert a finger into the tensioner receptacle in the cylinder block, push on the chain and take out the chain slack. Recheck all the timing marks to make sure all marks are still aligned properly as shown in **Figure 35**. If incorrect, reposition the cam chain on the sprockets.

14. Install the oil pipe (B, **Figure 15**) onto the left end of the camshaft journal holders so the white mark painted on the pipe is up. Install a new sealing washer behind each banjo bolt (A, **Figure 15**) and torque the bolts to the specification listed in **Table 3**.

15. Install the top cam chain guide (A, **Figure 14**), and torque the mounting bolts to the specification listed in **Table 3**.

16. Install the cam chain tensioner as described in this chapter.

17. Fill the pockets in the cylinder head (**Figure 36**) with approximately 50 cc (1.7 oz.) of clean engine oil.

18. After the tensioner is installed correctly, recheck the alignment as shown in **Figure 37**. If any of the alignment points are incorrect, repeat this procedure until *all* are correct.

> **CAUTION**
> *If there is any binding while rotating the crankshaft, **stop**. Determine the cause before proceeding.*

19. Use a 14 mm wrench on the starter clutch mounting bolt (A, **Figure 12**). Rotate the engine

clockwise, as viewed from the right side of the bike. Rotate the crankshaft several complete revolutions and check the operation of the valve train.

20. Adjust the valves as described in Chapter Three.

21. Install the spark plugs as described in Chapter Three.

22. Install the cylinder head cover as described in this chapter.

23. Install the engine as described in Chapter Five.

CAM CHAIN TENSIONER AND GUIDES

Cam Chain Tensioner
Removal/Inspection/Installation

Refer to **Figure 38**.

> *CAUTION*
> *The cam chain tensioner is a non-return type. The internal push rod will not return to its original position once it has moved out, even the slightest amount. After the tensioner mounting bolts are loosened, the tensioner assembly must be **completely removed** and the pushrod reset with a flat-blade screwdriver or the special locking tool (Suzuki part number 09917-62430). If the mounting bolts are loosened, do not simply retighten the mounting bolts. The pushrod has already moved out to an extended position, and it will exert excessive pressure on the chain leading to costly engine damage.*

1. Remove the fuel tank as described in Chapter Eight.

2A. On 1997-1998 models, remove the plug from the end of the tensioner.

2B. On 1999-on models, unscrew and remove the bolt and washer from the end of the tensioner.

3. Use a narrow flat-blade screwdriver and turn the inner adjuster *clockwise* to lock the spring tension.

4. Remove the mounting bolts and remove the cam chain tensioner and gasket (**Figure 39**) from the cylinder block. Remove the tensioner assembly.

5. Inspect the housing (A, **Figure 40**) for cracks or other damage. Replace the tensioner assembly if necessary.

6. Inspect the tensioner ratchet rack (B, **Figure 40**) for chipped or missing teeth. Check the plunger and rod end (C, **Figure 40**) for damage.

7. Use a narrow flat-blade screwdriver and turn the inner adjuster *clockwise* to lock the spring tension. Insert the small metal insert (**Figure 41**) to keep the spring tension locked.

8. Install a new gasket onto the tensioner.

9. Apply a light coat of ThreeBond TB1342, Loctite No. 242, or equivalent to the mounting bolt threads before installation.

10. To allow slack in the cam chain, perform the following:

    a. If in place, remove the starter clutch cover cap (A, **Figure 11**).

    b. Use a 14 mm wrench on the starter clutch mounting bolt (A, **Figure 12**) and rotate the engine *counterclockwise* 1/4 turn.

11. Install the tensioner housing and mounting bolts. Tighten the mounting bolts to the torque specification listed in **Table 3**.

12. Remove the small metal insert from the tensioner body.

13. Use a narrow flat-blade screwdriver and turn the inner adjuster *counterclockwise* to move the spring loaded tensioner rod out against the camshaft drive chain.

14. After the tensioner has been installed and expanded, check that there is proper tension on the chain. There should be no chain slack between both sprockets. It should be taut. If the chain can be easily moved up and down, the tensioner is not working properly or was installed incorrectly. Correct the problem at this time.

15A. On 1997-1998 models, install the end plug onto the end of the tensioner.

15B. On 1999-on models, install the bolt and washer onto the end of the tensioner. Tighten the bolt securely.

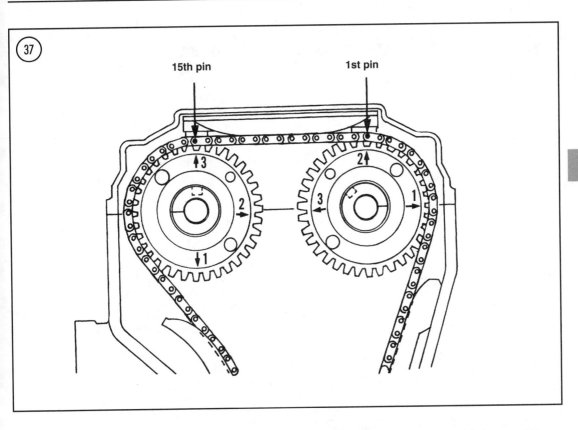

16. Install the fuel tank as described in Chapter Eight.

Cam Chain Guides
Removal/Inspection/Installation

Refer to **Figure 38**.
1. Remove the cylinder head as described in this chapter.
2. Remove the starter clutch assembly as described in Chapter Five.
3. Remove the signal generator assembly as described in Chapter Nine.
4. Pull straight up and withdraw the front cam chain guide (A, **Figure 42**).
5. Remove the bolt and washer (B, **Figure 42**) securing the rear chain guide. A second washer sits between the backside of the guide and the crankcase. Do not lose it.
6. Pull straight up and withdraw the rear chain guide (C, **Figure 42**).
7. Inspect both guides (**Figure 43**) for wear or damage, replace as necessary.
8. Make sure the cam chain is properly meshed with the timing sprocket on the crankshaft.

9. Install the rear cam chain guide into position.

10. Fit a washer onto the chain guide mounting bolt, and install the bolt (B, **Figure 42**) part way. Install the second washer behind the guide, and push the bolt the rest of the way through the guide and the inboard washer.

11. Tighten the bolt securely.

12. Install the front cam chain guide (A, **Figure 42**), and push it down until it seats on the crankcase bolt (D, **Figure 42**).

13. Install the signal generator assembly as described in Chapter Nine.

14. Install the starter clutch assembly as described in Chapter Five.

15. Install the cylinder head as described in this chapter.

CAM CHAIN

A continuous cam chain is used on all models. Do not cut the chain; replacement link components are not available.

CAM CHAIN AND TENSIONER

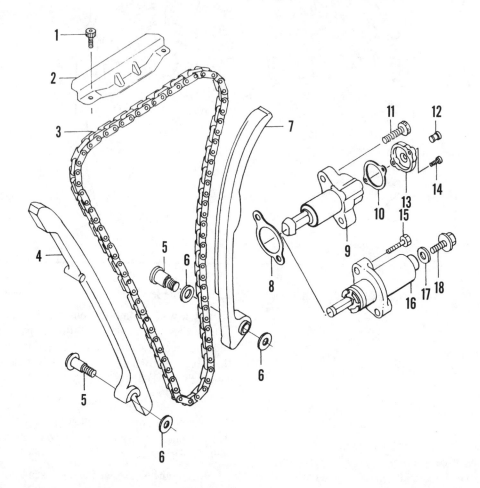

1. Bolt
2. Top chain guide
3. Cam chain
4. Front chain guide
5. Shoulder bolt
6. Washer

7. Rear chain guide
8. Gasket
9. Tensioner (1996-1998)
10. Gasket (1997-1998)
11. Bolt (1997-1998)
12. Plug (1997-1998)

13. Cap (1997-1998)
14. Screw (1997-1998)
15. Bolt (1999-on)
16. Tensioner (1999-on)
17. Washer (1999-on)
18. Bolt (1999-on)

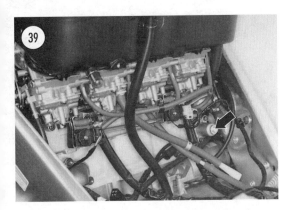

4

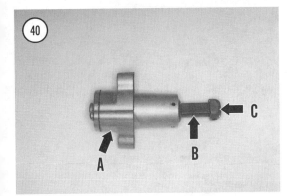

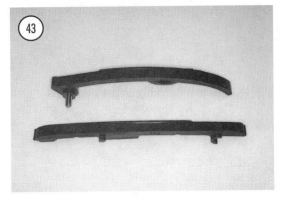

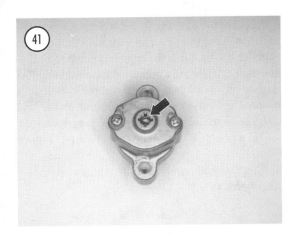

Removal/Installation

1. Remove the cylinder head as described in this chapter.

NOTE
The crankshaft timing sprocket is an integral part of the signal generator rotor.

2. Remove the signal generator assembly as described in Chapter Nine, and then remove the cam chain from the timing sprocket on the crankshaft.

3. Pull the cam chain up through the chain tunnel (**Figure 44**) in the cylinder block, and remove the chain.

4. Install the cam chain by reversing these removal steps.

Inspection

If the cam chain or chain guides show excessive wear, the chain tensioner may not be working prop-

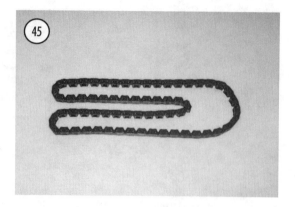

erly. Refer to *Cam Chain Tensioner Inspection* in this chapter.

1. Clean the cam chain in solvent. Blow it dry with compressed air.

2. Check the cam chain (**Figure 45**) for:
   a. Worn or damaged pins and rollers.
   b. Cracked or damaged side plates.

3. If the cam chain is excessively worn or damaged, inspect both camshaft sprockets (**Figure 46**) and the timing sprocket on the crankshaft (**Figure 47**) for the same wear conditions. If any of the sprockets show signs of wear or damage, replace them.

> *CAUTION*
> *Do not install a new chain over worn or damaged sprockets. Doing so will quickly wear the new chain.*

CYLINDER HEAD

Removal

1. Remove the engine as described in Chapter Five.

2. Remove the cylinder head cover (A, **Figure 48**) and both camshafts as described in this chapter.

3. Remove the banjo bolt and sealing washers (B, **Figure 48**) securing the upper oil hose fitting to the cylinder head. Unless the engine is going to be disassembled, leave the upper hose attached to the fitting on the crankcase. Place the banjo bolt in a reclosable plastic bag and secure the plastic bag over the open end of the oil hose to keep it clean.

4. Tie a piece of wire to the cam chain (A, **Figure 49**) and secure it to the exterior of the engine.

5. Unscrew and remove the cam chain stopper bolt (B, **Figure 49**).

> *CAUTION*
> *The valve lifters and shims can remain in the cylinder head if it is not going to be serviced. Do not allow the lifters and shims to fall out by turning the cylinder head over or on its side. If these parts fall out, they may be damaged and it will be impossible to return them to their original locations, making it necessary to adjust the valve clearances.*

6. If the cylinder head is going to be inspected and/or serviced, remove the valve lifters and shims

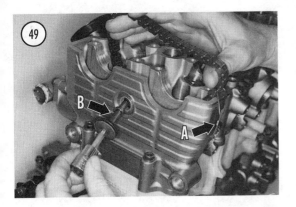

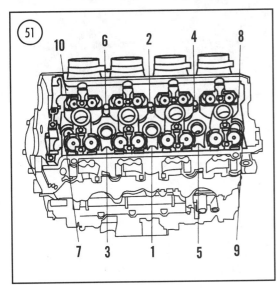

before removing the head. Refer to *Valve Lifter and Shim Removal and Installation* in this chapter.

7. Trace an outline of the cylinder head on a piece of cardboard. Punch holes in the cardboard and number them so they correspond to the bolt hole locations in the cylinder head.

8. On the right side, remove the three 6 mm bolts (**Figure 50**).

9. Use a 12 mm socket and long extension and loosen the cylinder head bolts in 2-3 stages. Loosen all ten bolts in the *reverse order* of the tightening sequence shown in **Figure 51**. Remove the bolts and washers and place them in the cardboard holder.

10. Break the cylinder head free from the head gasket by tapping around the perimeter with a soft faced mallet. If necessary, *gently* pry the cylinder head loose with a broad tipped screwdriver.

11. Lift the cylinder head straight up and off the cylinder block. Guide the cam chain through the opening in the cylinder head and retie the wire to the exterior of the engine. This prevents the chain from falling down into the crankcase.

12. Remove the cylinder head gasket and discard it. Watch for the two locating dowels from the cylinder block. If the dowels are loose, remove them, if tight, leave them in place.

13. Place a clean shop cloth into the cam chain tunnel, and then cover the cylinder block with another clean shop rag.

Inspection

1. If not already removed, remove the valve lifters and shims. Make sure to keep them in order so they can be reinstalled in their original locations. Refer to Step 6 in the cylinder head removal procedure.

2. Remove all traces of gasket residue from the cylinder head (**Figure 52**) and cylinder block mating surfaces. Do not scratch the gasket surfaces.

3. *Without removing the valves*, remove all carbon deposits from the combustion chamber (A, **Figure**

53). Use a fine wire brush dipped in solvent or make a scraper from hardwood. Take care not to damage the head, valves or spark plug threads.

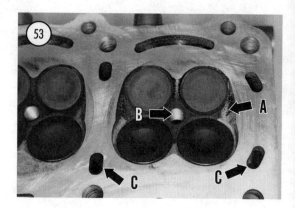

> *CAUTION*
> *Cleaning the combustion chamber with the valves removed can damage the valve seat surfaces. A damaged or even slightly scratched valve seat causes poor valve seating.*

4. Examine the spark plug threads (B, **Figure 53**) in the cylinder head for damage. If damage is minor or if the threads are dirty or clogged with carbon, use a spark plug thread tap (**Figure 54**) to clean the threads following the manufacturer's instructions. If thread damage is excessive, the threads can be restored by installing a steel thread insert. Thread insert kits can be purchased at automotive supply stores or the inserts can be installed by a Suzuki dealership or machine shop.

> *NOTE*
> *When using a tap to clean spark plug threads, coat the tap with an aluminum tap cutting fluid or kerosene.*

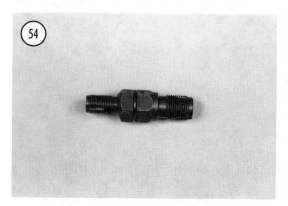

> *NOTE*
> *Aluminum spark plug threads are commonly damaged due to galling, cross-threading and overtightening. To prevent galling, apply an antiseize compound on the plug threads before installation and do not overtighten.*

5. After all carbon is removed from combustion chambers and valve ports, and the spark plug thread hole is repaired, clean the entire head in solvent. Blow it dry with compressed air.

6. Examine the crown on all four pistons. A crown should show no signs of wear or damage. If a crown appears pecked or spongy-looking, also check the spark plug, valves and combustion chamber for aluminum deposits. If these deposits are found, the cylinder is suffering from excessive heat caused by a lean fuel mixture or preignition.

7. Inspect the intake manifolds (**Figure 55**) for cracks or other damage that would allow unfiltered air to enter the engine. If necessary, remove the intake manifolds and install new O-rings between the intake manifold and the cylinder head. Install each intake manifold in its original location and tighten the screws securely.

8. Check for cracks in the combustion chambers, the intake ports (**Figure 55**) and the exhaust ports (A, **Figure 56**). A cracked head must be replaced if it cannot be repaired by welding.

9. Inspect the threads (B, **Figure 56**) on the exhaust pipe mounting bolts for damage. Clean up with an appropriate size metric tap if damaged.

10. Make sure all coolant passageways (C, **Figure 53**) are clear. If necessary, blow the passageways clear with compressed air.

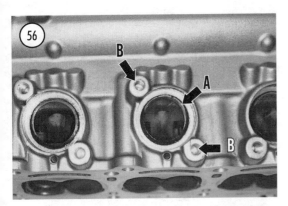

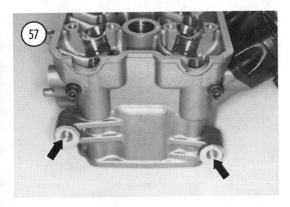

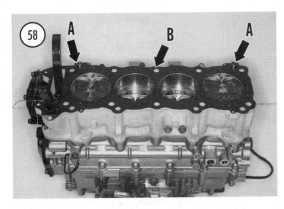

11. Run a tap through each threaded hole to remove any debris accumulation. Make sure the engine mounting bolt holes (**Figure 57**) are in good condition.

12. Thoroughly clean the cylinder head in solvent and then hot soap and water.

NOTE
If the cylinder head was bead blasted, grit in small crevices can be hard to remove. Any residual grit left in the engine will contaminate the oil and

cause premature wear. Repeatedly wash the cylinder head in a solution of hot soap and water to remove this debris.

13. After the head has been thoroughly cleaned, place a straightedge across the gasket surface at several points. Measure warp by attempting to insert a feeler gauge between the straightedge and cylinder head at each location. The maximum warp limit is listed in **Table 2**. A warped or nicked cylinder head surface could cause an air leak and result in overheating. If the warp limit exceeds the specification, the cylinder head must be resurfaced or replaced. Consult a Suzuki dealership or machine shop experienced in this type of work.

Installation

1. Remove the shop cloths from the cylinder block.
2. Make sure the cylinder head and cylinder block mating surfaces are clean of all gasket residue.
3. If removed, install the two locating dowels (A, **Figure 58**) into the rear corners of the cylinder block.
4. Install the new cylinder head gasket (B, **Figure 58**). Make sure all the gasket holes align with those in the cylinder block.
5. Position the cylinder head over the cylinder block and run the cam chain and its safety wire through the cam chain tunnel. Tie the safety wire to the exterior of the engine.
6. Carefully slide the cylinder head onto the engine, and seat the cylinder head onto the cylinder block. Make sure the locating dowels engage the cylinder head.
7. Pull up on the cam chain and make sure it is properly engaged with the crankshaft timing sprocket before continuing.
8. Make sure the cylinder head bolt, threads and washers are free of debris. Dirt on the bolt threads or washers may effect bolt torque.

CAUTION
Do not apply oil to the bolt threads. Apply oil only to the washers.

9. Remove one bolt at a time from the cardboard holder. Apply clean engine oil to each side of the washers prior to installation. Install the bolt and washer into the correct location in the cylinder

head. Start each bolt by hand to make sure it is not cross-threaded.

10. Using a 12 mm socket and long extension, tighten the cylinder head bolts in 2-3 stages. Tighten the bolts in the tightening sequence shown in **Figure 51**. Torque the bolts, in two stages, to the specification in **Table 3**.

11. On the right side, install the three 6 mm bolts (**Figure 50**). Torque the bolts to the specification in **Table 3**.

12. Pull up on the cam chain and install the cam chain stopper bolt (B, **Figure 49**). Use a new gasket on the stopper bolt, and tighten to the torque specification listed in **Table 3**.

13. Remove the safety wire from the cam chain (A, **Figure 49**).

14. If the valve lifters and shims were removed, install them at this time as described in *Valve Lifter and Shim Removal and Installation* later in this chapter.

15. Remove the plastic bag from the upper oil hose. Install a *new* sealing washer on each side of the oil hose fitting and install the banjo bolt (B, **Figure 48**). Tighten to the torque specification listed in **Table 3**.

16. Install both camshafts and the cylinder head cover (A, **Figure 48**) as described in this chapter.

17. Install the engine as described in this chapter.

VALVE LIFTERS AND SHIMS

Removal and Installation

Refer to **Figure 59** when servicing the valves.

If the cylinder head is going to be inspected and/or serviced, remove the valve lifters and shims before removing the head. To avoid mixing up the parts, do this procedure very systematically and only work with the lifters from one cylinder at a time.

1. Make a holder for the valve lifters and shims. Mark it with the cylinder number and the intake and exhaust side. The cylinders are numbered from left to right, 1-4. The left and right sides refer to the position of the parts as viewed by the rider siting on the seat facing forward.

2. Remove one set of the valve lifters (**Figure 60**) and the respective shims (**Figure 61**) and place both of them in the correct location in the holder.

3. Repeat this for all of the valve lifters and shims in this cylinder.

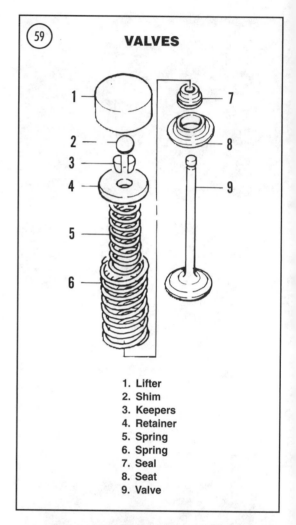

VALVES

1. Lifter
2. Shim
3. Keepers
4. Retainer
5. Spring
6. Spring
7. Seal
8. Seat
9. Valve

4. Repeat this process for the remaining three cylinders.

5. Inspect the valve lifters and shims for wear or heat damage. Service specifications for the outer diameter of the lifter and the inner diameter of the

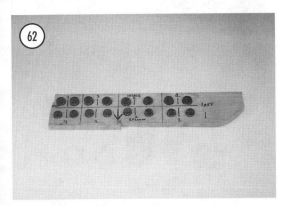

lifter receptacle in the cylinder head are not available. The lifter (with clean oil applied to its sides) should move up and down in the cylinder head receptacle with no binding or chatter. If the side of the lifter is scuffed or scratched, replace it.

> *NOTE*
> *To avoid mixing up the parts, perform Step 6 very systematically and work on one cylinder at a time. Position the holder containing the valve lifters and shims (**Figure 62**) with the same ori-*

entation as the cylinder head with the No. 1 cylinder components on the left side.

6. Working with one cylinder at a time, first install the shim onto the top of the valve keepers and make sure it is seated correctly.

7. Apply clean engine oil to the side of the valve lifter and install it.

8. Rotate the lifter to make sure it is seated correctly and rotates freely.

9. Install all shims and lifters into that cylinder, and then continue with the next cylinder.

VALVES AND VALVE COMPONENTS

Refer to **Figure 59**.

Complete valve service requires a number of special tools. The following procedures describe how to check for valve component wear and to determine what type of service is required. In most cases, valve troubles are caused by poor valve seating, worn valve guides and burned valves. A valve spring compressor will be required to remove and install the valves.

Valve Removal

1. Remove the cylinder head, valve lifters and shims as described in this chapter.

2. Protect the walls of the valve bore during valve removal by performing the following:
   a. Cut the bottom out of a plastic 35-mm film canister.
   b. Cut open the side of the canister so it is flexible.
   c. Insert the modified film canister between the valve assembly and the valve bore (**Figure 63**). The canister will prevent the valve spring compressor from damaging the bore during valve spring removal and installation.

3. Install a valve spring compressor (**Figure 64**) squarely over the valve spring retainer (**Figure 65**), and place the other end of tool against the valve head.

> *CAUTION*
> *To avoid loss of spring tension, do not compress the spring any more than necessary to remove the valve keepers.*

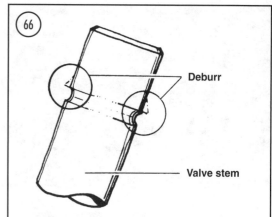

Deburr

Valve stem

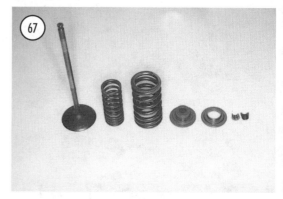

4. Tighten the valve spring compressor until the valve keepers separate from the valve stem. Lift the valve keepers out through the valve spring compressor with a magnet or needlenose pliers.

5. Gradually loosen the valve spring compressor and remove it from the cylinder head.

6. Remove the spring retainer and the two valve springs.

> *CAUTION*
> *Remove any burrs from the valve stem groove before removing the valve (Figure 66); otherwise the valve guide will be damaged as the valve stem passes through it.*

7. Remove the valve from the cylinder while rotating it slightly.

8. Remove the spring seat.

9. Pull the oil seal off of the valve guide. Discard the oil seal.

> *CAUTION*
> *All component parts of each valve assembly must be kept together (Figure 67). Place each set in a divided car-*

ton, into separate small boxes or into small reclosable plastic bags. Label each valve set. Identify a valve set by its cylinder number and either intake or exhaust valves. This will keep parts from getting mixed up and will make installation simpler. Do not intermix components from the valves or excessive wear may result.

10. Repeat Steps 3-9 and remove the remaining valves—keep all valve sets separate.

Valve Inspection

Refer to the troubleshooting chart in **Figure 68** when performing valve inspection procedures in this section. When measuring the valves and valve components in this section, compare the actual measurements to the new and wear limit specifications listed in **Table 2**. Replace parts that are out of specification or show damage as described in this section.

(68)

VALVE TROUBLESHOOTING

4

| Excessive valve deposits | **Check:**
- Worn valve guide
- Carbon buildup from incorrect engine tuning
- Carbon buildup from incorrect fuel delivery operation
- Dirty or gummed fuel
- Dirty engine oil |

| Valve sticking | **Check:**
- Worn valve guide
- Bent valve stem
- Deposits collected on valve stem
- Valve burning or overheating |

| Valve burning | **Check:**
- Valve sticking
- Cylinder head warped
- Valve seat distorted
- Valve clearance incorrect
- Incorrect valve spring
- Valve spring worn
- Worn valve seat
- Carbon buildup in engine
- Ignition or fuel delivery malfunction |

| Valve seat/face wear | **Check:**
- Valve burning
- Incorrect valve clearance
- Abrasive material on valve face and seat |

| Valve damage | **Check:**
- Valve burning
- Incorrectly installed or serviced valve guides
- Incorrect valve clearance
- Incorrect valve, spring seat and retainer assmbly
- Detonation caused by incorrect ignition and/or fuel delivery malfunction |

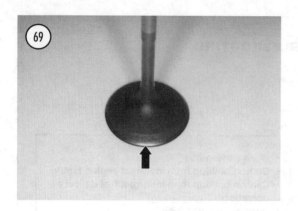

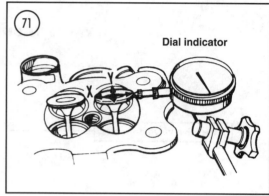

Dial indicator

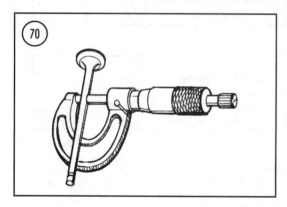

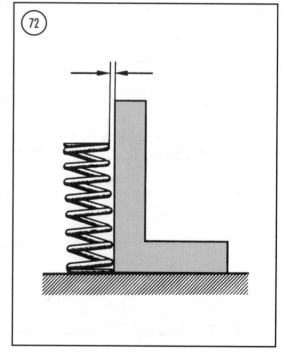

1. Clean valves in solvent. Do not gouge or damage the valve seating surface.

2. Inspect the valve face (**Figure 69**). Minor roughness and pitting can be removed by lapping the valve as described in this chapter. Excessive unevenness to the contact surface is an indication that the valve is not serviceable.

3. Inspect the valve stem for wear and roughness. Then measure the valve stem outside diameter with a micrometer (**Figure 70**).

4. Remove all carbon and varnish from the valve guides with a stiff spiral wire brush before measuring wear.

NOTE
If the required measuring tools are not available, proceed to Step 6.

5. Measure the valve guide inside diameter with a small hole gauge. Measure at the top, center and bottom positions. Then measure the small hole gauge and check against the dimension in **Table 2**.

6. If a small hole gauge is not available, insert each valve into its guide. Attach a dial indicator to the valve stem next to the head (**Figure 71**) and check the valve stem deflection. Hold the valve slightly off its seat and rock it sideways in two directions 90° to each other. If the valve stem deflection in either direction exceeds the service limit in **Table 2**, the guide is probably worn. However, as a final check, take the cylinder head to a Suzuki dealership or machine shop and have the valve guides measured.

7. Check the inner and outer valve springs as follows:

    a. Check each of the valve springs for visual damage.

    b. Use a square and visually check each spring for distortion or tilt (**Figure 72**).

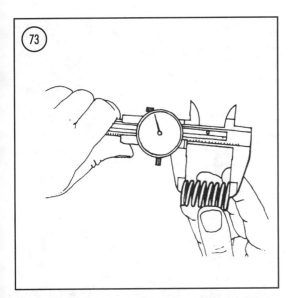

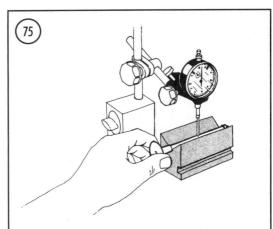

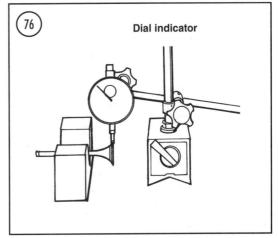

Dial indicator

c. Measure the valve spring free length with a vernier caliper (**Figure 73**) and check against the dimension in **Table 2**.

d. Repeat for each valve spring.

e. Replace defective springs as a set (inner and outer).

8. Check the valve spring seats and valve keepers for cracks or other damage.

9. Inspect the valve seats (**Figure 74**) in the cylinder head. If worn or burned, they may be reconditioned as described in this chapter. Seats and valves in near-perfect condition can be reconditioned by lapping with fine carborundum paste. Check as follows:

a. Clean the valve seat and corresponding valve mating areas with contact cleaner.

b. Coat the valve seat with layout fluid.

c. Install the valve into its guide. Using the valve lapping tool, tap the valve against the valve seat with a light rotating motion in both directions. See *Valve Lapping* in this chapter.

d. Lift the valve out of the guide and measure the seat width with a vernier caliper.

e. The seat width of each valve should be within the specifications listed in **Table 2** all the way around the seat. If the seat width is outside the specified range, regrind the seats as described in this chapter.

f. Remove all layout fluid residue from the seats and valves.

10. Check the valve stem runout with a V-block and dial indicator as shown in **Figure 75**. Replace the valve if the valve stem runout exceeds the service limit listed in **Table 2**.

11. Measure valve head radial runout with a dial indicator as shown in **Figure 76**. Replace the valve if the valve head radial runout exceeds the wear limit in **Table 2**.

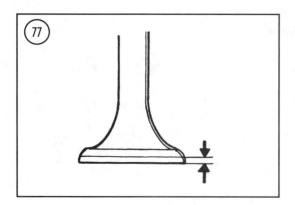

12. Measure the valve head thickness with a vernier caliper (**Figure 77**). Replace the valve if valve head thickness is less than the service limit in **Table 2**.

13. Measure the valve head out diameter with a vernier caliper. Compare the measurement to the specification in **Table 2**.

Valve Installation

1. Clean the end of the valve guide.

2. Oil the inside of the new oil seal and install it over the end of the valve guide. Push the seal down until it is completely seated on the cylinder head surface (**Figure 78**).

3. Install the spring seat (**Figure 79**) over the oil seal and push it down until it is completely seated on the cylinder head surface.

4. Coat the valve stem with molybdenum disulfide paste. Install the valve part way into the guide (**Figure 80**). Then, slowly turn the valve as it enters the oil seal and continue turning it until the valve is completely installed.

5. Position the valve springs with their *closer* wound coils (**Figure 81**) facing the cylinder head.

6. Install the outer valve spring (**Figure 82**) and make sure it is properly seated on the spring seat.

7. Install the inner valve spring (**Figure 83**) and make sure it is properly seated on the lower spring seat.

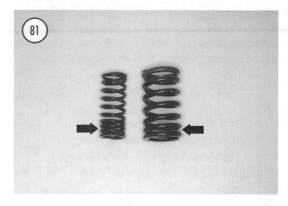

8. Install the spring retainer (**Figure 84**) on top of the valve springs.

9. Install the modified 35-mm film canister used during removal.

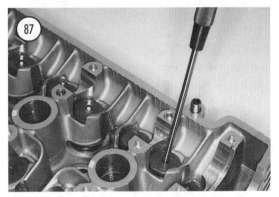

4

CAUTION
To avoid loss of spring tension, do not
compress the springs any more than
necessary to install the valve keepers.

10. Compress the valve springs with a valve spring compressor (**Figure 64**) and install the valve keepers (**Figure 85**).

11. Make sure both keepers are seated around the valve stem before releasing the compressor.

12. Slowly release tension from the compressor and remove it. After removing the compressor, inspect the valve keepers to make sure they are properly seated (**Figure 86**). Tap the end of the valve stem with a drift and hammer (**Figure 87**). This ensures that the keepers are properly seated.

13. Repeat Steps 1-12 for the remaining valves.

14. Install the shims and valve lifters as described in this chapter.

15 Install the cylinder head as described in this chapter.

16 After installing the cylinder head, adjust the valve clearance as described in Chapter Three.

Valve Guide Replacement

If the valve guide-to-valve stem clearance is excessive, replace the valve guides and valves. Special tools and experience are required to replace the valve guides. If these tools are not available, it is more economical to have this procedure performed by a machine shop.

Valve Seat Inspection

The most accurate method for checking the valve seat is to use a layout fluid, available from auto parts and tool stores. Layout fluids are used for locating high or irregular spots when checking or making close fits and when scraping bearing surfaces. Follow the manufacturer's directions.

> *NOTE*
> *Because of the close operating tolerances within the valve assembly, the valve stem and guide must be within tolerance; otherwise the inspection results will be inaccurate.*

1. Remove the valves as described in this chapter.
2. Clean the valve seat in the cylinder head and valve mating areas with contact cleaner.
3. Thoroughly clean off all carbon deposits from the valve face with solvent or detergent, and dry the valve thoroughly.
4. Spread a thin layer of layout fluid evenly on the valve face. Allow the fluid to air dry.
5. Moisten the end of a suction cup valve tool and attach it to the valve. Insert the valve into the guide.
6. Using the valve lapping tool, tap the valve against the valve seat with a light rotating motion in both directions.
7. Remove the valve and examine the impression left by the layout fluid. If the impression (on the valve or in the cylinder head) is not even and continuous and if the valve seat width (**Figure 88**) is not within the specified tolerance listed in **Table 2**, the valve seat must be reconditioned.
8. Closely examine the valve seat in the cylinder head (**Figure 74**). It should be smooth and even with a polished seating surface.
9. If the valve seat is good, install the valve as described in this chapter.
10. If the valve seat is not correct, recondition the valve seat(s).

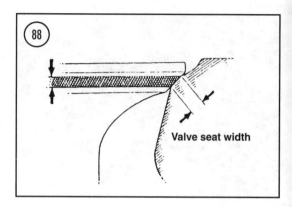

Valve seat width

11. Repeat for the other valves.

Valve Seat Reconditioning

Considerable expertise and specialized equipment are required to recondition valve seats. If these are not available, have the procedure performed by a machine shop that specializes in valve service.

Valve Lapping

Valve lapping is a simple operation which can restore the valve seal without machining if the amount of wear or distortion is not too great.

Perform this procedure only after determining that the valve seat width and outside diameter are within specifications. A lapping stick (**Figure 89**) is required.

1. Smear a light coat of fine grade valve lapping compound onto the seating surface of the valve.
2. Insert the valve into the cylinder head.
3. Wet the suction cup of the lapping stick and stick in onto the head of the valve. Spin the stick in both directions, while pressing it against the valve seat

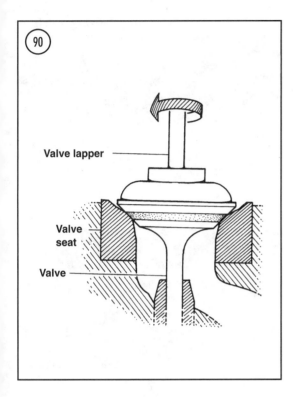

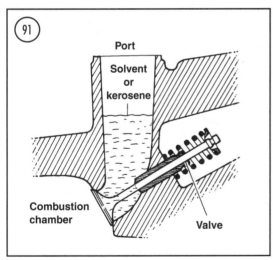

and lap the valve to the seat. See **Figure 90**. Every 5 to 10 seconds, rotate the valve 180° in the valve seat. Continue with this action until the mating surfaces on the valve and seat are smooth and equal in size.

4. Closely examine the valve seat in the cylinder head (**Figure 74**). It should be smooth and even with a polished seating ring.

5. Repeat Steps 1-4 for the other valves.

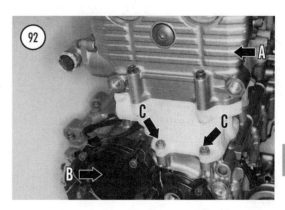

6. Thoroughly clean the valves and cylinder head in solvent or detergent and hot water to remove all valve grinding compound. Dry the components thoroughly.

> *CAUTION*
> *Any compound left on the valves or the cylinder head will contaminate the oil and cause premature engine wear.*

7. Install the valve assemblies as described in this chapter.

8. After completely the lapping and reinstalling the valves into the head, test the valve seal. Check the seal of each valve by pouring solvent into the intake and exhaust ports (**Figure 91**). There should be no leaking past the seat in the combustion chamber. If leakage occurs, the combustion chamber will appear wet. If fluid leaks past any of the seats, disassemble that valve assembly and repeat this procedure until there is no leakage.

> *NOTE*
> *This solvent test does not ensure long-term durability or maximum power. It merely ensures maximum compression will be available on initial start-up after reassembly.*

9. Apply a light coat of engine oil to all bare metal surfaces to prevent rust.

CYLINDER BLOCK

Removal

1. Remove the engine as described in Chapter Five.

2. Remove the cylinder head (A, **Figure 92**) as described in this chapter.

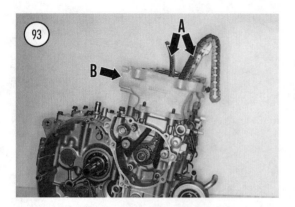

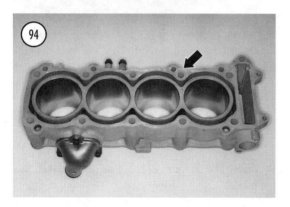

3. Remove the starter gear assembly (B, **Figure 92**) as described in Chapter Five.

4. Remove the signal generator as described in Chapter Nine.

5. Remove the cam chain tensioner and guides (A, **Figure 93**) as described in this chapter.

6. Disengage the cam chain from the crankshaft timing sprocket and remove the cam chain.

7. On the right side, remove the two cylinder base nuts (C, **Figure 92**) that secure the cylinder block to the crankcase.

8. Loosen the cylinder block (B, **Figure 93**) by tapping around its perimeter with a rubber or soft-faced mallet. If necessary, *gently* pry the cylinder block loose with a broad tipped screwdriver.

9. Pull the cylinder block straight up and off the crankcase. Remove and discard the base gasket. Watch for the two locating dowels between the cylinder block and crankcase. If they are loose, remove them.

10. If necessary, remove the pistons as described under *Piston Removal/Installation* in this chapter.

11. Cover the crankcase opening to prevent objects and debris from falling into the crankcase.

Inspection

Use a bore gauge and micrometer to accurately measure the cylinder bore. If these tools are not available, have the measurements performed by a Suzuki dealership or machine shop.

NOTE
The cylinder bores feature Suzuki's Composite Electro-chemical Material (SCEM) design. These chromed aluminum cylinders cannot be bored.

1. Remove all gasket residue from the cylinder block gasket surfaces (**Figure 94** and **Figure 95**). Both surfaces must be free of all residue.

2. If necessary, remove the bolts securing the coolant fitting (**Figure 96**) and remove the fitting and its O-ring.

3. Wash the cylinder block in solvent. Dry it with compressed air.

4. Check the locating dowel holes for cracks or other damage.

5. Check each cylinder bore (**Figure 97**) for scoring, rust or other visible damage.

6. Measure the cylinder bore inside diameter, taper

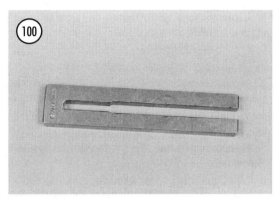

4

and out-of-round with a bore gauge (**Figure 98**) or inside micrometer. Measure the cylinder bore at the three positions, measured from the top surface, as shown in **Figure 99**. Measure in line with the piston pin and 90° to the pin. Check all measurements against the specifications in **Table 2**. If any measurement is out of specification, replace the cylinder block.

7. If the cylinder bore(s) is within specifications, determine piston-to-cylinder clearance as described in *Piston Clearance* in this chapter.

8. After the cylinder block has been thoroughly cleaned, place a straightedge across the cylinder head-to-cylinder mating surface at several points. Measure warp by attempting to insert a feeler gauge between the straightedge and cylinder at each location. Maximum warp is listed in **Table 2**. Warp or nicks in the cylinder block surface could cause a coolant leak and result in overheating. If warp exceeds the limit, resurface or replace the cylinder block. Consult a Suzuki dealership or machine shop experienced in this type of work.

9. Inspect the coolant inlet area for corrosion, wear or damage. Check the mounting bolt hole threads for damage. Clean them out with an appropriate size metric tap if necessary.

Installation

A set of piston holding fixtures (**Figure 100**) make installation of the cylinder block over the pistons safer and easier. It is possible to install the cylinder block without these tools, but it is more difficult and increases the chance of damage to the cylinder wall surfaces and the piston rings and skirts. A set of piston holding fixtures is available from a Suzuki dealership.

1. Clean the crankcase mating surface of gasket residue.

2. Check that the top and bottom of the cylinder block surfaces are clean of gasket residue.

3. Install the cylinder block locating dowels (A, **Figure 101**).

4. Install a new cylinder block base gasket (B, **Figure 101**). Make sure all holes align.

5. If removed, install the pistons as described in this chapter.

6. Make sure the transmission is in neutral.

7. If still installed, remove the cover from the alternator as described in Chapter Nine.

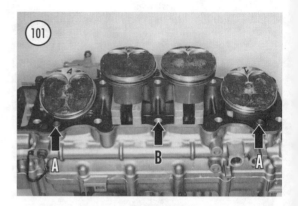

8. Make sure the cam chain properly meshes the timing sprocket on the crankshaft, then have an assistant pull up on the chain during the next step.

9. Using the alternator rotor, slowly rotate the engine *clockwise*, as viewed from the right side of the engine. Guide the No. 1 and No. 4 pistons down into the upper crankcase and rotate the engine until the pistons are positioned at BDC. This also positions the No. 2 and No. 3 pistons at TDC and makes cylinder block installation easier.

10. Check that all piston pin clips are installed and seated correctly.

11. Install the piston holding tool(s) (**Figure 102**) under the No. 2 and No. 3 pistons.

12. Lubricate the cylinder walls, pistons and rings liberally with clean engine oil before installation.

13. Carefully align the cylinder block with the two raised pistons.

14. Slowly slide the cylinder block down on the No. 2 and No. 3 pistons until it *lightly* bottoms out on the top piston rings.

15. To stabilize the cylinder block during installation over the pistons, install four cylinder head bolts at the corners of the cylinder (**Figure 103**). Hand-tighten the four bolts.

16. On the No. 2 and No. 3 pistons, compress each piston ring as it enters the cylinder bore. Slide the cylinder block over the piston rings (A, **Figure 104**).

> *CAUTION*
> *In the following step, do not damage the No. 2 and No. 3 pistons when the piston holding fixtures are removed.*

17. Support the cylinder block before removing the piston holding fixtures. Remove the piston holding fixtures (B, **Figure 104**).

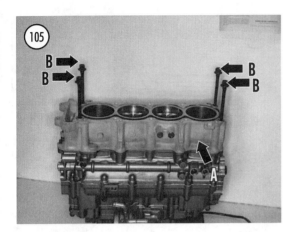

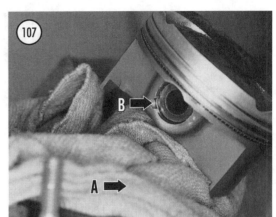

18. Slowly lower the cylinder block and insert the No. 1 and No. 4 pistons (C, **Figure 104**) into the cylinder bores. Compress each piston ring as it enters the cylinder bore. Slide the cylinder block over the piston rings.

19. Carefully push the cylinder block down until it bottoms on the upper crankcase (A, **Figure 105**). Make sure the locating dowels correctly engage the cylinder block.

20. Unscrew and remove the four cylinder head mounting bolts (B, **Figure 105**).

21. Use a piece of wire and pull the cam chain up through the top of the cylinder block chain cavity.

22. On the right side, install the two cylinder base nuts (C, **Figure 92**) that secure the cylinder block to the crankcase. Tighten the nuts to the torque specification listed in **Table 3**.

23. Install the cam chain so it engages the timing sprocket on the crankshaft.

24. Install the cam chain tensioner and guides (A, **Figure 93**) as described in this chapter.

25. Install the signal generator as described in Chapter Nine.

26. Install the starter gear assembly (B, **Figure 92**) as described in Chapter Five.

27. Install the cylinder head (A, **Figure 92**) as described in this chapter.

28. Install the engine as described in Chapter Five.

PISTON AND PISTON RINGS

The pistons are made of an aluminum alloy. The piston pin is made of steel and is a precision fit in the pistons. The piston pins are secured by a clip at each end.

Piston Removal

1. Remove the cylinder head and cylinder block as described in this chapter.

2. Mark the top of each piston with its identification number (1, 2, 3, 4). Start with the No. 1 cylinder on the left side and work across from left-to-right (**Figure 106**). The left and right sides refer to the position of the parts as viewed by the rider siting on the seat facing forward.

3. Block off the crankcase below the piston with clean shop cloth (A, **Figure 107**) to prevent the piston pin circlips from falling into the crankcase.

4. Before removing the piston, hold the rod tightly and rock the piston. Any rocking motion (do not confuse with the normal sliding motion) indicates wear on the piston pin, rod bushing, pin bore, or more likely, a combination of all three.

5. Remove the circlip (B, **Figure 107**) from one side of the piston pin bore.

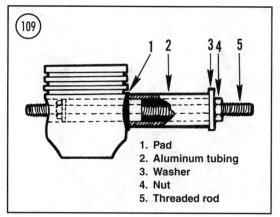

1. Pad
2. Aluminum tubing
3. Washer
4. Nut
5. Threaded rod

6. From the other side, push the piston pin (**Figure 108**) out of the piston by hand. If the pin is tight, use a homemade tool (**Figure 109**) and remove it. Do not drive the piston pin out. This action could damage the piston pin, connecting rod or piston.

7. Lift the piston off the connecting rod.

8. Repeat for the other three pistons.

9. Inspect the pistons as described in this chapter.

Piston Inspection

1. If necessary, remove the piston rings as described in this chapter.

2. Carefully clean the carbon from the piston crown (**Figure 110**) with a soft scraper or wire wheel mounted in a drill. Large carbon accumulations reduce piston cooling and result in detonation and piston damage. Renumber the piston as soon as it is cleaned.

> *CAUTION*
> *Be careful not to gouge or damage the piston when removing carbon. Never use a wire brush to clean the piston skirt or ring grooves. Do not attempt to remove carbon from the sides of the piston above the top ring or from the cylinder bore near the top. Removal of carbon from these two areas may cause increased oil consumption.*

3. After cleaning the piston, examine the crown. The crown should show no signs of wear or damage. If the crown appears pecked or spongy-looking, also check the spark plug, valves and combustion chamber for aluminum deposits. If these deposits are found, the engine is overheating.

4. Examine each ring groove (**Figure 111**) for burrs, dented edges or other damage. Pay particular

attention to the top compression ring groove. It usually wears more than the others. Because the oil rings are constantly bathed in oil, these rings and grooves wear little compared to compression rings and their grooves. If there is evidence of oil ring groove wear or if the oil ring assembly is tight and difficult to remove, the piston skirt may have collapsed due to excessive heat. Replace the piston.

5. Check the oil control holes (**Figure 112**) in the piston for carbon or oil sludge buildup. Clean the

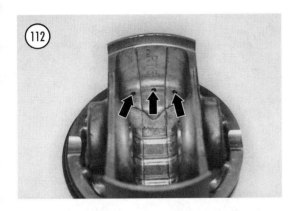

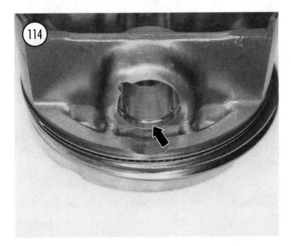

holes with wire and blow them clear with compressed air.

6. Check the piston skirt (**Figure 113**) for cracks or other damage. If a piston shows signs of partial seizure (bits of aluminum buildup on the piston skirt), it should be replaced to reduce the possibility of engine noise and further engine damage.

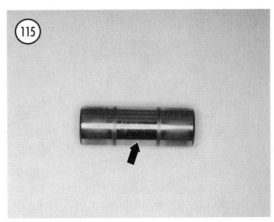

NOTE
If the piston skirt is worn or scuffed unevenly from side-to-side, the connecting rod may be bent or twisted.

7. Check the circlip groove (**Figure 114**) on each side for wear, cracks or other damage. If the grooves are questionable, check the circlip fit by installing a new circlip into each groove and then attempt to move the circlip from side-to-side. If the circlip has any side play, the groove is worn and the piston must be replaced.

8. Measure piston-to-cylinder clearance as described in *Piston Clearance* in this chapter.

9. If damage or wear indicate piston replacement, select a new piston as described under *Piston Clearance* in this chapter. If the piston, rings and cylinder are not damaged and are dimensionally correct, they can be reused.

Piston Pin
Inspection

1. Clean the piston pin in solvent, and dry it thoroughly.

2. Inspect the piston pin (**Figure 115**) for chrome flaking or cracks. Replace if necessary.

3. Oil the piston pin and install it into the connecting rod (**Figure 116**). Slowly rotate the piston pin and check for radial play.

4. Oil the piston pin and partially install it into the piston (**Figure 117**). Check the piston pin for excessive play (**Figure 118**).

5. Measure the piston pin outside diameter with a micrometer (**Figure 119**).

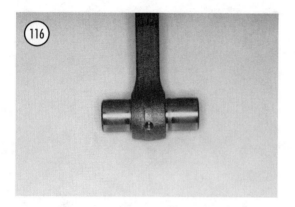

Measure in line with the piston pin and 90° to the pin. If the piston pin outside diameter is less than the service limit specified in **Table 2**, replace the piston pin.

6. Measure the inside diameter of the piston pin bore (**Figure 120**) with a small hole gauge. Measure the small hole gauge with a micrometer. If the measurement exceeds the service limit specified in **Table 2**, replace the piston.

7. Replace the piston pin and/or piston or connecting rod if necessary.

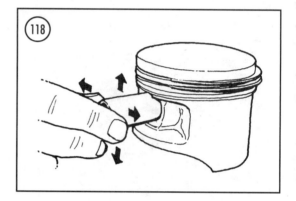

Piston Clearance

1. Make sure the piston skirt and cylinder wall are clean and dry.

2. Measure the cylinder bore with a bore gauge or inside micrometer (**Figure 121**). Measure the cylinder bore at the three positions, measured from the top surface, as shown in **Figure 99**. Measure in line with the piston pin and 90° to the pin. Record the bore inner diameter measurement.

3. Measure the piston outside diameter with a micrometer at a right angle to the piston pin bore. Measure up 15 mm (0.590 in.) from the bottom edge of the piston skirt (**Figure 122**).

4. Subtract the piston outside diameter from the largest bore diameter; the difference is piston-to-cylinder clearance. If the clearance exceeds the service limit specified in **Table 2**, replace the pistons and cylinder block.

Piston Installation

1. Make sure the transmission is in neutral.

2. If still installed, remove the cover from the alternator as described in Chapter Nine.

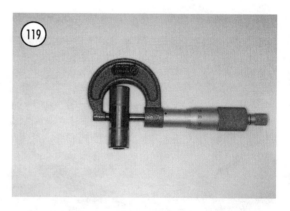

3. Make sure the cam chain properly meshes with the timing sprocket on the crankshaft, and then have an assistant pull the chain and hold it taut during the next step.

4. Using the alternator rotor, slowly rotate the engine *clockwise*, as viewed from the right side of the engine. Guide the No. 2 and No. 3 pistons down into the upper crankcase and rotate the engine until the pistons are positioned at BDC. This positions the No.1 and No.4 pistons at TDC and makes piston installation easier.

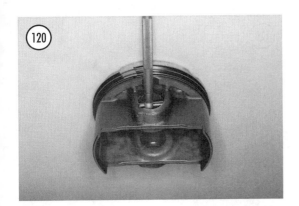

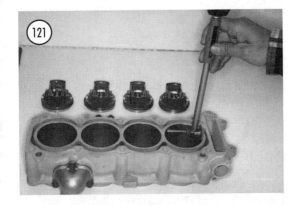

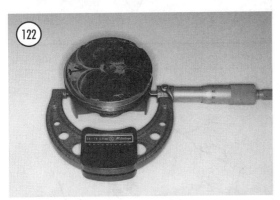

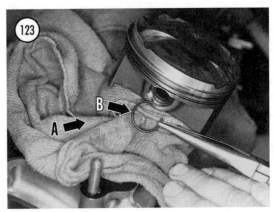

4

indexing mark is a small triangle. On 1998-on models, the indexing mark is a dot.

9. Align the piston pin with the hole in the connecting rod. Push the piston pin through the connecting rod (**Figure 108**) and into the other side of the piston until it is centered in the piston.

10. Place a clean shop cloth (A, **Figure 123**) under the piston to catch the piston pin should it work loose during installation.

11. Install a *new* piston pin circlip (B, **Figure 123**) into the other side of the pin boss. Make sure the circlip is seated correctly in the piston groove.

12. Repeat Steps 5-11 for the No. 1 piston.

13. Repeat Step 3 and Step 4 until the No. 2 and No. 3 connecting rods are at TDC.

14. Repeat Steps 3-11 for the No. 2 and No. 3 pistons.

15. If removed, install the piston rings as described in this chapter.

16. Install the cylinder block and cylinder head as described in this chapter.

**Piston Ring
Inspection and Removal**

The piston and ring assembly is a 3-ring type (**Figure 124**). The top and second rings are compression rings. The lower ring is an oil control ring assembly (consisting of two ring rails and an expander spacer).

When measuring the piston rings and piston in this section, compare the actual measurements to the new and service limit specifications in **Table 2**. Replace parts that are out of specification or show damage as described in this section.

5. Coat the connecting rod bushing, piston pin and No. 4 piston with molybdenum grease.

6. Install a *new* circlip into the side of the piston that faces the center line of the cylinder block. Make sure it is correctly seated in the piston groove.

7. Slide the piston pin into the piston until its end is flush with the piston pin boss.

8. Place the correct piston over the connecting rod so that the indexing mark on the piston crown faces the exhaust side of the engine. On 1997 models, the

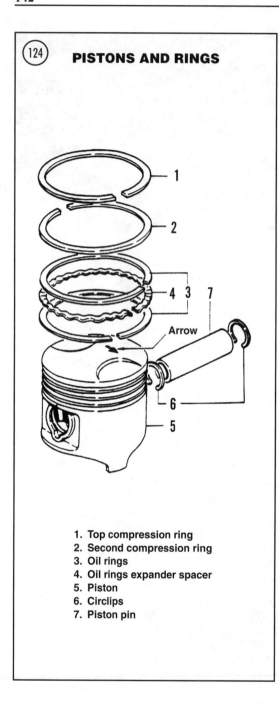

PISTONS AND RINGS

1. Top compression ring
2. Second compression ring
3. Oil rings
4. Oil rings expander spacer
5. Piston
6. Circlips
7. Piston pin

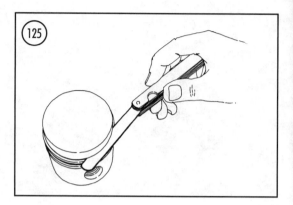

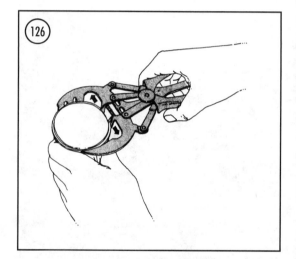

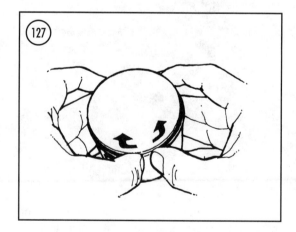

1. Measure the side clearance of each compression ring in its groove with a flat feeler gauge (**Figure 125**). If the clearance is greater than specified, replace the rings. If the clearance is still excessive with the new rings installed, replace the piston.

WARNING
The piston ring edges are sharp. Be careful when handling them.

NOTE
Store the old rings in the order they were removed.

2. Remove the compression rings with a ring expander tool (**Figure 126**) or by spreading the ring ends by hand (**Figure 127**).

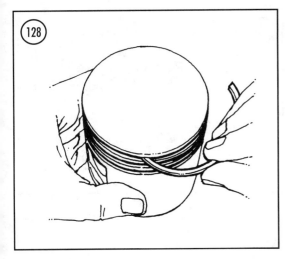

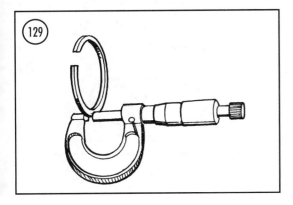

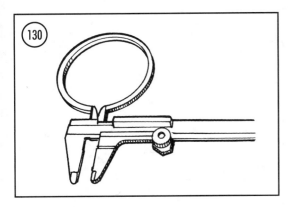

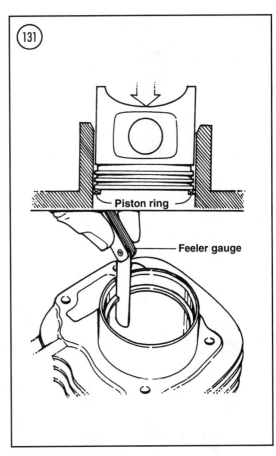

Feeler gauge

Piston ring

3. Remove the oil ring assembly by first removing the upper and then the lower ring rails. Then remove the expander spacer.

4. Using a broken piston ring, carefully remove carbon and oil residue from the piston ring grooves (**Figure 128**). Do not remove aluminum material from the ring grooves as this increases ring side clearance.

5. Measure each compression ring groove width with a vernier caliper. Measure each groove at several points around the piston. Replace the piston if any groove is outside the specified range.

6. Inspect grooves carefully for burrs, nicks or broken or cracked lands. Replace the piston if necessary.

7. Measure the thickness of each compression ring with a micrometer (**Figure 129**). If the thickness is less than specified, replace the ring(s).

8. Measure the free end gap with a vernier caliper (**Figure 130**). If the free end gap exceeds the service limit specified in **Table 2**, replace the ring(s).

9. Insert the ring into the bottom of the cylinder bore and square it with the cylinder wall by tapping it with the piston. Measure the installed end gap with a feeler gauge (**Figure 131**). Replace the rings if the end gap equals or exceeds service limit specified in **Table 2**. Also measure the end gap when installing new piston rings. If the gap on a new compression ring is smaller than specified, secure a

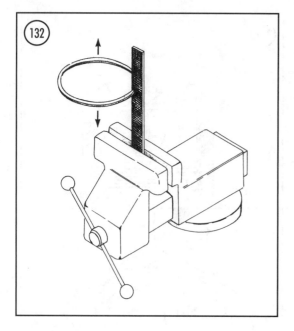

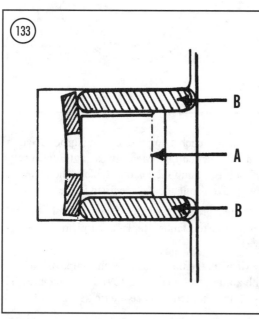

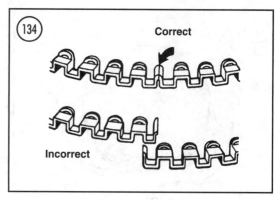

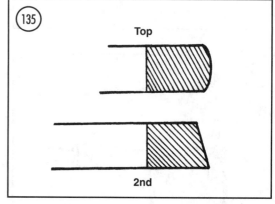

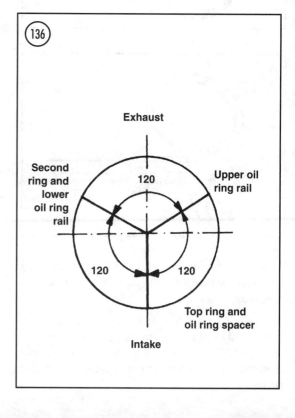

small file in a vise, grip the ends of the ring by hand and enlarge the gap (**Figure 132**).

Piston Ring Installation

1. Clean the piston and rings. Dry them with compressed air.

2. Install the piston rings as follows:

WARNING
The piston ring edges are sharp. Be careful when handling them.

NOTE
When installing aftermarket piston rings, follow the manufacturer's directions.

a. Install the oil control ring assembly into the bottom ring groove. Install the oil ring expander spacer first (A, **Figure 133**), and then install each ring rail (B, **Figure 133**). Make sure the ends of the expander spacer butt together (**Figure 134**). They should not overlap. If reassembling used parts, install the ring rails in their original positions.

b. Install the compression rings with a ring expander tool (**Figure 126**) or by carefully spreading the ring ends by hand (**Figure 127**).

c. Install the 2nd or middle compression ring with the manufacturer's RN mark facing up. This ring has a slight taper (**Figure 135**).

d. Install the top compression ring with the manufacturer's R mark facing up.

3. Make sure the rings are seated completely in their grooves all the way around the piston and that the end gaps are distributed around the piston as shown in **Figure 136**. To prevent compression from escaping past them, the ring gaps must not align.

4. If new parts were installed, follow the *Engine Break-In* procedure in Chapter Five.

Table 1 GENERAL ENGINE SPECIFICATIONS

Item	Specification
Engine type	4-stroke, DOHC, TCSS 4-valve head, inline 4 cylinders
Bore x stroke	65.5 x 44.5 mm (2.579 x 1.752 in.)
Displacement	600cc (36.6 cu. in.)
Compression ratio	12.0:1
Compression pressure	
Standard	1100-1500 kPa (160-218 psi)
Wear limit	900 kPa (131 psi)
Ignition system	
Ignition type	Electronic (CDI)
Ignition timing	5 B.T.D.C. at 1500 rpm
Firing order	1-2-4-3
Cooling system	Liquid
Lubrication system	Wet sump

Table 2 TOP END SPECIFICATIONS

Item	Standard mm (in.)	Wear limit mm (in.)
Camshaft		
Cam lobe height		
Intake		
CA models		
1997	33.992-34.048 (1.3383-1.3405)	33.70 (1.327)
1998-on	33.980-34.048 (1.3378-1.3405)	33.68 (1.326)
Non-CA modes		
1997	35.992-36.048 (1.4170-1.4192)	35.70 (1.406)
1998-on	36.660-36.728 (1.4433-1.4460)	36.36 (1.431)
	(continued)	

Table 2 TOP END SPECIFICATIONS (continued)

Item	Standard mm (in.)	Wear limit mm (in.)
Camshaft (continued)		
Exhaust		
1997	35.292-35.348 (1.3894-1.3917)	35.00 (1.378)
1998-on	34.780-34.848 (1.3693-1.3720)	34.48 (1.357)
Bearing oil clearance	0.032-0.066 (0.0013-0.0026)	0.150 (0.0059)
Journal outside diameter	23.959-23.980 (0.9433-0.9441)	–
Journal holder inside diameter	24.012-24.025 (0.9454-0.9459)	–
Camshaft runout	–	0.10 mm (0.004)
Valves and valve springs		
Valve clearance (cold)		
Intake	0.10-0.20 (0.004-0.008)	–
Exhaust	0.20-0.30 (0.008-0.012)	–
Valve stem outside diameter		
Intake	4.475-4.490 (0.1762-0.1768)	–
Exhaust	4.455-4.470 (0.1754-0.1760)	–
Valve stem deflection	–	0.35 (0.014)
Valve stem runout	–	0.05 (0.002)
Valve guide inside diameter	4.500-4.512 (0.1772-0.1776)	–
Valve stem-to-guide clearance		
Intake	0.010-0.037 (0.0004-0.0015)	
Exhaust	0.030-0.057 (0.0012-0.0022)	
Valve head diameter		
Intake	26.5 (1.04)	–
Exhaust	22.0 (0.87)	–
Valve head thickness	–	0.5 (0.02)
Valve head radial runout	–	0.03 (0.001)
Valve seat width	0.9-1.1 (0.035-0.043)	–
Valve seat cutter angle		
Intake	30, 45, 60	
Exhaust	15, 45, 60	
Valve spring free length		
Inner	–	36.80 (1.45)
Outer	–	39.8 (1.57)
Valve spring tension		
Inner	4.5 kg / 29.9 mm (9.9 lbs./ 1.18 in.)	–
Outer	18.3 kg / 33.4 mm (40.34 lbs./1.31 in.)	
Cylinder head warp	–	0.20 (0.008)
Cylinder		
Bore	65.500-65.515 (2.5787-2.5793)	Nicks or scratches
Warp	–	0.20 (0.008)
Compression pressure	1100-1500 kPa (156-213 psi)	900 kPa (128 psi)
Maximum difference between		
cylinders		200 kPa (28 psi)
Piston		
Outside diameter*	65.470-65.485 (2.5775-2.5781)	65.380 (2.5740)
Piston-to-cylinder clearance	0.025-0.035 (0.0010-0.0014)	0.12mm (0.0047 in.)
Piston-pin bore inside diameter	15.002-15.008 (0.5906-0.5909)	15.030 (0.5917)
Piston pin outside diameter		
1997	14.993-15.000 (0.5902-0.5906)	14.980 (0.5898)
1998-on	14.995-15.000 (0.5904-0.5906)	14.980 (0.5898)
Piston rings		
Ring-to groove clearance		
Top	–	0.18 (0.007)
Second	–	0.18 (0.007)
Ring thickness		
Top	0.97-0.99 (0.038-0.039)	–
Second	0.77-0.79 (0.030-0.031)	–

(continued)

Table 2 TOP END SPECIFICATIONS (continued)

Item	Standard mm (in.)	Wear limit mm (in.)
Piston rings (continued)		
Piston ring groove width		
Top	1.01-1.03 (0.040-0.041)	–
Second	0.81-0.83 (0.032-0.033)	–
Oil ring	1.51-1.53 (0.059-0.060)	–
Ring end gap (installed)		
Top	0.10-0.25 (0.004-0.010)	0.5 (0.02)
Second	0.10-0.25 (0.004-0.010)	0.5 (0.02)
Ring free gap		
1997		
First	Approx. 6.9 (0.27)	5.5 (0.22)
Second	Approx. 8.7 (0.34)	6.9 (0.27)
1998		
First	Approx. 6.2 (0.24)	4.9 (0.19)
Second	Approx. 8.0 (0.31)	6.4 (0.25)
1999-on		
First	Approx 5.4 (0.21)	4.3 (0.17)
Second	Approx. 5.9 (0.23)	4.7 (0.19)

*Measured 15 mm (0.590 in.) from skirt bottom.

Table 3 TOP END TIGHTENING TORQUE SPECIFICATIONS

Item	N•m	in.-lb.	ft.-lb.
Cam chain stopper bolt	14	–	10
Cam chain tensioner adjuster bolt	10	89	–
Cam chain tensioner mounting bolt	10	89	–
Camshaft holder bolt	10	89	–
Cylinder base nut	10	89	–
Cylinder head bolt			
6 mm	10	89	–
10 mm			
Initial	25	–	18
Final	43	–	32
Cylinder head cover bolt	14	–	10
Exhaust header bolt	23	–	17
Exhaust pipe mounting bolt	23	–	17
Exhaust pipe-to-muffler nut	26	–	19
Lower oil hose banjo bolt	25	–	18
Muffler mounting bolt	23	–	17
Oil pipe banjo bolt	10	89	–
Spark plug	12	106	–
Top cam chain guide mounting bolt	10	89	–
Upper oil hose banjo bolt	20	–	15
Valve timing inspection cap	23	–	17

Table 4 CAMSHAFT CODES

Year/model	Intake	Exhaust
1997		
California models	D	C
All other models	B	C
1998-on		
California	D	J
All other models	H	J

CHAPTER FIVE

ENGINE LOWER END

This chapter provides service procedures for lower end components. These include the crankcases, crankshaft and connecting rods, and the oil pump/lubrication system. This chapter also includes removal and installation procedures for the transmission and internal shift mechanism assemblies. However, service procedures for these assemblies are in Chapter Seven.

The specifications and bearing selection information are in **Tables 1-7** at the end of the chapter.

One of the most important aspects of a successful engine overhaul is preparation. Before removing the engine and disassembling the crankcase, degrease the engine and frame. Have all the necessary hand and special tools available. Make sure the work area is clean and well lit. Identify and store individual parts and assemblies in appropriate storage containers (**Figure 1**).

References to the left and right sides refer to the position of the parts as viewed by the rider siting on the seat facing forward, *not* how the engine sits on the workbench.

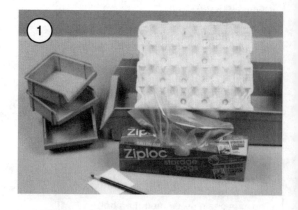

SERVICING ENGINE IN FRAME

The following components can be serviced with the engine mounted in the frame—(the frame is a great holding fixture, especially for breaking loose stubborn bolts and nuts):

1. External gearshift mechanism.
2. Clutch.
3. Oil pump.
4. Carburetor.
5. Alternator.

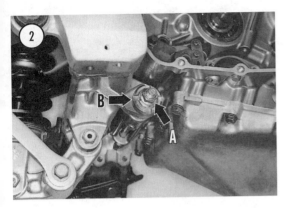

6. Starter motor and gears.

ENGINE

Removal

This procedure describes engine removal and installation. It may be easier in some cases to remove as many engine assemblies as possible before removing the lower end from the frame. Following this method reduces the weight of the engine and allows the frame to be used as a holding fixture. Disassembling the engine on the workbench without some type of holding fixture can be difficult and time consuming.

1. Securely support the bike on level ground.

2. Drain the engine oil and remove the oil filter as described in Chapter Three.

3. Drain the engine coolant as described in Chapter Three.

4. Disconnect the negative battery cable as described in Chapter Three.

5. Remove the fuel tank as described in Chapter Eight.

6. Remove the seats, lower fairing side panels, upper fairing and rear frame cover as described in Chapter Fifteen.

7. Remove the exhaust system as described in Chapter Four.

8. Remove the air box and carburetor assembly as described in Chapter Eight.

9. Disconnect the spark plug leads and secure them out of the way.

10. Remove the radiator assembly and coolant reservoir as described in Chapter Ten.

11. Remove the engine sprocket and drive chain from the engine as described in Chapter Eleven.

12. Disconnect the following electrical connectors:
   a. Engine ground cable: (black).
   b. Starter motor lead: (red).
   c. Alternator connector: three-pin (three black wires).
   d. Coolant temperature sensor lead: (black/green).
   e. Neutral switch connector: 1997 models two-pin (blue and pink); 1998-on, three-pin (blue, pink and black/white).
   f. Oil pressure switch connector: one-pin: (green/yellow wire).
   g. Signal generator connector: two-pin (black and green wires).
   h. Sidestand switch connector: two-pin (green and black/white wires).
   i. Speed sensor connector: three-pin (red, yellow and black wires).

13. If the engine requires disassembly, remove the following sub-assemblies:
   a. Alternator (Chapter Nine).
   b. Clutch (Chapter Six).
   c. Oil pump (this chapter).
   d. Starter motor (Chapter Nine).

14. Move all electrical wires, harnesses and hoses out of the way.

15. Place a floor jack underneath the engine. Raise the jack so the pad just rests against the bottom of the engine. Place a thick wooden block on the jack pad to protect the engine oil pan.

CAUTION
*Use a Suzuki special tool, Engine Mounting Thrust Adjuster Socket Wrench (part No. 09940-14980), to loosen the engine mounting thrust adjuster locknut (A, **Figure 2**) and mounting thrust adjuster (B, **Figure 2**, typical). Do not try to loosen these fasteners without this special wrench. The fasteners will be damaged. This tool is also required to tighten the fasteners to the correct torque specification during installation.*

NOTE
In Step 16 and Step 17, do not remove the lower and upper through bolts at this time. Leave them in place until the other fasteners are removed.

NOTE
The locknuts are self-locking and cannot be reused. Once removed they

must be replaced to retain their lock-
ing ability. Do not substitute another
type of locknut.

16. On the rear lower through bolt, perform the following:

    a. Remove the engine mounting nut from the
through bolt.

    b. Use the special tool and remove the rear
lower thrust adjuster locknut (**Figure 3**).

    c. Use the special tool and remove the thrust ad-
juster (**Figure 4**).

17. On the rear upper through bolt, perform the following:

    a. On the top surface of the rear crankcase,
loosen the pinch bolt (A, **Figure 5**).

    b. Insert a socket and extension through the
frame hole (B, **Figure 5**) and remove the
locknut (**Figure 6**)

18. On the right side, perform the following:

    a. Loosen the pinch bolts (A, **Figure 7**).

    b. Remove the two front upper mounting bolts
(B, **Figure 7**).

19. On the left side, remove the two front upper
mounting bolts (A, **Figure 8**).

20. Check to make sure the floor jack is still positioned correctly against the engine.

21. Block the front wheel so the bike cannot roll in
either direction.

22. Tie the front brake lever to the throttle grip to
keep the front brake applied.

NOTE
Due to the weight of the engine as-
sembly, a minimum of two people are
required to safely remove the engine
assembly from the frame.

23. Slowly withdraw the rear lower through bolt
(B, **Figure 8**) from the left side.

24. Have an assistant steady the engine assembly,
and then withdraw the rear upper through bolt (C,
Figure 8) from the left side.

25. Completely lower the jack (D, **Figure 8**) and
the engine from the frame.

26. Carefully remove the engine from the jack and
place the engine on a sheet of plywood or heavy
blanket.

27. Place the engine on a workbench.

28. While the engine is removed, check the engine
frame upper mounts (**Figure 9**) for cracks or other

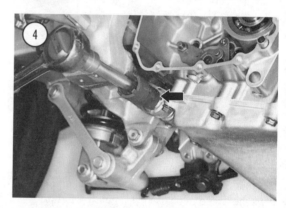

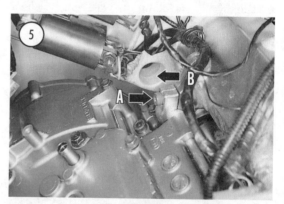

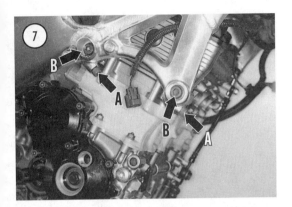

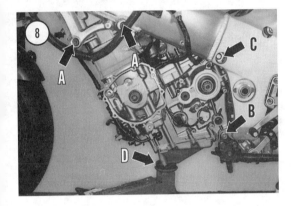

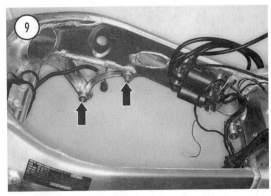

damage. Also check the mounting bolts for thread damage and repair them if necessary.

29. Remove corrosion from bolts and their threads with a wire wheel. Check the threads on all parts for wear or damage. Clean up with the appropriate size metric tap or die and clean with solvent.

30. Before installation, spray the engine mounting bolts with a rust inhibitor.

Installation

Installation is the reverse of removal. Follow the installation and tightening sequence described below. Do not torque any of the engine mounting fasteners until they all have been installed. Install all the engine mounting hardware finger-tight, and then torque the hardware to the specifications in **Table 2**.

1. Position the engine into the frame and align the rear upper and lower through bolt holes with the frame.

2. Install the rear upper (C, **Figure 8**) and lower (B, **Figure 8**) through bolts from the left side.

3. Install the locknut (**Figure 6**) onto the rear upper through bolt. Finger-tighten the nut at this time.

4. Perform the following on the rear lower through bolt:

   a. Install and finger-tighten the thrust adjuster (**Figure 4**).

   b. Install the thrust adjuster locknut (**Figure 3**).

5. On the left side, install and finger-tighten the front upper mounting bolts (A, **Figure 8**).

6. On the right side, install and finger-tighten the front upper mounting bolts (B, **Figure 7**).

7. On the rear lower through bolt, perform the following:

   a. Use the special tool and tighten the engine mounting thrust adjuster (**Figure 4**) to the torque specification listed in **Table 2**.

   b. Use the special tool and tighten the engine mounting thrust adjuster locknut (**Figure 3**) to the torque specification listed in **Table 2**.

   c. Tighten the rear lower engine mounting nut to the torque specification listed in **Table 2**.

8. Perform the following on the rear upper through bolt:

   a. Insert a socket and extension through the frame hole (B, **Figure 5**) and tighten the nut (**Figure 6**) to the torque specification listed in **Table 2**.

   b. On the top surface of the rear crankcase, tighten the pinch bolt (A, **Figure 5**) to the torque specification listed in **Table 2**.

9. On the left side, tighten the front upper mounting bolts (A, **Figure 8**) to the torque specification listed in **Table 2**.

10. On the right side, perform the following:

   a. Tighten the front upper mounting bolts (B, **Figure 7**) to the torque specification listed in **Table 2**.

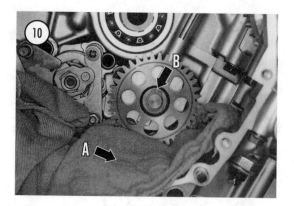

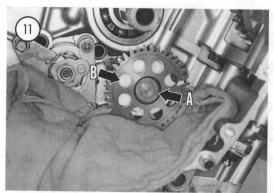

b. Tighten the engine mounting pinch bolts (A, **Figure 7**) to the torque specification listed in **Table 2**.

11. Assemble the engine by reversing Steps 2-13 of engine removal. Note the following:

a. Fill the engine with the recommended type and quantity of engine oil and coolant as described in Chapter Three.

b. Adjust the drive chain as described in Chapter Three.

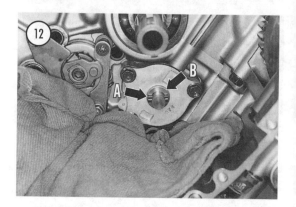

OIL PUMP

The oil pump is mounted behind the clutch on the right side of the engine. The oil pump can be removed with the engine mounted in the frame. Replacement parts are *not available* for the oil pump with the exception of the driven sprocket. If the oil pump is not operating properly, the entire oil pump assembly must be replaced.

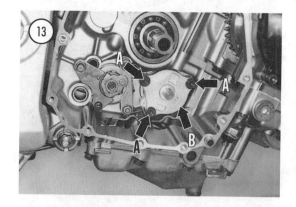

Removal/Disassembly

1. Remove the clutch as described in Chapter Six.

2. Place a clean shop cloth (A, **Figure 10**) into the crankcase opening to prevent any small parts from falling into the crankcase.

3. Remove the circlip (B, **Figure 10**) securing the driven sprocket.

4A. On 1997 models, remove the washer (A, **Figure 11**) and the sprocket (B, **Figure 11**).

4B. On 1998-on models, remove the sprocket (B, **Figure 11**). These models are not equipped with a washer between the sprocket and circlip.

5. Remove the pin (A, **Figure 12**) and washer (B, **Figure 12**).

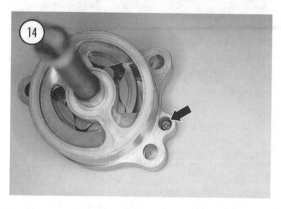

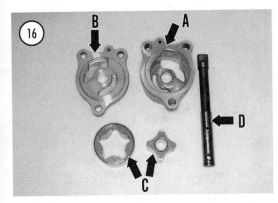

6. Remove the oil pump mounting screws (A, **Figure 13**).

7. Withdraw the oil pump assembly (B, **Figure 13**) and O-ring from the crankcase. Place the pump on a workbench for disassembly.

8. Remove the screw (**Figure 14**) securing the cover.

9. Remove the cover (**Figure 15**) from the pump body.

10. Remove the drive shaft as well as the inner and outer rotors from the body.

11. Inspect the oil pump as described in this chapter.

Oil Pump Inspection

1. Clean all parts in solvent and thoroughly dry them.

2. Inspect the oil pump body (A, **Figure 16**) and cover (B, **Figure 16**) for wear, cracks or damage. Check the inner wall for scuff marks.

3. Check the drive shaft bearing surface in the body for wear. Insert the shaft into the body, rotate the shaft and check for smooth operation.

4. Inspect the rotors (C, **Figure 16**) for abrasion, wear, cracks or damage.

5. Check the drive shaft (D, **Figure 16**) for binding or damage.

6. Check the drive shaft and pin (**Figure 17**). The pin must fit tightly in the shaft.

7. Inspect the oil pump driven sprocket for broken or chipped teeth (**Figure 18**).

8. Install the outer rotor into the body. Check the clearance between the outer rotor and the body with a flat feeler gauge (**Figure 19**). If the clearance exceeds the wear limit specified in **Table 1**, replace the oil pump.

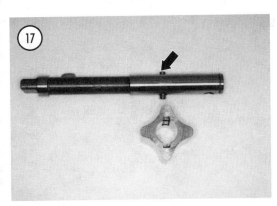

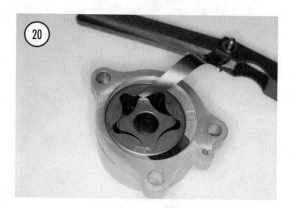

9. Install the inner rotor into the outer rotor. Check the clearance with a flat feeler gauge between the inner tip and the outer rotor (**Figure 20**). If the clearance exceeds the wear limit specified in **Table 1**, replace the oil pump.

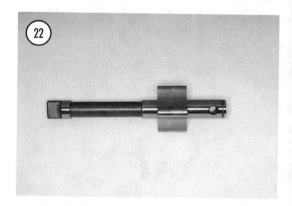

10. Remove the inner and outer rotors from the body.

Assembly/Installation

1. Apply clean engine oil to all parts before assembly.

2. If removed, install the drive pin into the drive shaft.

3. Position the inner rotor with the punch mark (**Figure 21**) facing out and install the inner rotor onto the drive shaft as shown in **Figure 22**.

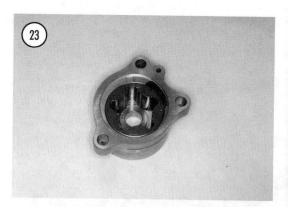

4. Position the outer rotor with the punch mark facing out and install the outer rotor into the body (**Figure 23**).

5. Install the drive shaft and inner rotor into the outer rotor and body (**Figure 24**). Make sure both punch marks face out.

6. Install the cover (**Figure 15**) onto the pump body and align the bolt holes.

7. Apply a small amount of threadlocking compound to the oil pump cover screw. Install the screw (**Figure 14**) and tighten it securely.

8. Install a new O-ring (A, **Figure 25**) onto the backside of the oil pump body.

9. Apply clean engine oil to the oil pump housing in the crankcase.

10. Rotate the drive shaft until the flats on the shaft end (B, **Figure 25**) are vertical.

11. Install the oil pump into the crankcase. Align the drive shaft flats with the water pump, and push

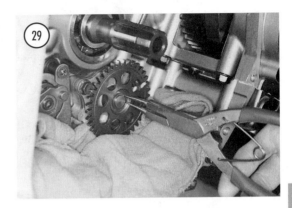

the oil pump into the crankcase until it stops against the crankcase surface.

12. Apply a small amount of threadlocking compound to the oil pump mounting screws. Install the screws (A, **Figure 13**) and tighten the screws to the torque specification listed in **Table 2**.

13. Place a clean shop cloth (A, **Figure 10**) into the crankcase opening to prevent any small parts from falling into the crankcase.

14. Install the washer (**Figure 26**) onto the drive shaft.

15. Install the pin (**Figure 27**) into the hole in the drive shaft, and center the pin.

16. Align the pin receptacle in the driven sprocket with the pin on the drive shaft and install the driven sprocket (A, **Figure 28**).

17. On 1997 models, install the washer (B, **Figure 28**) onto the drive shaft. The 1998-on models do not use a washer between the sprocket and circlip.

18. Install the circlip (**Figure 29**) securing the driven sprocket. Make sure the circlip is properly seated in the drive shaft groove (B, **Figure 10**).

19. Install the clutch as described in Chapter Six.

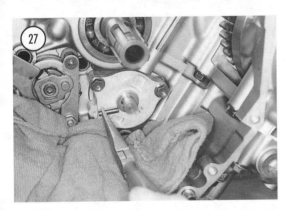

OIL PAN AND STRAINER

Removal/Inspection

NOTE
The oil pan and strainer can be removed with the engine installed in the frame as shown in Chapter Three during the strainer cleaning procedure. This procedure is shown with the engine removed for clarity.

1. Remove the lower fairing side panels as described in Chapter Fifteen.

2. Drain the engine oil as described in Chapter Three.

3. Remove the radiator as described in Chapter Ten.

4. Remove the exhaust system as described in Chapter Four.

5. Remove the oil pan bolts. A gasket washer is installed behind each of the three bolts (B, **Figure 30**) in the right rear cover of the oil pan. Make sure the gasket washer comes out with each bolt.

6. Remove the oil pan (A, **Figure 30**) and gasket. Do not lose the two locating dowels.

7. Remove the three oil inlet guide bolts (**Figure 31**), and remove the guide.

8. Remove the oil sump filter (**Figure 32**) from the crankcase.

9. If still in place, remove the oil sump gasket from the sump mount.

10. Remove the mounting bolts (A, **Figure 33**) securing the sump mount to the crankcase, and remove the sump mount (B, **Figure 33**).

11. Thoroughly clean all parts (**Figure 34**) in solvent, and dry them with compressed air.

NOTE
If the screen was contaminated with metal or clutch friction disc particles, clean as much of this contamination from the oil pan area of the lower crankcase as possible. Also clean any debris from the oil line.

12. Check the oil sump filter screen for debris buildup or damage. Thoroughly clean the oil inlet guide and screen with solvent, and dry them with compressed air. Inspect the screen for broken areas or damage and replace the oil sump filter if necessary.

13. Inspect the oil pan (**Figure 35**) for cracks or damage. Replace the pan if necessary.

Installation

1. Apply a small amount of ThreeBond No. TB1342 or equivalent to the threads of the sump mount bolts. Fit the sump mount (B, **Figure 33**) into place in the crankcase, and install the mounting bolts (A, **Figure 33**). Tighten the bolts securely.

2. Install a *new* gasket and the filter (**Figure 32**) onto the sump mount.

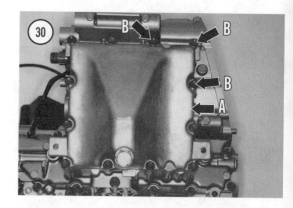

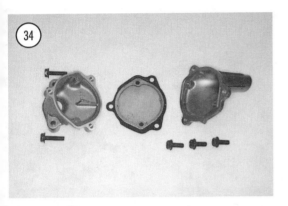

3. Install the oil inlet guide and tighten the oil inlet bolts securely (**Figure 31**).

4. Thoroughly clean off the gasket surface of the crankcase and oil pan of old gasket material. Clean the crankcase gasket surface with an aerosol parts cleaner.

5. If removed, install the locating dowels (A, **Figure 36**).

6. Apply a *small* amount of gasket sealer to the crankcase gasket surface, and fit the *new* gasket (B, **Figure 36**) to this surface.

7. Install the oil pan and oil pan bolts. Install the gasket washers under the three bolts (B, **Figure 30**) at the rear right corner of the oil pan. Tighten the oil pan bolts to the torque specification listed in **Table 2**.

8. Install the exhaust system as described in Chapter Eight.

9. Install the radiator as described in Chapter Ten.

10. Refill the engine oil as described in Chapter Three.

11. Start the engine and check for oil leaks. Turn the engine off.

12. Install the lower fairing side panels as described in Chapter Fifteen.

OIL PRESSURE REGULATOR

The oil pressure regulator valve is located inside the oil pan in the bottom to the crankcase.

Removal/Inspection/Installation

NOTE
There are no replacement parts for the valve. If damaged, the entire valve must be replaced.

1. Remove the oil pan as described in this chapter.

2. Unscrew the valve (**Figure 37**) from the crankcase.

3. To check the valve operation, use a piece of plastic rod or wood and push down on the piston within the valve. The piston must slide smoothly and return to the fully closed position when released. If piston operation is not smooth, clean the valve in solvent and thoroughly dry it with compressed air.

4. Repeat Step 3 to check valve operation. If cleaning does not solve the problem, replace the valve.

5. Use a small amount of threadlocking compound on the valve threads before installation.

6. Install the valve (**Figure 37**) and torque it to the specification listed in **Table 2**.

OIL COOLER

Oil Cooler
Removal/Installation

NOTE
The oil cooler and hoses can be removed with the engine installed in the frame. For clarity, some of the photographs in this procedure are shown with the engine removed.

1. Remove the lower fairing side panels as described in Chapter Fifteen.

2. Drain the engine oil as described in Chapter Three.

3. Remove the radiator as described in Chapter Ten.

4. Remove the exhaust system as described in Chapter Four.

5. Loosen the screws on the hose clamps (A, **Figure 38**).

6. Disconnect each hose (B, **Figure 38**) from the oil cooler and move them out of the way. Plug the ends to prevent any coolant from entering the oil cooler opening in the lower crankcase.

7. Place the oil drain pan under the oil cooler. Unscrew and remove the oil cooler mounting bolts (**Figure 39**) and remove the oil cooler.

8. Remove the oil cooler gasket (**Figure 40**). Install a *new* gasket every time the oil cooler is removed.

9. Check the coolant fittings for corrosion or leakage. Apply a *light* amount of air pressure onto one of the fittings to make sure the coolant is circulating through the oil cooler. The air should exit through the other fitting.

10. Install a *new* gasket (**Figure 40**) onto the crankcase. Make sure all holes are aligned correctly.

11. Install the oil cooler onto the lower crankcase and install the mounting bolts. Torque the oil cooler mounting bolts to the torque specification listed in **Table 2**.

12. Remove the plugs from the coolant hoses (B, **Figure 38**) and connect them onto the oil cooler fittings.

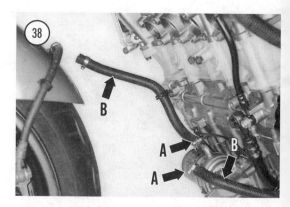

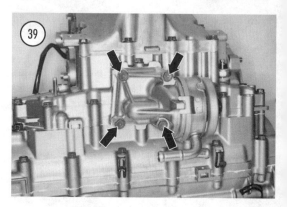

13. Tighten the screws on the hose clamps (A, **Figure 38**).

14. Install the exhaust system as described in Chapter Four.

15. Install the radiator as described in Chapter Ten.

16. Refill the engine oil as described in Chapter Three.

17. Refill the cooling system as described in Chapter Three.

18. Install the lower fairing side panels as described in Chapter Fifteen.

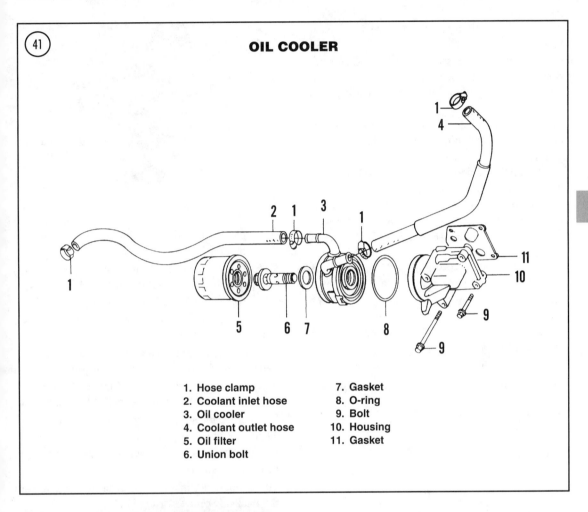

OIL COOLER

1. Hose clamp
2. Coolant inlet hose
3. Oil cooler
4. Coolant outlet hose
5. Oil filter
6. Union bolt
7. Gasket
8. O-ring
9. Bolt
10. Housing
11. Gasket

Disassembly/Assembly

Refer to **Figure 41** for this procedure.

NOTE
The oil cooler can be disassembled with the housing installed on the crankcase. For clarity, some of the photographs in this procedure are shown with the housing removed.

1. Remove the lower fairing side panels as described in Chapter Fifteen.

2. Drain the engine oil as described in Chapter Three.

3. Remove the exhaust system (A, **Figure 42**) as described in Chapter Four.

4. Remove the oil filter (B, **Figure 42**) as described in Chapter Three.

5. Loosen the screws on the hose clamps (A, **Figure 38**).

6. Disconnect each hose (B, **Figure 38**) from the oil cooler and move them out of the way. Plug the ends to prevent any coolant from entering the oil cooler opening in the lower crankcase.

7. Remove the banjo bolt (A, **Figure 43**) securing the oil cooler to the housing.

8. Remove the oil cooler (B, **Figure 43**) from the housing.

9. Inspect the O-ring seal for hardness and/or deterioration. Replace if necessary.

10. Apply a light coat of clean engine oil to the O-ring.

11. Install the oil cooler (B, **Figure 43**) onto the housing so the lug on the cooler (C, **Figure 43**) engages the raised tab on the housing (D, **Figure 43**).

12. Install the banjo bolt (A, **Figure 43**) and torque it to the specification listed in **Table 2**.

13. Remove the plugs and connect both hoses onto the oil cooler. Tighten the hose clamps securely.

14. Install the oil filter (B, **Figure 42**) as described in Chapter Three.

15. Install the exhaust system (A, **Figure 42**) as described in Chapter Four.

16. Refill the engine oil as described in Chapter Three.

17. Install the lower fairing side panels as described in Chapter Fifteen.

STARTER CLUTCH AND GEARS

Refer to **Figure 44**.

Removal

> *NOTE*
> *The starter clutch and gears can be removed with the engine installed in the frame. For clarity, this procedure is shown with the engine removed and partially disassembled.*

1. Remove the lower fairing side panels as described in Chapter Fifteen.

2. Remove the bolts securing the starter idler cover (A, **Figure 45**), and remove the cover and gasket. Account for the two locating dowels behind the cover. Note that one starter-idler-cover bolt (B, **Figure 45**) uses a gasket washer. Install a *new* gasket washer with this bolt during assembly.

3. Remove the spring washer, outer washer and starter idler gear No. 1.

4. Remove the shaft and the inner washer.

5. Remove the bolts securing the starter clutch cover (A, **Figure 46**), and remove the cover and gasket. Pay attention to the following:

    a. Do not lose the dowel(s) when removing the starter clutch cover. 1997 models have a sin-

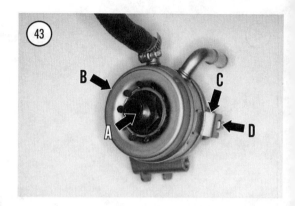

gle locating dowel being the cover; 1998-on models have two dowels.

    b. One starter-clutch-cover bolt (B, **Figure 46**) uses a gasket washer. Install a *new* gasket washer with this bolt during assembly.

6. Remove the spring washer, starter idler gear No. 2 and the shaft.

7. Hold the starter clutch with a clutch holding tool (Suzuki part No. 09920-34830, **Figure 47**) and loosen the starter clutch bolt (**Figure 48**). Remove the bolt and washer from the end of the crankshaft.

8. Remove the starter clutch gear and starter clutch as an assembly (**Figure 49**).

9. Slide the needle bearing and washer off the end of the crankshaft.

10. If removed, install the starter clutch gear into the backside of the starter clutch.

11. Try to rotate the starter clutch gear *counterclockwise*. It should rotate freely in this direction and lock in the clockwise direction.

12. If the starter clutch gear rotates in both directions or is locked up in both directions, replace the starter clutch as described in this chapter.

Inspection

1. Clean all parts in solvent and dry them with compressed air.

2. Inspect both starter idler gears (**Figure 50**) for wear or damaged teeth. Replace any gear as necessary. Insert the shaft into its respective gear and rotate the gear. If there is a noticeable amount of play, replace the gear(s) and shaft(s) as a set.

3. Inspect the starter clutch gear (A, **Figure 51**) for wear, chipped or missing teeth. Replace if necessary.

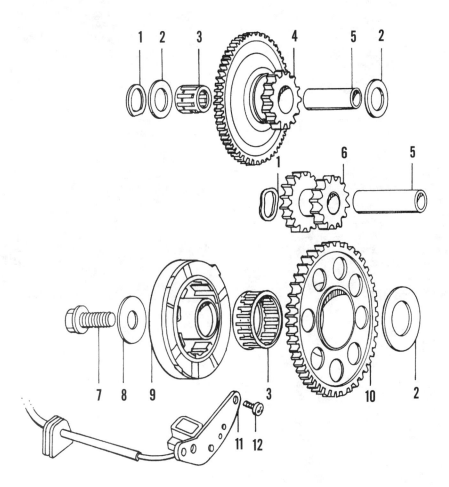

44

STARTER CLUTCH GEARS

5

1. Spring washer
2. Washer
3. Needle bearing
4. Starter idler gear No. 1
5. Shaft
6. Starter idler gear No. 2

7. Bolt
8. Washer
9. Starter clutch
10. Starter clutch gear
11. Signal generator
12. Screw

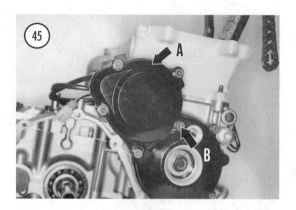

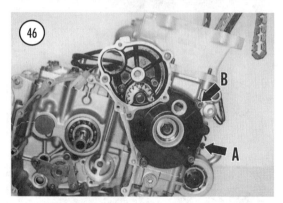

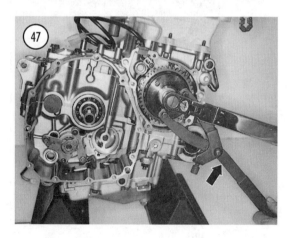

4. Inspect the needle bearing (B, **Figure 51**). The bearing must turn smoothly without excessive play or noise.

5. Inspect the starter clutch inner splines (A, **Figure 52**) where they mesh with the crankshaft.

6. Inspect the rollers (B, **Figure 52**) of the starter clutch for burrs, wear or damage. Replace if necessary.

7. Inspect the shaft bosses in the right crankcase for wear or damage.

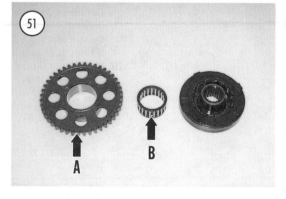

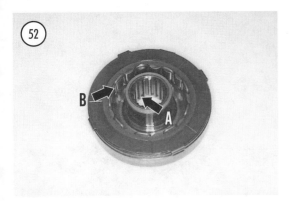

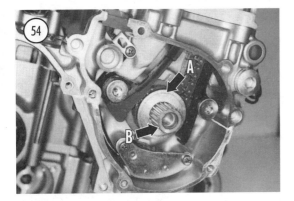

8. Inspect the shaft boss in the starter idler cover and in the starter clutch cover (**Figure 53**) for wear or damage.

Installation

1. Apply a light coat of clean engine oil to all sliding and rotating components.

2. Install the washer (A, **Figure 54**) and needle bearing (B, **Figure 54**) onto the crankshaft.

3. Align the engraved line mark (A, **Figure 55**) on the starter clutch with the punch mark on the crankshaft (B, **Figure 55**) and install the starter clutch gear and starter clutch onto the crankshaft.

4. Install the starter clutch bolt and washer (**Figure 48**) onto the crankshaft.

5. Hold the starter clutch with the clutch holding tool (**Figure 47**) and torque the starter clutch bolt to the specification listed in **Table 2**. Remove the tool.

6. Install the starter idler gear No. 2 (A, **Figure 56**) and its shaft, and then install the spring washer (**Figure 57**) onto the shaft.

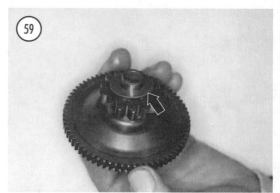

7. Apply a light coat of gasket seal to the areas where the mating surfaces of the crankcases meet (B, **Figure 56**).

8A. On 1997 models, install the locating dowel (A, **Figure 58**) and a *new* gasket (B, **Figure 58**).

8B. On 1998-on, install the two locating dowels (A and C, **Figure 58**) and new gasket (B, **Figure 58**).

9. Install the starter clutch cover (A, **Figure 46**) and the cover mounting bolts. Install a new gasket washer under the indicated bolt (B, **Figure 46**). Tighten the bolts securely.

10. Install the inner washer (**Figure 59**) onto the starter idler gear No. 1 and shaft.

11. Hold the inner washer in place and install starter idle gear No. 1 (A, **Figure 60**) and its shaft.

12. Install the outer washer (B, **Figure 60**) and the spring washer (**Figure 61**) onto the shaft.

13. Install the two locating dowels (A, **Figure 62**) and a *new* gasket (B, **Figure 62**).

14. Install the starter idler cover (A, **Figure 45**) and its mounting bolts. Include a *new* gasket washer under the indicated bolt (B, **Figure 45**). Tighten the bolts securely.

15. Install the lower fairing side panels as described in Chapter Fifteen.

CRANKCASE

The crankcase is a three-piece precision-cast aluminum alloy assembly. The upper, middle and lower sections are only available as a matched set. If one is damaged, all three must be replaced.

Do not hammer or pry on any of the projecting walls. Treat the sealing surfaces with extreme care. These areas are sealed with a gasket sealer; any small imperfections in the surfaces will cause oil leakage.

The following procedure has many references to the right and left sides of the engine. This refers to the engine while mounted in the frame, *not* as it sits on the workbench. Keep this in mind when the crankcase is upside down on the workbench.

Lower Crankcase, Transmission and Internal Shift Mechanism Disassembly

This procedure describes disassembly of the lower crankcase components and removal of the

e. Oil pump (this chapter).

f. Oil pan and strainer (this chapter).

g. Oil cooler (this chapter).

h. Engine sprocket (Chapter Eleven).

2. Remove the engine as described in this chapter.

3. Remove the cylinder head, cylinder block (A, **Figure 63**) and pistons as described in Chapter Four.

4. If still installed, remove the union bolt and sealing washers securing the upper oil hose (B, **Figure 63**) to the upper crankcase.

5. Remove the union bolts and sealing washers, and remove the lower oil hose (C, **Figure 63**).

6. Remove the two mounting screws (**Figure 64**) and remove the oil seal retainer.

7. Set the engine upright on the workbench. Support the engine on wooden blocks to loosen the bolts.

NOTE
To keep track of the crankcase bolts, draw the crankcase outline on a piece of cardboard, and then number and punch holes to correspond with each bolt location. After removal, insert the bolts in their appropriate locations. Leave any cable clamp on its respective bolt.

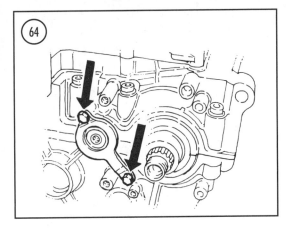

transmission shaft assemblies and the internal shift mechanism. Refer to Chapter Seven for transmission and internal shift mechanism service.

1. While the engine is still in the frame, remove all exterior engine assemblies as described in this chapter and related chapters:

a. Alternator (Chapter Nine).

b. Starter motor (Chapter Nine).

c. Starter clutch and gears (this chapter).

d. Clutch (Chapter Six).

8. Remove the crankcase bolts (**Figure 65**) on the rear of the upper crankcase. Following a crisscross pattern, loosen all the bolts in 2-3 stages, and then remove all of the bolts from the upper crankcase.

9. Turn the engine over and place it upside down on the workbench. Set the engine on wooden blocks to protect the connecting rods.

10. Remove the bolts from the front of the lower crankcase. Following a crisscross pattern, evenly loosen the lower crankcase bolts (A and B, **Figure**

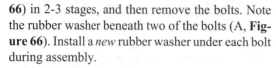

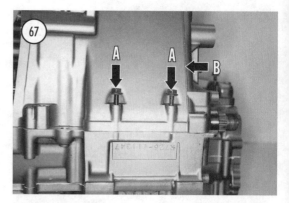

66) in 2-3 stages, and then remove the bolts. Note the rubber washer beneath two of the bolts (A, **Figure 66**). Install a *new* rubber washer under each bolt during assembly.

11. Loosen the two lower crankcase bolts (A, **Figure 67**) at the rear of the lower crankcase in 2-3 stages, and then remove the bolts.

NOTE
Do not loosen the bolts that secure the middle crankcase to the upper crankcase at this time.

12. Make sure all the lower crankcase bolts have been removed.

13. Tap around the perimeter of the sealing surfaces of the crankcase with a plastic soft-faced mallet and separate the lower crankcase from the middle crankcase.

CAUTION
*If it is necessary to pry the crankcases apart, do it very **carefully** to avoid damaging the gasket sealing surfaces. If damaged, it will result in an oil leak, requiring replacement of all three crankcase components.*

14. Lift the lower crankcase (B, **Figure 67**) off the middle crankcase.

15. If loose, remove the crankcase dowel pins at the front and the rear.

16. Carefully lift up and remove the countershaft (A, **Figure 68**) and mainshaft (B, **Figure 68**) assemblies from the middle crankcase. Store each assembly in a reclosable plastic bag. Seal and label the bags until it is time to service the assemblies.

17. Remove the transmission bearing locating C-rings from the middle crankcase. Do not remove the locating pins unless they are loose.

18. Turn the lower crankcase right ride up on the workbench.

19. Remove the external shift mechanism as described in Chapter Six.

20. Refer to **Figure 69** and remove the shift fork shafts and shift forks as follows:

NOTE
*The shift forks are not identical, and they are marked on one side. The marked side faces the right side of the crankcase. Before removing the shift forks, label them with a R (right), C (center) and L (left) to indicate their operating positions. See **Figure 70**.*

a. Slowly withdraw the front shift fork shaft and remove the center shift fork.

b. Slowly withdraw the rear shift fork shaft and remove the right and left shift forks.

21. Remove the shift drum from the right side.

22. Inspect the lower crankcase as described in this chapter.

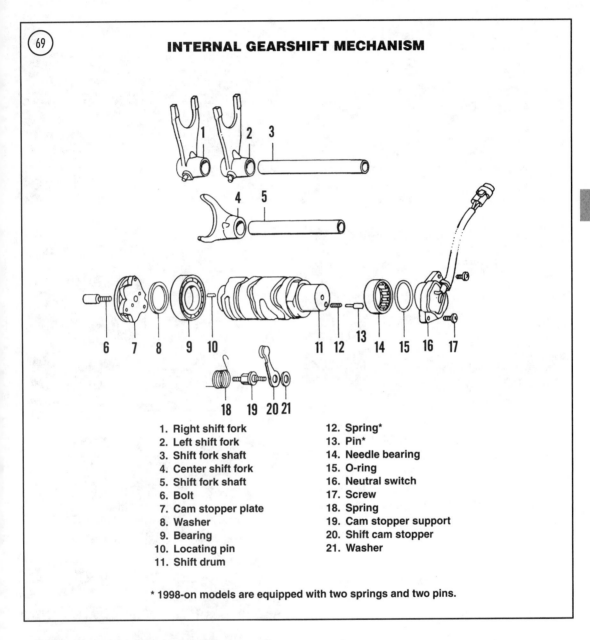

INTERNAL GEARSHIFT MECHANISM

1. Right shift fork
2. Left shift fork
3. Shift fork shaft
4. Center shift fork
5. Shift fork shaft
6. Bolt
7. Cam stopper plate
8. Washer
9. Bearing
10. Locating pin
11. Shift drum
12. Spring*
13. Pin*
14. Needle bearing
15. O-ring
16. Neutral switch
17. Screw
18. Spring
19. Cam stopper support
20. Shift cam stopper
21. Washer

* 1998-on models are equipped with two springs and two pins.

Lower Crankcase, Transmission and Internal Shift Mechanism Assembly

1. Set the middle and upper crankcase assembly upside down on the bench. Support the assembly on wooden blocks to protect the connecting rods.

2. If removed, install the front locating dowel (**Figure 71**) and rear locating dowel (**Figure 72**) into the middle crankcase.

3. Install *new* O-rings (**Figure 73**) into the five receptacles in the middle crankcase. Apply a light coat of clean engine oil to each O-ring.

4. Install the shift drum (**Figure 74**) from the right side of the lower crankcase. Push the shift drum in until it is completely seated in the lower crankcase (**Figure 75**), and then make sure it rotates freely.

5. Refer to **Figure 69** and install the shift fork shafts and shift forks into the lower crankcase by performing the following:

> *NOTE*
> *As noted during removal, the shift forks are not identical and are marked on one side. The marked side faces the right side of the crankcase. The shift fork shafts are identical and can be installed in either location. Refer to the R (right), C (center) and L (left) labels made during removal to indicate the original location (**Figure 70**) of each shift fork.*

a. Position the center shift fork (A, **Figure 76**) with the marked side facing the right side of the crankcase.

b. Insert the shift fork shaft (B, **Figure 76**) through the crankcase and shift fork. Push it in until it stops on the left side.

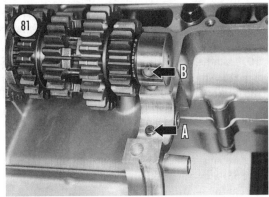

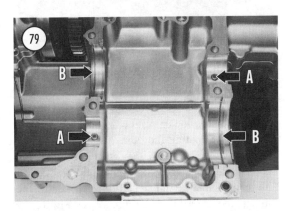

c. Position the right shift fork (A, **Figure 77**) with the marked side facing the right side of the crankcase.

d. Partially insert the shift fork (B, **Figure 77**) through the crankcase and the right shift fork, and then stop.

e. Position the left shift fork (C, **Figure 77**) with the marked side facing the right side of the crankcase.

f. Push the shift fork shaft (B, **Figure 77**) through the left shift fork (C, **Figure 77**). Push it in until it stops on the left side.

g. Move the shift forks into position and fit their guide pins into the shift drum grooves.

6. Install the external shift mechanism as described in Chapter Six.

7. On the middle crankcase, install the transmission bearing locating pins (**Figure 78**) if removed. See A, **Figure 79**.

8. Install the transmission bearing locating C-rings (B, **Figure 79**). Make sure they are properly seated in the crankcase groove.

NOTE
When installing the transmission shaft assemblies, the hole in each needle bearing must engage the locating pin in the middle crankcase. This ensures proper alignment of the transmission shafts to the crankcase.

9. Install the transmission mainshaft (**Figure 80**) as follows:

a. Align the needle bearing locating hole (A, **Figure 81**) with the locating pin (B, **Figure 81**) in the crankcase.

b. Install the mainshaft so its ball bearing properly engages in the C-ring (**Figure 82**) and its needle bearing engages the locating pin.

10. Install the transmission countershaft (A, **Figure 68**). Align the needle bearing locating hole with the locating pin in the middle crankcase, and install the countershaft so the ball bearing properly engages the C-ring and the needle bearing engages the locating pin.

11. Make sure the transmission shaft oil seals (**Figure 83**) are seated correctly in the crankcase.

12. Shift both transmission shafts into the NEUTRAL position. This will make shift fork engagement easier.

13. The lower crankcase is now ready to be joined onto the middle and upper crankcase assembly.

14. Make sure both crankcase sealing surfaces are free of old sealer material or other residue.

> *CAUTION*
> *When selecting a gasket sealer, avoid thick and hard setting materials. The coating must completely cover the entire mating surface, while being as thin as possible. If the sealer changes the crankcase alignment by being too thick, the bearing clearance will be excessive. This could result in engine damage.*

> *CAUTION*
> *When properly aligned, the lower crankcase half slides over the transmission shafts and seats against the middle crankcase. If the crankcases do not fit together completely, do not attempt to pull them together with the crankcase bolts. Separate the crankcases and determine the cause of the interference. Do not risk damaging the crankcases by forcing them together.*

15. Turn the lower crankcase upside down and slowly lower it onto the middle crankcase. Properly align the shift forks (**Figure 84**) with the grooves of their respective transmission gears. Push the lower crankcase down until it seats on the entire perimeter of the middle crankcase.

16. Join both halves and tap them together lightly with a plastic or soft-faced mallet. Do not use a metal hammer. It will damage the cases.

17. Before installing the crankcase bolts, slowly rotate the countershaft and shift the transmission through all of the gears. Make sure the shift forks are shifting each gear.

18. Remove the bolts from the cardboard template and install the lower crankcase mounting bolts. If the bolts are not all the same distance up from the bosses on the crankcase, they are not installed in the correct locations. Switch them around until they are all at the same height. Install *new* rubber washers under the two indicated bolts (A, **Figure 66**). Tighten all bolts finger-tight at this time.

19. Tighten the crankcase bolts at the front of the lower crankcase (A and B, **Figure 66**) in 2-3 stages in a crisscross pattern. Torque all the front lower crankcase bolts to the initial torque specification listed in **Table 2**, and then torque the bolts to the final torque.

20. Evenly tighten the crankcase bolts at the rear of the lower crankcase (A, **Figure 67**) in 2-3 stages. Torque the rear lower crankcase bolts to the initial torque specification listed in **Table 2**, and then torque the bolts to the final specification.

21. Turn the engine over and place it upright on the workbench.

NOTE
*Install **new** copper washers under the three bolts shown in **Figure 85** and **Figure 86**.*

22. At the rear of the upper crankcase, tighten the bolts (**Figure 65**) in 2-3 stages in a crisscross pattern. Torque all the upper crankcase bolts to the ini-

tial torque specification listed in **Table 2**, and then torque the bolts to the final specification.

23. Rotate the transmission shafts, crankshaft and, shift drum. Each assembly should turn smoothly. If a problem is detected, remove the crankcase mounting bolts, separate the crankcase components and correct the problem.

24. Install the oil seal retainer. Torque the two bolts (**Figure 64**) to the specification in **Table 2**.

25. Install the lower oil hose (C, **Figure 63**) onto the crankcase. Install new sealing washers on each side of the fitting, and then install the banjo bolts. Tighten the banjo bolts to the torque specification listed in **Table 2**.

26. Install the upper oil hose (B, **Figure 63**) onto the crankcase. Install new sealing washers on each side of the fitting, and then install the banjo bolt. Tighten the banjo bolt to the torque specification listed in **Table 2**.

27. Install the pistons, cylinder block (A, **Figure 63**) and cylinder head as described in Chapter Four.

28. Install the engine as described in this chapter.

29. Install all exterior engine assemblies as described in this chapter and related chapters:

    a. Alternator (Chapter Nine).
    b. Starter motor (Chapter Nine).
    c. Starter clutch and gears (this chapter).
    d. Clutch (Chapter Six).
    e. Oil pump (this chapter).
    f. Oil pan and strainer (this chapter).
    g. Oil cooler (this chapter).
    h. Engine sprocket (Chapter Eleven).

Upper and Middle Crankcase Disassembly

This procedure describes disassembly of the upper and middle crankcase components and removal of the crankshaft and connecting rod assembly.

1. Remove the lower crankcase from the upper and middle crankcase assembly as previously described in this chapter.

2. Remove the mainshaft and countershaft assemblies from the middle crankcase. Store each assembly in a reclosable plastic bag.

3. Place the crankcase assembly right side up on the workbench on wooden blocks.

NOTE
To keep track of the crankcase bolts, draw the crankcase outline on a piece of cardboard. Number and punch

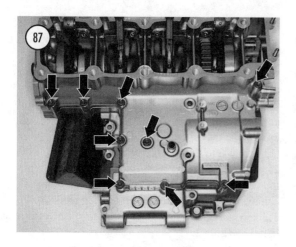

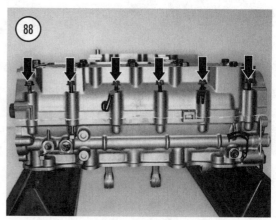

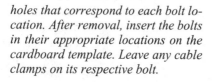

holes that correspond to each bolt location. After removal, insert the bolts in their appropriate locations on the cardboard template. Leave any cable clamps on its respective bolt.

4. Remove all the indicated bolts (**Figure 87**) at the rear of the upper crankcase. Follow a crisscross pattern and evenly loosen the bolts in 2-3 stages, and then remove the bolts.

5. To protect the connecting rod ends, turn the engine over and place it upside down on the workbench on wooden blocks.

6. Remove the crankcase bolts (**Figure 88**) from the front of the middle crankcase. Follow a crisscross pattern and evenly loosen the bolts in 2-3 stages, and then remove all bolts.

7. Refer to the raised numbers cast next to the remaining middle crankcase bolts (**Figure 89**), and evenly loosen the bolts in descending order. Loosen the bolts in 2-3 stages and then remove the crankcase bolts.

8. Make sure all of the crankcase bolts have been removed.

9. Tap around the perimeter of the sealing surfaces of the crankcase with a plastic or soft-faced mallet and separate the middle crankcase (**Figure 90**) from the upper crankcase.

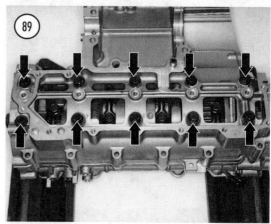

10. Lift the middle crankcase off the upper crankcase. Immediately turn the middle crankcase over and account for the main bearing inserts. If any have fallen out of position, attempt to return them to their original locations.

11. If loose, remove the crankcase dowel pins from the upper (**Figure 91**) or middle crankcase. Refer to **Figure 92** for dowel pin location on 1997 and 1998-on models.

12. Carefully lift and remove the crankshaft assembly (**Figure 93**) and the two thrust washers from the upper crankcase.

13. If the main bearing inserts are going to be removed, start with the left side and label the backside of each insert with a 1-5 and with upper (U) and lower (L) as it is removed.

14. Inspect the crankcases as described in this chapter.

15. Inspect the crankshaft/connecting rod assembly as described in this chapter.

CAUTION
*If it is necessary to pry the crankcases apart, do it very **carefully** to avoid damaging the gasket sealing surfaces. If damaged, it will result in oil leaks, requiring replacement of all three crankcase components.*

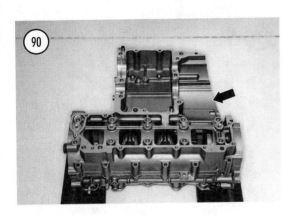

5

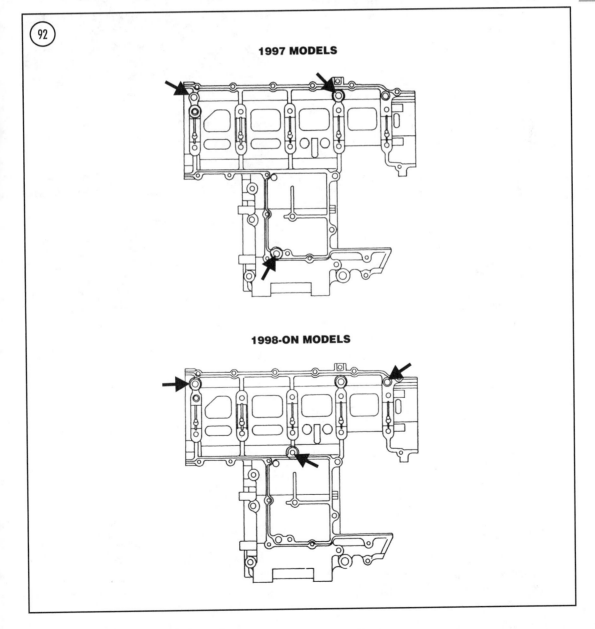

Upper and Middle Crankcase Assembly

1. If removed, install the crankcase dowel pins into the upper crankcase (**Figure 92**).

> *NOTE*
> *If reusing the old bearing inserts, make sure they are installed in their original locations as noted during removal.*

2. If removed, install the crankshaft main bearing inserts as follows:

   a. Make sure the bearing insert surfaces in both crankcase halves are clean. Check that the oil control hole at each journal is clear.

   b. Wipe both sides of the bearing insert with a lint-free cloth.

   c. Install the insert in the correct location and carefully press the insert into position by hand. Make sure the inserts are locked in place (**Figure 94**).

   d. Install all inserts in their correct locations (**Figure 95**).

3. Apply a light coat of molybdenum disulfide grease to the main bearing surfaces.

> *CAUTION*
> *Install both right and left thrust bearings with their oil grooves (**Figure 96**) facing out toward the crankshaft web.*

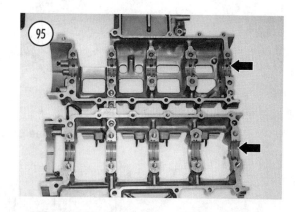

4. Apply a light coat of thick grease to the backside of the thrust bearings and install them onto the middle crankcase bearing support (**Figure 97**). Make sure to install both the right and left thrust bearings (**Figure 98**).

5. Guide the connecting rod ends through the openings in the upper crankcase, and install the crankshaft assembly (**Figure 93**) into the upper crankcase.

6. Check each end of the crankshaft to make sure it is properly seated in the crankcase.

7. The middle crankcase is now ready to be joined onto the upper crankcase assembly.

8. Make sure both crankcase sealing surfaces are free of old sealer material or other residue.

> *CAUTION*
> *When selecting a gasket sealer, avoid thick and hard setting materials. The coating must completely cover the en-*

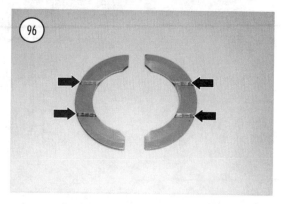

tire mating surface, while being as thin as possible. If the sealer changes the crankcase alignment by being too thick, the bearing clearance will be excessive. This could result in engine damage.

CAUTION
When properly aligned, the middle crankcase slides over the crankshaft assembly and seats against the upper crankcase. If the crankcases do not fit together completely, do not attempt to

pull them together with the crankcase bolts. Separate the components and determine the cause of the interference. Do not risk damaging the crankcases by forcing them together.

9. Turn the middle crankcase upside down and slowly lower it onto the upper crankcase. Properly align the crankshaft bearing inserts with the crankshaft. Push the middle crankcase down until it seats around the entire perimeter of the upper crankcase.

10. Join both halves and tap them together lightly with a plastic or soft-faced mallet. Do not use a metal hammer. It will damage the cases.

11. Remove the bolts from the cardboard template and install the middle crankcase mounting bolts (**Figure 88**). If the bolts are not all the same distance up from the bosses on the crankcase, they are not installed in the correct locations. Switch them around until they are all at the same height. Tighten all bolts finger-tight at this time.

12. Refer to the raised numbers cast next to the middle crankcase bolts. Tighten the crankcase bolts (**Figure 89**) in ascending order in 2-3 stages at the front of the upper crankcase. First tighten the bolts to the initial torque specification, and then the final torque specification listed in **Table 2**.

13. Turn the crankcase assembly over with the right side facing up on the workbench on wooden blocks to support it stationary.

NOTE
*Install a washer under the bolt on the right hand corner (A, **Figure 87**).*

14. Remove the bolts from the cardboard template and install the upper crankcase mounting bolts (**Figure 87**) in the correct locations. Install the wire clamps under the two bolts shown in **Figure 99**. Tighten all bolts finger-tight at this time.

15. Following a crisscross pattern, evenly tighten all the crankcase bolts (**Figure 87**) at the rear of the upper crankcase in 2-3 stages, and then tighten them to the torque specification listed in **Table 2**.

16. Turn the crankcase assembly over. Evenly tighten the crankcase bolts (**Figure 88**) at the front of the middle crankcase in 2-3 stages, and then torque the bolts to specification.

17. Install the lower crankcase onto the upper and middle crankcase assembly as previously described in this chapter.

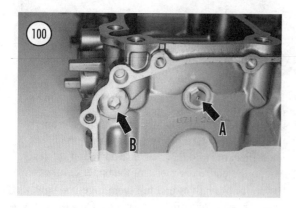

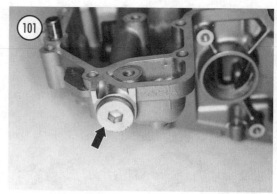

Crankcase Inspection

1. Clean all three crankcases, inside and out, and clean all crankcase bearings with cleaning solvent. Thoroughly dry all components with compressed air. Make sure there is no solvent residue left in the cases as it will contaminate the new engine oil.

2. Using a scraper, *carefully* remove any remaining sealer residue from all crankcase sealing surfaces.

3. Carefully check the sealing surface of all three crankcase components. Check for gouges or nicks that may lead to an oil leak.

4. Remove the oil jet (A, **Figure 100**) and the main oil gallery plug and washer (B, **Figure 100**) from the left end of the upper crankcase.

5. Remove the main oil gallery plug and washer (**Figure 101**) from the left side of the lower crankcase.

6. Apply compressed air to the oil gallery and blow out any accumulated residue. If necessary, rinse out the gallery with solvent, and once again apply compressed air to thoroughly clean out the gallery.

7. Install both oil gallery plugs with new sealing washers. Tighten them to the torque specification listed in **Table 2**.

8. Install the oil jet and tighten it to the torque specification listed in **Table 2**.

9. Remove the Allen bolt (A, **Figure 102**) securing the oil nozzle (B, **Figure 102**) and remove all four oil nozzles (**Figure 103**). Clean the oil passage in each oil nozzle with compressed air.

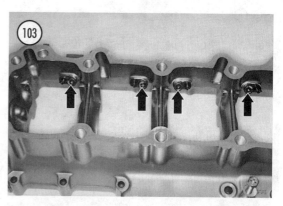

10. Install a new O-ring onto each oil nozzle, and install the nozzle. Apply ThreeBond No. TB1342 or equivalent to the threads of the Allen bolt, and tighten the bolt securely.

11. Clean all crankcase oil jets and passages (**Figure 104**) with compressed air.

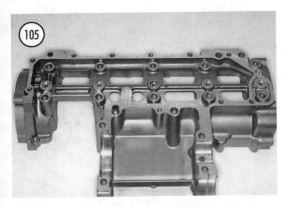

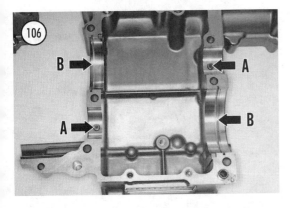

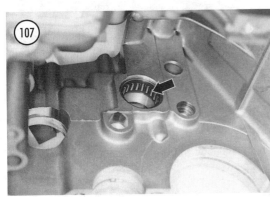

5

12. Inspect the cases (**Figure 105**) for cracks and fractures, especially in the lower areas where they are vulnerable to rock damage. Check the areas around the stiffening ribs, around bearing bosses and threaded holes for damage. If damage is found, have it repaired by a shop specializing in the repair of precision aluminum castings or replace the crankcases as a set.

13. Check the threaded holes in both crankcase halves for thread damage, dirt or oil buildup. If necessary, clean or repair the threads with a suitable size metric tap. Coat the tap threads with kerosene or an aluminum tap fluid before use.

14. Check the tightness of the shift lever stopper pin. Tighten it securely if necessary.

15. Make sure the oil control openings for the transmission needle bearings (A, **Figure 106**) are clear. Clean out with solvent and compressed air if necessary.

16. Check the transmission C-ring grooves (B, **Figure 106**) at each side of the crankcase for wear or damage.

17. Check the shift drum bearing (**Figure 107**) for wear. Rotate the inner race of the bearing by hand. The bearing must rotate freely with no signs of binding. If necessary, replace the bearing as described in this chapter.

18. Inspect the external oil hoses and banjo bolts (**Figure 108**) for wear or damage. Make sure the hoses and banjo bolts are clear by running solvent through them and then blowing through them with compressed air.

CRANKSHAFT

Removal/Installation

1. Remove the crankshaft/connecting rod assembly as described in *Upper and Middle Crankcase Disassembly* earlier in this chapter.

2. Remove the main bearing inserts (**Figure 95**) and label them so they can be installed in their original locations. Start with the left (alternator) side and label the backside of each insert with a 1-5 and with upper (U) and lower (L) as it is removed.

> *CAUTION*
> *If old bearing inserts are reused, they must be installed in their original locations.*

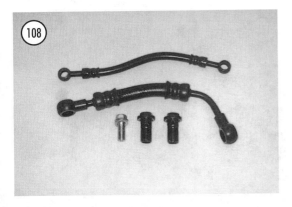

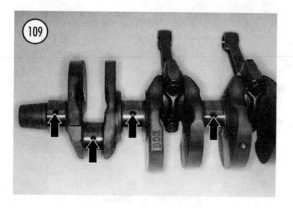

3. Inspect the crankshaft and main bearings as described in this chapter.

4. Install the crankshaft/connecting rod assembly as described in *Crankcase Assembly* in this chapter.

Crankshaft Inspection

1. Clean the crankshaft thoroughly with solvent. Clean the crankshaft oil passageways (**Figure 109**) with compressed air. If necessary, clean them with rifle cleaning brushes, and then flush the passageways with solvent. Dry the crankshaft with compressed air, and then lubricate all bearing surfaces with a light coat of engine oil.

2. Inspect each crankshaft main journal (A, **Figure 110**) and each connecting rod journal (B, **Figure 110**) for scratches, ridges, scoring, nicks or heat discoloration. Very small nicks and scratches may be removed with crocus cloth. Anything more serious must be referred to a machine shop.

3. If the surface finish on each crankshaft main bearing journal is satisfactory, measure the main journals with a micrometer for runout, taper and wear (**Figure 111**). Compare the measurements with the specifications listed in **Table 1**.

4. If the surface finish on each connecting rod journal is satisfactory, measure the journals with a micrometer (**Figure 112**) and check runout, taper and wear. Compare the measurements with the specifications listed in **Table 1**.

5. Inspect the crankshaft outer splines (A, **Figure 113**). If damaged, replace the crankshaft. If the crankshaft splines are damaged, also inspect the inner splines on the timing sprocket (**Figure 114**).

6. Inspect the teeth on the primary drive gear (B, **Figure 113**). If the primary drive gear is damaged, replace the crankshaft. If the gear is damaged, in-

spect the clutch outer housing gear. Refer to Chapter Six.

7. Check the tightness of the Torx bolts (**Figure 115**) securing the counterweight to the crankshaft. There are no torque specifications for the fasteners but they must be tightened securely. If the bolts are loose, remove them and apply a threadlocking compound to the bolt threads, and tighten them securely.

8. Measure crankshaft runout as follows:

a. Mount the crankshaft on two V-blocks.

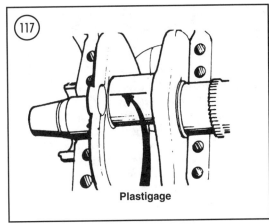

Plastigage

b. Position a dial indicator so its stem rests against one of the center bearing journals. Then zero the dial gauge.
c. Slowly turn the crankshaft while reading the dial gauge. Record the runout limit.
d. If the runout exceeds the service limit in **Table 1**, replace the crankshaft.

Crankshaft Main Bearing Clearance Measurement

1. Check each crankshaft main bearing insert (**Figure 116**) for evidence of wear, abrasion and scoring. If the bearing inserts are good, they may be reused. If any insert is questionable, replace the entire set.
2. Clean the bearing surfaces of the crankshaft and the bearing inserts for the crankshaft.
3. Place the upper crankcase half on a workbench upside down on two wooden or rubber blocks. This protects the protruding connecting rods after the crankshaft is installed.
4. If removed, install all existing crankshaft bearing inserts into the upper and middle crankcase halves in their original locations. Make sure they are locked into place.
5. Install the crankshaft assembly (**Figure 93**) into the upper crankcase half.
6. Place a piece of Plastigage over each crankshaft bearing journal. The Plastigage must be parallel to the crankshaft as shown in **Figure 117**. Do not place the Plastigage material over an oil hole in the crankshaft.

CAUTION
Do not rotate the crankshaft while the Plastigage is in place.

7. Position the middle crankcase half onto the upper crankcase half and set it down (**Figure 90**).

> *CAUTION*
> *When properly aligned, the middle crankcase slides over the crankshaft assembly and seats against the upper crankcase. If the crankcases do not fit together completely, do not attempt to pull them together with the crankcase bolts. Separate the crankcases and determine the cause of the interference. Do not damage the crankcase by forcing them together.*

8. Join both halves and lightly tap them together with a plastic or soft-faced mallet. Do not use a metal hammer. It will damage the cases.

9. Remove the bolts from the cardboard template and install the middle crankcase mounting bolts (**Figure 88**). If the bolts are not all the same distance up from the bosses on the crankcase, they are not installed in the correct locations. Switch them around until they are all at the same height. Tighten all bolts finger-tight at this time.

10. Refer to the raised numbers cast next to the middle crankcase bolts. Tighten the upper crankcase bolts (**Figure 89**) in ascending order in 2-3 stages. First tighten the bolts to the initial torque specification and then the final torque specification listed in **Table 2**.

11. Again, refer to the raised number on the crankcase, and loosen the bolts in descending order. Evenly loosen all bolts in 2-3 stages, and then remove the bolts.

12. Make sure all the crankcase bolts are removed.

13. Lift the middle crankcase off the upper crankcase. Immediately turn the middle crankcase over and account for the main bearing inserts. If any have fallen out of position, attempt to return them to their original locations.

14. Measure the width of the flattened Plastigage according to the manufacturer's instructions. Measure both ends of the Plastigage strip as shown in **Figure 118**. A difference of 0.025 mm (0.001 in.) or more indicates a tapered journal. Confirm with a micrometer as shown in **Figure 111**. Bearing clearance for new bearings is listed in **Table 1**.

15. If the widest part of the Plastigage exceeds the crankshaft journal oil clearance service limit specified in **Table 1**, install new bearings. Bearing selection is described below.

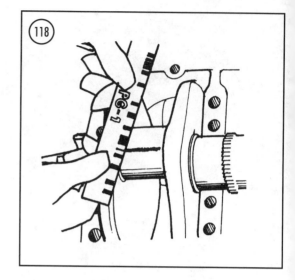

16. Remove all Plastigage material from the crankshaft journals.

17. If the bearing clearance is greater than specified, select new bearings as described in this chapter.

18. Remove the crankshaft assembly (**Figure 93**) from the upper crankcase half.

Crankshaft-to-Crankcase Main Bearing Selection

1. The crankshaft main bearing journal codes (A, B, and C) are stamped on the counterbalance web of the crankshaft. The codes coincide with the outside diameter of the main bearing journals as shown in **Figure 119**.

2. The crankcase inside journal codes (A or B) are stamped on the rear lower surface of the upper crankcase (**Figure 120**). These codes coincide with the inner diameter of the main bearing bosses in the crankcase.

3. Select new bearings by cross-referencing the crankshaft outside diameter codes (**Figure 119**) in the horizontal row of **Table 3** with the crankcase inside diameter codes (**Figure 120**) in the vertical column. The intersection of the appropriate row and column indicates the new bearing insert color. **Table 4** lists bearing color, part number and thickness. Always replace all 10 crankshaft bearing inserts as a set.

4. After installing new bearing inserts, recheck the clearance by repeating the *Crankshaft Main Bearing Clearance Measurement* procedure in this chap-

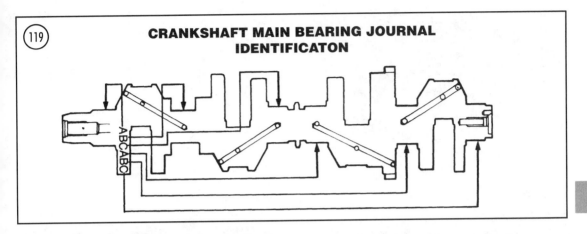

CRANKSHAFT MAIN BEARING JOURNAL IDENTIFICATON

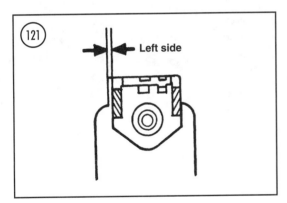

Left side

ter. If the clearance is still out of specification, either the crankshaft or the crankcase is worn beyond the service limit and requires replacement.

Crankshaft Thrust Clearance Inspection

1. Disassemble the crankcase as described in this chapter. Do not remove the crankshaft assembly from the upper crankcase.

2. Push the crankshaft assembly to the left side until there is no clearance between the crankshaft and the right thrust bearing.

3. Measure the thrust clearance (**Figure 121**) by inserting a flat feeler gauge between the crankshaft web thrust surface and the left thrust bearing as shown in **Figure 122**. Compare the reading to the crankshaft thrust clearance listed in **Table 1**.

4. If the thrust clearance is outside the specified range, perform the following.

    a. Remove the right thrust bearing and measure its thickness with a micrometer (**Figure 123**). Compare the reading to the bearing thickness specified in **Table 1**.

    b. If the thickness is within the specified range, reinstall the right thrust bearing and proceed to Step 5.

    c. If the thickness is less than specified, install a new right thrust bearing and repeat Step 2-4.

5. Remove the left thrust bearing.

6. Measure the left thrust bearing clearance by inserting a flat feeler gauge between the left surface of

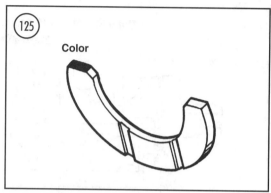

Color

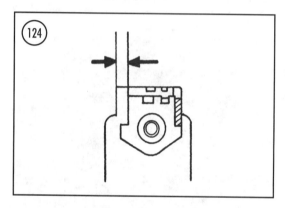

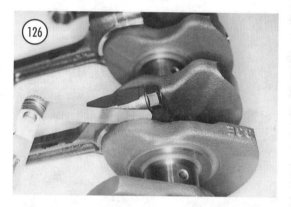

the crankcase and the machined surface of the crankshaft (**Figure 124**).

7. **Table 5** provides the left thrust bearing color code (**Figure 125**), part number and thickness. Refer to **Table 5** and use the clearance measured in Step 6 to select the correct left thrust bearing.

8. Install the new left thrust bearing, and then repeat Steps 2-4.

9. If the clearance cannot be brought into specification with the new thrust bearings, replace the crankshaft.

CAUTION
*Install both the right and left thrust bearings with their oil grooves (**Figure 96**) facing toward the crankshaft web.*

10. After adjusting the clearance, remove both thrust bearings and apply a coat of molybdenum disulfide grease to each side of both bearings. Install both bearings into the crankcase with their oil grooves facing toward the crankshaft web.

CONNECTING RODS

Removal/Installation

1. Remove the crankshaft/connecting rod assembly as described in *Upper and Middle Crankcase Disassembly* in this chapter.

2. Insert a flat feeler gauge between the connecting rod and the crankshaft machined surface (**Figure 126**). Compare the measurement to the connecting rod big end side clearance service limit in **Table 1**. Measure each connecting rod (**Figure 127**). If the

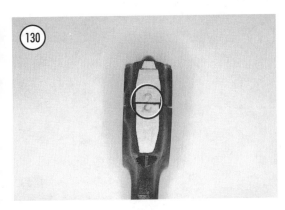

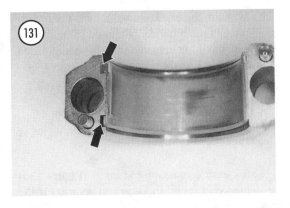

measurement is not within the service limit refer to *Connecting Rod Inspection* in this chapter to determine which component requires replacement.

3. Remove the connecting rod cap bolts (**Figure 128**), remove the cap and separate the rods from the crankshaft. Keep each cap with its original rod (**Figure 129**). The weight mark on the end of the cap should align with the mark on its connecting rod (**Figure 130**).

> *CAUTION*
> *If old bearing inserts are reused, they must be installed in their original locations. Keep each bearing insert in the connecting rod and cap. If they are removed, label the backside of each insert with a 1-4 that corresponds to the rod number and with rod (R) and cap (C) identification.*

4. Inspect the connecting rods and bearings as described in this chapter

5. If new bearing inserts are being installed, check the bearing clearance as described in this chapter.

6. Apply a light even coat of clean engine oil and molybdenum disulfide grease to the crankpin journals.

7. Make sure the inserts are locked into place (**Figure 131**). Apply clean engine and molybdenum disulfide grease oil to the bearing surface of both bearing inserts.

8. Install each connecting rod onto the crankshaft in the correct location and with the weight mark (**Figure 127**) facing toward the *rear* of the engine. Be careful not to damage the bearing surface of the crankshaft with the sharp edge of the connecting rod and upper insert.

9. Align the weight mark on the end of the cap with the mark on the rod and install the cap onto the rod. Push it on until it contacts the connecting rod.

10. Install the connecting rod cap bolts (**Figure 128**). Torque the bolts, in two stages, to the torque specifications listed in **Table 2**.

11. After installing the connecting rods and tightening the cap nuts correctly, rotate each connecting rod on the crankshaft and make sure there is no binding.

Connecting Rod Inspection

1. Check each connecting rod assembly (**Figure 129**) for obvious damage such as cracks or burns.

2. Make sure the small end oil hole (**Figure 132**) is open. Clean it out if necessary.

3. Measure the small end inside diameter with a small hole gauge (**Figure 133**) and measure the gauge with a micrometer. Replace the connecting rod if the small end inside diameter is worn to the wear limit specified in **Table 1**.

4. Check the piston pin (**Figure 134**) for chrome flaking or cracks. Replace the pin if necessary.

5. Check the piston pin where it contacts the surface of the small end (**Figure 132**) for wear or abrasion.

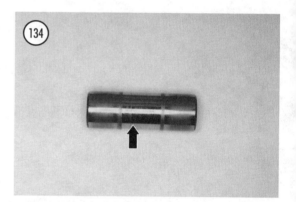

6. Oil the piston pin and install it in the connecting rod (**Figure 135**). Slowly rotate the piston pin and check for radial play.

7. Inspect the alignment of each connecting rod. If there is evidence of abnormal piston or cylinder wear, have the connecting rod inspected at a machine shop. Specialized equipment is required to accurately determine if a rod is bent or twisted.

8. Examine the bearing inserts (**Figure 136**) for wear, scoring or burned surfaces. They are reusable if in good condition. Make a note of the bearing color identification on the side of the insert if the bearing is to be discarded. A previous owner may have used undersize bearings.

9. If the connecting rod big end side clearance (*Connecting Rod Removal/Installation*) is greater than specified, perform the following:

    a. Measure the width of the connecting rod big end with a micrometer (**Figure 137**). If the width is less than the value specified in **Table 1**, replace the connecting rod assembly.

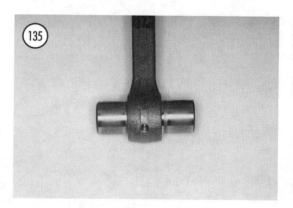

    b. Measure the crankpin width with a dial caliper or vernier caliper (**Figure 138**) and compare the measurement to the dimension listed in **Table 1**. If the width is greater than specified, replace the crankshaft.

Connecting Rod Bearing Clearance Measurement

1. Check each connecting rod insert (**Figure 136**) for evidence of wear, abrasion and scoring. If the

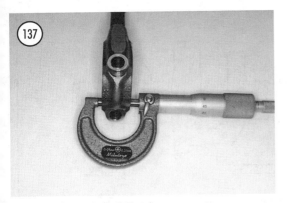

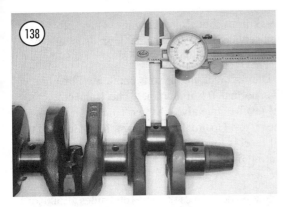

bearing inserts are good they may be reused. If any insert is questionable, replace all of the inserts as a set.

2. Clean the connecting rod bearing surfaces of the crankshaft (B, **Figure 110**) and check for damage as shown in **Figure 139**.

3. If removed, install the existing bearing inserts into the connecting rod and cap. Make sure they are locked into place (**Figure 131**).

4. Install the connecting rods onto the crankshaft in the correct location with the weight mark (**Figure 130**) facing the *rear* of the engine. Be careful to not damage the bearing surface of the crankshaft.

5. Place a piece of Plastigage over the rod journal. Make sure the Plastigage runs parallel to the crankshaft as shown in **Figure 140**. Do not place the Plastigage material over the oil hole in the crankshaft.

CAUTION
Do not rotate the crankshaft or the connecting rod while the Plastigage is in place.

6. Align the weight mark on the end of the cap with the mark on the rod (**Figure 127**) and install the cap. Install the bolts, and tighten them in two stages to the torque specifications listed in **Table 2**.

7. Loosen the cap bolts. Carefully lift the cap straight up and off the connecting rod.

8. Measure the width of the flattened Plastigage according to the manufacturer's instructions. Measure both ends of the Plastigage strip (**Figure 141**).

   a. A difference of 0.025 mm (0.001 in.) or more indicates a tapered journal. Confirm this with a micrometer as shown in **Figure 112**.

   b. If the connecting rod bearing clearance is greater than the wear limit specified in **Table 1**, select new bearings as described in this chapter.

9. Remove all of the Plastigage from the crankshaft rod journals.

Connecting Rod-to-Crankcase Bearing Selection

1. The connecting rod journals are identified by a code (1, 2 or 3) stamped into the counterbalance web on the crankshaft. The codes coincide with the crankpin journal outside diameter as shown in **Figure 142**.

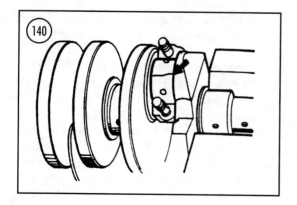

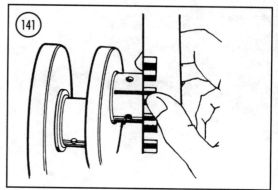

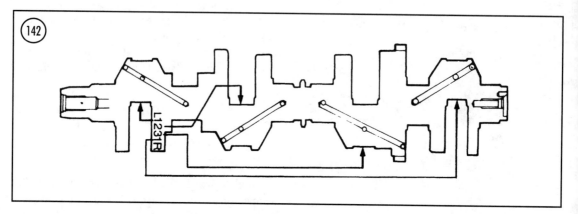

2. The connecting rods are coded with a weight number (1 or 2) marked on the side of the connecting rod (**Figure 130**). The codes coincide with the inside diameter of the connecting rod.

3. Select new bearings by cross-referencing the crankpin outside diameter code (**Figure 142**) in the row across the top of **Table 6** with the connecting rod inside diameter code (**Figure 130**) in the column down the left side of the table. The intersection of the appropriate row and column indicates the color of the new bearing inserts. **Table 7** lists the bearing color, part number and thickness. Always replace the bearing inserts as a set.

4. After installing new bearing inserts, recheck the clearance by repeating the *Connecting Rod Bearing Clearance Measurement* procedure. If the clearance is still out of specification, either the crankshaft or the connecting rod(s) is worn to the service limit and requires replacement.

ENGINE BREAK-IN

When replacing top end components or performing major lower end work, perform the engine break-in as though it were new. The performance and service life of the engine depends greatly on a careful and sensible break-in.

During break-in, oil consumption will be higher than normal. It is important to check and correct the oil level frequently (Chapter Three). Never allow the oil level to drop below the minimum level. If the oil level is low, the oil will become overheated resulting in insufficient lubrication and increased wear.

Suzuki designates the first 1000 miles (1,600 km) of vehicle operation as the break-in period. During the first 500 miles (800 km) of operation, do not exceed 6500 rpm. In the period between 500 and 1000 miles (800-1,600 km) of operation, do not exceed 10,000 rpm.

After the break-in period, change the engine oil and filter as described in Chapter Three. It is essential to perform this service to remove all the particles produced during break-in from the lubrication system. The small added expense is a smart investment that will pay off in increased engine life.

Table 1 LOWER END SPECIFICATIONS

Item	Standard mm (in.)	Wear limit mm (in.)
Connecting rod		
Small end inside diameter	15.010-15.018 (0.5909-0.5913)	15.040 (0.5921)
Big end side clearance	0.10-0.20 (0.004-0.008)	0.30 (0.010)
Big end width	20.95-21.00 (0.825-0.827)	
Connecting rod bearing		
clearance	0.032-0.056 (0.0013-0.0022)	0.080 (0.0031)
Crankshaft		
Crankpin width	21.10-21.15 (0.831-0.833)	–
Crankpin standard diameter	31.976-32.000 (1.2589-1.2598)	–
Code 1	31.992-32.000 mm (1.2595-1.2598 in.)	–
Code 2	31.984-31.992 mm (1.2592-1.2595 in.)	–
Code 3	31.976-31.984 mm (1.2589-1.2592 in.)	–
Crankpin oil clearance	0.032-0.056 mm (0.0013-0.0022 in.)	0.080 mm (0.0031 in.)
Crankshaft journal oil		
clearance		
1997	0.020-0.044 mm (0.0008-0.0017 in.)	0.080 mm (0.0031 in.)
1998-on	0.016-0.040 mm (0.0006-0.0016 in.)	0.080 mm (0.0031 in.)
Crankshaft journal standard		
diameter	33.976-34.000 mm (1.3376-1.3386 in.)	–
Code A	33.992-34.000 mm (1.3383-1.3386 in.)	–
Code B	33.984-33.992 mm (1.3380-1.3383 in.)	–
Code C	33.976-33.984 mm (1.3376-1.3380 in.)	–
Crankshaft runout	–	0.05 (0.002)
Crankshaft thrust clearance	0.055-0.110 (0.0022-0.0043)	–
Crankshaft thrust bearing		
thickness		
Right side	2.425-2.450 (0.0955-0.0965)	–
Left side	2.350-2.500 (0.0925-0.0984)	–
Oil pump		
Inner-to-outer rotor tip		
clearance		0.20 mm (0.008 in.)
Outer rotor to body clearance		0.35 mm (0.014 in.)
Oil pressure (hot)	200-500 kPa (28-71 psi) at 3000 rpm	

Table 2 LOWER END TORQUE SPECIFICATIONS

Item	N•m	in.-lb.	ft.-lb.
Alternator rotor bolt	120	–	89
Connecting rod cap bolt			
Initial	35	–	26
Final	67	–	49
Crankcase bolt			
Initial torque			
6 mm	6	53	–
8 mm	13	115	–
9 mm	18	–	13
Final torque			
6 mm	11	97	–
8 mm	24	–	18
9 mm	32	–	24
Engine mounting nut (rear lower)	79	–	58
Engine mounting nut (rear upper)	79	–	58
(continued)			

Table 2 LOWER END TORQUE SPECIFICATIONS (continued)

Item	N•m	in.-lb.	ft.-lb.
Engine mounting pinch bolt	23	–	17
Engine mounting thrust adjuster	10	89	–
Engine mounting thrust adjuster locknut	45	–	33
Engine sprocket nut	120	–	89
Lower oil hose banjo bolt	25	–	18
Mounting bolts (front engine upper)		–	
Left side (45 mm, 1.8 in. long)	55	–	41
Right side (55 mm, 2.2 in. long)	55	–	41
Oil cooler banjo bolt	73	–	54
Oil cooler mounting bolt	11	97	–
Oil drain bolt	28	–	21
Oil gallery plug			
M14	28	–	21
M16	40	–	29
Oil jet	5	44	–
Oil pan bolt	14	–	10
Oil pipe banjo bolt	10	89	–
Oil pressure regulator	28	–	21
Oil pressure switch	14	–	10
Oil pump mounting screw	10	89	–
Oil seal retainer bolt	10	89	–
Speedometer sensor rotor bolt	13	115	–
Starter clutch bolt	54	–	40
Starter clutch cover cap	11	97	–
Upper oil hose banjo bolt	20	–	15
Valve timing inspection cap	23	–	17

Table 3 CRANKSHAFT MAIN BEARING INSERT SELECTION

Crankshaft outer diameter code	A	B	C
Crankcase inner diameter code			
A	Green	Black	Brown
B	Black	Brown	Yellow

Table 4 CRANKSHAFT INSERT COLOR, PART NO., THICKNESS

1997 Models Color and part No.	Specification
Green 12229-31E50-0A0	1.486-1.490 (0.0585-0.0587)
Black 12229-31E50-0B0	1.490-1.494 (0.0587-0.0588)
Brown 12229-31E50-0C0	1.494-1.498 (0.0588-0.0590)
Yellow 12229-31E50-0D0	1.498-1.502 (0.0590-0.0591)
	(continued)

Table 4 CRANKSHAFT INSERT COLOR, PART NO., THICKNESS (continued)

1998-on Models Color and part No.	Specification (continued)
Green 12229-34E00-0A0	1.488-1.492 (0.0586-0.0587)
Black 12229-34E00-0B0	1.492-1.496 (0.0587-0.0589)
Brown 12229-34E00-0C0	1.496-1.500 (0.0589-0.0591)
Yellow 12229-34E00-0D0	1.500-1.504 (0.0591-0.0592)

Table 5 THRUST BEARING SELECTION

Clearance before inserting of left-hand side thrust bearing	Thrust bearing thickness	Color and part No.	Thrust clearance
2.560-2.585 mm (0.1008-0.1018 in.)	2.475-2.500 mm (0.0974-0.0984 in.)	White 12228-17E00-0F0	0.060-0.110 mm (0.0024-0.0043 in.)
2.535-2.560 mm (0.0998-0.1008 in.)	2.450-2.475 mm (0.0965-0.0974 in.)	Yellow 12228-17E00-0E0	0.060-0.110 mm (0.0024-0.0043 in.)
2.510-2.535 mm (0.0988-0.0998 in.)	2.425-2.450 mm (0.0955-0.0965 in.)	Green 12228-17E00-0D0	0.060-0.110 mm (0.0024-0.0043 in.)
2.485-2.510 mm (0.0978-0.0988 in.)	2.400-2.425 mm (0.0945-0.0955 in.)	Blue 12228-17E00-0C0	0.060-0.110 mm (0.0024-0.0043 in.)
2.460-2.485 mm (0.0969-0.0978 in.)	2.375-2.400 mm (0.0935-0.0945 in.)	Black 12228-17E00-0B0	0.060-0.110 mm (0.0024-0.0043 in.)
2.430-2.460 mm (0.0957-0.0969 in.)	2.350-2.375 mm (0.0925-0.0935 in.)	Red 12228-17E00-0A0	0.055-0.110 mm (0.0022-0-0.0043 in.)

Table 6 CONNECTING ROD BEARING INSERT SELECTION

Crankshaft outer diameter code	1	2	3
Connecting rod inner diameter code			
1	Green	Black	Brown
2	Black	Brown	Yellow

Table 7 CONNECTING ROD INSERT COLOR, PART NO., THICKNESS

Color and part No.	Specification
Green 12164-34E01-0A0	1.480-1.484 (0.0583-0.0584)
Black 12164-34E01-0B0	1.484-1.488 (0.0584-0.0586)
Brown 12164-34E01-0C0	1.488-1.492 (0.0586-0.0587)
Yellow 12164-34E01-0D0	1.492-1.496 (0.0587-0.0589)

CHAPTER SIX

CLUTCH AND EXTERNAL SHIFT MECHANISM

This chapter provides service procedures for the clutch, clutch release mechanism and external shift mechanism. Clutch specifications are in **Table 1** and **Table 2** at the end of the chapter.

The GSX-R600 clutch is a wet (operates in the engine oil) multi-plate design. The clutch assembly is located on the right side of the engine, with the hub splined to the transmission mainshaft and the outer housing geared to the crankshaft.

Release operation is accomplished via a pushrod/push piece assembly operating on the pressure plate. The pushrods pass through the transmission mainshaft and are activated by the clutch cable pulling on the clutch lifter mechanism mounted in the drive sprocket cover on the left side of the engine. This system does require routine adjustment (Chapter Three) to compensate for cable stretch.

EXTERNAL GEARSHIFT MECHANISM

The external gearshift mechanism is located on the right (clutch) side of the engine. Access to the internal gearshift mechanism requires removing the engine and splitting the crankcase as described in Chapter Five. Internal gearshift mechanism service is in Chapter Seven.

Removal

Refer to **Figure 1**.

1. Remove the seat as described in Chapter Fifteen.
2. Remove the lower fairing side panels from each side as described in Chapter Fifteen.
3. Remove the coolant reservoir as described in Chapter Ten.
4. Remove the engine sprocket cover as described in Chapter Eleven.
5. Remove the clutch assembly as described in this chapter.
6. On the left side of the engine, remove the circlip and washer (**Figure 2**) from the shift shaft.
7. On the right side of the engine, withdraw the shift shaft (A, **Figure 3**) from the crankcase. Reinstall the washer and circlip removed in Step 6 to avoid misplacing them.

NOTE
The following steps are shown with the engine removed and partially dis-

① **EXTERNAL GEARSHIFT MECHANISM**

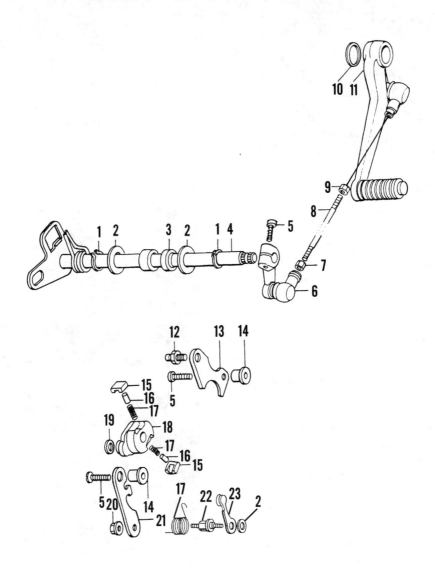

6

1. Circlip
2. Washer
3. Shift shaft seal
4. Shift shaft
5. Bolt
6. Shift lower arm
7. Nut (right-hand thread)
8. Shift link rod

9. Nut (left-hand thread)
10. Washer
11. Shift lever
12. Shift arm stopper bolt
13. Shift pawl lifter
14. Spacer
15. Pawl
16. Pin

17. Spring
18. Shift cam
19. Roller
20. Nut
21. Shift cam guide
22. Cam stopper support
23. Shift cam stopper

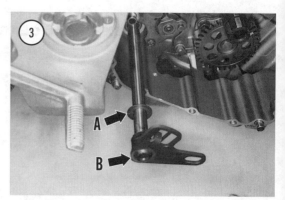

assembled for clarity. Engine re-moval is not necessary when servicing the external shift mechanism.

CAUTION
Some of the screws mentioned in the following procedures have a threadlocking compound applied to the threads. If the screws are difficult to loosen, use an impact driver and the correct size bit to loosen the screws. Do not try to loosen a stubborn screw with a screwdriver. This could damage the screw head slots making removal difficult.

8. Remove the nut (A, **Figure 4**) and the shift-cam-guide mounting bolt (B, **Figure 4**). Remove the shift cam guide (C, **Figure 4**), and then remove the spacer (D, **Figure 4**) located behind the guide's mounting bolt.

9. Remove the shift arm stopper bolt (A, **Figure 5**) and lower shift-pawl-lifter mounting screw (B, **Figure 5**). Remove the shift pawl lifter (C, **Figure 5**), and then remove the spacer (D, **Figure 5**) located behind the lifter's mounting screw.

NOTE
Remove the cam shifter assembly slowly. The small pawls, pins and springs are loose and will fall out during removal.

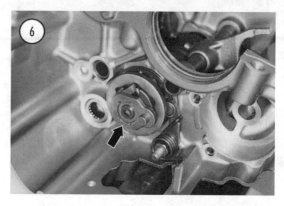

10. Remove the shift cam assembly (**Figure 6**) from the shift drum cam stopper plate. As soon as the pawls start to clear the cam stopper plate, hold them in place by hand to avoid losing the parts. Place the assembly into an aerosol can cap and place the cap into a plastic bag.

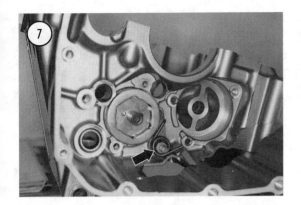

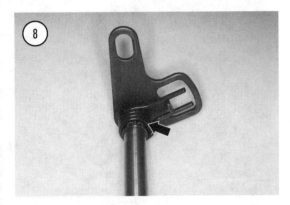

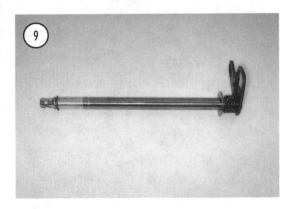

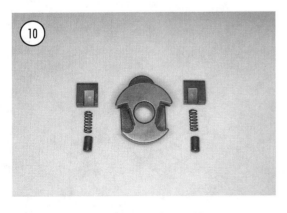

11. Remove the spring, the cam stopper support, shift cam stopper and washer (**Figure 7**) from the crankcase.

12. Inspect all parts as described in this chapter.

Inspection

1. Clean all parts in solvent, and dry them with compressed air.

2. Inspect the return spring (**Figure 8**) on the shift shaft assembly. Replace the spring if it is broken or weak.

3. Inspect the shift shaft assembly (**Figure 9**) for wear or damage (bent). Replace the shift shaft if necessary.

4. Disassemble the shift cam assembly (**Figure 10**), and inspect the pawls, springs and pins for wear or damage. Replace any worn or damaged parts.

5. Inspect the shift pawl lifter, shift cam guide, shift cam stopper and related parts (**Figure 11**) for wear or damage. Replace any worn or damaged parts.

6. Assemble the shift cam assembly as follows:

   a. Install the springs into the shift cam body.

   b. Position the pawl pins with the rounded end facing out and install them onto the springs.

   c. Install the pawls onto the pins and into the shift cam body.

   d. The pin grooves in the pawls are offset. When the pawls are installed correctly the wider shoulder must face toward the outside of the shift cam assembly (**Figure 12**).

   e. Hold the pawls in place and place the assembly into an aerosol can cap.

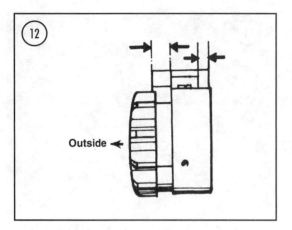

Outside

Installation

NOTE
Refer to Figure 13 for the correct ori-
entation of the shift cam stopper as-
sembly.

1. Install the shift cam stopper as follows:
   a. Apply ThreeBond TB 1342 or equivalent to the threads of the cam stopper support.
   b. Install the washer, shift cam stopper and cam stopper support (**Figure 14**) into the crankcase. Tighten the cam stopper support to the torque specification in **Table 2**.
   c. Move the shift cam stopper up against the shift drum, and then install the spring onto the stopper (A, **Figure 15**). The spring tang should press against the crankcase raised rib (B, **Figure 15**).

CAUTION
Apply a small amount of ThreeBond
TB1360 or Loctite No. 271 to the
screw threads before installation.

2. Remove the shift cam assembly from the aerosol can cap. Compress the spring-loaded shift pawls by hand (**Figure 16**). Install the shift cam assembly into the receptacle of the cam stopper plate. See **Figure 6**.

3. Install the spacer (**Figure 17**), and then the shift cam guide (C, **Figure 5**). While holding the spacer in place, install the shift-cam-guide mounting screw (B, **Figure 5**) and the shift arm stopper bolt (A, **Figure 5**). Tighten the stopper bolt to the torque specification listed in **Table 2**. Tighten the shift-cam-guide screw securely.

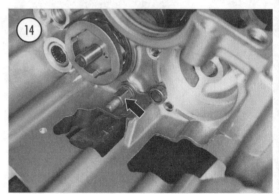

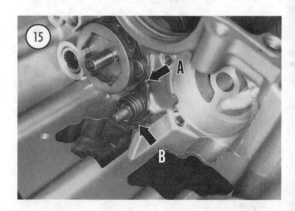

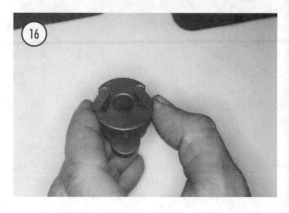

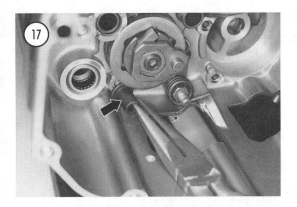

6

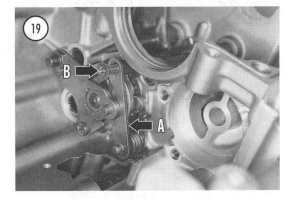

4. Install the spacer (**Figure 18**), the shift cam guide (A, **Figure 19**) and shift-cam-guide mounting bolt (B, **Figure 19**). Install the nut (A, **Figure 4**). Tighten the mounting bolt and nut securely.

5. Remove the circlip and washer from the left end of the shift shaft.

6. Make sure the washer (A, **Figure 3**) is in place on the right end of the shift shaft.

7. Apply clean engine oil to the shift shaft and install the shift shaft (A, **Figure 20**) part way into the crankcase.

8. Cover the crankcase opening with a clean shop cloth (B, **Figure 20**) so the roller does not drop into the crankcase during shift shaft installation.

9. Install the roller (C, **Figure 20**) onto the raised post on the shift cam.

10. Push the shift shaft until it stops against the crankcase. Make sure the arms of the shift shaft spring straddle the shaft arm stopper bolt (A, **Figure 21**) and the opening in the shift shaft arm engages the shift-cam roller (B, **Figure 21**). Remove the shop cloth.

11. On the left side of the engine, install the washer (**Figure 22**) and circlip (**Figure 2**) onto the end of the shift shaft. Make sure the circlip is properly seated in the shaft groove.

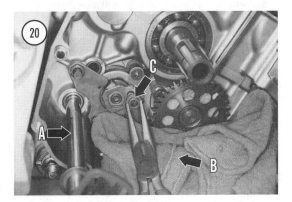

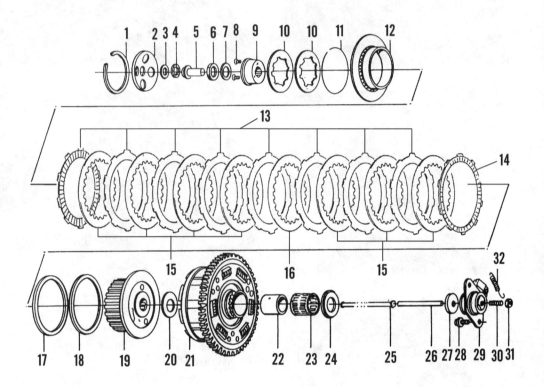

CLUTCH

1. Snap ring
2. Pressure plate lifter
3. Thrust washer
4. Thrust bearing
5. Push piece
6. Clutch sleeve nut
7. Lockwasher
8. Screw
9. Diaphragm spring holder
10. Diaphragm spring
11. Diaphragm spring seat
12. Pressure plate
13. Friction disc No. 1 (quantity 8)
14. Friction disc No. 2 (quantity 1)
15. Clutch plate No. 1 (quantity 7)
16. Clutch plate No. 2 (quantity 1)
17. Clutch plate washer
18. Clutch plate seat
19. Clutch hub
20. Outer thrust washer
21. Clutch outer housing
22. Collar
23. Needle bearing
24. Inner thrust washer
25. Clutch right side pushrod
26. Clutch left side pushrod
27. Oil seal
28. Screw
29. Release screw assembly
30. Adjust bolt
31. Locknut
32. Spring

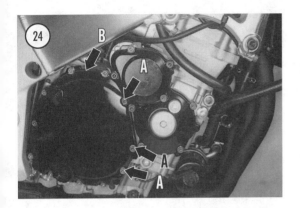

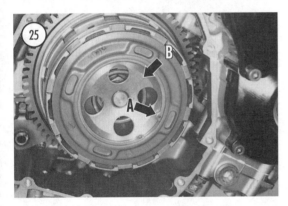

CLUTCH

6

Removal/Disassembly

Refer to **Figure 23**.

1. Remove the lower fairing side panels as described in Chapter Fifteen.

2. Drain the engine oil as described in Chapter Three.

> *NOTE*
> *This procedure is shown with the exhaust system removed for clarity. It is not necessary to remove the system when servicing the clutch.*

3. Shift the transmission into gear.

> *NOTE*
> *Use a grease pencil or tape to mark the location of the three clutch-cover bolts (A, Figure 24) that have sealing washers beneath them. The sealing washers must be installed behind these bolts during assembly. Also mark the location of the bolts with cable clamps beneath them.*

12. Install the clutch assembly as described in this chapter.

13. Install the engine sprocket cover as described in Chapter Eleven.

14. Install the coolant reservoir as described in Chapter Ten.

15. Install the lower fairing side panels as described in Chapter Fifteen.

16. Install the seat as described in Chapter Fifteen.

4. Remove the clutch cover bolts and the clutch cover (B, **Figure 24**). Watch for the two locating dowels behind the cover.

5. Remove the large circlip (A, **Figure 25**), and then remove the pressure plate lifter (B, **Figure 25**).

6. Remove the thrust washer, bearing and clutch push piece (**Figure 26**) from the end of the mainshaft.

7. Withdraw the clutch right-side push rod (**Figure 27**). If necessary, use a magnetic tool.

8. Install a clutch holding tool (**Figure 28**, Suzuki part No. 09920-34820) onto the pressure plate and loosen the clutch sleeve nut (**Figure 29**). Remove the tool, nut and lockwasher.

9. Remove the screws (A, **Figure 30**) and remove the diaphragm spring holder (B, **Figure 30**). Place the small screws and holder in a reclosable plastic bag to avoid misplacing them.

10. Remove the two diaphragm springs (**Figure 31**).

11. Remove the diaphragm spring seat and the pressure plate (**Figure 32**).

12. Install two 6 mm bolts into the center of the clutch hub.

13. Pull on the 6 mm bolts and withdraw the clutch hub, friction discs and clutch plates as an assembly.

14. Remove the outer thrust washer (**Figure 33**) from the mainshaft.

NOTE
*The crankshaft right outer counterweight must be rotated out of the way for the clutch outer housing gear to pass by it. **Figure 34** shows the clutch outer housing removed so the crankshaft counterweight can be seen.*

15. If necessary, use a 14 mm wrench on the starter clutch mounting bolt (**Figure 35**) to turn the engine. Rotate the engine *clockwise*, as viewed from the right side of the bike, until the counterweight is away from the crankcase opening (**Figure 34**).

CAUTION
*Do not try to remove the clutch outer housing without repositioning the crankshaft right counterweight (A, **Figure 36**) or before removing the collar and needle bearing. The coun-*

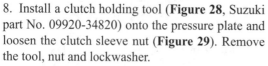

6

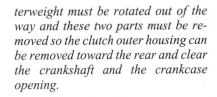

terweight must be rotated out of the way and these two parts must be removed so the clutch outer housing can be removed toward the rear and clear the crankshaft and the crankcase opening.

16. Remove the collar and needle bearing (**Figure 37**) from within the clutch outer housing and mainshaft.

17. Carefully remove the clutch outer housing along with the oil pump drive gear (**Figure 38**) from the mainshaft. The oil pump drive gear sits on the backside of the clutch outer housing. Be careful not to drop this gear when removing the clutch outer housing.

18. Remove the inner thrust washer (B, **Figure 36**) from the transmission mainshaft.

19. Remove the friction discs, clutch plates, clutch plate washer and clutch plate seat from the clutch hub. Keep all parts in their order of removal.

20. Inspect all components as described in this chapter.

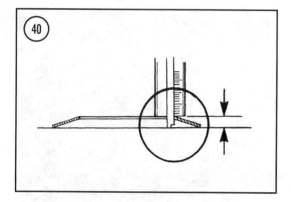

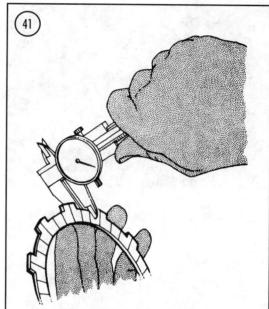

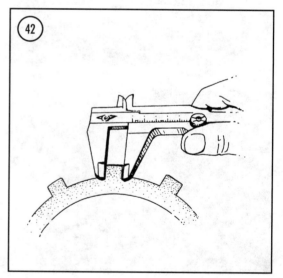

Inspection

Inspect all parts and replace any that are worn to the wear limit listed in **Table 1**.

1. Clean all clutch parts in a petroleum-based solvent such as kerosene, and thoroughly dry them with compressed air.

2. Check the diaphragm springs (**Figure 39**) for wear or distortion. Measure the free height of each diaphragm spring with a vernier caliper as shown in **Figure 40**. Replace any spring that is worn to the service limit.

3. Check the diaphragm spring holder for wear or damage.

4. Measure the thickness of each friction disc at several places around the disc as shown in **Figure 41**. If any measurement is outside the range specified in **Table 1**, replace all the friction discs.

5. Measure the width of all the claws on each friction disc as shown in **Figure 42**. If any claw width is worn to the service limit specified in **Table 1**, replace all the friction discs.

6. Check the clutch plates for surface damage from heat or lack of oil. Replace any plate that is damaged in any way.

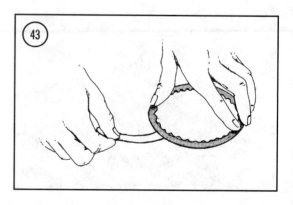

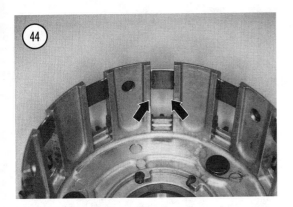

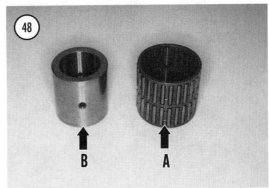

7. Check the clutch plates for warp with a flat feeler gauge and a surface plate or plate glass (**Figure 43**). If any plate is warped to the wear limit in **Table 1**, replace the *entire set* of clutch plates.

NOTE
If any of the friction discs or clutch plates require replacement, replace them as a set to retain maximum clutch performance.

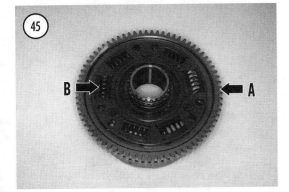

8. Inspect the slots (**Figure 44**) in the clutch outer housing for cracks, nicks or galling where they come in contact with the friction disc tabs. If excessive damage is evident on any slot, replace the housing.

9. Inspect the teeth of the primary driven gear (A, **Figure 45**) on the clutch outer housing for damage. Remove any small nicks with an oilstone. If damage is excessive, replace the clutch outer housing.

10. Inspect the damper springs (B, **Figure 45**). Replace the housing if they are sagged or broken.

11. Check the inner surface (A, **Figure 46**) of the clutch outer housing, where the needle bearing rides, for signs of wear or damage. Replace the clutch outer housing if necessary.

12. Inspect the teeth of the oil pump drive gear (B, **Figure 46**) for damage. Remove any small nicks with an oilstone.

13. Inspect the outer grooves (A, **Figure 47**) in the clutch hub. If there are any signs of wear or galling, replace the clutch hub.

14. Check the needle bearing (A, **Figure 48**). The bearing must turn smoothly without excessive play or noise. Replace the bearing if necessary.

15. Check the inner and outer surfaces of the spacer (B, **Figure 48**) for signs of wear or damage. Replace the spacer if necessary.

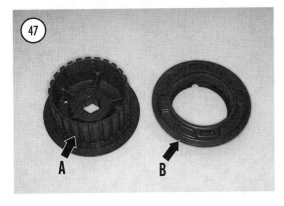

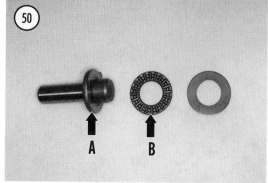

16. Install the spacer into the needle bearing (**Figure 49**). Rotate the spacer and check for wear. Replace either/or both parts if necessary.

17. Inspect the pressure plate (B, **Figure 47**) for wear or damage.

18. Check the clutch push piece (A, **Figure 50**) for wear or damage. Inspect the end that contacts the right push rod. Replace the push piece if necessary.

19. Check the clutch push piece bearing (B, **Figure 50**). Make sure it rotates smoothly. Replace the bearing if necessary.

20. Install the bearing and washer onto the push piece, and rotate them by hand. Make sure all parts rotate smoothly. Replace any worn part.

21. Inspect the push rods for straightness. Roll each rod on a surface plate or piece of plate glass. If the rod(s) is bent or deformed in any way, replace it. Otherwise, it may bind within the mainshaft, and cause erratic clutch operation.

Assembly/Installation

Refer to **Figure 23**.

1. Install the inner thrust washer (B, **Figure 36**) onto the transmission mainshaft. Make sure the beveled side (**Figure 51**) of the thrust washer faces in toward the transmission.

2. If removed, install the oil pump drive gear (**Figure 52**) into the backside of the clutch outer housing.

3. If necessary, rotate the crankshaft right outer counterweight (A, **Figure 36**) out of the way, so the clutch outer housing gear can pass by it. Use a 14 mm wrench on the starter clutch mounting bolt (**Figure 35**), and rotate the engine *clockwise*, as viewed from the right side of the bike, until the

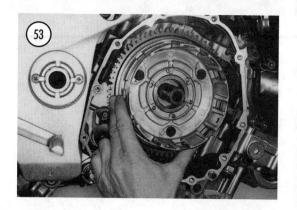

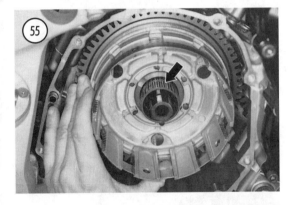

6

counter weight is rotated away from the crankcase opening (**Figure 34**).

4. Install the clutch outer housing onto the mainshaft (**Figure 53**). If necessary, use a scribe or thin screwdriver to slightly rotate the oil pump driven gear (**Figure 54**) back and forth until it properly engages the oil pump drive gear on the outer housing. Push the outer housing onto the mainshaft until it stops.

5. Apply clean engine oil to the needle bearing and install the needle bearing (**Figure 55**) into the outer housing. Push the needle bearing all the way into the housing.

6. Apply clean engine oil to the collar and install the collar onto the mainshaft and into the needle bearing (**Figure 56**).

7. Install the outer thrust washer (**Figure 33**) onto the mainshaft.

NOTE
If new friction discs and clutch plates are being installed, apply clean engine oil to all surfaces to avoid clutch lock up when the engine is started.

8. Assemble the components onto the clutch hub as follows:

    a. Install the clutch plate seat (**Figure 57**).

    b. Install the clutch plate washer (**Figure 58**) so the concave, or dished, side faces up. Push the clutch plate washer and clutch plate seat onto the hub until they stop.

9. Slide the clutch hub (**Figure 38**) onto the mainshaft. Push it on until it stops.

10. Install friction disc No. 2 (**Figure 59**) onto the clutch hub. The inside diameter of friction disc No. 2 is larger than the inside diameter of the other eight

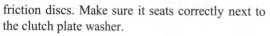

friction discs. Make sure it seats correctly next to the clutch plate washer.

11. Install a clutch plate (**Figure 60**) onto the clutch hub and then install a friction disc. Install a clutch plate, friction disc, another clutch plate and then another friction disc.

12. Next install clutch plate No. 2, which is thicker than the other seven clutch plates.

13. Install a friction disc and then a clutch plate. Continue alternating them, until all are installed. The last item installed should be a friction disc (**Figure 61**).

14. Refer to **Figure 23** to ensure all friction discs and clutch plates are installed in the correct order.

15. Install the pressure plate (**Figure 32**).

16. Install the diaphragm springs (**Figure 62**) so the concave or dished side faces in toward the transmission. Push the springs all the way on until they stop (**Figure 31**).

17. Install the diaphragm spring holder (B, **Figure 30**) until it bottoms in the clutch. Align the screw holes, and secure the holder in place with the mounting screws (A, **Figure 30**). Tighten the screws securely.

18. Install the lockwasher (**Figure 63**) and clutch nut (**Figure 29**).

19. Install the clutch holding tool (**Figure 28**) and tighten the clutch locknut (**Figure 64**) to the torque specification listed in **Table 2**. Use a centerpunch and hammer and stake the clutch nut onto the mainshaft.

20. Remove the special tool from the clutch hub.

NOTE
The right-side clutch pushrod is symmetrical so either end can be inserted into the mainshaft first.

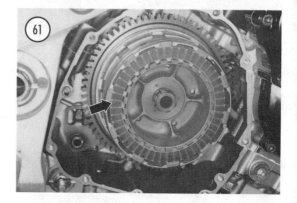

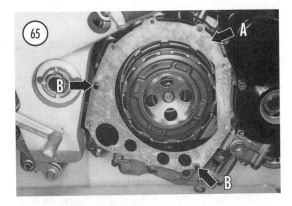

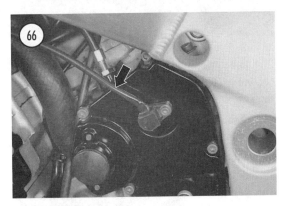

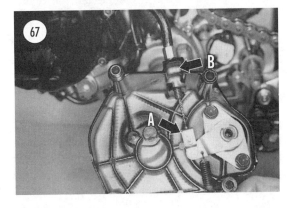

21. Install the clutch right-side pushrod (**Figure 27**) into the transmission shaft.

22. Install the clutch push piece, bearing and thrust washer (**Figure 26**) onto the end of the mainshaft.

23. Install the pressure plate lifter (B, **Figure 25**). Position the large circlip with the sharp edge facing out away from the engine. Install the large circlip (A, **Figure 25**) and make sure it is correctly seated within the groove in the pressure plate lifter.

24. Apply a light coat of ThreeBond No. 1104 gasket sealer or equivalent to the mating surfaces of the upper, middle and lower crankcases. This reduces the possibility of an oil leak.

25. Install a new gasket (A, **Figure 65**) and the two dowels (B, **Figure 65**).

26. Install the clutch cover (B, **Figure 24**) and the clutch cover bolts. Install a new gasket washer under the head of the front three bolts (A, **Figure 24**), and tighten the bolts securely.

27. Refill the engine oil as described in Chapter Three.

28. Install the lower fairing assembly as described in Chapter Fifteen.

CLUTCH LIFTER MECHANISM

The clutch lifter mechanism is located in the drive sprocket cover on the left side of the engine.

Removal/Installation

1. Remove the seat as described in Chapter Fifteen.

2. Remove the lower fairing side panels as described in Chapter Fifteen.

3. Remove the coolant reservoir as described in Chapter Ten.

4. Follow the electrical cable (**Figure 66**) from the speed sensor to the wiring harness, and disconnect the 3-pin speed sensor connector. This connector has three wires - orange/red, pink, black/white - on the harness side of the connector.

5. Partially remove the drive sprocket cover as described in Chapter Eleven. Do not lose the two locating dowels on the backside of the cover.

6. Turn the drive sprocket cover to gain access to the backside of the cover.

7. Disconnect the clutch cable (A, **Figure 67**) from the release screw assembly arm.

8. Remove the clutch cable and rubber grommet (B, **Figure 67**) from the engine sprocket cover and

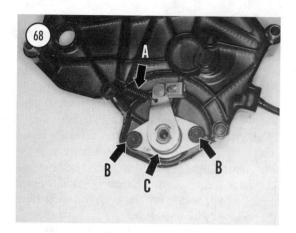

remove the cover. Do not lose the two locating dowels behind the cover.

9. Disconnect the spring (A, **Figure 68**) from the release screw assembly arm.

10. Remove the two mounting bolts (B, **Figure 68**) and the release screw assembly arm from the cover.

11. Remove the release screw assembly (C, **Figure 68**) from the cover.

12. Install by reversing these removal steps while noting the following:

    a. Securely tighten the release screw assembly bolts.

    b. If removed, install the locating dowels (**Figure 69**) into the cover.

    c. Adjust the clutch mechanism and cable as described in Chapter Three.

CLUTCH CABLE REPLACEMENT

1. Lubricate the new clutch cable, as described in Chapter Three.

2. Remove the seat as described in Chapter Fifteen.

3. Remove the lower fairing side panels as described in Chapter Fifteen.

4. Remove the coolant reservoir as described in Chapter Ten.

5. Remove the engine sprocket cover as described in Chapter Eleven.

6. Turn the engine sprocket cover to gain access to the backside of the cover.

7. Disconnect the clutch cable (A, **Figure 67**) from the release screw assembly arm.

8. Remove the cable and rubber grommet (B, **Figure 67**) from the engine sprocket cover.

9. Remove any cable ties securing the clutch cable to the frame.

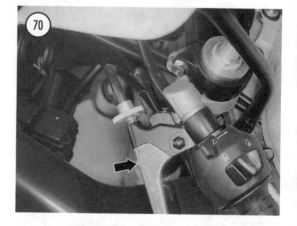

10. Tie a piece of heavy string onto the end of the old cable. Cut the string to a length that is longer than the new clutch cable.

11. Disconnect the clutch cable from the clutch lever (**Figure 70**).

12. Tie the lower end of the string to the frame or engine component.

13. Remove the old clutch cable by pulling it from the top (upper cable end). Continue until the cable is removed from the frame, leaving the attached piece of string in its mounting position.

14. Untie the string from the old cable and discard the old cable.

15. Tie the string onto the bottom end of the new clutch cable.

16. Slowly pull the string and cable to install the cable along the path of the original clutch cable. Continue until the clutch cable is correctly routed through the engine and frame. Untie and remove the string.

17. Visually check the entire length of the clutch cable as it runs through the frame and engine. Make sure there are no kinks or sharp bends. Straighten out if necessary.

18. Connect the upper cable end to the clutch lever.

19. Connect the lower end of the clutch cable to the release screw assembly (A, **Figure 67**).

20. Install any cable ties needed to secure the clutch cable to the frame.

21. Adjust the clutch cable as described in Chapter Three.

Table 1 CLUTCH SPECIFICATIONS

Item	Standard mm (in.)	Wear limit mm (in.)
Quantity		
Friction disc No. 1	8	–
Friction disc No. 2	1	–
Clutch plate No. 1	7	–
Clutch plate No 2.	1	–
Friction disc		
Thickness (No. 1 and No. 2)	2.92-3.08 (0.115-0.121)	–
Claw width (No. 1 and No. 2)		
1997	–	13.0 (0.521)
1998-on	13.7-13.8 (0.539-0.543)	12.9 (0.507)
Clutch plate warp (No. 1 and No. 2)	–	0.10 (0.004)
Clutch release screw setting	1/4 turns out	
Clutch diaphragm spring free height	–	2.9 (0.11)
Clutch lever free play	10-15 (0.4-0.6)	
Shift lever height	55 (2.2)	–

Table 2 CLUTCH AND GEARSHIFT MECHANISM TORQUE SPECIFICATIONS

Item	N•m	in.-lb.	ft.-lb.
Clutch hub nut	150	–	110
Shift arm stopper bolt	19	–	14
Shift lever clamp bolt	10	89	–
Cam stopper support	10	89	–

6

CHAPTER SEVEN

TRANSMISSION AND INTERNAL SHIFT MECHANISM

This chapter covers service to the transmission and internal gearshift assemblies. Removal of these two assemblies from the crankcase is covered in Chapter Five. Specifications are listed in **Table 1** and **Table 2** at the end of the chapter.

When the clutch is engaged, the mainshaft (input) is driven by the clutch hub, which is driven by the crankshaft primary drive gear/clutch outer housing. Power is transferred from the mainshaft through the selected gear combination to the countershaft (output), which drives the engine sprocket.

> *NOTE*
> *Suzuki terminology for the transmission shafts is different than most manufacturers. Suzuki refers to the input (main) shaft as the countershaft and the countershaft as the driveshaft. The procedures in this manual refer to the mainshaft as the mainshaft and the countershaft as the countershaft. Notice that this is opposite of Suzuki's parts information and keep this in mind when ordering replacement parts.*

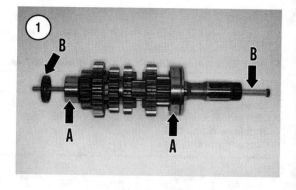

TRANSMISSION

Removal/Installation

Removal and installation of the transmission assembly is described in Chapter Five.

Preliminary Inspection

1. Clean and inspect the assemblies before disassembling them. Place the assembled shaft into a large can or plastic bucket, and thoroughly clean the assembly with a stiff brush and petroleum-based

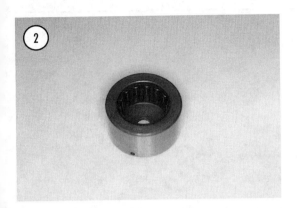

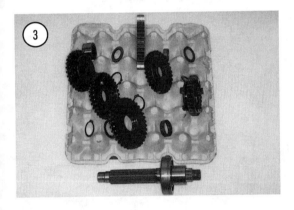

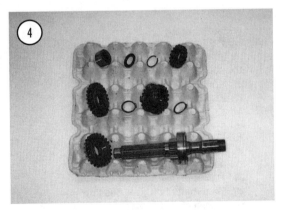

4. Rotate the transmission bearings by hand. Refer to A, **Figure 1** and **Figure 2**. Check for roughness, noise and radial play. Replace any bearing that is suspect.

5. Slide the clutch pushrods (B, **Figure 1**) into the mainshaft and check for binding. If binding occurs, check the pushrods for damage. Inspect the mainshaft tunnel for debris. Clean out the tunnel if necessary.

6. If the transmission shafts are satisfactory and are not going to be disassembled, apply assembly oil or engine oil to all components, and reinstall them into the crankcase as described in Chapter Five.

> *NOTE*
> *If disassembling a high mileage transmission, pay particular attention to any additional shims that may have been added by a previous owner. These may have been added to take up the tolerance of worn components and must be reinstalled in the same position since the shims have developed a wear pattern. If new parts are going to be installed these shims may be eliminated. This is something to determine upon assembly.*

Transmission Service Notes

1. After removing a part from the shaft, set it in an egg crate in the exact order of removal and with the same orientation the part had when installed on the shaft. This is an easy way to remember the correct relationship of all parts. Refer to **Figure 3** for the countershaft and **Figure 4** for the mainshaft.

2. The circlips fit tightly on the transmission shafts. It is recommended that all circlips be replaced during assembly.

3. Circlips will turn and fold over making removal and installation difficult. To ease replacement, open a circlip with a pair of circlip pliers while at the same time holding the back of the circlip with a pair of pliers and remove it. Repeat for installation.

Countershaft Disassembly

Refer to **Figure 5** for this procedure.

1. Place the assembled shaft into a large can or plastic bucket, and thoroughly clean the countershaft assembly with solvent and a stiff

solvent such as kerosene. Dry the assembly with compressed air or let it sit on rags to drip dry. Do this for the both shaft assemblies.

2. Visually inspect the components for excessive wear. Check the gear teeth for chips, burrs or pitting. Clean up minor damage with an oilstone. Replace any components with damage that can not be cleaned up.

3. Carefully check the engagement dogs. If any are chipped, worn, rounded or missing, replace the affected gear.

⑤

TRANSMISSION

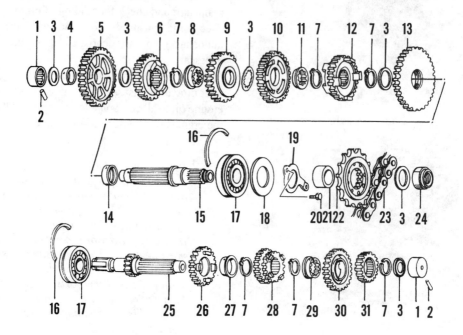

1. Needle bearing
2. Pin
3. Washer
4. Countershaft first gear bushing
5. Countershaft first gear
6. Countershaft fifth gear
7. Circlip
8. Countershaft fourth gear bushing
9. Countershaft fourth gear
10. Countershaft third gear
11. Countershaft third gear bushing
12. Countershaft sixth gear
13. Countershaft second gear
14. Countershaft second gear bushing
15. Countershaft
16. C-ring

17. Ball bearing
18. Oil seal
19. Oil seal retainer
20. Screw
21. Sprocket spacer
22. Engine sprocket
23. Drive chain
24. Engine sprocket nut
25. Mainshaft/first gear
26. Mainshaft fifth gear
27. Mainshaft fifth bear bushing
28. Mainshaft third/fourth combination gear
29. Mainshaft sixth gear bushing
30. Mainshaft sixth gear
31. Mainshaft second gear

brush. Dry it with compressed air or let it sit on rags to dry.

2. Slide off the needle bearing and washer.

3. Slide off the first gear and first gear bushing.

4. Slide off the washer and the fifth gear.

5. Remove the circlip.

6. Slide off the fourth gear and fourth gear bushing.

7. Slide off the washer.

8. Slide off the third gear and third gear bushing.

9. Remove the circlip.

10. Slide off the sixth gear.

11. Remove the circlip and slide off the washer.

12. Slide off the second gear and second gear bushing.

13. Keep the parts in the exact order of removal and with the same orientation they had while installed on the countershaft as shown in **Figure 3**.

14. Inspect the countershaft components as described in this chapter.

countershaft Assembly

1. Apply a light coat of clean engine oil to all sliding surfaces before installing any part.

2. Slide on the second gear bushing (A, **Figure 6**).

3. Install second gear so the engagement slots face out away from the ball bearing. (B, **Figure 6**).

4. Slide the washer onto the countershaft, and then install a new circlip. Make sure the circlip properly seats in the circlip groove.

5. Install sixth gear so the shift fork groove faces out away from second gear. (**Figure 7**).

6. Install the circlip (**Figure 8**) and make sure it is correctly seated.

7. Align the oil hole in the third gear bushing (A, **Figure 9**) with the countershaft oil hole (B, **Figure 9**) and slide the bushing onto the countershaft. This alignment is necessary for proper gear lubrication.

8. Install third gear so its engagement slots face in toward sixth gear (A, **Figure 10**).

9. Slide on the washer (B, **Figure 10**).

10. Install fourth gear (A, **Figure 11**) so its engagement slots face out away from third gear.

NOTE
Figure 12 is shown without fourth gear in place for clarity.

11. Align the oil hole in the fourth gear bushing (A, **Figure 12**) with the countershaft oil hole (B, **Figure**

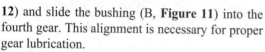

12) and slide the bushing (B, **Figure 11**) into the fourth gear. This alignment is necessary for proper gear lubrication.

12. Install a new circlip (**Figure 13**) and make sure it is correctly seated in the countershaft groove.

13. Install fifth gear (**Figure 14**) so the side with the short engagement dogs face out away from fourth gear.

14. Slide on the washer (A, **Figure 15**) and first gear bushing (B, **Figure 15**).

15. Install first gear (A, **Figure 16**) so its engagement slots face in toward fifth gear.

16. Install the washer (B, **Figure 16**) and the needle bearing (**Figure 17**).

17. Refer to **Figure 18** for correct placement of all gears. Make sure all circlips are correctly seated in the countershaft grooves.

18. Make sure each gear engages the adjoining gear properly where applicable.

Mainshaft Disassembly

Refer to **Figure 5**.

1. Place the assembled shaft into a large can or plastic bucket, and thoroughly clean it with solvent and a stiff brush. Dry the mainshaft assembly with compressed air or let it sit on rags to dry.

2. Slide off the needle bearing and seal.

NOTE
Slide the second and sixth gear down the mainshaft to gain access to the circlip securing second gear in place.

3. Release the circlip (**Figure 19**) from the mainshaft groove. Move the circlip down the shaft toward the third/fourth combination gear.

4. Slide the sixth and second gear down toward the third/fourth combination gear.

5. Secure the mainshaft vertically in a vise with soft jaws.

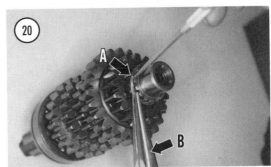

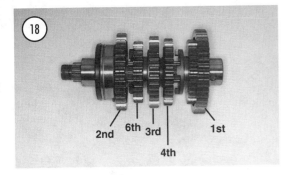

2nd 6th 3rd   1st

4th

11. Remove the circlip.

12. Slide off the fifth gear and the fifth gear bushing.

13. Keep the parts in the exact order of removal and with the same orientation they had while installed on the mainshaft as shown in **Figure 4**.

14. Inspect the mainshaft components as described in this chapter.

Mainshaft Assembly

1. Apply a light coat of clean engine oil to all sliding surfaces before installing any parts.

2. Install fifth gear onto the mainshaft so its engagement dogs face out away from first gear (A, **Figure 21**).

3. Slide the fifth gear bushing (B, **Figure 21**) into fifth gear.

4. Install a new circlip (**Figure 22**) and make sure it seats correctly in the mainshaft groove.

5. Slide the third/fourth combination gear onto the mainshaft so the larger fourth gear side (**Figure 23**) faces in toward fifth gear.

NOTE
The circlip installed in Step 6 must be positioned down on the shaft so the

NOTE
The circlip is very difficult to remove because it does not have notches at the end for the circlip pliers tips. Carefully pry the circlip from the mainshaft groove with a scribe.

6. Use a scribe to pry one end of the circlip out of the groove (A, **Figure 20**) and then grasp this end with needlenose pliers (B, **Figure 20**). Work around the shaft with the scribe, prying the circlip from the groove to remove it. Discard the circlip.

7. Slide off the second gear.

8. Slide off the sixth gear and the sixth gear bushing.

9. Remove the circlip.

10. Slide off the third/fourth combination gear.

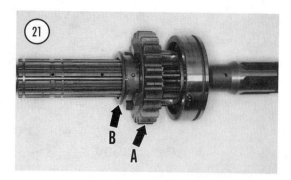

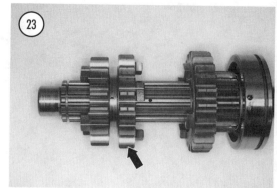

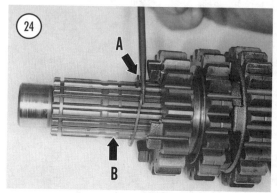

second gear circlip can be installed in
Step 10.

6. Slide a new circlip (A, **Figure 24**) onto the
mainshaft, but do *not* install it in its groove (B, **Figure 24**) at this time. Instead, slide the circlip down
toward the third/fourth combination gear.

7. Position the sixth gear bushing with the flange
side facing in toward the third/fourth combination
gear. Align the oil hole in the sixth gear bushing (A,
Figure 25) with the mainshaft oil hole (B, **Figure
25**), and slide the bushing down the mainshaft. This
alignment is necessary for proper gear lubrication.

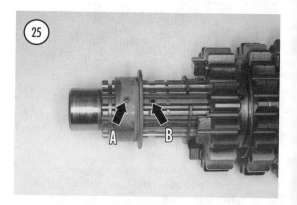

8. Install the sixth gear so its engagement dogs face
in toward the third/fourth combination gear. Slide
the sixth gear (**Figure 26**) onto the sixth gear bushing.

9. Install second gear (**Figure 27**) so the side with
the recess for the circlip and oil seal faces out away
from sixth gear.

10. Install the *new* circlip (**Figure 28**) and make
sure it seats correctly in the outermost groove in the
mainshaft (**Figure 29**).

11. Push the second and sixth gears toward the end
of the mainshaft.

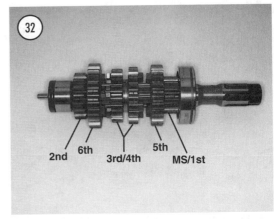

2nd 6th 3rd/4th 5th MS/1st

7

12. Move the circlip (**Figure 19**), installed on Step 6, into its correct groove in the mainshaft. Make sure it completely seats in the groove.

13. Slide on the oil seal (**Figure 30**) onto the mainshaft, and push it up against the circlip.

14. Install the needle bearing (**Figure 31**).

15. Refer to **Figure 32** for correct placement of all gears. Make sure all circlips are completely seated in the mainshaft grooves.

16. After assembling both transmission shafts, mesh the two assemblies together in the correct position (**Figure 33**). Make sure each gear combination properly engages. If any difficulty is encountered, determine the cause before installing the assembly into the crankcase.

Transmission Inspection

1. Check each gear for excessive wear, burrs, pitting, and chipped or missing teeth (A, **Figure 34**). Make sure the engagement dogs on the gears are in

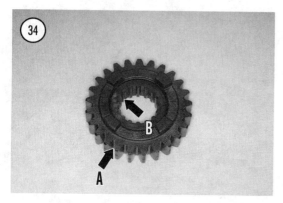

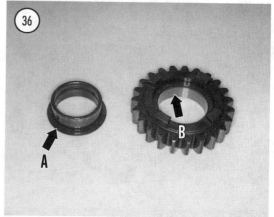

good condition. Also check the engagement slots (**Figure 35**) for wear or damage.

2. On splined gears, check the inner splines (B, **Figure 34**) for excessive wear or damage. Replace the gear if necessary.

3. Check each gear bushing (A, **Figure 36**) for excessive wear, pitting or damage. Replace the bushing if necessary.

4. On splined bushings, check the inner splines for excessive wear or damage. Replace if necessary.

5. On gears with bushings, inspect the inner surface of the gear (B, **Figure 36**) for wear, pitting or damage. Insert the bushing into the gear (**Figure 37**) and check for smooth operation.

6. Inspect the washers for bending wear or damage. Replace if necessary.

7. Inspect the shift fork-to-gear clearance as described in *Internal Gearshift Mechanism* later in this chapter.

NOTE
When replacing defective gears, it is recommended that the mating gear be

replaced also. Combining a new gear with an old gear will cause rapid wear to the new gear.

8. Make sure that all gears and bushings slide smoothly on their respective shaft splines.

NOTE
Replace all circlips every time the transmission is disassembled to ensure proper gear alignment. Do not expand a circlip more than necessary to slide it over the shaft.

9. Inspect the splines and the circlip grooves (A, **Figure 38**) on the countershaft. If any are damaged, replace the shaft.

10. Inspect the engine sprocket splines (B, **Figure 38**) and sprocket nut threads (C, **Figure 38**). If any spline is damaged, replace the shaft. If the threads have burrs or minor damage, clean them with a proper size metric thread die. If the threads are excessively worn, replace the countershaft.

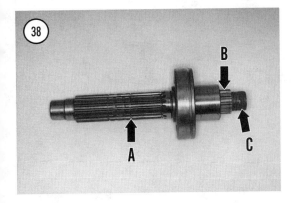

11. On the mainshaft, inspect the splines, the circlip grooves and the teeth of first gear (A, **Figure 39**). If any are damaged, replace the shaft.

12. Inspect the clutch hub splines (B, **Figure 39**) and clutch nut threads (C, **Figure 39**) of the mainshaft. If any spline is damaged, replace the shaft. If the threads have burrs or minor damage, clean them with a proper size metric thread die. If the threads are excessively worn, replace the mainshaft.

INTERNAL GEARSHIFT MECHANISM

Removal/Installation

Removal and installation of the internal gearshift mechanism is described in Chapter Five.

Inspection

Refer to **Figure 40**.

1. Clean all parts in solvent, and thoroughly dry them with compressed air.

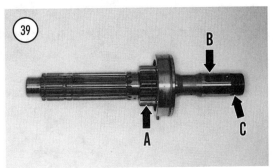

2. Inspect each shift fork for signs of wear or cracking. Check for any burned marks on the fingers of the shift forks (**Figure 41**). This indicates that the shift fork has come in contact with the gear. Replace the fork if the fork fingers have become excessively worn.

3. Check the bore of each shift fork and the shift fork shaft for burrs, wear or pitting. Replace any worn parts.

4. Install each shift fork onto its shaft (**Figure 42**) and make sure it moves freely on the shaft with no binding.

5. Check the guide pin (**Figure 43**) on each shift fork for wear or damage. Replace the shift fork(s) as necessary.

6. Roll each shift fork shaft on a surface plate or a piece of plate glass. If a shaft is bent, replace it.

7. Check the grooves in the shift drum (A, **Figure 44**) for wear or roughness. If any of the groove profiles have excessive wear or damage, replace the shift drum.

8. Inspect the cam gear locating pins and threaded hole in the end of the shift drum for wear or damage. Replace the shift drum if necessary.

9. Check the neutral switch contact plunger and spring for wear or damage. If the spring has sagged, replace it.

10. Check the shift drum bearing (B, **Figure 44**). Make sure it operates smoothly with no signs of wear or damage. Replace as necessary.

> *CAUTION*
> *Replace marginally worn shift forks. Worn forks can cause the transmission to slip out of gear, leading to serious damage.*

11. Install each shift fork into the groove in its respective gear. Use a flat feeler gauge and measure the clearance between the fork and the groove as

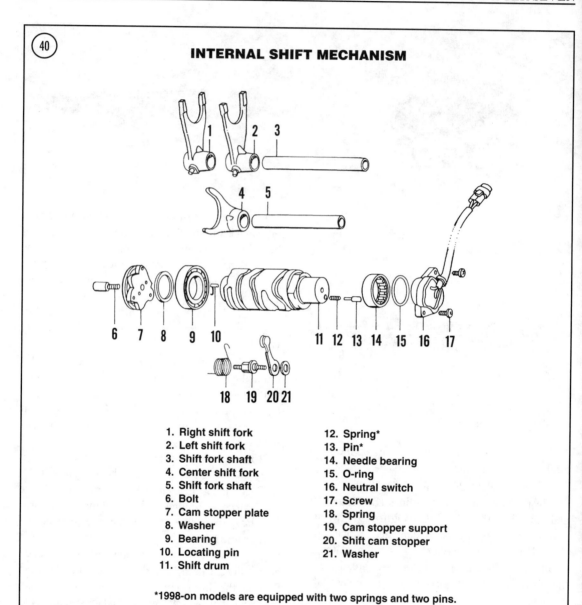

40

INTERNAL SHIFT MECHANISM

1. Right shift fork
2. Left shift fork
3. Shift fork shaft
4. Center shift fork
5. Shift fork shaft
6. Bolt
7. Cam stopper plate
8. Washer
9. Bearing
10. Locating pin
11. Shift drum

12. Spring*
13. Pin*
14. Needle bearing
15. O-ring
16. Neutral switch
17. Screw
18. Spring
19. Cam stopper support
20. Shift cam stopper
21. Washer

*1998-on models are equipped with two springs and two pins.

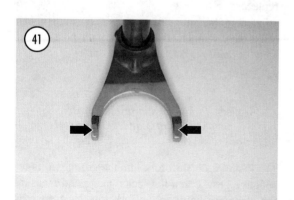

41

42

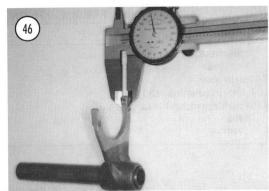

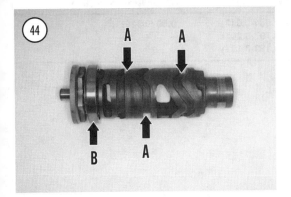

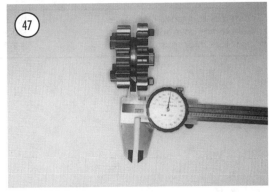

7

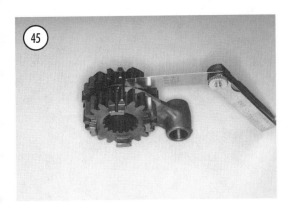

shown in **Figure 45**. If the shift fork-to-groove clearance exceeds the wear limit specified in **Table 2**, perform the following:

a. Measure the thickness of the shift fork fingers with a micrometer (**Figure 46**). Replace the shift fork if the width is outside the range specified in **Table 2**.

b. Use a vernier caliper to measure the width of the shift fork groove in the gear (**Figure 47**). Replace the gear if the groove width is outside the range specified in **Table 2**.

Table 1 TRANSMISSION SPECIFICATIONS

Item	Standard
Transmission gear ratios	
First gear	2.866 (43/15)
Second gear	
1997	2.058 (35/17)
1998-on	2.052 (39/19)
Third gear	1.650 (33/20)
Fourth gear	1.428 (30/21)
	(continued)

Table 1 TRANSMISSION SPECIFICATIONS (continued)

Item	Standard
Transmission gear ratios (continued)	
Fifth gear	1.285 (27/21)
Sixth gear	1.181 (26/22)
Primary reduction ratio	1.756 (72/41)
Secondary reduction ratio	
1997	2.812 (45/16)
1998-on	2.875 (46/16)

Table 2 INTERNAL SHIFT MECHANISM SPECIFICATIONS

Item	Standard mm (in.)	Wear limit mm (in.)
Shift fork-to-groove clearance	0.1-0.3 (0.004-0.012)	0.50 (0/020)
Shift fork groove width	5.0-5.1 (0.197-0.201)	–
Shift fork thickness	4.8-4.9 (0.189-0.193)	–

CHAPTER EIGHT

FUEL AND EMISSION CONTROL SYSTEMS

This chapter covers the service procedures for the fuel and emission systems. Air filter service is covered in Chapter Three. Carburetor specifications are listed in **Tables 1-5** at the end of the chapter.

The fuel system on the GSX-R600 consists of the fuel tank, vacuum fuel valve, four carburetors, a fuel pump/filter assembly, fuel pump relay and the air box.

The emission system components vary depending on the model. A crankcase breather system is used on all models. An evaporative emissions control system is used on California models. Models equipped with a PAIR (air supply) system are as follows:

1. California models from 1997-on.

2. U.S., Canada, Austria and Switzerland models from 1999-on.

> *WARNING*
> *Gasoline is a known carcinogen. It is extremely flammable and must be handled carefully. Wear latex gloves when working on components that may spill gasoline. If your skin comes in contact with gasoline, rinse it off immediately and then thoroughly wash with soap and warm water.*

CARBURETOR OPERATION

The carburetors atomize fuel and mix it in correct proportions with air that is drawn in through the air intake. At the primary throttle opening (idle), a small amount of fuel is siphoned through the pilot jet by the incoming air. As the throttle is opened further, the air stream begins to siphon fuel through the main jet and needle jet. As the tapered needle is lifted, it occupies progressively less area of the needle jet and thus increases the effective flow capacity of the jet. At full throttle, the carburetor venturi is fully open and the needle is lifted far enough to permit the main jet to flow at full capacity.

The choke circuit is a bystarter system in which the choke lever on the left handlebar opens an enrichment valve rather than closing a butterfly in the venturi area as on some carburetors. In the open position, the slow jet discharges a stream of fuel into the carburetor venturi, which enrichens the mixture.

On 1998 and later models, the main air system includes a soleniod valve. When the valve is opened, additional air flows into the venturi, which leans out the air/fuel mixture. The solenoid valve is operated by the CDI unit. It opens and closes the valve to provide the optimum air/fuel mixture for various operating conditions.

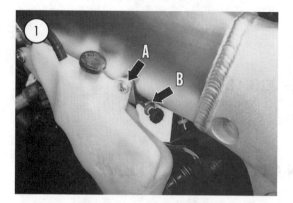

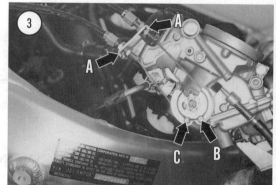

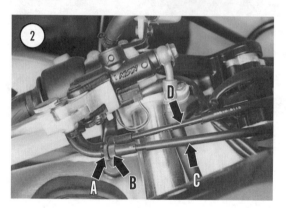

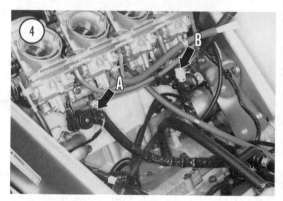

CARBURETOR

Removal/Installation

NOTE
Remove the four carburetors as an assembly. After removal from the engine, they can be separated if necessary.

1. Securely support the bike on level ground.
2. Remove the seats and the lower fairing side panels as described in Chapter Fifteen.
3. Disconnect the negative battery cable as described in Chapter Three.
4. Remove the fuel tank as described in this chapter.
5. Remove the air box as described in this chapter.
6. On the left side, remove the rear coolant-reservoir screw (A, **Figure 1**), and then remove the idle adjust knob bracket (B, **Figure 1**) from the frame. Move the idle adjust knob and bracket out of the way and reinstall the coolant reservoir screw.
7. At the throttle grip, loosen the throttle cable locknut (A, **Figure 2**) on the pull cable, and turn the adjuster (B, **Figure 2**) all the way into the switch as-

sembly to allow maximum slack in the pull cable (C, **Figure 2**). Repeat this procedure for the push cable (D, **Figure 2**).

NOTE
*In **Figure 3**, the carburetor assembly has been partially removed for photographic clarity. It is not necessary to remove the carburetor assembly to access the throttle wheel or throttle-cable mounting bracket.*

8. At the carburetor assembly, loosen both locknuts (A, **Figure 3**) securing the throttle cables to the mounting bracket.

NOTE
There are two throttle cables, one is the pull cable (accelerate) and the other one is the push cable (decelerate). These cables must be reinstalled in the correct position on the carburetor and connected to the correct position on the carburetor assembly throttle wheel.

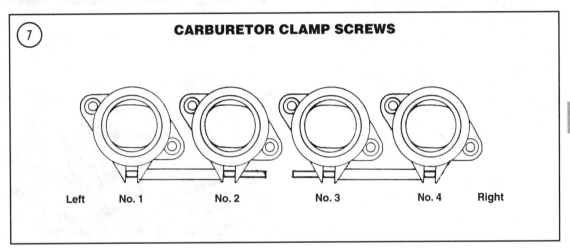

CARBURETOR CLAMP SCREWS

Left   No. 1   No. 2   No. 3   No. 4   Right

9. Disconnect the pull cable (B, **Figure 3**) from the throttle wheel on the carburetor and then disconnect the push cable (C, **Figure 3**). Disconnect each throttle cable from the bracket on the carburetor assembly. Move the cables out of the way.

10. On 1998-on models, disconnect the black electrical connector (A, **Figure 4**) from the left solenoid valve (for carb No. 2 and No. 3), and disconnect the white electrical connector (B, **Figure 4**) from the right solenoid valve (for carb No. 1 and No. 4).

11. Disconnect the electrical connector (**Figure 5**) from the throttle position sensor on the right side of the carburetor assembly.

12. On California models, disconnect the two evaporative emission hoses (**Figure 6**) from the fittings on the carburetor assembly.

NOTE
*Only two clamp screws secure the four carburetors to their respective intake manifolds. The outer screw secures the clamp on two adjacent intake manifolds. See **Figure 7**.*

13. On the right side, remove the cap from the frame, insert a long Phillips screwdriver (**Figure 8**) through the frame hole and loosen the clamp screw for the No. 3 and No. 4 carburetor intake manifolds.

14. On the left side, remove the cap from the frame, insert a long Phillips screwdriver through the frame

hole (**Figure 9**) and loosen the clamp screw for the No. 1 and No. 2 carburetor intake manifolds.

15. Lift the carburetor assembly straight up and free it from the cylinder head intake manifolds. Do not pull the assembly any farther than necessary. The choke cable is still connected to the carburetor assembly.

16. On the left side, disconnect the choke cable end (A, **Figure 10**) from the control linkage and release the cable elbow (B, **Figure 10**) from the carburetor assembly. Move the cable out of the way.

17. On U.K. models, unplug the electrical connector from each carburetor heater.

18. Check that all cables, hoses and electrical connectors are disconnected from the carburetor assembly. Remove the carburetor assembly.

19. Cover the intake manifolds with clean lint-free cloths (**Figure 11**) to prevent the entry of debris.

20. If any interconnecting hose (A, **Figure 12**) is disconnected during service, mark and label the hose and its fitting to ensure the hose will be reconnected to the correct fitting during assembly.

21. If the carburetor assembly is not going to be serviced, store it as follows:

  a. Attach a fuel line to the drain outlet (A, **Figure 13**) on each float bowl.

  b. Hold the carburetor assembly in its normal position.

  c. Open each drain screw (B, **Figure 13**) and drain the fuel from the float bowls into a suitable container. Dispose the fuel properly.

  d. Carefully and slowly shake the carburetor assembly to drain out as much fuel as possible.

  e. Close all four drain screws and remove the fuel hoses from the float bowl fittings.

  f. Place the carburetor assembly in a clean heavy-duty plastic bag and close it off to avoid moisture and debris contamination.

  g. Place the carburetor assembly, right side up, in a sturdy cardboard box. Set the box in a safe place away from any heating equipment or ignition source.

22. Install by reversing these removal steps.

  a. At the carburetor assembly, rotate the adjuster on each cable in either direction until the correct clearance shown in **Figure 14** is attained. Tighten the locknuts (A, **Figure 3**) securing each throttle cable to the mounting bracket.

  b. Adjust the throttle cables as described in Chapter Three.

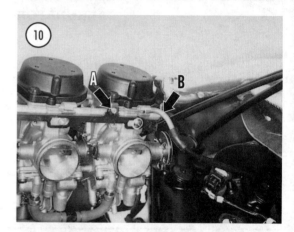

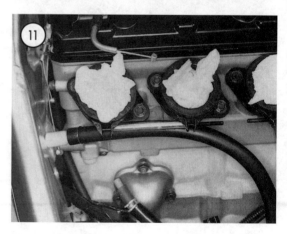

Carburetor Separation

The carburetors are joined by a lower mounting bracket and the inlet pipe holder plate. Almost all carburetor parts can be replaced without separating the carburetors. If the carburetors must be cleaned internally or if the pipe fittings must be replaced, separate the carburetors.

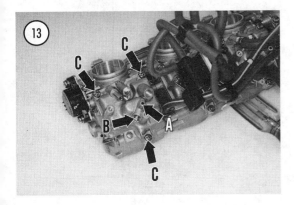

Refer to **Figure 15** for this procedure.

NOTE
The photographs in the following procedure show a carburetor assembly from a California model. The number of hoses and their fitting locations vary for carburetors found on other models.

1. Remove the carburetor assembly as described in this chapter.

2. Remove the two starter lever screws (A, **Figure 16**). Do not lose the washer behind each screw.

3. Carefully unhook the fingers of the starter lever from the starter plunger on each carburetor (B, **Figure 16**), and then remove the starter lever from the carburetor assembly.

4. Remove the upper carburetor connecting bolt (A, **Figure 17**) and lower carburetor connecting bolt (B, **Figure 17**).

5. Withdraw the carburetor connecting bolts, and remove the throttle cable bracket (C, **Figure 17**). Note the location of the spacers (**Figure 18**) on the

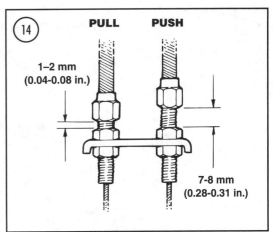

upper long bolt. Reinstall them in the correct location during assembly.

6. Remove the interconnecting hoses. Carefully mark and label each hose and its fitting while removing the hose. This ensures that each hose will be reconnected to the correct fitting during assembly. Refer to **Figure 19**.

7. Carefully pull the four carburetor bodies apart. Do not damage the control air hose.

8. Assemble the carburetors by reversing these removal steps while noting the following:

   a. Install new seals on the fuel hose connector set. Apply Suzuki Super Grease A (part No. 99000-25030) or equivalent to the seals before installing them.

   b. When assembling the carburetors, install the springs (A, **Figure 20**) and position the throttle levers (B, **Figure 20**) as shown.

   c. Place the carburetor outlet throats on a flat surface (piece of plate glass) to align the four carburetors.

   d. Carefully install the carburetor connecting bolts through the carburetor assemblies and spacers. Torque the carburetor connecting bolts to the specification in **Table 4**.

   e. Operate the starter lever and check for smooth operation.

Individual Carburetor Disassembly/Assembly

Refer to **Figure 21**.

To avoid accidentally mixing parts, disassemble, clean and reassemble one carburetor at a time.

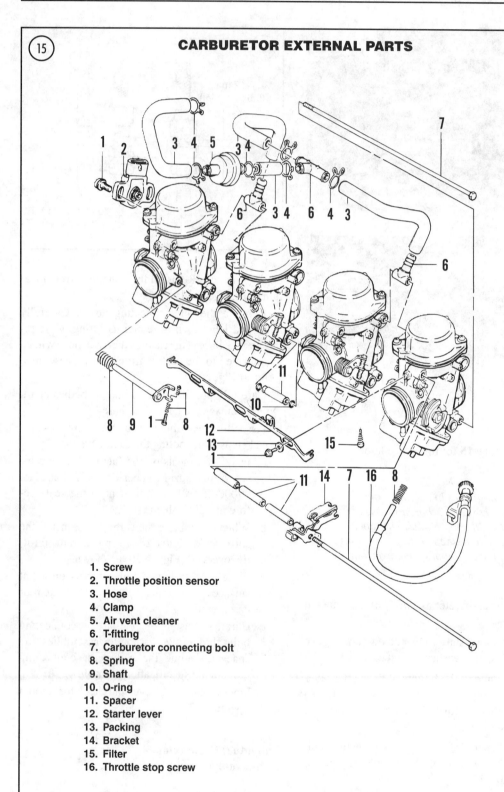

CARBURETOR EXTERNAL PARTS

1. Screw
2. Throttle position sensor
3. Hose
4. Clamp
5. Air vent cleaner
6. T-fitting
7. Carburetor connecting bolt
8. Spring
9. Shaft
10. O-ring
11. Spacer
12. Starter lever
13. Packing
14. Bracket
15. Filter
16. Throttle stop screw

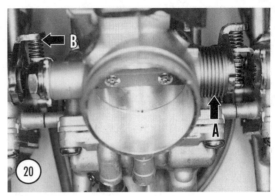

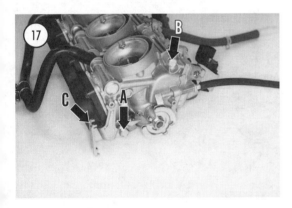

1. Remove the carburetor assembly as described in this chapter.

2. Disconnect the control air hoses (A, **Figure 22**) from their fittings on the carburetor assembly.

3. Remove the fuel hose (B, **Figure 22**), and remove the filter from the fuel hose fitting on the carburetor assembly.

4. Remove the two top cover screws (A, **Figure 23**) and the top cover (B, **Figure 23**).

5. Remove the spring (**Figure 24**) from the piston valve/diaphragm assembly, the piston valve/diaphragm (A, **Figure 25**) and the O-ring (B, **Figure 25**).

6. Turn the carburetor assembly over.

7. Remove the float bowl screws (C, **Figure 13**), and then remove the float bowl (A, **Figure 26**) and the float bowl O-ring (B, **Figure 26**).

8. Use needlenose pliers and carefully remove the float pivot pin (A, **Figure 27**) from the float and carburetor body.

9. Carefully pull straight up and remove the float assembly (B, **Figure 27**). Account for the needle valve (**Figure 28**) hanging from the float tang.

10. Unscrew and remove the main jet (**Figure 29**) and the main jet holder (**Figure 30**).

11. Unscrew and remove the pilot jet (A, **Figure 31**).

12. Remove the needle valve retaining screw (A, **Figure 32**), and then remove the needle valve (B, **Figure 32**).

13A. On U.S.A., California, Canada, Switzerland and Austria models, the pilot screw assembly is located under a plug (B, **Figure 31**) that is not to be removed. If removal is necessary, refer to *Pilot Screw* later in this chapter.

13B. On all other models, screw the pilot screw in until it *lightly seats* while counting and recording

CARBURETOR

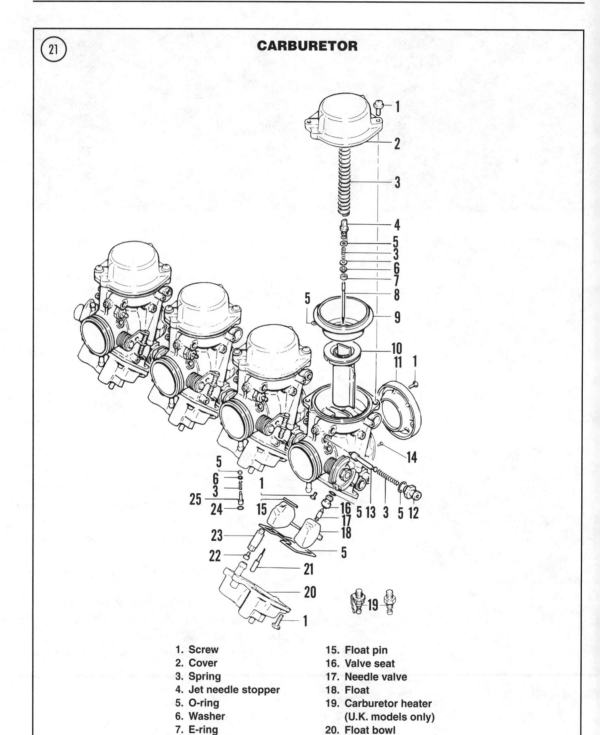

1. Screw
2. Cover
3. Spring
4. Jet needle stopper
5. O-ring
6. Washer
7. E-ring
8. Jet needle
9. Diaphragm
10. Piston valve
11. Funnel
12. Knob
13. Starter plunger
14. Pilot air jet
15. Float pin
16. Valve seat
17. Needle valve
18. Float
19. Carburetor heater
    (U.K. models only)
20. Float bowl
21. Pilot jet
22. Main jet
23. Main jet holder
24. Plug (U.S.A, California, Canada,
    Switzerland, and Austria models only
25. Pilot screw

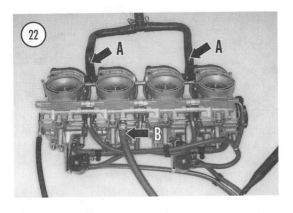

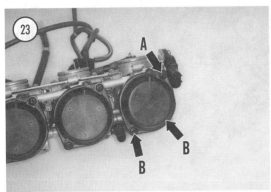

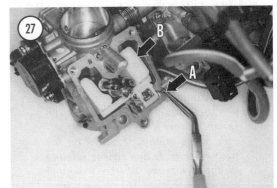

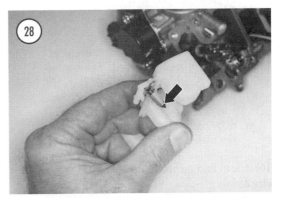

the number of turns. Reinstall the pilot screw to this same position during assembly. Unscrew and remove the pilot screw, spring, washer and O-ring.

14. To remove the pilot air jet, perform the following:

    a. Remove the screws (A, **Figure 33**) securing the funnel (B, **Figure 33**).

    b. Remove the funnel.

    c. Unscrew and remove the pilot air jet (C, **Figure 33**).

15. To disassemble the piston valve/diaphragm, perform the following:

    a. Using thin needlenose pliers, remove the jet needle stopper (**Figure 34**).

    b. Carefully remove the jet needle (**Figure 35**) from the piston valve.

NOTE
*The throttle position sensor (A, **Figure 36**) is preset by the manufacturer. Do not remove it. If removal is necessary, make alignment marks on the carburetor body and sensor relating to the centerline of the mounting screws (B, **Figure 36**) so the sensor can be installed in the **exact** same position.*

NOTE
*Further disassembly is neither necessary nor recommended. Do not remove the throttle shaft and butterfly assemblies (B, **Figure 12**). If these parts are damaged, replace the carburetor as these items are not available separately.*

16. Clean and inspect all parts as described in this chapter.

17. Assemble the carburetor by reversing these disassembly steps while noting the following:

    a. Make sure the washer and E-clip (**Figure 37**) are in place and installed on the jet needle.

    b. Position the jet needle stopper assembly with the spring end going in first (**Figure 34**). Push the stopper assembly down until it bottoms.

    c. Install the piston valve/diaphragm into the body, and seat it in the carburetor body. Make sure the small O-ring (B, **Figure 25**) is positioned correctly over the vent hole. Install the top cover, and torque the top-cover screws to the specification in **Table 4**.

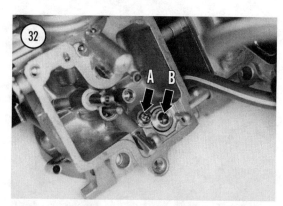

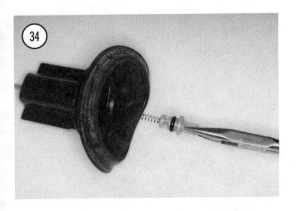

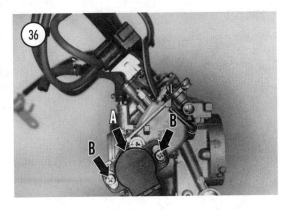

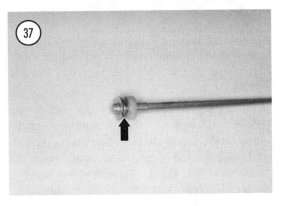

d. After the top cover has been installed, insert your finger through the venturi, and move the piston valve (D, **Figure 33**) up. The piston valve should slide back down immediately with no binding. If it binds or if the movement is sluggish, chances are the diaphragm did not seat correctly or is folded over. The diaphragm rubber is very soft and may fold over during spring and top cover installation.

e. When installing the float bowl, torque the float bowl screws to the specification in **Table 4**.

f. When installing the funnel, apply ThreeBond No. 1342 to the funnel screws, and torque the screws to the specification in **Table 4**.

g. Check and adjust the fuel level as described in this chapter.

h. After the assembly and installation are completed, adjust the carburetors as described in this chapter and in Chapter Three.

8

Cleaning and Inspection

> *CAUTION*
> *The carburetor bodies are equipped with plastic parts that cannot be removed. Do not dip the carburetor body, O-rings, float assembly, needle valve or piston valve/diaphragm into carburetor cleaner or other harsh solutions that can damage these parts. Suzuki does not recommend using a caustic carburetor cleaning solvent. Instead, clean the carburetors and related parts in a petroleum-based solvent or Simple Green. Then rinse in clean water.*

1. Initially clean all parts in a mild petroleum-based cleaning solution. Wash the parts in hot soap and water, and rinse them with cold water. Blow dry the parts with compressed air.

> *CAUTION*
> *If compressed air is not available, allow the parts to air dry or use a clean lint-free cloth. Do **not** use a paper towel to dry carburetor parts. The small paper particles could plug openings in the carburetor housing or jets.*

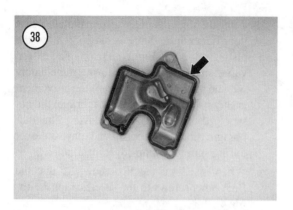

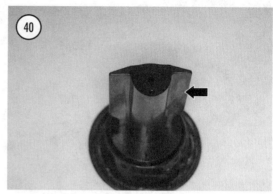

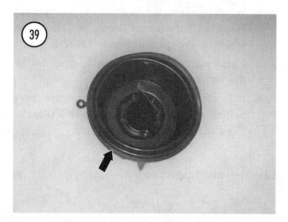

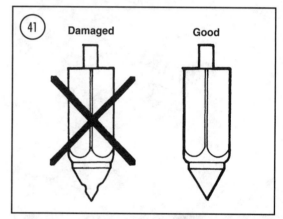

2. Allow the carburetors to dry thoroughly before assembly. Blow out the jets and the needle jet holder with compressed air.

> *CAUTION*
> *Do **not** use wire or drill bits to clean jets. Even minor gouges in the jet can alter flow rate and upset the air/fuel mixture.*

3. Inspect the float bowl O-ring gasket (**Figure 38**). Replace the O-ring if it has become hard or is starting to deteriorate.

4. Make sure the drain screw is in good condition and does not leak. Replace the drain screw if necessary.

5. Inspect the piston valve/diaphragm (**Figure 39**) for cracks, deterioration or other damage. Check the piston valve sides (**Figure 40**) for excessive wear. Install the piston valve into the carburetor body and move it up and down in the bore. The piston valve should move smoothly with no binding or excessive play. If there is excessive play, replace the piston valve and/or carburetor body.

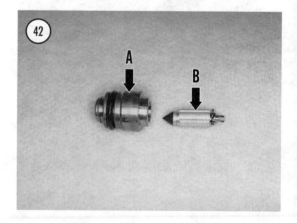

6. Inspect the needle valve tapered end for steps, uneven wear or other damage (**Figure 41**). Replace if damaged.

7. Inspect the needle valve seat (A, **Figure 42**) for steps, uneven wear or other damage. Inspect the O-ring on the needle valve for hardness or deterioration. Replace the O-ring as necessary. Insert the needle valve (B, **Figure 42**) and slowly move it back and forth checking for smooth operation. If ei-

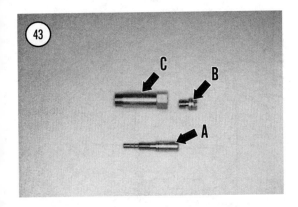

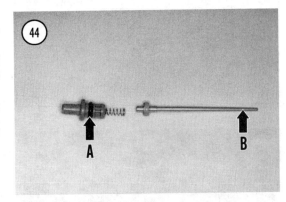

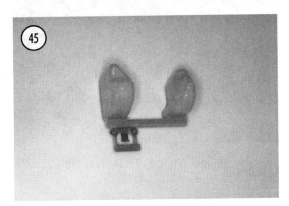

ther part is worn or damaged, replace both for maximum performance.

8. Inspect the pilot jet (A, **Figure 43**), main jet (B, **Figure 43**) and main jet holder (C, **Figure 43**). Make sure all holes are open and no part is worn or damaged. Replace worn parts.

9. Inspect the jet needle stopper assembly (A, **Figure 44**) for deterioration or damage. Check the small O-ring for deterioration, and replace it if necessary.

10. Inspect the jet needle tapered end (B, **Figure 44**) for steps, uneven wear or other damage. Replace if damaged.

11. If removed, inspect the pilot screw O-ring. Replace the O-ring if it has become hard or is deteriorating.

12. Inspect the float (**Figure 45**) for deterioration or damage. Place the float in a container of water and push it down. If the float sinks or if bubbles appear (indicating a leak), replace the float.

13. Make sure all openings in the carburetor housing are clear. Clean them out if they are plugged in any way, and then apply compressed air to all openings.

14. Check the top cover for cracks or damage, and replace it if necessary.

15. Make sure the throttle plate screws (B, **Figure 12**) are tight. Tighten if necessary.

16. Inspect the carburetor body for internal or external damage. If damaged, replace the carburetor assembly as the body cannot be replaced separately.

17. Move the throttle wheel (**Figure 46**) back and forth from stop-to-stop. The throttle lever should move smoothly and return under spring tension. If it does not move freely or if it sticks in any position, replace the carburetor housing.

PILOT SCREW

Removal/Installation
(U.S.A., California, Canada, Switzerland and Austria Models)

The pilot screws on these models are sealed. A plug has been installed at the top of the pilot screw bore to prevent tampering. The pilot screws do not require adjustment unless the carburetors are overhauled, the pilot screws are incorrectly adjusted, or if the pilot screws require replacement. The following procedure describes how to remove and install the pilot screws.

1. Set a stop 6 mm from the end of a 1/8 inch drill bit. See **Figure 47**.

2. Carefully drill a hole in the plug at the top of the pilot screw bore on the carburetor body as shown in **Figure 47**. Do not drill too deeply. The pilot screw will be difficult to remove if the head is damaged.

3. Screw a sheet metal screw into the plug, and pull the plug from the bore (B, **Figure 31**).

4. Screw the pilot screw in until it *lightly seats* while counting and recording the number of turns. Reinstall the pilot screw to the same position during assembly.

5. Remove the pilot screw, spring, washer and O-ring from the carburetor body.

6. Repeat for the other carburetors. Keep the components from each carburetor separate.

7. Inspect the O-ring and the end of the pilot screw. Replace the screw and/or O-ring if damaged or worn (grooved).

NOTE
*If the pilot screw was incorrectly adjusted, refer to the specifications in **Tables 1-3**.*

8. Install the pilot screws in the same position as noted during removal (Step 4) or to the specification listed in **Tables 1-3**.

9. Install new plugs by tapping them into place with a punch.

FUEL LEVEL

The fuel level in the carburetor float bowls is critical to performance. The fuel flow rate from the bowl up to the carburetor bore depends not only on the vacuum in the throttle bore and the size of the jets but also on the fuel level. Suzuki provides a specification for the fuel level measured from the top edge of the float bowl mounting screw boss on the carburetor body.

This measurement is more useful than a float height measurement because the actual fuel level can vary from carburetor-to-carburetor even when their floats are set at the same height. A fuel level gauge (Suzuki part No. 09913-10760) is required for this inspection procedure.

The fuel level is adjusted by bending the float arm tang in the proper direction.

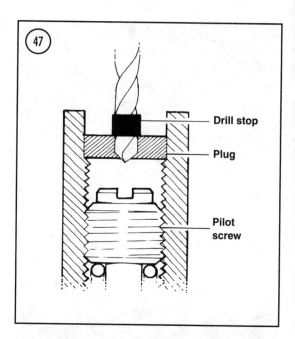

47

Drill stop

Plug

Pilot
screw

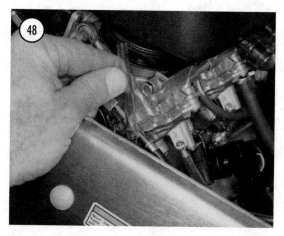

48

Inspection

Rough riding, a worn needle valve or bent float arm can cause the fuel level to change. To adjust the float level, perform the following.

WARNING
Some gasoline will drain from the carburetors during this procedure. Wipe up any spilled gasoline immediately. Work in a well-ventilated area at least 50 feet away from any open flame, including pilot lights in gas appliances. Do not allow anyone to smoke in the area.

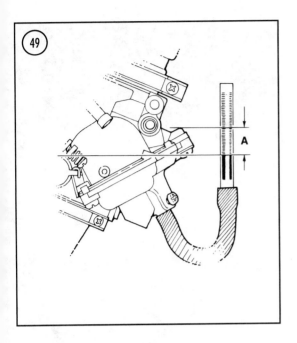

1. Check the tire pressure of both wheels as described in Chapter Three. If necessary, inflate the tires to the specified air pressure.

2. Securely support the bike in an upright position on *level ground*. Make sure the bike is in a true level position, front-to-back and side-to-side.

3. Raise and support the front of the fuel tank as described in this chapter.

4. Connect the fuel level gauge to the float bowl drain fitting on the No. 1 carburetor (**Figure 48**), and open the drain screw.

5. Hold the fuel level gauge against the carburetor so the top line is level with the mark on the carburetor (**Figure 49**).

6. Start the engine and let it run at idle speed for a few minutes.

7. Wait for the fuel in the gauge to settle. The fuel level on the gauge should equal the specification listed in **Tables 1-3**. Record the fuel level on the gauge and the carburetor number.

> *WARNING*
> *The engine is now hot and creates a potential fire hazard. Some gasoline will drain out when the fuel level gauge is removed from the float bowl. Place a shop cloth under the fuel level gauge to catch this fuel.*

8. Turn off the engine.

9. Close the drain screw and remove the fuel level gauge from the float bowl.

    a. If the fuel level is correct, repeat Steps 4-9 for the remaining carburetors.

    b. If the level is incorrect, adjust the float height as described in the following procedure.

10. If the fuel levels are within specification, lower the fuel tank and tighten the bolts securely.

11. Install the seats as described in Chapter Fifteen.

CARBURETOR FLOAT HEIGHT

Check and Adjustment

The needle valve and float maintain a constant fuel level in the carburetor float bowls. The carburetor assembly has to be removed and partially disassembled for this adjustment.

1. Remove the carburetor assembly as described in this chapter.

2. Remove the screws securing the float bowl (**Figure 50**) and remove the float bowl and the O-ring.

3. Hold the carburetor assembly so the float bowl mating surface is at a 45° angle to the workbench with the float arm just contacting the needle valve.

4. Measure the distance from the float bowl mating surface to the top of the float. The float height should be within the range specified in **Tables 1-3**. Record the float height and the carburetor number.

5. If the float height is incorrect, adjust it by performing the following:

    a. Use needle nose pliers and carefully remove the float pivot pin (A, **Figure 51**) from the float and carburetor body.

    b. Carefully pull straight up and remove the float assembly (B, **Figure 51**). Do not lose the needle valve (**Figure 28**) hanging on the float tang.

c. Carefully bend the float tang (**Figure 52**).

NOTE
Decreasing the float height raises the fuel level. Increasing the float height lowers the fuel level.

d. Install the needle valve onto the float tang and carefully install the float assembly straight down and into place on the carburetor body.

e. Install the float pivot pin and push it in until it is seated correctly.

6. Make sure the O-ring gasket is in place and correctly seats in the float bowl.

7. Install the float bowl and screws. Tighten the screws to the torque specification in **Table 4**.

THROTTLE POSITION SENSOR

Inspection/Adjustment

1. Remove the fuel tank as described in this chapter.

2. Disconnect the electrical connector (**Figure 53**) from the throttle position sensor.

3. Set an ohmmeter to the R × 1 K scale.

4. With the throttle lever fully closed, measure the resistance across the two outside terminals as shown in **Figure 54**. Record the measured value.

5. Compare the measurement to the fully closed resistance specified in **Table 5**.

   a. Replace the throttle position sensor if the resistance is outside the range specified in **Table 5**.

   b. If resistance is within specification, perform Step 6.

6. With the throttle lever in the wide open position, measure the wide open resistance across the two terminals as shown in **Figure 55**. Record this value.

7. Compare the wide open resistance to the fully closed resistance measured in Step 4.

   a. The wide open resistance should be 76 percent of the fully closed resistance. For example, if the fully closed resistance equals 5 K ohms, the wide open resistance should equal 3.8 K ohms (0.76 × 5 K = 3.8 K).

   b. If wide open resistance is not 76 percent of the fully closed resistance, remove the carburetor assembly as described in this chapter.

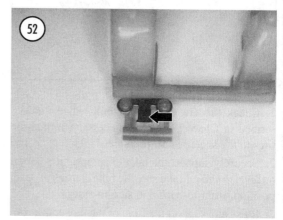

8. Loosen the throttle position sensor screws and slightly rotate the sensor. Repeat Step 7.

9. Continue adjusting the angle of the throttle position sensor until the wide-open resistance equals 76 percent of the fully closed resistance. When it does, tighten the throttle position sensor screws to the specification in **Table 4**.

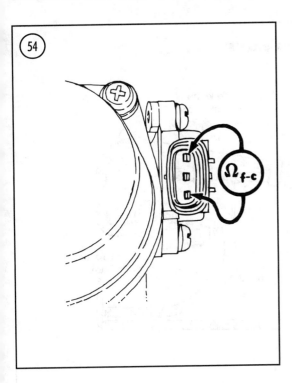

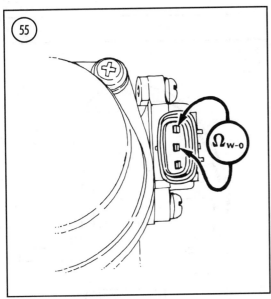

SOLENOID VALVE (1998-ON)

All 1998-on models are equipped with two solenoid valves that introduce additional air into the carburetors to provide optimum air/fuel mixture. Each solenoid valve controls the flow of air to two carburetors: The left valve (black connector) delivers air to carburetors No. 2 and No. 3. The right solenoid valve (white connector) provides additional air to carburetors No. 1 and No. 4. See **Figure 56**.

Removal/Installation

NOTE
The photographs show the carburetor assembly removed for clarity. The solenoid valves can be removed with the carburetors installed.

1. Remove the fuel tank as described in this chapter.
2. Disconnect the electrical connector from the solenoid valve.
3. Label the intake hose (A, **Figure 57**) and the output hose (B, **Figure 57**), and then remove them from the solenoid valve. Install these hoses onto the correct fittings during assembly.
4. Spread open the mounting tang on the solenoid valve, and lift the valve from the mounting bracket (C, **Figure 57**).
5. Installation is the reverse of removal. Make sure the hose from the air box (A, **Figure 57**) connects to the intake fitting on the solenoid valve and that the hose to the carburetor T-fitting (B, **Figure 57**) connects to the output fitting.

Inspection

1. Raise and support the fuel tank as described in this chapter.
2. Remove the electrical connector from the solenoid valve.
3. Use jumpers to momentarily apply battery voltage to the two electrical terminals on the solenoid valve (**Figure 58**). The solenoid should click when voltage is applied.
4. Reconnect the connector to the solenoid valve.
5. Repeat Steps 2-4 for the other solenoid valve.
6. Check the voltage of the left solenoid valve by performing the following:
   a. Backprobe the black connector and connect the voltmeter's positive test probe to the orange/white terminal and connect the negative test probe to the dark green terminal as shown in **Figure 59**.
   b. Start the engine and watch the voltmeter while gradually opening the throttle. The voltmeter reads battery voltage or higher

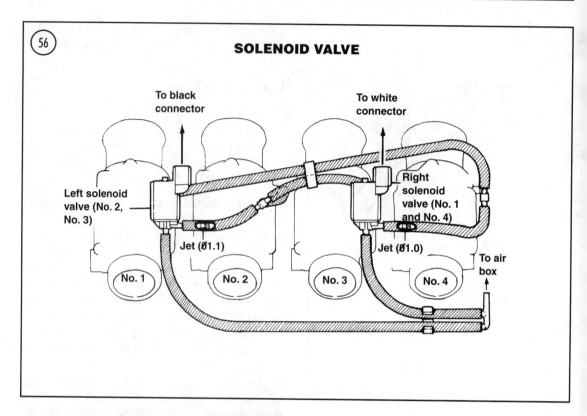

SOLENOID VALVE

To black connector

To white connector

Left solenoid valve (No. 2, No. 3)

Right solenoid valve (No. 1 and No. 4)

Jet (Ø1.1)

Jet (Ø1.0)

To air box

No. 1   No. 2   No. 3   No. 4

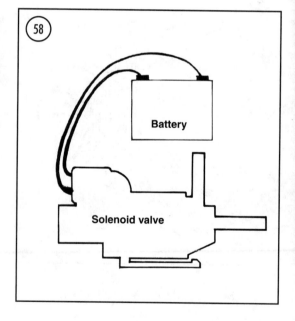

Battery

Solenoid valve

when the solenoid valve turns on, and it reads zero volts when the valve turns off. Note the engine speed when the solenoid valve turns on and off.

   c. Compare the test results to the specifications in **Table 5**.

7. Check the voltage of the right solenoid valve (for carburetors No. 1 and No. 4) by performing the following:

   a. Backprobe the white connector. Connect the voltmeter's positive test probe to the or-

ange/white terminal, and connect the negative test probe to the green terminal as shown in **Figure 60**.

   b. Start the engine and observe the voltmeter while gradually opening the throttle. The voltmeter reads battery voltage or higher

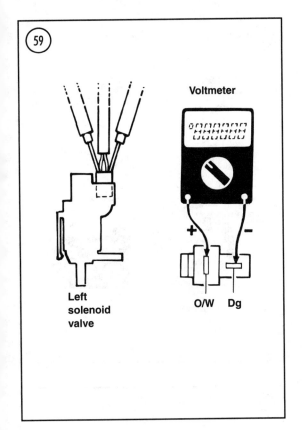

Left solenoid valve   O/W   Dg

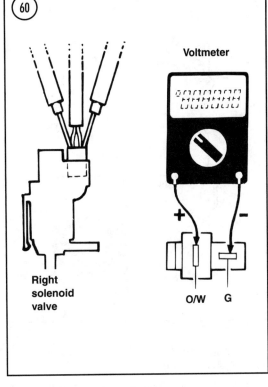

Right solenoid valve   O/W   G

8

when the solenoid valve turns on, and it reads zero volts when the valve turns off. Note the engine speed when the solenoid valve turns on and off.

8. Compare the test results to the specifications in **Table 5**.

   a. If both solenoid valves do not operate properly, check the electrical connectors and wiring between the solenoid valves and the CDI unit. If the wiring and connectors are acceptable, the CDI unit is probably defective. Have a Suzuki dealership test the unit.

   b. If one solenoid valve operates properly but the other does not, replace the defective solenoid valve.

CARBURETOR HEATER (U.K. MODELS)

Removal/Installation

1. Remove the fuel tank as described in this chapter.

2. Disconnect the electrical lead from the carburetor heater.

3. Unscrew and remove the carburetor heater from the bottom of the float bowl.

4. Repeat for the remaining carburetor heaters.

5. Installation is the reverse of removal. Note the following:

   a. Apply thermo grease (Suzuki part No. 99000-59029) to the tip of the carburetor heater.

   b. Torque the carburetor heater to the specification in **Table 4**.

Carburetor Heater Inspection

1. Remove the fuel tank as described in this chapter.

2. Disconnect the electrical lead from the carburetor heater on the bottom of the float bowl.

3. Check the resistance of the heater coil by performing the following:

   a. Set an ohmmeter to the R × 10 scale.

   b. Connect the ohmmeter negative test lead to the spade connector on the heater, and con-

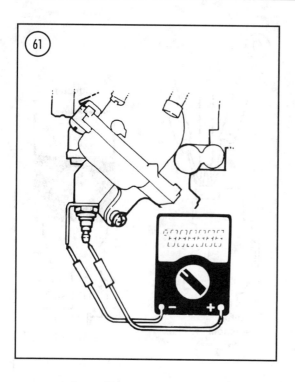

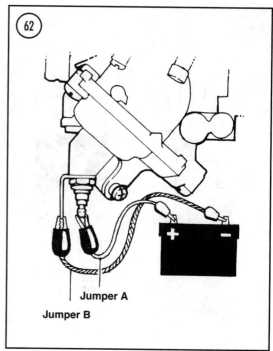

Jumper A

Jumper B

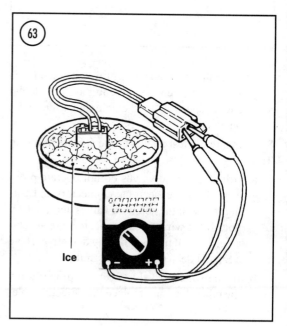

Ice

nect the positive test lead to the heater body as shown in **Figure 61**.

c. Replace the heater if the resistance is outside the range specified in **Table 5**.

> *CAUTION*
> *Electrical arcing may occur when connecting the jumpers in the following test. Connect the jumpers in the described order so any arcing takes place away from the carburetors.*

4. Use a battery to check the carburetor heater operation by performing the following:

a. Connect one end of jumper A to the battery positive terminal, and then connect the other end of jumper A to the carburetor body as shown in **Figure 62**.

b. Connect one end of jumper B to the spade connector on the carburetor heater, and then connect the other end of jumper B to the battery negative terminal.

> *CAUTION*
> *Do not touch the carburetor heater directly. It is hot.*

c. After 5 minutes, check the temperature of the float bowl by hand. It should be warm. Re-

place the carburetor heater if the float bowl does not heat up.

d. Disconnect the jumper B from the negative battery terminal and then from the carburetor heater. Then disconnect jumper A.

5. Repeat this test for the remaining carburetor heaters.

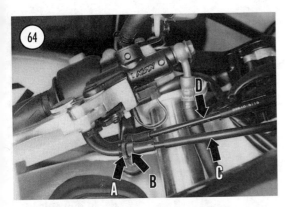

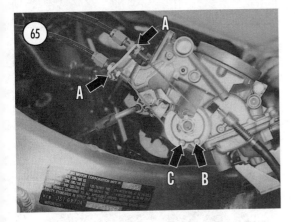

Carburetor Heater Thermo-Switch Inspection

1. Unplug the thermo-switch connector from the wiring harness.

2. Remove the thermo-switch and immerse it in a pan of ice.

3. After the switch has sat in the ice for approximately 5 minutes, check the continuity across the two terminals in the thermo-switch connector **Figure 63**.

4. The chilled switch should have zero or very low resistance. Replace the switch if it has infinite or very high resistance.

THROTTLE CABLE REPLACEMENT

NOTE
There are two throttle cables, one is the pull cable (accelerate) and the other is the push cable (decelerate). These cables must be reinstalled in the correct position on the carburetor and connected to the correct position on the throttle grip wheel.

1. Securely support the bike on level ground.

2. Remove the seat as described in Chapter Fifteen.

3. Remove each lower fairing side panel as described in Chapter Fifteen.

4. Disconnect the negative battery cable as described in Chapter Three.

5. Remove the fuel tank as described in this chapter.

6. Remove the air box as described in this chapter.

7. At the throttle grip, loosen the throttle cable locknut (A, **Figure 64**) and turn the adjuster (B, **Figure 64**) all the way into the switch assembly to allow maximum slack in the pull cable (C, **Figure 64**). Repeat this procedure for the push cable (D, **Figure 64**).

8. Remove the screws securing the right switch assembly together and separate the assembly halves.

9. Disconnect the throttle pull cable and disconnect the throttle push cable from the throttle grip.

NOTE
*In **Figure 65**, the carburetor assembly has been partially removed for photographic clarity. It is not necessary to remove the carburetor assembly to access the throttle wheel.*

10. At the carburetor assembly, loosen both locknuts (A, **Figure 65**) securing each throttle cable to the mounting bracket.

11. Disconnect the pull cable (B, **Figure 65**) from the throttle wheel on the carburetor and then disconnect the push cable (C, **Figure 65**). Disconnect each throttle cable from the bracket on the carburetor assembly. Move the cables out of the way.

12. Disconnect the throttle cable from any clips and/or cable ties that secure it to the frame.

13. Note how the cable is routed through the frame, and then remove it.

14. Lubricate the new cable as described in Chapter Three. Route the new cable along the same path noted in Step 13.

15. Reverse Steps 1-12 to install the new cables while noting the following:

    a. Connect the throttle push cable, then the pull cable onto the throttle grip and switch housing.

    b. Align the locating pin with the hole in the handlebar and install the switch onto the handlebar. Tighten the screws securely.

8

c. Connect the throttle pull cable (B, **Figure 65**) onto the front receptacle in the throttle wheel on the carburetor, and then install the push cable (C, **Figure 65**) from the rear receptacle in the throttle wheel on the carburetor.

d. Operate the throttle lever and make sure the carburetor throttle linkage is operating correctly with no binding. If operation is incorrect or there is binding, carefully check that the cables are attached correctly and there are no tight bends in either cable.

e. At the carburetor assembly, rotate the adjuster on each cable in either direction until the clearance shown in **Figure 66** is attained. Tighten the locknuts (A, **Figure 65**) securing each throttle cable to the mounting bracket.

f. Adjust the throttle cables as described in Chapter Three.

> *WARNING*
> *An improperly adjusted or incorrectly routed throttle cable can cause the throttle to hang open. This could cause a crash. Do not ride the vehicle until the throttle cable operation is correct.*

g. Start the engine and let it idle. Turn the handlebar from side to side and listen to the engine speed. Make sure the idle speed does not increase. If it does, the throttle cables are adjusted incorrectly or the throttle cable(s) is improperly routed. Find and correct the source of the problem before riding.

STARTER CABLE REPLACEMENT

1. Securely support the bike on level ground.
2. Remove the seat, and the lower and upper fairing assemblies as described in Chapter Fifteen.
3. Disconnect the negative battery cable as described in Chapter Three.
4. Remove the fuel tank as described in this chapter.
5. Remove the screws securing the left switch assembly (**Figure 67**) and separate the assembly halves.
6. Disconnect the starter lever and cable from the switch housing. Disconnect the starter cable end from the lever.
7. Remove the air box as described in this chapter.

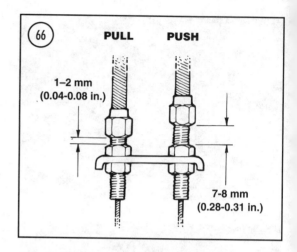

8. Partially remove the carburetor assembly to gain access to the choke cable as described in this chapter.
9. On the left side, disconnect the choke cable end from the control linkage (A, **Figure 68**) and release the cable elbow (B, **Figure 68**) from the carburetor assembly. Move the cable out of the way.
10. Disconnect the starter cable from any clips and/or cable ties securing it to the frame.
11. Note the path the starter cable follows through the frame. The new cable will have to be routed along the same path.
12. Lubricate the new cable as described in Chapter Three.
13. Reverse Steps 1-11 to install the new cable while noting the following:

a. Connect the cable and choke lever to the switch housing.

b. Align the switch housing locating pin with the hole in the handlebar and fit the switch in place on the handlebar. Tighten the screws securely.

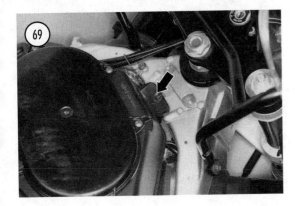

c. Operate the choke lever and make sure the link is operating correctly without binding. If the operation is incorrect or there is binding, carefully check that the cable is attached correctly and that there are no tight bends in the cable.

d. Start the engine and let it idle. Then turn the handlebar from side to side and listen to the engine. The engine speed should not increase when turning the handlebars. If it does, the cable is improperly routed. Correct the problem before riding.

AIR BOX

The air box is located under the fuel tank.

Removal/Installation

1. Securely support the bike on level ground.

2. Disconnect the negative battery cable as described in Chapter Three.

3. Remove the seat as described in Chapter Fifteen.

4. Remove the fuel tank as described in this chapter.

5. Remove the front bolt (**Figure 69**) securing the air box to the frame.

NOTE
Label each hose and its air-box fitting so the hose can be easily identified and reinstalled onto the correct fitting during assembly. The Lisle Vacuum Hose Identifiers (part No. 74600) were used to identify the components in the photographs. These color-coded plugs fit into the hoses and their related fittings for easy hose and fitting identification. They also plug the hoses and fittings so debris cannot enter.

6. Disconnect the crankcase ventilation hose (A, **Figure 70**) from the air box.

NOTE
The following models are equipped with the PAIR (air supply) system: all California models (1997-on), and 1999-on U.S., Canada, Austria and Switzerland models.

7. On models with a PAIR system, disconnect the PAIR cleaner hose (B, **Figure 70**) from the air box.

8. On 1998-on models, disconnect the control air hose (C, **Figure 70**) from the right side of the air box.

9. Loosen the screw (**Figure 71**) on each carburetor clamp.

10. Pull the air box straight up and off the carburetor assembly. Once the air box is free of the carburetors, move it rearward.

8

11. Disconnect the carburetor air vent hose (**Figure 72**) from the air box.

12. Remove the air box from the engine and frame.

13. Plug the carburetor inlets (**Figure 73**) to prevent debris from entering the carburetors.

14. Inspect the air box and the air inlet ducts (A, **Figure 74**) for cracks, wear or damage. If any damage is noted, replace the air box to avoid the possibility of unfiltered air entering the engine.

15. Inspect the air box-to-carburetor insulators (B, **Figure 74**) for hardness, deterioration or damage. Replace them as necessary.

16. Remove the drain plug (**Figure 75**) and clean out all residue from the plug and air box. Reinstall the drain plug.

17. Install by reversing the removal steps. Note the following:

   a. Make sure the lower section of the air box is correctly seated on each carburetor, and then securely tighten the screw (**Figure 71**) on each carburetor clamp. This prevents unfiltered air from entering the carburetors and causing engine damage.

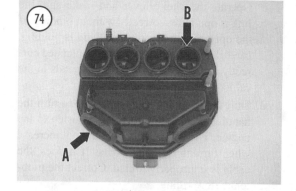

FUEL TANK

Raising/Supporting the Fuel Tank

1. Remove the seats as described in Chapter Fifteen.

2. Remove the fuel tank mounting bolts (**Figure 76**) from the front of the fuel tank.

3. Remove the fuel tank stay (**Figure 77**) from the tray under the rear seat.

4. Raise the front of the fuel tank, insert the crank end of the tank stay into the steering stem and insert

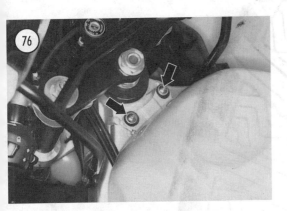

*sparks. Do not smoke or allow some-
one who is smoking in the work area.
Always work in a well ventilated area.
Wipe up any spills immediately.*

1. Securely support the bike on level ground.
2. Remove the seats as described in Chapter Fifteen.
3. Disconnect the negative battery cable as described in Chapter Three.
4. Remove the fuel tank mounting bolts (**Figure 76**) from the front of the tank.
5. Remove the fuel tank stay (**Figure 77**) from the tray under the rear seat.
6. Raise the front of the fuel tank, insert the crank end of the tank stay into the steering stem and insert the other end into one of the fuel tank mounts (**Figure 78**).
7. Disconnect the 4-pin fuel pump connector (**Figure 79**).

NOTE
Label the hoses and their fittings during removal so each hose can be installed on the correct fitting during assembly.

the other end into one of the fuel tank mounts (**Figure 78**).

Removal/Installation

WARNING
Some fuel may spill from the fuel tank hose when performing this procedure. Because gasoline is extremely flammable and explosive, perform this procedure away from all open flames (including appliance pilot lights) and

8. Disconnect the fuel hose (A, **Figure 80**) and the vacuum hose (B, **Figure 80**) from the fuel valve.
9. Disconnect the water drain hose (**Figure 81**) from the fitting on the right side of the tank.
10A. Disconnect the fuel tank breather hose from the fitting on the tank.
10B. On California models, disconnect the breather hose (A, **Figure 82**) from the rollover valve (B, **Figure 82**) on the left side of the fuel tank.
11. Remove the rear frame cover as described in Chapter Fifteen.

12. Remove the two bolts (**Figure 83**) securing the tank mounting bracket to the frame.

13. Note how the fuel tank breather and water hoses are routed through the frame. Reroute them along the same paths during assembly.

14. Carefully lift the fuel tank up and remove it from the frame. After the fuel tank has been inspected and serviced (if necessary), wrap the tank in a blanket or soft towels to protect the finish. Place the wrapped tank in a cardboard box, and store it in an area where it will not be damaged.

15. Plug the end of the fuel lines and vacuum lines with golf tees to prevent the entry of debris and loss of fuel from the hose.

16. Inspect the fuel tank as described in this chapter.

17. Install by reversing these removal steps while noting the following:

    a. Make sure to reconnect the fuel hose (A, **Figure 80**), vacuum hose (B, **Figure 80**) and water drain hose (**Figure 81**) to the correct fittings.

    b. On California models, connect the EVAP breather hose (A, **Figure 82**) to the fitting on the rollover valve (B, **Figure 82**).

    c. Check for fuel leakage at all hose connections after installation is completed.

    d. Tighten the fuel tank mounting bolts securely.

Inspection

1. Inspect the front rubber grommets on the mounting bracket for deterioration. Replace the grommets if necessary.

2. Inspect the rubber cushions and the vinyl trim strips for damage or deterioration, and replace if necessary.

3. Check the fittings (A, **Figure 84**) on the rear of the fuel tank for damage.

4. On California models, check the fitting on the rollover valve (B, **Figure 84**) for signs of damage.

5. Inspect the filler cap gaskets. If the cap gasket is damaged or deteriorating, replace the filler cap assembly. The gasket cannot be replaced separately. If the mounting flange gasket is damaged, replace it.

6. To remove the fuel filler cap, remove the screws and the filler cap assembly. Install the new filler cap and tighten the screws securely.

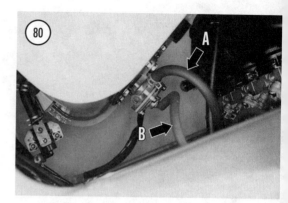

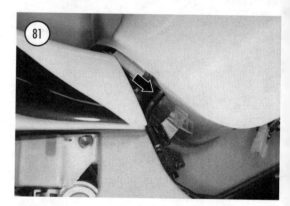

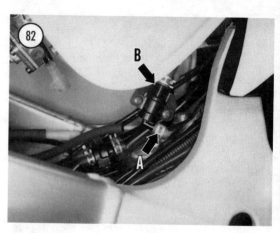

7. Inspect the entire fuel tank for leaks or damage. Repair or replace the fuel tank if any fuel leakage is found.

FUEL VALVE

Removal/Installation

1. Remove the fuel tank as described in this chapter. If not already drained, drain the tank and store

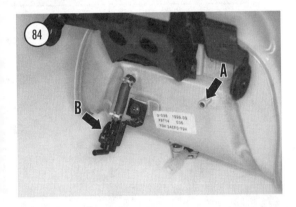

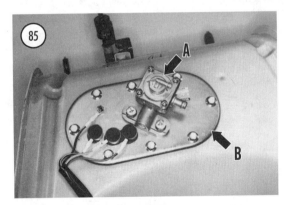

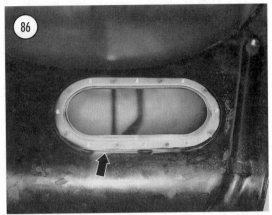

6. Fit a new O-ring seal onto the valve, and install the valve onto the base of the fuel pump. Tighten the screws securely.

7. Install the fuel tank as described in this chapter.

8. Check for fuel leakage at all hose connections after installation is completed.

8

FUEL PUMP AND FUEL FILTER

Removal/Installation

The fuel pump and fuel filter are attached to the fuel tank.

1. Remove the fuel tank as described in this chapter. If not already drained, completely drain the tank and store the fuel in an approved gasoline storage container. Place the container in a safe place.

2. Place several old blankets or soft towels on the workbench to protect the fuel tank finish.

3. Turn the fuel tank upside down on the workbench.

4. Remove the screws securing the fuel pump and fuel filter assembly (B, **Figure 85**) to the fuel tank.

5. Carefully withdraw the fuel pump and fuel filter assembly up and out of the fuel tank.

6. Remove the gasket. A new gasket must be installed every time the fuel pump and fuel filter assembly are removed.

7. Clean all gasket material and dirt from the gasket mating surface on the fuel tank (**Figure 86**).

8. Correctly align the bolt holes and install the *new* gasket (**Figure 87**) onto the fuel tank.

9. Install the fuel pump and fuel filter assembly onto the gasket as shown in **Figure 85**.

10. Install the mounting bolts.

the fuel in a can approved for gasoline storage. Place the container in a safe place.

2. Place several old blankets or soft towels on the work bench to protect the fuel tank.

3. Turn the fuel tank upside down on the work bench.

4. Remove the screws and washers securing the fuel valve (A, **Figure 85**) to the base of the fuel pump (B, **Figure 85**).

5. Remove the valve and the O-ring. Discard the O-ring seal. Install a new O-ring during assembly.

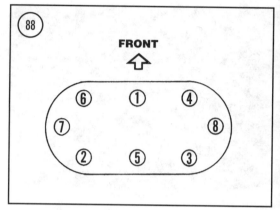

11. Hand-tighten the bolts in the sequence shown in **Figure 88** and then torque them to the specification in **Table 4**.

12. Partially refill the fuel tank and check for leakage. Correct any leaks at this time.

13. Install the fuel tank as described in this chapter.

Disassembly/Assembly

1. Remove the fuel pump and fuel filter assembly as previously described in this chapter.

2. Remove the fuel filter (A, **Figure 89**) from the fuel pump. Clean the filter with low pressure compressed air to remove any sediment and rust. Inspect the filter for any broken areas. Replace it as necessary.

3. Label all wires and connectors so they can be reinstalled in their original locations during assembly.

4. Remove the fuel-level-indicator switch from the base plate by performing the following:

    a. Disconnect the switch's two electrical leads (A, **Figure 90**).

    b. Remove the two mounting nuts (B, **Figure 90**) and lift the fuel-level-indicator switch from the base plate.

5. Remove the fuel pump from the base plate by performing the following:

    a. Remove the fuel pump electrical lead (C, **Figure 90**).

    b. Remove the mounting nut (D, **Figure 90**) and lift the fuel pump from the base plate.

6. Installation is the reverse of removal. Note the following:

    a. Make sure the hole on the filter side of the fuel pump assembly engages the indexing pin (B, **Figure 89**) on the base plate.

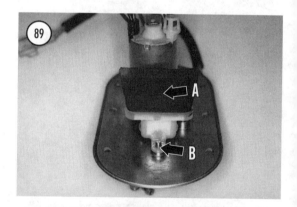

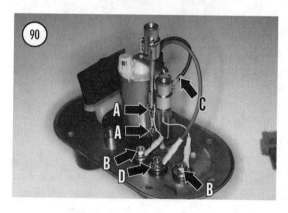

    b. Tighten the nuts securely and reconnect the electrical connectors.

7. Install the fuel pump and fuel filter assembly as previously described in this chapter.

PAIR (AIR SUPPLY) SYSTEM

The GSX-R600 PAIR system lowers emissions output by introducing secondary air into the exhaust ports. The introduction of air raises the exhaust tem-

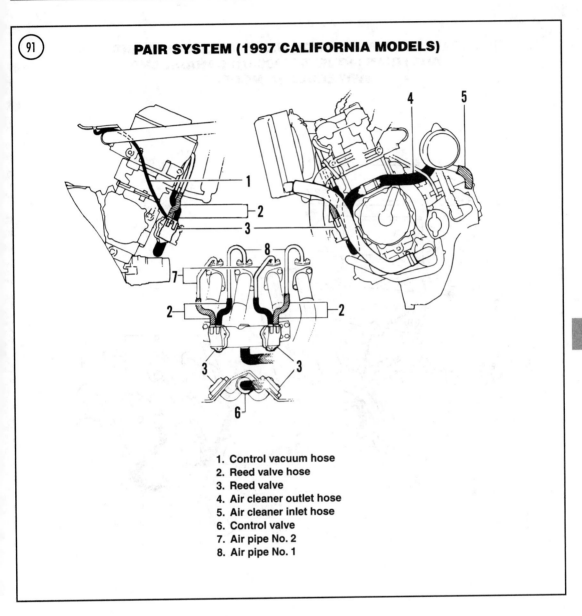

PAIR SYSTEM (1997 CALIFORNIA MODELS)

1. Control vacuum hose
2. Reed valve hose
3. Reed valve
4. Air cleaner outlet hose
5. Air cleaner inlet hose
6. Control valve
7. Air pipe No. 2
8. Air pipe No. 1

perature, which consumes some of the unburned fuel in the exhaust.

The PAIR system on 1997 California models consists of a control valve, two reed valves, an air cleaner, and the vacuum and outlet hoses (**Figure 91**).

The system on 1998-on California and 1999-on U.S., Canada, Austria and Switzerland models consists of two reed valves, PAIR air cleaner, and a control valve combined into a single PAIR valve assembly (**Figure 92**).

These systems use the momentary pressure variations created by the exhaust gas pulses to introduce additional air into the exhaust ports. During deceleration the control valve shuts off the airflow to the exhaust. This prevents exhaust backfire due to the rich mixture conditions on deceleration.

Removal/Installation
(1997-ON California Models, 1999-on U.S., Canada, Austria and Switzerland Models)

1. Remove the lower fairing side panels as described in Chapter Fifteen.
2. Remove the radiator as described in Chapter Ten.

92

PAIR SYSTEM (1998-ON U.S.A., CALIFORNIA AND AUSTRIAN MODELS, 1999-ON CANADA AND SWITZERLAND MODELS)

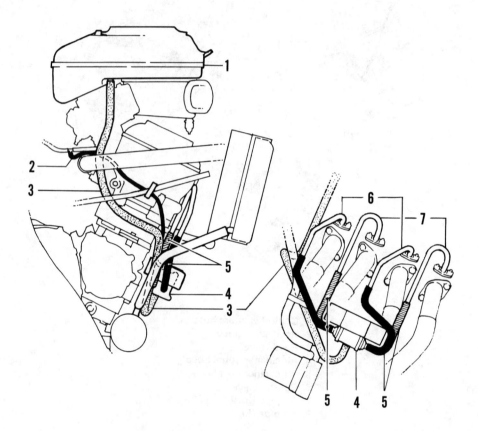

1. Air box
2. Vacuum hose
3. Air cleaner hose
4. Control valve
5. Control valve hose
6. Air pipe No. 2
7. Air pipe No. 1

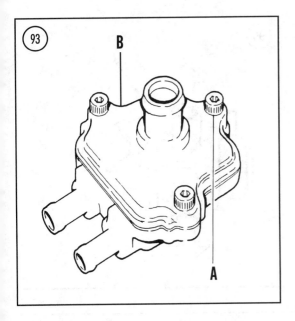

3. Remove the exhaust system as described in Chapter Four.

4. To remove only the hoses, loosen the hose clamps and disconnect the hose(s) from the fittings on the reed valve and the air pipe.

5A. On 1997 California models, remove the reed valve(s) by performing the following:
   a. Remove the screws securing the reed valve to the mounting bracket.
   b. Disconnect the control valve hose from the backside of the reed valve.
   c. Disconnect the reed valve hoses from the reed valve and remove the reed valve.
   d. Repeat for the other reed valve if necessary.
   e. Install by reversing these removal steps.

5B. On 1998-on California models and 1999-on U.S., Canada, Austria and Switzerland models; remove the PAIR valve assembly by performing the following:
   a. Disconnect the PAIR vacuum hose from the fitting on the top of the control valve.
   b. Disconnect the PAIR cleaner hose from the lower fitting on the control valve.
   c. Disconnect the four PAIR valve hoses from the outlets on each reed valve.
   d. Remove the two mounting screws, and lower the PAIR valve assembly from the mounting bracket.
   e. Lower the reed valve from the mounting bracket.
   f. Install by reversing these removal steps.

6. To remove the air pipe(s), perform the following:
   a. Disconnect the PAIR valve hose from the lower end of the air pipe.
   b. Remove the nuts securing the air pipe to the cylinder head.
   c. Remove the air pipe and gasket. Discard the gasket. Install a new one during assembly.
   d. Install by reversing these removal steps. Install a new gasket and tighten the nuts securely.

7. Install the exhaust system as described in Chapter Four.

8. Install the radiator as described in Chapter Ten.

9. Install the lower fairing side panels as described in Chapter Fifteen.

Inspection
(1997 California Models)

1. Inspect the reed valve by performing the following:
   a. Remove the cover screws (A, **Figure 93**) from the reed valve, and remove the cover (B).
   b. Remove the reed valve from the reed-valve body (**Figure 94**).
   c. Inspect the reed valve for carbon deposits. Replace the reed valve if deposits are found.
   d. Repeat Steps 1-3 for the other reed valve.

2. Inspect the control valve by performing the following:
   a. Blow air into the inlet port on the bottom of the control valve (**Figure 95**).
   b. Air should flow from the two control-valve outlet ports. Replace the control valve if it does not.
   c. Connect a vacuum pump to the vacuum fitting on the top of the control valve. See **Figure 96**.

> *CAUTION*
> *Vacuum pressure applied in the following step should not exceed the value specified in **Table 5**. The control valve could be damaged if excessive vacuum is applied.*

   d. Slowly apply vacuum to the control valve until the vacuum pressure is within the range specified in **Table 5**.

8

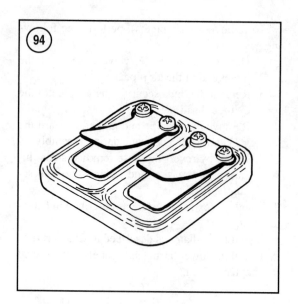

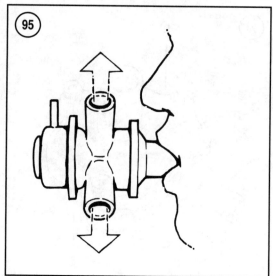

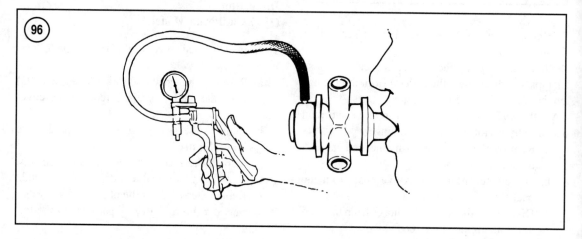

e. Blow into the control valve inlet port. Air should not flow from the outlet ports when the applied vacuum is within the vacuum pressure range specified in **Table 5**. If it does, replace the control valve.

Inspection
(1998-On California Models; 1999-On U.S., Canada, Austria and Switzerland Models)

1. Inspect the reed valve by performing the following:
   a. Remove the cover screws (A, **Figure 97**) from the reed valve, and remove the cover (B, **Figure 97**).
   b. Remove the reed valve (**Figure 94**) from the reed-valve body.

c. Inspect the reed valve for carbon deposits. Replace the reed valve if there are deposits.

d. Repeat Steps 1-3 for the other reed valve.

2. Inspect the control valve by performing the following:
   a. Blow air into the inlet port on the bottom of the control valve (**Figure 98**).
   b. Air should flow from the control-valve outlet ports. Replace the control valve if it does not.
   c. Connect a vacuum pump to the vacuum fitting on the top of the control valve. See **Figure 99**.

CAUTION
*Vacuum pressure applied in the following step should not exceed the value specified in **Table 5**. The control*

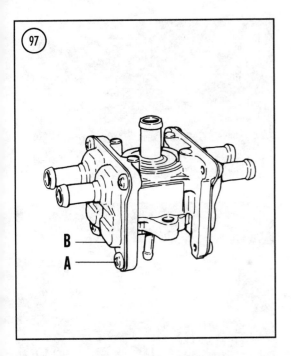

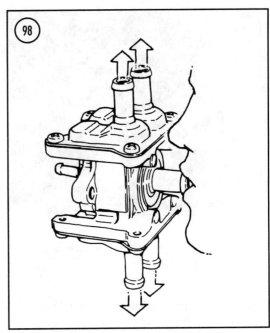

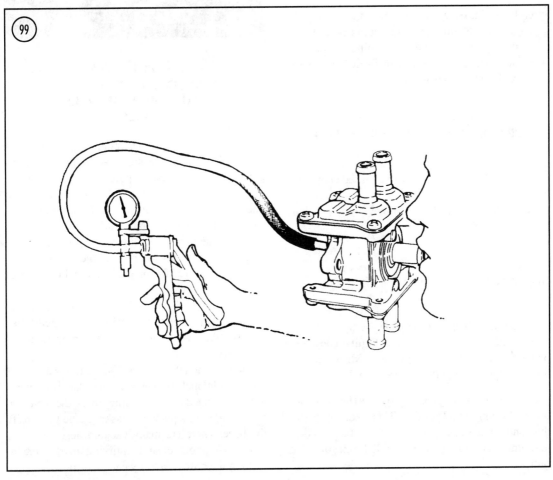

8

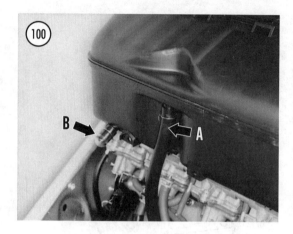

valve could be damaged if excessive vacuum is applied.

d. Slowly apply vacuum to the control valve until the vacuum pressure is within the range specified in **Table 5**.

e. Blow into the control valve inlet port. Air should not flow from the outlet ports when the applied vacuum is within the vacuum pressure range specified in **Table 5**. If it does, replace the control valve.

CRANKCASE BREATHER SYSTEM

All models are equipped with a closed crankcase breather system. This system routes crankcase vapors into the air box, and then they are drawn into the engine and burned.

Inspection and Cleaning

Inspect the breather hose from the upper crankcase to the air filter air box (A, **Figure 100**). Replace if it is cracked or deteriorated. Make sure the hose clamps are in place and are tight.

Remove the drain plug (B, **Figure 100**) from air box and drain out all residue. This cleaning procedure should be done more frequently if a considerable amount of riding is done at full throttle or in the rain.

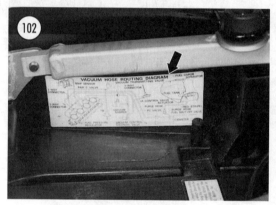

EVAPORATIVE EMISSION CONTROL SYSTEM (CALIFORNIA MODELS ONLY)

This system collects fuel system vapors in a charcoal canister when the engine is off. When the engine is started these vapors are routed to the carburetors, mixed with the intake charge and burned. The charcoal canister (A, **Figure 101**) is located on the right rear frame rail.

Due to the various manufacturing changes made during the years, always refer to the emission control label (**Figure 102**) on the inside right surface of the rear frame cover.

Make sure the hoses (B, **Figure 101**) are correctly routed and attached to the various components. See **Figure 103**. Inspect the hoses and replace any if necessary.

On most models, the hoses and fittings are color coded with labels or bands. If these labels or bands are deteriorated or are missing, mark the hose and the fitting with a piece of masking tape to identify the hose. There are many vacuum hoses on these models. Without clear identifying marks, reconnecting the hoses correctly can be difficult.

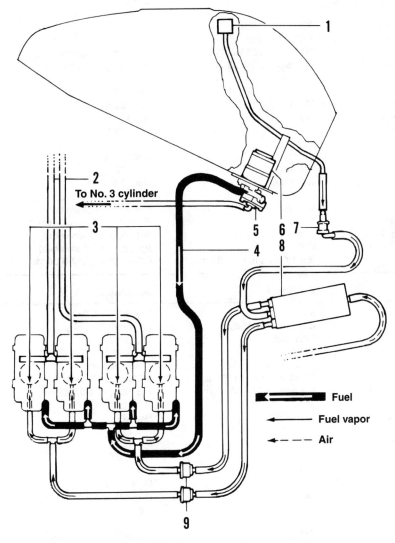

EVAPORATIVE EMISSION CONTROL SYSTEM (CALIFORNIA MODELS)

To No. 3 cylinder

→ Fuel
← Fuel vapor
←--- Air

1. Fuel-vapor separator
2. Air vent hose
3. Purge port
4. Fuel hose
5. Fuel valve
6. Fuel pump
7. Rollover valve
8. Canister
9. Purge control valve

Table 1 CARBURETOR SPECIFICATIONS (1997 MODELS)

Item	U.S.A., Switzerland, Canada, Austria	Belgium, France, Netherlands, Italy, Spain, U.K.
Carburetor model	Mikuni BDSR36	Mikuni BDSR36
Carburetor type	Constant velocity	Constant velocity
Bore size	36.5 mm	36.5 mm
Carburetor I.D.	34E1	34E0
Idle speed	–	1100-1300 rpm
U.S.A., Canada, Austria	1200-1400 rpm	–
Switzerland	1250-1400 rpm	–
Fuel level	15-16 mm (0.59-0.63 in.)	15-16 mm (0.59-0.63 in.)
Float height	6-8 mm (0.24-0.32 in.)	6-8 mm (0.24-0.32 in.)
Main jet		
Carburetor No. 1	No. 125	No. 125
Carburetor No. 2	No. 122.5	No. 122.5
Carburetor No. 3	No. 122.5	No. 122.5
Carburetor No. 4	No. 125	No. 122.5
Needle jet	P-0M	P-0
Jet needle	5DH20-53	5DH18-52-3
Throttle valve	No. 100	No. 100
Pilot jet	No. 12.5	No. 12.5
Pilot screw		
Carburetor No. 1	Preset	Preset (3 1/2 turns out)
Carburetor No. 2	Preset	Preset (2 1/2 turns out)
Carburetor No. 3	Preset	Preset (2 1/2 turns out)
Carburetor No. 4	Preset	Preset (3 1/2 turns out)
Throttle cable free play	0.5-1.0 mm (0.02-0.04 in.)	0.5-1.0 mm (0.02-0.04 in.)

Item	California	Australia
Carburetor model	Mikuni BDSR36	Mikuni BDSR36
Carburetor type	Constant velocity	Constant velocity
Bore size	36.5 mm	36.5 mm
Carburetor I.D.	34E3	34E4
Idle speed	1200-1400 rpm	1100-1300 rpm
Fuel level	15-16 mm (0.59-0.63 in.)	15-16 mm (0.59-0.63 in.)
Float height	6-8 mm (0.24-0.32 in.)	6-8 mm (0.24-0.32 in.)
Main jet		
Carburetor No. 1	No. 125	No. 125
Carburetor No. 2	No. 122.5	No. 122.5
Carburetor No. 3	No. 122.5	No. 122.5
Carburetor No. 4	No. 125	No. 122.5
Needle jet	P-0M	P-0
Jet needle	5DH20-53	5DH18-52-3
Throttle valve	No. 100	No. 100
Pilot jet	No. 12.5	No. 12.5
Pilot screw		
Carburetor No. 1	Preset	Preset (3 1/4 turns out)
Carburetor No. 2	Preset	Preset (2 1/4 turns out)
Carburetor No. 3	Preset	Preset (2 1/4 turns out)
Carburetor No. 4	Preset	Preset (3 1/4 turns out)
Throttle cable free play	0.5-1.0 mm (0.02-0.04 in.)	0.5-1.0 mm (0.02-0.04 in.)

Item	Brazil	Sweden, Finland, Norway, Germany
Carburetor model	Mikuni BDSR36	Mikuni BDSR36
Carburetor type	Constant velocity	Constant velocity
Bore size	36.5 mm	36.5 mm
Carburetor I.D.	34E5	34E2

(continued)

Table 1 CARBURETOR SPECIFICATIONS (1997 MODELS) (continued)

Item	Brazil	Sweden, Finland, Norway, Germany
Idle speed	1100-1300 rpm	1100-1300 rpm
Fuel level	15-16 mm (0.59-0.63 in.)	15-16 mm (0.59-0.63 in.)
Float height	6-8 mm (0.24-0.32 in.)	6-8 mm (0.24-0.32 in.)
Main jet		
Carburetor No. 1	No. 125	No. 125
Carburetor No. 2	No. 122.5	No. 122.5
Carburetor No. 3	No. 122.5	No. 122.5
Carburetor No. 4	No. 122.5	No. 122.5
Needle jet	P-0	P-0
Jet needle	5DH18-52-3	5DH18-52-3
Throttle valve	No. 100	No. 100
Pilot jet	No. 12.5	No. 12.5
Pilot screw		
Carburetor No. 1	Preset (3 1/2 turns out)	Preset (3 1/4 turns out)
Carburetor No. 2	Preset (2 1/2 turns out)	Preset (2 1/4 turns out)
Carburetor No. 3	Preset (2 1/2 turns out)	Preset (2 1/4 turns out)
Carburetor No. 4	Preset (3 1/2 turns out)	Preset (3 1/4 turns out)
Throttle cable free play	0.5-1.0 mm (0.02-0.04 in.)	0.5-1.0 mm (0.02-0.04 in.)

8

Table 2 CARBURETOR SPECIFICATIONS (1998 MODELS)

Item	U.S.A., Switzerland, Canada, Austria	Belgium, Netherlands, Italy, Spain, U.K.
Carburetor model	Mikuni BDSR36	Mikuni BDSR36
Carburetor type	Constant velocity	Constant velocity
Bore size	36.5 mm	36.5 mm
Carburetor I.D.	34E7	34E6
Idle speed	–	1100-1300 rpm
U.S.A., Canada, Austria	1200-1400 rpm	–
Switzerland	1250-1400 rpm	–
Fuel level	15-16 mm (0.59-0.63 in.)	15-16 mm (0.59-0.63 in.)
Float height	6-8 mm (0.24-0.32 in.)	6-8 mm (0.24-0.32 in.)
Main jet		
Carburetor No. 1	No. 135	No. 135
Carburetor No. 2	No. 132.5	No. 132.5
Carburetor No. 3	No. 132.5	No. 132.5
Carburetor No. 4	No. 135	No. 135
Needle jet	P-0M	P-0
Jet needle	5DHZ32	5DHZ31-3
Throttle valve	No. 100	No. 100
Pilot jet	No. 12.5	No. 12.5
Pilot screw		
Carburetor No. 1	Preset	Preset (3 turns out)
Carburetor No. 2	Preset	Preset (2 3/4 turns out)
Carburetor No. 3	Preset	Preset (2 3/4 turns out)
Carburetor No. 4	Preset	Preset (3 turns out)
Throttle cable free play	2.0-4.0 mm (0.08-0.16 in.)	2.0-4.0 mm (0.08-0.16 in.)

Item	California	Australia
Carburetor model	Mikuni BDSR36	Mikuni BDSR36
Carburetor type	Constant velocity	Constant velocity
Bore size	36.5 mm	36.5 mm
Carburetor I.D.	34E9	34EA

(continued)

Table 2 CARBURETOR SPECIFICATIONS (1998 MODELS) (continued)

Item	California	Australia
Idle speed	1200-1400 rpm	1100-1300 rpm
Fuel level	15-16 mm (0.59-0.63 in.)	15-16 mm (0.59-0.63 in.)
Float height	6-8 mm (0.24-0.32 in.)	6-8 mm (0.24-0.32 in.)
Main jet		
Carburetor No. 1	No. 135	No. 135
Carburetor No. 2	No. 132.5	No. 132.5
Carburetor No. 3	No. 132.5	No. 132.5
Carburetor No. 4	No. 135	No. 135
Needle jet	P-0M	P-0
Jet needle	5DH20-53	5DHZ31-3
Throttle valve	No. 100	No. 100
Pilot jet	No. 12.5	No. 12.5
Pilot screw		
Carburetor No. 1	Preset	Preset (3 turns out)
Carburetor No. 2	Preset	Preset (2 3/4 turns out)
Carburetor No. 3	Preset	Preset (2 3/4 turns out)
Carburetor No. 4	Preset	Preset (3 turns out)
Throttle cable free play	2.0-4.0 mm (0.08-0.16 in.)	2.0-4.0 mm (0.08-0.16 in.)

Item	France, Germany, Sweden, Finland, Norway
Carburetor model	Mikuni BDSR36
Carburetor type	Constant velocity
Bore size	36.5 mm
Carburetor I.D.	34E8
Idle speed	1100-1300 rpm
Fuel level	15-16 mm (0.59-0.63 in.)
Float height	6-8 mm (0.24-0.32 in.)
Main jet	
Carburetor No. 1	No. 135
Carburetor No. 2	No. 132.5
Carburetor No. 3	No. 132.5
Carburetor No. 4	No. 135
Needle jet	P-0
Jet needle	5DZ25-3
Throttle valve	No. 100
Pilot jet	No. 12.5
Pilot screw	
Carburetor No. 1	Preset (2 1/2 turns out)
Carburetor No. 2	Preset (2 turns out)
Carburetor No. 3	Preset (2 turns out)
Carburetor No. 4	Preset (2 1/2 turns out)
Throttle cable free play	2.0-4.0 mm (0.08-0.16 in.)

Table 3 CARBURETOR SPECIFICATIONS (1999-ON MODELS)

Item	U.S.A., Canada,	Belgium, Netherlands, Italy, Spain, U.K.
Carburetor model	Mikuni BDSR36	Mikuni BDSR36
Carburetor type	Constant velocity	Constant velocity
Bore size	36.5 mm	36.5 mm
Carburetor I.D.	34EC	34E6
Idle speed	1200-1400	1100-1300 rpm
Fuel level	15-16 mm (0.59-0.63 in.)	15-16 mm (0.59-0.63 in.)
Float height	6-8 mm (0.24-0.32 in.)	6-8 mm (0.24-0.32 in.)

(continued)

Table 3 CARBURETOR SPECIFICATIONS (1999-ON MODELS) (continued)

Item	U.S.A., Canada,	Belgium, Netherlands, Italy, Spain, U.K.
Main jet		
Carburetor No. 1	No. 132.5	No. 135
Carburetor No. 2	No. 130	No. 132.5
Carburetor No. 3	No. 130	No. 132.5
Carburetor No. 4	No. 132.5	No. 135
Needle jet	P-0M	P-0
Jet needle	5DH20-53	5DHZ31-3
Throttle valve	No. 100	No. 100
Pilot jet	No. 12.5	No. 12.5
Pilot screw		
Carburetor No. 1	Preset	Preset (3 turns out)
Carburetor No. 2	Preset	Preset (2 3/4 turns out)
Carburetor No. 3	Preset	Preset (2 3/4 turns out)
Carburetor No. 4	Preset	Preset (3 turns out)
Throttle cable free play	2.0-4.0 mm (0.08-0.16 in.)	2.0-4.0 mm (0.08-0.16 in.)

Item	California	Australia
Carburetor model	Mikuni BDSR36	Mikuni BDSR36
Carburetor type	Constant velocity	Constant velocity
Bore size	36.5 mm	36.5 mm
Carburetor I.D.	34EE	34EF
Idle speed	1200-1400 rpm	1200-1400 rpm
Fuel level	15-16 mm (0.59-0.63 in.)	15-16 mm (0.59-0.63 in.)
Float height	6-8 mm (0.24-0.32 in.)	6-8 mm (0.24-0.32 in.)
Main jet		
Carburetor No. 1	No. 132.5	No. 132.5
Carburetor No. 2	No. 130	No. 130
Carburetor No. 3	No. 130	No. 130
Carburetor No. 4	No. 132.5	No. 132.5
Needle jet	P-0M	P-0
Jet needle	5DH20-53	5DH20-53
Throttle valve	No. 100	No. 100
Pilot jet	No. 12.5	No. 12.5
Pilot screw		
Carburetor No. 1	Preset	Preset (4 turns out)
Carburetor No. 2	Preset	Preset (3 1/2 turns out)
Carburetor No. 3	Preset	Preset (3 1/2 turns out)
Carburetor No. 4	Preset	Preset (4 turns out)
Throttle cable free play	2.0-4.0 mm (0.08-0.16 in.)	2.0-4.0 mm (0.08-0.16 in.)

Item	Austria, Switzerland	France, Germany
Carburetor model	Mikuni BDSR36	Mikuni BDSR36
Carburetor type	Constant velocity	Constant velocity
Bore size	36.5 mm	36.5 mm
Carburetor I.D.	34E7	34E8
Idle speed	–	1100-1300 rpm
Austria	1200-1400 rpm	–
Switzerland	1250-1400 rpm	–
Fuel level	15-16 mm (0.59-0.63 in.)	15-16 mm (0.59-0.63 in.)
Float height	6-8 mm (0.24-0.32 in.)	6-8 mm (0.24-0.32 in.)
Main jet		
Carburetor No. 1	No. 135	No. 135
Carburetor No. 2	No. 132.5	No. 132.5
Carburetor No. 3	No. 132.5	No. 132.5
Carburetor No. 4	No. 135	No. 135

(continued)

8

Table 3 CARBURETOR SPECIFICATIONS (1999-ON MODELS) (continued)

Item	Austria, Switzerland	France, Germany
Needle jet	P-0M	P-0
Jet needle	5DHZ32	5DZ25-3
Throttle valve	No. 100	No. 100
Pilot jet	No. 12.5	No. 12.5
Pilot screw		
Carburetor No. 1	Preset (4 turns out)	Preset (2 1/2 turns out)
Carburetor No. 2	Preset (3 1/2 turns out)	Preset (2 turns out)
Carburetor No. 3	Preset (3 1/2 turns out)	Preset (2 turns out)
Carburetor No. 4	Preset (4 turns out)	Preset (2 1/2 turns out)
Throttle cable free play	2.0-4.0 mm (0.08-0.16 in.)	2.0-4.0 mm (0.08-0.16 in.)

Table 4 CARBURETOR TORQUE SPECIFICATIONS

Item	N•m	in.-lb.	ft.-lb.
Carburetor connecting bolt	5.0	44	–
Carburetor heater (U.K. models)	3.0	26	–
Float bowl screw	3.5	31	–
Fuel pump mounting bolts	3.0	26	–
Funnel screw	2.0	18	–
Main jet	1.8	16	–
Main jet holder	1.8	16	–
Pilot jet	1.0	9	–
Starter link screw	2.0	18	–
Throttle position sensor screws	3.5	31	–
Top cover screw	3.5	31	–
Valve seat retainer	1.0	9	–

Table 5 FUEL AND EMISSION CONTROL SYSTEM TEST SPECIFICATIONS

Item	Results
Carburetor heater coil resistance	12-18 ohms
Throttle position sensor	
Fully-closed resistance	3.5-6.5 k ohms
Wide-open resistance	76% of fully-closed reading
Solenoid valve	
Left solenoid valve (No. 2 and No. 3)	
At appoximately 2700 rpm	On, 12 volts
At appoximately 5000 rpm	Off, 0 volts
At appoximately 7300 rpm	On, 12 volts
At appoximately 10,000 rpm	Off, 0 volts
Right solenoid valve (No. 1 and No. 4)	
At appoximately 2700 rpm	On, 12 volts
At appoximately 4200 rpm	Off, 0 volts
At appoximately 5700 rpm	On, 12 volts
At appoximately 8800 rpm	Off, 0 volts
Solenoid valve 1999-on U.S.A., California, Canada and Australia models	
Left solenoid valve (No. 2 and No. 3)	
At appoximately 2700 rpm	On, 12 volts
At appoximately 4950 rpm	Off, 0 volts
At appoximately 7650 rpm	On, 12 volts
At appoximately 10,550 rpm	Off, 0 volts

(continued)

Table 5 FUEL AND EMISSION CONTROL SYSTEM TEST SPECIFICATIONS (continued)

Item	Results
Solenoid valve 1999-on U.S.A., California, Canada and Australia models (continued)	
Right solenoid valve (No. 1 and No. 4)	
At appoximately 2700 rpm	On, 12 volts
At appoximately 4050 rpm	Off, 0 volts
At appoximately 5800 rpm	On, 12 volts
At appoximately 9100 rpm	Off, 0 volts
PAIR Control Valve Vacuum Pressure	
1997 California models	47-73 kPa (350-550 mm Hg, 13.8-21.7 in. Hg)
1998-on California models	36-60 kPa (270-450 mm Hg, 10.6-17.7 in. Hg)
1999-on U.S.A., Canada, Austria and Switzerland models	36-60 kPa (270-450 mm Hg, 10.6-17.7 in. Hg)

8

CHAPTER NINE

ELECTRICAL SYSTEM

This chapter covers service and test procedures for most of the electrical systems. The battery, spark plugs and ignition timing are covered in Chapter Three. Electrical system specifications are listed in **Tables 1-3** at the end of the chapter. Wiring diagrams are located at the end of the book.

The systems included in this chapter are:

1. Charging.
2. Ignition.
3. Starting.
4. Lighting.
5. Cooling fan and switch.
6. Switches.
7. Various electrical components.

PRELIMINARY INFORMATION

Peak Voltage and Resistance Testing

Resistance readings vary with temperature. The resistance increases when the temperature increases and decreases when the temperature decreases.

Specifications for resistance are based on tests performed at a specific temperature [68° F (20° C)]. If a component is warm or hot let it cool to room temperature. If a component is tested at a temperature that varies from the specification test temperature, a false reading may result.

The manufacturer specifies using the Suzuki Multi Circuit Tester (part No. 09900-25008) and the peak voltage adapter for accurate resistance and voltage tests. Due to the specific resistance values of the semiconductors in this meter, using another meter may provide inaccurate results.

An equivalent tool is the Motion Pro IgnitionMate (part No. 08-0193). However, the test procedures in this chapter use the Suzuki Multi Circuit Tester. If an alternative meter is being used, follow that manufacturer's instructions.

Make sure the battery tester is in good condition. The battery of an ohmmeter is the source for the current that is applied to the circuit being tested. Accurate results depend on the battery having sufficient voltage.

All peak voltage specifications are *minimum* values. If the measured voltage meets or exceeds the specifications, the test results are acceptable. On some components the voltage may greatly exceed the minimum specification; this is normal.

> *NOTE*
> *When using an analog ohmmeter, always calibrate the meter between each resistance test by touching the test leads together and zeroing the meter.*

ELECTRICAL COMPONENT LOCATION

1. Turn signal relay
2. Left combination switch
3. Solenoid valve
4. Diode
5. Fuel pump relay
6. Main fuse (30 amp)
7. Fuel pump relay, sidestand relay and starter relay
8. Voltage regulator/rectifier
9. Spark plug cap/ignition coil
10. Alternator
11. Neutral switch and speed sensor
12. Sidestand switch
13. Battery

Component Replacement

Most parts suppliers do not accept returns on electrical components. If the exact cause of any electrical system malfunction has not been determined, do not attempt to remedy the problem with guesswork and unnecessary parts replacement. If possible, have the suspect component or system tested by a professional technician *before* purchasing electrical components.

Electrical Component/Connector Location and Service

The location of electrical connectors can vary between model years. The position of the connectors may have been changed during previous repairs. Always confirm the wire colors to and from the connector and follow the wiring harness to the various components when performing tests.

Moisture can enter many of the electrical connectors and cause corrosion, which may cause a poor electrical connection. This may result in component failure and a possible breakdown on the road. To prevent moisture from entering into the various connectors, disconnect them and after making sure the terminals are clean, pack the connector with dielectric grease. Do not use a substitute that may interfere with current flow. Dielectric grease is specifically formulated to seal the connector and not increase current resistance. For best results, the compound should fill the entire inner area of the connector. It is recommended that each time a connector is unplugged, that it be cleaned and sealed with dielectric grease.

An often overlook area when troubleshooting are the ground connections. Make sure they are corrosion free and tight. Apply dielectric grease to the terminals before reconnecting them.

Refer to **Figure 1** and **Figure 2** for component/connector location.

ELECTRICAL COMPONENT LOCATION

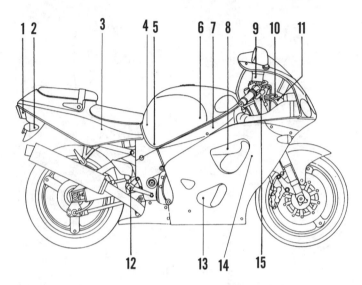

1. Taillight/brake light
2. Rear turn signal
3. CDI unit
4. Fuel pump and fuel level indicator switch
5. Diode
6. Starter motor
7. Engine coolant temperature gauge
8. Throttle position sensor

9. Right combination switch
10. Fuse panel
11. Combination meter
12. Rear brake light switch
13. Oil pressure switch
14. Cooling fan and cooling fan thermo switch
15. Front brake light switch

BATTERY NEGATIVE TERMINAL

Some of the component replacement procedures and some of the test procedures in this chapter require disconnecting the negative (–) battery cable as a safety precaution.

1. Turn the ignition switch OFF.

2. Remove the seat as described in Chapter Fifteen.

3. Remove the bolt and disconnect the negative battery cable (A, **Figure 3**) from the battery terminal.

4. Move the cable out of the way so it does not accidentally make contact with the battery terminal.

5. Once the procedure is completed, connect the negative battery cable to the terminal and tighten the bolt securely.

6. Install the seat as described in Chapter Fifteen.

CHARGING SYSTEM

The charging system consists of the battery, alternator and a voltage regulator/rectifier (**Figure 4**). Alternating current generated by the alternator is rectified to direct current. The voltage regulator

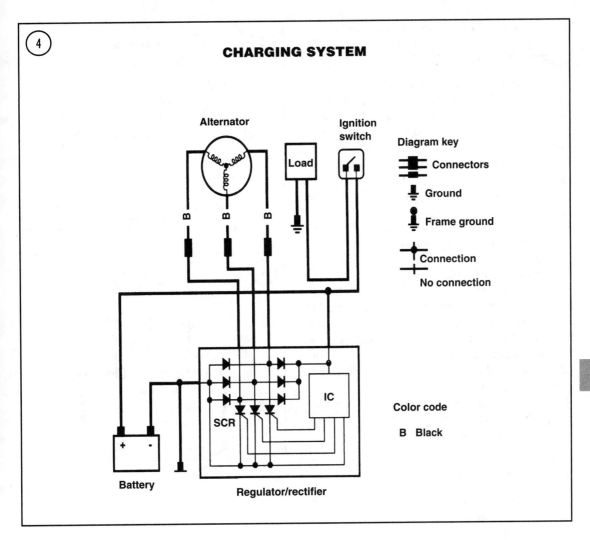

CHARGING SYSTEM

Alternator

Ignition switch

Load

Diagram key

Connectors

Ground

Frame ground

Connection

No connection

IC

SCR

Color code

B   Black

Battery

Regulator/rectifier

9

maintains the voltage to the battery and additional electrical loads at a constant voltage regardless of variations in engine speed.

A malfunction in the charging system generally causes the battery to remain undercharged. To prevent damage to the alternator and the regulator/rectifier when testing and repairing the charging system, note the following precautions:

1. Always disconnect the negative battery cable, as described in this chapter, before removing a component from the charging system.

2. When it is necessary to charge the battery, remove the battery from the motorcycle and recharge it as described in Chapter Three.

3. Inspect the physical condition of the battery. Look for bulges or cracks in the case, leaking electrolyte or corrosion buildup.

4. Check the wiring in the charging system for signs of chafing, deterioration or other damage.

5. Check the wiring for corroded or loose connections. Clean, tighten or reconnect as required.

Battery Drain (Current Draw) Test

Perform this test before performing the output test.

1. Turn the ignition switch OFF.

2. Remove the seat as described in Chapter Fifteen.

3. Disconnect the negative battery cable as described in this chapter.

CAUTION
Before connecting the ammeter into the circuit in Step 4, set the meter to its highest amperage scale. This prevents

a possible large current flow from damaging the meter or blowing the meter's fuse, if so equipped.

4. Connect the ammeter between the negative battery cable and the negative battery post (**Figure 5**). Switch the ammeter from its highest to lowest amperage scale while reading the meter. If the needle swings even the slightest amount, current is draining from the system. The battery will eventually discharge.

5. If the current drain is excessive, the probable causes are:

    a. Loose, dirty or faulty electrical system connectors in the charging system wiring harness.

    b. Short circuit in the system.

    c. Damaged battery.

6. Isolate the current drain to a specific circuit by removing the fuses one at a time and observing the ammeter. If the current flow stops when a fuse is removed, that is the effected circuit. Further isolation can be achieved by disconnecting the connectors within that circuit.

7. After the current drain problem has been repaired, disconnect the ammeter leads and reconnect the negative battery lead.

Charging System Output Test

Whenever charging system trouble is suspected, make sure the battery is fully charged and in good condition before going any further. Clean and test the battery as described in Chapter Three. Make sure all electrical connectors are tight and free of corrosion.

1. Start the engine and let it reach normal operating temperature. Shut off the engine.

2. Remove the front seat as described in Chapter Fifteen.

3. Connect a portable tachometer following the manufacturer's instructions.

4. Remove the red plastic cover from the positive battery terminal (B, **Figure 3**).

5. Turn the headlight dimmer switch to the HI position.

6. Restart the engine and let it idle.

7. Connect the positive test lead of a 0-25 DC voltmeter to the positive battery terminal, and connect the negative test lead to the negative battery terminal as shown in **Figure 6**.

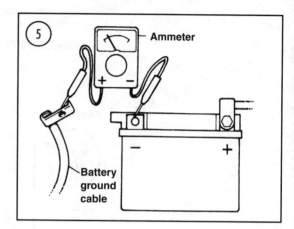

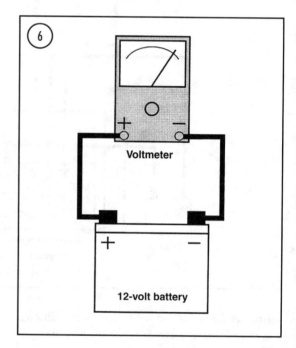

8. Increase engine speed to 5000 rpm. The voltage reading should be within the regulated voltage range specified in **Table 1**. If the voltage is outside the specified range, inspect the alternator and the voltage regulator as described in this chapter. The voltage regulator/rectifier is a separate unit from the alternator and can be replaced individually.

9. If the charging voltage is too high, the voltage regulator/rectifier is probably at fault.

10. After completing the test, shut off the engine and disconnect the voltmeter and portable tachometer.

11. Install the cover (B, **Figure 3**) on the positive battery cable.

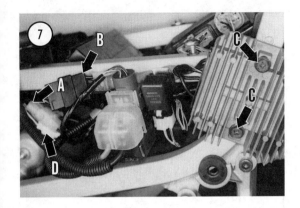

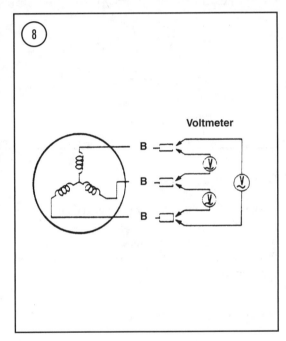

Voltmeter

5. Start the engine and let it idle.

NOTE
In Step 6 connect the voltmeter test leads to the alternator side of the electrical connector disconnected in Step 4.

6. Connect a 0-250 V (AC) voltmeter between each of the three terminals on the alternator side of the connector as shown in **Figure 8**.

7. Increase engine speed to 5000 rpm and check the voltage on the meter. The voltage should equal the no-load voltage specified in **Table 1**.

8. Repeat this test for the remaining terminals. Take a total of three readings.

9. If the voltage in any test is less than the specified no-load voltage, shut off the engine and check the charging system wiring harness and connectors for dirty or loose-fitting terminals. Clean and repair as required. If the wiring and connectors are good, the alternator is defective and must be replaced.

10. Disconnect and remove the voltmeter and portable tachometer.

11. Reconnect the alternator 3-pin connector (A, **Figure 7**). Make sure the connector is corrosion free and secure.

12. Install the rear frame cover, lower fairing side panel and the seats as described in Chapter Fifteen.

VOLTAGE REGULATOR/RECTIFIER

Testing

Suzuki specifies the use of the Suzuki Multi Circuit Tester (part No. 09900-25008) for testing the regulator/rectifier unit. If this tester is not available, have a Suzuki dealership test the unit.

NOTE
Before making this test, check the condition of the tester battery. To ensure an accurate reading, install a new battery.

12. Install the front seat as described in Chapter Fifteen.

Charging System No-Load Test

1. Remove both seats as described in Chapter Fifteen.

2. Remove the left lower fairing side panel and rear frame cover as described in Chapter Fifteen.

3. Connect a portable tachometer following the manufacturer's instructions.

4. Disconnect the alternator 3-pin electrical connector (A, **Figure 7**) on the left side of the rear frame member. If necessary, follow the electrical cable from the alternator stator assembly until the alternator connector is located.

1. Remove both seats as described in Chapter Fifteen.

2. Remove the left lower fairing side panel and rear frame cover as described in Chapter Fifteen.

3. Disconnect the regulator/rectifier 5-pin electrical connector (B, **Figure 7**).

4. Connect the Suzuki Multi Circuit Tester to the regulator/rectifier terminals (**Figure 9**) as indicated in **Figure 10**, and check the voltage across each pair of terminals.

5. If any voltage reading differs from the stated value, replace the regulator/rectifier unit as described in this chapter.

6. If the voltage regulator/rectifier is within specification, install the rear frame cover and both seats as described in Chapter Fifteen.

Voltage Regulator/Rectifier Removal/Installation

1. Remove both seats and rear frame cover as described in Chapter Fifteen.

2. Disconnect the negative battery lead as described in this chapter.

3. Disconnect the regulator/rectifier 5-pin electrical connector (B, **Figure 7**).

4. Remove the two mounting bolts (C, **Figure 7**) and remove the regulator/rectifier. Do not lose the spacers located between the voltage regulator/rectifier and the frame. Reinstall these spacers during assembly.

5. Carefully pull the electrical wiring harness out through the frame, noting its path, and remove the voltage regulator/rectifier assembly from the frame.

6. Install by reversing these removal steps while noting the following:

    a. Install the spacers between the voltage regulator/rectifier and the frame, and then tighten the mounting bolts securely.

    b. Make sure the electrical connector is tight and free of corrosion.

    c. Connect the negative battery lead.

ALTERNATOR

Alternators generate alternating current. The electrical system, however, requires direct current in order to recharge the battery and operate the electrical equipment.

The alternator consists, basically, of the stator winding and the rotor. The system produces current by the rotation of the magnetized rotor around the three stator coils. The resultant three-phase alternating current is then rectified by the voltage regulator/rectifier into direct current.

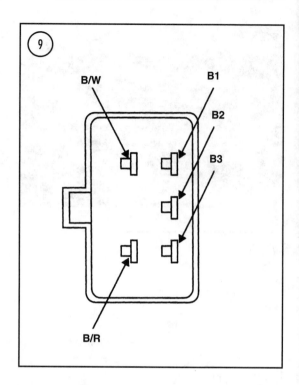

Rotor Testing

The rotor is permanently magnetized and cannot be tested except by replacing it with a known good one. The rotor can lose magnetism over time or from a sharp impact. If defective, replace the rotor. It cannot be re-magnetized.

Stator Coil Continuity Test

1. Remove both seats and rear frame cover as described in Chapter Fifteen.

2. Start the engine and let it reach normal operating temperature. Shut off the engine.

3. Disconnect the alternator 3-pin electrical connector (A, **Figure 7**).

4. Check the continuity between each of the terminals on the alternator side of the connector as shown in **Figure 11**. If using an analog ohmmeter, make sure to zero the meter.

5. There should be continuity between all three terminals. If not, the alternator is defective and must be replaced.

6. Next check for continuity between each terminal in the connector and ground. If there is continuity, one or more of the stator wires is shorted to ground. Replace the stator assembly.

REGULATOR/RECTIFIER TEST

⑩

		+ Probe of tester to:				
		B/R	B₁	B₂	B₃	B/W
− Probe of tester to:	B/R		0.4 ~ 0.7	0.4 ~ 0.7	0.4 ~ 0.7	0.5 ~ 1.2
	B₁	Approx. 1.5		Approx. 1.5	Approx. 1.5	0.4 ~ 0.7
	B₂	Approx. 1.5	Approx. 1.5		Approx. 1.5	0.4 ~ 0.7
	B₃	Approx. 1.5	Approx. 1.5	Approx. 1.5		0.4 ~ 0.7
	B/W	Approx. 1.5	Approx. 1.5	Approx. 1.5	Approx. 1.5	

B: Black, B/R: Black with red tracer, B/W: Black with white tracer

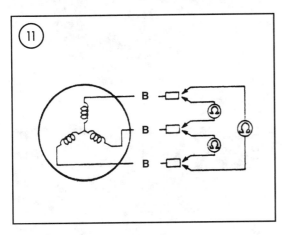

⑪

⑫

9

7. Disconnect and remove the ohmmeter.

8. Reconnect the alternator three-pin electrical connector. Make sure the connector is corrosion free and tight.

9. Install the rear frame cover and the seats as described in Chapter Fifteen.

Stator Assembly Removal/Installation

The stator assembly is located within the alternator cover.

1. Remove both seats and the rear frame cover as described in Chapter Fifteen.

2. Remove the left lower fairing side panel as described in Chapter Fifteen.

3. Disconnect the alternator three-pin electrical connector (A, **Figure 7**).

4. Remove the bolts securing the alternator cover (**Figure 12**) to the crankcase. A gasket washer is installed behind each of the two upper alternator-cover bolts. Install new gasket washers with each of these bolts during assembly.

5. Remove the alternator cover. Do not lose the two locating dowels behind the cover (A, **Figure 13**).

6. Carefully withdraw the wiring harness from the frame, while noting its path. Remove the alternator stator assembly and wiring harness from the frame.

7. Place several shop cloths on the workbench and turn the alternator cover upside down on these cloths.

8. Remove the screws and small metal clamps (A, **Figure 14**) securing the stator assembly wiring harness to the alternator cover. Note the location of

each of these metal clamps. Reinstall them in the same location during assembly.

9. Remove the bolts securing the stator assembly (B, **Figure 14**) to the cover. Carefully pull the rubber grommet (C, **Figure 14**) from the cover and remove the stator and ignition signal generator assembly from the cover.

10. Install by reversing these removal steps, noting the following:

a. Apply a light coat of ThreeBond TB1342 or equivalent to the mounting bolt threads before installation. Tighten the bolts securely.

b. Reinstall the small metal clamp (A, **Figure 14**) securing the stator assembly and wiring harness to the cover in the correct location. This clamp secures the wiring harness to the cover and away from the spinning rotor. If these wires come in contact with the rotor, they will be damaged.

c. Make sure the electrical connector is free of corrosion and is tight.

d. If removed, install the two locating dowels (A, **Figure 13**).

e. Apply a light coat of gasket sealer to the portion of the alternator-cover mating surfaces where the upper and lower crankcase halves meet (B, **Figure 13**).

f. Install a new gasket (A, **Figure 15**).

g. Install a new gasket washer with each of the alternator cover bolts at the two locations shown in B, **Figure 15**.

Rotor Removal/Installation

1. Remove the alternator stator assembly as described in this chapter.

2. Place a wrench on the flats of the rotor (A, **Figure 16**), and then loosen and remove the alternator rotor bolt (B, **Figure 16**).

> *CAUTION*
> *Do not attempt to remove the rotor without a puller. Doing so will ultimately lead to some form of damage to the engine and/or rotor. Pullers are available from part suppliers or dealerships (Suzuki part No. 09930-30450). If one is not available, have a dealership remove the rotor.*

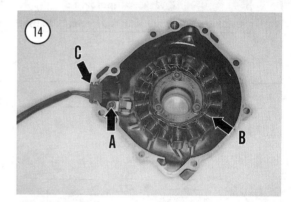

3. Install the rotor removal tool onto the threads of the rotor (**Figure 17**).

4. Hold the rotor with a suitable wrench. Turn the bolt or handle of the rotor removal tool until the rotor disengages from the crankshaft taper. Remove the rotor from the crankshaft.

CAUTION
If the rotor is difficult to remove, strike the end of the rotor removal tool (not the rotor because impact will damage it) firmly with a hammer.

CAUTION
Do not apply excessive pressure to the puller, this could strip the threads in the crankshaft. If the rotor is difficult to remove, have a Suzuki dealership perform the procedure.

5. Remove the rotor removal tool.

6. Inspect the inside of the rotor (**Figure 18**) for any metal debris that may have been picked up by the magnets. These small metal bits can damage the alternator stator assembly.

7. Install by reversing these removal steps while noting the following:

   a. Use aerosol parts cleaner to clean all oil residue from the crankshaft taper and the matching tapered surface in the rotor. This ensures a good tight fit between the rotor and the crankshaft.

   b. Apply a light coat of ThreeBond 1303 or equivalent to the mounting bolt threads before installation.

   c. Tighten the rotor bolt (**Figure 19**) to the torque specification listed in **Table 3**.

CAPACITOR DISCHARGE IGNITION SYSTEM

The GSX-R600 is equipped with a capacitor discharge ignition (CDI) system (**Figure 20**). The system consists of a signal generator, igniter unit, throttle position sensor, and four ignition coil/spark plug caps.

The signal generator portion of the system consists of a signal generator rotor on the crankshaft timing sprocket and the signal generator (or pickup coil). The throttle position sensor is mounted on the carburetor assembly.

As the crankshaft rotates, the pointer on the signal generator rotor passes the signal generator, which sends a signal to the igniter unit. The CPU (part of the igniter) uses this signal, input from the throttle position sensor and a stored digital data map to determine the optimum ignition timing for the operating conditions.

The system includes an rpm limiter. If the engine exceeds 13,400 rpm, the primary current to the ignition coil/spark plug caps is interrupted.

9

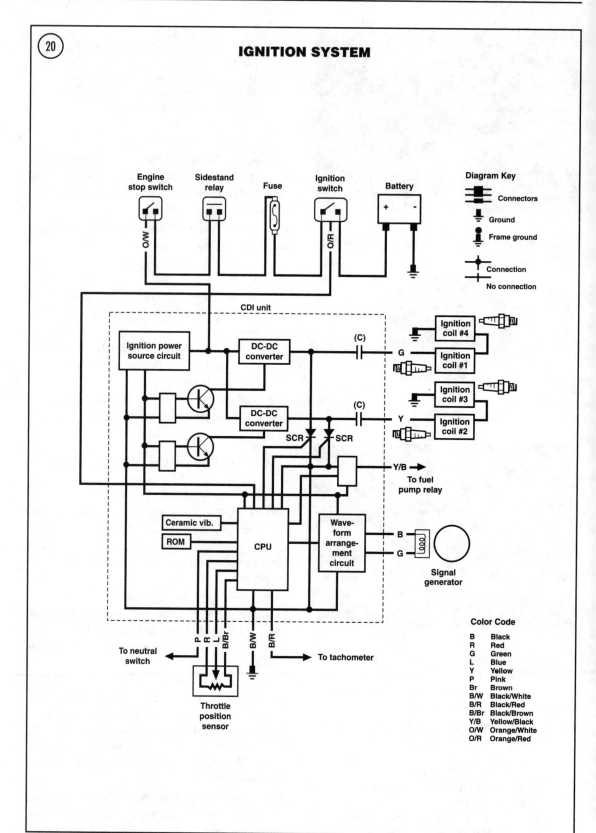

IGNITION SYSTEM

20

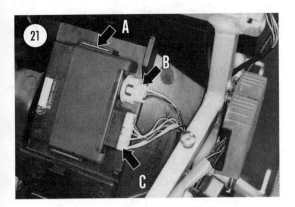

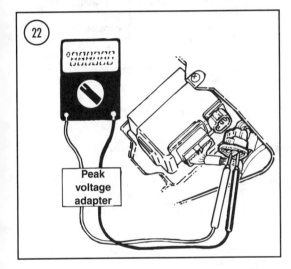

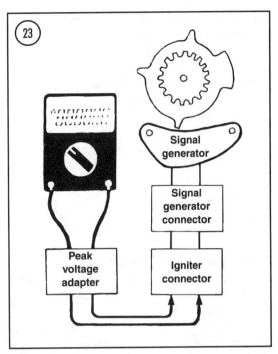

Ignition System Precautions

Certain measures must be taken to protect the ignition system. Damage to the semiconductors in the system may occur if any of the electrical connections are disconnected while the engine is running.

Troubleshooting

Refer to *Ignition System* in Chapter Two.

Signal Generator

Peak voltage test

Refer to *Preliminary Information* at the beginning of this chapter.

> *WARNING*
> *High voltage is present during ignition system operation. Do not touch*

ignition components, wires or test leads while the engine is running or cranking.

> *NOTE*
> *All peak voltage specifications are* ***minimum*** *values. If the measured voltage meets or exceeds the specifications, the test results are acceptable. On some components the voltage may greatly exceed the minimum specification; this is normal.*

1. Remove the front seat as described in Chapter Fifteen.

2. Disconnect the igniter connector (B, **Figure 21**) from the CDI unit.

3. Turn the tester's knob to voltage.

4. Connect the negative test probe to the green terminal on the connector, and connect the positive test probe to the black terminal. **Figure 22**.

5. Shift the transmission into neutral and turn the ignition switch ON.

6. Press the starter button and crank the engine for a few seconds and (**Figure 23**) record the highest reading.

7. If the signal generator peak voltage is less than the value specified in **Table 1**, check the peak volt-

age at the signal generator coupler (**Figure 24**) by performing the following:

   a. Remove the rear frame cover as described in Chapter Fifteen.

   b. Disconnect the 2-pin signal generator connector (D, **Figure 7**) from the main harness.

   c. Connect the negative test probe to the green terminal on the signal generator side of the connector, and connect the positive test probe to the black terminal. **Figure 25**.

   d. Shift the transmission into neutral and turn the ignition switch ON.

   e. Press the starter button and crank the engine for a few seconds and record the highest reading.

8. If the peak voltage measured at the signal generator connector is normal but the peak voltage at the igniter connector is less than the minimum specified value, replace the wiring.

9. If the peak voltage at both the signal generator connector and the igniter connector are less than the minimum value specified in **Table 1**, replace the signal generator.

10. If the tests are within specification, reconnect the electrical connector. Make sure the electrical connector is free of corrosion and is tight.

11. Install the rear frame cover and both seats.

Resistance test

   Refer to *Preliminary Information* at the beginning of this chapter.

1. Remove the seats and the rear frame cover as described in Chapter Fifteen.

2. Disconnect the 2-pin signal generator connector (D, **Figure 7**) from the main harness.

3. Set the ohmmeter to the R × 100 scale, and check the resistance between the black and green terminals in the signal generator side of the connector (**Figure 26**). If the signal generator coil resistance is outside the range specified in **Table 1**, replace the signal generator.

4. Check the continuity between the black terminal in the signal generator connector and ground (**Figure 26**). There should be no continuity (infinite resistance). If there is continuity, replace the signal generator.

5. If the tests are within specification, reconnect the electrical connector. Make sure the electrical connector is free of corrosion and is secure.

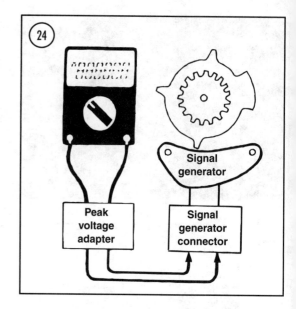

6. Install the rear frame cover and both seats.

Signal Generator Replacement

> *NOTE*
> *This procedure is shown with the engine removed from the frame for clarity.*

1. Remove the starter clutch assembly as described in Chapter Five.

2. Disconnect the 2-pin signal-generator connector (D, **Figure 7**) from the main harness.

> *NOTE*
> *Cover the crankcase opening with a piece of tape (**Figure 27**) to keep the screws from entering the crankcase.*

3. Remove the screws (A, **Figure 28**) securing the signal generator to the crankcase.

4. Remove the wire clip (B, **Figure 28**) and carefully pull the rubber grommet (C, **Figure 28**) out of the groove in the crankcase. Remove the signal generator and wiring from the engine and frame.

5. Remove the cam chain tensioner and chain guides as described in Chapter Four.

6. Disengage the cam chain from the timing sprocket on the crankshaft.

7. Remove the timing sprocket/signal generator assembly (A, **Figure 29**) from the crankshaft.

8. Inspect the signal generator rotor on the timing sprocket (**Figure 30**) for wear or damage. Replace

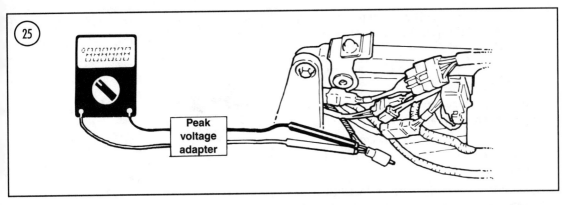

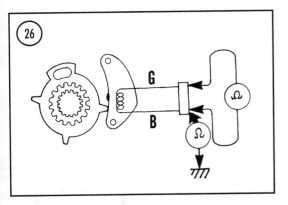

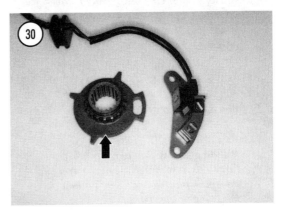

9

the timing sprocket/signal generator assembly if necessary.

9. Install by reversing these removal steps while noting the following:

CAUTION
In Step 9a, the alignment of the timing sprocket-to-crankshaft is critical because this determines the ignition timing. If the sprocket is installed incorrectly the timing will be off and the engine may not start.

a. Align the punch mark on the timing sprocket (B, **Figure 29**) with the punch mark on the end of the crankshaft (C, **Figure 29**).

b. Remove the tape (**Figure 27**) from the crankcase opening.

c. Apply a light coat of sealant to the crankcase groove before installing the rubber grommet.

d. Make sure the electrical connectors are free of corrosion and apply dielectric grease to the connector.

e. Securely couple the connector together.

f. Tighten the mounting bolts securely.

Ignition Coil/Spark Plug Cap Performance Test

1. Disconnect the ignition coil/plug cap and remove one of the spark plugs as described in Chapter Three.

> *CAUTION*
> *Do not ground the spark plug to the cylinder head cover, clutch cover, starter clutch cover, idler gear cover or the alternator cover. An electrical spark will damage these magnesium covers.*

2. Insert the spark plug into its cap and touch the spark plug base against the crankcase top to ground it. Position the spark plug so the electrode is in view.

> *WARNING*
> *If the engine is flooded, do not perform this test. Fuel ejected through the spark plug hole can be ignited by the firing of the spark plug.*

3. Turn the engine over with the electric starter. A fat blue spark should be evident across the spark plug electrode. If there is strong sunlight on the plug, shade the plug by hand. Repeat this test for the other three cylinders.

> *WARNING*
> *If necessary, hold onto the spark plug wire with a pair of insulated pliers. Do **not** hold the spark plug, wire or connector by hand. A serious electrical shock may result.*

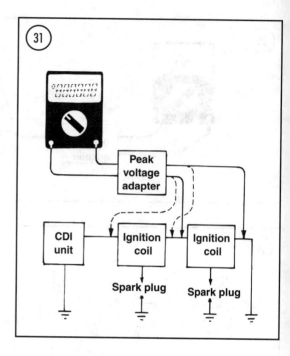

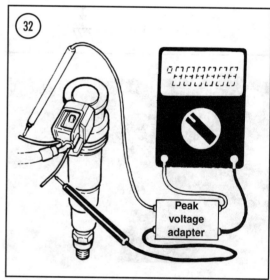

4. If a fat blue spark occurs, the ignition coil is good. If not, test the ignition coil as described below.

Ignition Coil

The GSX-R600 uses four ignition coils. Each ignition coil is an integral part of its spark plug cap.

Refer to *Preliminary Information* at the beginning of this chapter.

IGNITION COIL PRIMARY PEAK VOLTAGE TEST

(33)

At ignition coil/plug cap coupler		
Ignition coil/plug cap	Tester negative (-) probe	Tester positive (+) probe
No. 1	G	W/B
No. 2	Y	B
No. 3	B	B/W
No. 4	W/B	B/W

At CDI Unit		
Ignition coil/plug cap pair	Tester negative (-) probe	Tester positive (+) probe
No. 1 and No. 4	G	Ground
No. 2 and No. 3	Y	B

Ignition coil primary peak voltage test

1. Disconnect the ignition coil/plug caps and re-move all four spark plugs as described in Chapter Three.

2. Connect a new spark plug to each ignition coil /plug cap.

> *CAUTION*
> *Do not ground the spark plugs to the cylinder head cover, clutch cover, starter clutch cover, idler gear cover or the alternator cover. An electrical spark will damage these magnesium covers.*

3. Connect the electrical leads to the ignition coil/plug caps, and ground all four spark plugs to the crankcase.

> *CAUTION*
> *When backprobing the electrical connectors, use a probe with a small diameter. Large probes can damage the waterproof seal.*

4. To check the ignition coil primary peak voltage at the ignition coil/plug cap (**Figure 31**), perform the following:

   a. Turn the tester knob to voltage.

   b. Backprobe the electrical coupler of an ignition coil/spark plug cap (**Figure 32**).

   c. Refer to the chart in **Figure 33**, and connect the probes of the tester to the indicated terminals in the cap's electrical coupler.

   d. Shift the transmission into neutral and turn the ignition switch ON.

   e. Press the starter button and crank the engine for a few seconds and record the highest reading.

   f. Repeat substeps a-e for each of the remaining ignition coils.

   g. Compare the readings to the minimum ignition coil primary peak voltage specification is listed in **Table 1**. The individual peak voltage reading for each ignition coil can vary as long as the voltage meets or exceeds the specified minimum value.

   h. If the ignition coil primary peak voltage at the ignition coil/plug cap is less than the specified value, check the peak voltage at the CDI

9

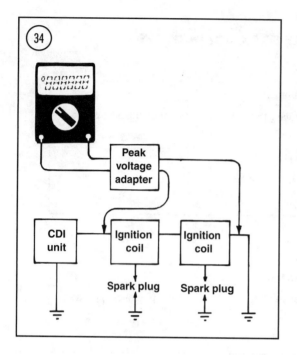

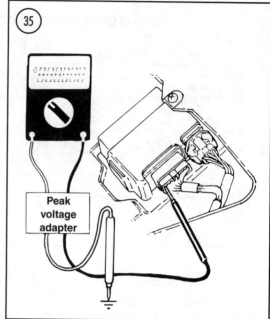

unit as described in Step 5. Refer to the ignition system diagnosis chart in Chapter Two.

5. To check the peak voltage at the CDI unit (**Figure 34**), perform the following:

  a. Make sure all four spark plugs are still grounded to the crankcase as described in Step 3.

  b. Make sure the tester's knob is turned to voltage.

  c. Refer to the chart in **Figure 33**. Connect the negative test probe to the indicated terminal in the CDI unit electrical connector and connect the positive test probe to ground (**Figure 35**).

  d. Shift the transmission into neutral and turn the ignition switch ON.

  e. Press the starter button and crank the engine for a few seconds and record the highest reading.

  f. Repeat substeps a-e for the other pair of ignition coils.

  g. Compare each reading to the minimum ignition coil primary peak voltage specification as listed in **Table 1**. The reading for each pair of ignition coils can differ from that of the other pair as long as the voltage meets or exceeds the specified minimum value.

  h. If the peak voltage at the CDI unit is less than the specified value, continue testing the ignition coil/plug cap, signal generator and CDI unit. Refer to the ignition system diagnosis chart in Chapter Two.

Ignition coil resistance test

Refer to *Preliminary Information* at the beginning of this chapter.

1. Remove both seats as described in Chapter Fifteen.

2. Remove the fuel tank as described in Chapter Eight.

3. Remove the air box as described in Chapter Eight.

4. Disconnect the negative battery cable as described in this chapter.

5. Carefully disconnect the electrical coupler (A, **Figure 36**) from each ignition coil/plug cap. Mark each coupler and ignition coil/plug cap in order to reinstall each one onto the correct spark plug during assembly.

6. The ignition coil/plug caps form a tight seal on the cylinder head cover and on the spark plugs. Grasp the ignition coil/plug cap (B, **Figure 36**), and twist it from side-to-side to break the seal. Then carefully pull the ignition coil/plug cap up and off the spark plug, and remove it from the cylinder head cover. If the ignition coil/plug cap is stuck to the plug, twist it slightly to break it loose.

7. Set an ohmmeter to the R × 1 scale, and measure the primary coil resistance between the positive and the negative terminals in the electrical connector of the ignition coil/plug cap (**Figure 37**). Compare the reading to the primary coil resistance specified in **Table 1**.

8. Set an ohmmeter to the R × 1000 scale, and measure the secondary coil resistance between the ignition coil/plug cap and the negative terminal in the electrical connector of the ignition coil/plug cap (**Figure 37**). Compare the reading to the secondary coil resistance specified in **Table 1**.

9. Repeat this step for the other three ignition coil/plug caps.

10. If the coil resistance does not meet (or come close to) either of these specifications, replace the coil. If the coil exhibits visible damage, replace it.

CAUTION
Do not use a plastic hammer or any type of tool to tap the ignition coil/plug cap assembly onto the spark plug. Striking the cap will cause damage. Only install the ignition coil/plug caps by hand.

NOTE
Push the ignition coil/plug cap all the way down to make full contact with the spark plug post. If each coil/cap does not make full contact with the spark plug, the engine may cut out at high engine speeds.

11. Refer to the marks made during removal and install each ignition coil/plug cap onto the correct spark plug. Press the ignition coil/plug cap onto the spark plug. Rotate the assembly slightly in both directions and make sure it is attached to the spark plug and at the sealing surface of the cylinder head cover.

12. Position the electrical connector receptacle on the ignition coil/plug cap so the No. 1 and No. 2 cylinders are facing toward each other and the No. 3 and No. 4 cylinders are facing toward each other.

13. Carefully connect the electrical coupler (A, **Figure 36**) onto each ignition coil/plug cap. Position the electrical coupler so it does not contact the raised portion of the cylinder head cover as shown in **Figure 38**.

14. Make sure the electrical connectors are free of corrosion and are on tight.

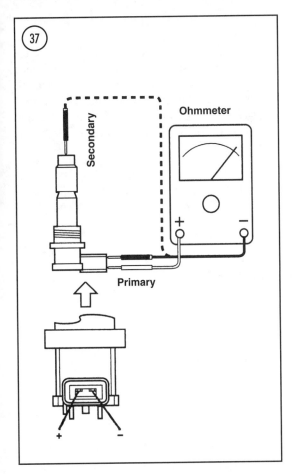

NOTE
In Step 7 and Step 8, the resistance specification is not as important as the fact that there is continuity between the terminals. If the ignition coil windings are in good condition, the resistance values will approximately equal the values specified in **Table 1***.*

15. Connect the negative battery lead as described in this chapter.

16. Install the air box and fuel tank as described in Chapter Eight.

17. Install both seats as described in Chapter Fifteen.

CDI Input Voltage Test

1. Remove the front seat as described in Chapter 15.

2. Connect the probes of a voltmeter to the orange/white terminal and the black/white terminal of the CDI 8-pin connector (C, **Figure 21**).

3. Turn the ignition switch ON, and check the voltage on the meter. It should read battery voltage.

Further testing of the CDI unit requires the Suzuki Digital Igniter Checker (part No. 09931-94490) and lead wire MODE 1-A4 (part No. 09931-61750) as well as the Suzuki Multi Circuit Tester (part No. 09900-25008). Refer testing of these units to a Suzuki dealership, as these tools are very expensive. If the signal generator and the ignition coils are working properly, then this simple check can be performed by the dealership to determine whether the CDI unit is defective.

CDI Unit Removal/Installation

1. Securely support the bike on the sidestand on level ground.

2. Remove both seats as described in Chapter Fifteen.

3. Disconnect the negative battery cable as described in this chapter.

4. Pull the CDI unit and rubber mount (A, **Figure 21**) up and off the mounting tabs on the rear fender.

5. Disconnect the two electrical connectors (B and C, **Figure 21**) from the unit.

6. Remove the CDI unit from the rubber mount. Place the CDI unit in a reclosable plastic bag, and place the unit in a box to protect it.

7. Install the CDI unit by reversing these removal steps while noting the following:

   a. Apply dielectric grease to the electrical connectors before reconnecting them. This helps seal out moisture.

   b. Make sure all electrical connectors are free of corrosion and securely coupled.

STARTING SYSTEM

The starting system (**Figure 39**) consists of the starter motor, starter gears, starter relay, clutch switch, sidestand switch, sidestand relay and the starter button. When the starter button is pressed, it engages the starter relay and completes the circuit allowing electricity to flow from the battery to the starter motor.

> *CAUTION*
> *Do not operate the starter for more than 5 seconds at a time. Let it cool approximately 10 seconds, before using it again.*

Troubleshooting

Refer to Chapter Two.

Starter
Removal/Installation

> *NOTE*
> *The starting gear system procedures are covered in Chapter Five.*

1. Securely support the bike on level ground.

2. Disconnect the negative battery cable as described in this chapter.

3. Remove the fuel tank and air box as described in Chapter Eight.

4. Pull back the rubber boot (A, **Figure 40**) from the starter motor electrical connector.

5. Remove the starter motor cable bolt and disconnect the starter motor cable from the starter.

6. Remove the two bolts (B, **Figure 40**) securing the starter to the crankcase.

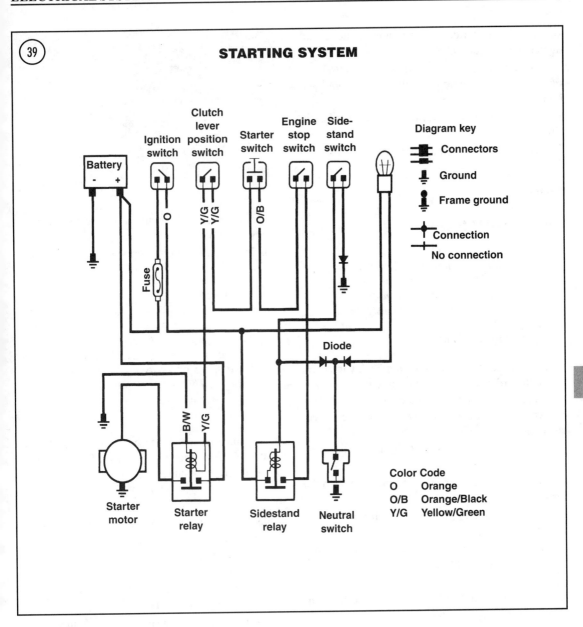

STARTING SYSTEM

39

Clutch lever position switch

Ignition switch

Battery
- +

Starter switch

Engine stop switch

Side-stand switch

Diagram key

Connectors

Ground

Frame ground

Connection

No connection

Fuse

Y/G Y/G

O/B

Diode

B/W Y/G

Starter motor

Starter relay

Sidestand relay

Neutral switch

Color Code
O   Orange
O/B   Orange/Black
Y/G   Yellow/Green

9

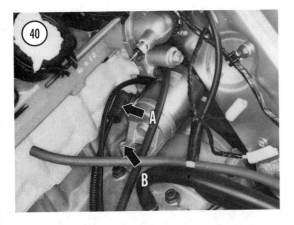

40

7. Pull the starter motor toward the left side, and then lift it up and out through the top of the frame.

8. Thoroughly clean the starter mounting pads on the crankcase and the mounting lugs on the starter motor.

9. Inspect the starter motor O-ring (A, **Figure 41**) in the right cover for hardness or deterioration. Replace the O-ring if necessary. Apply clean engine oil to the O-ring before installing the starter motor

10. Push the starter motor into the crankcase while guiding the starter motor sprocket onto the starter reduction gear.

11. Install the starter motor mounting bolts and tighten them securely.

12. Tighten the starter motor cable bolt to the specification in **Table 3** and press the rubber boot back into position.

13. Install the air box and fuel tank as described in Chapter Eight.

14. Connect the negative battery cable.

Disassembly

Refer to **Figure 42**.

> *NOTE*
> *Do not disassemble the starter motor unless absolutely necessary. Assembling this starter motor can be difficult. You must simultaneously hold four brushes in their holders while installing the armature.*

As the starter motor is disassembled, lay the parts out in the order of removal. When removing a part from the starter, set it next to the one previously removed. This is an easy way to remember the correct relationship of all parts.

1. Remove each case bolt (B, **Figure 41**) and its O-ring.

2. Remove the right cover (A, **Figure 43**) from the armature housing.

3. Slide the washers (B and C, **Figure 43**) off the armature shaft.

4. Slide the housing (**Figure 44**) off the armature.

5. Lift the armature (A, **Figure 45**) from the brush plate assembly in the left cover (B, **Figure 45**).

6. Remove the four brush springs (**Figure 46**) from their respective slots in the brush holder.

7. Remove the two brush mounting screws (A, **Figure 47**) and the two negative brushes (B, **Figure 47**).

8. Remove the brush holder (**Figure 48**) from the left cover. Leave the brush plate and positive brushes in the left cover.

> *CAUTION*
> *Do not immerse the wire windings in the case or the armature coil (A, **Figure 49**) in solvent because the insulation may be damaged. Wipe the windings with a cloth lightly moistened with solvent. Dry thoroughly.*

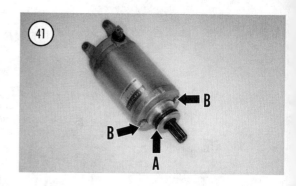

9. Clean all grease, dirt and carbon from all components.

10. Inspect all starter components as described in this chapter.

Assembly

> *NOTE*
> *In the next step, reinstall all parts in the same order as noted during removal. This is essential in order to insulate the brush assembly from the case.*

1. If removed, install the brush plate into the left cover. Make sure each hole (**Figure 50**) in the brush plate aligns with a threaded hole in the left cover.

2. Install the brush holder (**Figure 48**) into the left cover so the holes in the brush holder align with the holes in the brush plate and end cover.

3. Install each negative brush (B, **Figure 47**), and secure it in place with its mounting screw (A, **Figure 47**). Tighten the screw securely.

4. Apply molybdenum disulfide paste onto the small shaft (B, **Figure 49**) of the armature.

5. Install the four brush springs (**Figure 46**) by sliding each spring into its slot in the brush holder.

6. Slide each brush into its place in the brush holder.

> *NOTE*
> *Surgical clamps, such as hemostats, can be used to hold the brushes while installing the armature. If these are not available, have an assistant hold the brushes.*

7. Press each brush back into its holder so there is sufficient clearance for the commutator. Hold the armature upright, and insert the commutator end of

STARTER MOTOR

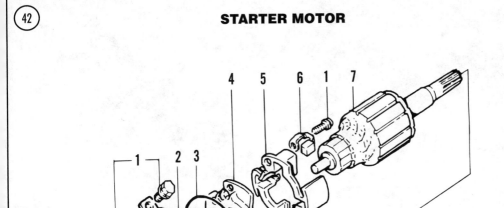

1. Bolt
2. Left cover
3. O-ring
4. Brush plate
5. Brush holder
6. Brush
7. Armature
8. Brush spring
9. Washer
10. Oil seal
11. Right cover
12. Case bolt
13. Armature housing

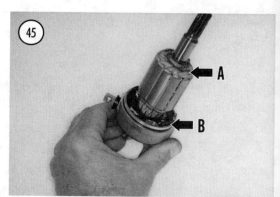

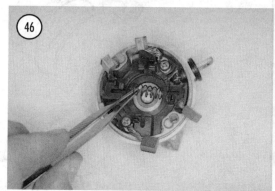

the armature (A, **Figure 49**) into the left cover (B, **Figure 45**). Do not damage the brushes during this step. Hold back the brushes as the commutator passes by them. Make sure each brush is in correct contact with the armature. Push the assembly down until it bottoms out.

8. Keep the assembly in this position and slowly rotate the armature coil assembly to make sure it rotates freely with the brushes in place.

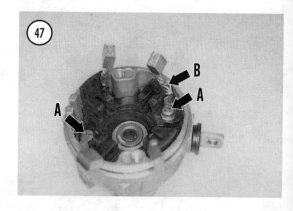

NOTE
Hold the armature coil and left cover together during the next step. The magnets within the armature housing will try to pull the armature out of the left cover and disengage the brushes.

9. Install the O-ring (**Figure 51**) onto the housing recess.

10. Install the housing over the armature coil assembly and onto the left cover (A, **Figure 52**). Align the case notch with the left cover notch (C, **Figure 52**).

11. Install the plain washer (C, **Figure 43**) onto the armature shaft.

12. Apply Suzuki Super Grease A (part No. 99000-25030) to the lips of the oil seal in the right cover, and install the armed washer into the cover.

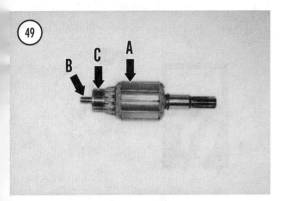

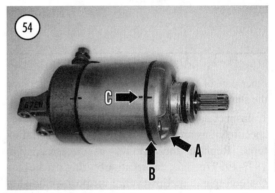

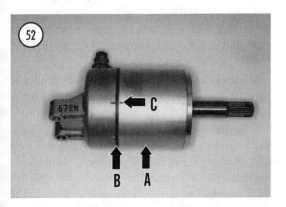

Align the washer arms with the slots in the cover as shown in **Figure 53**.

13. Install an O-ring onto the recess in the armature housing.

14. Install the right cover (A, **Figure 54**) onto the housing. Align the lines on the housing with the line on the cover.

15. Install the O-ring (D, **Figure 43**) onto the case bolts and apply a light coat of clean engine oil to each O-ring.

16. Install the case bolts (B, **Figure 41**) and tighten them securely. After the bolts are tightened, check the seams to ensure the end covers are pulled tight against the case.

Inspection

On 1997-1999 models, replacement parts are available for the starter motor, except for the positive brushes. If the positive brushes on these models require replacement, the brush plate must be replaced.

On 2000 models, the O-rings, washers, end covers, and oil seals can be purchased separately. If any

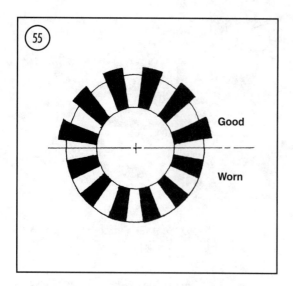

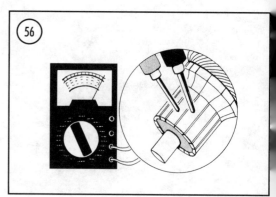

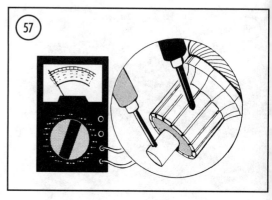

other part of the starter motor is defective, replace the starter motor.

1. Inspect each brush for abnormal wear. Service specifications are not available from the manufacturer. Replace the brushes as necessary. On 1997-1999 models, the negative brushes can be purchased separately. However, if the positive brushes are worn, replace the brush plate. On 2000 models, brushes are not available separately. Replace the left end cap if any brush is excessively worn.

2. Inspect the commutator (C, **Figure 49**). The mica in a good commutator is below the surface of the copper bars. On a worn commutator, the mica and copper bars may be worn to the same level (**Figure 55**). If necessary, have the commutator serviced by a electrical repair shop.

3. Check the entire length of the armature coil assembly for straightness or heat damage. Rotate the bearing and check for roughness or binding.

4. Inspect the armature shaft where it contacts the bushing (B, **Figure 49**). Check for wear, burrs or damage. If the armature is worn or damaged, replace the armature on 1997-1999 models. On 2000 models, replace the starter motor.

5. Inspect the commutator copper bars (C, **Figure 49**) for discoloration. If a pair of bars are discolored, grounded armature coils are indicated.

6. Use an ohmmeter and perform the following:

   a. Check for continuity between the commutator bars (**Figure 56**). There should be continuity (indicated resistance) between pairs of bars.

   b. Check for continuity between the commutator bars and the shaft (**Figure 57**). There should be no continuity (infinite resistance).

   c. If the armature fails either of these tests, replace the armature on 1997-1999 models. On 2000 models, replace the starter motor.

7. Inspect the oil seal (A, **Figure 58**) in the right cover for wear, hardness or damage. If the oil seal is worn or damaged, replace it on 2000 models. On 1997-1999 models, replace the right cover.

8. Inspect the O-ring (A, **Figure 41**) on the right cover for wear, hardness or damage. Replace the O-ring if necessary.

9. Inspect the needle bearing in the right cover. It must turn smoothly without excessive play or noise. Replace the cover as necessary.

10. Inspect the bushing in the left cover for wear or damage. The bushing cannot be replaced. If it is damaged, replace the left cover.

11. Inspect the magnets within the armature housing assembly. Make sure they have not picked up any small metal particles. If so remove them before assembly. Also inspect the armature housing for loose, chipped or damaged magnets.

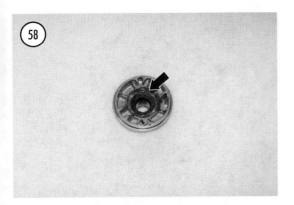

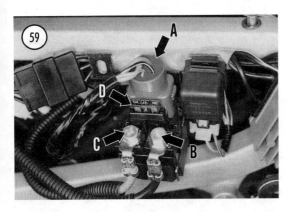

12. Inspect the brush holder and springs for wear or damage. If necessary, replace the holder or springs on 1997-1999 models. Replace the left cover on 2000 models.

13. Inspect both end covers for wear or damage. Replace either end cover if it is damaged.

14. Check the long case bolts for thread damage. Clean the threads with the appropriate size metric die if necessary. Inspect the O-ring seals for hardness, deterioration or damage. Replace as necessary.

STARTER RELAY

Starter Relay
Removal/Installation

1. Remove both seats and the rear frame cover as described in Chapter Fifteen.
2. Disconnect the negative battery cable as described in this chapter.
3. Remove the cover from the starter relay.
4. Disconnect the starter relay primary connector (A, **Figure 59**).
5. Disconnect the black starter motor lead (B, **Figure 59**) and the red battery lead (C, **Figure 59**) from the starter relay.
6. Install by reversing these removal steps while noting the following:
   a. Install both electrical red and black cables to the relay and tighten the nuts securely.
   b. Make sure the electrical connectors are on tight and that the rubber boot is properly installed to keep out moisture.
   c. Install the cover.

Troubleshooting

Refer to *Engine Starting System* in Chapter Two for starter relay test procedures.

LIGHTING SYSTEM

The lighting system consists of a headlight, taillight/brake light, license plate light, turn signals, instrument cluster indicator lights and assorted relays. **Table 2** lists replacement bulbs for these components.

Always use the correct wattage bulb as indicated in this section. A larger wattage bulb provides a dim light, and a smaller wattage bulb will burn out prematurely.

Headlight Bulb Replacement

> *CAUTION*
> *All models are equipped with quartz-halogen bulbs. Do not touch the bulb glass (**Figure 60**) with your fingers because traces of oil on the bulb will drastically reduce the life of the bulb. Clean any traces of oil or other chemicals from the bulb with a*

9

cloth moistened in alcohol or lacquer thinner.

> **WARNING**
> *If the headlight has just burned out or has just been turned off, it will be **hot**! Do not touch the bulb. Wait for the bulb to cool before removing it.*

1. Disconnect the electrical connector (A, **Figure 61**) by pulling it *straight out* from the back of the headlight assembly.

> **NOTE**
> *The following illustrations are shown with the headlight assembly removed from the upper fairing for clarity.*

2. Pull the tab at the base and remove the rubber dust cover (A, **Figure 62**). Check the rubber cover for tears or deterioration; replace it if necessary.
3. Unhook the light bulb retaining clip (**Figure 63**) and pivot it out of the way.
4. Remove the blown bulb.
5. Align the three tabs (**Figure 64**) on the new bulb with the notches in the headlight housing and install the bulb.
6. Hook the retaining clip (**Figure 64**) over the bulb to hold it in place.
7. Install the rubber cover so the TOP mark (B, **Figure 62**) on the cover sits at the top of the headlight assembly. Make sure the cover is correctly seated against the lens assembly and the bulb.
8. Correctly align the electrical plug terminals with the bulb and connect it to the bulb. Push it *straight on* until it bottoms on the bulb and the rubber cover. See A, **Figure 61**.
9. Check headlight operation.
10. Adjust the headlight as described in this chapter.

Position Bulb Replacement (All Models Except U.S.A., California, Canada and Australia)

1. Remove the screw securing the upper fairing center panel and remove the panel from the front of the motorcycle.
2. Reach into the upper fairing and rotate the position bulb socket assembly *counterclockwise*. Remove the bulb/socket assembly from the base of the headlight unit.

3. Remove the bulb from the socket and install a new bulb.

4. Insert the socket into the base of the headlight unit, rotate it *clockwise* and lock it in place.

5. Install the center panel into the upper fairing and tighten the screws securely.

Headlight Lens/Housing Removal/Installation

The headlight lens/housing assembly is removed along with the upper fairing as described in *Upper Fairing Removal/Installation* in Chapter Fifteen.

Inspect the headlight lens/housing (**Figure 65**) for damage and internal moisture. If damaged, replace the entire unit because there are no replacement parts available.

After the upper fairing is installed, adjust the headlight as described below.

Headlight Adjustment

Adjust the headlight horizontally and vertically according to local Department of Motor Vehicle regulations.

NOTE
There are four adjust screws, two for each headlight as shown in **Figure 66**.

1. Turn the handlebar to the full stop position opposite to the lens to be adjusted.

2. To adjust the headlight horizontally, use a short handle Phillips screwdriver and turn the upper Phillips screw (B, **Figure 61**) until the aim is correct.

3. To adjust the headlight vertically turn the lower Phillips screw (C, **Figure 61**).

4. Repeat for the other headlight if necessary.

Taillight/Brake Light and License Plate Bulb Replacement

1. Remove the rear seat as described in Chapter Fifteen.

2. Reach into the rear frame cover and rotate the bulb socket (**Figure 67**) counterclockwise and remove it from the housing.

3. Push the bulb into the socket, turn it counterclockwise and remove it.

4. Align the bulb pins with the bulb socket grooves. Push the bulb into the socket, turn it clockwise and release it. Check that the bulb is locked in the bulb socket.

5. Insert the bulb socket into the housing. Turn the bulb socket clockwise and lock it in place.

6. Repeat for the other bulb if necessary.

9

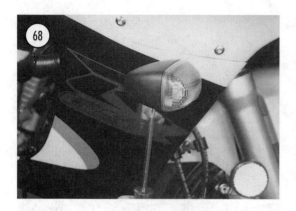

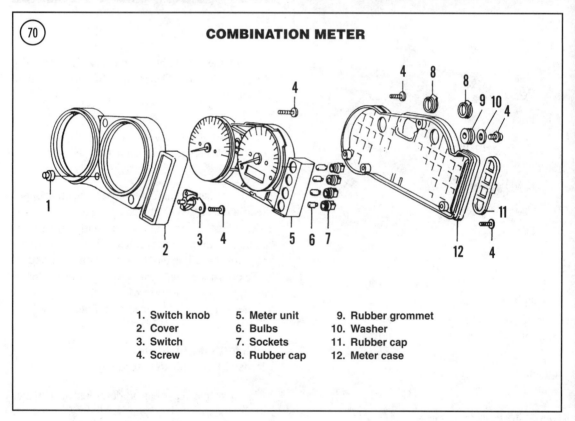

COMBINATION METER

1. Switch knob
2. Cover
3. Switch
4. Screw
5. Meter unit
6. Bulbs
7. Sockets
8. Rubber cap
9. Rubber grommet
10. Washer
11. Rubber cap
12. Meter case

7. Check taillight and brake light operation.

8. Install the rear seat as described in Chapter Fifteen.

Front and Rear Turn Signal
Bulb Replacement

1. Remove the lower screw (**Figure 68**) securing the lens to the housing.

2. Partially remove the lens (**Figure 69**) from the housing and turn it around.

3. Rotate the bulb socket counterclockwise and remove it from the lens.

4. Push the bulb in, turn it counterclockwise, and remove it from the bulb socket. Discard the blown bulb.

5. Align the bulb pins with the bulb socket grooves. Push the bulb into the socket, turn it clockwise and release it. Check that the bulb is locked in the bulb socket.

6. Insert the bulb socket into the housing. Turn the bulb socket clockwise and lock it in place.

7. Check the turn signal light operation.

8. Install the lens into the housing. Install and tighten the lower screw.

Combination Meter Indicator and Illumination Bulb Replacement

Refer to **Figure 70**.

1. Remove the upper fairing as described in Chapter Fifteen.

2. Remove the bulb socket covers (**Figure 71**) from the backside of the meter assembly.

3. Use needlenose pliers to carefully rotate the bulb/socket and remove it (**Figure 72**) from the printed circuit board on the meter assembly.

4. Install the bulb socket into the meter assembly. Rotate it until it is secure on the printed circuit board.

NOTE
If a new bulb does not work, check the printed circuit board for broken circuit strips on the board. Also check the bulb socket for corrosion.

5. Install the bulb socket covers (**Figure 71**) onto the backside of the meter assembly.

6. Install the upper fairing as described in Chapter Fifteen.

SWITCHES

Testing

Test switches for continuity with an ohmmeter (see Chapter One), or a test light at the switch connector plug by operating the switch in each of its operating positions and comparing the results with its switch operation diagram. For example, **Figure 73** shows a continuity diagram for an ignition switch. The horizontal lines indicate which terminals should show continuity when the switch is in that position. When the switch is in the PARK position, there should be continuity between the red and brown terminals. With the switch in the OFF position, there should be no continuity between any of the terminals.

When testing switches, refer to the appropriate continuity diagrams (**Figures 73-90**) and note the following:

1. First check the fuse as described in *Fuses* in this chapter.

2. Make sure the battery state of charge is acceptable (Chapter Three).

3. Disconnect the switch from the circuit or disconnect the negative battery cable before performing continuity tests.

CAUTION
Do not attempt to start the engine with the battery disconnected.

4. When separating two connectors, pull the connector housings and not the wires.

5. After isolating a defective circuit, check the connectors to make sure they are clean and properly connected. Check all wires going into a connector housing to make sure each wire is properly positioned and the wire end is not loose.

6. When reconnecting electrical connector halves, push them together until they click or snap into place.

73 IGNITION SWITCH (EXCEPT AUSTRALIA)

Position \ Color	R	O	Gr	Br	O/R	B/W
OFF						
ON	●—●		●—●		●—●	
P	●——————●					

76 DIMMER SWITCH

Position \ Color	Y/W	W	Y
HI		●——————●	
LO	●——————●		

74 IGNITION SWITCH (AUSTRALIA)

Position \ Color	R	O	O/Y	B/W
OFF				
ON	●—●		●—●	

77 TURN SIGNAL SWITCH

Position \ Color	G	Sb	B
L		●——————●	
PUSH			
R	●——————●		

75 LIGHTING SWITCH (1998-ON EXCEPT AUSTRALIA, CANADA AND U.S.)

Position \ Color	O/B	Gr	O/W	Y/W
OFF				
●	●	●—●		
ON	●—●		●—●	

78 PASSING LIGHT SWITCH (EXCEPT CANADA AND U.S.)

Position \ Color	O/R	Y
●		
PUSH	●——————●	

79 ENGINE STOP SWITCH

Position \ Color	O/B	O/W
●		
RUN	●——————●	

Right Handlebar Switch Housing Replacement

The right handlebar switch housing includes the following switches:

   a. Engine stop switch (A, **Figure 91**).

   b. Start button (B, **Figure 91**).

   c. Front brake light switch (electrical connectors only—the switch is separate).

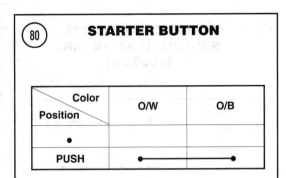

⑧⓪ STARTER BUTTON

Color Position	O/W	O/B
●		
PUSH	●———————●	

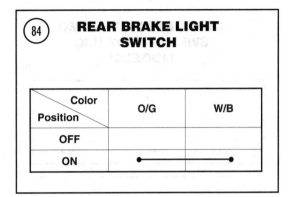

⑧④ REAR BRAKE LIGHT SWITCH

Color Position	O/G	W/B
OFF		
ON	●———————●	

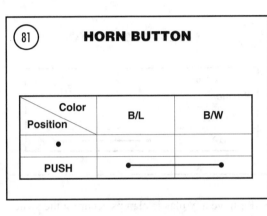

⑧① HORN BUTTON

Color Position	B/L	B/W
●		
PUSH	●———————●	

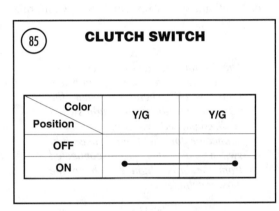

⑧⑤ CLUTCH SWITCH

Color Position	Y/G	Y/G
OFF		
ON	●———————●	

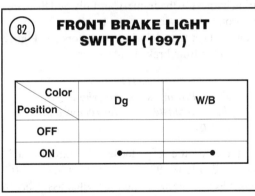

⑧② FRONT BRAKE LIGHT SWITCH (1997)

Color Position	Dg	W/B
OFF		
ON	●———————●	

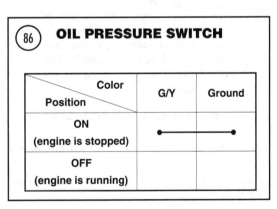

⑧⑥ OIL PRESSURE SWITCH

Color Position	G/Y	Ground
ON (engine is stopped)	●———————●	
OFF (engine is running)		

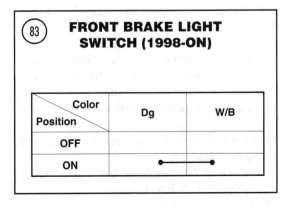

⑧③ FRONT BRAKE LIGHT SWITCH (1998-ON)

Color Position	Dg	W/B
OFF		
ON	●———————●	

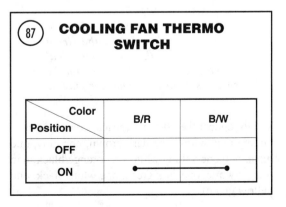

⑧⑦ COOLING FAN THERMO SWITCH

Color Position	B/R	B/W
OFF		
ON	●———————●	

9

CARBURETOR THERMO SWITCH (1997 U.K. MODELS)

(88)

Position \ Color	B	O/Y
OFF		
ON	•————————•	

CARBURETOR THERMO SWITCH (1998-ON U.K. MODELS)

(89)

Position \ Color	B	O/Y
OFF		
ON	•————————•	

d. Headlight switch (except U.S.A, California and Canada)

> *NOTE*
> *The 10-pin electrical connector also includes two wires for the front brake light switch. Therefore when the 10-pin connector for the right switch is disconnected, the 2-pin electrical connector for the front brake light switch must also be disconnected from the brake light switch on the master cylinder.*

> *NOTE*
> *The engine stop and headlight switches are not available separately. If one switch is damaged, replace the right switch housing assembly. The front brake light switch can be replaced independently.*

1. Disconnect the negative battery lead as described in this chapter.
2. Remove the fuel tank as described in Chapter Eight.
3. Remove the upper fairing as described in Chapter Fifteen.

> *NOTE*
> *The wiring color indicated in this procedure are for the colors on the wiring harness side of the 10-pin electrical connector. Some of the colors on the switch side of the connector may be different.*

4. Disconnect the 10-pin electrical connector containing nine wires (one dark brown, one gray, one black/red, one yellow/white, one orange/black, one orange/white, one dark green, one white/black, one yellow/green).

SIDESTAND SWITCH

(90)

Position \ Color	G	B/W
DOWN		
UP	•————————•	

5. Remove any plastic clamps securing the switch wiring harness to the frame. Carefully pull the wires out through the opening in the headlight housing.
6. Disconnect the two wire connectors (A, **Figure 92**) from the front brake light switch.

> *NOTE*
> *The following steps are shown with the front master cylinder removed for clarity.*

7. At the throttle grip, loosen the throttle cable locknut (B, **Figure 92**) and turn the adjust nut (C, **Figure 92**) all the way into the switch assembly to allow maximum slack in both cables. Perform this on both the pull (D, **Figure 92**) and push (E, **Figure 92**) cables.
8. Remove the screws securing the right switch assembly together and separate the switch assembly.
9. Disconnect the throttle pull cable, and then the throttle push cable from the throttle grip.
10. Remove the switch assembly from the handlebar and frame.
11. Install by reversing these removal steps while noting the following:

a. Connect the throttle cables onto the throttle grip and switch housing.

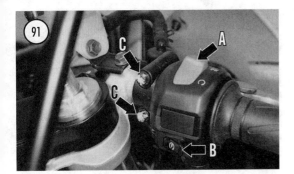

e. Passing button (non-U.S.A., California and Canada models).

NOTE
The 12-pin electrical connector also includes two wires for the clutch switch. Therefore when the 12-pin connector for the left switch is disconnected, the 2-pin electrical connector for the clutch switch must also be disconnected from the switch on the clutch lever.

NOTE
The three switches located within the left handlebar switch housing are not available separately. If one switch is damaged, replace the left switch housing assembly. The clutch switch is a separate unit and can be replaced independently.

1. Disconnect the negative battery lead as described in this chapter.
2. Remove the fuel tank as described in Chapter Eight.
3. Remove the upper fairing as described in Chapter Fifteen.

NOTE
The wiring color indicated in this procedure are for the colors on the wiring harness side of the 12-pin electrical connector. Some of the wiring colors on the switch side of the connector may be different.

4. Disconnect the 12-pin electrical connector, containing the following wires: one black/blue, one black/white, one light green, one light blue, one black, one black/red, one black/green (Australia, Canada, California, U.K. and U.S.A. models only),

b. Align the locating pin with the hole in the handlebar and install the switch onto the handlebar.
c. Install the screws and tighten them securely.
d. Make sure the electrical connectors are free of corrosion and secure.
e. Check the operation of each switch mounted in the right handlebar switch housing.
f. Operate the throttle lever and make sure the throttle linkage is operating correctly—without binding. If operation is incorrect or if there is binding, carefully check that the cable is attached correctly and there are no tight bends in the cable.
g. Adjust the throttle cables as described in Chapter Three.

Left Handlebar Switch Housing Replacement

The left handlebar switch housing includes the following switches:
a. Headlight dimmer switch (A, **Figure 93**).
b. Turn signal switch (B, **Figure 93**).
c. Horn button (C, **Figure 93**).
d. Clutch switch (electrical connectors only—the switch is separate).

9

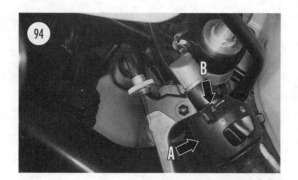

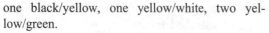

one black/yellow, one yellow/white, two yellow/green.

5. Remove any plastic clamps securing the switch wiring harness to the frame. Carefully pull the wires out through the opening in the headlight housing.

6. Remove the screws securing the left switch assembly together and separate the switch assembly (A, **Figure 94**).

7. Disconnect the choke lever and cable (B, **Figure 94**) from the switch housing.

8. Remove the switch assembly.

9. Install by reversing these removal steps while noting the following:

   a. Connect the choke cable and lever to the switch housing.

   b. Align the locating pin with the hole in the handlebar. Install the switch onto the handlebar and tighten the screws securely.

   c. Make sure the electrical connectors are free of corrosion and are tight.

   d. Check the operation of each switch mounted in the left switch housing.

   e. Operate the choke lever and make sure the linkage is operating correctly without binding. If operation is incorrect or if there is binding, carefully check that the cable is attached correctly and that there are no tight bends in the cable.

Ignition Switch Replacement

1. Disconnect the negative battery cable as described in this chapter.

2. Remove the upper fork bridge and ignition switch assembly as described in Chapter Twelve.

3. Place the upper fork bridge upside down on the work bench.

4. Remove the Torx bolts securing the ignition switch to the bottom of the upper fork bridge.

5. Install a new ignition switch and tighten the Torx bolts securely.

6. Install the upper fork bridge as described in Chapter Twelve.

7. Make sure the electrical connectors are free of corrosion and secure.

Neutral Switch Test

1. Remove both seats as described in Chapter Fifteen.

2. Remove the rear frame cover as described in Chapter Fifteen.

3. Disconnect the neutral-switch connector (A, **Figure 95**) at the harness connector on the left side of the rear frame.

   a. On 1997 models, the neutral switch connector is a two-pin electrical connector with one blue and one pink wire.

   b. On 1998-on models, the neutral-switch connector is a three-pin electrical connector with one blue, one pink and one black/white wire.

4. Shift the transmission into neutral.

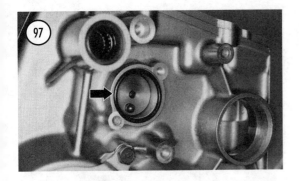

5. Connect an ohmmeter to the switch side of the electrical connector. Check that there is continuity between the blue terminal and ground.

6. Shift the transmission into any gear. There should be no continuity.

7. If the switch fails either of these tests, replace the switch.

8. If the switch tests good, reconnect the electrical connector.

9. Install the rear frame cover and both seats as described in Chapter Fifteen.

Neutral Switch Replacement

The neutral switch, or gear position switch, is mounted on the left crankcase below the drive sprocket.

1. Remove the drive sprocket cover as described in Chapter Eleven.

2. Remove both seats as described in Chapter Fifteen.

3. Remove the rear frame cover as described in Chapter Fifteen.

4. Disconnect the neutral-switch connector (A, **Figure 95**) at the harness connector on the left side of the rear frame.

5. Remove the mounting screws and the neutral switch (**Figure 96**) from the crankcase. Remove the O-ring behind the neutral switch.

6. Installation is the reverse of these removal steps while noting the following:

    a. Before installation, clean the switch contacts.

    b. Install a *new* O-ring (**Figure 97**). Lubricate the O-ring with Suzuki Super Grease A or equivalent.

    c. Install the switch and tighten the mounting screws securely.

    d. Check switch operation with the transmission in neutral and reverse.

Oil Pressure Switch Test

As soon as the ignition switch is turned ON, the low oil pressure symbol in the display should flicker and the indicator light should turn on. As soon as the engine is started, the symbol and the indicator light should go out. If there is a problem within the oil pressure system or if the oil pressure drops under the normal operating pressure range, the symbol flickers and indicator light turns on and stays on.

If the warning light is not operating correctly or does not come on when the ignition switch is in the ON position (engine not running), perform the following test. The oil pressure switch (**Figure 98**) is mounted on the right side of the lower crankcase below the starter clutch assembly.

1. Check the engine oil level as described in Chapter Three. Add oil if necessary.

2. Remove the lower fairing side panels as described in Chapter Fifteen.

3. Disconnect the electrical connector from the oil pressure switch (**Figure 98**).

4. Turn the ignition switch to the ON position.

5. Connect a jumper wire from the electrical connector to ground. The oil pressure warning light should come on.

6. If the light does not come on,

    a. Check the oil pressure warning light bulb. Replace the bulb if necessary.

    b. Also check the wiring from the switch to the warning light assembly and between the light and the junction box.

    c. If the bulb and wiring are good, replace the switch as described below.

9

Oil Pressure Switch Replacement

The oil pressure switch is mounted on the right side of the lower crankcase below the starter clutch assembly (**Figure 98**).

1. Remove the lower fairing as described in Chapter Fifteen.
2. Disconnect the electrical connector from the oil pressure switch.
3. Unscrew and remove the oil pressure switch (**Figure 98**) from the crankcase.
4. Installation is the reverse of these steps. Note the following:
   a. Apply a light coat of silicone sealant to the switch threads before installation.
   b. Install the switch securely.

Sidestand Switch Test

1. Remove both seats as described in Chapter Fifteen.
2. Remove the rear frame cover as described in Chapter Fifteen.
3. Disconnect the neutral-switch connector (A, **Figure 95**) at the harness connector on the left side of the rear frame.
4. Disconnect the 2- pin sidestand connector (B, **Figure 95**) at the harness connector on the left side of the rear frame.

NOTE
If a Suzuki Multi Circuit Tester is not available perform Step 6.

5A. Test the diode in the sidestand switch with a Suzuki Multi Circuit Tester or equivalent by performing the following:
   a. Set the test knob to diode test.
   b. Connect the test leads to the terminals in the switch side of the connector as shown in **Figure 99**.
   c. Move the sidestand to the up position and read the voltage on the meter.
   d. Move the sidestand to the down position and read the voltage on the meter.
   e. If the voltage is outside the range specified in **Figure 99**, replace the sidestand switch.
5B. If a Suzuki Multi Circuit tester or equivalent is not available, test the continuity of the sidestand switch by performing the following:

SIDESTAND SWITCH TEST

Color Position	G (+ probe)	B/W (- probe)
UP	0.4—0.6 V	0.4—0.6 V
DOWN	1.4—1.5 V	1.4—1.5 V

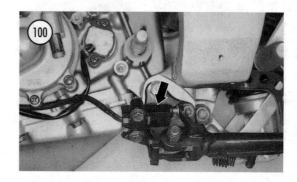

   a. Connect an ohmmeter to the terminals in the switch side of the connector terminals.
   b. Move the sidestand to the up position. The meter should show continuity.
   c. Move the sidestand to the down position. The meter should show no continuity.
   d. If the switch fails either of these tests, replace it.
6. Reconnect the electrical connectors and install all removed items.

Sidestand Switch Replacement

1. Remove the left lower fairing side panel as described in Chapter Fifteen.
2. Place the bike on a suitable jack or wooden blocks on level ground.
3. Disconnect the sidestand connector as described in the previous procedure.
4. Move the sidestand to the up position.
5. Remove the two bolts securing the sidestand switch (**Figure 100**) to the sidestand and remove the switch.
6. Install a new switch. Apply ThreeBond No. TB1342 to the mounting bolts and tighten them securely.

7. Move the sidestand from the raised to lowered position and check that the switch plunger has moved in.

8. Make sure the electrical connectors are free of corrosion and secure.

9. Install the lower fairing as described in Chapter Fifteen.

COMBINATION METER

Removal/Installation

1. Remove the upper faring and headlight lens assembly as described in Chapter Fifteen.

2. Disconnect the combination meter 16-pin electrical connector (A, **Figure 101**).

3. Remove the screws (B, **Figure 101**) securing the combination meter to the front fairing mounting bracket.

4. Remove the combination meter and store it carefully.

5. Install the combination meter onto the mounting bracket and tighten the screws securely.

6. Make sure the 16-pin electrical connector is free of corrosion, and connect it to the meter.

7. Install the upper fairing and headlight lens assembly as described in Chapter Fifteen.

Combination Meter Test

1. Remove the upper faring and headlight lens assembly as described in Chapter Fifteen.

2. Disconnect the combination meter 16-pin electrical connector (A, **Figure 101**).

3. Use an ohmmeter to check the continuity between the related terminals shown in **Figure 102**.

4. If continuity does not exist between any indicated pair of terminals, inspect the related indicator bulb for that circuit. Replace the bulb as necessary

and recheck the continuity. If the bulb is working, replace the meter assembly.

Engine Coolant Temperature Meter/Indicator Test

The liquid crystal display (LCD) and the light emitting diode (LED) in the tachometer provide engine coolant information. Check their operation by performing the following.

1. Raise and support the fuel tank as described in Chapter Eight.

2. Disconnect the green/yellow wire from the oil pressure switch (**Figure 98**).

3. Disconnect the black/green wire from the engine coolant temperature gauge (**Figure 103**).

4. Turn the ignition switch ON and check the LCD in the tachometer (**Figure 104**). It should display three dashes (- - -).

5. Connect a 9.56 k ohm resistor between the black/green wire and a good engine ground. The LED in the tachometer should go out and the tachometer's LCD should display *50° C or 122° F*.

6. Connect a 0.50 ohm resistor between the black/green wire and a good engine ground. The LED in the tachometer should turn on and the LCD should flash *130° C or 266° F*.

7. Connect a jumper between the black/green lead and a good engine ground. The LED in the tachometer should turn on and the LCD should flash *HI*.

8. If the meter fails one or more of the tests in Steps 4-7, replace the combination meter.

Fuel Level Indicator Test

1. Raise and support the fuel tank as described in Chapter Eight.

2. Disconnect the 4-pin fuel-pump connector (**Figure 105**).

3. Turn the ignition switch ON. The fuel level indicator should turn on for approximately three seconds after the ignition is turned on.

4. Use a jumper wire to connect the black/white terminal on the harness side of the connector to the red/black terminal on the harness side. The fuel level indicator light should flash.

5. Disconnect the jumper and watch the fuel level indicator light. It should go out approximately six seconds after disconnecting the jumper.

9

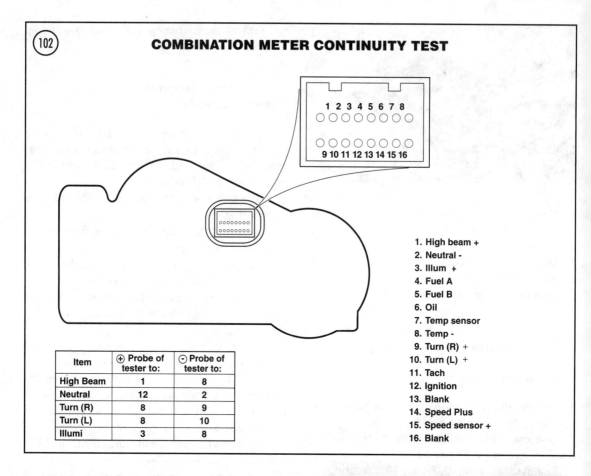

COMBINATION METER CONTINUITY TEST

1 2 3 4 5 6 7 8
9 10 11 12 13 14 15 16

Item	⊕ Probe of tester to:	⊙ Probe of tester to:
High Beam	1	8
Neutral	12	2
Turn (R)	8	9
Turn (L)	8	10
Illumi	3	8

1. High beam +
2. Neutral -
3. Illum +
4. Fuel A
5. Fuel B
6. Oil
7. Temp sensor
8. Temp -
9. Turn (R) +
10. Turn (L) +
11. Tach
12. Ignition
13. Blank
14. Speed Plus
15. Speed sensor +
16. Blank

6. Use the jumper wire to connect the black/white terminal on the harness side of the connector to the black/green terminal on the harness side. The fuel level indicator light should turn on.

7. Disconnect the jumper and watch the fuel level indicator light. It should go out approximately six seconds after disconnecting the jumper.

8. If the fuel level indicator does not function as described above, check the fuel level indicator bulb. If the bulb is good, replace the combination meter.

Fuel Level Indicator Switch Test

1. Remove the fuel pump assembly from the fuel tank, and remove the fuel level indicator from the fuel pump assembly. Refer to the fuel pump removal and disassembly procedures in Chapter Eight.

2. Connect a 12 volt battery and a 3.4 watt test bulb to the fuel level indicator as shown in **Figure 106**. The test light should turn on several seconds after the connection has been made.

3. With the battery and test lamp still connected, immerse the fuel level indicator switch into water as shown in **Figure 106**. The test light should go out.

4. Connect the battery and the test bulb to the fuel level indicator as shown in **Figure 107**. The test light should turn on several seconds after the connection has been made.

5. With the battery and test lamp still connected, immerse the fuel level indicator switch into water as shown in **Figure 107**. The test light should go out.

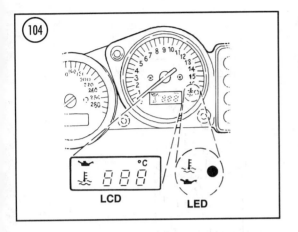

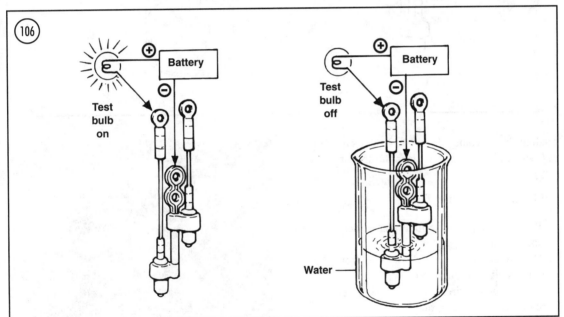

6. Replace the fuel level indicator switch if it fails any of these tests.

Speedometer, Odometer and Tripmeter Inspection

If the speedometer, odometer or tripmeter does not function properly, inspect the speed sensor and the connections. If the sensor and connections are good, replace the combination meter.

Speed Sensor Test

1. Remove the left fairing side panel as described in Chapter Fifteen.

2. Follow the speed sensor lead (A, **Figure 108**) to the wiring harness, and disconnect the 3-pin speed sensor connector.

3. Remove the speed sensor mounting bolt (B, **Figure 108**) and the speed sensor.

4. Connect the negative battery terminal to the black/white terminal in the sensor side of the connector and connect the positive battery terminal to the sensor's orange/white terminal.

5. Connect a 10 K ohm resistor to the orange/red and pink terminals on the sensor side of the connector and check the voltage across the resistor as shown in **Figure 109**.

6. Touch the pick-up surface of the sensor with a screwdriver and watch the voltmeter. The voltage

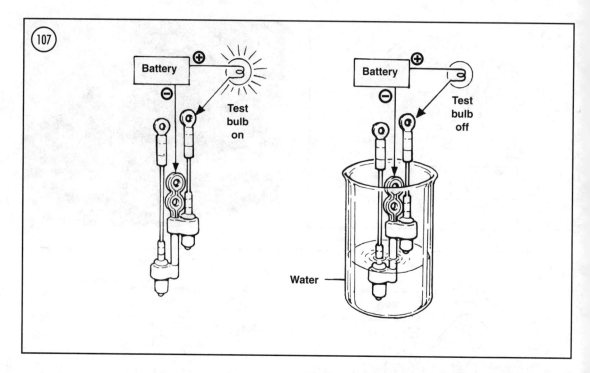

reading should change from 0 to 12 volts or from 12 to 0 volts. If it does not, replace the sensor.

Oil Pressure Indicator Test

1. Raise and support the fuel tank as described in Chapter Eight.
2. Disconnect the green/yellow wire from the oil pressure switch (**Figure 98**).
3. Use a jumper wire to connect the green/yellow wire to a good engine ground.
4. Turn the ignition switch on and watch the oil pressure indicator. It should turn on.
5. If the indicator does not turn on, check the wiring and connectors between the oil pressure switch and the meter. If they are good, replace the combination meter.

HORN

Test

1. Disconnect the negative battery cable as described in Chapter Three.
2. Remove the left fairing side panel as described in Chapter Fifteen.
3. Disconnect the electrical connectors (A, **Figure 110**) from the horn.

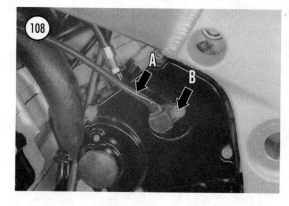

4. Connect a 12 volt battery to the horn terminals. The horn should sound.
5. If it does not, replace the horn.

Removal/Installation

1. Disconnect the negative battery cable as described in Chapter Three.
2. Remove the upper fairing as described in Chapter Fifteen.
3. Disconnect the electrical connectors (A, **Figure 110**) from the horn.
4. Remove the nut (B, **Figure 110**) securing the horn to the mounting bracket.
5. Remove the horn.

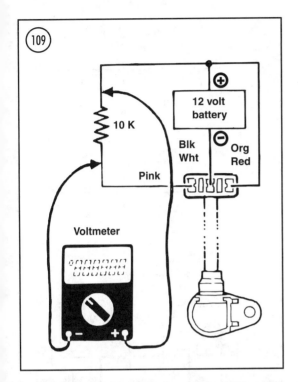

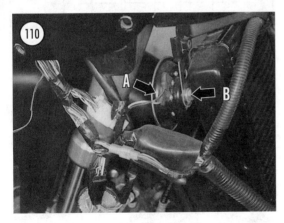

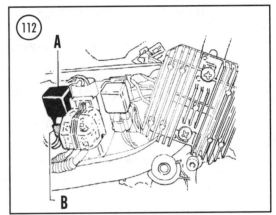

6. Install by reversing these removal steps while noting the following:

   a. Make sure the electrical connectors are free of corrosion and are tight.

   b. Test the horn to make sure it operates correctly.

RELAYS

On 1998-on models, the turn-signal relay, sidestand relay, and diode are combined into a single component, called the relay assembly (A, **Figure 111**), located beside the left air intake. If the turn-signal relay, sidestand relay or the diode is faulty in these models, replace the relay assembly.

Relay Assembly Replacement (1998-On)

1. Remove the relay assembly (A, **Figure 111**) from the mounting clip.
2. Disconnect the electrical connector from the relay assembly.
3. Connect the connector to a new relay assembly.
4. Fit the relay assembly onto the mounting clip.

Sidestand Relay Test
(1997 Models)

1. Disconnect the negative battery cable as described in this chapter.
2. Remove the seats and rear frame cover as described in Chapter Fifteen.
3. Pull straight up and remove the sidestand relay (A, **Figure 112**) from the rubber mount on the rear frame.

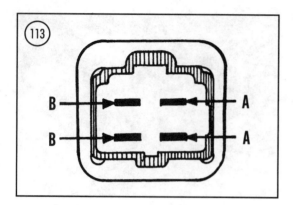

4. Disconnect the electrical connector (B, **Figure 112**) from the relay.

5. Connect a 12 volt battery to the A terminals on the relay (**Figure 113**).

6. Use an ohmmeter and check for continuity between the B terminals on the relay. There should be continuity.

7. If the relay fails this test, replace it. If the relay tests good, reconnect the electrical connector and install the relay onto the rubber mount on the rear frame.

Sidestand Relay Test
(1998-On)

1. Disconnect the negative battery cable as described in this chapter.

2. Pull straight up and remove the relay assembly (A, **Figure 111**) from the frame clip.

3. Disconnect the electrical connector from the relay assembly.

4. Apply 12 volts to the relay by connecting the negative side of the battery to the C terminal in the relay assembly and connect the positive battery terminal to the D terminal. See **Figure 114**.

5. Use an ohmmeter to check the continuity between terminals D and E on the relay assembly. There should be continuity.

6. Replace the relay assembly if there is no continuity.

Turn Signal Relay Test

If the turn signal light does not light, first look for a blown bulb. If the bulbs are good, check the turn signal switch as described in this chapter and check

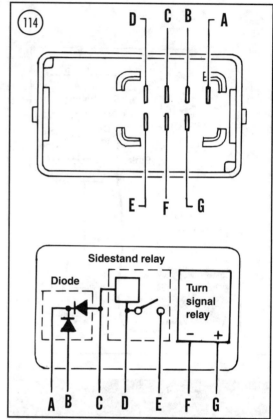

all electrical connections within the turn signal circuit.

If all of these areas test well, replace the turn signal relay on 1997 models. On 1998-on models, replace the relay assembly.

Turn Signal Relay Replacement
(1997 Models)

1. Turn the handlebar all the way to the left to gain access to the relay.

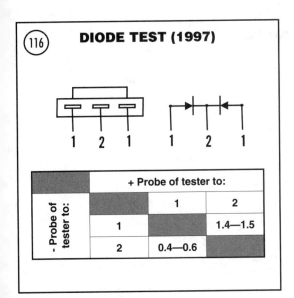

DIODE TEST (1997)

	+ Probe of tester to:	
	1	2
− Probe of tester to: 1		1.4—1.5
− Probe of tester to: 2	0.4—0.6	

sure the voltage across the diode terminals indicated in **Figure 116**.
5. Replace the diode if any reading is outside the range specified in **Figure 116**.

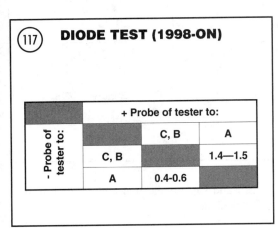

DIODE TEST (1998-ON)

	+ Probe of tester to:	
	C, B	A
− Probe of tester to: C, B		1.4—1.5
− Probe of tester to: A	0.4-0.6	

Diode Test (1998-On)

1. Remove the relay assembly as described above in this chapter.
2. Set the Suzuki Multi Circuit Tester (part No. 09900-25008) or equivalent to diode test, and measure the voltage across the diode terminals indicated in **Figure 117**. Also see **Figure 114**.
3. Replace the relay assembly if any measurement is outside the range specified in **Figure 117**.

Fuel Pump Relay
Removal/Testing/Installation

1. Disconnect the negative battery cable as described in this chapter.
2. Remove the seats and rear frame cover as described in Chapter Fifteen.
3. Pull straight up and remove the fuel pump relay (A, **Figure 118**) from the rubber mount on the rear frame.
4. Disconnect the electrical connector (B, **Figure 118**) from the relay.
5. Connect a 12-volt battery to the A terminals on the relay (**Figure 113**).
6. Use an ohmmeter and check for continuity between the B terminals on the relay. There should be continuity.
7. If the relay fails this test, replace the relay. If the relay tests good, reconnect the electrical connector and install the relay onto the rubber mount on the rear frame.

2. Unhook the turn signal relay (**Figure 115**) from the frame clip.
3. Disconnect the turn signal relay electrical connector and remove the relay.
4. Reconnect the connector to the relay and install the relay onto the frame clip.

Diode Test (1997 Models)

1. Raise and support the fuel tank as described in Chapter Eight.
2. Locate the diode beneath the fuel tank on the left side of the motorcycle.
3. Disconnect and remove the diode from the harness connector.
4. Set the Suzuki Multi Circuit Tester (part No. 09900-25008) or equivalent to diode test, and mea-

9

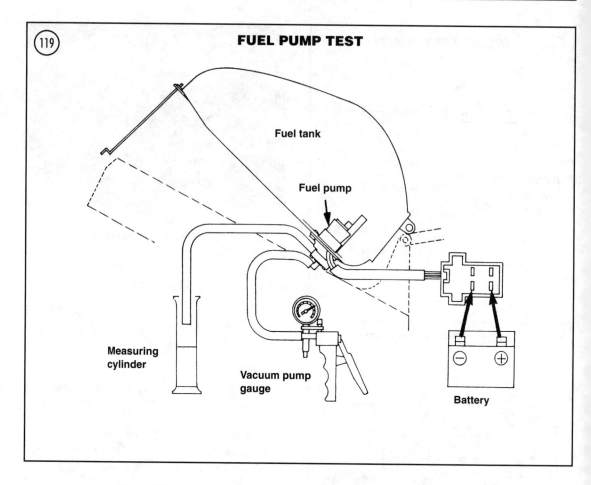

FUEL PUMP TEST

Fuel tank

Fuel pump

Measuring
cylinder

Vacuum pump
gauge

Battery

FUEL PUMP

> *WARNING*
> *Gasoline is a known carcinogen, and*
> *extremely flammable. Handle it care-*
> *fully. Wear latex gloves when working*
> *on components that may leak gaso-*
> *line. If your skin comes in contact with*
> *gasoline, rinse it off immediately and*
> *thoroughly wash the area with soap*
> *and warm water.*

Operation Inspection

Refer to **Figure 119**.
1. The battery must be fully charged, otherwise these test results may be inaccurate. Check the battery as described in Chapter Three.
2. The fuel tank must be filled with more than 1.5 gal. (5 liters) of gasoline.
3. Remove the seats as described in Chapter Fifteen.

4. Lift and support the fuel tank as described in Chapter Eight.

> *NOTE*
> *In Step 5 use a graduated beaker ca-*
> *pable of holding more than 1 U.S.*
> *quart (0.88 Imp. qt.) of gasoline.*

5. Disconnect the fuel hose (A, **Figure 120**) from the carburetor assembly and place the loose end into a graduated beaker. Secure the beaker so it does not tip over during this test.

6. Disconnect the fuel valve vacuum hose (B, **Figure 120**) from the carburetor assembly. Leave the hose attached to the shutoff valve.

> *CAUTION*
> *Use only a hand-operated vacuum*
> *pump. Do not apply a high vacuum to*
> *the fuel valve. The high vacuum will*
> *damage the valve.*

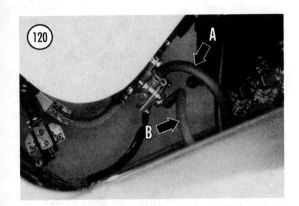

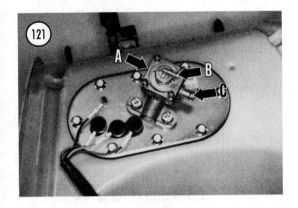

7. Connect a hand-operated vacuum pump to the vacuum hose (B, **Figure 120**) that is connected to the fuel valve vacuum port.

8. Disconnect the 4-pin fuel-pump electrical connector (**Figure 105**).

9. Using jumper cables with small alligator clips, connect a 12 volt battery power to the fuel pump electrical connector as follows:

    a. Connect the negative battery lead to the black/white terminal.

    b. Connect the positive battery lead to the yellow/red terminal.

10. Apply a vacuum (1.89 psi/13.3 kPa) to the fuel valve and measure the amount of gasoline discharged in 1 minute.

11. The fuel pump should discharge 1.06 U.S. qt/min. (0.88 Imp. qt/min.) during this test. If the test yielded less than this amount, inspect the fuel pump by performing the following:

    a. Remove the fuel pump assembly as described in Chapter Eight and check for a dirty and/or clogged fuel filter.

    b. Inspect the fuel valve as described in the following procedure.

    c. If the fuel filter is not clogged and/or if the fuel valve is good, replace the fuel pump as described in Chapter Eight.

12. If the fuel pump tests good, disconnect the battery jumper cables and disconnect the hand-operated vacuum pump.

13. Reconnect the fuel and vacuum hoses to the carburetor. Make sure the hoses are connected to the correct fittings on the valve and carburetor.

14. Remove the prop stay and lower the fuel tank. Install the two bolts and tighten securely.

15. Install the seats as described in Chapter Fifteen.

Fuel Valve Inspection

1. Remove the fuel tank as described in Chapter Eight.

2. Remove the screws and washers securing the fuel valve (A, **Figure 121**) to the base of the fuel pump.

> *CAUTION*
> *Use only a hand-operated vacuum pump. Do not apply a high vacuum to the fuel valve. The high vacuum will damage the valve.*

3. Connect a hand-operated vacuum pump to the vacuum port (B, **Figure 121**) on the fuel valve.

4. Connect a short piece of hose to the fuel port (C, **Figure 121**).

5. Apply a vacuum (1.89 psi/13.3 kPa) to the fuel valve and blow through the piece of hose into the fuel port.

6. Air should flow out of the inlet side of the valve where the gasoline normally enters the valve from the fuel tank.

7. If air does not flow out, the fuel valve is defective and must be replaced.

8. If the fuel valve tests good, reinstall it onto the fuel tank and tighten the screws securely.

9. Install the fuel tank as described in Chapter Eight.

COOLING SYSTEM

Fan Motor Test

    Use an ammeter and a fully charged 12-volt battery for this test.

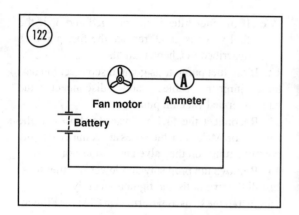

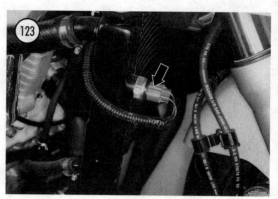

1. Remove the radiator as described in Chapter Ten.

2. Use jumper wires to connect the battery to the motor side of the 2-pin fan motor connector. Also connect an ammeter in line as shown in **Figure 122**.

3. The fan should operate when power is applied. Replace the fan assembly if the motor does not operate.

4. With the motor running at full speed, monitor the ammeter and note the load current. Replace the fan assembly if the load current exceeds the specification in **Table 1**.

Thermostatic Fan Switch Testing

The thermostatic fan switch controls the radiator fan according to the engine coolant temperature.

1. Remove the fan switch (**Figure 123**) from the radiator as described in Chapter Ten.

2. Fill a beaker or pan with water, and place it on a stove or hot plate.

3. Mount the fan switch so that the temperature sensing tip and the threaded portion of the body are submerged as shown in A, **Figure 124**.

> *NOTE*
> *The thermometer and the fan switch must not touch the container sides or bottom. If either does, it will result in a false reading.*

4. Place a thermometer (B, **Figure 124**) in the pan of water (use a cooking thermometer that is rated higher than the test temperature).

5. Attach the ohmmeter leads to the fan switch terminals as shown in A, **Figure 124**. Check the resistance as follows:

   a. Gradually heat the water.

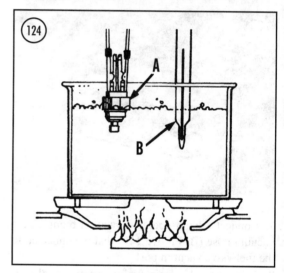

   b. When the temperature reaches 221° F (105° C), the meter should read continuity (switch on).

   c. Gradually reduce the heat.

   d. When the temperature lowers to approximately 212° F (100° C), the meter should not read continuity (switch off).

6. Replace the fan switch if it failed to operate as described in Step 5.

7. If the fan switch tests good, install the fan switch onto the radiator as described in Chapter Ten.

Coolant Temperature Gauge Testing

1. Remove the coolant temperature gauge sensor (**Figure 103**) from the thermostat housing as described in Chapter Ten.

2. Fill a beaker or pan with water, and place it on a stove or hot plate.

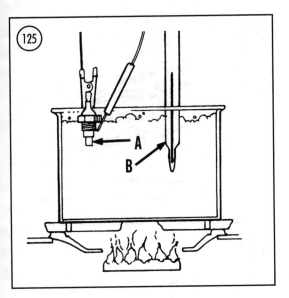

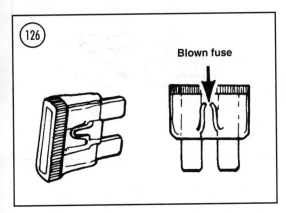

Blown fuse

3. Mount the coolant temperature gauge sensor so the temperature sensing tip and the threaded portion of the body are submerged as shown in A, **Figure 125**.

NOTE
The thermometer and the coolant temperature gauge sensor must not touch the container sides or bottom. If either does, it will result in a false reading.

4. Place a thermometer (B, **Figure 125**) in the pan of water (use a cooking thermometer that is rated higher than the test temperature).

5. Attach one ohmmeter lead to the water temperature sensor terminal and the other to the body as shown in A, **Figure 125**. Check the resistance as follows:

   a. Gradually heat the water.

b. Refer to the specifications in **Table 1** and note the resistance of the sensor when the water temperature reaches the specified value. Take a total of four readings.

   c. Replace the sensor if any reading does not equal the specified resistance at the specified temperature.

6. If the coolant temperature sensor tests good, install the sensor onto the thermostat housing as described in Chapter Ten.

FUSES

Replacement

All models are equipped with a single 30-amp main fuse (C, **Figure 118**) that is located next to the starter relay. The remaining fuses are located in the auxiliary fuse panel (B, **Figure 111**) located on the inside of the left air pipe.

If there is an electrical failure, first check for a blown fuse. A blown fuse will have a break in the element (**Figure 126**).

Whenever the fuse blows, determine the reason for the failure before replacing the fuse. Usually, the trouble is a short circuit in the wiring. This may be caused by worn-through insulation or a disconnected wire shorted to ground. Check by testing the circuit the fuse protects.

1. To replace the main fuse, perform the following:

   a. Remove the seats and rear frame cover as described in Chapter Fifteen.

   b. Remove the starter relay cover.

   c. Using needlenose pliers, pull the fuse (C, **Figure 118**) out and visually inspect it.

   d. Install a new fuse and push it in all the way until it bottoms out.

2. To remove the auxiliary fuses, perform the following:

   a. Remove the Phillips screw and open the fuse panel top cover.

   b. Locate the blown fuse and install a new one of the same amperage. See B, **Figure 111**.

NOTE
Always carry spare fuses.

   c. There are two spare fuses (10A and 15A) located in the fuse panel.

9

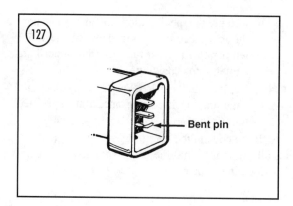

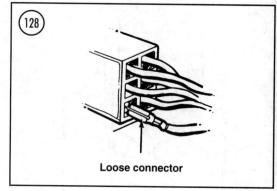

Loose connector

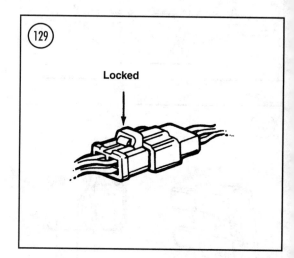

Locked

WIRING AND CONNECTORS

Circuit and Wiring Check

Many electrical troubles can be traced to damaged wiring or to contaminated or loose connectors.

1. Inspect all wiring for fraying, burning and any other visual damage.

2. Check the main fuse and make sure it is not blown. Replace it if necessary.

3. Check the individual fuse(s) for each circuit. Make sure it is not blown. Replace it if necessary.

4. Inspect the battery as described in Chapter Three. Make sure it is fully charged and that the battery electrical cable connectors are clean and securely attached to the battery terminals.

5. Connectors can be serviced by disconnecting and cleaning them with an aerosol electrical contact cleaner. After a thorough cleaning, pack multipin electrical connectors with dialectic grease to help seal out moisture.

6. Disconnect each electrical connector in the suspect circuit and check that there are no bent metal pins on the male side of the electrical connector (**Figure 127**). A bent pin will not contact the female end of the connector and this will cause an open circuit.

7. Check each female end of the connector. Make sure the metal connector on the end of each wire (**Figure 128**) is pushed all the way into the plastic connector. If not, carefully push them in with a narrow-blade screwdriver.

8. Push the connectors together and make sure they are fully engaged and locked together (**Figure 129**).

9. Never pull the electrical wires when disconnecting an electrical connector. Pull the connector plastic housing instead.

NOTE
Step 10 checks the continuity of individual circuits.

10. Check wiring continuity as follows:

   a. Disconnect the negative battery cable as described in this chapter.

   b. If using an analog ohmmeter, always touch test leads together and zero the needle according to manufacturer's instructions. An analog meter will yield false readings if it is not properly zeroed.

   c. Attach the test leads to the circuit to be tested.

   d. There should be continuity (indicated low resistance). If there is no continuity (infinite resistance), there is an open in the circuit.

WIRING DIAGRAMS

The wiring diagrams are at the end of the book.

Table 1 ELECTRICAL SYSTEM SPECIFICATIONS

Battery	
Type	FTX9-BS Maintenance free (sealed)
Capacity	12 volt 8 amp hour
Alternator	
Type	Three-phase AC
No-load voltage (when engine is cold)	55 volts (AC) at 5000 rpm
Maximum output	378 watts at 5000 rpm
Regulated voltage (charging voltage)	13.5-15.0 volts at 5000 rpm
Coil resistance	0.3 ohms
Ignition System	
Type	CDI
Firing order	1-2-4-3
Ignition timing	5 B.T.D.C. at 1500 rpm
Signal generator	
Coil resistance (pickup coil resistance)	50-200 ohms
Peak voltage	0.4 V
Ignition coil resistance	
Primary	0.07-0.11 ohms
Secondary	4.5-6.9 k ohms
Ignition coil primary peak voltage	
At ignition coil/plug cap	100 V or greater
At CDI connector	200 V or greater
Starter relay resistance	3-5 ohms
Fuse size	
Headlight (high and low beam)	15 amp
Turn signal	15 amp
Ignition	10 amp
Taillight	10 amp
Main	30 amp
Coolant temperature gauge resistance	
At 50° C (122° F)	Approximately 9.56 k ohms
At 100° C (212° F)	Approximately 2.78 k ohms
At 120° C (248° F)	Approximately 0.69 k ohms
At 130° C (266° F)	Approximately 0.50 k ohms
Thermostatic fan switch operating temperature	
Off-On	Approximately 105° C (221° F)
On-Off	Approximately 100° C (212° F)
Radiator fan load current (maximum)	5 amps

9

Table 2 REPLACEMENT BULBS

Item	Voltage/wattage
Headlight (high/low beam)	
U.S.A., California, Canada, Australia, U.K.	12 V 55/50 W x 2
Austria, Belgium, Brazil, France, Finland, Germany, Italy, Netherlands, Norway, Spain, Sweden, Switzerland	12 V 55/55 W
Position light	
Austria, Belgium, Brazil, France, Finland, Germany, Italy, Netherlands, Norway, Spain, Sweden, Switzerland, U.K.	12 V 5 W
Tail/brake light	12 V 5/21 W x 2
Turn signal	12 V 21 W
Tachometer light	12 V 1.7 W
Speedometer light	12 V 1.7 W
Neutral indicator light	12 V 1.7 W
High beam indicator light	12 V 1.7 W
Turn signal indicator light	12 V 1.7 W
Fuel indicator light	12 V 1.7 W

Table 3 ELECTRICAL SYSTEM TORQUE SPECIFICATIONS

Item	N•m	in.-lb.	ft.-lb.
Alternator rotor bolt	120	–	89
Engine coolant temperature gauge	9	80	–
Starter motor cable bolt	3	26	–

CHAPTER TEN

COOLING SYSTEM

This chapter covers repair and replacement procedures for the radiator and cap, thermostat, electric fan and coolant reservoir. Routine maintenance operations are described in Chapter Three. Cooling system specifications are listed in **Table 1** and **Table 2** at the end of this chapter.

> **WARNING**
> *Do not remove the radiator cap or any cooling system component that is under pressure when the engine is hot. The coolant is very hot and under pressure. Severe scalding could result if the coolant comes in contact with your skin. The cooling system must be cool before removing any system component.*

> **WARNING**
> *If the engine is warm or hot, the fan may come on (even with the ignition off). Never work around the fan until the engine is completely cool.*

> **WARNING**
> *Antifreeze is an environmental toxic waste. Do not dispose of it by flushing*

down a drain or pouring it onto the ground. Place old antifreeze into a suitable container and dispose of it properly. Do not store coolant where it is accessible to children or animals.

> **CAUTION**
> *When adding coolant or refilling the system use a mixture of ethylene glycol antifreeze formulated for aluminum engines and distilled water. Do not use only distilled water (even if freezing temperatures are not expected), the antifreeze inhibits internal engine corrosion and provides lubrication for moving parts.*

TEMPERATURE WARNING SYSTEM

A coolant temperature meter/oil pressure indicator LCD display is located in the tachometer (**Figure 1**). When the ignition switch is turned ON, the LCD displays a test pattern of assorted numbers for three seconds. If the coolant temperature is less than 40° C (104° F), the display indicates three dashes (– – –). If the coolant temperature is above 120° C

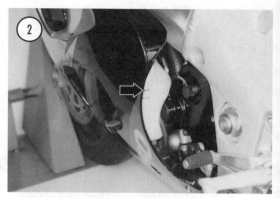

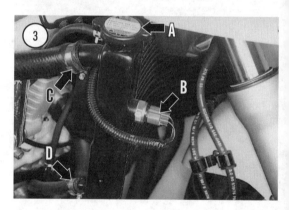

(248° F), the display flickers and the indicator light within the tachometer face comes on. If the coolant temperature is over 123° C (254° F), the display will flash HI and the LED remains on.

If the display continues to indicate HI after the engine as been started and run for a short period of time, turn the engine off and allow it to cool down. Determine the cause of the overheating condition before operating the motorcycle. Make sure the coolant level is at the FULL mark on the reservoir (**Figure 2**). Do not add coolant to the radiator.

HOSES AND CLAMPS

After removing any cooling system component, inspect the adjoining hose(s) to determine if replacement is necessary. Hoses deteriorate with age and should be inspected carefully for conditions that may cause them to fail. The possibility of a hose failing should be taken seriously. Loss of coolant causes the engine to overheat and spray from a leaking hose can injure the rider. Observe the following when servicing hoses:

1. Make sure the cooling system is cool before removing any coolant hose or component, including the radiator cap (**Figure 3**).

2. Use original equipment replacement hoses; they are formed to a specific shape and dimension for correct fit.

3. Do not use excessive force when removing a hose from a fitting. Refer to *Removing Hoses* in Chapter One.

4. If the hose is difficult to install onto the fitting, soak the hose in hot water to make it more pliable. Do not use any lubricant when installing hoses.

5. Inspect the hose clamps for damage. Always use the screw adjusting type hose clamps.

6. With the hose correctly installed, position the clamp approximately .50 in (12.8 mm) from the end of the hose and tighten the clamp.

COOLING SYSTEM INSPECTION

1. Run the engine until it reaches operating temperature. While the engine is running a pressure surge should be felt when the water pump outlet hose (**Figure 4**) is squeezed.

2. If steam is observed at the muffler outlet, the head gasket might be damaged. If enough coolant leaks into a cylinder(s), the cylinder could hydrolock and prevent the engine from being cranked. Coolant may also be present in the engine oil. If the oil visible in the oil level gauge (located on the right crankcase cover) is foamy or milky-looking, there is coolant in the oil. If so, correct the problem before returning the bike to service.

CAUTION
If the engine oil is contaminated with coolant, change the oil and filter after

repairing the cooling system. Refer to Chapter Three.

3. Check the radiator for clogged or damaged fins. If more than 15 percent of the radiator fin area is damaged, repair or replace the radiator.

4. Check all coolant hoses for cracks or damage. Replace all questionable parts. Make sure all hose clamps are tight, but not so tight that they cut the hoses. Refer to *Hoses and Clamps* in this chapter.

5. Pressure test the cooling system as described in Chapter Three.

COOLANT RESERVOIR

Removal/Installation

1. Support the bike on level ground on the sidestand.

2. Remove the left lower fairing side panel as described in Chapter Fifteen.

3. Disconnect the overflow hose (A, **Figure 5**) from the reservoir.

4. Remove the reservoir mounting bolts (B, **Figure 5**).

5. Disconnect the reservoir inlet hose (C, **Figure 5**) from the fitting at the base of the reservoir and place a finger over the hose fitting. Remove the reservoir.

6. Pull the coolant reservoir away from the frame and remove it.

7. Remove the fill cap and drain any residual coolant from the reservoir. Dispose of the coolant properly.

8. If necessary, clean the inside of the reservoir with a liquid detergent. Thoroughly rinse the reservoir with clean water. Make sure to remove all detergent residue from the reservoir.

9. Install by reversing these removal steps.

RADIATOR AND RADIATOR FAN

WARNING
Whenever the engine is warm or hot, the fan may start even with the ignition switch turned OFF. Never work around the fan or touch the fan until the engine and coolant are completely cool.

Removal/Installation

Refer to **Figure 6**.

1. Remove the upper and lower fairings as described in Chapter Fifteen.

2. Remove the fuel tank as described in Chapter Eight.

3. Drain the cooling system as described in Chapter Three.

4. Disconnect the negative battery cable as described in Chapter Three.

5. Disconnect the radiator cooling fan 2-pin electrical connector.

6. Disconnect the electrical connector from the thermostatic switch (B, **Figure 3**) on the upper right side of the radiator.

NOTE
Even though the cooling system has been drained, some residual coolant remains in the radiator and hoses. Place a drain pan under each hose as it is removed and wipe up any spilled coolant.

10

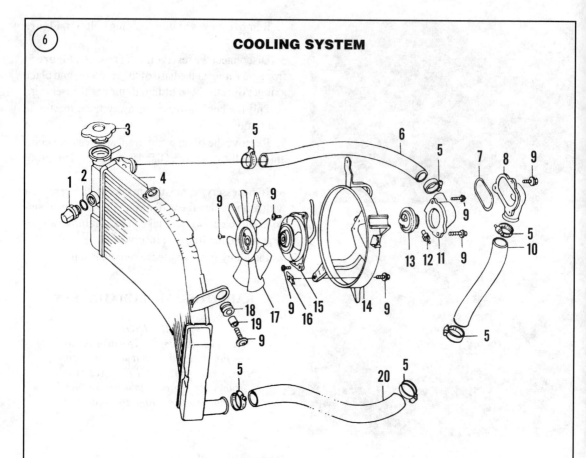

COOLING SYSTEM

1. Cooling fan thermo switch
2. O-ring
3. Radiator cap
4. Radiator
5. Hose clamp
6. Upper hose
7. O-ring seal
8. Coolant fitting
9. Bolt
10. Middle hose

11. Thermostat housing
12. Coolant temperature sensor
13. Thermostat
14. Fan shroud
15. Fan motor
16. Special nut
17. Fan blade
18. Rubber grommet
19. Collar
20. Lower hose

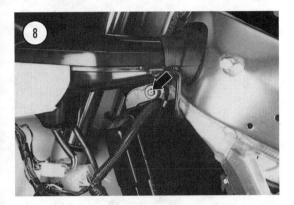

7. On the lower left side, loosen the hose clamp on the lower hose (**Figure 7**). Move the clamp back onto the hose and off of the radiator fitting. Remove the hose from the fitting and plug the end of the hose.

> *WARNING*
> *Coolant is very slippery if spilled on concrete or a similar surface. Do not walk on spilled coolant—wipe it off the floor immediately. Also wipe off any coolant that may get onto the soles of your shoes.*

8. On the right side, loosen the hose clamp on the upper hose (C, **Figure 3**) and the lower hose (D, **Figure 3**). Move each clamp back onto its hose and off of the radiator fitting. Remove each hose from the radiator and plug the hose end.

9. Remove the upper radiator-mounting bolt and collar (**Figure 8**) from each side of the radiator.

10. Remove the lower radiator mounting bolt and collar (**Figure 9**).

11. Carefully remove the radiator from the frame without contacting the front fender.

12. Inspect the radiator as described in this chapter.

13. Install by reversing these removal steps while noting the following:

    a. Replace all radiator hoses if they are deteriorating or are damaged in any way as described in this chapter.

    b. Make sure the damper is in place on each radiator mount.

    c. Torque the radiator mounting bolts to the specification in **Table 2**.

    d. Make sure the cooling fan and thermostatic switch electrical connections are free of corrosion and secure.

    e. Refill the cooling system with the recommended type and quantity of coolant as described in Chapter Three.

Radiator Inspection

1. Remove the radiator fan assembly (A, **Figure 10**) for inspection as described in this chapter.

2. On models so equipped, remove the protective screen from the front of the radiator.

3. If compressed air is available, use short spurts of air directed to the *backside* (B, **Figure 10**) of the radiator core to blow out debris.

10

4. Flush off the exterior of the radiator with a garden hose on low pressure. Spray both the front and the back to remove all debris. Carefully use a whisk broom or stiff paint brush to remove any stubborn dirt from the cooling fins.

CAUTION
Do not press hard on the cooling fins
or tubes.

5. Carefully straighten out any bent cooling fins (**Figure 11**) with a broad tipped screwdriver or putty knife.

6. Check for cracks or leakage (usually a moss-green colored residue) at all hose fittings (A, **Figure 12**) and both side tank seams (**Figure 13**).

7. To prevent oxidation of the radiator, touch up any areas where the paint is worn off. Use a quality spray paint and apply several *light* coats. Do not apply heavy coats as this cuts down on the cooling efficiency of the radiator.

8. Inspect the rubber dampers (B, **Figure 12**) in the radiator mounts. Replace any that are damaged or starting to deteriorate.

9. Check for leaks at the thermo fan switch (C, **Figure 12**), and make sure the switch is securely installed in the radiator. Tighten the switch if necessary.

RADIATOR FAN

Removal/Installation

Replacement parts for the fan assembly are not available. If the fan motor is defective, replace the entire fan assembly.

Refer to **Figure 6** for this procedure.

1. Remove the radiator as described in this chapter.

2. Place a blanket or large towels on the workbench to protect the radiator.

3. Remove the screws securing the fan shroud (A, **Figure 10**) to the radiator and carefully detach the fan assembly from the radiator.

4. Test the radiator fan motor as described in Chapter Nine.

5. Install by reversing these removal steps.

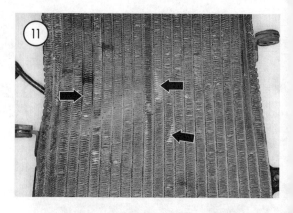

THERMOSTAT

Removal/Installation

Refer to **Figure 6**.

1. Remove the seat as described in Chapter Fifteen.

2. Remove the lower fairing as described in Chapter Fifteen.

3. Remove the fuel tank and air filter air box as described in Chapter Eight.

4. Remove the carburetor assembly as described in Chapter Eight.

5. Drain the cooling system as described in Chapter Three.

6. Disconnect the electrical connector from the engine coolant temperature gauge sensor (A, **Figure 14**).

7. Loosen the hose clamp (B, **Figure 14**) and move the clamp off the fitting. Disconnect the hose from the thermostat housing.

8. Remove the screws securing the thermostat cover (C, **Figure 14**) and remove the cover and gasket.

9. Remove the thermostat from the thermostat housing.

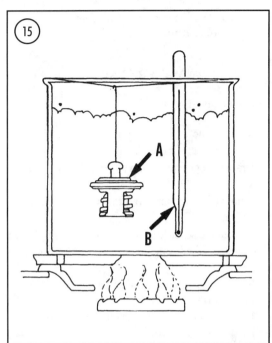

10. If necessary, test the thermostat as described in this chapter.

11. Inspect the thermostat for damage and make sure the spring has not sagged or broken. Replace the thermostat if necessary.

12. Clean the inside of the thermostat housing of any debris or old coolant residue. Make sure the opening leading to the hose is clear.

13. Install by reversing these removal steps while noting the following:

    a. Inspect the cover gasket. Replace it if necessary.

    b. Position the thermostat with the air bleed hole positioned toward the top of the cover.

    c. Apply Suzuki Super Grease A or equivalent to the rubber seat on the thermostat.

    d. Tighten the thermostat housing bolts to the specification in **Table 2**.

    e. Refill the cooling system with the recommended type and quantity of coolant as described in Chapter Three.

Testing

Test the thermostat to ensure proper operation. Replace the thermostat if it remains open at normal room temperature or stays closed after the specified temperature has been reached during the test procedure.

> *NOTE*
> *The thermometer and the thermostat must not touch the container sides or bottom. If either does, it will result in a false reading.*

Suspend the thermostat and thermometer in a pan of water (**Figure 15**). Use a cooking thermometer that is rated higher than the test temperature. Gradually heat the water and continue to gently stir the water until it reaches the temperature listed in **Table 1**. At this temperature the thermostat valve should open.

> *NOTE*
> *Valve operation is sometimes sluggish; it usually takes 3-5 minutes for the valve to operate properly and to open completely. If the valve fails to open, replace the thermostat (it cannot be serviced). Make sure to replace*

10

it with a thermostat of the same temperature rating.

WATER PUMP

Removal/Installation

1. Remove the left lower fairing side panel as described in Chapter Fifteen.

2. Drain the cooling system as described in Chapter Three.

3. Remove the coolant reservoir as described in this chapter.

4. Loosen the screw on the inlet hose clamp. Move the clamp off the fitting on the water pump and onto the hose.

5. Remove the inlet hose (**Figure 16**) from the water pump fitting.

6. Loosen the oil cooler hose clamp (A, **Figure 17**) and move the clamp off the fitting.

7. Remove the oil cooler hose (B, **Figure 17**) from the water pump fitting.

8. Remove the drive sprocket cover as described in Chapter Thirteen.

9. Loosen the hose clamp on the outlet hose and move the clamp off the fitting.

10. Remove the outlet hose (**Figure 4**) from the water pump outlet fitting.

11. Remove the two bolts (A, **Figure 18**) securing the water pump (B, **Figure 18**) and withdraw the water pump from the crankcase.

12. Inspect the water pump as described in this chapter.

13. Install by reversing these removal steps while noting the following:

   a. Install a new O-ring seal onto the water pump and apply a light coat of Suzuki Super Grease A or equivalent to the O-ring.

   b. Align the water pump shaft notch with the raised tab on the oil pump shaft, then install the water pump into the crankcase. If necessary, slightly reposition the shaft to achieve correct alignment. Push the water pump in until it is completely seated and the bolt holes are aligned. Tighten the water pump mounting bolts to the specification in **Table 2**.

   c. Make sure all hose clamp screws are tight.

   d. Refill the cooling system as described in Chapter Three.

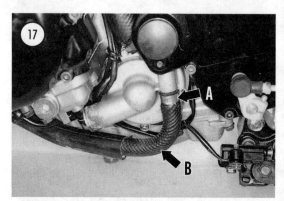

   e. Start the engine and check for leaks before installing the lower fairing.

Disassembly/Inspection/Assembly

Refer to **Figure 19**.

1. Remove the mounting screws (**Figure 20**), and the cover from the base.

2. Thoroughly clean the water pump base and cover in solvent to remove all old coolant residue.

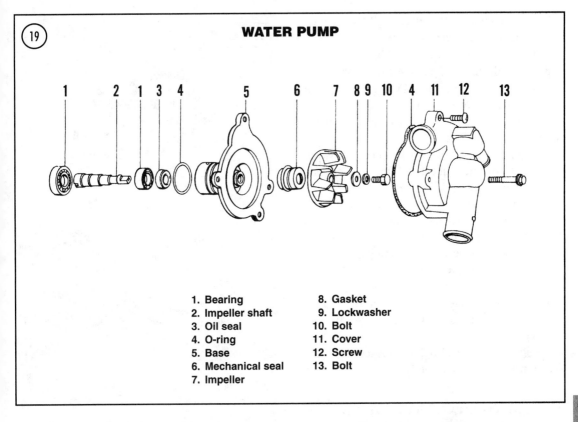

WATER PUMP

1. Bearing
2. Impeller shaft
3. Oil seal
4. O-ring
5. Base
6. Mechanical seal
7. Impeller
8. Gasket
9. Lockwasher
10. Bolt
11. Cover
12. Screw
13. Bolt

10

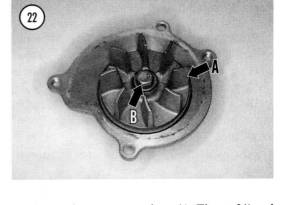

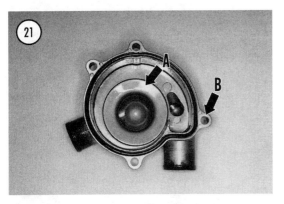

3. Inspect the water pump base (A, **Figure 21**) and cover (B, **Figure 21**) for wear or damage.

4. Turn the impeller shaft, and check the bearing for excessive noise or roughness. If the bearing operation is rough, replace the water pump.

5. Check the impeller blades (A, **Figure 22**) for corrosion or damage. If corrosion is excessive or if the blades are cracked or broken, replace the impeller as follows:

   a. Remove the impeller bolt (B, **Figure 22**) and washer.

b. Lift the impeller (**Figure 23**) off the impeller shaft and out of the base.

c. Remove the impeller shaft (**Figure 24**).

d. Install the impeller shaft into the base.

e. Install a new impeller (**Figure 25**), washer and bolt. Tighten the nut securely.

6. If the water pump has been leaking, replace the mechanical seal as follows:

a. Use a flat blade screwdriver and carefully pry out the old mechanical seal from the backside of the impeller (**Figure 26**).

b. Clean the seal receptacle in the impeller.

c. Use a socket that matches the outside diameter of the new mechanical seal (**Figure 27**), and drive the new seal into the impeller until it bottoms (**Figure 28**).

7. Remove the O-ring from the cover.

8. Install a *new* O-ring seal (4, **Figure 19**) into the cover. Apply Suzuki Super Grease A or equivalent to the O-ring.

9. Install the cover and tighten the screws to the torque specification in **Table 2**.

THERMOSTATIC FAN SWITCH

Removal/Installation

1. Remove the right lower fairing side panel as described in Chapter Fifteen.

2. Drain the cooling system as described under *Coolant Change* in Chapter Three.

3. Disconnect the electrical connector (**Figure 29**) from the thermostatic fan switch on the right side of the radiator.

4. Unscrew the thermostatic fan switch from the radiator.

5. If necessary, test the switch as described in Chapter Nine.

6. Install by reversing these removal steps while noting the following:

a. Install a new O-ring. Apply a light coat of Suzuki Super Grease A or equivalent to the O-ring.

b. Install the switch and torque it to the specification in **Table 2**.

c. Refill the cooling system as described in Chapter Three.

d. Start the engine and check for leaks before installing the lower fairing.

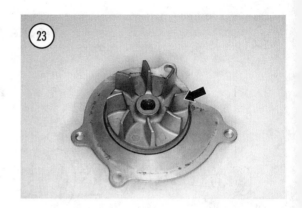

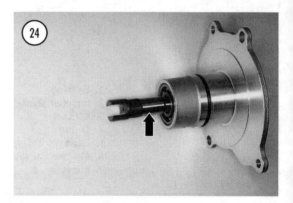

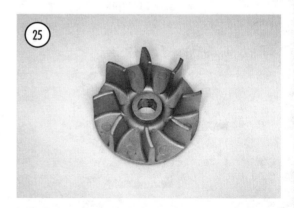

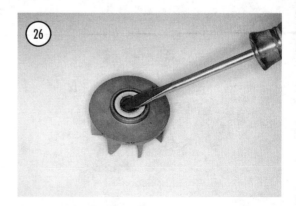

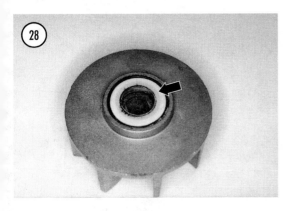

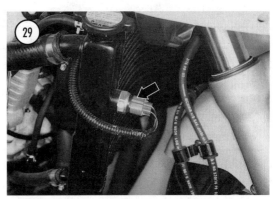

COOLANT TEMPERATURE GAUGE

Removal/Installation

1. Remove the seat as described in Chapter Fifteen.
2. Remove the fuel tank and air box as described in Chapter Eight.
3. Remove the carburetor assembly as described in Chapter Eight.

4. Drain the cooling system as described under *Coolant Change* in Chapter Three.

5. Disconnect the electrical connector from the engine coolant temperature gauge sensor (A, **Figure 14**).

6. Place a small container under the sensor to catch the coolant that drains out.

7. Unscrew the temperature sensor from the thermostat housing cover and remove it.

8. Install by reversing these removal steps while noting the following:

   a. Apply a light coat of Suzuki Bond 1207B or equivalent sealant to the sensor threads before installation.

   b. Tighten the switch to the specification in **Table 2**.

   c. Refill the cooling system as described in Chapter Three.

   d. Start the engine and check for leaks before installing the lower fairing.

10

Table 1 COOLING SYSTEM SPECIFICATIONS

Item	Specification
Coolant type	Antifreeze/coolant compatable with aluminum radiator. Mixed with distilled water at 50:50 ratio.
Coolant capacity	2.5 L (2.7 U.S. qt., 2.2 Imp qt.)
Thermostat valve opening temperature	74.5-78.5° C (166.1-173.3° F)
Thermostat valve lift	Over 7.0 mm at 90° C (over 0.28 in. at 194° F)
Radiator cap valve opening pressure	110 kPa (15.6 psi)

Table 2 COOLING SYSTEM TORQUE SPECIFICATIONS

Item	N•m	in.-lb.	ft.-lb.
Coolant temperature gauge sensor	9	80	–
Impeller bolt	8	71	–
Thermostatic fan switch	17	–	12
Thermostat housing bolt	10	89	–
Radiator mounting bolt	6	53	–
Water pump cover screw	6	53	–
Water pump mounting bolt	6	53	–

CHAPTER ELEVEN

WHEELS, TIRES AND DRIVE CHAIN

This chapter describes repair and maintenance procedures for the front and rear wheels, tires and the drive chain.

Specifications are in **Table 1** and **Table 2** at the end of the chapter.

BIKE STAND

Many procedures in this chapter require that the bike be supported with a wheel off the ground. A motorcycle front end stand (**Figure 1**) or swing arm stand does this safely and effectively. Before purchasing or using a stand, check the manufacturer's instructions to make sure it is designed for the GSX-R600. If the bike or stand requires any adjustment or the installation of accessories (tie-downs), perform the required modification(s) before lifting the bike. When using a bike stand, have an assistant standing by.

> *CAUTION*
> *Regardless of the method used to lift a bike, make sure the motorcycle is properly supported before walking away from it.*

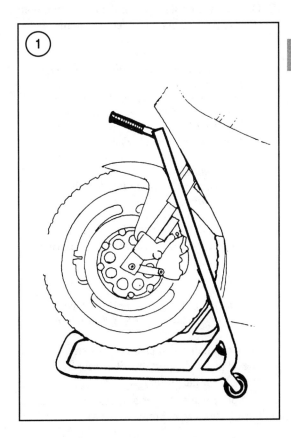

FRONT WHEEL

Removal

> *CAUTION*
> *Use care when removing, handling and installing a wheel with disc brake rotors. The rotors can easily be damaged by side impacts due to their thin design. A rotor that is not true will cause brake pulsation. Protect the rotors if the wheels are being transported for tire service. The rotors cannot be machined to repair excessive runout.*

1. Place the bike on the sidestand.
2. Remove the lower fairing from each side as described in Chapter Fifteen.
3. Shift the transmission into gear to prevent the bike from rolling in either direction while the bike is on a jack or wooden blocks.
4. On the right fork leg, loosen both axle pinch bolts (A, **Figure 2**), and then loosen the front axle (B, **Figure 2**).
5. On the left fork leg, loosen the axle pinch bolts (A, **Figure 3**) securing the spacer nut in place.

> *NOTE*
> *Insert a piece of vinyl tubing or wood between the pads of each caliper once the caliper is removed. That way, if the brake lever is inadvertently squeezed, the pistons will not be forced out of the cylinder. If this does happen, the caliper may have to be disassembled to reseat the pistons and the system will have to be bled. By using a spacer, bleeding the brake is not necessary when installing the wheel.*

6. Remove both brake calipers as described in Chapter Fourteen.

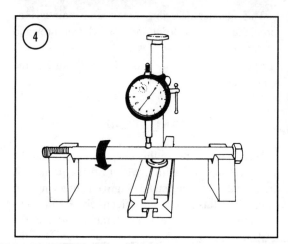

> *CAUTION*
> *If using a jack, place a piece of wood on the jack pad to protect the oil pan.*

7. Place a suitable size jack or wooden blocks under the oil pan to support the bike securely with the front wheel off the ground.
8. Completely unscrew the axle from the spacer nut on the left fork leg and remove the axle.

9. Pull the wheel down and forward and remove the wheel from the front fork.
10. Remove the spacer nut (B, **Figure 3**) from the left fork leg.

> *CAUTION*
> *Do not set the wheel down on the disc surface as it may get scratched or warped. Set the tire sidewalls on two wooden blocks.*

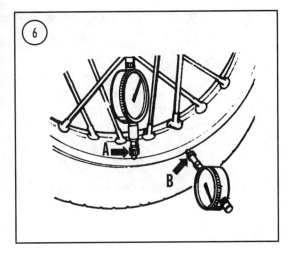

11. Inspect the wheel as described in this chapter.

Inspection

1. Remove any corrosion from the front axle with a piece of fine emery cloth. Clean the axle with solvent, and then wipe the axle clean with a lint-free cloth.

2. Set the axle on V-blocks and place the tip of a dial indicator in the middle of the axle (**Figure 4**). Rotate the axle and check its runout. If axle runout exceeds the specification listed in **Table 1**, replace the axle. Do not attempt to straighten it.

3. Check the disc brake bolts (**Figure 5**) for tightness on each side. Refer to **Table 2**, and tighten if necessary.

4. Check rim runout as follows:
   a. Measure the radial (up and down) runout of the wheel rim with a dial indicator (A, **Figure 6**). If runout exceeds the specification listed in **Table 1**, check the wheel bearings.

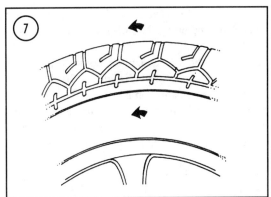

   b. Measure the axial (side to side) runout of the wheel rim with a dial indicator (B, **Figure 6**). If runout exceeds the specification listed in **Table 1**, check the wheel bearings.
   c. Replace the front wheel bearings as described in *Front and Rear Hubs* in this chapter.

5. Inspect the wheel rim for dents, bending or cracks. Check the rim and rim sealing surface for scratches that are deeper than 0.5 mm (0.01 in.). If any of these conditions are present, replace the rim.

6. Inspect the brake pads (Chapter Fourteen).

Installation

1. Make sure the bearing surfaces of each fork slider, the spacer nut and the axle are free from burrs and nicks.

2. Install the spacer nut (B, **Figure 3**) into the left fork leg and hand-tighten the clamp bolts.

3. Correctly position the wheel so the directional arrow (**Figure 7**) points in the direction of normal wheel rotation.

4. Apply a light coat of grease to the front axle.

5. Position the wheel between the fork legs, lift the wheel and insert the front axle through the right fork leg, the wheel hub and into the spacer nut.

6. Screw the axle (B, **Figure 2**) into the left fork leg spacer nut, and tighten the axle securely.

7. Tighten the spacer nut pinch bolts (A, **Figure 3**) to the torque specification listed in **Table 2**.

8. Install both brake calipers as described in Chapter Fourteen.

9. Remove the jack or wooden block(s) from under the oil pan.

10. Have an assistant apply the front brake and tighten the axle (B, **Figure 2**) to the torque specification listed in **Table 2**.

11

11. Apply the front brake, push down hard on the handlebars and pump the fork four or five times to seat the front axle.

12. Tighten the front axle pinch bolts (A, **Figure 2**) to the torque specification listed in **Table 2**.

13. Shift the transmission into neutral.

14. Roll the bike back and forth the several times. Apply the front brake as many times as necessary to make sure the brake pads seat against the brake disc correctly.

15. Place the bike on the sidestand.

16. Install the lower fairing onto each side as described in Chapter Fifteen.

REAR WHEEL

Removal

1. Remove the lower fairing from each side as described in Chapter Fifteen.

2. On U.S.A, California and Canada models, remove the cotter pin (A, **Figure 8**) from the rear axle nut. A *new* one must be installed during assembly.

3. Have an assistant apply the rear brake, and then loosen the axle nut (B, **Figure 8**).

4. Block the front wheel to prevent the bike from rolling in either direction while the bike is on a jack or wooden blocks.

CAUTION
If using a jack, place a piece of wood on the jack pad to protect the oil pan.

5. Place a suitable size jack or wooden blocks under the oil pan to support the bike securely with the rear wheel off the ground.

WARNING
If the bike has just been run, the muffler will be very HOT. If possible, wait for the muffler to cool down. If not, protect yourself accordingly.

6. Loosen the adjuster locknut (A, **Figure 9**), then loosen the adjuster (B, **Figure 9**) on each side of the swing arm to allow maximum slack in the drive chain.

7. Remove the rear axle nut (B, **Figure 8**). On non-U.S.A, California and Canada models, remove the washer.

8. Remove the rear axle (C, **Figure 9**) from the right side of the motorcycle. The adjuster blocks

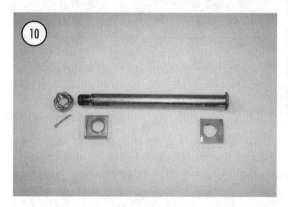

will come off when the rear axle is withdrawn. The adjuster blocks are not interchangeable. Mark them with an R (right) and L (left) so they will be installed on the correct side.

9. To avoid misplacing parts, reinstall the adjuster blocks and nut onto the rear axle (**Figure 10**).

NOTE
Insert a piece of vinyl tubing or wood into the caliper in place of the brake disc. That way, if the bake pedal is inadvertently pressed, the pistons will

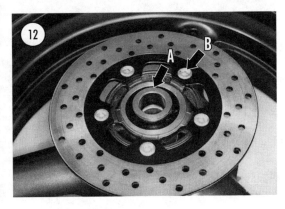

not be forced out of the cylinders. If this does happen, the caliper may have to be disassembled to reseat the pistons and the system will have to be bled. By using a spacer, bleeding the brake is not necessary when installing the wheel.

10. Lower the rear caliper, caliper carrier and torque link. Suspend the caliper from the frame with a bunjee cord or piece of wire so there is no strain on the hydraulic hose.

11. Push the wheel forward and remove the drive chain (C, **Figure 8**) from the rear sprocket.

12. Pull the wheel rearward, and remove the wheel from the swing arm.

13. Remove each spacer from the left (A, **Figure 11**) and right (A, **Figure 12**) sides of the wheel.

> *CAUTION*
> *Do not set the wheel down on the disc surface as it may get scratched or warped. Set the sidewalls on two wooden blocks.*

14. Inspect the wheel as described in this chapter.

Inspection

> *NOTE*
> *The rear wheel hub is equipped with a single seal that is located on the right side of the hub. The other seal is located in the rear coupling assembly on the left side.*

1. If still in place, remove the left (A, **Figure 11**) and right (A, **Figure 12**) axle spacers from the hub.

2. Clean the axle and spacers in solvent to remove all old grease and dirt. Make sure all axle contact surfaces are clean and free of dirt and old grease before installation. If these surfaces are not cleaned, the axle may be difficult to remove later on.

3. Place the axle on V-blocks and place the tip of a dial indicator in the middle of the axle (**Figure 4**). Rotate the axle and check the runout. If axle runout exceeds the specification listed in **Table 1**, replace the axle. Do not attempt to straighten it.

4. Check the disc brake bolts for tightness (B, **Figure 12**). Refer to **Table 2** and retighten if necessary.

5. Check the rear sprocket nuts (B, **Figure 11**) for tightness. Refer to **Table 2** and retighten if necessary.

6. Check rim runout as follows:

   a. Measure the radial (up and down) runout of the wheel rim with a dial indicator (A, **Figure 6**). If runout exceeds the specification listed in **Table 1**, check the wheel bearings.

   b. Measure the axial (side to side) runout of the wheel rim with a dial indicator as (B, **Figure 6**). If runout exceeds the specification listed in **Table 1**, check the wheel bearings.

   c. Replace the rear wheel and/or rear coupling bearings as described in *Front and Rear Hubs* in this chapter.

7. Inspect the wheel rim for dents, bending or cracks. Check the rim and rim sealing surface for scratches that are deeper than 0.5 mm (0.01 in.). If any of these conditions are present, replace the rim.

8. Inspect the brake pads (Chapter Fourteen).

Installation

1. Make sure all axle contact surfaces on the swing arm and axle spacers are free of dirt and small burrs.

2. Apply a light coat of grease to the axle, bearings, spacers and grease seal.

3. Make sure the left (A, **Figure 11**) and right (B, **Figure 12**) axle spacers are installed on each side of the rear hub.

4. Position the wheel into place and roll it forward. Install the drive chain onto the rear sprocket.

5. Remove the vinyl tubing or piece of wood from the brake caliper.

6. Move the rear brake caliper and bracket assembly onto the disc. Make sure the right axle spacer is still in place.

7. Install the drive chain adjuster onto the right end of the axle and position it with the large pad (**Figure 13**) facing forward. Position the flats on the rear axle into the flats on the drive chain adjuster.

8. Raise the rear wheel up and into alignment with the swing arm. From the right side of the motorcycle insert the rear axle (C, **Figure 9**) through the swing arm, the caliper bracket, the rear wheel and out through the left side of the swing arm. Push the axle all the way in until it bottoms in the swing arm.

9. On non-U.S.A. California and Canada models, install the washer.

10. Install the rear axle nut (B, **Figure 8**). Hand-tighten the nut at this time.

11. Adjust the drive chain as described in Chapter Three.

12. Torque the axle nut to the specification in **Table 2**, and tighten each adjust locknut securely.

13. On U.S.A., California and Canada models, install a *new* cotter pin onto the rear axle nut (A, **Figure 8**) and bend both ends over completely.

14. Remove the jack or wooden block(s) from under the oil pan. Remove the blocks from the front wheel.

15. Roll the bike back and forth several times. Apply the rear brake as many times as necessary to make sure the brake pads are seated against the brake disc correctly.

16. Place the bike on the sidestand.

17. Install the lower fairing on each side as described in Chapter Fifteen.

REAR COUPLING AND REAR SPROCKET

Removal/Disassembly/Assembly/Installation

1. Remove the rear wheel as described in this chapter.

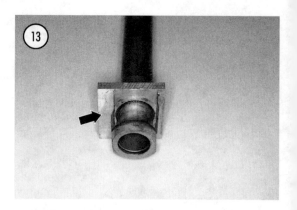

2. If still in place, remove the left axle spacer (A, **Figure 11**).

3. If the rear sprocket is going to be removed, loosen and remove the nuts (B, **Figure 11**) securing the rear sprocket to the rear coupling at this time.

> *NOTE*
> *If the rear coupling assembly is difficult to remove from the hub, tap on the backside of the sprocket (from the opposite side of the wheel through the wheel spokes) with the wooden handle of a hammer. Tap evenly around the perimeter of the sprocket until the coupling assembly is free of the hub and the rubber dampers.*

4. Pull straight up and remove the rear coupling assembly from the rear hub.

5. Remove the inner retainer (A, **Figure 14**) from the rear coupling assembly.

6. If necessary, remove the rear sprocket nuts (B, **Figure 11**) and separate the rear sprocket from the rear coupling.

7. Install by reversing these removal steps while noting the following:

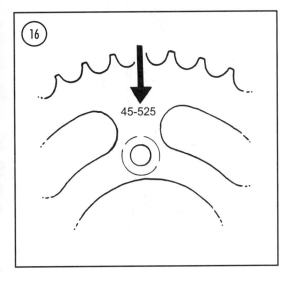

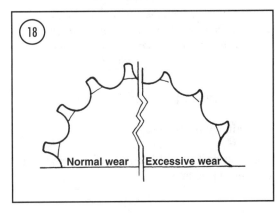

a. Align the rear coupling bosses (B, **Figure 14**) with the rubber damper receptacles (A, **Figure 15**) and install the rear coupling.

b. If removed, install the rear sprocket so the side with the stamping (**Figure 16**) faces out away from the rear coupling.

CAUTION
On a new machine or after a new rear sprocket has been installed, check the torque on the rear sprocket nuts after 10 minutes of riding and after each 10 minute riding period until the nuts have seated to the new sprocket and remain tight. Failure to keep the sprocket nuts correctly tightened will destroy the rear hub.

c. Tighten the rear sprocket nuts to the torque specification listed in **Table 2** after the assembly has been reinstalled in the rear wheel.

Inspection

1. Inspect the rubber dampers (B, **Figure 15**) for damage or deterioration. If damaged, replace as a complete set.

2. Inspect the raised webs (**Figure 17**) in the rear hub. Check for cracks or wear. If any damage is visible, replace the rear wheel.

3. Inspect the rear coupling assembly for cracks or damage, replace if necessary.

4. Inspect the rear sprocket teeth. If the teeth are worn (**Figure 18**), replace the rear sprocket as described in this chapter.

CAUTION
If the rear sprocket requires replacement, also replace the engine sprocket and the drive chain. Never install a new drive chain over worn sprockets or a worn drive chain over new sprockets. The old part wears out the new part prematurely.

5. If the rear sprocket requires replacement, also inspect the drive chain (Chapter Three) and engine

sprocket (this chapter). They also may be worn and need replacing.

6. Inspect the bearing for excessive axial play and radial (**Figure 19**). Replace the bearing if it has an excess amount of free play.

7. On a non-sealed bearing, check the balls for wear, pitting or excessive heat (bluish tint). Turn the inner race by hand. The bearing must turn smoothly without excessive play or noise. Replace a questionable bearing. When replacing the bearing, compare the new and old bearings to ensure a match.

> *NOTE*
> *Fully sealed bearings are available from many bearing specialty shops. Fully sealed bearings provide better protection from dirt and moisture.*

FRONT AND REAR HUBS

Preliminary Inspection

Inspect each wheel bearing before removing it from the wheel hub.

> *CAUTION*
> *Do not remove the wheel bearings for inspection purposes. The bearings will be damaged during removal. Remove the wheel bearings only if replacing them.*

1. Perform Steps 1-3 of *Disassembly* in the following procedure.

2. Turn each bearing by hand. The bearings must turn smoothly with no roughness.

3. Inspect the play of the inner race of each wheel bearing. Check for excessive axial play and radial play (**Figure 19**). Replace the bearing if it has an excess amount of free play.

4. On non-sealed bearings, check the balls for wear, pitting or excessive heat (bluish tint). Replace the bearings if necessary; always replace as a complete set. When replacing the bearings, compare the new and old bearings to ensure a match.

> *NOTE*
> *Fully sealed bearings are available from many bearing specialty shops. Fully sealed bearings provide better protection from dirt and moisture that may get into the hub.*

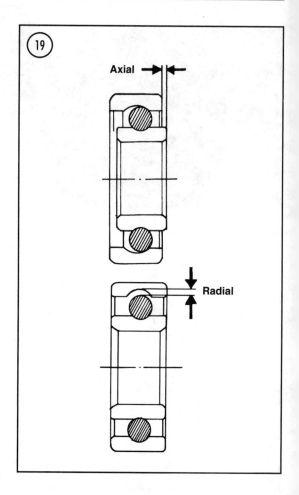

Disassembly

This procedure applies to both the front (**Figure 20**) and rear (**Figure 21**) wheel and hub assemblies. Where differences occur they are identified.

1A. Remove the front wheel as described in this chapter.

1B. Remove the rear wheel as described in this chapter.

2. On the rear wheel, if still in place, remove the spacer (A, **Figure 12**) from the brake disc side of the hub.

3. Carefully pry out the seals (A, **Figure 22**) with a large screwdriver. Place a shop cloth under the screwdriver to protect the hub. Install *new* seals during assembly.

4. If necessary, remove the bolts (B, **Figure 22**) securing the brake disc and remove the disc.

5. Before proceeding further, inspect the wheel bearings (**Figure 23**) as described in this chapter. If they must be replaced, proceed as follows.

FRONT WHEEL AND HUB

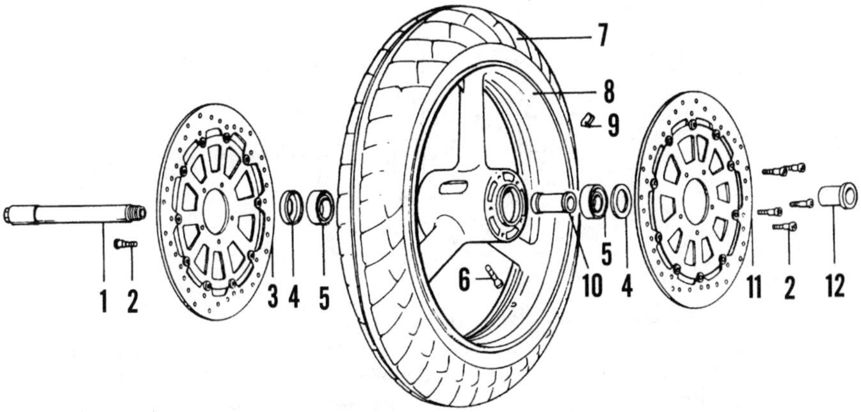

1. Front axle
2. Bolt
3. Brake disc
4. Seal
5. Bearing
6. Valve stem
7. Tire
8. Wheel
9. Balance weight
10. Distance collar
11. Brake disc
12. Special nut

11

WARNING
*Wear safety glasses while removing
the wheel bearings.*

6A. If the special tools are not used, perform the following:

a. To remove the right and left bearings and distance collar, insert a soft aluminum or brass drift into one side of the hub.

b. Push the distance collar over to one side and place the drift on the inner race of the lower bearing.

c. Tap the bearing out of the hub with a hammer, working around the perimeter of the inner

race (**Figure 24**). Remove the bearing and distance collar.

d. Repeat for the bearing on the other side.

NOTE
The Kowa Seiki Wheel Bearing Remover set can be ordered by a Suzuki dealership through K & L Supply Co. in Santa Clara, CA.

6B. To remove the bearings with the Kowa Seiki Wheel Bearing Remover set, perform the following:

a. Select the correct size remover head tool and insert it into the bearing.

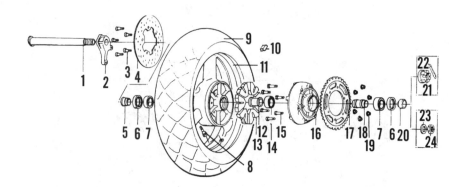

REAL WHEEL AND HUB

1. Rear axle
2. Caliper carrier
3. Bolt
4. Brake disc
5. Spacer
6. Seal
7. Bearing
8. Valve stem
9. Tire
10. Balance weight
11. Wheel
12. Distance collar
13. Rubber cushions
14. Bearing
15. Bolt
16. Rear coupling
17. Driven sprocket
18. Inner retainer
19. Nuts
20. Spacer
21. Nut (U.S. and Canada models)
22. Cotter pin (U.S. and Canada models)
23. Washer
24. Nut

b. Turn the wheel over and insert the remover shaft into the backside of the adapter. Tap the shaft and force it into the slit in the adapter (**Figure 25**). This will force the adapter against the bearing inner race.

c. Tap on the end of the shaft with a hammer and drive the bearing out of the hub. Remove the bearing and the distance collar.

d. Repeat for the bearing on the other side.

7. Clean the inside and the outside of the hub with solvent. Dry with compressed air.

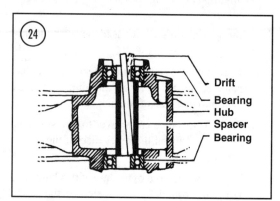

Drift
Bearing
Hub
Spacer
Bearing

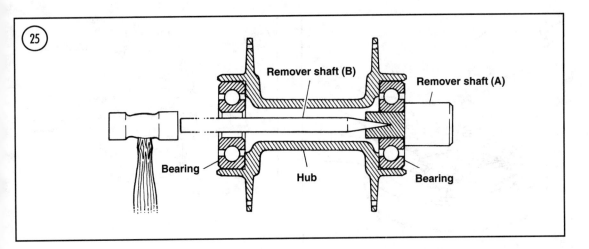

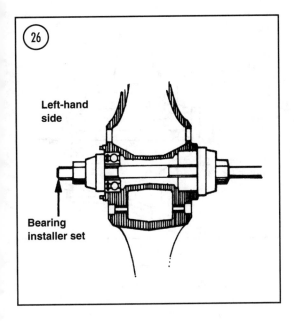

Assembly

> *CAUTION*
> *Always reinstall **new** bearings. The bearings are damaged during removal and must not be reused.*

> *NOTE*
> *Replace bearings as a set. If any one bearing in a wheel is worn, replace all the bearings in that wheel. On the front wheel, replace both wheel bearings. On the rear wheel replace both wheel bearings as well as the rear coupling bearing.*

1. On non-sealed bearings, pack the bearings with water-proof bearing grease. To pack the bearings, spread some grease in the palm of your hand and scrape the open side of the bearing across your palm until the bearing is completely packed full of grease. Spin the bearing a few times to determine if there are any open areas; repack if necessary.

2. Blow any dirt or foreign matter out of the hub before installing the new bearings.

3. Apply a light coat of wheel bearing grease to the bearing seating areas of the hub. This makes bearing installation easier.

> *CAUTION*
> *Install non-sealed bearings with the single sealed side facing outward. Tap the bearings squarely into place and tap on the outer race only. Applying pressure to the inner race will damage the bearing. Be sure the bearings are completely seated.*

4A. A special Suzuki tool set-up (part No. 09924-84510) can be used to install the *front wheel bearings* as follows:

    a. Install the left bearing into the hub first.

    b. Set the left bearing with the sealed side facing out, and install the bearing installer as shown in **Figure 26**.

    c. Tighten the bearing installer (**Figure 27**) and pull the left bearing into the hub until it is completely seated. Remove the bearing installer.

    d. Turn the wheel over (right side up) on the workbench and install the distance collar.

11

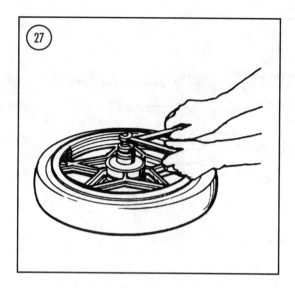

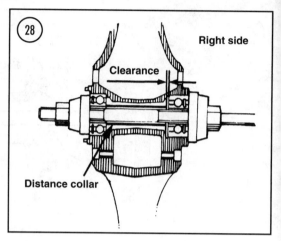

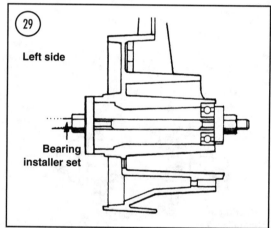

e. Set the right bearing into the hub with the sealed side facing out, and install the bearing installer as shown in **Figure 28**.

NOTE
Suzuki does not provide a specification for the clearance between the bearing and the distance collar. The important thing is that these two parts are not pressed up against each other.

f. Tighten the bearing installer and pull the right bearing into the hub until there is a *slight* clearance between the inner race and the distance collar.

g. Remove the bearing installer.

4B. A special Suzuki tool set-up (part No. 09924-84510) can be used to install the *rear wheel bearings* as follows:

a. Install the right bearing into the hub first.

b. Set the right bearing into the hub with the sealed side facing out and install the bearing installer as shown in **Figure 29**.

c. Tighten the bearing installer (**Figure 27**) and pull the right bearing into the hub until it is completely seated. Remove the bearing installer.

d. Turn the wheel over (left side up) on the workbench and install the distance collar.

e. Set the left bearing into the hub with the sealed side facing out and install the bearing installer as shown in **Figure 30**.

NOTE
Suzuki does not provide a specification for the clearance between the bearing and the distance collar. The important thing is that these two parts are not pressed up against each other.

f. Tighten the bearing installer and pull the left bearing into the hub until there is a *slight* clearance between the inner race and the distance collar.

g. Remove the bearing installer.

4C. If special tools are not used, perform the following:

a. On the front wheel, install the left bearing first; on the rear wheel, install the right bearing first.

b. Using a socket that matches the outer race diameter, tap the first bearing (left bearing on front wheel; right bearing on rear wheel)

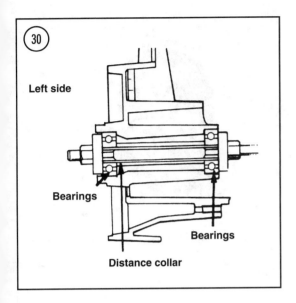

Left side

Bearings

Bearings

Distance collar

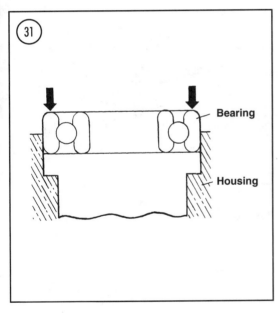

Bearing

Housing

squarely into place in the hub. Tap on the outer race only (**Figure 31**). Do not tap on the inner race or the bearing might become damaged. Make sure the bearing is completely seated.

c. Turn the wheel over on the workbench and install the distance collar.

NOTE
Suzuki does not provide a specification for the clearance between the bearing and the distance collar. The

important thing is that these two parts are not pressed up against each other.

   d. Use the same tool set-up and drive the second bearing (right bearing on the front wheel; left bearing on the rear wheel) into the hub until there is a *slight* clearance between the inner race and the distance collar.

5. If the brake disc was removed, perform the following:

   a. Apply a small amount of a locking compound such as ThreeBond No. TB1360 or Loctite No. 271 to the brake disc bolt threads before installation.

   b. Install the brake disc. Tighten the brake disc bolts (B, **Figure 22**) to the torque specifications listed in **Table 2**.

6. On the rear wheel, install the spacer into the brake disc side of the hub.

7A. Install the front wheel as described in this chapter.

7B. Install the rear wheel as described in this chapter.

WHEELS

Wheel Balance

An unbalanced wheel is unsafe. Depending upon the degree of imbalance and the speed of the motorcycle, the rider may experience anything from a mild vibration to a violent shimmy that could lead to a loss of control.

The balance weights attach to the rim on the GSX-R600. Weight kits are available from motorcycle dealerships. These kits contain test weights and strips of adhesive backed weights that can be cut to the desired weight and attached to the rim.

Before attempting to balance the wheel, make sure the wheel bearings are in good condition and properly lubricated and that the brakes do not drag. The wheel must rotate freely.

NOTE
When balancing the wheels, do so with the brake disc(s) and the rear coupling attached. These components rotate with the wheel and they affect the balance.

1A. Remove the front wheel as described in this chapter.

11

1B. Remove the rear wheel as described in this chapter.

2. Mount the wheel on a fixture such as the one shown in **Figure 32** so the wheel can rotate freely.

3. Spin the wheel and let it coast to a stop. Mark the tire at the lowest point with chalk or light colored crayon.

4. Spin the wheel several more times. If the wheel keeps coming to rest at the same point, it is out of balance.

5. Attach a test weight to the upper (or light) side of the wheel.

6. Experiment with different weights until the wheel, when spun, comes to rest at a different position each time.

7. Remove the test weight, thoroughly clean the rim surface, then install the correct size weight onto the rim. Make sure it is secured in place so it does not fly off when riding.

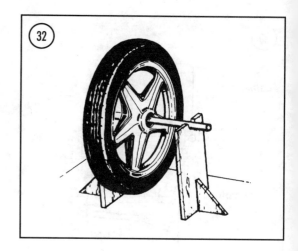

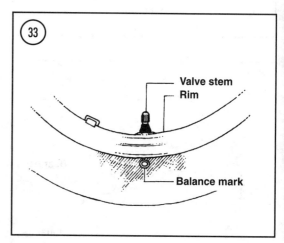

TIRES

Tire Safety

Tire wear and performance is greatly effected by tire pressure. Have a good tire gauge on hand and make a habit of frequently checking tire pressure. Maintain the tire inflation pressure recommended in **Table 1** for original equipment tires. If using another tire brand, follow their recommendation.

Follow a sensible break in period when running on new tires. When tires are new they exhibit significantly less adhesion ability. Do not subject a new tire to hard cornering, hard acceleration or hard braking for the first 100 miles (160 km).

TUBELESS TIRE CHANGING

The original equipment cast alloy wheels are designed for use with tubeless tires only. These wheels can easily be damaged during tire removal. Take special care to avoid scratching and gouging the outer rim surface, especially when using tire irons. Insert scraps of leather between the tire iron and the rim to protect the rim from damage.

When removing a tubeless tire, take care not to damage the tire beads, inner liner of the tire or the wheel rim flange. Use tire levers or flat-handle tire irons with rounded heads.

Tire Removal

CAUTION
Suzuki recommends that the tires be removed with a tire changer. Due to the large and rigid tires, tire removal with tire irons can be difficult and result in rim damage. On the other hand, a pneumatic tire changer can easily break the beads loose as well as remove and install the tire without damaging the cast wheel. The following procedure is provided if this alternative is not chosen.

CAUTION
To avoid damage when removing the tire, support the wheel on two blocks of wood so the brake discs or the rear sprocket does not contact the floor.

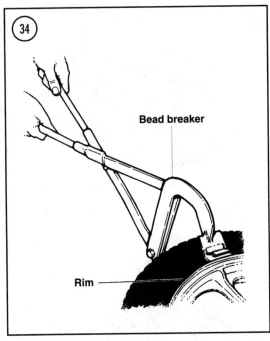

Bead breaker

Rim

NOTE
To make tire removal easier, warming the tire will make it softer and more pliable. Place the wheel and tire assembly in the sun. If possible, place the wheel assembly in a completely closed vehicle. At the same time, place the new tire in the same location.

1A. Remove the front wheel as described in this chapter.

1B. Remove the rear wheel as described in this chapter.

2. If not already marked by the tire manufacturer, mark the valve stem location on the tire (**Figure 33**), in order to install the tire in the same location for easier balancing.

3. Remove the valve core from the valve stem and deflate the tire.

NOTE
*Removal of tubeless tires from their rims can be very difficult because of the exceptional tight tire bead-to-rim seal. Breaking the bead seal may require the use of a special tool (**Figure 34**). If the seal does not break loose, take the wheel to a motorcycle repair shop and have them break it loose on a tire changing machine.*

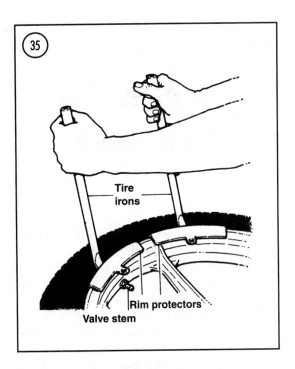

Tire irons

Rim protectors
Valve stem

CAUTION
The inner rim and bead area are the sealing surfaces on the tubeless tire. Do not scratch the inside of the rim or damage the tire bead.

4. Press the entire bead on both sides of the tire away from the rim and into the center of the rim.

5. Lubricate both beads with soapy water.

CAUTION
*Use rim protectors (**Figure 35**) or insert scraps of leather between the tire iron and the rim to protect the rim from damage.*

NOTE
*Use only quality tire irons without sharp edges (**Figure 36**). If necessary, file the ends of the tire irons to remove rough edges.*

6. Insert a tire iron under the top bead next to the valve stem (**Figure 37**). Force the bead on the opposite side of the tire into the center of the rim and pry the bead over the rim with the tire iron.

7. Insert a second tire iron next to the first iron to hold the bead over the rim. Then work around the tire with the first tire iron, prying the bead over the rim (**Figure 38**).

11

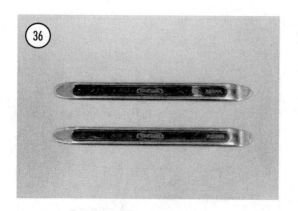

8. Stand the wheel upright. Insert a tire iron between the second bead and the side of the rim that the first bead was pried over (**Figure 39**). Force the bead on the opposite side from the tire iron into the center of the rim. Pry the back bead off the rim working around as with the first bead.

9. Inspect the valve stem seal. It is advisable to replace the valve stem when replacing the tire.

10. Remove the old valve stem and discard it. Inspect the valve stem hole (**Figure 40**) in the rim. Remove any dirt or corrosion from the hole and wipe it dry with a clean cloth. Install a new valve stem and make sure it properly seats in the rim.

11. Carefully inspect the tire and wheel rim for any damage as described in the following.

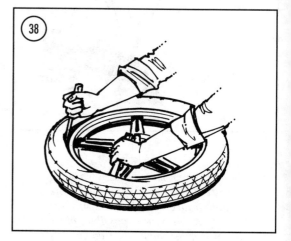

Tire and Wheel Rim Inspection

1. Wipe off the inner surfaces of the wheel rim. Clean off any rubber residue or any oxidation.

> *WARNING*
> *Carefully consider whether a tire should be replaced. If there is any doubt about the quality of the existing tire, replace it with a new one. Do not take a chance on a tire failure at any speed.*

2. If any one of the following are observed; replace the tire with a new one:

   a. A puncture or split with a total length or diameter exceeding 6 mm (0.24 in.).

   b. A scratch or split on the side wall.

   c. Any type of ply separation.

   d. Tread separation or excessive abnormal wear pattern.

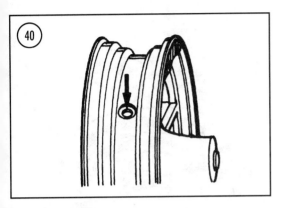

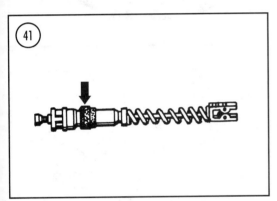

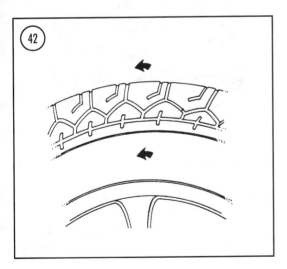

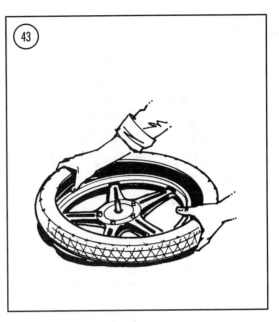

3. Inspect the valve stem hole in the rim. Remove any dirt or corrosion from the hole, and wipe it dry with a clean cloth.

Tire Installation

1. Inspect the valve stem core rubber seal (**Figure 41**) for hardness or deterioration. Replace the valve core if necessary.

2. A new tire may have balancing rubbers inside. These are not patches and must be left in place. Most tires are marked with a colored spot near the bead (**Figure 33**) that indicates a lighter point on the tire. This should be placed next to the valve stem.

3. Lubricate both beads of the tire with soapy water.

4. When installing the tire on the rim, make sure the correct tire, either front or rear is installed on the correct wheel. Also, install the tire so the direction arrow faces the normal direction of wheel rotation (**Figure 42**).

5. If remounting the old tire, align the mark made in Step 2 of *Removal* with the valve stem. If installing a new tire, align the colored stop near the bead (indicating the lightest point of the tire) with the valve stem. See **Figure 33**.

6. Place the backside of the tire onto the rim so the lower bead sits in the center of the rim while the upper bead remains outside the rim. (**Figure 43**). Work around the tire in both directions and press the

e. Tread depth of less than the minimum value specified (**Table 1**) for original equipment tires. Aftermarket tire tread depth minimum may vary.

f. Scratches on either sealing bead.

g. The cord is cut in any place.

h. Flat spots in the tread from skidding.

i. Any abnormality in the inner liner.

11

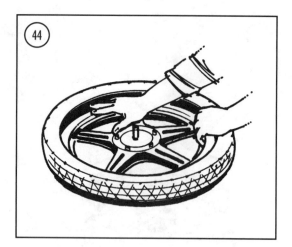

lower bead, by hand, into the center of the rim (**Figure 44**). Use a tire iron for the last few inches of bead (**Figure 45**).

7. Press the upper bead into the rim opposite the valve stem. Working on both sides of this initial point, pry the bead into the rim with a tire tool, and work around the rim to the valve stem (**Figure 46**). If the tire wants to pull up on one side, either use another tire iron or a knee to hold the tire in place. The last few inches are usually the toughest to install. If possible, continue to push the tire into the rim with by hand. Relubricate the bead if necessary. If the tire bead wants to pull out from under the rim use both knees to hold the tire in place. If necessary, use a tire iron for the last few inches.

8. Bounce the wheel several times, rotating it each time. This forces the tire bead against the rim flanges. After the tire beads are in contact with the rim, inflate the tire to seat the beads.

9. Place an inflatable band around the circumference of the tire. Slowly inflate the band until the tire beads are pressed against the rim. Inflate the tire enough to seat it. Deflate the band and remove it.

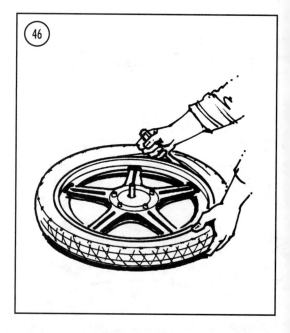

> *WARNING*
> *In the next step, never exceed 400 kPa*
> *(56 psi) inflation pressure as the tire*
> *could burst causing severe injury.*
> *Never stand directly over a tire while*
> *inflating it.*

10. After inflating the tire, check to see that the beads are fully seated and that the rim lines are the same distance from the rim all the way around the tire. If the beads are seated, deflate the tire and lubricate the rim and beads with soapy water.

11. Reinflate the tire to the required pressure as listed in **Table 1**. Install the valve stem cap.

12. Balance the wheel as described in this chapter.

13A. Install the front wheel as described in this chapter.

13B. Install the rear wheel as described in this chapter.

TIRE REPAIRS

> *NOTE*
> *Changing or patching on the road is*
> *very difficult. A can of pressurized tire*
> *sealant may inflate the tire and seal*

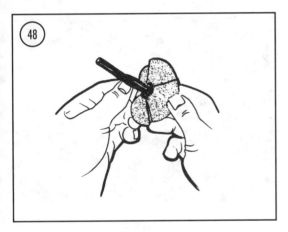

the hole, but this is only a temporary fix.

WARNING
Do not install an inner tube inside a tubeless tire. The tube will cause an abnormal heat buildup in the tire.

Tubeless tires have the word TUBELESS molded into the sidewall and the rims have SUITABLE FOR TUBELESS TIRES or equivalent (**Figure 47**) cast on them.

If the tire is punctured, remove it from the rim, inspect the inside of the tire, and apply a combination plug/patch from inside the tire (**Figure 48**). Never attempt to repair a tubeless motorcycle tire using a plug or cord patch applied from outside the tire. This type of repair might be acceptable for automobiles, but they are not safe on a motorcycle tire, especially on a high-performance bike like the GSX-R600.

After repairing a tubeless tire, do exceed 30 mph (50 kph) for the first 24 hours. Do not exceed 80 mph (130 kph) and never race (canyon or other-

wise) on a repaired tubeless tire. The patch could work lose because of tire flex and heat—resulting in a serious accident.

Repair

Do not rely on a plug or cord patch applied from outside the tire. Use a combination plug/patch applied from inside the tire (**Figure 48**).

1. Remove the tire from the wheel rim as described in this chapter.
2. Inspect the rim inner flange. Smooth any scratches on the sealing surface with emery cloth. If a scratch is deeper than 0.5 mm (0.020 in.), replace the wheel.
3. Inspect the tire inside and out. Replace a tire if any of the following conditions are found:
   a. A puncture larger than 6 mm (1/4 in) diameter.
   b. A punctured or damaged side wall.
   c. More than two punctures in the tire.
   d. Tread depth less than the minimum value specified in **Table 1**.
   e. Ply or tread separation.
   f. Flat spots.
   g. Scratches on the bead.
   h. Cuts in the cord.
4. Apply the plug/patch following the manufacturer's instructions with the patch kit.

DRIVE CHAIN

Removal/Installation

1. Remove the swing arm as described in Chapter Thirteen.
2. Remove the engine sprocket cover as described in this chapter.
3. Slide the drive chain off the engine sprocket and remove it from the motorcycle.
4. Installation is the reverse of removal.

SPROCKETS

Inspection

Refer to *Drive Chain and Sprocket Wear Inspection* in Chapter Three.

11

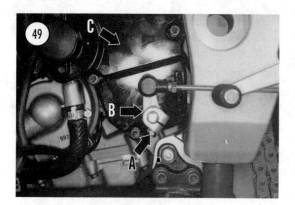

Engine Sprocket Cover and Engine Sprocket Removal

NOTE
The engine sprocket cover must be partially removed to gain access to the engine sprocket.

1. Place the bike on the sidestand on level ground.
2. Remove the seat as described in Chapter Fifteen.
3. Remove the lower fairing assembly as described in Chapter Fifteen.
4. Remove the coolant reservoir as described in Chapter Ten.
5. Remove the engine sprocket cover by performing the following:
   a. Remove the gearshift lever bolt (A, **Figure 49**) and slide the gearshift lever (B, **Figure 49**) from the shift shaft. Reinstall the bolt to avoid loosing it.

CAUTION
If the cover is not going to be completely removed, suspend the cover by the clutch release cable, not by the speedometer sensor rotor electrical harness. Rest the cover on the frame or engine.

   b. Remove the five engine sprocket cover bolts and the cover (C, **Figure 49**) from the crankcase. Move the cover out of the way and rest it on the frame or engine. Do not lose the locating dowels behind the cover.
6. Remove the drive chain from the engine sprocket. If necessary, create some slack in the drive chain by performing the following:
   a. On U.S.A., California and Canada models, remove the cotter pin (A, **Figure 50**) from the

rear axle nut. Install a *new* one during assembly.

   b. Loosen the axle nut while an assistant is applying the rear brake (B, **Figure 50**).

   c. Loosen the chain adjuster locknut (A, **Figure 51**), then loosen the adjuster (B, **Figure 51**) on each side of the swing arm.

   d. Push the wheel forward to create the necessary slack in the drive chain.

7. Remove the bolt (A, **Figure 52**) securing the speedometer rotor (B, **Figure 52**) to the countershaft, and remove the rotor. Place the rotor and the mounting bolt in a reclosable plastic bag to avoid misplacing them.

8. Hold the engine sprocket with a clutch holding tool (A, **Figure 53**) and loosen the engine sprocket nut.

9. Remove the engine sprocket nut (**Figure 54**) and washer.

10. Remove the engine sprocket (**Figure 55**) from the countershaft.

11. If necessary, remove the engine sprocket spacer (**Figure 56**) from the countershaft.

**Engine Sprocket Cover and
Engine Sprocket Installation**

1. If removed, install the engine sprocket spacer (**Figure 56**) onto the countershaft.

2. Slide the engine sprocket (**Figure 55**) onto the countershaft. Push the sprocket onto the shaft until it bottoms.

3. Install the washer and the engine sprocket nut (**Figure 54**).

4. Hold the engine sprocket with a clutch holding tool (A, **Figure 53**), and torque the engine sprocket nut (B) to the specification in **Table 2**.

5. Install the speedometer rotor (B, **Figure 52**) and mounting bolt onto the countershaft. Tighten the speedometer rotor bolt (A, **Figure 52**) to the torque specification listed in **Table 2**.

6. Set the drive chain onto the engine sprocket.

7. Install the engine sprocket cover as follows:

   a. Apply a small amount of Suzuki Super Grease A or equivalent to the clutch release mechanism (**Figure 57**) where it contacts the clutch push rod.

   b. If removed, install the locating dowels (**Figure 58**) into the cover.

11

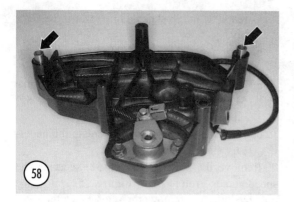

c. Install the engine sprocket cover (C, **Figure 49**) and its five mounting bolts. Tighten the bolts securely.

d. If removed, install the shift shaft bushing (**Figure 59**) onto the shift shaft.

e. Install the gearshift lever (B, **Figure 49**) onto the shift shaft. Check that the top of the shift pedal lever is 55 mm (2.2 in.) below the top surface of the footrest. If necessary, adjust the shift pedal as described in Chapter Three.

f. Install the gearshift lever bolt (A, **Figure 49**), and tighten it securely.

8. Install the coolant reservoir as described in Chapter Ten.

9. Install the lower fairing assembly as described in Chapter Fifteen.

10. Install the seat as described in Chapter Fifteen.

11. Adjust the chain tension as described in Chapter Three.

**Rear Sprocket
Removal/Installation**

Refer to *Rear Coupling and Rear Sprocket Removal/Disassembly/Assembly/Installation* in this chapter.

Table 1 WHEELS, TIRES AND DRIVE CHAIN SPECIFICATIONS

Item	Specification
Wheel rim size	
Front	J17 x MT 3.50
Rear	J17 x MT 5.50
Rim runout limit	
Axial	2.0 mm (0.08 in.)
Radial	2.0 mm (0.08 in.)
Axle runout limit	
Front	0.25 mm (0.010 in.)
Rear	0.25 mm (0.010 in.)
Tire Size	
Front	120/70 ZR17 (58W)
Rear	180/55 ZR17 (73W)
Tire tread minimum depth	
Front	1.6 mm (0.06 in.)
Rear	2.0 mm (o.08 in.)
Tire pressure (cold)*	
Front	
Solo	250 kPa (36 psi)
Rider and passenger	250 kPa (36 psi)
	(continued)

Table 1 WHEELS, TIRES AND DRIVE CHAIN SPECIFICATIONS (continued)

Item	Specification
Tire pressure (cold)* (continued)	
Rear	
Solo	250 kPa (36 psi)
Rider and passenger	250 kPa (36 psi)
Drive Chain	
Type	Takasago RK525SMOZ2 (108 links, continuous)
21-pin length	319.4 mm (12.6 in.)
Chain slack	20-30 mm (0.8-1.2 in.)

*Tire inflation pressure is for original equipment tires. Aftermarket tires may require different inflation pressure. The use of tires other than those specified by Suzuki may cause instability.

Table 2 WHEELS, TIRES AND DRIVE CHAIN TORQUE SPECIFICATIONS

Item	N•m	in.-lb.	ft.-lb.
Brake disc bolt	23	–	17
Engine sprocket nut	120	–	89
Front axle nut	100	–	74
Front axle pinch bolt	23	–	17
Rear axle nut	100	–	74
Rear sprocket nut	60	–	44
Spacer nut pinch bolt	23	–	17
Speedometer rotor bolt	13	115	–

11

CHAPTER TWELVE

FRONT SUSPENSION AND STEERING

This chapter describes repair and maintenance procedures for the front fork and steering components. Front wheel removal, front hub service, tire changing, tire repair and wheel balancing are covered in Chapter Eleven. Front suspension specifications are listed in **Table 1** and **Table 2** at the end of the chapter.

HANDLEBAR

The individual front handlebars mount onto the fork tubes below the bottom surface of the upper fork bridge. It is necessary to lower the fork leg to remove a particular handlebar. Service one handlebar at a time. Lower one fork leg, remove, service and reinstall that specific handlebar assembly, and then remove and service the other handlebar assembly.

> *NOTE*
> *This procedure covers complete removal and installation of the handlebar assembly on each side. If only one handlebar assembly requires re-*

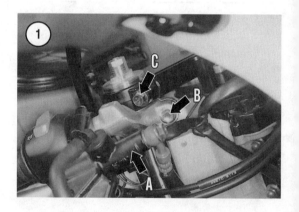

moval, only use that portion of the procedure.

Removal/Installation

1. Remove the front wheel as described in Chapter Eleven.

2. Remove the front fender as described in Chapter Fifteen.

3. Remove both lower fairing side panels as described in Chapter Fifteen.

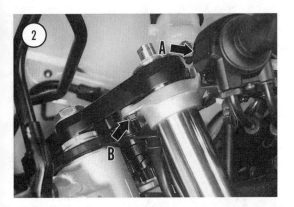

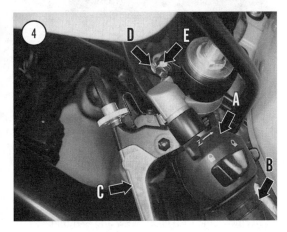

d. Loosen the handlebar clamp bolt (B, **Figure 1**).

e. Loosen the upper fork bridge clamp bolt (C, **Figure 1**) and the two lower fork bridge clamp bolts (**Figure 3**).

f. Lower the right fork leg until its top is below the handlebar mounting bracket, or completely remove the fork leg.

g. Remove the handlebar mounting bolt (B, **Figure 2**) and the right handlebar assembly from the upper fork bridge.

5. To remove the left handlebar, perform the following:

a. Remove the left switch assembly (A, **Figure 4**) as described in Chapter Nine.

b. Remove the left hand grip (B, **Figure 4**) as described in this chapter.

c. Loosen the clutch lever assembly clamp bolt and remove the clutch lever assembly (C, **Figure 4**).

d. Loosen the handlebar clamp bolt (D, **Figure 4**).

e. Loosen the upper fork bridge clamp bolt (E, **Figure 4**) and the two lower fork bridge clamp bolts (**Figure 5**).

f. Lower the left fork leg until its top is below the handlebar mounting bracket, or completely remove the fork leg.

g. Remove the handlebar mounting bolt (**Figure 6**) and the left handlebar assembly from the upper fork bridge.

6. Install by reversing these removal steps while noting the following:

a. Tighten the handlebar mounting bolt to the torque specification listed in **Table 2**.

b. Slide the fork leg assembly into position until the top of the fork tube sits 3.2 mm (0.13 in.)

4. To remove the right handlebar, perform the following:

a. Remove the front brake master cylinder (A, **Figure 1**) as described in Chapter Fourteen.

b. Tie the master cylinder assembly to the frame, keeping the front brake master cylinder and reservoir in an upright position to prevent air from entering into the system.

c. Remove the right switch assembly (A, **Figure 2**) as described in Chapter Nine.

12

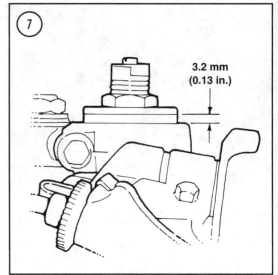

above the top surface of the upper fork bridge (**Figure 7**).

NOTE
A torque adapter (Chapter One) is necessary to torque the lower fork bridge clamp bolts.

c. Tighten the handlebar clamp bolt, the upper fork bridge clamp bolts and the lower fork bridge clamp bolts to the torque specifications listed in **Table 2**.

WARNING
After installation is completed, make sure that when the brake lever is applied it does not come in contact with the throttle grip assembly. If it does, the brake fluid may be low in the reservoir; refill it as necessary. Refer to Front Disc Brakes in Chapter Fourteen.

d. Adjust the throttle operation as described in Chapter Three.

e. Check the operation of both switch assemblies.

Inspection

Check the handlebar bolt holes and the entire mounting bracket for cracks or damage. Replace a bent or damaged handlebar immediately. If the bike has been involved in a crash, thoroughly examine both handlebars, the steering stem and front fork for any signs of damage or misalignment. Correct any problem immediately.

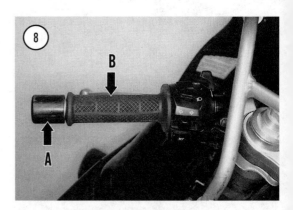

HANDLEBAR LEFT GRIP REPLACEMENT

NOTE
The right grip is part of the throttle grip assembly and cannot be replaced separately.

1. Remove the trim cap, screw and weight (A, **Figure 8**) from the end of the handlebar.

2. Slide a thin screwdriver between the left grip (B, **Figure 8**) and handlebar. Spray electrical contact cleaner into the opening under the grip.

3. Pull the screwdriver out and quickly twist the grip to break its bond with the handlebar, and then slide the grip off.

4. Clean the handlebar of all rubber or sealer residue.

5. Install the new grip following the manufacturer's directions. Apply an adhesive, such as

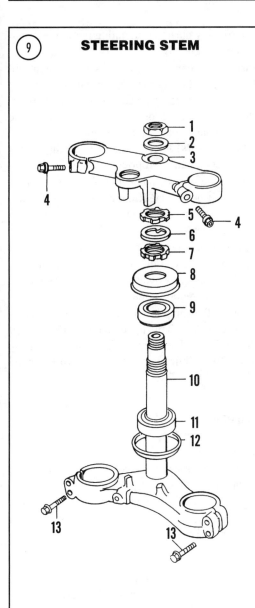

9 STEERING STEM

1. Steering stem cap nut
2. Washer
3. Upper fork bridge
4. Bolt
5. Steering stem locknut
6. Washer
7. Bearing adjusting nut
8. Dust seal
9. Upper bearing
10. Steering stem
11. Lower bearing
12. Grease seal
13. Bolt

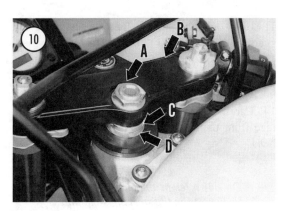

ThreeBond Griplock, between the grip and handlebar. When applying an adhesive, follow the manufacturer's instructions for drying time before operating the bike.

STEERING HEAD AND STEM

Removal

Refer to **Figure 9**.

1. Remove the front wheel as described in this chapter.

2. Remove the front fork as described in this chapter.

3. Remove the handlebar assemblies as described in this chapter.

4. Remove the right- and left-hand switch assembly wiring harness from the guide on the steering head portion of the frame.

5. Disconnect the ignition switch 6-pin electrical connector from the main wiring harness behind the radiator.

6. Remove the ignition switch wiring from the wire clamp.

7. Remove the steering stem head nut and washer (A, **Figure 10**).

8. Remove the upper fork bridge (B, **Figure 10**) and ignition switch wiring harness.

9. Loosen the steering stem locknut (C, **Figure 10**) with a spanner wrench. Remove the locknut.

10. Loosen the bearing adjust nut (D, **Figure 10**) with a spanner wrench.

NOTE
Support the weight of the steering stem while removing the bearing adjust nut or the assembly will drop out of the steering head.

12

11. Hold onto the steering stem and remove the bearing adjust nut (D, **Figure 10**).

12. Gently lower the steering stem assembly out of the frame.

13. Remove the dust seal from the top of the frame.

14. Carefully remove the upper bearing and inner race from the upper bearing race in the steering head.

CAUTION
Do not attempt to remove the lower bearing from the steering stem unless the bearing is going to be replaced. The bearing is pressed onto the steering stem and will be damaged during removal.

Inspection

1. Clean the upper and lower bearings in a bearing degreaser. Make certain the bearing degreaser is compatible with the rubber covers on each bearing. Hold onto the bearing so it does not spin and thoroughly dry both bearings with compressed air. Make sure all solvent is removed from the lower bearing still installed on the steering stem.

2. Wipe the old grease from the outer races located in the steering head, and then clean the outer races with a rag soaked in solvent. Thoroughly dry the races with a lint-free cloth.

3. Check the steering stem outer races for pitting, galling and corrosion. If any race is worn or damaged, replace the race(s) and bearing as an assembly as described in this chapter.

4. Check the welds around the steering head for cracks and fractures. If any damage is found, have the frame repaired at a competent frame shop or welding service.

5. Check the balls for pitting, scratches or discoloration indicating wear or corrosion. Replace the bearing if any balls are less than perfect.

6. If the bearings are in good condition, pack them thoroughly with Suzuki Super Grease A or an equivalent water-proof bearing grease. To pack the bearings, spread some grease in the palm of your hand and scrape the open side of the bearing across your palm until the bearing is packed completely full of grease. Spin the bearing a few times to determine if there are any open areas; repack if necessary.

7. Thoroughly clean all mounting parts in solvent. Dry them completely.

8. Inspect the cap nut, washer, steering stem nut and bearing adjust nut for wear or damage. Inspect the threads. If necessary, clean them with an appropriate size metric tap or replace the nut(s). If the threads are damaged, inspect the appropriate steering stem thread(s) for damage. If necessary, clean the threads with an appropriate size metric die.

9. Inspect the steering stem nut washer for damage. Replace it if necessary. If damaged, check the underside of the steering stem nut for damage. Replace it as necessary.

10. Inspect the steering stem and the lower fork bridge for cracks or other damage. Make sure the fork bridge clamping areas are free of burrs and the bolt holes are in good condition.

11. Inspect the upper fork bridge for cracks or other damage. Check both the upper and lower surface of the fork bridge. Make sure the fork bridge clamping areas are free of burrs and the bolt holes are in good condition.

Installation

Refer to **Figure 9**.

1. Make sure the steering head outer races are properly seated and clean.

2. Apply an even, complete coat of Suzuki Super Grease A or equivalent to the steering head outer races, to both bearings, and to the dust seal and cap nut.

NOTE
The fork receptacles in the steering stem are offset and must face toward the front of the bike. This is necessary for proper alignment with the fork receptacles in the upper fork bridge.

3. Install the upper bearing into the race in the top of the steering head.

4. Position the steering stem with the fork receptacles facing toward the front of the bike. Carefully slide the steering stem up into the frame. Take care not to dislodge the upper bearing. If this happens reseat the bearing.

5. Pack the under side of the dust seal with grease. Install the bearing cover and bearing adjust nut (D, **Figure 10**) and perform the following:

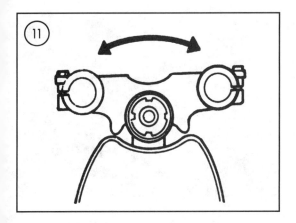

a. Tighten the bearing adjust nut to the torque specification listed in **Table 2**.

b. Turn the steering stem from side to side 5 to 6 times to help seat the ball bearings.

NOTE
In substep c, the adjustment amount varies from bike to bike. After loosening the adjust nut the 1/4 to 1/2 turn, there must be no play detected in the steering stem.

c. Loosen the adjust nut 1/4 to 1/2 turn.

6. Once again, turn the steering stem from side to side 5 to 6 times (**Figure 11**). The steering stem should move freely with no looseness or stiffness. If necessary, repeat Step 5 and 6 as necessary until the steering stem moves properly.

7. Align the tab on the washer with the steering stem groove and install the washer.

8. Install the steering stem locknut (C, **Figure 10**). Tighten it to the torque specifications listed in **Table 2**.

9. Install the upper fork bridge (B, **Figure 10**) onto the steering stem.

10. Install the washer and the steering stem head nut (A, **Figure 10**). Tighten the head nut finger-tight at this time.

NOTE
Perform Steps 11-15 in this order to ensure proper upper and lower fork bridge-to-fork alignment.

11. Temporarily slide the fork tubes into position until they are just above the top surface of the upper fork bridge. Tighten the lower fork bridge clamp bolts securely.

12. Temporarily install the front axle into the fork legs and tighten the axle nut securely.

13. Tighten the lower fork bridge clamp bolts to the torque specification listed in **Table 1**.

14. Tighten the steering stem head nut to the torque specification listed in **Table 1**.

15. Remove the front axle. Loosen the lower fork bridge clamp bolts, and slide the fork tubes out from the fork bridge.

16. Install the handlebar assemblies as described in this chapter.

17. Install the front fork assemblies as described in this chapter.

18. Check the movement of the front fork and steering stem assembly. The steering stem must turn freely from side to side but without any binding or free play when the fork legs are moved fore and aft.

19. Reposition the ignition switch wiring onto the wire clamp.

20. Connect the ignition switch 6-pin electrical connector to the main wiring harness behind the radiator.

21. Reposition the right- and left-hand switch assembly wiring harness to the guide on the steering head portion of the frame.

22. Install the front wheel as described in this chapter.

STEERING HEAD BEARING RACE REPLACEMENT

The upper and lower bearing outer races must not be removed unless they are going to be replaced. These races are pressed into place and will be damaged during removal. If removed, replace both the outer race along with the bearing at the same time. Never reuse an outer race that has been removed. It is no longer true and will damage the ball bearings if reused.

NOTE
The following procedure describes simple home techniques to remove the bearing races. If removal is difficult, do not chance damage to the motorcycle or new bearing races. Have the task performed by a qualified specialist.

1. Remove the steering stem as described in this chapter.

12

2. Insert an aluminum drift into the steering head and carefully tap the lower race out from the inside (**Figure 12**). Repeat for the upper race.

3. Chill the new bearing races in a freezer for a few hours to shrink the outer diameter of the race as much as possible.

4. Clean the race seats (**Figure 13**) in the steering head. Check for cracks or other damage.

5. Insert the new race into the steering head with the tapered side facing out (**Figure 14**), and square the race with the race bore (**Figure 15**).

> *CAUTION*
> *To avoid damage to the races and to the race seats in the steering head, install the races as described below.*

6. Assemble a puller tool as shown in **Figure 16**. The block mounted at the bottom of the threaded rod is used as a T-handle to hold the rod stationary when the bearing race is being installed from the opposite end. Two nuts locked together can be used as a substitute for the handle block. Two or more *thick* washers are also required. The outer diameter of the washers must be greater than the outer diameter of the bearing races.

> *CAUTION*
> *When installing the bearing outer races with the threaded rod or similar tool, do not let the rod or tool contact the face of the bearing race and damage it.*

7. To install the upper race, insert the puller through the bottom of the steering stem. Seat the lower washer or plate against the steering stem.

8. At the top of the steering stem, slide the large washer down and seat it squarely on top of the bearing race. Install the required washers and coupling nut onto the rod.

9. Hand-tighten the coupling nut and center the washer on the upper bearing race.

10. Hold the threaded rod to prevent it from turning and tighten the coupling nut with a wrench (**Figure 17**). Continue to tighten the coupling until the race is completely drawn into the steering head. Remove the puller assembly and inspect the bearing race. It should be bottomed in the steering head as shown in **Figure 18**.

11. Turn the special tool over and repeat this procedure for the lower bearing race.

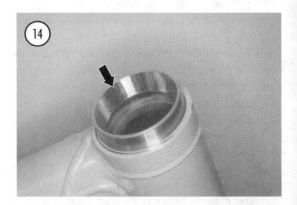

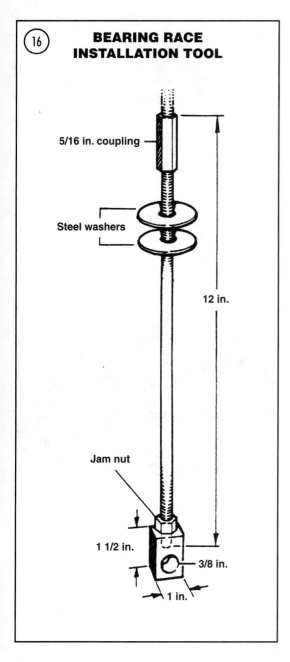

BEARING RACE INSTALLATION TOOL

5/16 in. coupling

Steel washers

12 in.

Jam nut

1 1/2 in.

3/8 in.

1 in.

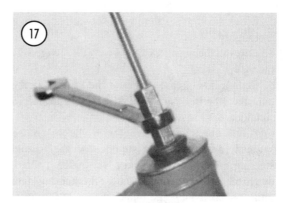

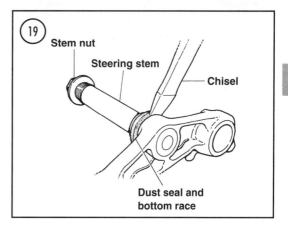

Stem nut

Steering stem

Chisel

Dust seal and bottom race

12

STEERING STEM BEARING REPLACEMENT

Do not remove the steering stem lower bearing and lower seal unless they are going to be replaced. The lower bearing can be difficult to remove. If you cannot remove it as described in this procedure; take the steering stem to a dealership service department and have them remove it and reinstall a new bearing and seal.

Never reinstall a lower bearing that has been removed. It is no longer true and will damage the rest of the bearing assembly if reused.

1. Install the steering stem bolt onto the top of the steering stem to protect the threads.

2. Loosen the lower bearing from the shoulder at the base of the steering stem with a chisel as shown in **Figure 19**. Slide the lower bearing and grease seal off the steering stem. Discard the lower bearing and the grease seal.

3. Clean the steering stem with solvent, and dry it thoroughly.

4. Position the new grease seal with the flange side facing up.

5. Slide a new grease seal, and the lower bearing onto the steering stem until it stops on the raised shoulder.

6. Align the lower bearing with the machined shoulder on the steering stem. Slide the Suzuki steering bearing installer (part No. 09925-18010), or a piece of pipe (**Figure 20**) over the steering stem until it seats against the inner portion of the *inner* race of the lower bearing. Drive the lower bearing onto the steering stem until it bottoms.

7. Pack the balls with wheel bearing grease.

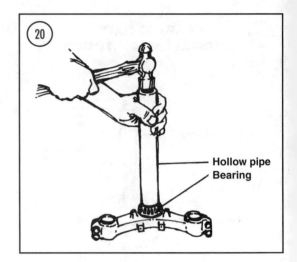

FRONT FORK

Front Fork Service

Before suspecting major trouble, drain the front fork oil and refill the fork with the proper type and quantity fork oil as described in this chapter. If there is still trouble, such as poor damping, a tendency to bottom or top out, or leaking around the oil seals; follow the service procedures in this section.

To simplify fork service and to prevent the mixing of parts, remove, service and install the fork legs individually.

Removal

> *NOTE*
> *For fork assembly removal only, do not perform Step 4. This step is only necessary if the fork is going to be disassembled for service.*

1. Remove the lower fairing side panels from each side as described in Chapter Fifteen.

2. Remove the front wheel as described in Chapter Eleven.

3. Remove the front fender as described in Chapter Fifteen.

4. If the fork assembly is going to be disassembled, perform the following:

    a. Place a drain pan under the fork slider as some fork oil may drain out.

    b. Hold the boss on the slider with an adjustable wrench, and slightly loosen (just break it loose) the damper rod Allen bolt at the base of

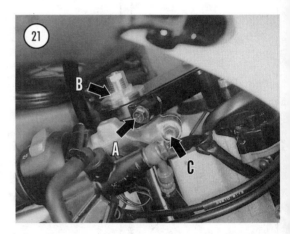

the slider. If the bolt is loosened too much, fork oil may start to drain out of the slider.

    c. Loosen the upper fork bridge clamp bolt (A, **Figure 21**).

    d. Loosen the cap bolt (B, **Figure 21**).

5. If not loosened in Step 4, loosen the upper fork bridge clamp bolt (A, **Figure 21**).

6. Loosen the handlebar clamp bolt (C, **Figure 21**).

7. Loosen the lower fork bridge clamp bolts (**Figure 22**).

8. Carefully lower the fork assembly out of the lower and upper fork bridges. It may be necessary to rotate the fork tube slightly while pulling it down and out. Take the fork assembly to a workbench for service. If the fork is not going to be serviced, wrap it in a bath towel or blanket to protect the surface from damage.

9. If the Allen and cap bolts were loosened in Step 4, place the fork assembly in a drain pan. Keep it up-

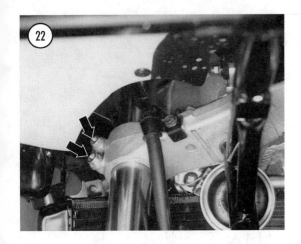

right to avoid spilling fork oil through the top of the fork tube.

10. If both fork tube assemblies are going to be removed, mark them with an R (right side) and L (left side) so the assemblies will be reinstalled on the correct side.

Installation

NOTE
If both fork assemblies are removed, make sure to install the fork assembly on the correct side of the bike. Refer to the marks made in Step 10 of Removal.

1. Slowly install the fork tube into the lower fork bridge, and then the upper fork bridge.

2. Slide the fork tube assembly into position until the top of the fork tube is located 3.2 mm (0.13 in.) above the top surface of the upper fork bridge (**Figure 7**).

3. Tighten the lower fork bridge clamp bolts (**Figure 22**) to the torque specification listed in **Table 2**.

4A. If the fork was disassembled for service, perform the following:

   a. Tighten the cap bolt (B, **Figure 21**) to the torque specification listed in **Table 2**.

   b. Tighten the upper fork bridge clamp bolt (A, **Figure 21**) to the torque specification listed in **Table 2**.

   c. Tighten the damper rod Allen bolt at the base of the slider to the torque specification listed in **Table 2**.

4B. If the fork was not disassembled, tighten the upper fork bridge clamp bolt (A, **Figure 21**) to the torque specification listed in **Table 2**.

5. Tighten the handlebar clamp bolt (C, **Figure 21**) to the torque specification listed in **Table 2**.

6. Install the front fender as described in Chapter Fifteen.

7. Install the front wheel as described in Chapter Eleven.

8. Install the lower fairing onto each side as described in Chapter Fifteen.

Disassembly

Refer to **Figure 23**.

1. If the damper rod Allen bolt was not loosened during the fork removal sequence, perform the following:

   a. Secure the fork slider horizontally in a vise with soft jaws.

   b. Have an assistant compress the fork tube into the slider. This places additional pressure on the damper rod to keep it from rotating while loosening the Allen bolt.

   c. Use an Allen wrench and impact wrench to loosen the damper rod Allen bolt on the bottom of the slider. Do not remove the Allen bolt and gasket from the slider at this time as the fork is still full of fork oil.

2. Secure the fork vertically in a vise with soft jaws. Completely unscrew the fork cap bolt from the fork tube. Lift the cap and piston rod from the cartridge assembly as shown in **Figure 24**.

3. Hold the spring adjuster (A, **Figure 24**) with a wrench and loosen the inner rod lock nut (B, **Figure 24**).

4. Remove the fork cap assembly (**Figure 25**) from the fork tube. Do not disassemble the fork cap assembly unless the spring preload adjuster or the rebound damping adjuster is not working properly. Refer to the procedure later in this chapter.

5. Remove the spring retainer (A, **Figure 26**), the washers (B, **Figure 26**) and spacer (C, **Figure 26**) from the fork tube.

6. Remove the fork spring.

7. Turn the fork assembly upside down and drain the fork oil into a suitable container. Pump the fork several times by hand to expel most of the remaining oil, and then pump the piston rod to expel oil from the cartridge. Dispose of the fork oil properly.

12

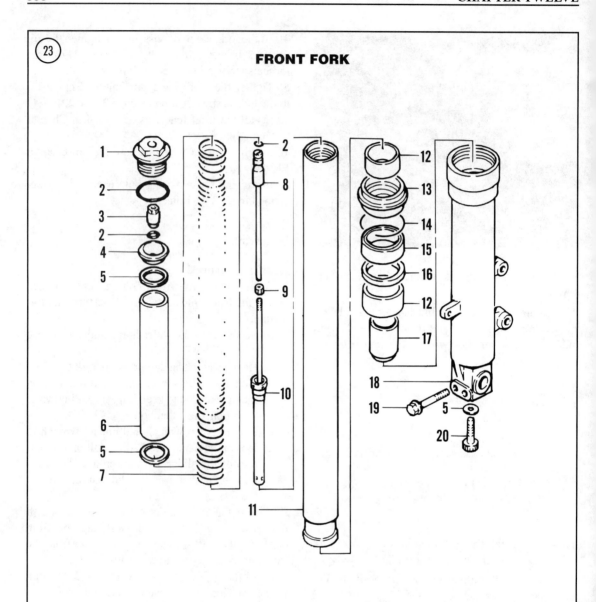

FRONT FORK

1. Cap bolt
2. O-ring
3. Spring adjuster
4. Spring retainer
5. Washer
6. Spacer
7. Fork spring
8. Rebound damping adjuster
9. Nut
10. Cartridge
11. Fork tube
12. Bushing
13. Dust seal
14. Circlip
15. Oil seal
16. Spacer
17. Oil lock piece
18. Slider
19. Bolt
20. Allen bolt

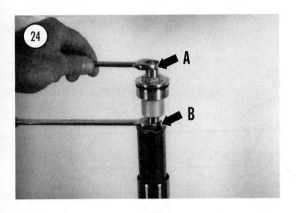

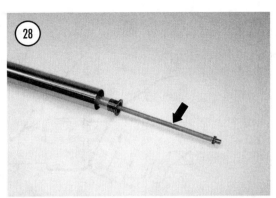

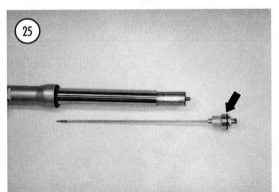

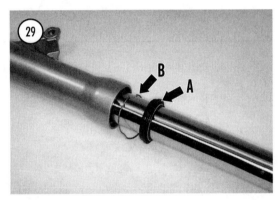

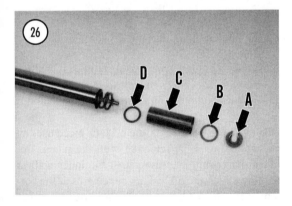

8. Remove the damper rod Allen bolt (A, **Figure 27**) and the washer (B, **Figure 27**).

> *NOTE*
> *The spring is fixed to the cartridge body. Do not attempt to remove it.*

9. Remove the cartridge assembly (**Figure 28**) from the fork leg.

10. Pry the dust seal (A, **Figure 29**) from the slider, and move it up the fork tube.

11. Remove the circlip (B, **Figure 29**) from its seat in the slider, and move it up the fork tube.

12. Secure the fork slider horizontally into a vise with soft jaws.

> *NOTE*
> *It may be necessary to slightly heat the area on the slider around the oil seal before removal. Heat the area with a rag soaked in hot water. Do not apply a flame directly to the fork slider.*

13. There is an interference fit between the bushing in the fork slider and the bushing on the fork tube. In

12

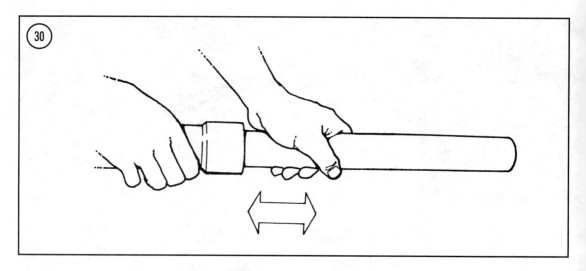

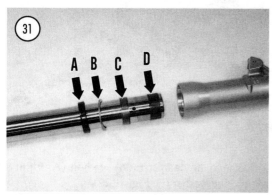

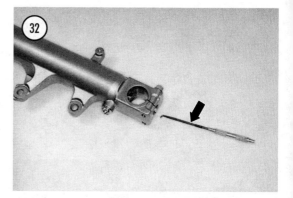

order to remove the fork tube from the slider, pull hard on the fork tube using quick in-and-out strokes (**Figure 30**) and withdraw the fork tube from the slider. Doing so also pulls the oil seal (A, **Figure 31**), spacer (B, **Figure 31**) and the slider bushing (C, **Figure 31**) from the slider.

> *NOTE*
> *Do not remove the fork tube bushing (D, **Figure 31**) unless it is going to be replaced. Inspect it as described in this chapter.*

14. Slide the oil seal (A, **Figure 31**), spacer (B, **Figure 31**) and the slider bushing (C, **Figure 31**) from the fork tube.

15A. On 1997 models, remove the oil lock piece from the bottom of the fork slider.

> *CAUTION*
> *On 1998-on models, remove the oil lock piece and its O-ring before wash-*

ing the slider with solvent. The solvent may cause the O-ring to swell, making it much more difficult to remove.

15B. On 1998-on models, the oil lock piece uses an O-ring that must be removed with the piece. Because the O-ring presses against the inner wall in the fork slider, the oil lock piece remains at the bottom of the slider when the cartridge assembly is being removed. The oil lock piece cannot be removed until it has been moved off the bottom of the slider. Remove the oil lock piece from these models by performing the following:

  a. Insert a 1 in. dowel down the fork tube and into the oil lock piece. Make sure the dowel fits snuggly into the oil lock piece.

  b. Rock the dowel back and forth, and walk the oil lock piece up into the slider.

  c. Once the oil lock piece is off its seat in the slider, insert a hooked tool that is approximately 8 in. long (**Figure 32**) through the Al-

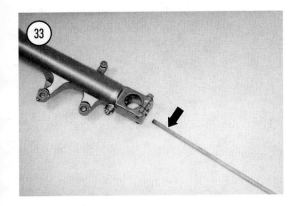

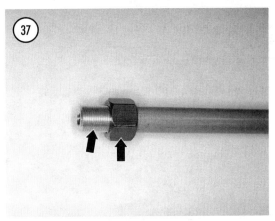

len bolt hole, and push the oil lock piece and its O-ring further up into the slider. Take care not to scratch the sides of the slider.

d. Use a 3/16 in. wooden dowel (**Figure 33**) to push the oil lock piece and its O-ring up and out of the slider.

e. Remove and discard the oil-lock-piece O-ring (A, **Figure 34**). Install a new one during assembly.

16. On 1998-on models, remove the compression adjuster (**Figure 35**) from the fork slider.

17. Inspect the components as described in this chapter.

Inspection

CAUTION
Do not clean the cartridge in solvent. It is extremely difficult to remove all the solvent from the cartridge, and this solvent contaminates the fork oil. Instead, wipe the cartridge with a clean cloth, and set it aside for inspection and assembly.

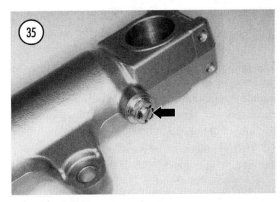

1. Thoroughly clean all parts, except the cartridge, in solvent and dry them. Check the fork tube for signs of wear or scratches.

2. Check the cartridge assembly for straightness and damage (**Figure 36**). Manually move the inner rod in and out of the cartridge. It should move smoothly.

3. Check the threads and nut (**Figure 37**) at the top of the cartridge assembly for damage. Clean the threads with an appropriate size metric tap and/or die if necessary.

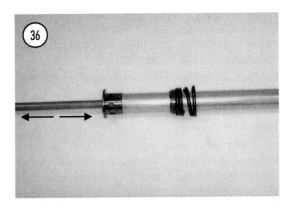

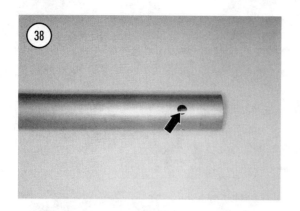

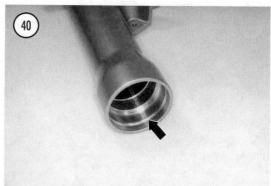

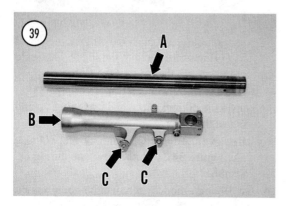

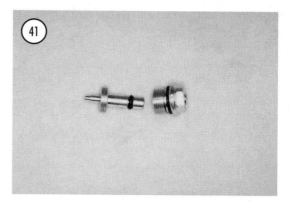

4. Make sure the oil hole (**Figure 38**) in the cartridge assembly is clear. Clean it if necessary.

5. Check the fork tube (A, **Figure 39**) for straightness. If bent or excessively scratched, replace it.

6. Inspect the threads in the top of the fork tube for wear or damage. Clean the threads with the appropriate size metric tap if necessary.

7. Check the slider (B, **Figure 39**) for dents or exterior damage that may cause the fork tube to stick. Replace the slider if necessary.

8. Inspect the inner surfaces (**Figure 40**) in the slider for damage or burrs. Pay particular attention to the circlip groove and the sealing surface. Clean the slider if necessary.

9. Inspect the brake caliper mounting bosses (C, **Figure 39**) on the slider for cracks or other damage. If damaged, replace the slider.

NOTE
Consider replacing the slider bushings whenever a fork is disassembled.

10. Inspect the slider bushing (C, **Figure 31**) and fork tube bushing (D, **Figure 31**). If either is scratched or scored, replace it. If the copper base

material shows on approximately 3/4 of the total bushing surface, too much of the Teflon coating has worn off. Replace the bushing.

11. To replace the fork tube bushing, open the bushing slot with a screwdriver, and slide the bushing off the fork tube. Lubricate a new bushing with fresh fork oil, open its slot slightly and slide the bushing onto the fork tube slot.

12. Inspect the compression adjuster needle for damage. Also inspect the bolt threads on the compression adjuster (**Figure 41**) for wear or damage. Clean the bolt threads with the appropriate size metric die if necessary.

13. Inspect the O-rings on the compression adjuster. Replace the compression adjuster if either O-ring is worn, cracked or swollen.

14. Measure the uncompressed length of the fork spring as shown in **Figure 42**. Replace the spring if it has sagged to less than the wear limit specified in **Table 1**.

15. Replace any parts that are worn or damaged. Simply cleaning and reinstalling unserviceable components does not improve the performance of the front suspension.

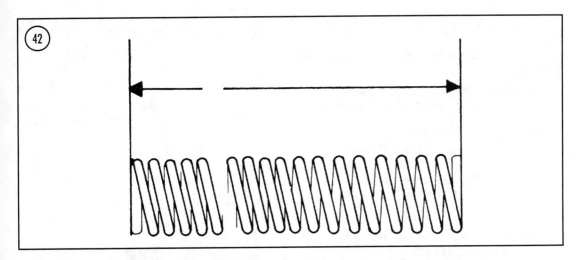

Assembly

1. Coat all parts with fresh SAE 10W fork oil before installation.

2. On 1998-on models, install the compression adjuster into the fork slider (**Figure 35**). Torque the adjuster to the specification listed in **Table 2**.

> *NOTE*
> *On 1997 models, the oil lock piece is installed with the cartridge assembly.*

3. On 1998-on models, install the oil lock piece by performing the following:

   a. Lubricate a towel with SAE 10W fork oil and push the towel into the slider to lubricate the inner wall.

   b. Lubricate a new O-ring (**Figure 34**) and install it onto the oil lock piece.

   c. Set the oil lock piece squarely into the slider so the end with the O-ring faces down into the slider. Carefully push the oil lock piece part-

way into the slider (**Figure 43**). Make sure the O-ring does not tear or turn inside out.

   d. Use the cartridge assembly to push the oil lock piece into the slider until the piece seats in the bottom of the slider (**Figure 44**).

   e. Remove the cartridge assembly from the slider.

4. Slide the cartridge through the fork tube. On 1997 models, install the oil lock piece onto the end of the cartridge (**Figure 45**).

5. Install the fork tube into the slider. On 1998-on models, make sure the end of the cartridge seats into the oil lock piece.

6. Secure the slider horizontally in a vise with soft jaws, and install the Allen bolt and washer into the end of the slider. Tighten the Allen bolt to the torque specification in **Table 2**. If necessary, temporarily install the fork spring with the tapered end down into the slider, the two washers, spacer and cap bolt. Remove them once the Allen bolt has been torqued.

12

7. Secure the fork vertically in a vise with soft jaws.

8. Install the slider bushing and spacer by performing the following:

   a. Slide the slider bushing (A, **Figure 46**) and the spacer (B, **Figure 46**) down the fork tube.

> *NOTE*
> *Fork seal drivers (**Figure 47**) can be purchased from a number of after-market suppliers. Measure the outside diameter of the fork tube, and purchase a driver with the same diameter.*

   b. Drive the bushing into the slider with a fork seal driver (**Figure 47**).

   c. Drive the bushing into place until it is completely seated into the recess in the slider.

> *NOTE*
> *To avoid damaging the fork seal and dust seal, place a piece of plastic wrap over the end of the fork tube, and coat it thoroughly with fork oil.*

9. Install the oil seal by performing the following:

   a. Lubricate the oil seal with fork oil.

   b. Slide the oil seal (**Figure 48**) down the fork tube. Make sure the manufacturer's marks face up.

   c. Drive the seal into the slider with the fork seal driver (**Figure 47**).

   d. Drive the seal until the circlip groove in the slider is visible above the top of the oil seal.

10. Slide the circlip (B, **Figure 29**) down the fork tube, and install it into the slider. Make sure the circlip is completely seated in the circlip groove in the slider.

11. Slide the dust seal (A, **Figure 29**) down the fork tube, and seat it in the slider (**Figure 49**).

12. Fill the fork with oil, set the oil level and complete fork assembly as described in *Fork Oil Adjustment* below.

Fork Oil Adjustment

1. Secure the fork vertically in a vise with soft jaws.

2. Push the fork tube into the slider until the tube bottoms. Compress the cartridge damper rod until it also bottoms (**Figure 50**).

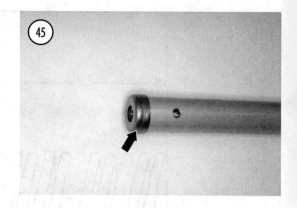

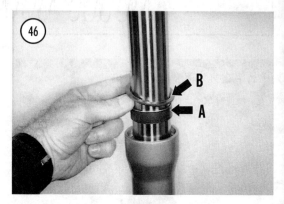

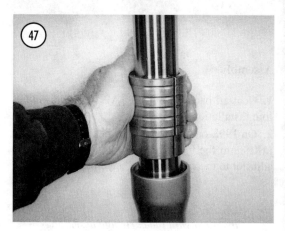

> *NOTE*
> *It is possible to bleed the cartridge without an inner rod holder, but the tool simplifies the procedure. If a tool is not available, use a nut (inner metric thread 12 × 1.0) that is approximately 2 in. long.*

3. Install the inner rod holder (Suzuki part No. 09940-52841) or equivalent onto the cartridge damper rod (**Figure 51**).

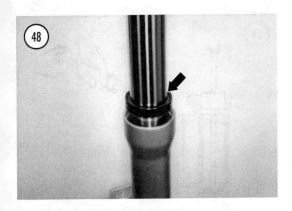

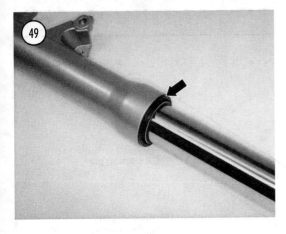

4. Refer to **Table 1**, and add the recommended amount of fork oil to the fork assembly.

> NOTE
> *During the bleeding procedure, the fork oil level must remain above the top of the cartridge assembly. If the oil level drops below this level, air may enter the cartridge nullifying the bleeding procedure.*

5. Bleed the air from the cartridge by performing the following.

   a. Keep the fork assembly in a vertical position during bleeding.

   b. Use the inner rod holder to *slowly* move the cartridge assembly up and down its full travel.

   c. Repeat this at least 10 times or until the fork oil is free of bubbles.

   d. If necessary, add additional fork oil until the oil is almost level with the top of the compressed fork tube.

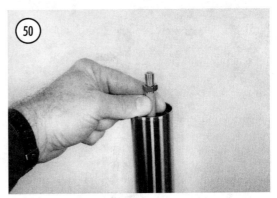

   e. Hold the slider and slowly move the fork tube up and down several stokes or until bubbles do not come from the oil.

   f. Secure the fork assembly in this vertical position for 5-10 minutes to allow any additional trapped air to escape. Tap the side of the fork assembly to break away any bubbles adhered to the side of the fork.

6. Set the fork oil level by performing the following:

   a. Hold the fork assembly vertical and fully compress the fork tube.

   b. Use an accurate ruler, the Suzuki oil level gauge (part No. 09943-74111) or equivalent to set the oil level to the value listed in **Table 1**. Refer to **Figure 52**.

> NOTE
> *An oil level measuring devise can be fabricated as shown in **Figure 53**. Fill the fork with a few cc more than the required amount of oil. Position the lower edge of the hose clamp against the top edge of the fork tube and draw out the excess oil. Oil is sucked out until the level reaches the small diameter hole. A precise oil level can be achieved with this simple device.*

   c. Allow the oil to settle completely and recheck the oil level measurement. Adjust the oil level if necessary.

   d. Remove the special tools.

7. Fully extend the fork tube.

8. Position the fork spring with the tapered end (**Figure 54**) going in first and install the fork spring.

9. Grasp the inner rod holder and compress the fork spring. Install a washer (B, **Figure 55**), spacer (C, **Figure 55**), the second washer and the spring re-

12

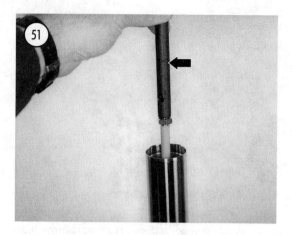

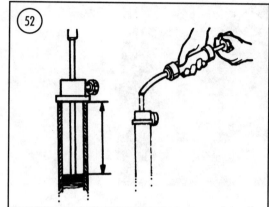

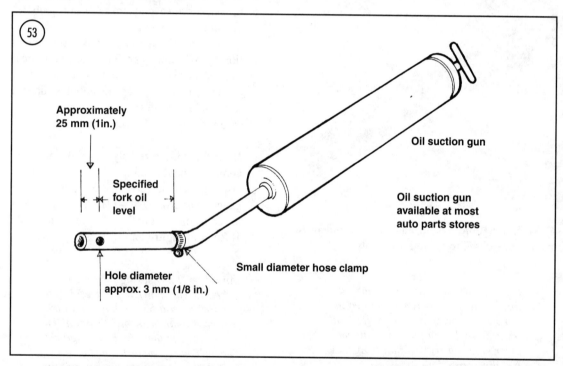

Approximately
25 mm (1in.)

Specified
fork oil
level

Hole diameter
approx. 3 mm (1/8 in.)

Small diameter hose clamp

Oil suction gun

Oil suction gun
available at most
auto parts stores

tainer (A, **Figure 55**). Make sure the spring retainer is seated beneath the damper rod locknut.

10. Unscrew and remove the inner rod holder (**Figure 51**) from the cartridge assembly.

11. Hold onto the cartridge assembly and thread the locknut all the way down until it stops (**Figure 56**).

12. Check the height of the rebound damping adjuster. The piston rod must extend 1.5 mm (0.06 in.) above the top surface of the adjuster as shown in **Figure 57**. Make any necessary adjustment.

13. Screw the cap bolt assembly onto the cartridge assembly until the rebound damping force adjuster seats on the inner rod. See **Figure 58**.

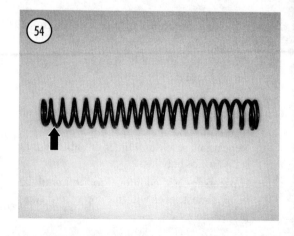

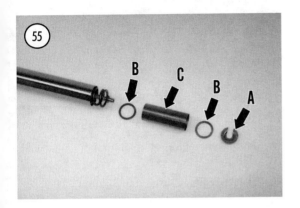

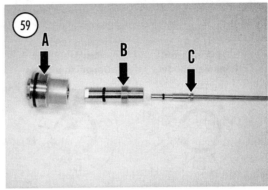

14. Install an open end wrench on the flats on the cap bolt (A, **Figure 58**) and another onto the damper rod locknut (B, **Figure 58**).

15. Hold onto the cap bolt and tighten the damper rod locknut to the torque specification listed in **Table 2**. Remove the wrenches.

16. Pull the fork tube up against the cap bolt and screw the cap bolt into the fork tube. Tighten the cap bolt securely. Do not tighten it to the final torque at this time.

17. Install the fork assemblies as described in this chapter and tighten the cap bolt to the torque specification listed in **Table 2**.

18. Adjust the spring preload and rebound damping as described in this chapter.

FORK CAP BOLT

Disassembly/Inspection

Disassembly of the fork cap bolt is only necessary if the spring preload adjuster and/or the damping force adjuster is not working properly. If either adjuster is stiff or does not rotate, then the assembly must be disassembled and cleaned.

All of the components within the fork cap bolt can be replaced individually. Suzuki does not provide any new or service limit specifications for any of these parts. If any show signs wear or damage, replace them.

1. Remove the fork cap assembly as described in *Front Fork Disassembly*.

2. Remove the fork cap (A, **Figure 59**) from the rebound damping adjuster (B, **Figure 59**).

3. Remove the damping adjuster from the piston rod (C, **Figure 59**).

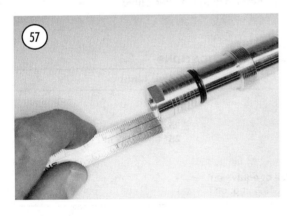

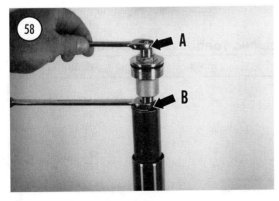

12

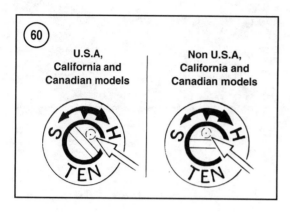

U.S.A,
California and
Canadian models

Non U.S.A,
California and
Canadian models

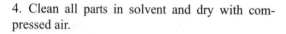

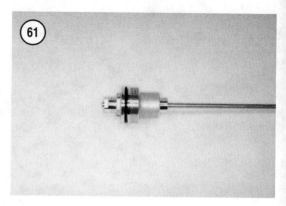

4. Clean all parts in solvent and dry with compressed air.

5. Inspect the rebound damping force adjuster, cap bolt and spring rebound adjuster for wear or damage.

6. Inspect the threaded portion of the damping force adjuster for damage. Clean up with an appropriate size metric die if necessary.

7. Replace the O-ring on the fork cap, rebound damping adjuster, and piston rod.

Assembly

1. Thread the rebound damping adjuster onto the piston rod until the rod extends 1.5 mm (0.06 in.) above the top of the damping adjuster (**Figure 57**).
2. Adjust the rebound damping adjuster so the punch mark is at the position shown in **Figure 60**.
3. Thread the fork cap onto the rebound damping adjuster (**Figure 61**).
4. Install the fork cap assembly into the fork tube as described in *Front Fork Assembly*.
5. Adjust the spring preload and rebound damping as described in Chapter Three.

Table 1 FRONT SUSPENSION SPECIFICATIONS

Item	Specification	Wear Limit
Front fork stroke	120 mm (4.7 in.)	–
Fork spring free length		
1997	–	252 mm (9.9 in.)
1998-on	266.6 mm (10.5 in.)	261 mm (10.3 in.)
Front fork oil level	110 mm (4.3 in.)	–
Fork oil		
Viscosity	Suzuki No. 10 fork oil or equivalent	–
Capacity per leg	533 ml (18.0 U.S. oz., 18.8 Imp. oz.)	–

Table 2 FRONT SUSPENSION AND STEERING TORQUE SPECIFICATIONS

Item	N•m	in.-lb.	ft.-lb.
Bearing adjust nut	45	–	33
Compression adjuster	18	–	13
Damper rod Allen bolt	35	–	26
Damper rod locknut	20	–	15
Fork bridge clamp bolt (lower)	23	–	17
Fork bridge clamp bolt (upper)	23	–	17
Fork cap bolt	35	–	26

(continued)

Table 2 FRONT SUSPENSION AND STEERING TORQUE SPECIFICATIONS (continued)

Item	N•m	in.-lb.	ft.-lb.
Front axle nut	100	–	74
Front axle pinch bolt	23	–	17
Handlebar clamp bolt	23	–	17
Handlebar mounting bolt	10	89	–
Steering stem head nut	90	–	66
Steering stem locknut	80	–	59

12

CHAPTER THIRTEEN

REAR SUSPENSION

This chapter covers procedures for the rear suspension components. Wheel removal, hub and tire service is covered in Chapter Eleven. Specifications for the rear suspension are listed in **Table 1** and **Table 2** at the end of the chapter.

The link-type suspension consists of a single adjustable shock absorber, a shock-lever and tie-rod assembly, and aluminum swing arm.

The swing arm and shock linkage pivot in caged bearings. For maximum service life, all pivot joints must be disassembled, inspected and lubricated frequently.

SHOCK ABSORBER

Removal/Installation

Refer to **Figure 1**.

1. Remove the lower fairing side cover from each side as described in Chapter Fifteen.
2. Support the bike securely with the rear wheel off the ground. If a bike stand or jack is not available, place wooden block(s) under the engine.
3. Remove the rear wheel as described in Chapter Eleven.
4. Loosen the mounting hardware at the forward tie rod mount (A, **Figure 2**) and rear tie rod mount (B, **Figure 2**).
5. Remove the bolts (**Figure 3**) and collars that secure the chain slider to the swing arm.
6. Remove the rear tie rod nut.
7. Pull the lower rail (A, **Figure 4**) of the chain slider down, and remove the rear tie rod bolt (B, **Figure 4**) from the pivot boss on the swing arm.
8. Remove the lower shock mounting bolt (**Figure 5**), and separate the lower shock mount from the shock lever.

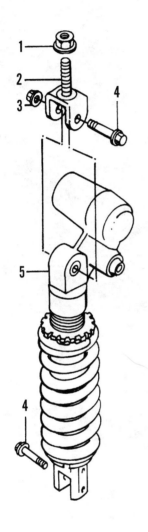

SHOCK ABSORBER

1. Nut
2. Upper mounting bracket
3. Nut
4. Bolt
5. Shock absorber

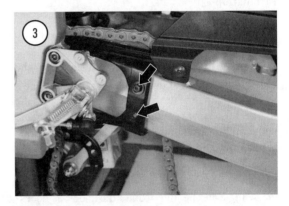

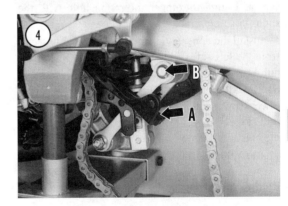

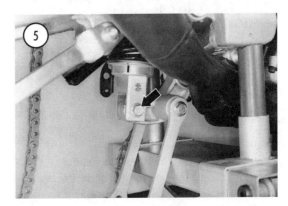

13

9. Remove the upper shock mounting bolt (**Figure 6**).

10. Lower the shock absorber from the shock bracket in the frame, and remove the shock through the large hole in the swing arm.

11. If necessary, remove the shock bracket nut (**Figure 7**) and lower the shock bracket from the frame.

12. Inspect the shock absorber as described in this chapter.

Installation

1. Clean the mounting bolts and nuts in solvent, and dry them thoroughly.

2. Apply a light coat of waterproof grease to the shock absorber upper and lower mounts.

3. If removed, fit the shock bracket in place in the frame. Position the bracket so the side with the white mark faces the frame. Install the shock bracket nut (**Figure 7**), and torque the nut to the specification in **Table 2**.

4. Carefully insert the shock absorber up through the swing arm opening. Rotate the shock as necessary and align the upper mounting hole with the shock absorber bracket in the frame.

5. Install the upper shock mounting bolt (**Figure 6**) from the left side of the motorcycle and install the nut. Finger-tighten the nut at this time.

6. Move the shock lever up into the shock absorber lower mount and install the lower shock mounting bolt (**Figure 5**) from the right side. Finger-tighten the bolt at this time.

7. Raise the tie rods into place on either side of the swing arm pivot boss. Install the rear tie rod bolt (B, **Figure 4**) from the left side, and then install the nut.

> *CAUTION*
> *Do not overtighten the lower shock mounting bolt. This bolt threads directly into the shock absorber. If the threads become damaged, replace the shock absorber.*

8. Tighten the upper shock mounting nut, the lower shock mounting bolt, and both tie rod nuts to the torque specifications in **Table 2**.

9. Raise the lower rail of the chain slider (A, **Figure 4**) into place on the swing arm. Install the collars and the mounting bolts (**Figure 3**) and secure

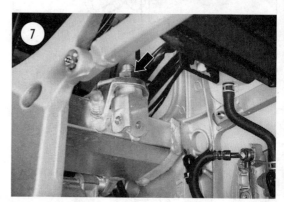

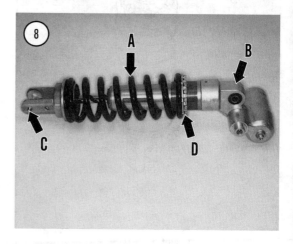

the slider to the swing arm. Tighten the bolts securely.

10. Install the rear wheel as described in this chapter.

11. Take the bike off the jack or stand, push down on the rear of the bike to make sure the linkage is operating correctly with no binding.

12. Install the lower fairing side covers as described in Chapter Fifteen.

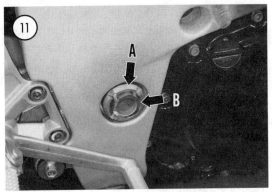

5. On 1998-on models, rotate the compression damping force adjuster (**Figure 9**) from one stop to another. The adjuster should rotate freely and engage the detent at each stop.

6. Rotate the rebound damping force adjuster (**Figure 10**) from one stop to another. Check that the adjuster rotates freely and that it engages the detent at each stop.

7. If any of these areas are damaged, replace the shock absorber.

SWING ARM

Swing Arm Bearing
Preliminary Inspection

The condition of the swing arm bearings can greatly affect the handling of the bike. Worn bearings causes wheel hop, pulling to one side under acceleration and pulling to the other side during braking. To check the condition of the swing arm bearings, perform the following steps.

1. Remove the rear wheel as described in this chapter.

2. Remove the rear tie rod mounting hardware (B, **Figure 4**), and lower the tie rods away from the swing arm. The tie rods do not have to be completely removed.

3. On the right side, make sure the swing arm pivot locknut nut (A, **Figure 11**) is tight.

4. On the left side, make sure the pivot nut (**Figure 12**) is tight.

5. The swing arm is now free to move under its own weight.

NOTE
Have an assistant steady the bike when performing Step 6 and Step 7.

Inspection

No replacement parts are available for the original equipment shock absorber. If any part of the shock absorber is defective, replace the shock absorber assembly.

WARNING
The shock absorber contains highly compressed nitrogen gas. Do not tamper with or attempt to open the housing. Do not place it near an open flame or other extreme heat. Do not weld on the frame near the shock. Do not dispose of the unit yourself. Take it to a Suzuki dealership where it can be deactivated and disposed of properly.

1. Inspect the shock absorber for oil leaks.

2. Check the spring (A, **Figure 8**) for cracks or other damage.

3. Inspect the upper (B, **Figure 8**) and lower (C, **Figure 8**) mounts for wear or damage. If necessary, replace the upper bushing.

4. Make sure the spring preload locknut and adjust nut (D, **Figure 8**) are tight.

13

6. Grasp both ends of the swing arm and attempt to move it from side to side in a horizontal arc. If more than a slight amount of movement is felt, the bearings are worn and must be replaced.

7. Grasp both ends of the swing arm and move it up and down. The swing arm should move smoothly with no binding or abnormal noise from the bearings. If there is binding or noise, the bearings are worn and must be replaced.

8. Move the swing arm and the tie rods into position. Install the rear tie rod bolt from the left side. Install the tie rod nut, and tighten it to the torque specification listed in **Table 2**.

9. Install the rear wheel as described in this chapter.

Removal

Refer to **Figure 13**.

1. Remove the seats and the lower fairing side panels from each side as described in Chapter Fifteen.

2. Remove the rear wheel as described in Chapter Eleven.

3. Remove the muffler as described in Chapter Four. Wrap a plastic bag around the exhaust pipe to keep contaminants out of the exhaust system.

4. Remove the chain guide (**Figure 14**) from the swing arm.

5. Remove the rear caliper as described in Chapter Fourteen. Place the loose end of the brake hose in a reclosable plastic bag and close it.

6. Unhook the brake hose from the two clamps (A, **Figure 15**) on top of the swing arm, and carefully pull the rear brake hose out from the guide (B, **Figure 15**) on the inside surface of the swing arm.

7. Remove the lower shock mounting bolt (A, **Figure 16**).

8. Remove the tie rod nut (A, **Figure 2**) from the forward tie rod mount, and pull the tie rod bolt (B, **Figure 16**) from the right side of the motorcycle. Separate the tie rods from the shock lever.

9. Remove the mounting nut from the upper shock mount, and pull the mounting bolt (**Figure 6**) from the left side of the motorcycle.

10. On the right side, use the Suzuki Swing Arm Pivot Thrust Adjuster Socket Wrench, (part No. 09940-14970) and remove the pivot locknut (A, **Figure 11**).

11. Tie the end of the swing arm to the frame or place a box under the end of the swing arm and support it securely.

12. Hold the pivot shaft (B, **Figure 11**) with a 27 mm socket.

13. On the left side, use a 36 mm socket to remove the pivot nut (**Figure 12**) and washer.

14. From the left side, carefully tap the pivot shaft out of the frame and swing arm. Pull the pivot shaft (**Figure 17**) from the right side of the frame.

15. Lower the swing arm from the frame or from the box. Do not lose the dust seal from either side of the swing arm pivot.

16. Remove the shock absorber from the hole in the swing arm. See **Figure 18**.

17. Rotate the swing arm and remove its left arm from the drive chain.

18. If the swing arm bearings are not going to be serviced, place a strip of duct tape over each pivot. This protects the bearing assemblies and prevents the loss of any small parts.

19. Inspect the swing arm as described in this chapter. Lubricate all bearings as described in this chapter.

Installation

> *NOTE*
> *Swing arm installation can be accomplished alone; however, the task is much easier with the aid of another person.*

1. Lubricate the swing arm and shock linkage bearings, the pivot bolts and collars with waterproof grease before installation.

> *NOTE*
> *Refer to **Figure 13** for the correct installation direction for the pivot bolts. To ensure maximum performance and*

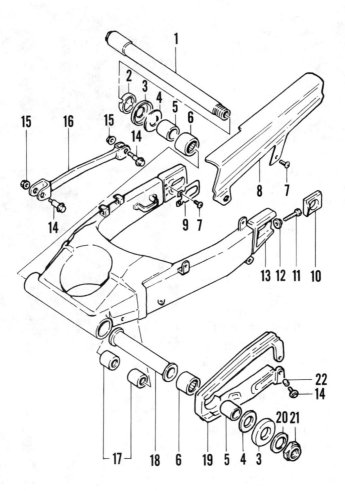

13

SWING ARM

1. Pivot bolt
2. Pivot locknut
3. Dust seal
4. Thrust washer
5. Bushing
6. Needle bearing
7. Screw
8. Chain guard
9. Plate
10. Chain adjuster
11. Chain adjuster bolt
12. Chain adjuster locknut
13. Swing arm
14. Bolt
15. Nut
16. Torque arm
17. Needle bearing
18. Spacer
19. Chain slider
20. Washer
21. Pivot nut
22. Collar

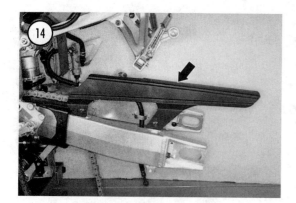

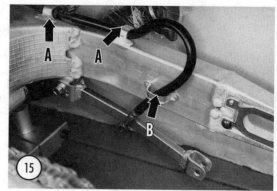

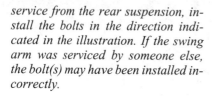

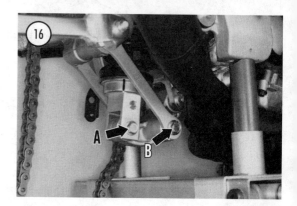

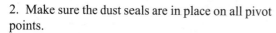

service from the rear suspension, install the bolts in the direction indicated in the illustration. If the swing arm was serviced by someone else, the bolt(s) may have been installed incorrectly.

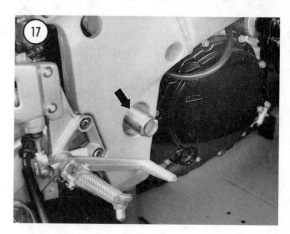

2. Make sure the dust seals are in place on all pivot points.

3. Secure the rear brake hose above the swing arm mount in the frame so the hose will not be pinched.

4. Insert the left arm of the swing arm between the drive chain, and set the swing arm in place beneath the frame. See **Figure 18**.

5. Set the shock absorber into the hole in the swing arm as shown in **Figure 18**.

6. Raise the swing arm, and install it between the frame pivots. Align the notch on the left side of the chain slider with the frame boss. From the right side of the motorcycle, install the swing arm pivot shaft (**Figure 17**) through the frame and the swing arm pivots.

7. Loosely install the washer and pivot nut (**Figure 19**) onto the left end of the pivot shaft.

8. Position the upper shock mount within the shock bracket. Install the upper shock mounting bolt from the left side of the motorcycle, and finger-tighten the mounting nut.

9. Set the thrust clearance by tightening the swing arm pivot fasteners in the order described below. Tighten each fastener to the torque specification listed in **Table 2**.

   a. Torque the swing arm pivot shaft (B, **Figure 11**).

   b. Hold the pivot shaft with a 27 mm socket, and torque the pivot nut (**Figure 12**) to specification.

   c. Use the Suzuki Swing Arm Pivot Thrust Adjuster Socket Wrench, (part No. 09940-14970) and torque the pivot locknut (A, **Figure 11**) to the specification.

10. After tightening all of the fasteners in Step 9, move the swing arm up and down and check for smooth movement. If the swing arm is tight or loose, then the fasteners in Step 9 were either tightened in the wrong sequence or to the incorrect torque specification; repeat Step 9.

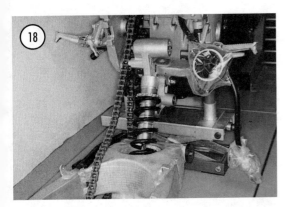

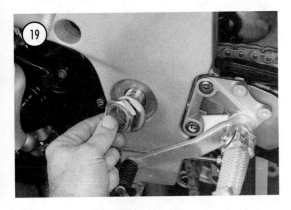

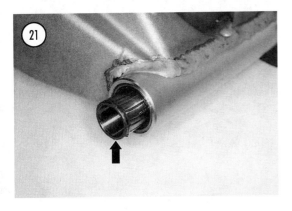

11. Align each tie rod with the center mount on the shock lever. Install the tie rod bolts from the right side of the motorcycle (B, **Figure 16**) and install the forward tie-rod nut. Torque the nut to the specification in **Table 2**.

12. Align the lower shock mount with the rear mount on the shock lever, and install the lower shock mounting bolt (A, **Figure 16**). Install the bolt from the right side of the motorcycle, and torque the bolt to the specification in **Table 2**.

13. Route the rear brake hose across the swing arm and through the guide (B, **Figure 15**) on the swing arm. Make sure the hose is secured under the two clamps (A, **Figure 15**) on top of the swing arm.

14. Install the chain guard (**Figure 14**) onto the swing arm. Tighten the bolts securely.

15. Install the rear brake caliper as described in Chapter Fourteen.

16. Install the muffler as described in Chapter Four.

17. Install the rear wheel as described in Chapter Eleven.

18. Adjust the chain as described in Chapter Three.

19. Bleed the brakes as described in Chapter Fourteen.

20. Install the lower fairing panels and seats as described in Chapter Fifteen.

Disassembly

Refer to **Figure 13**.

1. Remove the swing arm assembly as described in this chapter.

2. If still in place, remove the dust seal and thrust washer (**Figure 20**) from each side of the swing arm pivot.

3. Remove the bushing (**Figure 21**) from each needle bearing.

> *NOTE*
> *The tie rods are symmetrical and can be installed on either side of the shock lever. After prolonged use, they will develop a unique wear pattern and should be reinstalled on the same side. Before removing the tie rods, mark them with an L (left) or R (right) so they can be reinstalled on the correct side of the shock lever.*

13

4. Remove the tie-rod mounting nut (A, **Figure 22**) and bolt, and remove the tie rods (B, **Figure 22**) from the swing arm.

5. Remove the pivot collar (A, **Figure 23**) from the pivot boss (B, **Figure 23**) on the swing arm.

6. If necessary, remove the bolts and collars (**Figure 24**) and remove the chain slider from the swing arm.

7. If necessary, remove the mounting hardware and the torque arm (C, **Figure 23**) from the swing arm.

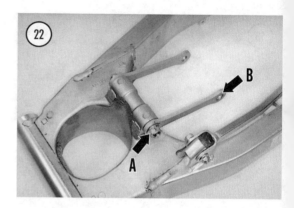

Inspection

1. Wash the bolts, collar and bushings in solvent, and thoroughly dry them.

2. Inspect the pivot collar and bushings for wear, scratches or score marks.

3. Check the bolts for straightness. If a bolt is bent it will restrict the movement of the swing arm.

4. Inspect the swing arm pivot bearings as follows:

   a. Use a clean lint-free rag and wipe off surface grease from the pivot area needle bearings.

   b. Turn each bearing (**Figure 25**) by hand. The bearing should turn smoothly without excessive play or noise. Check the rollers for wear, pitting or rust.

   c. Inspect the bushings for wear, scratches or score marks.

   d. Reinstall the bushing (**Figure 21**) into the bearings and slowly rotate each bushing. The bushings must turn smoothly without excessive play or noise.

   e. Remove the bushings.

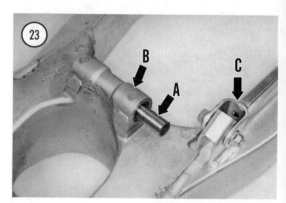

5. Inspect the tie-rod pivot boss (B, **Figure 23**) on the swing arm as follows:

   a. Use a clean lint-free rag and wipe off surface grease from the needle bearings.

   b. Turn each bearing by hand. The bearing should turn smoothly without excessive play or noise. Check the rollers for wear, pitting or rust.

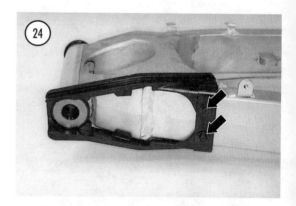

   c. Insert the collar (A, **Figure 23**) into each bearing and slowly rotate the collar. It should turn smoothly without excessive play or noise.

   d. Remove the collar.

6. Replace any worn or damaged bearing as described in *Swing Arm Needle Bearing Replacement* in this chapter.

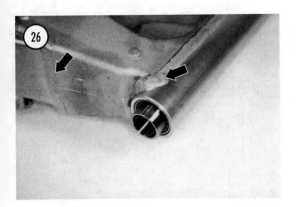

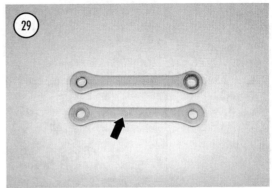

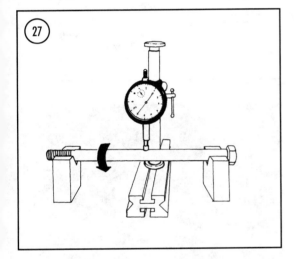

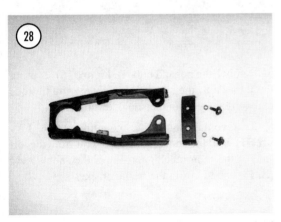

7. Check the welded sections (**Figure 26**) on the swing arm for cracks or fractures.

8. Inspect the drive chain adjuster washer, bolt and locknut on each side for wear or damage. If necessary, replace any damaged part(s).

9. Check the pivot shaft for straightness with V-blocks and a dial indicator (**Figure 27**). Replace

the pivot shaft if the runout equals or exceeds the service limit specified in **Table 1**.

10. Inspect the drive chain slider (**Figure 28**) for wear or damage, replace as necessary.

Assembly

1. If removed, install the torque arm (C, **Figure 23**) onto the swing arm. Install the forward torque arm bolt and nut, and torque the nut to the specification in **Table 2**.

2. If removed, install the chain slider onto the swing arm. Secure it in place with the bolts and collars (**Figure 24**). Tighten the bolts securely.

3. Lubricate the following parts with grease:
    a. Needle bearings.
    b. Pivot collars and bushings.

4. Install the pivot collar (A, **Figure 23**) into the tie-rod pivot boss (B, **Figure 23**) on the swing arm. Make sure the ends of the collar are flush with the end of each needle bearing.

5. Install the tie rods (B, **Figure 22**) onto the swing arm.
    a. Use the marks made before removal to reinstall each tie rod onto its original side (left or right).
    b. Install each tie rod so the side with the inner diameter stamp (**Figure 29**) faces the outboard side of the swing arm.
    c. Secure the tie rods to the swing arm with the tie rod bolts and nut (A, **Figure 22**). Torque the nut to the specification in **Table 2**.

6. Install the bushing (**Figure 21**) into the needle bearing on each side of the swing arm pivot.

7. Install the thrust washer and dust seal onto each side of the swing arm pivot. Push the dust seal on until it is completely seated.

13

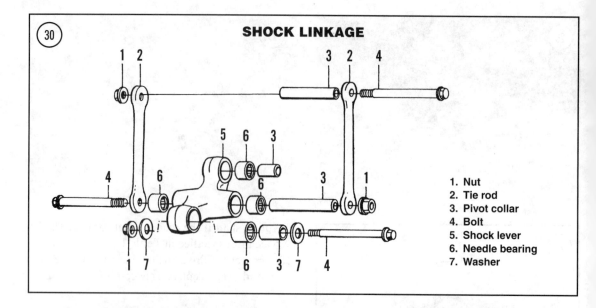

SHOCK LINKAGE

1. Nut
2. Tie rod
3. Pivot collar
4. Bolt
5. Shock lever
6. Needle bearing
7. Washer

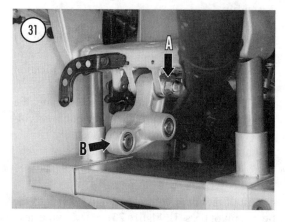

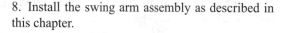

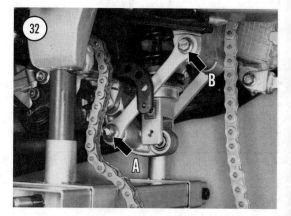

8. Install the swing arm assembly as described in this chapter.

SHOCK LINKAGE

Removal

Refer to **Figure 30**.

1. Remove the seats and the lower fairing side panels from each side as described in Chapter Fifteen.

2. Remove the rear wheel as described in Chapter Eleven.

3. Remove the muffler or complete exhaust system as described in Chapter Four.

4. Remove the bolt (A, **Figure 16**) securing the lower shock mount to the shock lever.

5. Remove the nut and bolt (B, **Figure 16**) securing the tie rods to the shock lever. Swing the tie rods rearward away from the shock lever.

6. Remove the shock lever mounting nut (A, **Figure 31**). Pull the shock lever pivot bolt from the left side of the motorcycle, and lower the shock lever (B, **Figure 31**) from the frame bracket.

Installation

1. Apply grease to the pivot points on the lower end of the shock absorber and to the frame mounting boss.

2. Position the shock lever (B, **Figure 31**) correctly and align the shock-lever forward mount within the frame bracket. Insert the shock lever pivot bolt from

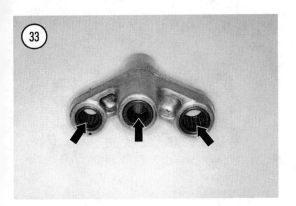

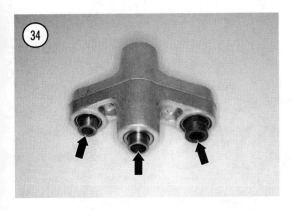

b. Torque the tie-rod mounting nut (A, **Figure 32**) to specification.

c. Torque the shock lever mounting nut (A, **Figure 31**) to specification.

7. Install the muffler as described in Chapter Four.

8. Install the rear wheel as described in Chapter Eleven.

9. Install the lower fairing side panels and seats as described in Chapter Fifteen.

Inspection

1. Inspect the shock lever pivot bearings as follows:

a. Remove the pivot collars from the pivot.

b. Use a clean lint-free rag and wipe off surface grease from the pivot needle bearings (**Figure 33**).

c. Turn each bearing by hand. The bearing should turn smoothly without excessive play or noise. Check the rollers for wear, pitting or rust.

d. Reinstall the pivot collars (**Figure 34**) into the bearings and slowly rotate each pivot collar. The collars must turn smoothly without excessive play or noise.

e. Remove the pivot collars.

f. If the needle bearings must be replaced, refer to *Shock Lever Needle Bearing Replacement* in this chapter.

2. Inspect the pivot collars (**Figure 35**) for wear and damage. Replace each collar as necessary.

3. Inspect the rocker arm for cracks or damage. Replace as necessary.

4. Inspect the tie rods (**Figure 36**) for bending, cracks or damage. Replace as necessary.

the left side. Loosely install the mounting nut (A, **Figure 31**), but do not tighten it at this time.

3. Move the shock lever up, and align the lever rear pivot with the shock absorber lower mount. Loosely insert the shock mounting bolt (A, **Figure 16**) from the right side. Finger-tighten the bolt at this time.

4. Rotate the tie rods forward, and align their mounting holes with the center pivot on the shock lever.

5. Install the tie rod bolt (B, **Figure 16**) from the right side of the motorcycle, and loosely install the tie-rod mounting nut.

> *CAUTION*
> *Do not overtighten the lower shock mounting bolt. This bolt threads directly into the shock absorber. If the threads become damaged, replace the shock absorber.*

6. Refer to **Table 2** and tighten the mounting hardware to the indicated torque specification. Tighten the fasteners in the following order:

a. Torque the lower shock mounting bolt (A, **Figure 16**) to specification.

13

5. Clean the pivot bolts and nuts in solvent. Check the bolts for straightness. If a bolt is bent, it will restrict the movement of the rocker arm.

6. Before installing the pivot collars, coat the inner surface of the bearings with molybdenum disulfide grease.

BEARING REPLACEMENT

Swing Arm Needle Bearing Replacement

Do not remove the swing arm needle bearings unless they must be replaced. The needle bearings are pressed onto the swing arm. A set of blind bearing pullers is required to remove the needle bearings. The needle bearings can be installed with a homemade tool.

> *NOTE*
> *If the needle bearings are replaced, replace the pivot bushings at the same time. These parts should always be replaced as a set.*

1. If still installed, remove the dust seals, thrust washers and pivot bushings from the needle bearings as described in this chapter.

> *NOTE*
> *In the following steps, the bearing puller grabs the inner surface of the bearing and then withdraws it from the pivot boss in the swing arm.*

2. Insert the bearing puller through the needle bearing and expand it behind the bearing.

3. Using sharp strokes of the slide hammer, withdraw the needle bearing from the pivot boss.

4. Remove the bearing puller and the bearing.

5. Withdraw the spacer located between the bearings.

6. Repeat for the bearing on the other side.

7. Remove the special tool.

8. Repeat Steps 2-7 for the shock lever pivot bearings on the bottom of the swing arm.

9. Thoroughly clean out the inside of the pivot bore with solvent, and dry it with compressed air.

10. To make bearing installation easier, apply a light coat of grease to the exterior of the new bearings and to the inner circumference of the pivot bore.

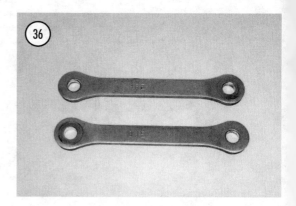

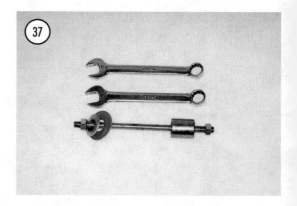

> *NOTE*
> *Install one needle bearing at a time. Make sure the bearing is entering the pivot boss squarely, otherwise the bearing and the pivot boss may be damaged.*

11. Position the bearing with the manufacturer's marks facing out.

> *NOTE*
> *The bearing can be easily installed using a homemade tool consisting of a piece of threaded rod, two thick washers, two nuts, a socket that matches the outer race diameter, and two wrenches as shown in* **Figure 37**.

12. Locate and square the new bearing in the pivot bore. Assemble the homemade tool through the pivot bore so the socket presses against the bearing. See **Figure 38**.

13. Hold the nut adjacent to the socket (A, **Figure 39**).

14. Tighten the nut on the opposite side (B, **Figure 39**) and pull the bearing into the pivot bore. Pull the

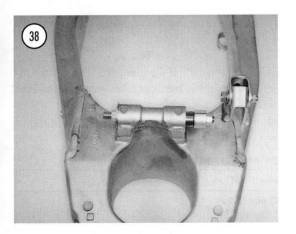

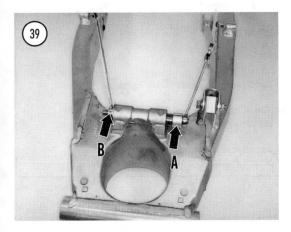

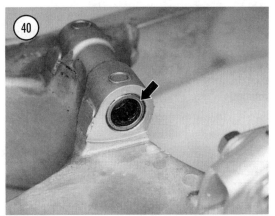

bearing until it is flush with the outer surface of the pivot boss (**Figure 40**).

15. Disassemble the tool and reinstall it on the opposite side, then repeat for the other bearing.

16. Remove the tool.

17. Make sure the bearings are properly seated. Turn each bearing by hand, it should turn smoothly.

18. Lubricate the new bearings with grease.

19. Repeat for the other set of bearings in the swing arm.

Shock Lever Needle Bearing Replacement

Do not remove the shock lever needle bearings unless they must be replaced. The needle bearings are pressed onto the shock lever. A set of blind bearing pullers is required to remove the needle bearings. The needle bearings can be installed with a homemade tool, or socket and hammer.

NOTE
If the needle bearings are replaced, replace the pivot collars at the same time. These parts should always be replaced as a set.

1. If still installed, remove the pivot collars.

NOTE
In the following steps, the bearing puller grabs the inner surface of the bearing and then withdraws it from the pivot areas of the swing arm.

2. Insert the bearing puller through the needle bearing and expand it behind the front bearing.

3. Using sharp strokes of the slide hammer, withdraw the needle bearing from the front pivot hole.

NOTE
The bearings are different sizes. Mark the bearings front, center and rear as they are removed. The center two bearings are identical.

4. Remove the special tool and the bearing.

5. At the center pivot area, repeat Step 2 and Step 3 for the bearing on each side.

6. Repeat Step 2 and Step 3 for the rear bearing.

7. Thoroughly clean out the inside of the pivot bores with solvent. Dry them with compressed air.

8. To make bearing installation easier, apply a light coat of grease to the exterior of the new bearings and to the inner circumference of the pivot bores.

9. Locate and square the new bearing in the pivot bore.

13

10. Install the bearings with an appropriate size drift or socket that matches the outer race diameter. Tap the bearings into place.

11. Check that the bearing is properly seated. Turn each bearing by hand. The bearing should turn smoothly.

12. Lubricate the needles of the new bearing with a waterproof bearing grease.

13. Repeat for the other bearings.

14. Before installing the pivot collars, coat the inner surface of the bearings with grease. Install the pivot collars as described in this chapter.

Table 1 REAR SUSPENSION SPECIFICATIONS

Item	Specification
Rear wheel travel	133 mm (5.2 in.)
Swing-arm pivot-shaft runout wear limit	0.3 mm (0.01 in.)
Shock absorber	
Gas pressure	1000 kPa (145 psi)
Spring length	
1997	193.9 mm (7.6 in.)
1998-on	195.4 mm (7.7 in.)
Shock absorber damping adjuster	
1997	
Rebound damping	At punch mark (approx. 1 1/8 turns out)
Compression damping	
U.S.A., California and Canada models	At punch mark (approx. 7/8 turns out)
Non U.S.A., California and Canada models	At punch mark (approx. 3/4 turns out)
1998-on	
Rebound damping	At punch mark (approx. 1 turn out)
Compression damping	At punch mark (approx. 1 3/8 turns out)

Table 2 REAR SUSPENSION TORQUE SPECIFICATIONS

Item	N•m	in.-lb.	ft.-lb.
Shock absorber			
Bracket nut	115	–	85
Mounting bolt/nut (upper and lower)	50	–	37
Tie rod nut			
Tie rod to shock lever mount	78	–	58
Tie rod to swing arm mount	78	–	58
Shock lever mounting nut	78	–	58
Torque arm bolt/nut			
Front	28	–	21
Rear	35	–	26
Swing arm			
Pivot nut	100	–	74
Pivot locknut	90	–	66
Pivot shaft	15	–	11

CHAPTER FOURTEEN

BRAKES

This chapter covers service, repair and replacement procedures for the front and rear brake systems. Brake specifications are located in **Table 1** and **Table 2** at the end of this chapter.

The brake system consists of dual discs up front and a single disc mounted in the rear.

BRAKE SERVICE

The disc brake system transmits hydraulic pressure from the master cylinders to the brake calipers. This pressure is transmitted from the caliper(s) to the brake pads, which grip both sides of the brake disc(s) and slow the motorcycle. As the pads wear, the pistons move out of the caliper bores to automatically compensate for wear. As this occurs the fluid level in the reservoir goes down. This must be compensated for by occasionally adding fluid.

The proper operation of this system depends on a supply of clean brake fluid (DOT 4) and a clean work environment when any service is being performed. Any tiny particle of debris that enters the system can damage the components and cause poor brake performance.

Brake fluid is hygroscopic (easily absorbs moisture) and moisture in the system will reduce brake performance. It is a good idea to purchase brake fluid in small containers and discard any small quantities that remain. Small quantities of fluid will quickly absorb the moisture in the container. Use only fluid clearly marked DOT 4. If possible, use the same brand of fluid. Do not replace the fluid with DOT 5 (silicone) fluid. It is not possible to remove all of the old fluid and DOT 5 is not compatible with other types. Silicone type fluids used in systems for which they were not designed will cause internal seals to swell and deteriorate. Do not reuse drained fluid and discard old fluid properly.

Proper service also includes carefully performed procedures. Do not use any sharp tools inside the master cylinders or calipers or on the pistons. Any damage to these components could cause a loss in the systems ability to maintain hydraulic pressure. If there is any doubt about having the ability to correctly and safely service the brake system, have a profession technician perform the task.

Consider the following when servicing the brake system:

1. The hydraulic components rarely require disassembly. Make sure it is necessary.

2. Keep the reservoir covers in place to prevent the entry of moisture and debris.

3. Clean parts with an aerosol brake cleaner or isopropyl alcohol. Never use petroleum based sol-

14

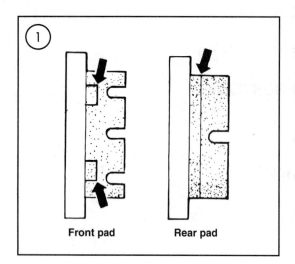

Front pad   Rear pad

*parts when servicing any component
still installed on the bike.*

FRONT BRAKE PAD REPLACEMENT

vents on internal brake system components. They
will cause seals to swell and distort.

4. Do not allow brake fluid to contact plastic,
painted or plated parts. It will damage the surface.

5. Dispose of brake fluid properly.

6. If the hydraulic system has been opened (not including the reservoir cover) the system must be bled
to remove air from the system. Refer to *Brake
Bleeding* in this chapter.

7. The manufacturer does not provide wear limit
specifications for the caliper and master cylinder assemblies. Use good judgement when inspecting
these components or consult a professional technician for advice.

> *WARNING*
> *Do not add to or replace the brake
> fluid with Silicone (DOT 5) brake
> fluid. It is not compatible with the sys-
> tem and may cause brake failure.*

> *WARNING*
> *Whenever working on the brake sys-
> tem, do **not** inhale brake dust. It may
> contain asbestos, which can cause
> lung injury and cancer. Wear a
> facemask that meets OSHA require-
> ments for trapping asbestos particles,
> and wash hands and forearms thor-
> oughly after completing the work.*

> *WARNING*
> ***NEVER** use compressed air to clean
> any part of the brake system. This will
> release the harmful brake pad dust.
> Use an aerosol brake cleaner to clean*

Pad wear depends greatly on riding habits and
conditions. Frequently check the pads for wear. If
either pad is worn to the wear limit shown in **Figure
1**, replace the brake pads.

To maintain even brake pressure on the disc, always replace both pads in a caliper at the same time.
Also, replace both pads in *both front brake calipers*
at the same time. If any front brake pad is worn to
the wear limit, replace all four front brake pads as a
set. It is not necessary to disconnect the brake hose
from a caliper during brake pad replacement. Disconnect the hose only when servicing the brake caliper.

> *CAUTION*
> *Check the pads more frequently as the
> pad thickness approaches the wear
> limit line (**Figure 1**). On some pads,
> the limit line is very close to the metal*

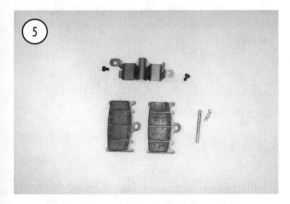

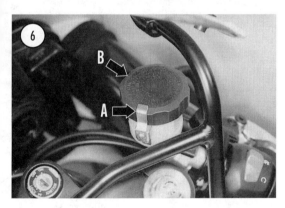

4. Remove the small bolts (A, **Figure 2**) securing the brake pad spring to the caliper.

5. Remove the brake pad spring (B, **Figure 2**).

6. Use needlenose pliers and remove the clip (**Figure 3**), and then withdraw the pad pin (A, **Figure 4**) from the caliper.

7. Remove both brake pads from the caliper assembly.

8. Clean the pad recess and the end of both sets of pistons with a soft brush. Do not use solvent, a wire brush or any hard tool that would damage the cylinders or pistons.

9. Carefully remove any rust or corrosion from the disc.

10. Thoroughly clean the pad spring, screws, pad pin and clip of any corrosion or road dirt.

11. Check the friction surface (**Figure 5**) of the new pads for any foreign matter or manufacturing residue. If necessary, clean the pads with an aerosol brake cleaner.

NOTE
When purchasing new pads, check with the parts supplier to make sure the friction compound of the new pads is compatible with the disc material. Remove any roughness from the backs of the new pads with a fine-cut file.

12. Repeat Steps 4-11 and remove the brake pads in the other caliper assembly.

13. When new pads are installed in the calipers, the master cylinder brake fluid level will rise as the caliper pistons are repositioned. Perform the following:

   a. Clean the top of the master cylinder of all debris.

   b. Cover the fairing and other parts sitting beneath the master cylinder to protect them from brake fluid spills.

   c. Remove the mounting screw and move the retaining clip (A, **Figure 6**) off the top cover.

   d. Remove the top cover (B, **Figure 6**), diaphragm plate and diaphragm from the master cylinder reservoir.

   e. Temporarily install both old brake pads into the caliper and seat them against the pistons.

   f. Grasp the caliper and brake pad with a large pair of slip-joint pliers and squeeze the piston back into the caliper. Pad the caliper with a shop cloth to prevent scuffing it. Repeat for

backing plate. If pad wear happens to be uneven for some reason, the backing plate could come in contact with the disc and cause damage.

1. Review the *Brake Service* information earlier in this chapter.

2. Place the bike on the sidestand on level ground.

3. Place a spacer between the brake lever and the throttle grip and secure it in place. That way if the brake lever is inadvertently squeezed, the pistons will not be forced out of the cylinders.

14

each side until the pistons are completely in the caliper. Constantly check the reservoir and make sure the fluid does not overflow. Draw out excess fluid if necessary.

g. The pistons should move freely. If they do not, remove and service the caliper as described in this chapter.

h. Remove the old brake pads.

i. Repeat this process for the other caliper.

14. Install the outboard pad (C, **Figure 4**) and the inboard pad (B, **Figure 4**) into the caliper. Carefully push them into the caliper until they bottom.

15. Insert the pad pin (A, **Figure 4**) through the caliper. Push it through both brake pads until it stops.

16. Install the clip (**Figure 3**) through the hole in the pad pin. Make sure it seats correctly.

17. Install the pad spring (B, **Figure 2**). Secure the spring in place with the two mounting screws (A, **Figure 2**).

18. Remove the spacer from the front brake lever.

19. Pump the front brake lever to reposition the brake pads against the brake disc. Roll the bike back and forth and continue to pump the brake lever as many times as it takes to refill the cylinders in the calipers and correctly locate the brake pads against the disc.

> *NOTE*
> *To control the small flow of hydraulic fluid, punch a small hole into the seal of a new container of brake fluid next to the edge of the pour spout. This helps eliminate spillage especially when adding fluid to the very small reservoirs.*

> *WARNING*
> *Use brake fluid clearly marked DOT 4 from a sealed container. Other types may vaporize and cause brake failure. Always use the same brand of brake fluid. Do not intermix brake fluid brands. Many brands are not compatible. Do not intermix silicone based (DOT 5) brake fluid as it can cause brake component damage leading to brake system failure.*

20. Refill the master cylinder reservoir, if necessary, to maintain the correct fluid level as indicated on the side of the reservoir. Install the diaphragm and plate. Install the top cover, and tighten it securely.

21. Move the reservoir top cover retaining clip back into position and tighten the mounting screw securely.

> *WARNING*
> *Do not ride the motorcycle until the brakes are operating correctly with full hydraulic advantage. If necessary, bleed the brake as described in this chapter.*

22. Bed the pads in gradually for the first 2-3 days of riding by using only light pressure as much as possible. Immediate hard application glazes the new friction pads and greatly reduces their effectiveness.

FRONT CALIPER

Removal/Installation

Refer to **Figure 7**.

> *CAUTION*
> *Do not spill any brake fluid on the front fork or front wheel. Brake fluid is caustic and will destroy the finish on any plastic, painted or plated surface. Use soapy water to wash off any spilled brake fluid immediately.*

> *CAUTION*
> *During the following procedure, do not allow the pistons to come in contact with the brake disc. If this happens the pistons may damage the disc during caliper removal.*

> *NOTE*
> *By performing Step 1b, compressed air may not be necessary for piston removal during caliper disassembly.*

1. If the caliper assembly is going to be disassembled for service, perform the following:

> *NOTE*
> *By performing Step 1b, compressed air may not be necessary for piston removal during caliper disassembly.*

a. Remove the brake pads as described in this chapter.

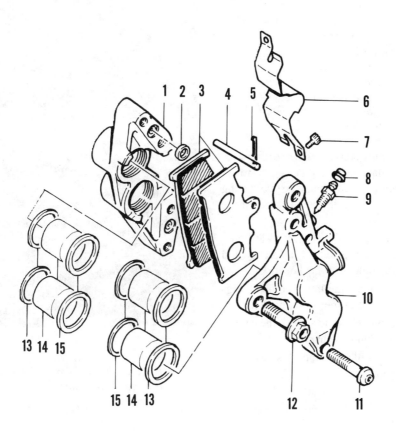

⑦

FRONT BRAKE CALIPER

1. Inboard caliper body half
2. O-ring
3. Brake pad
4. Pad pin
5. Clip
6. Pad spring
7. Screw
8. Cap
9. Bleed valve
10. Outboard caliper body half
11. Caliper housing bolt
12. Caliper mounting bolt
13. Piston seal
14. Piston
15. Dust seal

14

b. Slowly apply the brake lever to push the pistons part way out of the caliper assembly for ease of removal during caliper service.

c. Loosen the four caliper housing bolts (A, **Figure 8**).

NOTE
*The upper hose (A, **Figure 9**) and the crossover hose (B, **Figure 9**) attach to the right caliper. Consequently, the banjo bolt on the right caliper (C, **Figure 9**) is longer than the banjo bolt on the left caliper.*

d. Remove the banjo bolt (B, **Figure 8**) and sealing washers attaching the brake hose(s) to the caliper assembly. There should be two sealing washers on the left caliper and three on the right.

e. Place the loose end of the brake hose(s) in a reclosable plastic bag to prevent brake fluid from dribbling onto the wheel or fork.

2. Remove the two caliper mounting bolts (C, **Figure 8**), and lift the brake caliper from the disc.

3. If necessary, disassemble and service the caliper assembly as described in this chapter.

4. Install by reversing these removal steps while noting the following:

a. Carefully install the caliper assembly onto the disc being careful not to damage the leading edge of the brake pads.

b. Install the two caliper mounting bolts (C, **Figure 8**) and secure the brake caliper to the front fork. Torque the caliper mounting bolts to the specification listed in **Table 2**.

NOTE
*Make sure to install both brake hoses (A and B, **Figure 9**) onto the right caliper as well as the banjo bolt (C, **Figure 9**).*

c. If removed, install the brake hose onto the caliper. Install a new sealing washer on each side of the brake hose fitting(s) and install the banjo bolt (B, **Figure 8**). Install two new sealing washers on the left caliper. Install three new sealing washers on the right caliper. Tighten the banjo bolt to the torque specification listed in **Table 2**.

d. Bleed the brakes as described in this chapter.

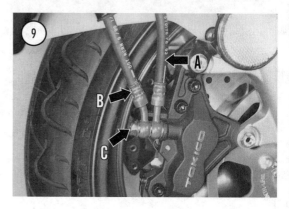

WARNING
Do not ride the motorcycle until there is certainty that the brakes are operating properly.

Disassembly

Refer to **Figure 7**.

1. Remove the caliper and brake pads as described in this chapter.

2. Remove the four caliper housing bolts (A, **Figure 8**) loosened during the removal procedure.

3. Separate the caliper body halves. Remove and discard the two O-rings (A, **Figure 10**). Install new O-rings during assembly.

NOTE
If the pistons were partially forced out of the caliper body during removal, Steps 4-6 may not be necessary. If the pistons or caliper bores are corroded or very dirty, a small amount of compressed air may be necessary to completely remove the pistons from the bores.

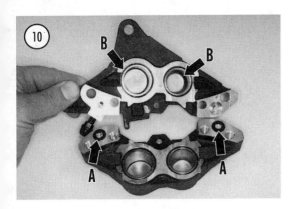

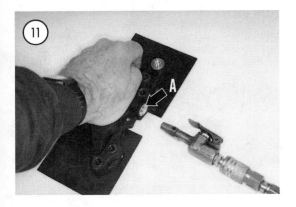

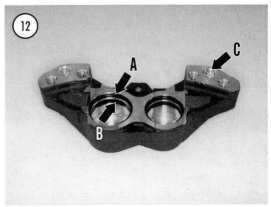

5. The spacer will prevent the first piston from coming out so that both pistons can be driven from their respective bores.

d. Remove each piston by hand from its bore.

7. Repeat Steps 4-6 for the other caliper body half.

CAUTION
In the following step, do not use a sharp tool to remove the dust and piston seals from the caliper cylinders. Do not damage the cylinder surface.

8. Use a piece of wood or plastic scraper and carefully push the dust seal (A, **Figure 12**) and the piston seal (B, **Figure 12**) in toward the caliper cylinder and out of their grooves. Remove the dust and piston seals from both cylinders in each caliper half.

9. If necessary, unscrew and remove the bleed valve assembly.

10. Inspect the caliper assembly as described in this section.

Inspection

1. Clean both caliper body halves and pistons with an aerosol brake cleaner or isopropyl alcohol. Thoroughly dry the parts with compressed air.

2. Make sure the fluid passageways in the base of the piston bores are clear. Apply compressed air to the openings to make sure they are clear. Clean out the passages if necessary.

3. Make sure the fluid passageways (C, **Figure 12**) in the caliper body halves are clean. Apply compressed air to the openings to make sure they are clear. Clean them if necessary.

4. Tighten the bleed valve.

WARNING
In the next step, the piston may shoot out of the caliper body with considerable force. Keep hands and fingers out of the way. Wear shop gloves and safety goggles when using compressed air to remove the pistons.

5. Place the caliper body face down on a rubber mat to partially seal the fluid passages. Press the caliper firmly into the mat, and apply the air pressure in short spurts to the hydraulic passageway on the caliper body (**Figure 11**). Repeat this process for the other caliper body half. Use a service station air hose if an air compressor is not available.

6. If only one piston comes out of the caliper body, perform the following:

a. Push this piston back into the caliper body, and set the caliper body face down on the mat.

b. Place a plastic or a wooden spacer under the piston that came out.

c. Press the caliper firmly into the mat, and apply air to the banjo fitting as described in Step

14

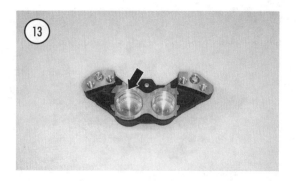

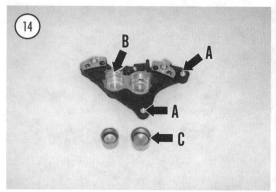

4. Inspect the piston and dust seal grooves (**Figure 13**) in both caliper bodies for damage. If any groove is damaged or corroded, replace the caliper assembly.

5. Inspect the banjo bolt threaded hole (A, **Figure 11**) in the outer caliper body. If worn or damaged, clean out with a metric thread tap or replace the caliper assembly.

6. Inspect the bleed valve threaded hole in the caliper body. If worn or damaged, clean the threads with a metric tap or replace the caliper assembly.

7. Inspect the bleed valve. Apply compressed air to the opening and make sure it is clear. If necessary, clean it out. Install the bleed valve, and tighten it to the torque specification listed in **Table 2**.

8. Inspect both caliper bodies for damage. Check the caliper mounting bolt hole threads (A, **Figure 14**) for wear or damage. Clean the threads with an appropriate size metric tap or replace the caliper assembly.

9. Inspect the cylinder walls (B, **Figure 14**) and pistons (C, **Figure 14**) for scratches, scoring or other damage.

10. Measure the cylinder bores with a bore gauge (**Figure 15**) or vernier caliper. Refer to the specification listed in **Table 1**.

11. Measure the outside diameter of the pistons with a micrometer (**Figure 16**) or vernier caliper. Refer to the specification listed in **Table 1**.

Assembly

> *WARNING*
> *Never reuse old dust seals or piston seals. Very minor damage or age deterioration can effect brake performance.*

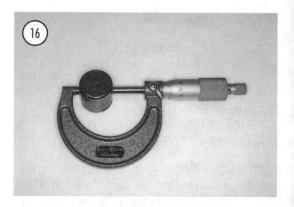

1. Soak the new dust and piston seals in clean DOT 4 brake fluid.

2. Coat the piston bores and pistons with clean DOT 4 brake fluid.

3. Carefully install the new piston seals (B, **Figure 12**) into the lower grooves in each cylinder. Make sure the seals are properly seated in their respective grooves.

4. Carefully install the new dust seals (A, **Figure 12**) into the upper grooves. Make sure all seals are properly seated in their respective grooves.

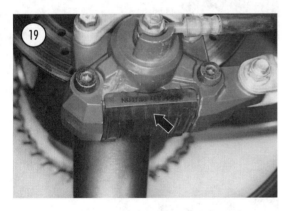

5. Repeat Step 3 and Step 4 for the other caliper body half.

6. Position the pistons with the open ends facing out and install the pistons into the caliper cylinders (B, **Figure 10**). Push the pistons in until they bottom.

7. Repeat Step 6 for the other caliper body half. Make sure all pistons are installed correctly.

8. Coat the *new* O-rings in DOT 4 brake fluid and install the O-rings (A, **Figure 10**) into place in the inboard caliper half.

9. Set the two inside caliper housing bolts in place in the outboard caliper half (**Figure 17**). Lower the outboard caliper half over the inboard caliper half,

and turn the two inner housing bolts into place in the inboard caliper half.

10. Install the remaining two caliper housing bolts (**Figure 18**), and tighten the bolts securely. The caliper housing bolts will be torqued to specification after the caliper has been installed on the fork.

11. If removed, install the bleed valve assembly. Tighten it to the torque specification listed in **Table 2**.

12. Install the caliper and brake pads as described in this chapter.

13. Tighten the four caliper housing bolts (A, **Figure 8**) to the torque specification listed in **Table 2**.

14. Bleed the brake as described in this chapter.

REAR BRAKE PAD REPLACEMENT

Pad wear depends greatly on riding habits and conditions. Check the pads for wear before each ride.

To maintain even brake pressure on the disc, always replace both pads in the caliper at the same time. It is not necessary to disconnect the brake hose from the caliper during brake pad replacement. Disconnect the hose only when servicing the brake caliper.

1. Read the information listed in *Brake Service* in this chapter.

2. Place the bike on the sidestand on level ground.

3. To prevent the rear brake pedal from being applied, tie the end of the pedal up to the frame. That way if the brake pedal is inadvertently pressed, the pistons will not be forced out of the cylinders.

4. Squeeze the sides of the pad cover and remove the cover (**Figure 19**).

5. Remove the clip (**Figure 20**), and then withdraw the pad pins (**Figure 21**) from the caliper. Remove the anti-rattle springs.

14

6. Withdraw both brake pads and shims from the caliper assembly.

7. Clean the pad recess and the end of both pistons with a soft brush. Do not use solvent, a wire brush or any hard tool that would damage the cylinders or pistons.

8. Carefully remove any rust or corrosion from the disc.

9. Thoroughly clean any corrosion or road dirt from the anti-rattle springs, pad pins and clip.

10. Check the friction surface of the new pads for any debris or manufacturing residue. If necessary, clean the pads with an aerosol brake cleaner.

11. When new pads are installed in the calipers, the rear master cylinder brake fluid level will rise as the caliper pistons are repositioned. Remove the hydraulic fluid from the master cylinder reservoir by performing the following:

a. Remove the rear frame cover as described in Chapter Fifteen.

b. Clean the top of the master cylinder reservoir of all dirt and foreign matter.

c. Remove the top cover mounting screws and the top cover and diaphragm (**Figure 22**).

d. Temporarily install one of the old brake pads into the caliper and seat it against the piston.

e. Press the pad against the piston, and slowly push the caliper piston all the way into the caliper. Constantly check the reservoir to make sure brake fluid does not overflow. Remove fluid, if necessary, to prevent any overflow.

f. The piston should move freely. If it does not, remove and service the caliper as described in this chapter.

g. Remove the old brake pad and repeat this process for the piston on the other side.

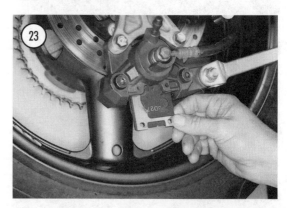

12. Install the shims onto the new brake pads so the closed end of the shim faces the rear of the bike as shown in **Figure 23**.

13. Install the outboard brake pad (**Figure 24**) and the inboard pad (**Figure 25**) into the caliper.

14. Install the anti-rattle spring (A, **Figure 26**) in place on both brake pads.

15. Position the front pad pin (B, **Figure 26**) so its clip hole faces down, and then insert the front pad pin through the caliper and into both pads. Make sure the pad pin is positioned above the anti-rattle springs in order to hold them in place.

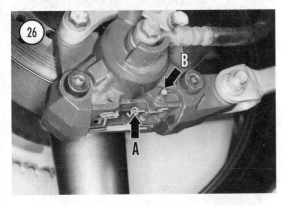

21. Pump the rear brake pedal to reposition the brake pads against the brake disc. Roll the bike back and forth and continue to pump the brake pedal as many times as it takes to refill the cylinders in the caliper and correctly locate the brake pads against the disc.

NOTE
To control the flow of brake fluid, punch a small hole into the seal of a new container of brake fluid next to the edge of the pour spout. This helps eliminate fluid spills especially while adding fluid to the very small reservoir.

WARNING
Use brake fluid clearly marked DOT 4 from a sealed container. Other types may vaporize and cause brake failure. Always use the same brand of brake fluid. Do not intermix brands. They may not be compatible. Also do not intermix silicone based (DOT 5) brake fluid. It can cause brake component damage leading to brake system failure.

22. Refill the master cylinder reservoir, if necessary, to maintain the correct fluid level as indicated on the side of the reservoir. Install the diaphragm and the top cover. Install the screws and tighten them securely.

WARNING
Do not ride the motorcycle until the brakes are operating correctly with full hydraulic advantage. If necessary, bleed the brake as described in this chapter.

23. Bed the pads in gradually for the first 2-3 days of riding by using only light pressure as much as possible. Immediate hard application glazes the new friction pads and greatly reduces the effectiveness.

16. Install the rear pad pin through the caliper and into both pads. Make sure the pad pin is positioned above the anti-rattle springs and the clip hole faces down.

17. Push the pins into the caliper until they bottom.

18. Slide the pin clip fingers (**Figure 20**) through the hole in both pins, push the clip into the caliper until the clip locks onto the pins (**Figure 27**).

19. Install the pad cover (**Figure 19**) and make sure it is locked in place.

20. Untie the rear brake pedal.

REAR BRAKE CALIPER

Removal/Installation

CAUTION
Do not spill any brake fluid on the rear wheel or swing arm. Brake fluid

14

will destroy the finish on any plastic, painted or plated surface. Wash off any spilled brake fluid immediately. Use soapy water, and rinse the area completely.

CAUTION
In the following procedure, do not allow the pistons to contact the brake disc. If this happens the pistons may damage the disc during caliper removal.

NOTE
By performing substep b, compressed air may not be necessary for piston removal during caliper disassembly.

1. If the caliper assembly is going to be disassembled for service, perform the following:
   a. Remove the brake pads as described in this chapter.
   b. Apply the brake pedal to push the pistons partially out of the caliper assembly for ease of removal during caliper service.
   c. Loosen the caliper housing bolts (A, **Figure 28**).
   d. Place a drain pan under the rear caliper and remove the union bolt and sealing washers (B, **Figure 28**) securing the brake hose to the caliper assembly.
   e. Place the loose end of the brake hose in a reclosable plastic bag to prevent the entry of debris and prevent brake fluid from leaking onto the bike.

2. Remove the torque arm nut and bolt (C, **Figure 28**), and separate the torque arm from the caliper.

3. Remove the caliper mounting bolts (D, **Figure 28**), and lower the caliper from the caliper carrier and brake disc.

4. If necessary, disassemble and service the caliper assembly as described in this chapter.

5. Install by reversing these removal steps while noting the following:
   a. Install the caliper assembly onto the disc being careful not to damage the leading edge of the brake pads.
   b. Install the caliper mounting bolts (D, **Figure 28**), and tighten them to the torque specification listed in **Table 2**.

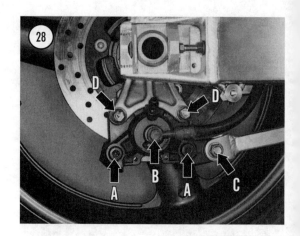

c. Secure the torque arm to the rear caliper. Tighten the torque arm nut (C, **Figure 28**) to the torque specification listed in **Table 2**.
d. Install a new sealing washer to each side of the brake hose fitting and install the banjo bolt (B, **Figure 28**). Tighten the banjo bolt to the torque specification listed in **Table 2**.
e. Bleed the brake as described in this chapter.

WARNING
Do not ride the motorcycle until the brakes are operating properly.

Disassembly

Refer to **Figure 29**.

1. Remove the rear caliper and brake pads as described in this chapter.

2. Remove the two caliper housing bolts (**Figure 30**) loosened during the removal procedure.

3. Separate the caliper body halves. Remove the O-rings (**Figure 31**) and discard them. Install new O-rings every time the caliper is disassembled.

NOTE
If the pistons were partially forced out of the caliper body during removal, Steps 4-6 may not be necessary. If the pistons or caliper bores are corroded or very dirty, a small amount of compressed air may be necessary to completely remove the pistons from the body bores.

4. Place a piece of soft wood or folded shop cloth over the end of the piston and the caliper body. Turn

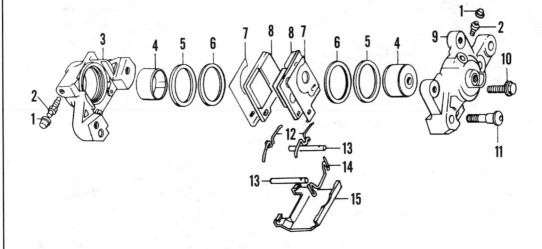

REAR BRAKE CALIPER

1. Cap
2. Bleed valve
3. Inboard caliper half
4. Piston
5. Piston seal
6. Dust seal
7. Shim
8. Pads
9. Outboard caliper half
10. Caliper mounting bolt
11. Caliper housing bolts
12. Anti-rattle springs
13. Pad pin
14. Clip
15. Pad cover

14

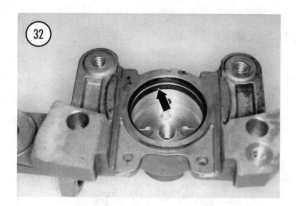

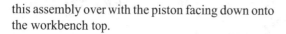

this assembly over with the piston facing down onto the workbench top.

> *WARNING*
> *In the next step, the piston may shoot out of the caliper body with considerable force. Keep hands and fingers out of the way. Wear shop gloves and safety goggles when using compressed air to remove the pistons.*

5. Apply the air pressure in short spurts to the hydraulic fluid passageway and force the piston out of the caliper bore. Remove the piston from the bore. Repeat for the other caliper body half. Use a service station air hose if an air compressor is not available.

> *CAUTION*
> *In the following step, do not use a sharp tool to remove the dust and piston seals from the caliper cylinders. Do not damage the cylinder surface.*

6. Use a piece of wood or a plastic scraper and carefully push the dust seal and the piston seal (**Figure 32**) in toward the caliper cylinder and out of their grooves. Remove the dust and piston seals from the other caliper half and discard all seals.

7. If necessary, remove the bleed valve (A, **Figure 33**).

8. Inspect the caliper assembly as described in this section.

Inspection

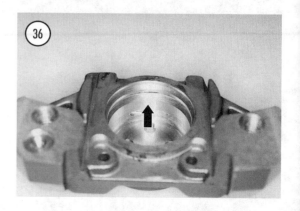

1. Clean both caliper body halves and pistons with an aerosol brake cleaner or isopropyl alcohol. Dry the parts with compressed air.

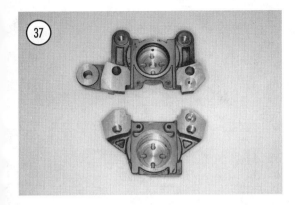

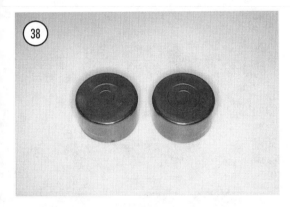

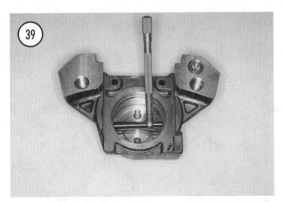

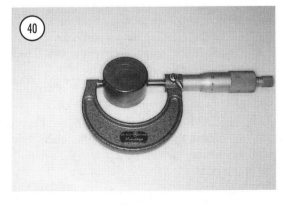

2. Make sure the fluid passageways (**Figure 34**) in the base of the cylinder bores are clean. Apply compressed air to the openings to make sure they are clear. Clean them if necessary.

3. Make sure the fluid passageways (**Figure 35**) in the caliper body halves are clear. Apply compressed air to the openings to make sure they are clear. Clean them if necessary.

4. Inspect the piston and dust seal grooves (**Figure 36**) in both caliper bodies for damage. If damaged or corroded, replace the caliper assembly.

5. Inspect the banjo bolt threaded hole (B, **Figure 33**) in the outer caliper body. If worn or damaged, dress the threads with a metric tap or replace the caliper assembly.

6. Inspect the bleed valve threaded hole in the inboard caliper body. If worn or damaged, dress the threads with a metric tap or replace the caliper assembly.

7. Inspect the bleed valve. Apply compressed air to the opening and make sure it is clear. Clean the valve if necessary. Install the bleed valve into the caliper body, and tighten the valve to the torque specification listed in **Table 2**.

8. Inspect both caliper bodies (**Figure 37**) for damage. Check the threads of the caliper mounting hole for wear or damage. Clean the threads with an appropriate size metric tap or replace the caliper assembly.

9. Inspect the cylinder walls and pistons (**Figure 38**) for scratches, scoring or other damage.

10. Measure the cylinder bores with a bore gauge (**Figure 39**) or vernier caliper. Refer to the specification listed in **Table 1**.

11. Measure the outside diameter of the pistons with a micrometer (**Figure 40**) or vernier caliper. Refer to the specification listed in **Table 1**.

14

Assembly

> *WARNING*
> *Never reuse old dust seals or piston seals. Very minor damage or age deterioration can effect brake performance.*

1. Soak the new dust and piston seals in fresh DOT 4 brake fluid.

2. Coat the piston bores and pistons with clean DOT 4 brake fluid.

3. Carefully install the new piston seal into the lower groove.

4. Carefully install the new dust seal into the upper groove. Make sure all seals are properly seated in their respective grooves (**Figure 32**).

5. Repeat Step 3 and Step 4 for the other caliper body half.

6. Position the piston with the open end facing out, and install the piston into the caliper cylinder. Push the piston in until it bottoms.

7. Repeat Step 6 for the other caliper body half (**Figure 41**). Make sure both pistons are installed correctly.

8. Coat the *new* O-rings with DOT 4 brake fluid, and install the O-ring (**Figure 31**).

9. Make sure the O-ring is still in place and assemble the caliper body halves.

10. Install the two caliper housing bolts (**Figure 30**) and tighten them securely. They will be tightened to the correct torque value after the caliper is installed on the rear caliper bracket.

11. Install the bleed valve, and tighten it to the torque specification listed in **Table 2**.

12. Install the caliper and brake pads as described in this chapter.

13. Tighten the two caliper housing bolts (A, **Figure 28**) to the torque specification listed in **Table 2**.

14. Bleed the brake as described in this chapter.

FRONT MASTER CYLINDER

Removal

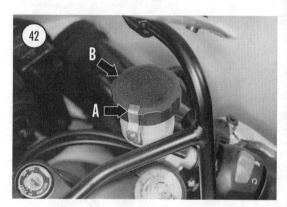

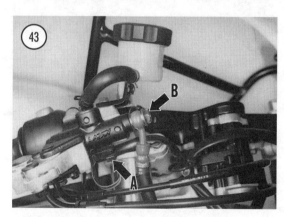

CAUTION
Cover the fuel tank and front fairing with a heavy cloth or plastic tarp to protect them from accidental brake fluid spills. Brake fluid destroys the finish on any plastic, painted or plated surface. Immediately wash any spilled brake fluid from the motorcycle. Use soapy water, and rinse the area completely.

1. Clean the top of the master cylinder of all debris.

2. Remove the clip mounting screw and move the reservoir-cap retaining clip (A, **Figure 42**) from the top cover.

3. Remove the top cover (B, **Figure 42**), diaphragm plate and diaphragm from the master cylinder reservoir.

4. If a shop syringe is available, draw all the brake fluid out of the master cylinder reservoir. Temporarily reinstall the diaphragm, plate and cover. Tighten the cover finger-tight.

5. Disconnect the brake light switch electrical connector (A, **Figure 43**) from the brake switch.

6. Place a rag beneath the banjo bolt, (B, **Figure 43**) and remove the bolt. Separate the brake hose from the master cylinder. Do not lose the two sealing washers, one from each side of the brake hose fitting.

7. Place the loose end of the brake hose in a reclosable plastic bag to prevent brake fluid from leaking onto the motorcycle. Tie the loose end of the hose up to the handlebar

8. Remove the bolt (**Figure 44**) securing the master cylinder reservoir to the bracket on the upper fork bridge.

9. Remove the master cylinder clamp bolts (A, **Figure 45**) and the clamp (B, **Figure 45**).

10. Remove the master cylinder and reservoir assembly from the handlebar.

11. Drain any residual brake fluid from the master cylinder and reservoir. Dispose of the fluid properly.

12. If the master cylinder and reservoir are being removed and are not going to be serviced, place them in a reclosable plastic bag to protect them from debris.

Installation

1. Position the front master cylinder onto the right handlebar and align the mating surface with the handlebar punch mark.

2. Position the clamp with the UP mark facing up, and install the master cylinder clamp bolts (A, **Figure 45**). Tighten the upper mounting bolt first, then the lower bolt leaving a gap at the bottom. Tighten the bolts to the torque specification listed in **Table 2**.

> *NOTE*
> *If the reservoir was removed from the master cylinder for service, the hose may have to be repositioned on the master cylinder to prevent any binding on the hose.*

3. Install the remote reservoir onto the upper fork bridge and tighten the mounting bolt securely (**Figure 44**).

4. Install the brake hose onto the master cylinder. Install a new sealing washer onto each side of the hose fitting, and torque the banjo bolt (B, **Figure 43**) to the specification in **Table 2**.

5. Reconnect the front brake light switch electrical connectors (A, **Figure 43**) onto the brake switch. Make sure the electrical connectors are locked into place.

6. Refill the master cylinder and reservoir and bleed the brake system as described in this chapter.

Disassembly

Refer to **Figure 46**.

1. Remove the master cylinder and reservoir assembly as described in this chapter.

2. Release the hose clamp (A, **Figure 47**) and disconnect the interconnect hose (B) from the master cylinder. Drain any residual brake fluid from both assemblies. Dispose of the fluid properly.

3. Remove the nut (A, **Figure 48**) and pivot bolt securing the hand lever to the master cylinder body. Remove the hand lever (B, **Figure 48**).

4. Remove the screw (A, **Figure 49**) securing the front brake switch. Apply the brake lever to move the lever actuating pad away from the switch plunger, and remove the switch (B, **Figure 49**).

5. Slide the rubber cap (**Figure 50**) up and away from the circlip on the hose connector port on the master cylinder.

6. Using circlip pliers, remove the internal circlip (A, **Figure 51**) and the hose connector (B, **Figure 51**) from the master cylinder body.

7. Remove the O-ring (**Figure 52**) from the body.

14

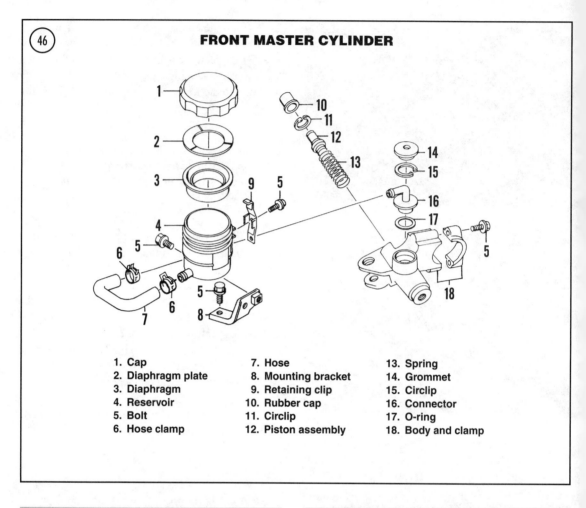

FRONT MASTER CYLINDER

1. Cap
2. Diaphragm plate
3. Diaphragm
4. Reservoir
5. Bolt
6. Hose clamp
7. Hose
8. Mounting bracket
9. Retaining clip
10. Rubber cap
11. Circlip
12. Piston assembly
13. Spring
14. Grommet
15. Circlip
16. Connector
17. O-ring
18. Body and clamp

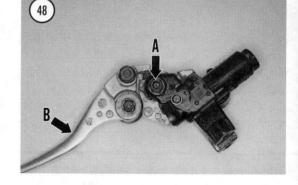

8. Remove the rubber boot (**Figure 53**) from the cylinder bore on the master cylinder.

9. Press the piston (**Figure 54**) into the cylinder bore, and use circlip pliers to remove the internal circlip (A, **Figure 55**).

10. Remove the piston assembly (B, **Figure 55**) and the spring from the cylinder bore.

Inspection

1. Clean all parts with an aerosol brake cleaner or isopropyl alcohol. Inspect the cylinder bore surface and piston contact surfaces for wear or damage. If less than perfect, replace the master cylinder assembly. The body cannot be replaced separately.

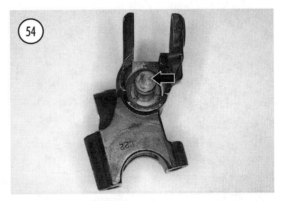

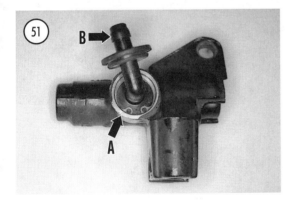

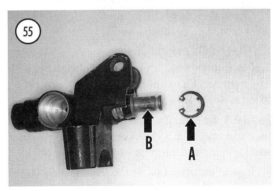

14

2. Inspect the piston cups (**Figure 56**) for wear and damage. If less than perfect, replace the piston assembly. The individual cups cannot be replaced.

3. Measure the cylinder bore with a bore gauge (**Figure 57**) or vernier caliper. Refer to the specification listed in **Table 1**.

4. Make sure the fluid passage (**Figure 58**) in the bottom of the master cylinder body is clear. Clean it if necessary.

5. Inspect the piston contact surface (A, **Figure 59**) for wear and damage. If less than perfect, replace the piston assembly.

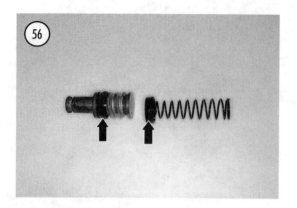

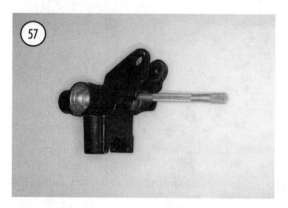

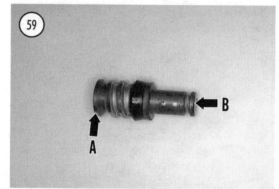

6. Check the end of the piston (B, **Figure 59**) for wear caused by the hand lever. If worn, replace the piston assembly.

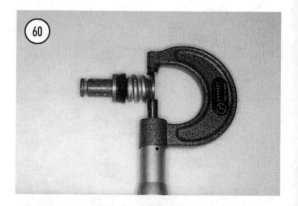

7. Measure the outside diameter of the piston with a micrometer (**Figure 60**). Refer to the specification listed in **Table 1**.

8. Check the hand lever pivot lugs (**Figure 61**) on the master cylinder body for cracks or elongation. If damaged, replace the master cylinder assembly.

9. Inspect the pivot hole in the hand lever. If worn or elongated replace the lever.

10. Inspect the threads in the cylinder bore (**Figure 62**) for the banjo bolt. If worn or damaged, clean the threads with a metric thread tap or replace the master cylinder assembly.

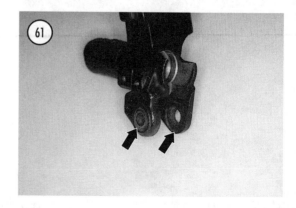

11. Inspect the hose connector and circlip (**Figure 63**) for damage and deterioration. Replace either part as necessary.

12. Check the top cover, diaphragm and diaphragm plate (**Figure 64**) for damage and deterioration; replace as necessary.

13. Inspect the adjuster on the hand lever. If worn or damaged, replace the hand lever as an assembly.

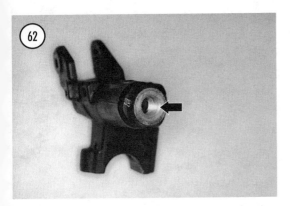

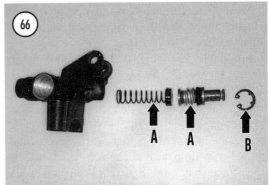

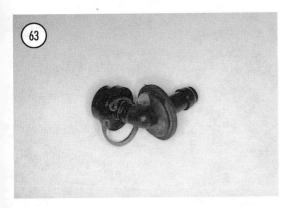

14. Check the reservoir and interconnect hose (**Figure 65**) for damage and deterioration and replace as necessary.

Assembly

Refer to **Figure 46**.

1. Soak the new cups and the new piston assembly in fresh DOT 4 brake fluid for at least 15 minutes to make them pliable. Coat the inside of the cylinder bore with fresh brake fluid before the assembly of parts.

2. If removed, install the primary cup onto the spring and onto the piston cup (**Figure 56**).

> *CAUTION*
> *When installing the piston assembly, do not allow the cups to turn inside out as they will be damaged and allow brake fluid leakage within the cylinder bore.*

3. Position the spring with the tapered end facing the piston.

4. Install the spring, primary cup and piston assembly (A, **Figure 66**) into the cylinder bore. Push them in until they bottom in the cylinder.

5. Press the piston assembly into the cylinder, and install the circlip (B, **Figure 66**). Make sure it is correctly seated in the groove, and then slide on the rubber boot (**Figure 53**).

6. Install a new O-ring into the interconnect port (**Figure 52**) in the master cylinder body.

7. Seat the connector (B, **Figure 51**) into the interconnect port and install the circlip. Make sure the circlip is properly seated in the groove (A, **Figure 51**).

14

8. Move the rubber cap down into position above the circlip, and seat it onto the interconnect port (**Figure 50**).

9. Install the hand lever (B, **Figure 48**), bolt and nut (A, **Figure 48**). Tighten the bolt and nut securely, and then make sure the hand lever operates freely within the master cylinder. There should be no binding.

10. Apply the brake lever to move the lever actuating pad away from the brake switch area. Install the front brake switch (B, **Figure 49**) and screw (A, **Figure 49**). Tighten the mounting screw securely.

11. Release the brake lever and make sure the switch plunger moves in and out with no binding.

12. Install the interconnect hose (B, **Figure 47**) onto the connector on the master cylinder. Secure the hose in place with the hose clamp (A, **Figure 47**).

13. Install the master cylinder as described in this chapter.

REAR MASTER CYLINDER

Removal

> *CAUTION*
> *Cover the swing arm and rear wheel with a heavy cloth or plastic tarp to protect them from accidental brake fluid spills. Brake fluid destroys the finish on any plastic, painted or plated surface. Wash any spilled brake fluid off these surfaces immediately. Use soapy water, and rinse the area completely.*

1. Remove the seats as described in Chapter Fifteen.

2. Remove the frame side cover as described in Chapter Fifteen.

3. Clean all debris from the top of the master cylinder reservoir.

4. Remove the top cover mounting screws, and remove the top cover (A, **Figure 67**) and diaphragm.

5. If a shop syringe is available, draw all the brake fluid out of the master cylinder reservoir.

6. Attach a hose to the bleed valve on the rear caliper and open the bleed valve.

7. Place the end of the hose over a container and let the brake fluid drain out into the container. Slowly apply the rear brake pedal several times to expel

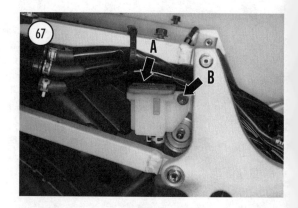

most of the brake fluid from the rear hose and the master cylinder. Dispose of this brake fluid properly. Never reuse brake fluid.

8. Remove the hose and close the bleed valve.

9. Remove the bolts (**Figure 68**) securing the footrest guard and remove the guard. Reinstall the bolts to hold the master cylinder in place temporarily.

10. Remove the reservoir mounting bolt (B, **Figure 67**).

11. Remove the cotter pin from the end of the clevis pin (A, **Figure 69**), and then withdraw the clevis pin securing the master cylinder pushrod to the brake pedal. Do not lose the washer behind the pushrod yoke.

12. Loosen, but do not remove, the banjo bolt (**Figure 70**) securing the brake hose to the inboard side of the master cylinder.

13. Remove the bolts (B, **Figure 69**) securing the master cylinder to the footpeg bracket. Move the master cylinder and reservoir part way out of the frame.

14. Place several rags under the banjo bolt and brake hose at the top of the master cylinder to catch any residual brake fluid.

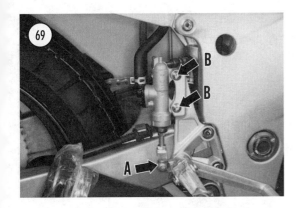

15. Unscrew the banjo bolt securing the brake hose to the top of the master cylinder. Remove the sealing washer from each side of the hose fitting.

16. Remove the hose and place the loose end in a reclosable plastic bag to keep debris out of the system. Tie the loose end of the hose up to the frame.

17. Remove the master cylinder and reservoir assembly.

18. If the master cylinder and reservoir will not be serviced, place them in a reclosable plastic bag to protect them from debris.

19. Wash any spilled brake fluid immediately.

Installation

1. Correctly position the brake hose onto the top of the master cylinder. Place a sealing washer onto each side of the brake hose fitting and install the banjo bolt. Tighten the banjo bolt finger-tight.

2. Install the reservoir up through the rear frame and move the master cylinder into the correct position. Align the mounting hole in the reservoir with the mount on the frame and install the mounting bolt (B, **Figure 67**). Tighten the bolt securely.

3. Install the master cylinder onto the backside of the footpeg bracket and temporarily install the mounting bolts (B, **Figure 69**). Finger-tighten the bolts.

4. Align the master cylinder pushrod yoke with the brake pedal, and install the clevis pin (A, **Figure 69**) through both parts. Slide the washer over the end of the clevis pin. Install a *new* cotter pin, and bend the ends over completely.

5. Remove the bolts (B, **Figure 69**) and install the footrest guard. Reinstall the master cylinder mounting bolts (**Figure 68**). Torque them to the specification in **Table 2**.

6. Torque the banjo bolt (**Figure 70**) to the specification in **Table 2**.

7. Bleed the rear brake as described in this chapter.

8. Install the frame side cover and seats as described in Chapter Fifteen.

Disassembly

Refer to **Figure 71**.

1. Remove the rear master cylinder and reservoir assembly as described in this chapter.

2. Release the hose clamp (A, **Figure 72**) and disconnect the hose (B, **Figure 72**) from the fitting on the master cylinder.

3. Remove the connector mounting screw (A, **Figure 73**) and the connector (B, **Figure 73**) from the master cylinder. Remove the O-ring (**Figure 74**) from the hose port on the master cylinder.

4. Slide the rubber boot (A, **Figure 75**) down the pushrod and out of the way.

5. Using circlip pliers, remove the internal circlip (B, **Figure 75**) securing the pushrod assembly in the master cylinder body.

6. Withdraw the pushrod assembly, the piston assembly and spring from the master cylinder body.

7. Pour out any residual brake fluid and discard it. *Never* reuse hydraulic fluid.

8. If necessary, loosen the master-cylinder-rod locknut (A, **Figure 76**), and then remove the push rod yoke (B, **Figure 76**) and nut from the pushrod.

Inspection

1. Clean all parts in isopropyl alcohol or with an aerosol brake cleaner.

14

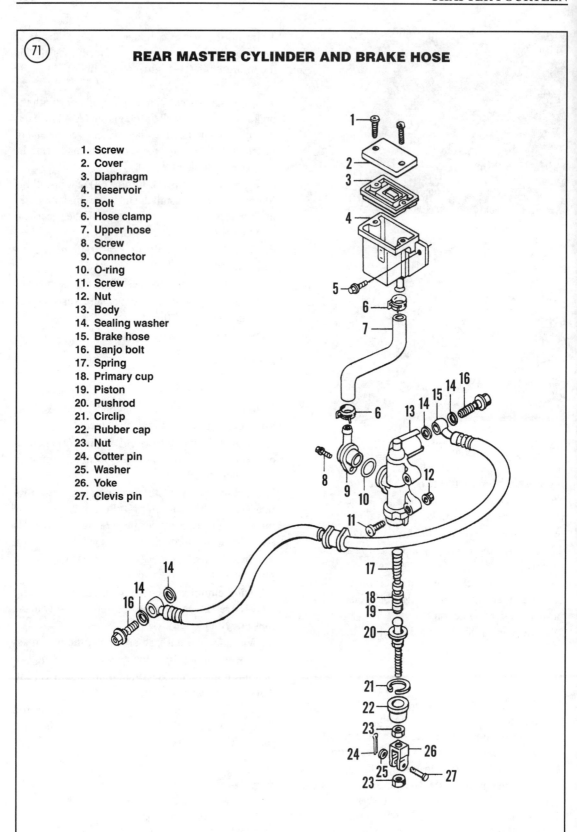

REAR MASTER CYLINDER AND BRAKE HOSE

1. Screw
2. Cover
3. Diaphragm
4. Reservoir
5. Bolt
6. Hose clamp
7. Upper hose
8. Screw
9. Connector
10. O-ring
11. Screw
12. Nut
13. Body
14. Sealing washer
15. Brake hose
16. Banjo bolt
17. Spring
18. Primary cup
19. Piston
20. Pushrod
21. Circlip
22. Rubber cap
23. Nut
24. Cotter pin
25. Washer
26. Yoke
27. Clevis pin

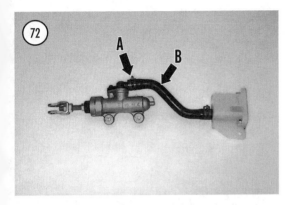

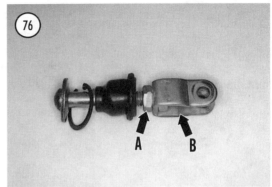

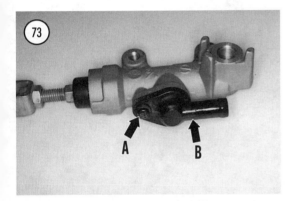

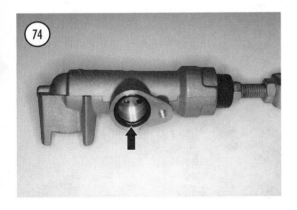

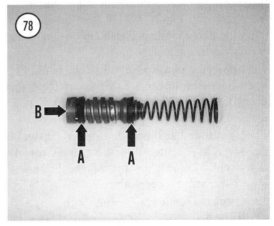

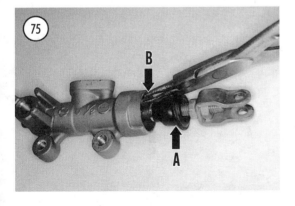

14

2. Inspect the cylinder bore surface (**Figure 77**). If it is less than perfect, replace the master cylinder assembly. The body cannot be replaced separately.

3. Inspect the piston cups (A, **Figure 78**) for wear and damage. If less than perfect, replace the piston assembly. The cups cannot be replaced separately.

4. Check the end of the piston (B, **Figure 78**) for wear caused by the pushrod. If worn, replace the piston assembly.

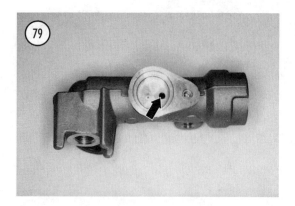

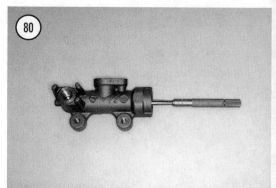

5. Make sure the fluid passage way (**Figure 79**) in the master cylinder body is clear. Clean it if necessary.

6. Measure the cylinder bore with a bore gauge (**Figure 80**) or vernier caliper. Refer to the specification listed in **Table 1**.

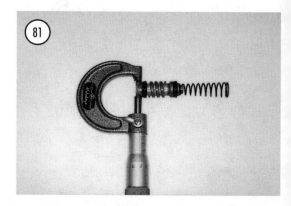

7. Measure the outside diameter of the piston with a micrometer (**Figure 81**). Refer to the specification listed in **Table 1**.

8. Check the entire master cylinder body (A, **Figure 82**) for wear or damage. If damaged in any way, replace the master cylinder assembly.

9. Inspect the banjo bolt threads in the master cylinder body (B, **Figure 82**). If worn or damaged, clean the threads with a thread tap or replace the master cylinder assembly.

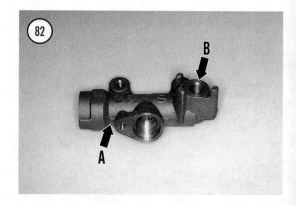

10. Inspect the piston push rod assembly (A, **Figure 83**) for wear or damage. Make sure the rubber boot (B, **Figure 83**) is in good condition. Replace the boot if necessary.

11. Inspect the banjo bolt threads for damage. If damaged, clean the threads with a metric thread die or replace the bolt. Make sure the brake fluid hole is clear. Clean it out if necessary.

12. Check the connector for damage.

13. Remove the cover and diaphragm (**Figure 84**) from the reservoir. Check all components for damage and deterioration. Replace worn components as necessary.

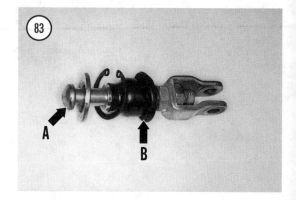

14. Inspect the reservoir and hose (**Figure 85**) for wear or deterioration. Replace worn parts as necessary.

Assembly

Refer to **Figure 71**.

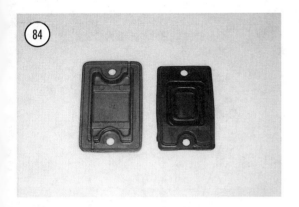

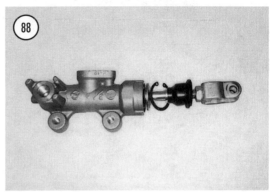

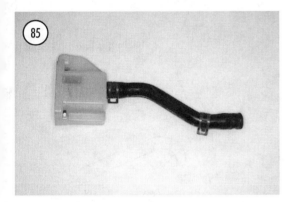

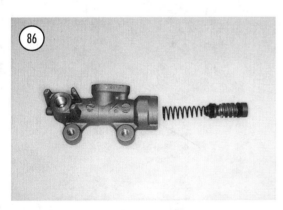

1. Soak the new cups in clean DOT 4 brake fluid for at least 15 minutes to make them pliable. Install the new cups onto the new piston assembly.

2. Coat the inside of the cylinder bore with clean DOT 4 brake fluid before the assembly of parts.

CAUTION
When installing the piston assembly, do not allow the cups to turn inside out as they will be damaged and allow brake fluid leakage within the cylinder bore.

3. Position the spring with the tapered end facing the piston assembly (**Figure 86**). Install the spring and piston assembly into the cylinder together (**Figure 86**). Push the piston assembly all way in until it bottoms in the cylinder (**Figure 87**).

4. Install the pushrod assembly (**Figure 88**) and push the piston cup assembly all the way into the cylinder.

5. Hold the pushrod assembly in this position, and install the circlip. Make sure the circlip is correctly seated in the groove.

6. Slide the rubber boot up into the body so it completely seats in the cylinder (**Figure 89**). This is necessary to keep out dirt and moisture.

7. If removed, install the yoke and nut onto the pushrod. Do not tighten the locknut at this time as the brake pedal must be adjusted.

8. Install a *new* O-ring (**Figure 74**) into the hose port in the master cylinder body. Apply a light coat of fresh brake fluid to the O-ring.

9. Make sure the O-ring is still in place, and install the reservoir hose connector (B, **Figure 73**) onto the master cylinder. Secure the connector in place with the mounting screw (A, **Figure 73**). Tighten the screw securely.

14

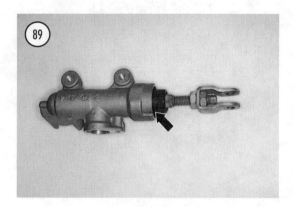

10. Install the master cylinder as described in this chapter.

11. Adjust the brake pedal height as described in Chapter Three.

BRAKE HOSE REPLACEMENT

Front Brake Hoses

Refer to **Figure 90** for this procedure.

> *CAUTION*
> *Cover the front fender with a heavy cloth or plastic tarp to protect it from accidental brake fluid spills. Brake fluid destroys the finish on plastic, painted or plated surfaces. Immediately wash spilled brake fluid off the motorcycle. Use soapy water, and rinse the area completely.*

1. Remove the upper fairing as described in Chapter Fifteen.

2. Remove the mounting screw from the retaining clip (A, **Figure 91**) and move the retaining clip from the top cover.

3. Remove the top cover (B, **Figure 91**), diaphragm plate and diaphragm from the master cylinder reservoir.

> *NOTE*
> *Place a shop cloth under the banjo bolts and brake hose fittings to catch any spilled brake fluid that might leak out during the procedure.*

4. On the left side, perform the following:

  a. Remove the banjo bolt (A, **Figure 92**) and sealing washers securing the brake hose to the left caliper.

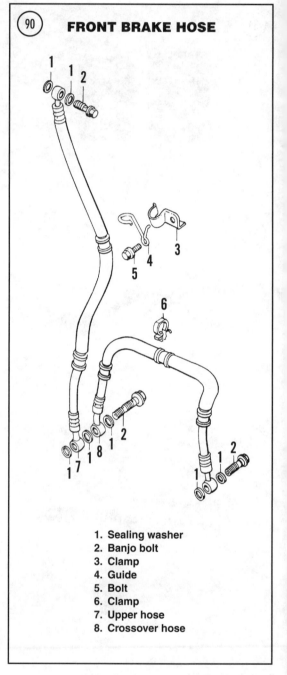

FRONT BRAKE HOSE

1. Sealing washer
2. Banjo bolt
3. Clamp
4. Guide
5. Bolt
6. Clamp
7. Upper hose
8. Crossover hose

  b. Place the end of the brake hose over a container and let the brake fluid drain out into the container. Apply the front brake lever several times to force the fluid out of the brake hose. Dispose of this brake fluid properly—never reuse brake fluid.

  c. Carefully release the hose clamp (B, **Figure 92**) from the front fender.

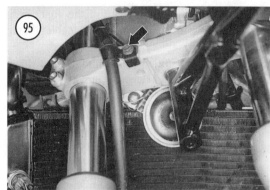

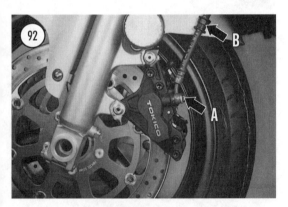

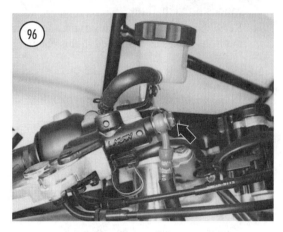

5. On the right side, perform the following:

   a. Remove the banjo bolt (C, **Figure 93**) and the three sealing washers securing the cross-over brake hose (B, **Figure 93**) and the upper brake hose (A, **Figure 93**) to the right caliper.

   b. Place the end of the brake hoses over a container and let the brake fluid drain out into the container. Apply the front brake lever several times to force the fluid out of the brake hose. Dispose of this brake fluid properly—never reuse brake fluid.

   c. Disconnect the cross-over hose (A, **Figure 94**) and the upper brake hose (B, **Figure 94**) from the clamp on the front fender.

6. Carefully remove the cross-over hose (A, **Figure 94**) from the calipers and front fender.

7. Remove the clamp (**Figure 95**) from the right side of the lower fork bridge, and release the upper brake hose from the clamp and hose guide.

8. Remove the banjo bolt (**Figure 96**) and sealing washers securing the upper brake hose to the master cylinder.

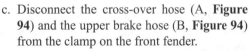

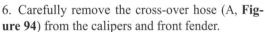

14

9. Carefully pull the lower end of the upper hose down and out from behind the throttle cables on the right side.

10. Wash off any spilled brake fluid that may have leaked out of the hoses during removal.

11. Install new hoses in the reverse order of removal while noting the following:

    a. Install new sealing washers on each side of the hose fittings. Make sure to use three sealing washers when securing the two brake hoses to the right brake caliper.

    b. Tighten the banjo bolts to the torque specifications listed in **Table 2**.

    c. Refill the master cylinder reservoir and bleed the front brakes as described in this chapter.

Rear Brake Hose

Refer to **Figure 71**.

> *NOTE*
> *The reservoir hose replacement procedure is covered under **Rear Master Cylinder** in this chapter.*

> *CAUTION*
> *Cover the surrounding area with a heavy cloth or plastic tarp to protect the components from brake fluid spills. Brake fluid destroys the finish on any plastic, painted or plated surface. Wash spilled brake fluid off any of these surfaces immediately. Use soapy water, and rinse the area completely.*

1. Remove the frame side cover as described in Chapter Fifteen.

2. Remove the rear wheel as described in Chapter Eleven.

3. Perform Steps 1-16 of *Rear Master Cylinder Removal* and disconnect the brake hose from the master cylinder.

> *NOTE*
> *Place a shop cloth under the banjo bolts and brake hose fittings to catch any spilled brake fluid that will leak out in the following steps.*

4. Remove the banjo bolt (**Figure 97**) and sealing washers attaching the brake hose to the rear caliper

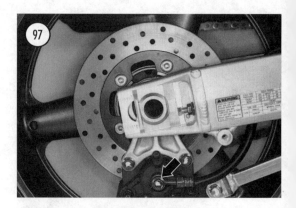

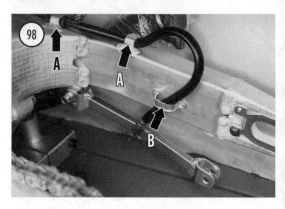

assembly. Do not lose the sealing washer from each side of the hose fitting.

> *NOTE*
> *Figure 98 is shown with the rear wheel removed for clarity. It is not necessary to remove the wheel for this procedure.*

5. Unhook the brake hose from the two clamps (A, **Figure 98**) on top of the swing arm.

6. Carefully pull the rear of the brake hose out from the guide (B, **Figure 98**) on the inner surface of the swing arm, and remove the brake hose.

7. Install a new hose, new sealing washers and banjo bolts in the reverse order of removal while noting the following:

    a. Install new sealing washers on each side of the brake hose fittings.

    b. Tighten the banjo bolts to the torque specifications listed in **Table 2**.

    c. Make sure the brake hose is correctly installed through the guide (B, **Figure 98**) on the swing arm so it does not touch the rear wheel.

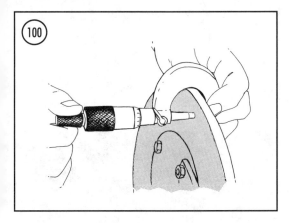

wear limit listed in **Table 1**, use the specification on the disc when inspecting it.

When servicing the brake discs, do not have the discs machined to compensate for any warp. The discs are thin and machining only reduces their thickness, causing them to warp quite rapidly. If the disc is warped, the brake pads may be dragging on the disc due to a faulty caliper and causing the disc to overheat. Overheating can also be caused when there is unequal pad pressure on the sides of the disc.

Four main causes of unequal brake pad pressure are:

   a. The floating caliper is binding on the caliper mounting bracket shafts, thus preventing the caliper from floating side to side on the disc.

   b. The brake caliper piston seals are worn or damaged.

   c. The small master cylinder relief port is plugged.

   d. The primary cup on the master cylinder piston is worn or damaged.

NOTE
It is not necessary to remove the wheel to measure the disc thickness. The measurement can be performed with the wheel installed or removed from the bike.

1. Measure the thickness of the disc at several locations around the disc with a vernier caliper or a micrometer (**Figure 100**). The disc must be replaced if the thickness in any area is less than that specified in **Table 1** (or the MIN dimension stamped on the disc).

2. Make sure the disc mounting bolts are tight before running this check. Check the disc runout with a dial indicator as shown in **Figure 101**.

NOTE
When checking the front disc, turn the handlebar all the way to one side, and then to the other side.

3. Slowly rotate the wheel and watch the dial indicator. If the runout exceeds that listed in **Table 1**, replace the disc.

4. Clean the disc of any rust or corrosion, and wipe it clean with lacquer thinner. Never use an oil-based solvent that may leave an oil residue on the disc.

   d. Refill the master cylinder reservoir and bleed the rear brake system as described in this chapter.

BRAKE DISC

The brake discs are separate from the wheel hubs and can be removed once the wheel is removed from the bike.

Inspection

It is not necessary to remove the disc from the wheel to inspect it. Small nicks and marks on the disc are not important, but radial scratches deep enough to snag a fingernail reduce braking effectiveness and increase brake pad wear. If these grooves are evident and the brake pads are wearing rapidly, replace the disc.

The specifications for the standard and wear limits are listed in **Table 1**. The minimum (MIN) thickness is stamped on the disc face (**Figure 99**). If the specification stamped on the disc differs from the

14

5. On front brake discs, inspect all fasteners (A, **Figure 102**) between the outer and the inner rings of the disc. If any are loose or damaged, replace the disc.

Removal/Installation

1. Remove the front or rear wheel as described in Chapter Eleven.

> *NOTE*
> *Insert a piece of wood or vinyl tube between the pads in the caliper(s). This way, if the brake lever or pedal is inadvertently applied, the pistons will not be forced out of the cylinders. If this does happen, the caliper might have to be disassembled to reseat the pistons and the system will have to be bled. By using the wood or vinyl tube in place of the disc, it will not be necessary to bleed the system when installing the wheel.*

> *CAUTION*
> *Do not set the wheel down on the disc surface, as it may get scratched or warped. Set the wheel on two wooden blocks.*

2. Remove the bolts (**Figure 103**) securing the brake disc to the hub and remove the disc.

3. Install by reversing these removal steps while noting the following:

   a. On a disc so marked, position the disc so the arrow (B, **Figure 102**) points in the direction of tire rotation.

> *WARNING*
> *The disc bolts are specifically designed for the application. If replacement bolts are required, make sure to use the original equipment type. Never compromise the brake system by using a substandard bolt that may not properly secure the disc to the hub.*

   b. Use a small amount of a locking compound such as ThreeBond No. TB1303 on the brake disc bolts before installation.

   c. Tighten the disc mounting bolts to the torque specification listed in **Table 2**.

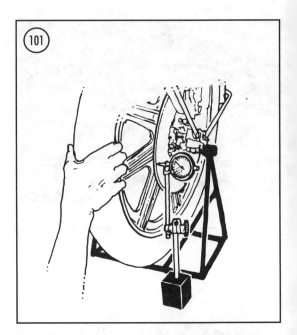

BRAKE BLEEDING

Bleeding the brakes removes air from the brake system. Air in the brakes increases brake lever or pedal travel, and it makes the brakes feel soft or spongy. Under extreme circumstances, it can cause complete loss of brake pressure.

The brakes can be bled manually or with the use of a brake bleeding tool. The manual method is described here. If there is a vacuum pump or other brake bleeding tool available, follow the instructions that came with the tool.

Only use fresh DOT 4 brake fluid when bleeding the brakes. Do not reuse old brake fluid and do not use DOT 5 (silicone based) brake fluid. Brake fluid will damage the finish on most surfaces. Protect the motorcycle from accidental spills by covering the

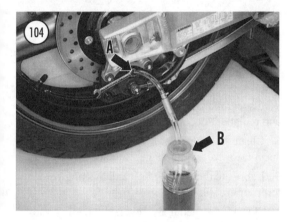

the top cover, diaphragm plate (front reservoir only) and the diaphragm from the reservoir.

5. Add brake fluid to the reservoir until the fluid level is about 10 mm (3/8 in.) below the top. Loosely install the diaphragm and the cover. Leave them in place during this procedure to prevent the entry of dirt.

6. Apply the front brake lever or the rear brake pedal until it stops, and hold it in this position.

7. Open the bleed valve (A, **Figure 104**) with a wrench. Let the brake lever or pedal move to the limit of its travel, and then close the bleed valve. Do not release the brake lever (or brake pedal) while the bleed valve is open.

8. Pump the brake lever or pedal a few times and then release it.

NOTE
As break fluid enters the system, the level in the reservoir drops. Add brake fluid as necessary to keep the fluid level 10 mm (3/8 in.) below the reservoir top so air will not be drawn into the system.

9. Repeat Steps 6-8 until the brake fluid flowing from the hose is clear and free of air. If the system is difficult to bleed, tap the master cylinder or caliper with a soft mallet.

10. Test the feel of the brake lever or pedal. It should feel firm and offer the same resistance each time it is operated. If the lever or pedal feels soft, air is still trapped in the system. Continue bleeding.

11. When bleeding is complete, disconnect the hose from the bleed valve. Torque the caliper bleed valve to the torque specification in **Table 2**.

12. If necessary, add brake fluid to the master cylinder to correct the fluid level.

13. Install the diaphragm, diaphragm plate (front reservoir only) and top cap. Make sure the cap is secured in place.

NOTE
Do not ride the bike until both brakes and the brake light are working properly.

areas beneath the calipers and master cylinders with a tarp. Immediately clean up any spilled brake fluid. Wash the affected parts with soapy water, and completely rinse the area with plenty of clean water.

NOTE
The rear caliper is equipped with two bleed valves, one for each caliper body half. Bleed the inner caliper body half first, and then the outer caliper half.

1. Check that all banjo bolts in the system are tight.

2. Remove the dust cap from the bleed valve on the caliper assembly.

3. Connect a length of clear tubing to the bleed valve. Place the other end of the tube into a clean container (B, **Figure 104**). Fill the container with enough fresh brake fluid to keep the end submerged. The tube should be long enough so its loop can be higher than the bleed valve to prevent air from being drawn into the caliper during bleeding.

4. Clean all dirt or foreign matter from the top of the front or rear master cylinder reservoir. Remove

14. Test ride the bike slowly at first to make sure the brakes are operating properly.

14

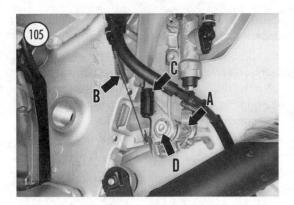

REAR BRAKE PEDAL

Removal/Lubrication/Installation

NOTE
This procedure is shown with the rear wheel and swing arm removed for photographic clarity. It is not necessary to remove either of these components but it does allow more working room.

1. Remove the cotter pin (A, **Figure 105**) and the washer from the back end of the clevis pin that secure the master cylinder pushrod to the brake pedal.
2. Withdraw the clevis pin (**Figure 106**) and separate the pushrod yoke from the brake pedal.
3. Unhook the rear brake light switch spring (B, **Figure 105**) from the brake pedal.
4. Use locking pliers and disconnect the pedal return spring (C, **Figure 105**) from the brake pedal.

5. Remove the footpeg bolt (D, **Figure 105**) from the inboard side of the mounting bracket.
6. Remove the footpeg and rear brake pedal assembly. Do not lose the washer between the brake pedal and the footpeg mounting bracket.
7. Inspect the brake pedal for fractures or damage and replace if necessary.
8. Clean the footpeg bolt with solvent, and then inspect it for wear or damage. Replace if necessary.
9. Lubricate the footpeg bolt and bushing with waterproof grease.
10. Install the pedal by reversing these removal steps while noting the following:
    a. Tighten the footpeg bolt securely.
    b. Install a new cotter pin and bend the ends over completely.
    c. Adjust the rear brake pedal height as described in Chapter Three.

Table 1 BRAKE SPECIFICATIONS

Item	Standard mm (in.)	Wear limit mm (in.)
Brake fluid	DOT 4	–
Brake disc runout (front and rear)	–	0.30 (0.16)
Brake disc thickness		
1997		
Front	4.3-4.7 (0.169-0.185)	4.0 (0.16)
Rear	4.8-5.2 (0.189-0.205)	4.5 (0.18)
1998-on		
Front	4.8-5.2 (0.189-0.205)	4.5 (018)
Rear	4.8-5.2 (0.189-0.205)	4.5 (018)
	(continued)	

Table 1 BRAKE SPECIFICATIONS (continued)

Item	Standard mm (in.)	Wear limit mm (in.)
Front master cylinder		
Cylinder bore	14.000-14.043 (0.5512-0.5529)	–
Piston diameter	13.957-13.984 (0.5495-0.5506)	–
Front caliper		
Cylinder bore		–
Leading	27.000-27.076 (1.0630-1.0660)	–
Trailing	30.230-30.306 (1.1902-1.1931)	–
Piston diameter		
Leading	26.920-26.970 (1.0598-1.0618)	–
Trailing	30.150-30.200 (1.1870-1.1890)	–
Rear master cylinder		
Cylinder bore	12.700-12.743 (0.5000-0.5017)	–
Piston diameter	12.657-12.648 (0.4983-0.4994)	–
Rear caliper		
Cylinder bore	38.180-38.256 (1.5031-1.5061)	–
Piston diameter	38.098-38.148 (1.4999-1.5019)	–
Brake pedal height	55 (2.2)	–

Table 2 BRAKE TORQUE SPECIFICATIONS

Item	N•m	in.-lb.	ft.-lb.
Brake disc bolt			
Front	23	–	17
Rear	35	–	26
Brake hose banjo bolt (front and rear)	23	–	17
Caliper bleed valve (front and rear)	8	71	–
Front caliper mounting bolt	39	–	29
Front caliper housing bolt	23	–	17
Front master cylinder clamp bolt	10	89	–
Rear caliper mounting bolt	26	–	19
Rear caliper housing bolt	33	–	24
Rear master cylinder mounting bolt	10	89	–
Rear master-cylinder-rod locknut	18	–	13
Torque arm bolt/nut			
Front	28	–	21
Rear	35	–	26

14

CHAPTER FIFTEEN

BODY AND FRAME

This chapter contains removal and installation procedures for the body panels and the sidestand.

Whenever a body or frame member is removed, reinstall all mounting hardware (i.e. small brackets, bolts, nuts, rubber bushings, metal collars, etc.) onto the removed part so they will not be misplaced. Frequent changes during the model year make it possible that the way it attaches to the frame may differ slightly from the one in this chapter.

The fairing and frame cover parts are easily damaged and expensive to replace. After each part is removed from the bike, wrap it in a blanket or towel, and place it in a cardboard box. Store it in an area where it will not be damaged.

SEATS

Removal/Installation

1. Park the bike on the sidestand on level ground.
2. To remove the rear seat, perform the following:
   a. On the left side of the frame cover, insert the ignition key into the lock and turn it clockwise.
   b. Lift the front of the rear seat (A, **Figure 1**), pull the seat forward until it clears the frame retainers, and remove the seat.

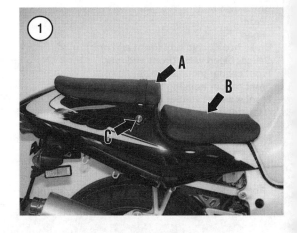

3. To remove the front seat, perform the following:
   a. Carefully lift up on a rear corner of the seat.
   b. Remove the mounting bolt (**Figure 2**). Repeat this on the other side.
   c. Pull the seat (B, **Figure 1**) rearward, lift the front of the seat, and remove it.

> *WARNING*
> *Do **not** try to repair damaged retaining hooks. These hooks are molded into the seat base and must be solid with no fractures or cracks in order to safely secure the seat. A repaired hook may create a false sense of security*

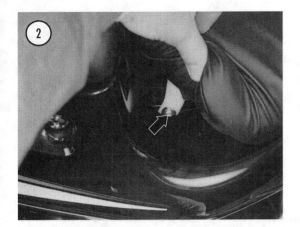

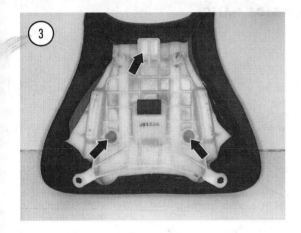

b. Push the front of the seat down until it locks in place.

c. Check that the seat is firmly locked in place.

WARNING
After the seats are installed, pull up firmly and move them from side to side to make sure they are securely locked into place. If the seats are not correctly locked into place, they may slide to one side or the other when riding the bike. This could lead to the loss of control and a possible accident.

FRONT FENDER

Removal/Installation

1. Place the bike on the sidestand on level ground.
2. Remove the front wheel as described in Chapter Eleven.

NOTE
It is not necessary to disconnect the brake hoses from the caliper assemblies.

3. Remove the brake hoses from the front fender as follows:

   a. On the left side, carefully release the hose clamp (**Figure 4**) from the front fender.

   b. On the right side, disconnect the cross-over hose (A, **Figure 5**) and the upper brake hose (B, **Figure 5**) from the clamps on the front fender.

4. Remove the two screws securing each side of the front fender to the fork slider. Remove the screw (A,

that may lead to a seat working loose during a ride.

4. Inspect the plastic base on the underside of each seat for cracks or damage. Make sure all molded retaining hooks and mounting tabs (**Figure 3**) are not damaged. If damaged, replace the seat(s).

5. To install the front seat, perform the following:

   a. Insert the rear of the seat into the frame cover opening.

   b. Slide the front hook into the seat retainer on the frame. Make sure the front hook is positioned correctly.

   c. Carefully lift up on the rear corner of the seat and align the bolt holes with the frame. Install the mounting bolt (**Figure 2**), and tighten it securely. Repeat for the other side.

   d. Check that the seat is firmly locked in place.

6. To install the rear seat, perform the following:

   a. Slide the rear hooks into the seat retainers on the frame.

15

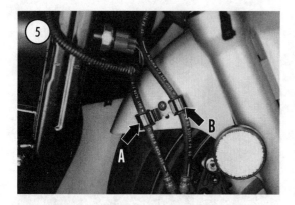

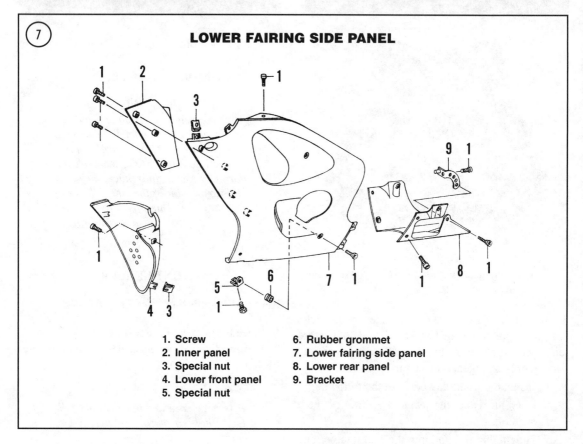

LOWER FAIRING SIDE PANEL

1. Screw
2. Inner panel
3. Special nut
4. Lower front panel
5. Special nut
6. Rubber grommet
7. Lower fairing side panel
8. Lower rear panel
9. Bracket

Figure 6), two washers and a spacer from the front mount on each side of the fender. Remove the screw and washer (B, **Figure 6**) from the rear mount on each side.

5. Carefully pull the front fender forward and out from between the fork.

6. Inspect the fender for damage, cracks or fractures.

7. Install by reversing these removal steps while noting the following:

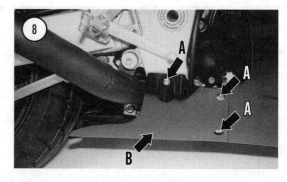

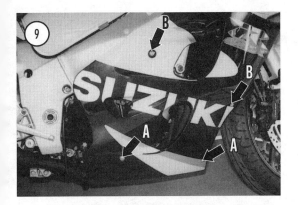

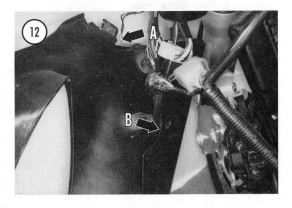

a. Install the spacer and two washers with the front mounting screw (A, **Figure 6**).

b. Install a single washer with the rear screw (B, **Figure 6**) on each side.

c. Tighten the screws securely, but do not overtighten them. The plastic fender may fracture if the screws are overtightened.

FAIRING LOWER SIDE PANELS

Removal/Installation

Refer to **Figure 7**.

1. Place the bike on the sidestand on level ground.

2. Remove the screws (A, **Figure 8**) on both sides securing the lower rear panel to the lower side panel and mounting brackets. Remove the lower rear panel (B, **Figure 8**).

3. Remove the screws securing the lower front panel to one of the lower side panels. The lower front panel can remain attached to the other lower side panel or it can be removed if necessary.

4. Remove the two lower screws (A, **Figure 9**) and the two upper screws (B, **Figure 9**) that secure the lower side panel in place.

5. Have an assistant hold onto the panel, and then remove the top screws (**Figure 10**).

6. When removing the right lower side panel, perform the following:

a. Pull the side panel from the frame and expose the electrical connectors.

b. Depress the tab on the 2-pin front-turn-signal electrical connector (**Figure 11**), and disconnect the connector from the main harness.

c. Remove the side panel from the motorcycle.

7. When removing the left lower side panel, perform the following:

a. Pull the side panel from the frame and expose the electrical connectors.

b. Depress the tab on the 2-pin front-turn-signal electrical connector (A, **Figure 12**), and disconnect the connector from the main harness.

NOTE
*Note how the wiring harness is routed between the inner panel (**Figure 12**) and the left lower side panel. Reroute the harness along the same path during assembly.*

15

⑬

UPPER FAIRING AND BRACKET

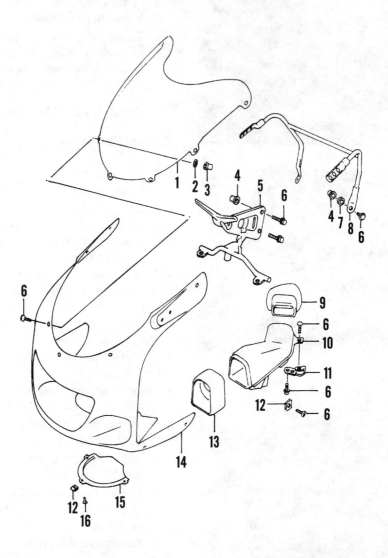

1. Windshield
2. Washer
3. Special nut
4. Nut
5. Upper fairing mounting bracket
6. Bolt
7. Grommet
8. Rear view mirror mounting bracket
9. Rear rubber boot
10. Air intake duct
11. Bracket
12. Special nut
13. Front rubber boot
14. Upper fairing
15. Lower lid
16. Screw

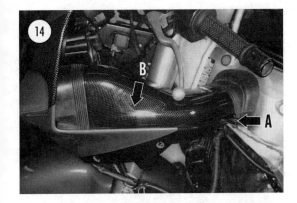

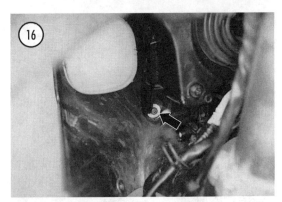

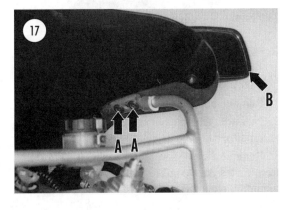

c. Remove one of the screws that connects the inner panel (B, **Figure 12**) to the inside of the lower front panel. Remove the screw at the point where the wiring harness passes between these two panels.

d. Pull the wiring harness from between the inner panel and the left side panel. Once the wiring harness is clear, remove the lower side panel.

8. Install by reversing these removal steps. Tighten the screws securely, but do not overtighten them. The plastic panels may fracture if the hardware is overtightened.

UPPER FAIRING

Removal/Installation

Refer to **Figure 13**.

1. Remove the fairing lower side panel on each side as previously described in this chapter.

2. Remove the screw (A, **Figure 14**) securing the air intake duct to the frame. Remove the air intake duct and rubber boots (B, **Figure 14**). Place clean shop cloths into the intake openings in the air box to prevent the entry of small parts and debris.

3. Working under the headlight area next to the left air intake pipe, locate and disconnect the four electrical connectors.

4. Remove the upper screw (**Figure 15**) and lower screw (**Figure 16**) on each side that secures the headlight assembly to the upper fairing.

5. Place several towels or blankets on top of the front fender to protect it should the upper fairing drop down onto it during removal and installation.

6. Remove the bolts (A, **Figure 17**) securing the rear view mirror (B, **Figure 17**). Remove both mirror assemblies and rubber cushion.

7. Carefully pull the upper fairing forward and off the mounting brackets. The headlight will remain with the upper fairing mounting bracket, held in place only by the electrical wiring harness.

8. Disconnect the electrical wiring harness and remove the headlight assembly from the upper fairing mounting bracket.

9. Store the upper fairing and headlight in a safe place.

10. To remove the upper fairing mounting bracket, perform the following:

15

a. Release the right- and left-hand combination switch electrical wiring harness from the clamp on the steering head.

b. On 1997 models, the turn signal relay is mounted onto the left side of the upper fairing mounting bracket. Disconnect the connector from the relay.

c. Disconnect the electrical connector (**Figure 18**) from the backside of the instrument cluster.

d. Remove the bolts and nuts (**Figure 19**) securing the mounting bracket to the frame. Carefully move the upper fairing bracket and instrument cluster assembly forward making sure all electrical connectors have been disconnected. Remove the assembly from the bike.

11. Install by reversing these removal steps while noting the following:

a. Install the air intake ducts onto the frame and make sure the rear rubber boot is positioned correctly on the air box.

b. Make sure the air intake duct front boot is indexed into the air intake horn on the upper fairing (**Figure 20**).

c. Make sure to install the rubber cushion under the rearview mirror before installation of the nuts.

d. Make sure all electrical connectors are secure and corrosion free.

e. Tighten all screws and bolts securely. Do not overtighten them. The plastic fairing may fracture if the hardware is overtightened.

Inspection

1. Inspect all components for damage, cracks or fractures. Check each mounting hole for elongation or fractures from overtightening of fasteners.

2. Examine the raised post, on parts so equipped, for damage or cracks.

3. Repair or replace any damaged part.

4. Check the air intake ducts for cracks or damage and replace them if necessary.

5. If removed, inspect the mounting bracket for bending or other damage. Replace it if necessary.

REAR FRAME COVER

Removal/Installation

Refer to **Figure 21**.

1. Remove both seats as described in this chapter.

2. Remove the two front center screws (**Figure 22**) and special nuts.

3. Remove the side screw and washer (C, **Figure 1**) from each side. Do not lose the collar located in the mounting receptacle of the frame cover.

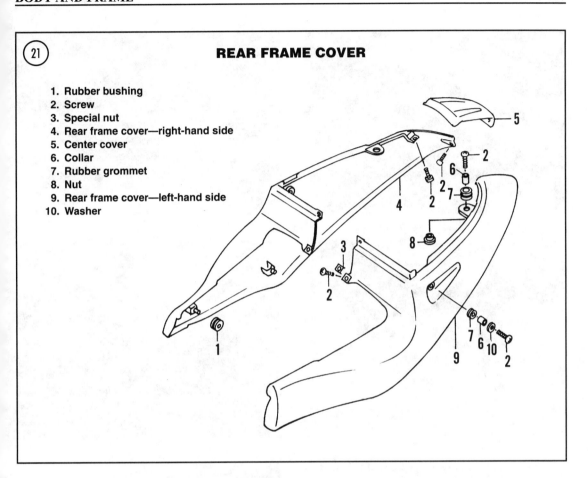

REAR FRAME COVER

1. Rubber bushing
2. Screw
3. Special nut
4. Rear frame cover—right-hand side
5. Center cover
6. Collar
7. Rubber grommet
8. Nut
9. Rear frame cover—left-hand side
10. Washer

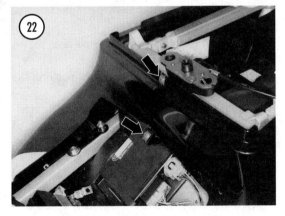

4. Remove the two top screws (**Figure 23**). Do not lose the collar and large washers located in the mounting receptacle of the cover.

5. Remove the rear screw and washer (**Figure 24**) on each side of the taillight.

6. Carefully pull out the front arm of each side to release the two posts from the rubber grommets on the frame mounts.

7. Carefully spread out the front portions of the cover, move the cover assembly rearward and remove it from the frame.

8. Install by reversing these removal steps while noting the following:

   a. Apply a light coat of liquid detergent to the rubber grommets on the frame mounts to ease the installation of the side cover posts. Press

15

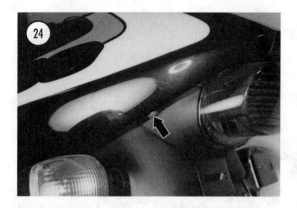

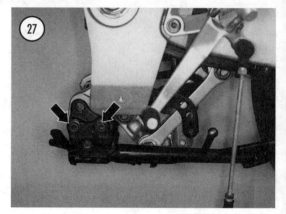

the side cover only in the areas of the posts to avoid damage to the side cover.

b. Tighten the screws and bolts securely, but do not overtighten them. The plastic frame cover may fracture if fasteners are overtightened.

SIDESTAND

Removal/Installation

1. Remove the lower rear panel and both lower fairing side panels as described in this chapter.

2. Place the bike on a suitable jack or wooden blocks on level ground.

3. To replace only the springs, perform the following:

    a. Place the sidestand in the raised position. This places the return springs in their relaxed position.

    b. Use locking pliers and disconnect the springs from the mounting bracket post. Remove both springs.

NOTE
The sidestand is removed in **Figure 25** *for clarity.*

    c. Reinstall the springs onto the posts as shown in **Figure 25**.

4. To remove the sidestand assembly, perform the following:

    a. Locate the two-pin sidestand-switch electrical connector (one green wire, one black/white wire) and disconnect the connector.

    b. Remove the bolts securing the sidestand switch (**Figure 26**) and remove the switch.

    c. Remove the springs as previously described.

NOTE
Figure 27 *shows the engine removed for clarity.*

    d. Remove the bolts (**Figure 27**) securing the sidestand mounting bracket to the frame.

    e. Remove the sidestand.

5. Check the sidestand for damage and make sure the pivot bolt is tight.

6. Inspect the spring mounting posts for cracks or damage.

7. Apply clean engine oil to the pivot area.

8. Correctly position the sidestand in the frame, install the bolts, and tighten them securely.

9. Move the sidestand up and down to check for freedom of movement.

10. Install the sidestand switch and reconnect the sidestand switch electrical connector to the wiring harness. Make sure the connector is free of corrosion and is tight.

11. Remove the jack or wooden blocks.

12. Install the lower fairing side panels as described in this chapter.

INDEX

16

16

WIRING DIAGRAMS

1997 U.S.A, CALIFORNIA AND CANADA MODELS

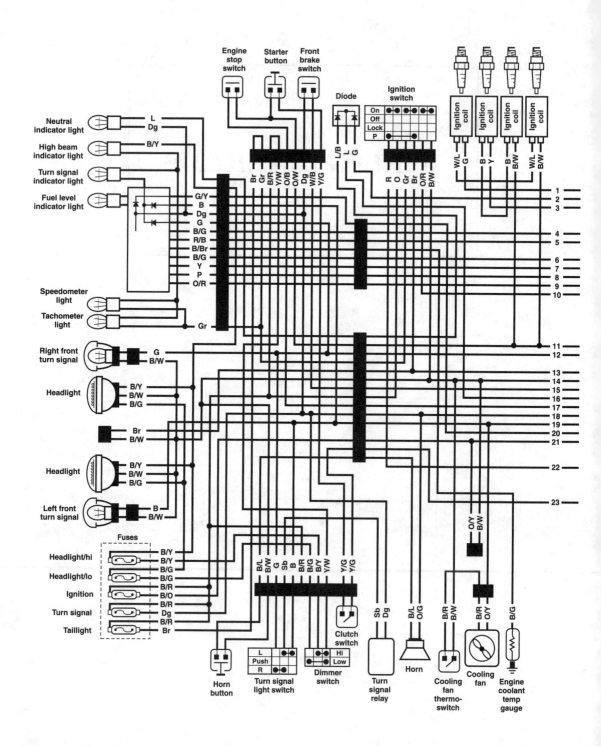

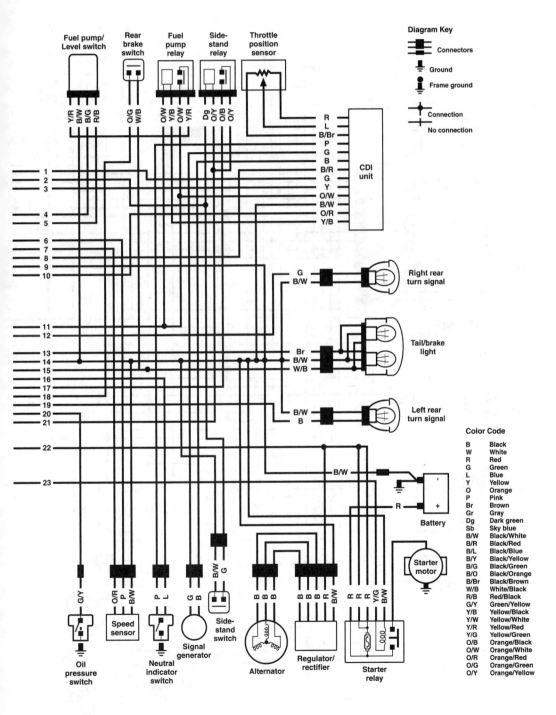

1997 U.K. MODELS

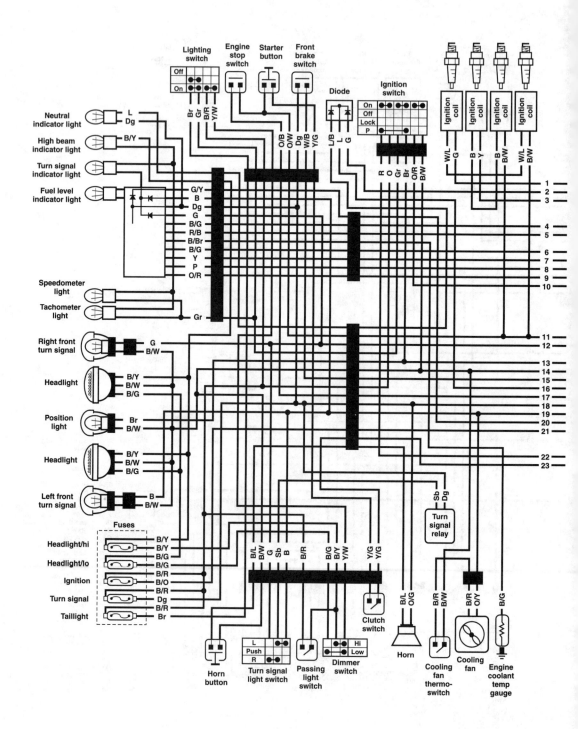

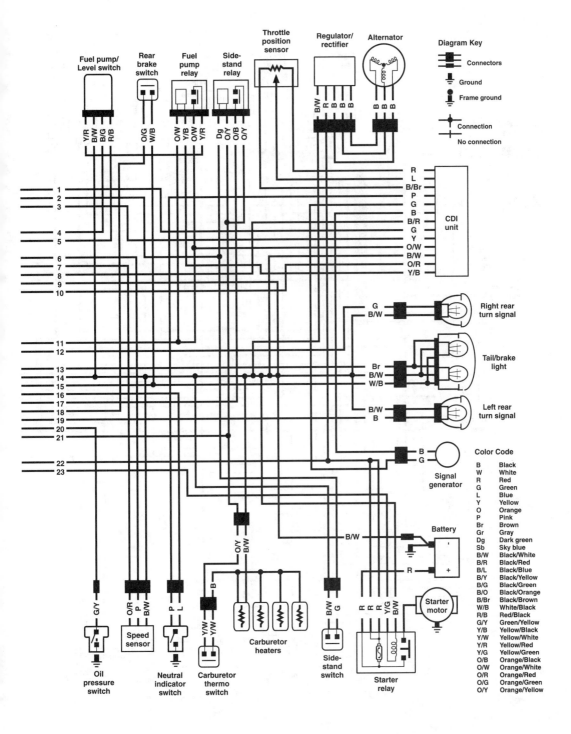

1997 AUSTRALIA MODELS

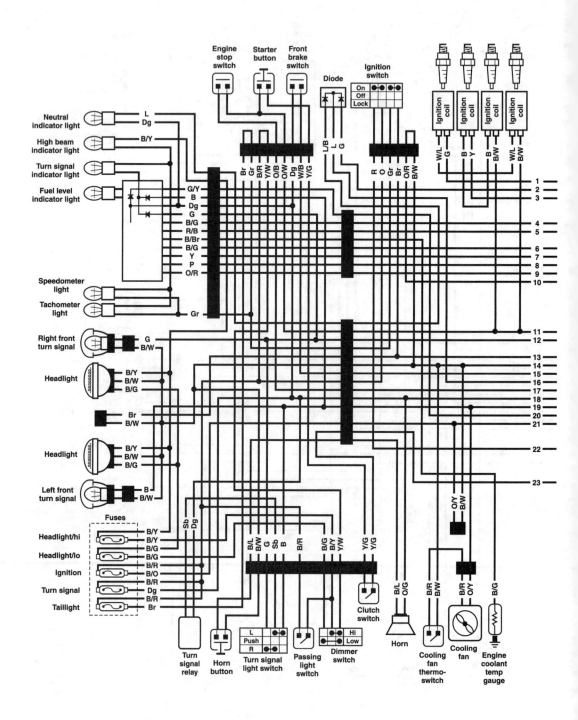

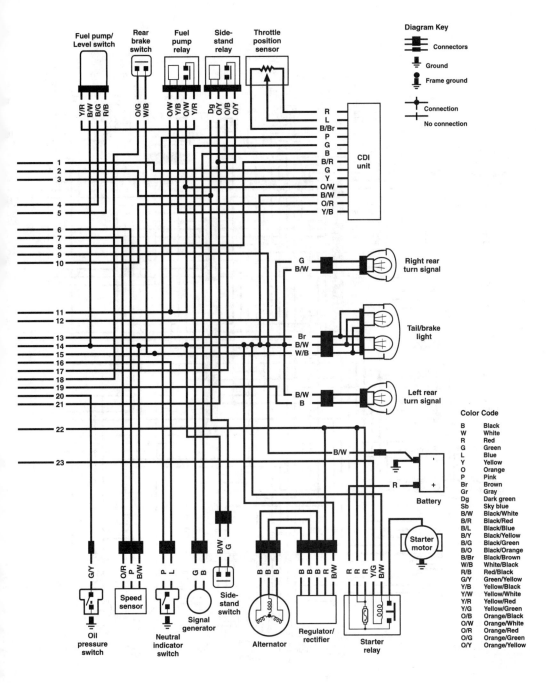

Diagram Key

Connectors
Ground
Frame ground
Connection
No connection

Fuel pump/Level switch
Rear brake switch
Fuel pump relay
Side-stand relay
Throttle position sensor

CDI unit

Right rear turn signal

Tail/brake light

Left rear turn signal

Battery

Starter motor

Oil pressure switch
Speed sensor
Neutral indicator switch
Signal generator
Side-stand switch
Alternator
Regulator/rectifier
Starter relay

Color Code

B	Black
W	White
R	Red
G	Green
L	Blue
Y	Yellow
O	Orange
P	Pink
Br	Brown
Gr	Gray
Dg	Dark green
Sb	Sky blue
B/W	Black/White
B/R	Black/Red
B/L	Black/Blue
B/Y	Black/Yellow
B/G	Black/Green
B/O	Black/Orange
B/Br	Black/Brown
W/B	White/Black
R/B	Red/Black
G/Y	Green/Yellow
Y/B	Yellow/Black
Y/W	Yellow/White
Y/R	Yellow/Red
Y/G	Yellow/Green
O/B	Orange/Black
O/W	Orange/White
O/R	Orange/Red
O/G	Orange/Green
O/Y	Orange/Yellow

17

1997 AUSTRIA, BELGIUM, BRAZIL, FRANCE, GERMANY, ITALY, NETHERLANDS, SPAIN AND SWITZERLAND MODELS

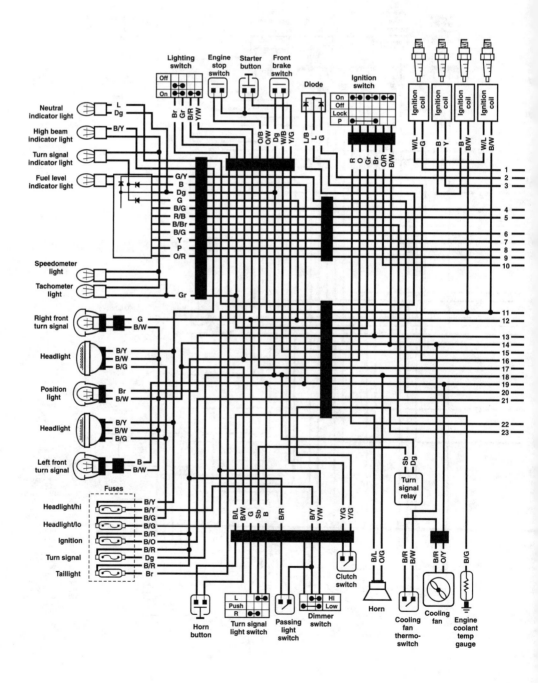

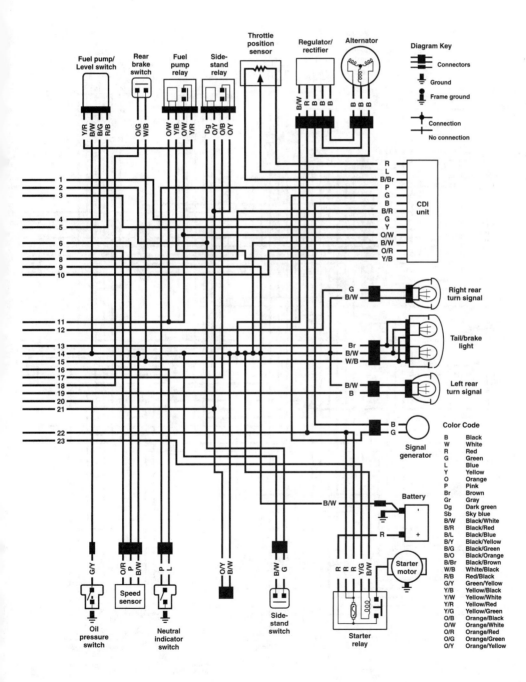

17

1998-ON U.S.A., CALIFORNIA AND CANADA MODELS

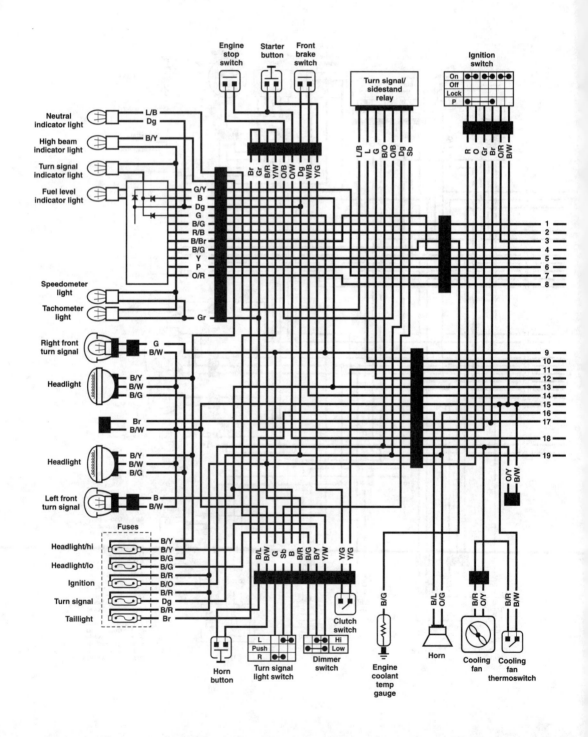

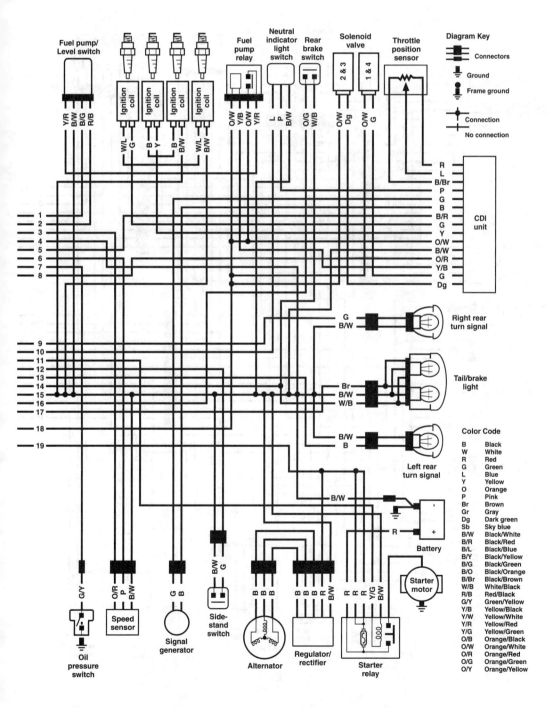

17

1998-ON U.K. MODELS

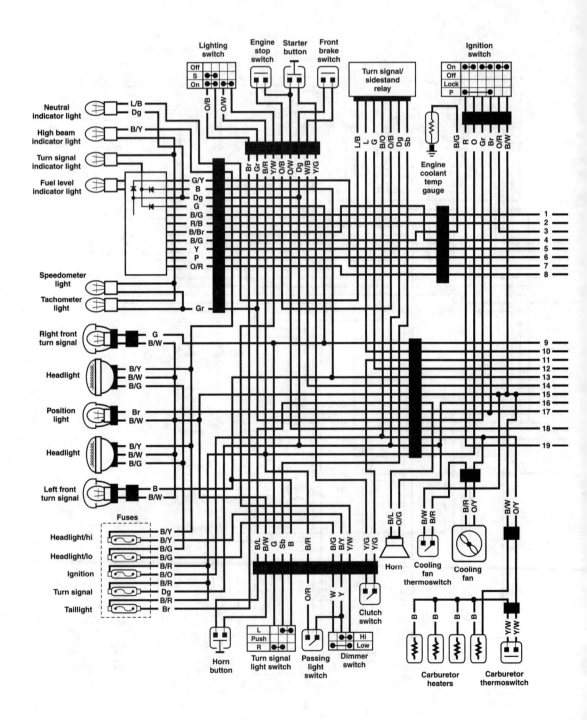

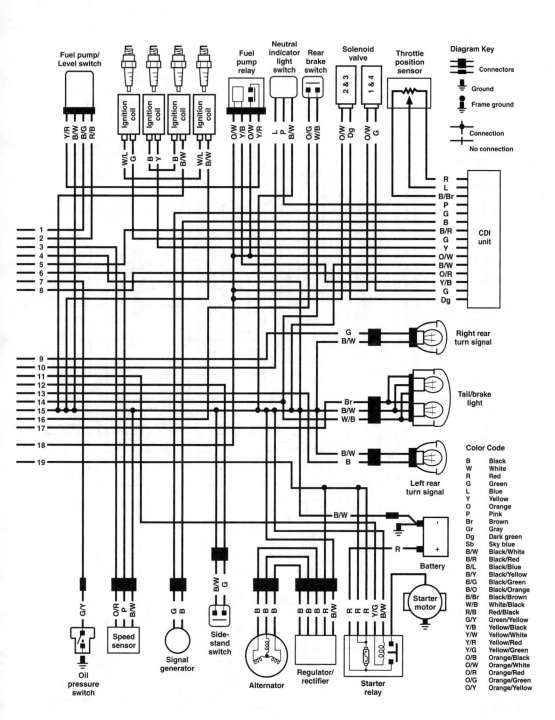

1998-ON AUSTRALIA MODELS

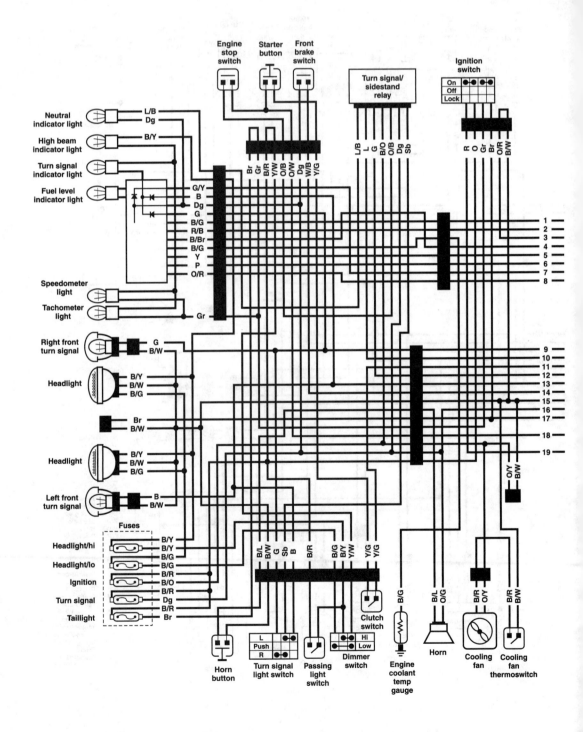

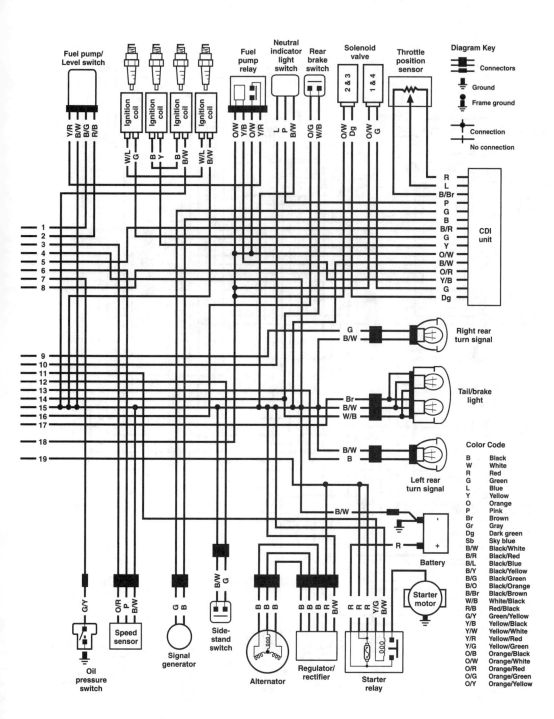

1998-ON AUSTRIA, BELGIUM, BRAZIL, FRANCE, GERMANY, ITALY, NETHERLANDS, SPAIN AND SWITZERLAND MODELS

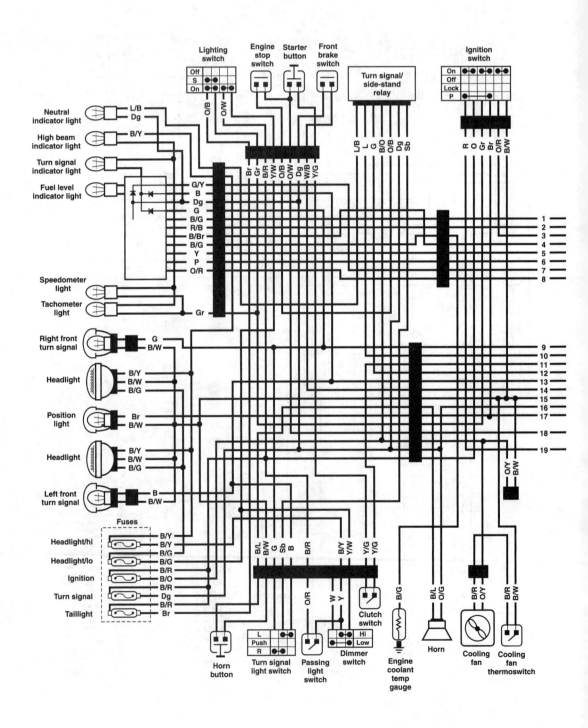

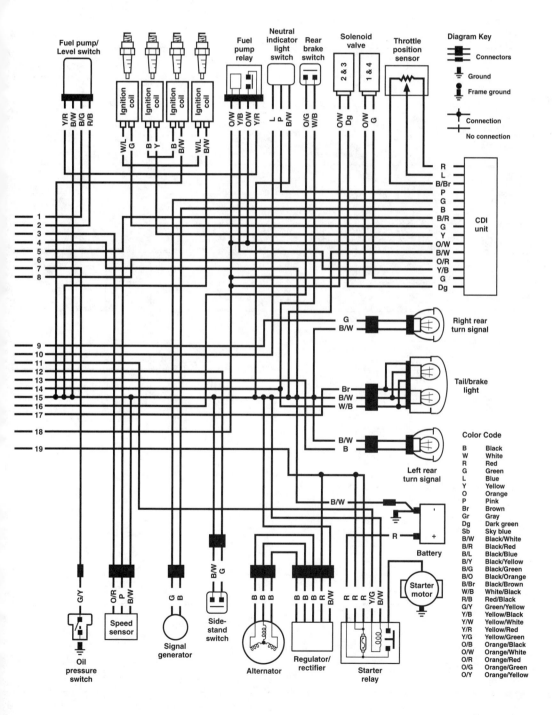

MAINTENANCE LOG

Service Performed	Mileage Reading				
Oil change (example)	2,836	5,782	8,601		